Reading Greek

GRAMMAR AND EXERCISES

SECOND EDITION

First published in 1978, *Reading Greek* has become a best-selling one-year introductory course in ancient Greek for students and adults. It combines the best of modern and traditional language-learning techniques and is used widely in schools, summer schools and universities across the world. It has also been translated into several foreign languages. This volume provides full grammatical support together with numerous exercises at different levels. For the second edition the presentations of grammar have been substantially rewritten to meet the needs of today's students and the volume has been completely redesigned, with the use of colour. Greek–English and English–Greek vocabularies are provided, as well as a substantial reference grammar and language surveys. The accompanying *Text and Vocabulary* volume contains a narrative adapted entirely from ancient authors in order to encourage students rapidly to develop their reading skills, while simultaneously receiving a good introduction to Greek culture.

THE JOINT ASSOCIATION OF CLASSICAL TEACHERS' GREEK COURSE

Reading Greek

GRAMMAR AND EXERCISES

SECOND EDITION

CAMBRIDGE
UNIVERSITY PRESS

CAMBRIDGE
UNIVERSITY PRESS

University Printing House, Cambridge CB2 8BS, United Kingdom

Cambridge University Press is part of the University of Cambridge.

It furthers the University's mission by disseminating knowledge in the pursuit of education, learning and research at the highest international levels of excellence.

www.cambridge.org
Information on this title: www.cambridge.org/9780521698528

First edition published 1978
Twenty-sixth reprint 2006
Second edition published 2007
18th printing 2022

Printed in the United Kingdom by TJ Books Limited, Padstow Cornwall

A catalogue record for this publication is available from the British Library

ISBN 978-0-521-69852-8 Paperback

Contents

---

[1] Bold numbers refer to the grammatical paragraph sections.

Γράμματα μαθεῖν δεῖ καὶ μαθόντα νοῦν ἔχειν
Menander

Preface

This book is written to be used in step with *Reading Greek (Text)* of the Joint Association of Classical Teachers' Greek Course. In it will be found:

A: Section-by-section grammatical explanations and exercises to support the reading of the twenty sections of the *Text* (pp. 1–368). While we recommend that the *Text* is tackled before students turn to the grammar and exercises, no harm will be done by taking a different view.

B: A *Reference Grammar*, which summarises and sometimes expands upon the essential features of the grammar met in the Course (pp. 369–464).

C: A number of *Language Surveys* which look in detail at some of the more important features of the language (pp. 465–496).

D: A Total Vocabulary of all words that should have been learnt – this has been appended to the *Text* as well – followed by a list of proper names (pp. 497–520).

E: A vocabulary for the English-Greek exercises (pp. 521–528).

F: Indices to the grammar and to Greek words (pp. 529–543), originally constructed by Professor W. K. Lacey and his students at the University of Auckland, New Zealand and here revised.

It would be impracticable to produce an exhaustive grammar of the whole Greek language. We have therefore concentrated attention on its most common features. Students and teachers should bear in mind that the first aim of this grammar is to help students to translate from Greek into English.

> Peter Jones
> Newcastle on Tyne
> October 2006

Acknowledgements to the original edition of *Reading Greek* (1978)

Reading Greek was developed by a Project Team (Dr P.V. Jones, Dr K.C. Sidwell and Miss F.E. Corrie) under the guidance of a Steering Committee and Advisory Panel made up as follows:

Steering Committee: Professor J.P.A. Gould (Bristol University) (Chairman); M.G. Balme (Harrow School); R.M. Griffin (Manchester Grammar School); Dr J.T. Killen (Joint Treasurer, Jesus College, Cambridge); Sir Desmond Lee (Joint Treasurer, President, Hughes Hall, Cambridge); A.C.F. Verity (Headmaster, Leeds Grammar School); Miss E.P. Story (Hughes Hall, Cambridge).

Advisory Panel: G.L. Cawkwell (University College, Oxford); Dr J. Chadwick (Downing College, Cambridge); Professor A. Morpurgo Davies (Somerville College, Oxford); Sir Kenneth Dover (President, Corpus Christi College, Oxford); Professor E.W. Handley (University College, London); B.W. Kay (HMI); Dr A.H. Sommerstein (Nottingham University); Dr B. Sparkes (Southampton University); G. Suggitt (Headmaster, Stratton School); A.F. Turberfield (HMI). The Committee and Panel met in full session three times a year during the period 1974-8 while the Course was being developed, but also divided up into sub-committees to give specific help to the Project Team on certain aspects of the Course, as follows:

Text: K.J.D.; E.W.H.

Grammar: J.C.; A.M.D.; A.H.S. (who, with K.J.D., have kindly made individual contributions to the Reference Grammar and Language Surveys).

Exercises: M.G.B.; R.M.G.; A.C.F.V.

Background: G.L.C.; J.P.A.G.; B.S.

Dissemination: B.W.K.; H.D.P.L.; E.P.S.; G.S.; A.F.T.

We have also been guided by a number of overseas scholars who have used, or given advice on, the Course, as follows:

J.A. Barsby (Dunedin, New Zealand); S. Ebbesen (Copenhagen, Denmark); B. Gollan (Queensland, Australia); Professor A.S. Henry (Monash, Australia); Drs D. Sieswerda (Holland); Professor H.A. Thompson (Princeton, U.S.A.).

We would like to stress the immense debt of gratitude which we all owe to the Steering Committee, Advisory Panel and our overseas advisers. But we would also like to make it clear that the final decisions about every aspect of the Course and any errors of omission and commission are the sole responsibility of the Team.

We gratefully acknowledge the help and advice of Professor D. W. Packard (Chapel Hill, N. Carolina, U.S.A.) on the use of the computer in analysing and printing Greek; and of Dr John Dawson of the Cambridge University Literary and Linguistic Computing Laboratory, who made available to us the resources of the Computer Centre for printing and analysing draft material in the early stages of the Project.

We have learnt a great deal from members of the Team who produced the Cambridge Latin Course, and are extremely grateful to them for help, especially in the early stages of the Project. If we have produced a Course which takes a more traditional view of language-learning, our debt to many of the principles and much of the practice which the C.L.C. first advocated is still very great.

Finally, our best thanks go to all the teachers in schools, universities and adult education centres both in the U.K. and overseas who used and criticised draft materials. We owe an especial debt of thanks to the organisers of the J.A.C.T. Greek Summer School in Cheltenham, who allowed us to use our material at the School for the three years while the Course was being developed.

> Peter V. Jones (Director)
> Keith C. Sidwell (Second Writer)
> Frances E. Corrie (Research Assistant)

The second edition of *Reading Greek* (2007)

The main features of the revised course

Reading Greek was originally written on the assumption that its users would know Latin. *Tempora mutantur* – it has now been revised on the assumption that they do not, and in the light of the experiences of those using the course over nearly thirty years. While the overall structure of the course and its reading matter remain the same, the most important changes are:

Text

1. The running and learning vocabularies are now in the *Text*, on the same pages as the Greek to which they refer. The *Text* also has the total Greek-English Learning Vocabulary at the back, as does the *Grammar*.
2. There are indications throughout the *Text* of what grammatical material is being introduced and at what point; and there are cross-references to the sections of *The World of Athens* (second edition) relevant to the story-line and issues under discussion.

    As a result of these changes, the Text *can now act as a stand-alone 'revision' reader for anyone who has a basic grasp of ancient Greek, whatever beginners' course they have used. The second half of the* Text *in particular, starting with its carefully adapted extracts from the extremely important legal speech against the woman Neaira and leading on to Plato and an introduction to the dialects of Herodotus and Homer, makes an ideal introduction to some superb literature and central social, cultural, historical and philosophical issues relating to the ancient Greek world.*

3. Various aspects of the cultural and historical background of the *Text* are discussed from time to time *in situ*.

4. The original Section Five has been split into two sections, Five and Six. As a result, there are now twenty sections to the course.

Grammar

The *Grammar* has been completely re-written and re–designed. The aim has been to make its lay-out and content more user-friendly:

1. There is an introduction to some basics of English grammar and its terminology, and its relation to ancient Greek.

2. Explanations are clearer and fuller, composed for those who have never learnt an inflected language, and the lay-out more generous on the eye.

3. Brief, usually one-word, *Exercises* accompany the explanations of each new item of grammar. *If the teacher so chooses*, these can be used to provide instant feed-back on the student's grasp of the new material.

4. Declensions go down, not across, the page and the 'shading' of cases has been abandoned.

Acknowledgements

The revision was conducted under the aegis of a sub-committee of the Joint Association of Classical Teachers' Greek Committee, the body that invented the idea of the Project and oversaw it from its inception in 1974. The sub-committee consisted of Professor David Langslow (University of Manchester, chairman), Dr Peter Jones (Course Director), Dr Andrew Morrison (University of Manchester), James Morwood (Wadham College, Oxford), Dr James Robson (Open University), Dr John Taylor (Tonbridge School), Dr Naoko Yamagata (Open University), Dr James Clackson (Jesus College, Cambridge) and Adrian Spooner (Management Consultant).

The sub-committee met roughly once a term for two years and took decisions that affected every aspect of the second edition. It concentrated particularly on the *Grammar*. Sections 1–2 were revised in the first instance by Dr Andrew Morrison, Sections 3–9 by Dr James Robson and Sections 10–20 by Dr Peter Jones, while the Language Surveys were revised by Professor David Langslow. Members of the sub-committee read and commented on virtually everything. Professor Brian Sparkes (University of Southampton) again advised on the illustrations. We are grateful to the students and tutors at the 2006 JACT Greek Summer School in Bryanston for giving a thorough testing to the first half of the revised course in draft form, especially to Anthony Bowen (Jesus College, Cambridge); and to Dr Janet Watson for work on the proofs.

Cambridge University Press has given its full backing to the revision. Dr Michael Sharp patiently discussed and met with most of our requests, Peter Ducker solved the complicated design problems with elegance and ingenuity and Dr Caroline Murray expertly oversaw the computerisation of the text.

Dr Peter Jones as Director carries final responsibility for this second edition.

Peter Jones
Newcastle on Tyne
September 2006

Abbreviations

abs.(olute)
acc.(usative)
act.(ive)
adj.(ective)
adv.(erb)
aor.(ist)
art.(icle)
aug.(ment)
cf. (= confer) (Latin: 'compare')
comp.(arative)
cond.(itional)
conj.(ugated, ugation)
contr.(acted, action)
dat.(ive)
decl.(ension)
def.(inite)
del.(iberative)
dir.(ect)
f.(eminine)
fut.(ure)
gen.(itive)
imper.(ative)
impf. (= imperfect)
inc.(luding)
ind.(icative)
indec(linable)
indef.(inite)
indir.(ect)
inf.(initive)
irr.(egular)
lit.(erally)

m.(asculine)
mid.(dle)
n.(euter)
nom.(inative)
opt.(ative)
part.(iciple)
pass.(ive)
perf.(ect)
pl.(ural)
plup.(erfect)
prep.(osition)
pres.(ent)
prim.(ary)
pron.(oun)
q.(uestion)
redupl.(icated, ication)
rel.(ative)
s.(ingular)
sc.(ilicet) (Latin: 'that is to say')
sec.(ondary)
seq.(uence)
sp.(eech)
subj.(unctive)
sup.(erlative)
tr.(anslate)
uncontr.(acted)
unfulf.(illed)
vb. (= verb)
voc.(ative)

1st, 2nd, 3rd *refer to persons of the verb, i.e.*
　　　　1st s. = 'I' (sometimes 1s.)
　　　　2nd s. = 'you' (sometimes 2s.)

3rd s. = 'he, she, it' (sometimes 3s.)
1st pl. = 'we' (sometimes 1pl., etc.)
2nd pl. = 'you'
3rd pl. = 'they'

A Grammar, Vocabularies and Exercises for Sections One–Twenty

Introduction

Alphabet and pronunciation

A	α	(alpha) pronounced '*cup*' or '*calm*'
B	β	(beta) pronounced 'b' as in English
Γ	γ	(gamma) a hard 'g', like '*got*'
Δ	δ	(delta) a clean* 'd', like '*dot*'
E	ε	(epsilon) short 'e' like 'p*e*t'
Z	ζ	(zeta) like 'wi*sd*om'
H	η	(eta) pronounced as in 'h*air*'
Θ	θ	(theta) – blow a hard* 't' ('*t*are')
I	ι	(iota) like 'b*i*n' or like 'b*ead*'
K	κ	(kappa) a clean* 'k' like 's*k*in'
Λ	λ	(lambda) like '*l*ock'
M	μ	(mu) like '*m*ock'
N	ν	(nu) like '*n*et'
Ξ	ξ	(xi) like 'bo*x*'
O	ο	(omicron) a short 'o', like 'p*o*t'
Π	π	(pi) a clean* 'p', like 's*p*ot'
P	ρ	(rho) a rolled 'r', like '*rr*at'
Σ	σ ς	(sigma) a soft 's', like '*s*ing'
T	τ	(tau) a clean 't', like 's*t*ing'
Υ	υ	(upsilon) French 'l*u*ne' or German 'M*ü*ller'
Φ	φ	(phi) – blow a hard* 'p', like '*p*ool'
X	χ	(khi) – blow a hard* 'c', like '*c*ool'
Ψ	ψ	(psi) as in 'la*ps*e'
Ω	ω	(omega) like 's*aw*'

* 'Clean' indicates no 'h' sound; 'blow hard' indicates plenty of 'h' aspiration (e.g. φ as in 'top-hole').

Diphthongs

αι as in 'h*igh*'
αυ as in 'h*ow*'
οι as in 'b*oy*'
υι as in French 'h*ui*t'

1

Digraphs

ει (*fiancé*) and ου (b*oo*) are single sounds
εὐ- pronounce both elements *separately*

Double-consonants

γγ as in 'fi*ng*er'; γ is sounded as *ng* in γκ , γχ , γξ , and γμ.
ττ as 'ra*t-t*rap', λλ as 'who*ll*y', should be dwelt on.

Sigma and iota subscript

Observe that ς is used at the *end* of words, while σ is used elsewhere (e.g. στάσις, 'revolt'). Sometimes ι is printed *underneath* a preceding α (ᾳ), η (ῃ) and ω (ῳ), when it is called 'iota subscript' (Latin, 'written under'). It is always written 'adscript' in capitals, e.g. τίμη → TIMHI.

Breathings

■ *'Rough' breathing*

All words that begin with a vowel have a breathing. ' above a lower-case vowel, or in front of a capital, indicates the *presence* of an 'h' sound, e.g. ὅρος = *horos* ('marker'), ὁπλίτης = *hoplitēs* ('hoplite'), Ἑλλάς = *Hellas* ('Greece').

■ *'Smooth' breathing*

' above a lower-case vowel, or in front of a capital, indicates the *absence* of 'h' sound, e.g. ὄρος = *oros* ('mountain'), ἄτομος = *atomos* ('atom').

■ *Diphthongs*

Note that, on a diphthong and digraph, the breathing comes on the *second* vowel, e.g. Αἰσχυλος, Aeschylus.

Punctuation

Greek uses **;** for a question-mark (?) and · for a colon (:) or semi-colon (;). Otherwise, punctuation is as in English.

Vowel-length

Diphthongs and the vowels η and ω are always pronounced long; o and ε are always pronounced short. A macron is used to indicate where α, ι, υ are pronounced long (ᾱ, ῑ, ῡ) in learning vocabularies, total vocabularies and tables in the *Grammar*. A vowel with a circumflex accent ~ or iota subscript ͺ is long, needing no macron to mark it.

* Further information on the whole subject of alphabet and pronunciation is given in the *Reference Grammar*.

Transliteration

Most Greek letters convert simply into English, e.g. β and τ become 'b' and 't'.

But some are not so obvious. Note in particular:

ζ = sd *or* z

γγ = ng

η = e

θ = th

κ = *c or* k

-ον = -um *or* -on

-ος = -us *or* -os

υ = y *or* u

χ = ch *or* kh

ψ = ps

EXERCISES

1. Write the following Greek words (which you will meet in Section 1) in their English form:*

   Βυζάντιον   Παρθενών

   Δικαιόπολις   Χίος

   Εὔβοια   ἀκρόπολις

   Ζηνόθεμις   ἐμπόριον

   Ἡγέστρατος

   * You will see these words have accents. They are explained at **343**, **344–8**.

2. Write the following English words in their Greek form:
   (a) for a word that *begins* with a vowel, mark the 'smooth' breathing *over the vowel*, e.g. ēlectron = ἠλεκτρον
   (b) for a word that begins with an 'h', write the vowel which follows 'h' and then mark the *rough* breathing *over it* . Thus *historia* = ἱστορια.
   (c) diphthongs place the breathing over the *second* vowel, e.g. *eugenēs* = εὐγενης.

   drama, panthēr, crocus, geranium, hippopotamus, ibis, asbestos, charactēr, scēnē, Periclēs, Sophoclēs, Euripidēs, *Hippocratēs, comma, cōlon, Sōcratēs, Zeus, Artemis, *Hēraclēs, asthma, dyspepsia, cinēma, orchēstra, mēlon, iris.

   * With English *capital* 'H', write the vowel which follows the H as a capital, and put the 'rough' breathing *before* it, e.g. Homēros, Ὁμηρος (Homer).

Grammatical introduction

This section introduces some basic terms of grammar for you when translating from Greek into English. The grammar of a language explains simply how it works, and it does this by using various technical terms, the most important of which are introduced below.

Those who are familiar with these terms (e.g. because they have already studied Latin) should nevertheless read **6–7** for its introduction to some basic principles of Greek.

BASIC TERMS

Below you will find some of the basic technical terms of grammar.

Noun

'The <u>woman</u> persuades the <u>man</u>.'

1. In this sentence 'woman' and 'man' are NOUNS. Nouns name things or people, e.g. potato, telephone, Chloe, honesty, courage. Cf. 'The <u>dog</u> pursues <u>Charlotte</u>.'

Gender

2. Gender is a grammatical term and has nothing to do with males and females. Nouns come in three 'genders' in Greek – MASCULINE, FEMININE and NEUTER. Compare French or Spanish, which have two genders, masculine and feminine: 'le soleil' and 'el sol' ['the sun' in French and Spanish] are MASCULINE, but 'la lune' and 'la luna' ['the moon'] are FEMININE. The gender of a noun in a given language DOES NOT CHANGE. So 'the moon' is ALWAYS feminine in Spanish and French.

Verb and clause

'The woman <u>persuades</u> the man.'

3. (a) The word 'persuades' is a VERB. Verbs are usually 'action-words' – bring, win, walk, complain: 'I *bring*', 'you *win*', 'they *complain*'. They can also express a state: 'she *is*', 'he *remains*'. The verb tells us what is being done or happening in a sentence: 'The dog <u>pursues</u> Charlotte.' All the verbs quoted here are FINITE verbs. This means they have a person ('I', 'he' etc.), a TENSE (all referring to present time in the examples given) and a MOOD (here 'indicative': they indicate something is the case. See p.369(iv)).
   (b) Sentences often contain numbers of CLAUSES. Each clause has a FINITE verb in it, e.g. 'When Chloe left, although she forgot her glasses, she did not return to pick them up.' The finite verbs here are 'left', 'forgot', 'return' – but not 'pick'.

(c) We define these clauses in relation to each other. 'SUBORDINATE' clauses are introduced by words like 'when', 'although', 'so that', 'if', 'because', 'since' and so on. When you have removed all the subordinating clauses, you are left with the MAIN CLAUSE and the MAIN VERB (or verbs). In the example in (b), 'return' is the main verb.

Definite article

'The woman persuades the man.'

4. 'The' is what is known as the DEFINITE ARTICLE in English. As we shall see when we meet the definite article (def. art.) in Greek in the grammar for Section 1 A–B, it plays an extremely important role in translation from Greek into English.

Subject and object

'The woman persuades the man.'

5. The SUBJECT of the sentence above is 'the woman' – the woman is doing the persuading. The subject, in grammar, is the person or thing doing the action of the verb. This is very important. The subject is NOT what the sentence is about, but is the person or thing performing the verb: 'I bring the potatoes,' 'She wins the cup,' 'The dog pursues Charlotte.'

The OBJECT of the sentence above is 'the man' – the woman is persuading the man. The object is the person or thing on the receiving end of the verb. Examples: 'You bite the apple,' 'Toby likes sport,' 'The dog pursues Charlotte.'

WORD SHAPE AND WORD ORDER

6. One of the most important differences between Greek and English is that in English it is the *order* of the words which tells you what a sentence means, but in Greek it is the changing *shape* of the words. For example, in English the following two sentences mean very different things:

'The woman persuades the man.'

'The man persuades the woman.'

The difference in meaning between these two sentences lies in the *word order*. This tells you who or what is doing the persuading. In the first 'the woman' comes before 'persuades' and this tells you the woman is persuading. In the second 'the man' comes before 'persuades' and so it is the man who is persuading.

Now read the following two sentences in Greek:

ἡ γυνὴ πείθει τὸν ἄνθρωπον.
| | | | |
'The woman persuades the man.'

τὴν γυναῖκα   πείθει   ὁ ἄνθρωπος
| | | | |
'The woman   persuades the   man.'

Both sentences have the same word order in Greek: woman – persuades – man. But the *meaning* is quite different: the first means 'The woman persuades the man,' but the second, despite the order of the words, in fact means 'The man persuades the woman'. What is going on? How can we tell which is which?

– In Greek it is the *shape of the words* which tells you what job any word is doing and therefore what a sentence as a whole means – in this case, who is persuading whom. The changes to words in Greek usually (but not always) come at the *end* of words.

Now look at the changes of *word shape* in the two sentences given above. You will observe that ἡ γυνὴ contrasts with τὴν γυναῖκα, and τὸν ἄνθρωπον with ὁ ἄνθρωπος. The reason is as follows:

– In the first sentence 'the woman' is the *subject* (the woman is doing the persuading) and the Greek form for 'the woman-as-subject' is ἡ γυνή.
– In the second, she is the *object* (she is on the receiving end of the persuasion) and the Greek form for that is τὴν γυναῖκα (now you know where 'gynaecology' comes from).
– In the same way, 'the man' is the subject in the second sentence and the Greek form is ὁ ἄνθρωπος;
– but when he is the object in the first sentence, the Greek is τὸν ἄνθρωπον.
– Notice also how the def. art. changes as well: it is ὁ (masculine) or ἡ (feminine) when its noun is the *subject*, but τόν (masculine) or τήν (feminine) when its noun is the *object*.

> ▶ **RULE:** pay close attention at all times to the changes in word shape in Greek. There are also examples of changing word shapes in English, usually left-overs from an earlier period. For example:

– 'I', 'he' and 'she' are the *subject shapes* of the sentence;
– 'me', 'him' and 'her' the shapes for the object and everything else.
– So 'There is a dispute between me, him and her', not 'between I, he and she'.

CASE: SUBJECT AND OBJECT

7. Look at the following sentences in English (and note that, while in English we say 'Hegestratos', in Greek it is common to say '*the* Hegestratos'):

'[The] Hegestratos sees [the] Sdenothemis.'

'[The] Sdenothemis chases the sailors.'

'The woman persuades [the] Hegestratos.'

What are the SUBJECTS in each of these sentences? What are the OBJECTS? Now examine the same sentences in Greek:

ὁ Ἡγέστρατος ὁρᾷ τὸν Ζηνόθεμιν.

ὁ Ζηνόθεμις διώκει τοὺς ναύτας.

ἡ γυνὴ πείθει τὸν Ἡγέστρατον.

What are the differences between the Greek for '[the] Hegestratos' when Hegestratos is SUBJECT and when he is OBJECT? What form would '[the] Zenothemis' have if he were the SUBJECT?

Case

The grammatical term for these different word shapes is CASE. Nouns in Greek have a different shape, a different CASE, according to whether they are subject or object in a sentence.

We have already met several examples of different cases in Greek:

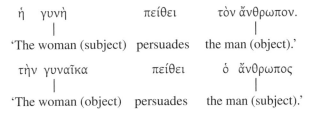

The cases in Greek have different names:

The case of the subject is the NOMINATIVE case.
The case of the object is the ACCUSATIVE case.

ἡ γυνὴ is the nominative of 'the woman' in Greek, and τὴν γυναῖκα is the accusative. 'The woman' has the shape ἡ γυνὴ, the nominative case, when it is the subject of a sentence (e.g. when the woman persuades someone), but when 'the woman' is the object of a sentence (e.g. when someone persuades the woman), it has the shape τὴν γυναῖκα, the accusative.

Other cases and word shapes of verbs will be explained later.

Grammar for Section 1A–B

In this section you cover:
- The definite article 'the', ὁ ἡ τό
- The principle of 'agreement'
- Adjectives like καλός καλή καλόν
- The vocative case

VOCABULARY CHECK

Ensure you know the meaning of:

ἆρα	ἔπειτα	τίς;
δέ	καί	ὦ
δεῦρο	σύ	
ἐγώ	τε . . . καί	

VOCABULARY NEEDED FOR 9 (p.9)

βαίνω I go
βαίνει he/she/it goes
ἐν Βυζαντίῳ in
  Byzantium
ἡ γῆ the land
τὴν γῆν the land

ἐστιν is
ὁ ἡ τό the
ὁ ναύτης the sailor
οἱ ναῦται the sailors
ὁρῶσι [they] see
τὸ πλοῖον the ship

ὁ ῥαψῳδός the rhapsode
τὸν ῥαψῳδόν the rhapsode

'DECLENSION' OF THE DEFINITE ARTICLE

8. We have met several examples of the def. art. in Greek, which corresponds to 'the' in English: τὸ πλοῖον, 'the ship', ὁ κυβερνήτης, 'the helmsman', οἱ ναῦται, 'the sailors'. Here is the def. art. set out in the traditional pattern common to all adjectives and nouns (called a 'declension'), showing how def. art. 'declines':

The definite article ὁ, ἡ, τό, 'the'

	Singular		
	m.	*f.*	*n.*
Nominative	ὁ	ἡ	τό
Accusative	τόν	τήν	τό
Genitive	τοῦ	τῆς	τοῦ
Dative	τῷ	τῇ	τῷ

The definite article ὁ, ἡ, τό, 'the' *(continued)*			
	Plural		
	m.	*f.*	*n.*
Nominative	οἱ	αἱ	τά
Accusative	τούς	τᾱς	τά
Genitive	τῶν	τῶν	τῶν
Dative	τοῖς	ταῖς	τοῖς

You have already met the nominative and accusative cases. We shall be concentrating on these for the moment. But you can see that there are two other cases, the genitive (often meaning 'of') and dative (often meaning 'to', 'for' or 'by').

▶ **It is essential that you learn all these forms now.** Their functions will be fully discussed later. The cases will often be referred to in their shortened forms as nom., acc., gen. and dat.

The principle of agreement

9. Translate the following sentences:

ὁ ῥαψῳδὸς βαίνει.

τὸ πλοῖόν ἐστιν ἐν Βυζαντίῳ.

οἱ ναῦται ὁρῶσι τὴν γῆν καὶ τὸν ῥαψῳδόν.

What marks the SUBJECT in each of them? What marks the OBJECT (note there is no object in the first two sentences)? The reason the article is ὁ when 'the rhapsode' is the SUBJECT and τόν when 'the rhapsode' is the OBJECT is that the article changes to AGREE with the noun with which it is linked. That is to say, it changes form according to:

- the GENDER of its noun (i.e. whether the noun is masculine, feminine or neuter – remember the GENDER of a noun never changes),
- the CASE its noun is in (e.g. nom. if it is the subject),
- and the NUMBER of the noun (i.e. whether it is SINGULAR or PLURAL).

If the noun with which the article is linked is MASCULINE, NOM., and SINGULAR, the article will *also* be MASCULINE, NOM., and SINGULAR. This is what we mean by saying the article is 'agreeing' with its noun. So:

ἡ γυνὴ πείθει τὸν ἄνθρωπον. ('The woman persuades the man.')

'The woman' = ἡ γυνή when 'the woman' is the subject, because ἡ γυνή is FEMININE, NOM., SINGULAR. What would be the form of the def. art. if 'the woman' were the *object*?

ἆρα ἀκούεις καὶ σὺ τὸν ψόφον; ('Do you also hear the noise?')

'The noise' = <u>τὸν</u> ψόφον when 'the noise' is the object, because ψόφον is MASCULINE, ACC., SINGULAR. What would be the form of the def. art. if 'the noise' were the *subject*?

οἱ ναῦται εἰσβαίνουσιν εἰς τὸ πλοῖον. ('The sailors go onto the ship.')

'The sailors' = <u>οἱ</u> ναῦται when 'the sailors' are the subject, because ναῦται is MASCULINE, NOM., PLURAL. What would the form of the def. art. be if 'the sailors' were the *object*?

ποῦ ἐστιν ἡ ἀκρόπολις; ('Where is the Acropolis?')

'The Acropolis' = <u>ἡ</u> ἀκρόπολις when 'the Acropolis' is the subject, because ἀκρόπολις is FEMININE, NOM., SINGULAR. What would the form of the def. art. be if 'the Acropolis' were the *object*?

The def. art. is your *anchor* in the sentence:

> ▶ See οἱ, and you know the noun it goes with is subject, plural, masculine.
> ▶ See τόν, and you know the noun it goes with is object, singular, masculine, and so on.
> ▶ So even if you do not know how the NOUN changes, the def. art. will tell you exactly the function in the sentence of the noun it agrees with.

See how useful the def. art is by doing the following examples. You have not yet met or learned any of the nouns involved, though you can have a guess at their meaning. But you can tell a great deal about them by the preceding def. art. So, using each word's def. art. as your guide to the answer, write down the GENDER, CASE, and NUMBER (where possible) of each:

τὴν πόλιν (cf. 'political')	τῆς δημοκρατίας
τὸν βασιλέα (cf. 'basil', king of herbs)	τῷ Ὁμήρῳ
οἱ γέροντες (cf. 'gerontologist')	τῶν ἀτόμων
τὰς τριήρεις (cf. 'trireme')	ταῖς τέχναις

Would τὴν πόλιν be SUBJECT or OBJECT in a sentence?
What about οἱ γέροντες?
The def. art. tells you this even if you have learnt nothing at all about the noun or the ways it changes.

> ▶ **RULE:** always PAY THE CLOSEST ATTENTION to the def. art.: it will tell you immediately the function of the noun to which it is

attached. Those who have studied Latin, which does *not* have a def. art., will realise how enormously helpful this is.

EXERCISE

1A–B: 1. Name the GENDER, CASE, and NUMBER (where possible) of the following def. art. + noun combinations (guess again at the meaning of the nouns):

1. τῇ σκηνῇ
2. ἡ δημοκρατία
3. τὸ νεῦρον
4. τοῦ σκελετοῦ
5. τοὺς ὀφθαλμούς
6. τὸ ἆσθμα
7. τοῖς δεσπόταις
8. τῶν σπόγγων
9. τὰ κρανία
10. τῆς τραγῳδίας

VOCABULARY NEEDED FOR 11

ἡ ἀκρόπολις the acropolis
καλός καλή καλόν beautiful, fine; good
τὸ νεώριον the dockyard
ὁ Παρθενών the Parthenon

ADJECTIVES

10. So far you have met two Greek ADJECTIVES (i.e. a 'describing-word', e.g. red, brave, tall, honest). They are 'the' and καλός, 'fine, beautiful'. καλός declines (see **8**) as follows:

καλ-ός -ή -όν, 'fine, beautiful, good'

Singular

	m.	*f.*	*n.*
Nom.	καλ-ός	καλ-ή	καλ-όν
Acc.	καλ-όν	καλ-ήν	καλ-όν
Gen.	καλ-οῦ	καλ-ῆς	καλ-οῦ
Dat.	καλ-ῷ	καλ-ῇ	καλ-ῷ
Vocative	καλ-έ		

Plural

	m.	*f.*	*n.*
Nom.	καλ-οί	καλ-αί	καλ-ά
Acc.	καλ-ούς	καλ-άς	καλ-ά
Gen.	καλ-ῶν	καλ-ῶν	καλ-ῶν
Dat.	καλ-οῖς	καλ-αῖς	καλ-οῖς

▶ Observe that a new case has been added, the VOCATIVE (voc.). It is used when addressing people ('O man'). In many cases, the nom. and voc. forms are identical; so it is added to the declension *only where it is different from the nom.* Its function will be fully discussed later (see **22**).

Agreement of adjectives

11. Observe how καλός changes in each of these sentences:

ὡς <u>καλός</u> ἐστιν ὁ Παρθενών.

<u>καλή</u> δὲ ἡ ἀκρόπολις.

ὡς <u>καλόν</u> ἐστι τὸ νεώριον.

Why does it change? For the same reason that the def. art. does: the form of καλός changes to AGREE with its noun in GENDER, CASE, and NUMBER.

● In the sentences above, Παρθενών is MASCULINE, NOM., SINGULAR, so the definite article has the form ὁ (which itself tells us all of this information), and the adjective has the form καλός, which is MASCULINE, NOM., SINGULAR.

● Contrast this with ἀκρόπολις, which is FEMININE, NOM., SINGULAR, so that its definite article has the form ἡ and its adjective the form καλή, which is *also* FEMININE, NOM., SINGULAR (it AGREES with its noun in GENDER, CASE, NUMBER).

▶ In other words, just like def. art. ὁ ἡ τό, the endings of καλός change according to the GENDER, CASE, and NUMBER of its accompanying noun.

Observe how similar the endings of καλ-ός -ή -όν are to the def. art., making it easy to learn if you know ὁ ἡ τό.

▶ There is an important lesson here: learn one set of forms in ancient Greek and you will be able to apply them across many others.

From now on, masculine, feminine and neuter will be denoted by m., f., and n.; and singular and plural by s. and pl.

EXERCISE

1A–B: 2. Write the correct form of καλ-ός -ή -όν for the following nouns (remember you can tell their GENDER, CASE, and NUMBER from their def. art.), e.g. τὸν – ψόφον = τὸν καλὸν ψόφον. See if you can remember the meaning of any of the nouns:

1. ὁ – κυβερνήτης	6. τὴν – ἀκρόπολιν
2. τὸ – πλοῖον	7. τὸν – Παρθενῶνα
3. τοῦ – ἔργου	8. ταῖς – βοαῖς
4. τὰς – Ἀθήνας	9. τῷ – πλοίῳ
5. τοῖς – ἀνθρώποις	10. τῇ – ἀκροπόλει

SUMMARY LEARNING VOCABULARY FOR SECTION 1A–B

The *Summary Learning Vocabularies*, which occur from time to time throughout the *Grammar* for revision and testing purposes, contain all the words now needing to be learned. Some you should have learned already from the *Running Vocabularies*; others will have been used in the *Exercises*. The words listed in these places will be used extensively in the ensuing *Revision Exercise*

ἀκρόπολις, ἡ	acropolis
ἆρα	indicates a question
βαίνω (βα-)*	I come, go, walk
γῆ, ἡ	land
δέ	and, but
δεῦρο	over here
ἐγώ	I (sometimes emphatic)
ἔπειτα	then, next
καί	and, also
καλ-ός ή όν	beautiful, fine, good
ναύτης, ὁ	sailor
νεώριον, τό	dockyard
ὁ ἡ τό	the
Παρθενών, ὁ	the Parthenon
πλοῖον, τό	vessel, ship
ῥαψῳδός, ὁ	rhapsode
σύ	you (s.)
τε ... καί...	A and B, both A and B
τίς	who? what?
ὦ	O (addressing someone)

*Asterisked words contain very important alternative stems (in brackets) which must be learned now. Their significance will be explained later. Stems are parts of words that do not change.

TAKING STOCK
1. Can you decline ὁ and καλός?
2. Do you understand the principles of agreement between noun and adjective?

Grammar for Section 1C–D

In this section you cover:
- Verbs ending in -ω (present 'tense', indicative 'mood', active 'voice')
- Tense, mood, voice, person and number
- Compound verbs (with prefixes)
- The imperative [command/order] 'mood'
- The vocative case

VOCABULARY CHECK

Ensure you know the meaning of:

ἀληθῆ	ἡμεῖς	οὖν
ἀλλά	μή	τί;
βαίνω	οἱ ναῦται	ὑμεῖς
γάρ	οὐ, οὐκ, οὐχ	ὡς
ἔγωγε	οὐδέν	

VOCABULARY NEEDED FOR THE EXERCISES

ἀκούω I hear, listen
βλέπω I look (at)
διώκω I pursue
εἰσβαίνω I go [onto], on board

καταβαίνω I descend, go/come down
μένω I remain, wait for
φεύγω I run off, flee

VERBS IN -ω

12. CONJUGATION is the technical term for a set of verb forms (cf. 'declension', **8**). Here is the conjugation of βαίνω 'I go/am going/do go', in the present indicative active:

βαίνω 'I go/am going/do go'

Stem	Ending	Meaning	Description
βαίν-	ω	'I go', 'I am going'	first person s. (1 s.)
βαίν-	εις	'you go', 'you are going'	second person s. (2 s.)
βαίν-	ει	'he/she/it goes' (etc.)	third person s. (3 s.)
βαίν-	ομεν	'we go'	first person pl. (1 pl.)
βαίν-	ετε	'you go'	second person pl. (2 pl.)
βαίν-	ουσι(ν)	'they go'	third person pl. (3 pl.)

Form and use of verbs

In the technical description 'Present indicative active':

▶ 'Present' shows the *tense* (other 'tenses' are e.g. future, 'I shall – ', imperfect 'I was -ing', etc.)

▶ 'Indicative' shows the *mood* (in this case, it *indicates* that something is happening; the other 'moods' are imperative, infinitive, subjunctive, and optative)

▶ 'Active' shows the *voice* (that it is the subject *doing* the action; the two other 'voices' are 'middle' and 'passive').

■ *Tense*

13. Verbs (in Greek and in English) have different TENSES, that is, sets of different forms which show *when* the action of the verb takes place, in the past, present, or future. For example, in English, 'I go' is in the present tense, but 'I went' is in the past tense, 'I shall go' is in the future. The forms of βαίνω conjugated here are the present tense of the Greek verb 'to go'.

■ *Mood*

14. Verbs also have different 'moods': the 'indicative' tells you something is *indicated* as occurring (or, with the negative οὐ, οὐκ, οὐχ, not occurring!), the 'imperative' expresses a command ('learn this!'), and so on.

■ *Voice*

15. The 'active' voice tells you that the subject is doing the action ('Charlotte is carrying the book'); the 'passive' voice that something is being done to the subject ('the book is being carried'). The passive voice will be met and learned later.

■ *Person and number*

16a. The forms of a verb differ according to NUMBER, that is whether the verb is s. or pl., and PERSON. There are three persons:

first person	'I', s. 'we', pl.
second person	'you', s. and pl. (Greek uses different forms for s. and pl. 'you'.)
third person	'he/she/it', s., 'they', pl.

In English we indicate the PERSON of a verb by using a pronoun like 'I' or 'you', but in Greek it is the ENDING of the verb which tells you the person:

βαίν-εις	'you go' (or 'go-you' as a Greek would hear it)
βαίν-ουσι	'they go' ('go-they')

All verbs ending in -ω like βαίνω follow the same pattern of endings. We have met ἀκούω, βλέπω, φεύγω, μένω and διώκω. Once you have mastered βαίνω, you will know the endings of all of these other verbs also (indeed, most verbs in Greek). The golden rule again: learn one set of forms, and you can apply them to many other sets.

■ *'Thematic' verbs*

16b. All -ω verbs are also 'thematic'. A 'thematic' verb is one consisting of stem + 'thematic' vowel + person endings. The 'thematic' vowels are:

1s.	-o-	1pl.	-o-
2s.	-ε-	2pl.	-ε-
3s.	-ε-	3pl.	-o-

This o ε ε o ε o pattern will recur elsewhere.

■ *Compound verbs*

17. In Greek you can make COMPOUND VERBS from simple verbs like βαίνω by adding a prefix. We have seen some examples of this:

εἰσ-βαίνω   'I go <u>into, on board</u>' ('into-go-I')

κατα-βαίνω   'I go <u>down</u>' ('down-go-I')

The endings for these compound verbs are the same as for simple βαίνω. Look out for compounds of other simple Greek verbs you meet. The basic meaning is usually close to, but different from, that of the simple verb. Cf. English 'import', 'export', 'transport', 'deport', 'report', etc.

EXERCISES

1C–D: 1. Translate into English:

1. οὐκ ἀκούεις	6. βαίνουσι
2. βλέπομεν	7. οὐ βλέπετε
3. μένουσιν	8. ἀκούει
4. οὐ φεύγει	9. φεύγεις
5. διώκεις	10. μένει

1C–D: 2. Translate into Greek. Remember one Greek word will often correspond to several English words for the same action (e.g. 'you are going' = βαίνεις). In this exercise, all the answers are one word in Greek:

1. They hear	6. He is running for it
2. She is looking at	7. They chase
3. You (pl.) pursue	8. You (s.) look at
4. I am going	9. We are waiting
5. They do not remain	10. He does not hear

IMPERATIVE

18. The imperative 'mood' is the form of a verb which is used to express orders or commands, e.g. 'stop!' in English.

βαῖνε	**'go!'**

βαῖν-ε	'go!'	s. (telling one person to go)
βαίν-ετε	'go!'	pl. (telling more than one person to go)

Form and use of imperatives

19. Translate and observe the differences between the following two Greek sentences:

> ὁ Ζηνόθεμις <u>βαίνει</u>.

> ὦ Ζηνόθεμι, <u>βαῖνε</u>.

While βαίνει is the indicative 'mood', showing that Sdenothemis is going, βαῖνε is in the imperative 'mood', ordering him to go. Again, all regular verbs ending in -ω follow this pattern of imperative endings.

■ *An ambiguity*

20. You may have noticed a problem here. The pl. *imperative* mood, βαίνετε is identical to that of the second person pl. *indicative* mood. So βαίνετε could mean either 'go!' (pl.) or 'you (pl.) are going'. Only the context can give you the right answer. For 'mood', see p. 369 (iv).

■ *Ordering someone not to*

21. In Greek, to make an imperative negative, i.e. to tell someone NOT to do something, put μή before the imperative:

μὴ βαῖνε	'do not go!' (s.)
μὴ βαίνετε	'do not go!' (pl.)

> ▶ So: the imperative is a 'mood', expressing an order (negative μή); and the 2pl. imperative and 2pl. indicative, having identical forms, need to be distinguished by context.

VOCATIVE CASE

22. In the sentence ὦ Ζηνόθεμι, βαῖνε, the form Ζηνόθεμι is in the VOC. case.

> ▶ The VOC. is the 'calling' CASE – used when someone is being called or addressed (cf. 'Play it again, Sam'). Its form is frequently identical to the nom. (see **10**).

The voc. is often prefaced with ὦ in Greek, and is usually found with IMPERATIVES (as βαῖνε above) or second-person verbs (e.g. βαίνεις and βαίνετε, 'you are going'). The voc. is sometimes distinguished from the nom. in the s.; in the pl., nom. and voc. are *always* the same, e.g.

οἱ <u>ναῦται</u> τὸν Ἡγέστρατον διώκουσιν.

ὦ <u>ναῦται</u>, διώκετε.

EXERCISE

1C–D: 3. Translate into English (specify whether the imperative is s. or pl. – unless you think the imperative mood is not being used …):

1. βαῖνε	6. μὴ βλέπετε
2. βλέπε	7. καταβαίνετε
3. ὦ ναῦται, διώκετε	8. βαίνετε
4. ἄκουε	9. ὦ Ἡγέστρατε, μὴ μένε
5. φεύγετε	10. μὴ εἰσβαίνετε

SUMMARY LEARNING VOCABULARY FOR SECTION 1C–D

ἀκούω	hear, listen
ἀληθῆ	the truth
ἀλλά	but, alternatively
βλέπω	look (at)
γάρ	for, because
διώκω	chase, pursue
ἔγωγε	I at least/at any rate
εἰσβαίνω (εἰσβα-)*	enter, board
ἡμεῖς	we
καταβαίνω (καταβα-)	go/come down
μένω (μεινα-)	remain, wait for
μή	don't!
οὐ, οὐκ, οὐχ	no, not
οὐδέν	nothing
οὖν	so, then, really, therefore
τί	what?
ὑμεῖς	you (pl.)
φεύγω	flee, run away/off
ὡς	how!

TAKING STOCK
1. Can you confidently conjugate βαίνω?
2. Do you know the imperative forms and their negative?

---

*Learn now the stems in brackets. They will come into play later on.

Grammar for Section 1E–F

In this section you cover:
- 'Contract' verbs (-άω, -έω, -όω): present indicative and imperative
- Rules of 'contract'
- Adverbs (' -ly')

VOCABULARY CHECK

Ensure you know the meaning of:

μέν . . . δέ   ποῖ;   σεαυτόν
οἴμοι   ποῦ;

VOCABULARY NEEDED FOR THE EXERCISES

ἀκρῑβ-ῶς accurately, closely   καλῶς finely, beautifully
βαθέως deeply   ὁράω see
βοηθέω help, run to help   ποιέω make, do
δηλόω show, reveal   σαφῶς clearly
κακῶς badly, evilly

'CONTRACT' VERBS

23. Verbs ending in -ω like βαίνω are the 'normal' Greek verbs which we met
in the Grammar for 1C–D. Verbs whose stem (the part that does not change)
ends in a vowel, like ὁρά-ω, 'I see', have slightly different endings. These are
called CONTRACTED or CONTRACT verbs. There are three types, named
after the vowels in which their original stem ended. These are:

>   α-contracts (e.g. ὁρά-ω);
>
>   ε-contracts (e.g. ποιέ-ω, 'I do/make'); and
>
>   o-contracts (e.g. δηλό-ω, 'I show').

They will be shown *uncontracted* (that is, with that vowel still present) in the
vocabularies.
Note that contraction is confined to verbs whose stem ends in α-, ε- or o-. So
verbs like κελεύ-ω or κλαί-ω are NOT contract verbs, but take endings like
βαίν-ω.

Forming contract verbs

24. Note that the *uncontracted* forms are given first in each of the three columns
(it is, of course, the *contracted* forms you will be using to read and write).

ὁρά-ω→ὁρ-ῶ 'I see', ποιέ-ω→ποι-ῶ 'I make, do', δηλό-ω→ δηλ-ῶ 'I show'

	α-contract		ε-contract		o-contract	
1s.	ὁρά-ω →	ὁρ-ῶ	ποιέ-ω →	ποι-ῶ	δηλό-ω →	δηλ-ῶ
2s.	ὁρά-εις →	ὁρ-ᾷς	ποιέ-εις →	ποι-εῖς	δηλό-εις →	δηλ-οῖς
3s.	ὁρά-ει →	ὁρ-ᾷ	ποιέ-ει →	ποι-εῖ	δηλό-ει →	δηλ-οῖ
1pl.	ὁρά-ομεν →	ὁρ-ῶμεν	ποιέ-ομεν →	ποι-οῦμεν	δηλό-ομεν →	δηλ-οῦμεν
2pl.	ὁρά-ετε →	ὁρ-ᾶτε	ποιέ-ετε →	ποι-εῖτε	δηλό-ετε →	δηλ-οῦτε
3pl.	ὁρά-ουσι →	ὁρ-ῶσι	ποιέ-ουσι →	ποι-οῦσι	δηλό-ουσι →	δηλ-οῦσι

Rules of contract

25. In early Greek, such verbs were *uncontracted*. But over time the contract vowel began to blend with the endings to produce a new-look ending, which you can see above. It is rather like English 'I've', 'he's', 'they're'. The pattern of the contractions is entirely predictable, according to the following table. To use it, find the first vowel in the left-hand column and the second in the top row – where they intersect is the contraction which you get when these two vowels come together *in that order*. For example, α + ε = α, while ε + α = η.

	α	ε	ει	ι	η	ῃ	o	ου	οι	ω	ῳ
α	α	α	ᾳ	αι	α	ᾳ	ω	ω	ῳ	ω	ῳ
ε	η	ει	ει	ει	η	ῃ	ου	ου	οι	ω	ῳ
o	ω	ου	οι	οι	ω	οι	ου	ου	οι	ω	ῳ

■ *A learning strategy for contracts*

On the grounds that learning the whole chart off by heart could well induce contractions, two options are available:

(a) Learn just the contractions relevant to this tense, i.e.

1. α + o/ου/ω = ω,   α + ε/ει = α (ι goes subscript)
2. ε + ω = ω,   ε + ε/ει = ει,   ε + o/ου = ου
3. o + ω = ω,   o + ε/o/ου = ου, anything with iota = οι

(b) Learn the contract verbs as mere variations on verbs ending in -ω like βαίνω. Compare their endings in the present indicative active below with those of βαίνω:

	Uncontracted βαίν-	**α-contract** ὁρά-	**ε-contract** ποιέ-	**o-contract** δηλό-
1s.	βαίν-ω	ὁρ-ῶ	ποι-ῶ	δηλ-ῶ
2s.	βαίν-εις	ὁρ-ᾷς	ποι-εῖς	δηλ-οῖς
3s.	βαίν-ει	ὁρ-ᾷ	ποι-εῖ	δηλ-οῖ
1pl.	βαίν-ομεν	ὁρ-ῶμεν	ποι-οῦμεν	δηλ-οῦμεν
2pl.	βαίν-ετε	ὁρ-ᾶτε	ποι-εῖτε	δηλ-οῦτε
3pl.	βαίν-ουσι(ν)	ὁρ-ῶσι(ν)	ποι-οῦσι(ν)	δηλ-οῦσι(ν)

▶ Again, the golden rule applies: when you have learnt the contracted forms of ὁρά-ω, ποιέ-ω and δηλό-ω, you will be able to recognise and form the present indicative active of *all* contract verbs.

EXERCISES

1E–F: 1. Translate into English:

1. ὁρᾷς	6. βοηθεῖς
2. ὁρᾷ	7. δηλοῖς
3. ὁρῶσιν	8. ποιεῖς
4. ποιοῦμεν	9. δηλοῦτε
5. δηλοῦσιν	10. βοηθεῖ

1E–F: 2. Translate into Greek (n.b. one-word answers throughout):

1. They see	6. He makes
2. She makes	7. They do
3. You (pl.) do	8. You (s.) show
4. I show	9. We see
5. They are helping	10. He is doing

1E–F: 3. Write the contracted form of the following verbs (you do not need to know what the verbs mean):

1. τιμά-ω	6. ἀσθενέ-ει
2. γαμέ-εις	7. ἐλευθερό-ομεν
3. οἰκέ-ουσι	8. ἐξαπατά-ει
4. σιγά-ομεν	9. νοσέ-ω
5. ἀσεβέ-ετε	10. τιμά-ετε

CONTRACT IMPERATIVES

26. Contract verbs also have imperatives. You will be able to predict what those forms will be by using the chart at **25** above. But consult the following chart, again comparing contracts with βαίνω:

	ὅρα 'see!',	ποίει 'do!/make!',	δήλου 'show!'
uncontracted	α-contracts	ε-contracts	o-contracts
s. βαῖν-ε	ὅρ-α 'see!'	ποί-ει 'do!/make!'	δήλ-ου 'show!'
pl. βαίν-ετε	ὁρ-ᾶτε 'see!'	ποι-εῖτε 'do!/make!'	δηλ-οῦτε 'show!'

■ *Accent on ε-contract imperatives*

27. Pay particular attention to the accent on imperative s. active ποίει ('do!'). This distinguishes it from the third person s. indicative active ποιεῖ ('he/she/it does').

EXERCISES

1E–F: 4. Translate into English:

1. ὅρα	6. μένε
2. ποίει	7. βαίνετε (two translations)
3. ποιεῖ	8. ποιεῖς
4. ὁρᾷ	9. μὴ δήλου
5. μὴ δηλοῦτε	10. δηλοῖ

1E–F: 5. Translate into Greek:

1. Do not wait! (pl.)	6. He makes
2. Chase! (s.)	7. Do not do! (s.)
3. Show! (pl.)	8. He sees
4. Do not hear! (s.)	9. See! (s.)
5. Help! (s.)	10. Do not go! (s.)

ADVERBS

28. In English, adverbs usually end in '-ly' – actuall̲y, normall̲y, beautifull̲y, quickl̲y, slowl̲y. They tell you *how* or *in what way* the action of a verb is done, or they *modify* (i.e. make a difference to) an adjective. For example:

- 'He played *beautifully*' tells you *how* someone *played* (verb);
- '*Extremely* cold' tells you *how* cold (adjective) it is.

Forming adverbs

29. Adverbs in Greek *do not change form*. Observe how these adverbs are formed from adjectives and deduce the rule:

Adjective	Gen. masc. pl.	Adverb
καλ-ός 'fine/beautiful'	καλ-ῶν	καλ-ῶς 'finely/beautifully'
κακ-ός 'bad/evil'	κακ-ῶν	κακ-ῶς 'badly/evilly'
σαφ-ής 'clear'	σαφ-ῶν	σαφ-ῶς 'clearly'
βαθ-ύς 'deep'	βαθ-έων	βαθ-έως 'deeply'
ἀκριβ-ής 'accurate'	ἀκρῑβ-ῶν	ἀκρῑβ-ῶς 'accurately'

▶   The rule, then, is that adverbs (which do not change their forms) are mostly formed by substituting ς for the ν at the end of the m. gen. pl. form of the adjective. So most adverbs end with -ῶς or -έως.

SUMMARY LEARNING VOCABULARY FOR SECTION 1E–F

ἀκρῑβ-ῶς	accurately, closely
βαθέως	deeply
βοηθέω	help, run to help
δηλόω	show, reveal
κακῶς	badly, evilly
καλῶς	finely, beautifully
μέν ... δέ ...	on the one hand ... on the other
οἴμοι	alas! Oh dear!
ὁράω	see
ποῖ;	to where?
ποιέω	make, do
ποῦ;	where (at)?
σαφῶς	clearly
σεαυτόν	yourself (s.)

TAKING STOCK
1. Can you conjugate ὁράω in its contracted forms in the present, with the imperative forms?
2. Can you repeat the exercise with ποιέω?
3. Do you know what an adverb is, and how to form one?

Grammar for Section 1G

In this section you cover:
- Nouns like ἄνθρωπος ('man', 2a) and ἔργον ('work', 2b)
- Patterns of 'declension'
- Neuter nouns as subject or object
- Adjectives like ἡμέτερος ἡμετέρᾱ ἡμέτερον
- Prepositions like 'towards', 'from', 'in'
- Particles and their position; enclitics
- Translating English into Greek

VOCABULARY NEEDED FOR THE EXERCISES

ὁ ἄνθρωπος the man; fellow
δύω sink
τὸ ἔργον the task, work, job; duty
τὸ ἐμπόριον the market-hall,
   trading-post
ἡμέτερος -ᾱ -ον our(s)

κακός ή όν bad, evil; cowardly;
   lowly, mean
ὁ κυβερνήτης the captain, helmsman
ὁ λέμβος the boat, life-boat
σῶος ᾱ ον safe

NOUNS: TYPES 2A AND 2B

30. Like def. art. and adjectives, all nouns in Greek – words like ἄνθρωπος 'man'
and ἔργον 'work' – change shape in accordance with their function in the
sentence (e.g. subject or object, s. or pl.). Here are the declensions (see **8** for
this term) of two very common types of noun, labelled 2a and 2b:

ἄνθρωπος, ὁ 'man/fellow' (2a)

	s.	pl.
Nom.	ἄνθρωπ-ος	ἄνθρωπ-οι
Acc.	ἄνθρωπ-ον	ἀνθρώπ-ους
Gen.	ἀνθρώπ-ου	ἀνθρώπ-ων
Dat.	ἀνθρώπ-ῳ	ἀνθρώπ-οις
Voc.	ὦ ἄνθρωπ-ε	

ἔργον, τό 'task/duty/job/work' (2b)

	s.	pl.
Nom.	ἔργ-ον	ἔργ-α
Acc.	ἔργ-ον	ἔργ-α
Gen.	ἔργ-ου	ἔργ-ων
Dat.	ἔργ-ῳ	ἔργ-οις

The declensions

31. Broadly speaking, there are THREE DECLENSIONS in Greek.

- stems in α- (Type 1)
- stems in o- (Type 2)
- all the rest (Type 3)

Each DECLENSION or TYPE has a number of sub-types, reflecting slight differences in the endings used (these sub-types will be called 1a–d, 2a and b, and 3a–h).

▶ *All* TYPE 2a nouns follow the same pattern as ἄνθρωπος, while *all* TYPE 2b nouns follow the pattern of ἔργον: the golden rule, again.

■ *2a nouns*

32. The endings of the cases of TYPE 2a nouns like ἄνθρωπος are very similar to those of the masc. and neut. def. art. (**8**), and the m. forms of the adjective καλός (**10**). Most TYPE 2a nouns are m., though there are a few feminines and some (e.g. ἄνθρωπος) which are m. or f.

■ *2b nouns*

33. Again, the endings of TYPE 2b nouns are similar to those of the neuter def. art. and the neuter forms of καλός. TYPES 2a and 2b therefore have very similar endings – only nom. and voc. s., and nom., voc., and acc. pl. are different. TYPE 2b nouns are all neuter. N. nouns are often inanimate, or regarded as effectively inanimate, e.g. τὸ νεώριον and τὸ ἐμπόριον (what do these two nouns mean?) and some diminutive, perhaps affectionate, like παιδίον 'child, slave' (!).

Neuter nouns

■ *Subject or object?*

34. Consider the following sentences:

τὸ πλοῖον δύει ὁ Ἡγέστρατος.

τὸ πλοῖόν ἐστιν ἐν Βυζαντίῳ.

Is τὸ πλοῖον SUBJECT or OBJECT in the first sentence? What about the second sentence?
The nom. and acc. s. and nom. and acc. pl. of *all* n. nouns and adjectives are *identical*. Therefore:

▶ Only the context of the sentence will tell you whether the noun in question is subject or object; if it is not immediately clear what the meaning is, you will have to try both.
▶ Nor will the def. art. help here, because that too follows the n. 'rule': τό is nom. and acc. s., and τά nom. and acc. pl.

■ *Neuter pl. subjects*

35. Examine these two sentences:

> τὰ ἐμπόριά ἐστι καλά.
>
> τὰ πλοῖα βαίνει.

What is the subject in the first sentence? Is it s. or pl.? Is the verb s. or pl.? Ask the same questions of the second sentence.

> ▶ The conclusion? N. pl. subjects (normally) take a s. verb, as in our examples above.

EXERCISES

1G: 1. Write the correct form of ἄνθρωπος or ἔργον for the following def. art. + adjective combinations. Check the *gender* of the def. art. + adj. to determine which noun to put with them. Sometimes you can give *two* answers:

1. τὸν καλόν –	5. τῷ κακῷ –
2. τῶν κακῶν –	6. τοὺς κακούς –
3. οἱ καλοί –	7. τῷ καλῷ –
4. τοῖς σώοις –	8. τὸ σῶον –

1G: 2. Write the correct form of the verb in brackets in the following sentences:

1. τὰ νεώρια (are) καλά.
2. οἱ ἄνθρωποι (chase) τοὺς ναύτας.
3. τὰ ἐμπόρια (make) τοὺς λέμβους.
4. ὁ κυβερνήτης (sees) τὸν ἄνθρωπον.
5. τὰ ἐμπόρια (are) κακά.

ADJECTIVES

36. There is another type of adjective very similar to adjectives like καλός. Adjectives of the ἡμέτερ-ος type have exactly the same endings as καλός in the m. and n. s. and pl., and the f. pl. They only differ in the f. s., where they have α instead of η:

ἡμέτερος -ᾱ -ον 'our(s)'

	m.	*s.* *f.*	*n.*
Nom.	ἡμέτερ-ος	ἡμετέρ-ᾱ	ἡμέτερ-ον
Acc.	ἡμέτερ-ον	ἡμετέρ-ᾱν	ἡμέτερ-ον
Gen.	ἡμετέρ-ου	ἡμετέρ-ᾱς	ἡμετέρ-ου
Dat.	ἡμετέρ-ῳ	ἡμετέρ-ᾳ	ἡμετέρ-ῳ

ἡμέτερος -ᾱ -ον 'our(s)' *(continued)*

	pl.		
	m.	*f.*	*n.*
Nom.	ἡμέτεροι	ἡμέτεραι	ἡμέτερα
Acc.	ἡμετέρους	ἡμετέρᾱς	ἡμέτερα
Gen.	ἡμετέρων	ἡμετέρων	ἡμετέρων
Dat.	ἡμετέροις	ἡμετέραις	ἡμετέροις

■ *The ι, ρ, ε rule*

37. If an adjective ends in -ος in the m. nom. s. and its stem ends in ι, ρ, ε, it will follow the pattern of ἡμέτερος (i.e. it will have α instead of η in the f. s.). For example, the f. nom. s. of ὑμέτερ-ος, 'your(s)', is ὑμετέρ-ᾱ, like ἡμετέρ-ᾱ, because its stem ends in ρ.

Check you understand this by forming all the f. s. forms for the following nouns:

ἀλλότρι-ος, 'someone else's, alien'
ἀνδρεῖ-ος, 'manly'
κακ-ός 'evil'
ἰσχῡρ-ός, 'strong, powerful'

EXERCISES

1G: 3. Translate the following phrases into Greek, using the correct form of the def. art., adjective and noun, e.g. '[the] our man' (nom.) – ὁ ἡμέτερος ἄνθρωπος:

1. The fine land (acc.)   5. The beautiful tasks (nom.)
2. [The] our tasks (dat.)   6. [The] our boat (dat.)
3. The evil men (gen.)   7. The fine market-places (gen.)
4. [The] our men (acc.)   8. The evil men (dat.)

1G: 4. Add the correct form of the noun ἄνθρωπος to the following Greek phrases and specify the CASE and NUMBER of the article, adjective and noun, e.g. ὁ καλός – ἄνθρωπος, nom. s.:

1. τὸν ἡμέτερον –   4. τοῖς ἡμετέροις –
2. τῶν καλῶν –   5. τοῦ καλοῦ –
3. τοὺς ἡμετέρους –

PREPOSITIONS

38. PREPOSITIONS are words like 'in', 'on', 'below', 'towards', 'to', followed by a noun, e.g. 'in the house', 'to the beach':

- They can indicate place or movement;
- They can express a relationship in terms of time (e.g. 'after'); or
- They can indicate something more abstract like cause (e.g. 'because of').

In Greek, they are always followed by nouns or pronouns in the acc., gen., or dat. For example: εἰς + ACC. means 'into', so εἰς τὴν θάλατταν means 'into the sea' (you can tell θάλατταν is acc. from the def. art. τήν).

- When a preposition is followed by a particular case, it is said to 'take' or 'govern' that case (so εἰς + acc. = εἰς 'takes' the acc.).
- When a noun or pronoun goes into this case because of a preposition, it is said to be 'governed' by it (e.g. τὴν θάλατταν is 'governed' by εἰς in the phrase above).

Other prepositions we have met, together with the cases they take, are:

- ▶ πρός + ACC., 'towards', e.g. πρὸς τὴν γῆν, 'towards the land'
- ▶ ἀπό + GEN., 'away from', e.g. ἀπὸ τοῦ πλοίου, 'away from the ship'
- ▶ ἐκ + GEN., 'out of/from', e.g. ἐκ τοῦ πλοίου, 'from the ship'
- ▶ ἐν + DAT., 'in', e.g. ἐν τῇ θαλάττῃ, 'in the sea'

Some prepositions may govern more than one case and differ in meaning depending on the case being taken, e.g. while πρός + ACC. means 'towards' (see above), πρός + GEN. means 'in the name of', 'from', 'under the protection of'. For the moment, however, we will meet prepositions taking one case only.

- ▶ In general, it is important to think carefully about the meaning of the preposition. For example, the meaning of 'in' in 'Get in the boat!' is different from that in 'she swims in the sea' – the former εἰς, the latter ἐν.

EXERCISES

1G: 5. Translate into English:

1. ἐν τοῖς ἐμπορίοις	6. ἀπὸ τῶν πλοίων
2. εἰς τὰ πλοῖα	7. πρὸς τὰ ἐμπόρια
3. ἐν τῷ ἔργῳ	8. εἰς τὸ πλοῖον
4. ἀπὸ τῶν ἀνθρώπων	9. ἐν τοῖς λέμβοις
5. ἐκ τοῦ ἐμπορίου	10. πρὸς τοὺς ἀνθρώπους

1G: 6. Translate into Greek:

1. Out of the ship	5. Towards the life-boat
2. Into the life-boat	6. Into the ship
3. Away from the man	7. Towards the men
4. In the ships	8. Into the markets

PARTICLES

39. You will have noticed several short Greek words such as ἀλλά, γάρ, γε, δέ, οὖν and so on. We have usually translated these with an English equivalent, such as 'but' for ἀλλά or 'for' for γάρ. Nevertheless the resulting translation can often seem a bit unnatural in English, because particles often indicate gesture, intonation, facial expression or attitude (e.g. ἀμαθής γ᾽ εἶ, 'why, you *are* stupid!') and this cannot necessarily be reproduced by a word-for-word translation. To get your translation to sound natural in English, you will often have to change it after the first attempt. You can also sometimes use exclamation marks, inverted commas, etc. to capture the tone of the particle.

'First-position' particles

40. There are three particles which normally come first in the sentence or part of the sentence to which they belong. These are:

- ἆρα which introduces a question when there is no interrogative word like 'Who, What, Why?' (e.g. ἆρα τοὺς ἀνθρώπους ὁρᾷς; lit. '[question] the men you see?', 'do you see the men?')
- ἀλλά 'but'
- καί 'and', 'even', 'actually'

'Postpositive' particles

41. Most of the other particles you will meet for now are 'postpositive', lit. 'after-placed', and usually come *second* in the sentence or clause to which they belong, e.g.

- γάρ, γε, δέ, μέν, οὖν, τε.

Enclitics

42. Two of these 'postpositive' particles – γε and τε – are *also* enclitics ('on-leaning'). These are words which have accents, but they give them to the *previous* word if possible. Thus they can alter the accentuation of the preceding word [*Reference Grammar,* 264ff.]. Note the following points:

   a. Like postpositives, enclitics cannot come first in a sentence or clause.
   b. Other enclitics you have met are με and εἰμί, 'I am' in the present indicative (but not second person s.).
   c. Most particles, even those which cannot come first in a sentence or clause, are *not* enclitics. For more on enclitics see [*Reference Grammar*, **34.7.**].

μέν **and** δέ

43. Two of the most important particles are often found together in parallel, coordinated sentences or clauses. These are μέν and δέ.

   a. These are often used to draw a contrast between two ideas or halves of a sentence:

   καταβαίνει μὲν οὖν ὁ κυβερνήτης, ἀναβαίνουσι δὲ οἱ ναῦται.

   'So the captain goes *down*, but the sailors go *up*.'

Here the contrast between the two halves of the sentence, indicated by μέν… δέ in the Greek – '*down* goes the captain, *up* go the sailors' – is translated in English by 'but'.

   b. Another useful way of translating μέν and δέ is by using 'while' to introduce one of the clauses, as in:

   ὁ μὲν Δικαιόπολις φεύγει, οἱ δὲ ναῦται διώκουσιν.

   '*While* Dikaiopolis runs away, the sailors give chase', or 'Dikaiopolis runs away while …'

   c. It is also possible to translate μέν … δέ by using 'on the one hand…, on the other hand…'. This, while useful as a literal way of translating the Greek, usually sounds strained in English.

   d. Sometimes the contrast drawn by Greek using μέν … δέ is not at all strong, e.g.

   καλὸς μὲν ὁ Παρθενών, καλὴ δὲ ἡ ἀκρόπολις.

   'The Parthenon is beautiful and the Acropolis is beautiful.'

Here it is worth observing that μέν … δέ … δέ … δέ … δέ … δέ (etc.) is used to construct a (usually uncontrasted) list: 'A and B and C and D and E', etc.

SUMMARY LEARNING VOCABULARY FOR SECTION 1G

ἀναβαίνω (ἀναβα-)*	go up
ἄνθρωπος, ὁ	man; fellow
ἀπό + gen.	away from
ἀποθνῄσκω (ἀποθαν-)	die
ἀποχωρέω	go away, depart
γε	at least, at any rate
διὰ τί	why?
δύω	sink
εἰς + acc.	to, into, onto
ἐκ, ἐξ + gen.	out of
ἐλθέ	come! go!
ἐμπόριον, τό	market-hall, trading-post
ἐν + dat.	in
ἔργον, τό	task, work, job; duty
ἔχω (σχ-)	have, hold
ἡμέτερος -ᾱ -ον	our(s)
θάλαττα, ἡ	sea
κακός ή όν	bad, evil; cowardly; lowly, mean
κυβερνήτης, ὁ	captain, helmsman
λέγω (εἰπ-)	say
λέμβος, ὁ	boat, life-boat
νῦν	now
πλέω (πλευσα-)	sail
πρός + acc.	towards
ῥίπτω	throw, hurl
σῴζω	save, keep safe
σῶος ᾱ ον	safe
σωτηρίᾱ, ἡ	safety, salvation
φίλος, ὁ	friend
φίλος ή όν	dear, friendly, one's own
φροντίζω	think; worry

TAKING STOCK
1. Can you decline ἄνθρωπος and ἔργον?
2. Can you explain how ἡμέτερος declines differently from καλός?
3. Can you instantly give the meanings of πρός, ἀπό, ἐκ and ἐν?
4. Can you instantly recall the meanings of ἀκούω, ἀποθνῄσκω, βλέπω, διώκω, κακός, λέγω, μένω, ὁράω, φεύγω, φίλος?

*Remember to learn the bracketed forms too!

REVISION EXERCISES FOR 1A–G

In the Revision Exercise sections of *Reading Greek*, summing up largish chunks of grammar, you will find exercises divided into five sections:

A – VOCABULARY-BUILDING: these build up your vocabulary by getting you to think about the meaning of words based on those you have already met. These are provided for Sections 1–11 only.

B – WORD SHAPE: these get you practising the changing forms of nouns, pronouns, adjectives and verbs.

C – SYNTAX: these get you practising how to use these changing forms in sentences.

D – ENGLISH INTO GREEK: these help you practise writing Greek, which is an excellent way of mastering the Greek you are learning. In the first four Sections there are 'guide'-sentences to get you started. There is also an introduction 'Writing in Greek' at pp. 365–6.

E – TEST EXERCISE: these come usually at the end of Sections, and test grammar and vocabulary from the section just completed. They should be done as written exercises, without help from vocabulary or grammar, after all the other work on a section has been completed. There is a guide on how to tackle Test Exercises at pp. 366–7.

A – VOCABULARY-BUILDING

Translate the words in the left-hand column and use them to translate those in the right-hand column.

βαίνω	ἐκβαίνω
διώκω	ἐκδιώκω
θάλαττα	θαλάττιος α ον
κυβερνήτης	κυβερνῶ
ναύτης	ναυτικός ή όν
ὁρῶ	εἰσορῶ
φεύγω	ἀποφεύγω

B – WORD SHAPE*

1. Translate each word, then give the pl. form, e.g. a 1st person s. will become 1st person pl., etc.

   βαίν-εις, βλέπ-ω, ποι-εῖ, ὁρ-ᾷ, βοήθ-ει (check the accent, and compare ποι-εῖ)

2. Translate each word, then give the s. form (there may be more than one!):

   φροντίζ-ετε, κατα-βαίν-ουσι, ἀνα-βαίν-ομεν, ὁρ-ᾶτε, ἀπο-χωρ-εῖτε

3. Fit the appropriate form of the def. art. to the following nouns:

   ἄνθρωπ-οι, ψόφ-οις, πλοῖ-α, λέμβ-ῳ, νεώρι-ον (2b), ἀνθρώπ-ων

4. Use the information provided by the def. art. to put the adjective and the noun into the correct form:

   a. ὁ καλ- ἄνθρωπ-
   b. τὰ καλ- νεώρι-
   c. τῷ καλ- ἐμπορί-
   d. τοῖς καλ- ἀνθρώπ-
   e. τὸν καλ- ἄνθρωπ-

C – SYNTAX

For each of the examples, translate the Greek sentence and then write what the Greek would be for the word(s) in italics (there is no need to translate the English sentence into Greek):

1. ὁ Ἡγέστρατος ὁρᾷ τὴν ἀκρόπολιν.
   We see *Hegestratos*.

2. οἱ ναῦται διώκουσι τὸν Ζηνόθεμιν.
   Sdenothemis pursues the ships.

3. ὁ Δικαιόπολις τοὺς ἀνθρώπους σῴζει.
   The man rescues us.

---

* Never hyphenate your answers to exercises.

4. ὁ κυβερνήτης δηλοῖ τοὺς λέμβους.
   The life-boat is not in the harbour.

5. οἱ ἄνθρωποι οὐχ ὁρῶσι τοὺς λέμβους.
   We chase *the men*.

D – ENGLISH INTO GREEK

Translate these pairs of sentences (there are tips on writing in Greek given at pp. 365–6):

1. ὁ Ζηνόθεμις βαίνει εἰς τὸ πλοῖον.
   The man runs off towards the boat.

2. τὸν Ἡγέστρατον οὐχ ὁρῶσιν οἱ ναῦται.
   Hegestratos does not see the men.

3. ἆρα οὐχ ὁρᾷς σὺ τὴν ἀκρόπολιν;
   Do you (s.) also see the men?

4. δεῦρο ἔλθετε καὶ βλέπετε.
   Come and help (pl.)! Chase the man! Do not run away!

5. οἱ ἄνθρωποι ἀναβαίνουσιν.
   The friends are not waiting.

E – TEST EXERCISE ONE A–G

Translate into English (n.b. underlined words are given in the vocabulary below):

ἀποχωρεῖ μὲν τὸ πλοῖον ἀπὸ τῆς Εὐβοίας, πλεῖ δὲ πρὸς τὸν Πειραιᾶ. ὁ μὲν Ζηνόθεμις βλέπει πρὸς <u>τὴν γῆν</u>. ὁ δὲ Ἡγέστρατος <u>κάτω</u> μένει καὶ <u>καταδύει</u> τὸ πλοῖον. <u>πέλεκυν</u> γὰρ ἔχει ὁ ἄνθρωπος. ἄνω δέ εἰσιν ὁ κυβερνήτης καὶ ὁ Δικαιόπολις. βλέπουσι δὲ πρὸς τὴν γῆν καὶ ὁρῶσι τά τε <u>νεώρια</u> καὶ τὸν Παρθενῶνα. ἀλλὰ <u>ἐξαίφνης</u> ἀκούουσι τὸν <u>ψόφον</u>. ἔπειτα δὲ καταβαίνουσιν.

ΚΥΒΕΡΝΗΤΗΣ	τίς ποιεῖ τὸν ψόφον; ἆρα ὁρᾷς, ὦ Δικαιόπολι;
ΔΙΚΑΙΟΠΟΛΙΣ	ναί· ὁρῶ ἔγωγε· ὁ γὰρ Ἡγέστρατος τὸν ψόφον ποιεῖ. πέλεκυν γὰρ ἔχει ἐν <u>τῇ δεξιᾷ</u>.
ΚΥΒ.	μὴ μένετε, ὦ ναῦται, ἀλλὰ βοηθεῖτε καὶ διώκετε τὸν ἄνθρωπον.

ὁ μὲν Ἡγέστρατος φεύγει <u>κάτωθεν</u>, ὁ δὲ Ζηνόθεμις ἄνω μένει. οἱ μὲν ναῦται ἀναβαίνουσι κάτωθεν. οἱ δὲ ἄνθρωποι τοὺς ναύτας σαφῶς ὁρῶσι καὶ ῥίπτουσιν <u>ἑαυτοὺς</u> εἰς τὴν θάλατταν. εἰς τὴν μὲν θάλατταν φεύγουσιν οἱ ἄνθρωποι, ἐν δὲ τῇ θαλάττῃ ἀποθνήσκουσιν.

Vocabulary (in the order it occurs in the text)

τὴν γῆν	the land
κάτω	below

καταδύω	cause to sink, sink
πέλεκυν	axe (acc.)
νεώριον, τό	dockyard (2b)
ἐξαίφνης	suddenly
ψόφος, ὁ	noise (2a)
τῇ δεξιᾷ	his right hand
κάτωθεν	from below
ἑαυτούς	themselves (as 'reflexive' object, e.g. 'they hurt *themselves*')

Grammar for Section 1H–J

> In this section you cover:
> - Verbs εἰμί 'I am' and οἶδα 'I know'
> - Complement and ellipse with εἰμί
> - Adjectives used as nouns
> - More particles

VOCABULARY CHECK

Ensure you know the meaning of:

δῆλος, ὅτι, παίζω, σαφῶς, γιγνώσκω, ἔργον, ἀεί, ἄριστος, εἰμί, οἶδα, ναῦς

VOCABULARY NEEDED FOR EXERCISES

τὰ ναυτικά lit. 'the naval-things', naval matters
τὰ στρατηγικά lit. 'the army-leader's-things', leadership, generalship
τὰ στρατιωτικά lit. 'the soldier's-things', military matters

IRREGULAR VERBS

44. Just as in English, French, Spanish and many other languages, some common verbs in Greek are irregular. Here is the present tense of two of the most common irregular verbs, εἰμί, 'I am' (i.e. the Greek verb 'to be'), and οἶδα, 'I know':

εἰμί, 'I am'

εἰμί	'I am'	first person s.
εἶ	'you are'	second person s.
ἐστί(ν)	'he/she/it is'	third person s.
ἐσμέν	'we are'	first person pl.
ἐστέ	'you are'	second person pl.
εἰσί(ν)	'they are'	third person pl.

οἶδα, 'I know'

οἶδα	'I know'	first person s.
οἶσθα	'you know'	second person s.
οἶδε	'he/she/it knows'	third person s.
ἴσμεν	'we know'	first person pl.
ἴστε	'you know'	second person pl.
ἴσασι(ν)	'they know'	third person pl.

The complement: 'same case before and after'

45. The verb 'to be', in English and Greek, is often used to describe someone or something by linking it to an adjective, e.g.:

'The *man* is *good*.'

ἡ θάλαττά ἐστι κακή, 'The *sea* is *evil*.'

Since the adjective is describing the subject, it goes in the NOM. case in Greek, AGREEING with the subject. In the Greek sentence above ἡ θάλαττα is the subject of ἐστί, so it goes in the nom. case; and so does the adjective κακή, describing ἡ θάλαττα.

▶ To put it very crudely – but helpfully – the verb 'to be' takes the *same case before and after*, which usually means the *nom.*

46. The verb 'to be' can also be used to link the subject to another NOUN, which also goes in the NOM., e.g.

'The *man* is the *captain*.'

ὁ ῥαψῳδός ἐστιν Ἴων, 'The *rhapsode* is *Ion*.'

The SUBJECT in sentences such as these is usually marked by having the def. art. – ἡ θάλαττα and ὁ ῥαψῳδός. Both the adjective and the noun to which it is linked by the verb 'to be' are called the COMPLEMENT (= 'completion'; cf. compliment, 'congratulation').

No complementary def. art.

47. In Greek, the complement does not normally have a def. art. Look at these two sentences:

ὁ Ὅμηρός ἐστι ῥαψῳδὸς ἄριστος.

ῥαψῳδὸς ἄριστός ἐστιν ὁ Ὅμηρος.

Both sentences mean 'Homer is the best rhapsode,' and in both cases the SUBJECT of ἐστί is ὁ Ὅμηρος, as indicated by the def. art.

▶ So, with the verb 'to be', def. art. will go with the subject; the complement will not have one.

Omission of verb 'to be'

48. Quite often the verb 'to be' is omitted from a sentence (a feature called 'ellipse'). So if you find a sentence without a verb, try some form of εἰμί, e.g.

Μέμνων καλός 'Memnon handsome.'

Supply ἐστί, giving 'Memnon *is* handsome.' The Greek here is an example of the many common 'καλός inscriptions' on Greek pots, the complement καλός complimenting a young man on his good looks (and omitting ἐστί 'is'). See *Text* p. 103, ὁ παῖς καλός 'the youth [is] handsome'.

EXERCISES

1H–J: 1. Translate into English:

1. ἐστί (translate three ways)	6. εἶ
2. ἴσμεν	7. οἶσθα
3. ἐστέ	8. εἰσίν
4. ἴστε	9. εἰμί
5. ἐσμέν	10. ἴσασι

1H–J: 2. Translate into Greek:

1. I know	6. She knows
2. You are (s.)	7. We are
3. They are	8. It is
4. She is	9. He knows
5. They know	10. You are (pl.)

ADJECTIVES AS NOUNS

Neuter 'things'

49. The stem πολλ- means 'many, much'. πολλ-ά is its n. pl. form: the -α ending is like the n. pl. def. art. τ-ά, the noun ἔργ-α and the n. pl. adjective καλ-ά. (Remember the nom., voc., and acc. pls. of neuter articles, nouns and adjective generally end in -α).

In this n. pl. form, πολλά means 'many *things*'.

In a similar way, the adjective στρατηγικός, means 'of a general', but in the n. pl. with a def. art., τὰ στρατηγικά, literally 'things to do with a general', it means 'a general's business', or 'generalship'.

▶ This use of the n. pl. of an adjective, especially when linked with the def. art., is very common, e.g.:

τὰ ναυτικά lit. the naval-things, i.e. 'naval matters'

τὰ στρατιωτικά lit. the military-things, 'military matters'

▶ The n. s. can also be used as an *abstract* noun. τὸ καλόν, 'the beautiful thing', comes to mean 'beauty'.

Masculine and feminine 'people'

50. The def. art. can, in fact, be used in this way with adjectives in *all* genders and numbers. When m., it will refer to men, and when f., to women, e.g.

> ἡ καλή, 'the beautiful [f. s.] woman'

> οἱ σοφοί, 'the wise [m. pl.] men, wise men (in general), the wise'

English plays the same game, e.g. 'The clever [= 'clever people'] are not always wise.'

PARTICLES

τε…τε **and** τε…καί

51. The combinations of particles τε…τε and τε…καί link two words or phrases together ('both…and'), e.g.

> ὅ τε Δικαιόπολις καὶ ὁ ῥαψῳδός, '[The] both Dikaiopolis and the rhapsode.'

> ὁρᾷ τε ὁ ἄνθρωπος καὶ οὐχ ὁρᾷ, 'The man [both] sees and does not see.'

Note the position of τε in these phrases – it goes *after* the FIRST item it will link with the next (between article and noun in the first example), while καί comes *before* the SECOND item.

> ▶ In other words, τε in this usage waves a flag saying 'another item coming up'.

Remember, τε is an ENCLITIC (**42**)

EXERCISES

1H–J: 3. Translate into English:

1. οἶσθα τά τε ναυτικὰ καὶ τὰ στρατηγικά.
2. πολλὰ ἴσμεν τε καὶ ὁρῶμεν.
3. ἐστέ τε καὶ οὐκ ἐστέ.
4. ἴστε πολλά.
5. ἆρα τά τε στρατιωτικὰ καὶ τὰ στρατηγικὰ ἴσασιν;

1H–J: 4. Translate into Greek:

1. They know much.
2. He is and he is not.
3. He does not know generalship.
4. I know and I do not know naval and military matters.
5. We are and we know.

SUMMARY LEARNING VOCABULARY FOR SECTION 1H–J

ἀεί	always
ἄριστος η ον	best; very good
γιγνώσκω (γνο-)	know; think; resolve
δῆλος η ον	clear; obvious
εἰμί	I am (= verb 'to be')
Ἕλλην, ὁ	Greek
ἔμπειρος ον*	skilled, experienced
ἤ	or
μῶρος ᾱ ον	stupid; foolish
ναί	yes
ναῦς, ἡ	ship
οἶδα	know
ὅτι	that
παίζω (πρός + acc.)	play; joke (at)
περί	(+ acc.) about
πολλά	many things (acc.)
πῶς γὰρ οὔ;	of course
στρατηγός, ὁ	general (2a)
τὰ ναυτικά	lit. 'the naval-things', naval matters
τὰ στρατηγικά	lit. 'the leader's-things', leadership, generalship
τὰ στρατιωτικά	lit. 'the soldier's-things', military matters

*This adjective uses the same endings in the m. and f.

TAKING STOCK

1. Be certain that you can conjugate εἰμί and οἶδα in the present.
2. Do you understand the idea of a 'complement'?
3. In what ways are adjectives used as nouns in Greek?
4. What are the alternative stems of ἔχω, λέγω, βαίνω, ἀποθνήσκω?

REVISION EXERCISES FOR 1H–J

A – VOCABULARY-BUILDING

1. From the words in the left-hand column deduce the meaning of those on the
   right:

ἀποχωρῶ	περιχωρῶ
βαίνω	περιβαίνω
δῆλος	δηλῶ
εἰμί	ἔνειμι
Ἕλλην	Ἑλληνικός ή όν
μένω	περιμένω
στρατηγός	στρατηγῶ

B – WORD SHAPE

1. Translate each verb, then change to the s. or pl. form as appropriate:

   ἐστέ, γιγνώσκει, οἶσθα, ἐστί, ἴσασι, παῖζε, εἰμί, ἴσμεν

C – SYNTAX

1. Translate these sentences:

   a. ὁ ῥαψῳδός ἐστιν Ἕλλην.
   b. ὁ Ἕλλην ἐστὶ ῥαψῳδός.
   c. στρατηγοὶ ἄριστοί εἰσιν οἱ ῥαψῳδοί.
   d. μῶρός ἐστιν ὁ ῥαψῳδός.
   e. κυβερνήτης ὁ ῥαψῳδός.
   f. ῥαψῳδός ἐστιν ὁ κυβερνήτης.

D – ENGLISH INTO GREEK

If you need a reminder of how to tackle this exercise, look at pp. 365–6.

Translate these pairs of sentences:

1. δῆλόν ἐστιν ὅτι ὁ Δικαιόπολις παίζει πρὸς τὸν ῥαψῳδόν.
   It is clear that the rhapsode knows many things.

2. ἔμπειρός εἰμι ἐγὼ περὶ πολλά.
   You are not experienced in the job.

3. οἱ ῥαψῳδοί εἰσι στρατηγοὶ ἄριστοι.
   The best general is a rhapsode.

4. ἆρ' οὐκ οἶσθα ὅτι ὁ ἄνθρωπος παίζει ἀεί;
   Doesn't he know that the rhapsode is speaking accurately?

5. ἔμπειρος μὲν οὐκ εἶ, μῶρος δέ.
   But I am not a fool; I know a lot.

E – TEST EXERCISE ONE H–J

Translate into English:

τὸ μὲν οὖν πλοῖον πλεῖ πρὸς τὸν Πειραιᾶ. οἱ δὲ ναῦται οὐκ ἴσασι ποῦ ἐστι τὸ πλοῖον. ἐρωτῶσιν οὖν τὸν κυβερνήτην ποῦ ἐστιν. ὁ μὲν κυβερνήτης λέγει ὅτι ἐγγὺς τοῦ λιμένος ἐστὶ τὸ πλοῖον. ἐξαίφνης δὲ ὁ ῥαψῳδὸς ὁμηρίζει. καὶ δῆλόν ἐστιν ὅτι πολλὰ γιγνώσκει περὶ Ὁμήρου ὁ ἄνθρωπος. ὁ δὲ Δικαιόπολις παίζει πρὸς τὸν ῥαψῳδόν.

ΔΙΚΑΙΟΠΟΛΙΣ   ἆρα γιγνώσκεις τὰ ῥαψῳδικά, ὦ ῥαψῳδέ;
ΡΑΨΩΙΔΟΣ   πῶς δὲ οὔ; γιγνώσκω δὲ καὶ τὰ στρατηγικά.
ΔΙΚ.   τί λέγεις; ῥαψῳδὸς γὰρ εἶ καὶ οὐ στρατηγός.
ΡΑΨ.   ἆρα οὐκ οἶσθα ὅτι ὁ ἀγαθὸς ῥαψῳδός ἐστιν ἅμα καὶ
               στρατηγὸς ἀγαθός;
ΔΙΚ.   οὔκ, ἀλλὰ οἶδα ὅτι σὺ μῶρος εἶ, ὦ ῥαψῳδέ. σὺ μὲν γὰρ
               ῥαψῳδὸς εἶ τῶν Ἑλλήνων ἄριστος καὶ ἔμπειρος περὶ τοῦ
               Ὁμήρου. περὶ δὲ τὰ στρατηγικὰ οὐκ ἔμπειρος εἶ, οὐδὲ
               οἶσθα οὐδὲν ἀκριβῶς.

Vocabulary

ἐγγὺς τοῦ λιμένος	near the harbour
ἐξαίφνης	suddenly
ὁμηρίζω	recite Homer
ἀγαθός ή όν	good
ἅμα	at the same time
τῶν Ἑλλήνων	of the Greeks
περί	about
οὐδέ	and…not

Grammar for Section 2A–D

> In this section you cover:
> - 'Middle' verbs in -ομαι (middle 'voice': present and imperative)
> - 'Contract' middle verbs in -άομαι, -έομαι, -όομαι (present and imperative)
> - Nouns like βοή (1a), ἀπορίᾱ (1b), θάλαττα (1c), ναύτης, νεᾱνίᾱς (1d)
> - The genitive case, 'of'
> - 'Sandwich' and 'repeated article' constructions
> - Prepositions governing accusative and dative cases

VOCABULARY CHECK

Ensure you know the meaning of:
παρά, ἀγαθός, νικάω, τέλος, ἐμός, λόγος, σκοπέω, ἀναχωρέω, ἐπειδή, ἐπί, ταχέως, ὥσπερ

VOCABULARY NEEDED FOR EXERCISES

ἀπορί-ᾱ, ἡ perplexity
βο-ή, ἡ shout
γίγν-ομαι happen, be made, be born
δουλό-ομαι enslave
ἔρχ-ομαι go, come

θεά-ομαι observe, watch
μάχ-ομαι fight
τόλμ-α, ἡ daring, courage
φοβέ-ομαι be afraid of, fear

MIDDLE VERBS (-ομαι)

52. Most of the verbs we have met so far have followed the CONJUGATION (or pattern) of βαίν-ω, ending -ει in the third person s., -ουσι in the third person pl. and so on (see βαίνω, **12**). But you have also met verbs with different endings:

> ἡ μὲν ναῦς πρὸς τὸν Πειραιᾶ βραδέως ἔρχ-εται.
>
> 'The ship goes slowly towards the Piraeus.'
>
> ὑπὲρ τῆς ἐλευθερίας μάχ-ονται οἱ Ἀθηναῖοι.
>
> 'The Athenians fight for the sake of freedom.'
>
> οἱ Ἕλληνες ταχέως ἐπὶ τοὺς Μήδους ἐπέρχ-ονται.
>
> 'The Greeks swiftly attack [against] the Persians.'

- These verbs are called 'middle' verbs (the technical term is the middle 'voice', in contrast with the active 'voice').
- Verbs in the middle 'voice' end in -ομαι in the first person s. (compare βαίν-ω).
- We have met, for example, ἔρχομαι, γίγνομαι, μάχομαι, φοβέομαι, θεάομαι.

Here is the CONJUGATION of ἔρχομαι, 'I go', set out in full for the present indicative middle forms. This is the pattern that all uncontracted middle verbs follow in the present indicative tense (so, e.g., γίγνομαι, 'I become', and μάχομαι, 'I fight', follow this pattern).

Middle indicative

ἔρχομαι 'I go, am going'

ἔρχ-ομαι	'I go', 'I am going'	first person s.
ἔρχ-ῃ (-ει)	'you go', 'you are going'	second person s.
ἔρχ-εται	'he/she/it goes/is going'	third person s.
ἐρχ-όμεθα	'we go', 'we are going'	first person pl.
ἔρχ-εσθε	'you go', 'you are going'	second person pl.
ἔρχ-ονται	'they go', 'they are going'	third person pl.

Middle imperative

ἔρχου 'go!'

ἔρχ-ου (s.), 'go!'
ἔρχ-εσθε (pl.), 'go!'

■ *Form*

(a) Middle forms have two patterns of ending: this one – worth remembering in these terms because it will recur – is:

-μαι -σαι -ται -μεθα -σθε -νται

These endings are added to the thematic vowels: ο ε ε ο ε ο (see **16b**).

(b) You will immediately (and rightly) demand to know where the -σαι has got to in the 2s. Here, then, is another useful hint. In Greek, in certain circumstances, a σ between vowels ('intervocalic sigma') disappears. The 2s form was once ἔρχ-ε-σαι. The σ disappeared leaving ἔρχε-αι. This then contracted into ἔρχῃ, sometimes ἔρχει.

CONTRACTED MIDDLE VERBS

53. We have also met some contracted middle verbs, which follow the same rules of contraction as contracted active verbs (see **23–5**).

● Just as with active contracted verbs, there are three different types of contracted middle verbs, α-contracts, ε-contracts and ο-contracts.

> ● All regular middle α-contracts follow the pattern of θεάομαι, all regular middle ε-contracts follow the pattern of φοβέομαι, all regular o-contracts follow the pattern of δουλό-ομαι, as given below:

Present indicative middle

θεῶμαι, 'I watch, am watching'

α +	-ομαι	→	θε-ῶμαι	'I watch'
α +	-η	→	θε-ᾷ	'you watch'
α +	-εται	→	θε-ᾶται	'he/she/it watches'
α +	-ομεθα	→	θε-ώμεθα	'we watch'
α +	-εσθε	→	θε-ᾶσθε	'you watch'
α +	-ονται	→	θε-ῶνται	'they watch'

φοβοῦμαι, 'I fear, am fearing'

ε +	-ομαι	→	φοβ-οῦμαι	'I fear'
ε +	-η	→	φοβ-ῇ	'you fear'
ε +	-εται	→	φοβ-εῖται	'he/she/it fears'
ε +	-ομεθα	→	φοβ-ούμεθα	'we fear'
ε +	-εσθε	→	φοβ-εῖσθε	'you fear'
ε +	-ονται	→	φοβ-οῦνται	'they fear'

δουλοῦμαι, 'I enslave (for myself), make X my slave'

o +	-ομαι	→	δουλ-οῦμαι	'I enslave'
o +	-η	→	δουλ-οῖ	'you enslave'
o +	-εται	→	δουλ-οῦται	'he/she/it enslaves'
o +	-ομεθα	→	δουλ-ούμεθα	'we enslave'
o +	-εσθε	→	δουλ-οῦσθε	'you enslave'
o +	-ονται	→	δουλ-οῦνται	'they enslave'

Present imperative middle

54. Using the rules of contraction, you can also predict what the imperative forms must be for middle α-, ε- and o-contracts:

α-contracts: θεῶ (s.), 'watch!'

α + -ου → θε-ῶ (s.), 'watch!'
α + -εσθε → θε-ᾶσθε (pl.), 'watch!'

ε-contracts: φοβοῦ (s.), 'fear!'

ε + -ου → φοβ-οῦ (s.), 'fear!'
ε + -εσθε → φοβ-εῖσθε (pl.), 'fear!'

o-contracts: δουλοῦ (s.), 'enslave!'

o + -ου → δουλ-οῦ (s.), 'enslave!'
o + -εσθε → δουλ-οῦσθε (pl.), 'enslave!'

Note that, as with active verbs (**20**), the second person pl. indicative form is the same as the pl. imperative.

EXERCISES

2A–D: 1. Translate into English:

1. γίγνεται (translate three ways)	8. ἔρχεσθε καὶ μάχεσθε (translate two ways)
2. οὐκ ἐρχόμεθα	9. φοβεῖται
3. δουλοῦνται	10. δουλοῦται
4. μάχονται	11. θεᾶται
5. μὴ μάχου	12. φοβῇ
6. δουλούμεθα	13. οὐ θεῶμαι
7. ἔρχου	14. δηλοῖ

2A–D: 2. Translate into Greek using middle verbs:

1. Do not watch (pl.)	7. We go
2. They are going	8. They fear
3. He does not fear	9. She enslaves
4. You become (pl.)	10. She watches
5. You (pl.) enslave	11. They do not become
6. I fear	12. You go (s.)

NOUNS TYPES 1A, 1B, 1C, 1D

55. Here are some more types of noun, which we have categorised as TYPES 1a, 1b, 1c (all f.) and 1d (m.).

TYPE 1a nouns have endings in s. and pl. exactly like the f. def. art. (see **8**).

βοή, ἡ, 'shout' (1a)

	s.	*pl.*
Nom.	βο-ή	βο-αί
Acc.	βο-ήν	βο-άς
Gen.	βο-ῆς	βο-ῶν
Dat.	βο-ῇ	βο-αῖς

---

56. TYPE 1b nouns like ἀπορί-α:

- Replace the -η with -α (pronounced LONG) all the way through the s. This is because their stem ends in ρ, ε, or ι (see **37**), i.e. they follow the same rule which you have already learnt for adjectives in -ος whose stems end in ρ, ε, ι (e.g. such as ἡμέτερ-ος, f. ἡμετέρ-ᾱ);

> • *Usually* have a long final α in the nom./voc. and acc. s., and always have a long α in the gen. and dat. s. and acc. pl.

ἀπορία, ἡ, 'perplexity' (1b)

	s.	*pl.*
Nom.	ἀπορί-ᾱ	ἀπορί-αι
Acc.	ἀπορί-ᾱν	ἀπορί-ᾱς
Gen.	ἀπορί-ᾱς	ἀπορι-ῶν
Dat.	ἀπορί-ᾳ	ἀπορί-αις

---

57. TYPE 1c nouns like θάλαττα:

> • Show -α in the ending of the nom. and acc. s. (pronounced short);
> • Switch to η in the gen. (-ης) and dat. s. (-ῃ: contrast TYPE 1b nouns);
> • Usually have a stem ending in σ or a double consonant: but note τόλμ-α-ης 'daring' (1c).

θάλαττᾰ, ἡ, 'sea' (1c)

	s.	*pl.*
Nom.	θάλαττ-ᾰ	θάλαττ-αι
Acc.	θάλαττ-ᾰν	θαλάττ-ᾱς
Gen.	θαλάττ-ης	θαλαττ-ῶν
Dat.	θαλάττ-ῃ	θαλάττ-αις

---

58. Type 1d nouns:

> • Are all *masculine*; but
> • Take endings which look suspiciously f., except for the gen. s. in -ου: nothing for it but to learn it accurately.
> • Some 1d nouns end in nom. -ας, e.g. νεανί-ας, 'young man'.
> • You will, however, observe that the pl. endings of ALL type 1 nouns follow exactly the same pattern, and that they are also the same as the f. pl. endings of adjectives like καλός [**10**].

ναύτης, ὁ, 'sailor' (1d)

	s.	*pl.*
Nom.	ναύτη-ς	ναῦτ-αι
Acc.	ναύτ-ην	ναύτ-ᾱς
Gen.	ναύτ-ου	ναυτ-ῶν
Dat.	ναύτ-ῃ	ναύτ-αις
Voc.	ναῦτ-ᾰ	

νεᾱνίᾱς, ὁ, 'young man' (1d)

	s.	pl.
Nom.	νεᾱνί-ᾱς	νεᾱνί-αι
Acc.	νεᾱνί-ᾱν	νεᾱνί-ᾱς
Gen.	νεᾱνί-ου	νεᾱνι-ῶν
Dat.	νεᾱνί-ᾳ	νεᾱνί-αις
Voc.	νεᾱνί-ᾱ	

EXERCISES

2A–D: 3. Decide which of the five nouns above can agree with each def. art.
below (gender will tell you) and then choose the right case and number to
make them agree:

1. τόν
2. τῶν
3. ταῖς
4. ἡ
5. τούς
6. αἱ
7. τοῖς
8. ὁ
9. τήν
10. τῷ

2A–D: 4. Change s. to pl. and vice-versa:

1. τὴν βοήν
2. τοῖς ναύταις
3. αἱ τόλμαι
4. τῆς ἀπορίας
5. ὁ ναύτης
6. ταῖς βοαῖς
7. τὰς τόλμας
8. τοὺς νεανίας

GENITIVE CASE

Meaning

59. The gen. case has a wide range of functions, and very often it is equivalent to
the English 'of':

τῶν ἀνθρώπων, 'of the men'; τῶν ἔργων, 'of the deeds'

■ Form

60. Observe the form of the gen. pl. of some of the words you have met, e.g.

ἀνθρώπων, τῶν, καλῶν, τολμῶν, ἀποριῶν

They all end in -ων.

▶ In fact, *all* nouns and adjectives end in -ων in the gen. pl. – as you will
find out (though, of course, not all words which end in -ων are gen. pl.).

'Sandwich' and 'repeated article' constructions

61. Notice the position of the gen. in the following sentences, all meaning 'the
ship of the men':

τὸ πλοῖον τῶν ἀνθρώπων 'the ship of-the men'

τὸ τῶν ἀνθρώπων πλοῖον 'the of-the men ship'

τὸ πλοῖον τὸ τῶν ἀνθρώπων 'the ship the [one] of-the men'

τῶν ἀνθρώπων τὸ πλοῖον 'of-the men the ship'

■ 'Sandwich'

The normal order is τὸ τῶν ἀνθρώπων πλοῖον, with the gen. coming BETWEEN article and noun, as in the following sentence (the 'sandwich'-construction):

> ὁρῶ τὸ τῶν ἀνθρώπων πλοῖον, 'I see the [of] the men ship.' (in answer to the question, 'What are you doing?')

■ 'Repeated article'

If the question had instead been, 'Whose ship do you see?', the order would have been as follows (the 'repeated article'-construction):

> τὸ πλοῖον ὁρῶ τὸ τῶν ἀνθρώπων, 'It is the men's ship I see.' (lit. 'The ship I see the [one] of the men.')

The def. art. is repeated here (in the n., to agree with πλοῖον, to specify which ship it is that is being seen).

■ Other uses of the 'sandwich' and 'repeated article' construction

62. This use of the def. art. is seen with other phrases which do not involve the gen., e.g.

> τὰ πράγματα τὰ περὶ Σαλαμῖνα, 'the events around Salamis' (lit. 'the events the [ones] around Salamis')

Here again, the article is repeated to specify which events are being referred to. But it is also possible to extend phrases without repeating the def. art., e.g. by using the 'sandwich'-construction we saw above (where a gen. came BETWEEN article and noun):

> τὰ περὶ Σαλαμῖνα πράγματα, 'the around Salamis events'

■ Article + preposition constructions

63. In Greek the def. art. can be used to extend phrases in a way similar to its use with adjectives to make nouns (**49**). Examine the following phrases:

> τὰ περὶ Σαλαμῖνα, 'the [n. pl., i.e.] things/events around Salamis'
>
> οἱ ἐν Σαλαμῖνι, 'the [m. pl., i.e.] men in Salamis/those in Salamis'
>
> αἱ ἐν τῷ Πειραιεῖ, 'the [f. pl., i.e.] women in the Piraeus'

In these phrases the def. art. + prepositional phrase is being used as an equivalent of a noun.

Prepositions governing the accusative

64. Note the following prepositions, all of which have the given meanings when they take the acc. case:

παρά + ACC.	'along, alongside'
ἐπί + ACC.	'against', 'at', 'to attack'
διά + ACC.	'because of'

Prepositions governing the dative

65. The DATIVE is the last of the cases in Greek, the different possible word shapes a noun, adjective, pronoun or article can have. You have been learning the dative forms of the types of nouns and adjectives we have introduced, and you have met the dat. used with the preposition ἐν, 'in', 'on' or 'among', as in the following phrases:

ἐν τῇ θαλάττῃ, 'in/on the sea'
ἐν τῇ δεξιᾷ, 'in his/her right hand'
ἐν Βυζαντίῳ, 'in Byzantium'

EXERCISES

2A–D: 5. Revise the prepositions taking the GENITIVE at **38** and translate into English:

1. διὰ τὸν πόλεμον.
2. ἐπὶ τοὺς βαρβάρους.
3. παρὰ τὸ πλοῖον.
4. ἀπὸ τῶν φίλων.
5. διὰ τοὺς ναύτας.
6. παρὰ τοὺς Ἀθηναίους.
7. ἐπὶ τοὺς πολεμίους.
8. διὰ τὴν ναυμαχίαν.
9. διὰ τὴν ἀπορίαν.
10. ἐκ τῶν στρατιῶν.
11. παρὰ τὸν ἄνθρωπον.
12. ἀπὸ τῶν Ἀθηναίων.

2A–D: 6. Translate into Greek:

1. Because of the shouts.
2. Out of the boats.
3. Alongside the friends.
4. At/against the army.
5. Because of freedom.
6. Alongside the goddesses.
7. Because of the agreements.
8. Away from the enemy.
9. At/against the men.
10. Because of the victory.

EXERCISE USING THE DATIVE (OR NOT)

2A–D: 7. Write the correct form of the article between preposition and noun and translate the resulting phrase:

ἐν __ βαρβάροις.　　　εἰς __ γῆν.
ἐν __ ναυμαχίᾳ.　　　ἐν __ Πειραιεῖ.
ἐν __ ἔργῳ.

SUMMARY LEARNING VOCABULARY FOR SECTION 2A–D

ἀγαθός ή όν	good, noble, courageous	κάλλιστος η ον	most/very fine/beautiful/good
Ἀθηναῖος, ὁ	Athenian (2a)	λόγος, ὁ	story, tale (2a)
ἅμα	at the same time	μάχομαι (μαχεσα-)	fight
ἀναχωρέω	retreat	ναυμαχίᾱ, ἡ	naval battle (1b)
ἀπορέ-ω	be at a loss; have no resources	νῑκάω	win, defeat
ἀπορί-ᾱ, ἡ	perplexity, lack of provisions (1b)	νίκη, ἡ	victory, conquest (1a)
αὖθις	again	ὁμόνοια, ἡ	agreement, harmony (1b)
βάρβαρος, ὁ	barbarian, foreigner (2a)	ὅσος η ον	how great!
βέβαιος (ᾱ) ον	secure	οὐκέτι	no longer
βραδέως	slowly	οὕτω(ς)	thus, so, in this way
διά	(+ acc.) because of	παρά	(+ acc.) along, alongside
διέρχομαι (διελθ-)	go through, relate	πίπτω (πεσ-)	fall, die
δουλό-ομαι	enslave, make X a slave	πολέμιοι, οἱ	the enemy (2a)
		πολέμιος ᾱ ον	hostile, enemy
ἐλευθερίᾱ, ἡ	freedom (1b)	πόλεμος, ὁ	war (2a)
ἐλεύθερος α ον	free	πότερον … ἤ	whether … or
ἐλευθερόω	free, set free	προσέρχομαι (προσελθ-)	advance, go/come towards
ἐμός ή όν	my; mine		
ἐπειδή	when	σιωπά-ω	be silent
ἐπέρχομαι (ἐπελθ-)	go against, attack	σκοπέ-ω	look (at), consider
ἐπί (+ acc.)	at, against, to attack	στρατιᾱ́, ἡ	army (1b)
		ταχέως	quickly
ἔρχομαι (ἐλθ-)	go, come	τέλος	in the end, finally
ἡδέως	with pleasure, happily	τι	a, something
		τόλμα, ἡ	daring (1c)
ἤδη	by now, now, already	τολμάω	dare, be daring, undertake
ἡσυχάζω	be quiet, keep quiet	φοβέομαι	fear, be afraid (of)
ἡσυχίᾱ, ἡ	quiet, peace (1b)	ψευδῶς	falsely
θεᾱ́, ἡ	goddess (1b)	ὥσπερ	like, as
θεᾱ́-ομαι	observe, watch		

TAKING STOCK
1. Show that you can conjugate ἔρχομαι and φοβοῦμαι by heart, with imperative forms.
2. Rattle through the declensions of ἀπορίᾱ, θάλαττα and ναύτης, with definite article attached.

REVISION EXERCISES FOR SECTION 2

A – VOCABULARY BUILDING
Deduce the meaning of the words on the right from those on the left:

ἀληθῆ	ἡ ἀλήθεια
ἀκριβῶς	ἡ ἀκρίβεια
ἄνθρωπος, ὁ	ἡ ἄνθρωπος
βοή	βοῶ (α-contract)
ἔμπειρος	ἡ ἐμπειρία
ἔργον	ἐργάζομαι
ἡδέως	ἥδομαι, ἡ ἡδονή
κακός	ἡ κακία
μάχομαι	ὁ μαχητής, ἡ μάχη, ἄμαχος ον
μῶρος	ἡ μωρία
ναῦς/μάχομαι	ναυμαχῶ (ε-contract)
νίκη/νικάω	ἀνίκητος ον
ποιέω	ὁ ποιήτης
πόλεμος	ὁ πολεμήτης, πολεμῶ (ε-contract)
σιωπάω	ἡ σιωπή
στρατιά	ὁ στρατός, στρατεύω, ὁ στρατιώτης
τολμάω	ὁ τολμητής, ἄτολμος ον, ἀτολμῶ (ε-contract)
φίλος	φιλῶ (ε-contract), ἡ φιλία
φοβέομαι	ὁ φόβος
ψευδῶς	ψεύδομαι

B – WORD SHAPE
1. Translate each verb, then change to s. or pl. as appropriate:

   διερχόμεθα, μάχεται, φοβῇ, θεῶνται, δουλοῦσθε, θεᾶσθε, προσέρχεται, φοβοῦνται, φοβοῦμαι, γίγνονται, ἐπέρχῃ, μάχεσθε

2. Add the correct form of the def. art. to these nouns:

   ναύτης, τόλμαν, ναύτῃ, βοάς, νῖκαι, ναυτῶν, στρατιάν, κυβερνήταις, νίκην, ἀπορία

3. Put in the correct form of adjective and noun:

   1. ἡ καλλίστ- βο-
   2. αἱ ἐμ- βο-
   3. τῇ ἐμ- ἀπορί-
   4. τὴν πολεμί- βο-
   5. ταῖς καλ- νίκ-

C – SYNTAX
1. 'The war of the Athenians' = ὁ πόλεμος ὁ τῶν Ἀθηναίων/ὁ τῶν Ἀθηναίων πόλεμος. Put together the following groups of words in the same patterns, and translate:

a. τὰ ἔργα + τῶν Περσῶν

b. ἡ στρατιά + τῶν βαρβάρων

c. ἡ βοή + ἐν τῷ λιμένι

d. οἱ ναῦται + ἐν τῷ πλοίῳ

e. τὸ πλοῖον + τῶν πολεμίων

D – ENGLISH INTO GREEK

If you need a reminder of how to tackle this exercise, look at p. 365ff.

Translate these pairs of sentences:

1. ἡ ναῦς πρὸς τὴν ναυμαχίαν προσέρχεται.
   The sailors converse with the rhapsode.

2. ὁ ἄριστος ῥαψῳδὸς ἀεὶ καλλίστους ποιεῖ τοὺς λόγους.
   The captain relates with pleasure our sea-battle.

3. ἔπειτα μάχονται μὲν οἱ Ἀθηναῖοι, φοβοῦνται δὲ οἱ τῶν Περσῶν στρατηγοί.
   Finally the Athenians are victorious, while the Athenians' enemies are falling.

4. μὴ ἀναχωρεῖτε, ὦ φίλοι, ἀλλὰ μάχεσθε.
   Do not be afraid, sailors, but fight and become free.

5. ἴσμεν ὅτι προσέρχεται ἡ τῶν Ἑλλήνων στρατιά.
   You (pl.) know that the Persians' generals are retreating.

E – TEST EXERCISE TWO

Translate into English:

ἐπειδὴ οὖν προσέρχονται ἡ τῶν Περσῶν στρατιὰ καὶ τὸ ναυτικόν, οἱ Ἀθηναῖοι ταχέως εἰσβαίνουσιν εἰς τὰς ναῦς καὶ πρὸς τὴν Σαλαμῖνα πλέουσιν. ἔπειτα δὲ οἵ τε Ἀθηναῖοι καὶ οἱ ἄλλοι Ἕλληνες ἡσυχάζουσι. τέλος δὲ ἀφικνεῖται τὸ τῶν Περσῶν ναυτικόν, καὶ ἐπειδὴ νὺξ γίγνεται, ἔνθα καὶ ἔνθα βραδέως πλέουσιν αἱ νῆες. καὶ ἐπειδὴ γίγνεται ἡ ἡμέρα, οἱ μὲν Πέρσαι προσέρχονται ταχέως ἐπὶ ναυμαχίαν, οἱ δὲ Ἕλληνες ἀποροῦσι καὶ φοβοῦνται. τέλος δὲ οὐκέτι φοβοῦνται, ἀλλὰ τολμῶσι, καὶ ἐπέρχονται ἐπὶ τοὺς βαρβάρους. μάχονται οὖν εὐκόσμως καὶ νικῶσι τοὺς βαρβάρους. οἱ μὲν οὖν βάρβαροι φεύγουσι, φεύγει δὲ καὶ ὁ Ξέρξης. οὕτως οὖν ἐλεύθεροι γίγνονται οἱ Ἕλληνες διὰ τὴν ἀρετήν.

Vocabulary

ναυτικόν, τό	fleet, navy (2b)
ἀφικνέομαι	arrive
νύξ, ἡ	night (nom.)
ἔνθα καὶ ἔνθα	this way and that
ἡμέρα, ἡ	day (1b)
εὐκόσμως	in good order
ἀρετή, ἡ	courage

Grammar for Section 3A–B

In this section you cover:
- Type 3a nouns: λιμήν and νύξ (3a)
- Personal pronouns: ἐγώ, σύ, ἡμεῖς, ὑμεῖς

VOCABULARY CHECK

Ensure you know the meaning of:
ἀφικνέομαι, κίνδῡνος, ἰδού, χωρέω, δεινός, οἰκίᾱ, φαίνομαι

VOCABULARY TO BE LEARNED

ἀνήρ (ἀνδρ-), ὁ man (3a)
γείτων (γειτον-), ὁ neighbour (3a)
λαμπάς (λαμπαδ-), ἡ torch (3a)
λιμήν (λιμεν-), ὁ harbour (3a)
νύξ (νυκτ-), ἡ night (3a)
παῖς (παιδ-), ὁ child, son, boy, slave (3a)
πατρίς (πατριδ-), ἡ fatherland (3a)
σωτήρ (σωτηρ-), ὁ saviour (3a)

THIRD DECLENSION NOUNS

66. So far you have met nouns classified as types 1 or 2 (or 1st and 2nd declension). The endings of these nouns show very helpful similarities with the definite article and adjectives like καλός, and their genders can for the most part be predicted.

There is a further group of nouns, type 3 nouns, which decline in another way. Here are two examples of type 3 nouns laid out in full: ὁ λιμήν, 'harbour', and ἡ νύξ, 'night'.

	ὁ λιμήν (λιμεν-), **'harbour'** (3a)		ἡ νύξ (νυκτ-), **'night'** (3a)	
	s.	*pl.*	*s.*	*pl.*
Nom.	λιμήν	λιμέν-ες	νύξ	νύκτ-ες
Acc.	λιμέν-α	λιμέν-ας	νύκτ-α	νύκτ-ας
Gen.	λιμέν-ος	λιμέν-ων	νυκτ-ός	νυκτ-ῶν
Dat.	λιμέν-ι	λιμέσι(ν) [< λιμέν-σι(ν)]	νυκτ-ί	νυξί(ν) [< νυκτ-σί(ν)]

Important features of 3rd declension nouns

■ *Gender*

67. (a) The gender of 3rd declension nouns is not generally predictable from the *ending*. This means that you must be especially careful to learn the gender along with the noun. Nevertheless, there are patterns, for example:

> ▶ Nouns classified as type 3a are either m. or f., but never n.;
> ▶ Nouns classified as types 3b, 3c and 3f are always neuter.

■ *Stem*

(b) The noun's STEM is generally *not obvious from the nom. s.*

> ▶ When you learn a new noun, you must therefore also learn its stem – ὁ λιμήν (λιμέν-), 'harbour', ὁ ἀνήρ (ἀνδρ-), 'man', ἡ λαμπάς (λαμπαδ-), 'torch', and so on.

This is the only way for you to be able to spot the noun when it occurs in a form *different* from the nom. s. (In time, you will find that you are often able to predict a noun's stem from its nom. s. form and *vice versa*: this will come with experience.)

■ *Genitive singular*

(c) In dictionaries and word lists, you will usually find the nom. s. form of a noun listed along with its gen. s. and gender, e.g. λιμήν, λιμένος (m.) (or simply λιμήν ένος [m.]).
The gen. form enables you to see:

> ● The stem of the noun (i.e. λιμεν-); and
> ● That it is a type 3 noun (because of the ending, -ος).
> ● You will also find other nouns listed in this way, e.g. ἄνθρωπος ου (m.), 'man' and θάλαττα ης (f.), 'sea'.

■ *Vocative*

(d) The vocative of λιμήν and νύξ (both s. and pl.) are the same as the equivalent nom. forms: on the vocatives of other type 3a nouns see **204**.

■ *Noun-types*

(e) There are a number of different types of 3rd declension noun, of which 3a is the most common. In *Reading Greek*, 3rd declension nouns are classified as types 3a–h (you will meet types 3b–h in future sections).

> ● But you must be aware that when you look up a word in a dictionary you will not find these conventions employed: instead, you will have to

> deduce its type – 3a, 3b, etc. – from the way the noun is listed, i.e. its nom. and gen. forms and its gender.

■ *Accusative singular*

(f) 3a nouns ending in -ις (usually feminine) generally have an acc. s. in -ιν, e.g. χάρις (χαριτ-), 'grace', acc. s. χάριν, but otherwise follow the same pattern as λιμήν and νύξ. Note that πατρίς (acc. πατρίδα) is an exception.

■ *Knowing the endings*

(g) As you can see, the endings are very different from those of 1st and 2nd declension nouns. These type 3 endings are found extremely commonly in Greek, and it will be important to master them now.

(h) The dat. pl. of ἀνήρ (ἀνδρ-) 'man' is ἀνδράσι(ν), and its vocative ἄνερ.

EXERCISES

3A–B: 1. Taking all the 3a nouns listed in the learning vocabulary at the start of this section, and paying close attention to stem and gender, attach as many as you can to the following forms of the definite article:

1. τόν	5. τούς
2. οἱ	6. αἱ
3. τάς	7. τήν
4. ἡ	8. ὁ

3A–B: 2. Provide the correct form of the noun to agree with the definite article (for the stems, see the list above):

1. τῆς (πατρίς)	5. τοῖς (λιμήν)
2. τῶν (παῖς)	6. τῶν (γείτων)
3. τοῦ (σωτήρ)	7. ταῖς (νύξ)
4. τῷ (ἀνήρ)	8. τῇ (λαμπάς)

3A–B: 3. Translate into Greek using the nouns listed in the learning vocabulary at the start of this section and the following prepositions: διά, εἰς, ἐπί, παρά, πρός.

1. Alongside the harbour	6. Into the harbours
2. Into the fatherland	7. Against the neighbour
3. At/against the men	8. Because of the night
4. Towards the neighbours	9. At/against the children
5. Because of the child	10. Because of the fatherland

PERSONAL PRONOUNS
ἐγώ, 'I'; σύ, 'YOU' (S.); ἡμεῖς, 'WE'; ὑμεῖς, 'YOU' (PL.)

68. Learn the following pronouns:

s.

	ἐγώ '**I/me**'	σύ '**you**' (*s.*)
Nom.	ἐγώ	σύ
Acc.	με *or* ἐμέ	σέ
Gen.	μου *or* ἐμοῦ	σοῦ
Dat.	μοι *or* ἐμοί	σοί

pl.

	ἡμεῖς '**we/us**'	ὑμεῖς '**you**' (*pl.*)
Nom.	ἡμεῖς	ὑμεῖς
Acc.	ἡμᾶς	ὑμᾶς
Gen.	ἡμῶν	ὑμῶν
Dat.	ἡμῖν	ὑμῖν

Form and use

(a) Note that ἐμέ, ἐμοῦ, ἐμοί and σέ, σοῦ, σοί are emphatic forms, με, μου, μοι and σε, σου, σοι unemphatic, e.g. 'He is watching me' (με); 'Whom is he watching? Me!' (ἐμέ). The *unaccented* forms of these pronouns are 'enclitics': see **42**.

(b) Note the emphatic usage of the nom. forms, often implying a strong contrast with someone or something else. So:

- βαίνω means 'I am going'; but
- βαίνω ἐγώ means '*I* am going', and will probably be set in opposition to something/one else, equally emphatic e.g. σὺ δὲ μένεις 'but *you* are staying put'.

EXERCISES

3A–B: 4. Translate:

1. ἡμεῖς μὲν μαχόμεθα, ὑμεῖς δὲ ἡσυχάζετε.
2. ὁρῶ σὲ ἐγώ, σὺ δ' οὐχ ὁρᾷς ἐμέ.
3. ἐν ὑμῖν ἐστιν ἡ ἡμετέρα σωτηρία, οὐκ ἐν ἡμῖν.
4. τίς ὑμῶν ἢ τίς ἡμῶν φοβεῖται τοὺς ἄνδρας;
5. ἡ ἐλευθερία ἡ ὑμετέρα ἐν ἐμοί ἐστιν.
6. ὑμᾶς μὲν νικῶσιν οἱ κακοί, ἡμᾶς δὲ οὔ.
7. μὴ ἡμᾶς διώκετε, ὦ ἄνδρες.
8. ἀποθνῄσκομεν μὲν ἡμεῖς, σὺ δὲ οὐδὲν ποιεῖς ἀλλὰ ἡμᾶς θεᾷ.

3A–B: 5. Translate the italicised words:

1. Can they see *us*?
2. *You* (pl.) are foolish, *we* are intelligent.

3. Our safety is *in me*.
4. They go *towards you* (s.).
5. They come *from you* (pl.).
6. Which *of us* is free?
7. They cannot find *me* or *you* (s.).
8. Their freedom is *in us*.

TAKING STOCK

1. It is essential that you are confident you know the endings of 3rd declension nouns. Can you decline λιμήν and νύξ?
2. Explain the importance of finding the stems of 3rd declension nouns. Can you give the 'stems' of: ἀνήρ, γείτων, παῖς, and πατρίς?
3. Can you decline in full the personal pronouns ἐγώ and σύ?
4. Of what verbs are these the alternative stems – ἀφικ-, φαν-, μειν-, ἐλθ-, μαχεσ-?

REVISION EXERCISES FOR SECTION 3A–B

A VOCABULARY-BUILDING

1. Deduce the meaning of the words on the right from those on the left:

ἀνήρ	ἀνδρεῖος α ον
γῆ + ἔργον	ὁ γεωργός, γεωργέω
γιγνώσκω	ἀγνοέω
ἐκεῖσε	ἐκεῖ, ἐκεῖθεν
ἔμπειρος	ἄπειρος ον
θεάομαι	ἡ θέα, ὁ θεατής, τὸ θέατρον
θόρυβος	θορυβέω
ὁ κίνδυνος	κινδυνεύω, ἀκίνδυνος ον
μανθάνω	ὁ μαθητής
οἰκία	οἰκεῖος α ον
ὅπλα	ὁ ὁπλίτης
παῖς	ἡ παιδεία, παιδεύω, ἀπαίδευτος
φαίνομαι	φανερός (α) ον

B WORD SHAPE

1. Change nom. to acc.:

a. ὁ ἔμπειρος ἀνήρ
b. ἡ κακὴ νύξ
c. ὁ σῶος παῖς
d. ἡ καλὴ πατρίς

2. Change acc. to nom.:

a. τὸν ἀγαθὸν γείτονα
b. τὴν καλλίστην λαμπάδα
c. τὸν πολέμιον λιμένα
d. τὴν ἐλευθέραν πατρίδα

3. Change the phrases from question 1 into the gen. case and the phrases from question 2 into the dat. case.

C SYNTAX

Translate the phrases in exercises B 1 and 2 above.

Grammar for Section 3C–E

> In this section you cover:
> ● Adjectives/pronouns: οὗτος, ἐκεῖνος
> ● Adjectives: πολύς, μέγας
> ● Irregular nouns: ναῦς, Ζεύς
> ● Negatives

> VOCABULARY CHECK
>
> Ensure you know the meaning of:
> ἄλλος, γῆ, εἰπέ, λαμβάνω, λόγος, μανθάνω, τέχνη, ἔτι, καλέω, τρέχω, εὔχομαι, κελεύω

ADJECTIVES/PRONOUNS
οὗτος, 'THIS'; ἐκεῖνος, 'THAT'

69. The Greek words for 'this' and 'that' can be used as:

> ● *Adjectives*, in which case they will agree with a noun ('*this* ship', '*that* harbour'); or
> ● On their own as *pronouns*, when they will mean 'he', 'she', 'it', etc., depending on form and context.

Thus:

ἆρα οὐχ ὁρᾷς ἐκεῖνα τὰ πυρά;   'Do you not see *those* fires' (*adjective*)?

ἐπειδὴ οὗτος κελεύει, ἡ ναῦς ἀποπλεῖ.   'When *he* orders, the ship sails away' (*pronoun*).

Cf. on adjectives used as nouns, **49–50**.
Here are the declensions of οὗτος and ἐκεῖνος in full:

οὗτος αὕτη τοῦτο **'this', 'he, she, it'**

s.

	m.	*f.*	*n.*
Nom.	οὗτ-ος	αὕτ-η	τοῦτ-ο
Acc.	τοῦτ-ον	ταύτ-ην	τοῦτ-ο
Gen.	τούτ-ου	ταύτ-ης	τούτ-ου
Dat.	τούτ-ῳ	ταύτ-ῃ	τούτ-ῳ

οὗτος αὕτη τοῦτο **'this'**, **'he, she, it'** *(continued)*

pl.

	m.	*f.*	*n.*
Nom.	οὗτ-οι	αὗτ-αι	ταῦτ-α
Acc.	τούτ-ους	ταύτ-ᾱς	ταῦτ-α
Gen.	τούτ-ων	τούτ-ων	τούτ-ων
Dat.	τούτ-οις	ταύτ-αις	τούτ-οις

Form

(a) As with the definite article, all forms except the nom. m. and f. s. and pl. begin with τ-.

(b) Note especially the n. forms τοῦτο and ταῦτα and the f. gen. pl.: τούτων.

(c) It may be helpful to observe the rule that α/η in the ending goes with -αυ- in the stem, whereas o/ω in the ending goes with -ου- in the stem.

ἐκεῖνος ἐκείνη ἐκεῖνο **'that'**, **'he, she, it'**

s.

	m.	*f.*	*n.*
Nom.	ἐκεῖν-ος	ἐκείν-η	ἐκεῖν-ο
Acc.	ἐκεῖν-ον	ἐκείν-ην	ἐκεῖν-ο
Gen.	ἐκείν-ου	ἐκείν-ης	ἐκείν-ου
Dat.	ἐκείν-ῳ	ἐκείν-ῃ	ἐκείν-ῳ

pl.

	m.	*f.*	*n.*
Nom.	ἐκεῖν-οι	ἐκεῖν-αι	ἐκεῖν-α
Acc.	ἐκείν-ους	ἐκείν-ᾱς	ἐκεῖν-α
Gen.	ἐκείν-ων	ἐκείν-ων	ἐκείν-ων
Dat.	ἐκείν-οις	ἐκείν-αις	ἐκείν-οις

Usage

■ *'This, that'*

70. When οὗτος and ἐκεῖνος are used as adjectives they must, of course, agree with the noun which they are describing. Observe closely how Greek does this:

οὗτος ὁ ναύτης	or	ὁ ναύτης οὗτος	'this sailor'
ταῦτα τὰ ἔργα	or	τὰ ἔργα ταῦτα	'these deeds'
ἐκείνη ἡ βοή	or	ἡ βοὴ ἐκείνη	'that shout'

In other words, unlike English, Greek says (literally) either 'this the sailor', or 'the sailor this', all the words agreeing. Greek never sandwiches οὗτος and ἐκεῖνος between the definite article and the noun to make 'the this sailor'.

■ *'He, she, it'*

71. οὗτος and ἐκεῖνος are regularly used on their own, as third person pronouns, to mean 'this man', 'that woman', 'that thing', etc. and are usually best translated 'he', 'she', 'it', 'they', etc., depending on context.

οὗτος ἀφικνεῖται	'this [m., i.e. man] is approaching' (or '*he* is approaching')
ἐκεῖναι τρέχουσιν	'those [f., i.e. women] are running' (or '*they* are running')
τοῦτο ποιεῖ	'he is doing this [n., i.e. thing]' (or 'he is doing *it*')

■ *οὑτοσί and ἐκεινοσί*

72. Both οὗτος and ἐκεῖνος can occur in forms ending in -ῑ́, e.g. ἐκεινοσί, τουτονί, etc. This intensifies the pronouns so that they mean 'this man *here*', 'that woman *there*', etc.

EXERCISES

3C–E: 1. Add the correct form of οὗτος ὁ to the following nouns and translate:

1. λιμένα	6. ἄνδρας
2. λαμπάδες	7. ἔργον
3. γείτων	8. νύκτες
4. παῖδας	9. σωτῆρες
5. πατρίδα	10. ὅπλα

3C–E: 2. Add the correct form of ἐκεῖνος ὁ to the following nouns and translate:

1. λιμένες	6. ἄνδρες
2. λαμπάδας	7. σωτήρ
3. γείτονα	8. νύκτες
4. παῖδες	9. ἔργον
5. πατρίς	10. πυρά

3C–E: 3. Add the correct forms of οὗτος ὁ and ἐκεῖνος ὁ to the following nouns:

1. γείτονος	5. ἀνδράσι
2. λαμπάδι	6. πατρίδος
3. παίδων	7. νυξί
4. λιμένι	8. ἔργων

'MANY' AND 'GREAT': πολύς, μέγας

73. πολύς (πολλ-), 'many, much', and μέγας (μεγαλ-), 'great', decline just like καλός except for the four forms underlined:

πολύς πολλή πολύ (πολλ-), **'many, much'**

s.

	m.	*f.*	*n.*
Nom.	<u>πολύς</u>	πολλ-ή	<u>πολύ</u>
Acc.	<u>πολύν</u>	πολλ-ήν	<u>πολύ</u>
Gen.	πολλ-οῦ	πολλ-ῆς	πολλ-οῦ
Dat.	πολλ-ῷ	πολλ-ῇ	πολλ-ῷ

pl.

	m.	*f.*	*n.*
Nom.	πολλ-οί	πολλ-αί	πολλ-ά
Acc.	πολλ-ούς	πολλ-άς	πολλ-ά
Gen.	πολλ-ῶν	πυλλ-ῶν	πολλ-ῶν
Dat.	πολλ-οῖς	πολλ-αῖς	πολλ-οῖς

μέγας μεγάλη μέγα (μεγαλ-), **'big, great'**

s.

	m.	*f.*	*n.*
Nom.	<u>μέγας</u>	μεγάλ-η	<u>μέγα</u>
Acc.	<u>μέγαν</u>	μεγάλ-ην	<u>μέγα</u>
Gen.	μεγάλ-ου	μεγάλ-ης	μεγάλ-ου
Dat.	μεγάλ-ῳ	μεγάλ-ῃ	μεγάλ-ῳ

pl.

	m.	*f.*	*n.*
Nom.	μεγάλ-οι	μεγάλ-αι	μεγάλ-α
Acc.	μεγάλ-ους	μεγάλ-ᾱς	μεγάλ-α
Gen.	μεγάλ-ων	μεγάλ-ων	μεγάλ-ων
Dat.	μεγάλ-οις	μεγάλ-αις	μεγάλ-οις

EXERCISES

3C–E: 4. Add the correct form of πολύς to the following nouns, and translate:

1. λιμένας   5. ὅπλα
2. λαμπάδες   6. νύκτας
3. γείτονες   7. ἀπορία
4. πόλεμος

3C–E: 5. Add the correct form of μέγας to the following nouns, and translate:

1. λιμένα   4. ἔργον
2. λαμπάς   5. πατρίδας
3. γείτονες   6. ἀνήρ

3C–E: 6. Add the correct forms of πολύς and μέγας to the following nouns:

1. λιμένος
2. ἀνθρώπῳ
3. λαμπάδος
4. λόγων
5. ἔργοις
6. ἀπορίᾳ

IRREGULAR NOUNS
ἡ ναῦς, 'SHIP'; ὁ Ζεύς, 'ZEUS'

74. Learn the two following irregular nouns:

	ὁ Ζεύς, **'Zeus'**	ἡ ναῦς, **'ship'**	
		s.	*pl.*
Nom.	Ζεύς	ναῦς	νῆες
Acc.	Δί-α	ναῦν	ναῦς
Gen.	Δι-ός	νεώς	νεῶν
Dat.	Δι-ί	νηί	ναυσί(ν)
Voc.	ὦ Ζεῦ	ὦ ναῦ	

Form

The endings of ὁ Ζεύς, 'Zeus', are the same as for regular type 3a nouns: it is classed as irregular because of the unusual change in its stem.

EXERCISE

3C–E: 7. Translate into Greek using the following prepositions: διά, εἰς, ἐπί, παρά, πρός.

1. Because of (the) Zeus
2. Alongside the ships
3. Into the ship
4. Towards (the) Zeus
5. Against the ships

NEGATIVES

75. (a) A series of negatives with the simple negative (οὐ or μή) *first* in the clause reinforces the negative, e.g.

οὐκ ἀφικνεῖται οὐδείς	'nobody comes'
οὐκ ἀφικνεῖται οὐδεὶς οὐδέποτε	'no one ever comes'
μὴ λέγε μηδέν	'don't say anything at all'

(b) Where the simple negative *follows* a compound negative, they create a positive, e.g.

οὐδεὶς οὐκ ἀφικνεῖται	'nobody does not come', i.e. 'everyone comes'

76. (a) As we have already seen, Greek often leaves out the verb 'to be' if it can be assumed from the context (**48**). Likewise, other words can be left out if they are understood easily from the context, e.g.

ἆρα οὐ μελετῶσιν οἱ Λακεδαιμόνιοι;	'Don't the Spartans practise?'
οὔκ, ἀλλὰ ἡμεῖς κωλύομεν.	'No, (but instead) we prevent (*understand* 'them').'

(b) Observe that what appears in Greek as an adjective may best be translated into English as an adverb, e.g.

ἥσυχος καθεύδει ὁ δεσπότης	'The master is sleeping *peacefully.*' (lit. 'peaceful')

(c) You saw earlier how adjectives can be used as nouns in Greek by the addition of the definite article (**49**), e.g.

τὰ στρατηγικά	'military matters'
τὰ ναυτικά	'naval matters'

In fact, nearly all Greek adjectives can be used as nouns (cf. **50**). Observe the following:

ὁ κακός	'the evil man'
οἱ πολέμιοι	'the enemy'
αἱ βάρβαροι	'the barbarian women' (see note on p. 401)
τὸ καλόν	'the beautiful (thing)', i.e. 'beauty'

Remember, though, that when οὗτος and ἐκεῖνος are used as *pronouns* (meaning 'he', she', 'it', etc.) the definite article is *not* used.

SUMMARY LEARNING VOCABULARY FOR SECTION 3A–E

ἄγε	come!
ἀλλήλους	each other, one another (2a)
ἄλλος η ο	other, the rest of
ἀνήρ (ἀνδρ-), ὁ	man (3a)
ἀφικνέομαι (ἀφῑκ-)	arrive, come
βοάω	shout (for)
γείτων (γειτον-), ὁ	neighbour (3a)
δεινός ή όν	terrible, dire, clever
δή	then, indeed
ἐγγύς	(+gen.) near, nearby
ἐγώ	I
εἰπέ	speak! tell me!
ἐκεῖνος ἐκείνη ἐκεῖνο	that

SUMMARY LEARNING VOCABULARY FOR SECTION 3A–E
(CONTINUED)

ἐμβαίνω (ἐμβα-)	embark
ἐπειδή	when, since, because
ἐρωτάω (ἐρ-)	ask
ἔτι	still, yet
εὖ	well
εὐχή, ἡ	prayer (1a)
εὔχομαι	pray
Ζεύς (Δι-), ὁ	Zeus
ζητέω	look for, seek
ἡμεῖς	we
θεάομαι	watch, gaze at
θόρυβος, ὁ	noise, din, hustle and bustle (2a)
θύρᾱ, ἡ	door (1b)
θυσίᾱ, ἡ	a sacrifice (1b)
θύω	sacrifice
ἰδού	look! here! hey!
καθεύδω	sleep
καλέω	call, summon
κατά	(+acc.) in, on, by, according to
κελευστής, ὁ	boatswain (1d)
κελεύω	order
κίνδῡνος, ὁ	danger (2a)
Λακεδαιμόνιος, ὁ	Spartan (2a)
λαμβάνω (λαβ-)	take, capture
λαμπάς (λαμπαδ-), ἡ	torch (3a)
λιμήν (λιμεν-), ὁ	harbour (3a)
λόγος, ὁ	word, speech; story, tale (2a)
μανθάνω (μαθ-)	learn, understand
μέγας μεγάλη μέγα (μεγαλ-)	big, great
ναυτικός ή όν	naval
νῆσος, ἡ	island (2a)
νύξ (νυκτ-), ἡ	night (3a)
οἰκίᾱ, ἡ	house (1b)
οἴκαδε	homewards
οἴκοι	at home
ὅπλα, τά	weapons, arms (2b)
οὐδέ	and not, not even
οὗτος αὕτη τοῦτο	this
οὑτοσί αὑτηί τουτί	this here
παῖς (παιδ-), ὁ	child, son, boy, slave (3a)

SUMMARY LEARNING VOCABULARY FOR SECTION 3A–E
(CONTINUED)

πατρίς (πατριδ-), ἡ	fatherland (3a)
πόθεν;	from where?
πολύς πολλή πολύ (πολλ-)	many, much
πορεύομαι	march, journey, go
πυρά, τά	fire-signal (2b)
σπένδω	pour a libation
σπεύδω	hurry
σπονδή, ἡ	a libation (1a)
σύ	you (s.)
σωτήρ (σωτηρ-), ὁ	saviour (3a)
τέχνη, ἡ	skill, art, expertise (1a)
τρέχω (δραμ-)	run
τριήραρχος, ὁ	trierarch (2a)
ὑμεῖς	you (pl.)
φαίνομαι (φαν-)	appear, seem
χωρέω	go, come

TAKING STOCK

1. Can you explain when οὗτος and ἐκεῖνος are used as adjectives and when as pronouns, and what the difference in meaning is?
2. Do you know what the stems of πολύς and μέγας are, and which of the forms are 'irregular'?
3. Can you conjugate ναῦς and Ζεύς?

REVISION EXERCISES FOR SECTION 3C–E

A VOCABULARY-BUILDING

1. Group the words in this list together which seem to share common roots, then translate:

οὕτως	βοηθέω	κελεύω	ὑμέτερος	σπένδω	ἐκεῖσε
ἔνδον	βοή	ἔμπειρος	εὔχομαι	ἡμεῖς	βοάω
ὑμεῖς	σπονδή	οὗτος	κελευστής	εὐχή	ἐκεῖνος
ἐμπειρία	ἡμέτερος	κατακελεύω	ἐν	θέω	

B WORD SHAPE

1. Change nom. to acc.:

   a. οὗτος ὁ ἀνήρ
   b. ταῦτα τὰ ἔργα
   c. αὕτη ἡ λαμπάς
   d. αἱ βοαὶ αὗται
   e. οὗτοι οἱ λιμένες

2. Change acc. to nom.:

   a. τοῦτον τὸν γείτονα
   b. ταύτας τὰς λαμπάδας
   c. τὰ πυρὰ ταῦτα
   d. τὴν πατρίδα ταύτην
   e. τούτους τοὺς ἄνδρας

3. Insert the appropriate form of μέγας or πολύς:

   a. (μέγας) ἐστὶ τὸ ἔργον.
   b. οἱ ἄνδρες (πολύς) ἐμπειρίαν ἔχουσιν εἰς τὰ ναυτικά.
   c. ὁ κυβερνήτης πρὸς (μέγας) λιμένα κυβερνᾷ.
   d. ὁ ναύτης (πολύς) καὶ δεινὰ ὁρᾷ.

C SYNTAX
Translate the answers to exercises B 1–3 above.

D ENGLISH INTO GREEK
Translate these pairs of sentences:

1. ὁ οὖν κυβερνήτης πρὸς τὴν Σαλαμῖνα ταχέως βλέπει.
   And so the ship sails slowly towards that harbour.

2. μέγας μὲν γὰρ ὁ κίνδυνος ὁ τῶν Ἀθηναίων, πολὺς δὲ ὁ τῶν ἀνδρῶν θόρυβος.
   For there is much din, a lot of shouting and many men appear.

3. ἆρ' οὐκ οἶσθα πότερον ἐκεῖνοι ναυταί εἰσιν ἢ οὔ;
   I don't know whether that fellow is a general or not.

4. οὗτος ὁ ἀγαθὸς κυβερνήτης οὐκ ἀκούει ταύτας τὰς βοάς.
   That stupid rhapsode is afraid of these Spartans.

5. ἐκεῖνος μὲν γὰρ μῶρος περὶ πολλά, οὗτος δὲ περὶ οὐδέν.
   For while those women are cowardly about many things, this woman is not.

E TEST EXERCISE THREE C–E
Translate into English:

> ἡ μὲν ναῦς αὕτη πλεῖ παρὰ τὴν νῆσον, ὁ δὲ Δικαιόπολις λαμπάδα ὁρᾷ ἐν
> τῇ νήσῳ. ὁ δὲ κυβερνήτης εὖ οἶδεν ὅτι οὐκ ἔστι λαμπάς, ἀλλὰ τὰ πυρά.
> σπεύδει οὖν εἰς τὸν λιμένα· δηλοῖ γὰρ ἐκεῖνα τὰ πυρὰ ὅτι οἱ πολέμιοι
> ἐπέρχονται ἐπὶ τοὺς Ἀθηναίους. οἱ δὲ ἄνδρες οἱ ἐν τῷ λιμένι θεῶνται
> 5 ἐκεῖνα τὰ πυρὰ καὶ οἴκαδε τρέχουσιν ἐπὶ τὰ ὅπλα. ἴσασι γὰρ ὅτι μέγας
> ὁ κίνδυνος. φόβος δὲ μέγας λαμβάνει τὸν ῥαψῳδόν. φοβεῖται γὰρ τοὺς
> Λακεδαιμονίους. οἱ δὲ ναῦται λέγουσιν ὅτι Ἀθηναῖοι μὲν κρατοῦσι κατὰ
> θάλατταν, Λακεδαιμόνιοι δὲ κατὰ γῆν. καὶ Λακεδαιμόνιοι οὐ ῥᾳδίως
> μανθάνουσι τὴν ναυτικὴν τέχνην. ἐπειδὴ οὖν τὸ πλοῖον ἀφικνεῖται
> 10 εἰς τὸν λιμένα, ὁ Δικαιόπολις καὶ ὁ ῥαψῳδὸς πορεύονται πρὸς τὰς
> ναῦς. καὶ δῆλόν ἐστιν ὅτι αἱ νῆες αὗται ἐπέρχονται ἐπὶ ναυμαχίαν. οἱ
> μὲν γὰρ κελευσταὶ ζητοῦσι τοὺς τριηράρχους, ἐκεῖνοι δὲ καθεύδουσι
> ἥσυχοι. τέλος δὲ οἱ τριήραρχοι οὗτοι ἀφικνοῦνται εἰς τὸν λιμένα καὶ
> ἐμβαίνουσιν. ἔπειτα τὰς θυσίας θύουσι καὶ τὰς σπονδὰς σπένδουσι καὶ
> 15 ἀνάγονται.

Vocabulary

ἀνάγομαι   set sail, put out to sea

EXERCISE

Answer the following questions using the passage above. Give the line numbers of each word you identify.

1. Find two more examples of prepositional phrases like παρὰ τὴν νῆσον (l.1) which are made up of a preposition plus a noun in the acc. case.
2. Find three examples of verbs in the third person pl.
3. Find two examples of nouns which are in the acc. because they are the direct object of a verb, and state the verb of which each is the object.
4. Find an example of an adjective which is (a) m. s. nom., (b) f. s. acc., (c) n. s. nom.

Grammar for Section 4A–B

In this section you cover:
- Types 3b, c, e, f nouns: πρᾶγμα, πλῆθος, πόλις, πρέσβυς, ἄστυ
- Adjectives: εὔφρων
- Adjectives/pronouns: τις, τίς, οὐδείς
- Present participles: ὤν

VOCABULARY CHECK

Ensure you know the meaning of:
γυνή, κρατέω, ὀλίγος, διαφθείρω, θεός, κωλύω, νόμος, τῑμάω, φέρω, φόβος

VOCABULARY NEEDED FOR EXERCISES

ἄστυ, τό city (of Athens) (3f)
εὔφρων, εὖφρον (εὔφρον-) well-disposed
κακοδαίμων κακόδαιμον (κακόδαιμον-) unlucky, dogged by an evil daimon
οἴκησις, ἡ dwelling (3e)
οὐδείς οὐδεμία οὐδέν (οὐδεν-) no; no one, nothing
πλῆθος, τό number, crowd; the people (3c)
πόλις, ἡ city (state) (3e)
πρᾶγμα (πρᾱγματ-), τό thing; matter; affair; (pl.) troubles (3b)
σκεύη, τά gear, furniture (3c)
τάξις, ἡ battle-array, order, rank (3e)
τίς τί (τίν-) who? what?
τις τι (τιν-) a, a certain; someone

THIRD DECLENSION NOUNS
πρᾶγμα (3B), πλῆθος (3C), πόλις (3E), πρέσβυς (3E), ἄστυ (3F)

Type 3b nouns

77. Type 3b nouns are all neuter, and most end in -μα. Their stem is commonly a verb stem, and the noun has a *passive* sense – thus πράττω (πραγ-) 'I do', πρᾶγμα 'thing done', 'deed':

πρᾶγμα (πρᾱγματ-), τό **'deed, thing, matter' (3b)**

	s.	*pl.*
Nom.	πρᾶγμα	πρᾱ́γματ-α
Acc.	πρᾶγμα	πρᾱ́γματ-α
Gen.	πρᾱ́γματ-ος	πρᾱγμάτ-ων
Dat.	πρᾱ́γματ-ι	πρᾱ́γμασι(ν)

■ *Form*

> Be careful not to confuse 3b nouns with the few 1c nouns which end in -μα,
> e.g. ἡ τόλμα, 'daring'. A small number of type 3b nouns do not end in -μα,
> e.g. τὸ πῦρ, 'fire'.

Type 3c nouns

78. These are all neuter, and end in -ος:

πλῆθος, τό **'number, crowd, the people' (3c)**	
	s.	*pl.*
Nom.	πλῆθ-ος	πλήθ-η
Acc.	πλῆθ-ος	πλήθ-η
Gen.	πλήθ-ους	πληθ-ῶν
Dat.	πλήθε-ι	πλήθε-σι(ν)

■ *Form*

- Be careful not to confuse type 3c nouns like τὸ πλῆθος with type 2a nouns like ὁ ἄνθρωπος, 'man': the *gender* here makes all the difference.
- Also be careful not to mistake nom. and acc. pl. of type 3c nouns (e.g. τὰ πλῆθη) for the nom. s. of type 1a nouns like βοή, 'shout'.
- Note the presence of -ε- in the stem of this noun, which has contracted with 'regular' type 3a endings: i.e. the -ους ending was once -εος, -η was once -εα and -ῶν was once -έων.
- Note also that the -ους ending may be acc. pl. of 2a nouns, or the gen. s. of 3c nouns.

Type 3e nouns

79. These all end in -ις (f.) or -υς (m.):

πόλις, ἡ **'city-state' (3e)**	
	s.	*pl.*
Nom.	πόλι-ς	πόλεις
Acc.	πόλι-ν	πόλεις
Gen.	πόλε-ως	πόλε-ων
Dat.	πόλε-ι	πόλε-σι(ν)
Voc.	ὦ πόλι	

πρέσβυς, ὁ **'old man'** ; *pl.* **'ambassadors' (3e)**	
	s.	*pl.*
Nom.	πρέσβυ-ς	πρέσβεις
Acc.	πρέσβυ-ν	πρέσβεις
Gen.	πρέσβε-ως	πρέσβε-ων
Dat.	πρέσβε-ι	πρέσβε-σι(ν)
Voc.	ὦ πρέσβυ	

■ *Form*

- Note, once more, the presence of -ε- in the stem of this noun, which has contracted with 'regular' type 3a endings: i.e. the -εις ending of the nom. pl. is a contraction of ε-ες. (The acc. pl. form is borrowed from the nom.)
- πρέσβυς is unusual in that it has a different meaning in the s. and pl. The Greek for 'ambassador' (s.) would be ὁ πρεσβευτής and 'old men' (pl.) οἱ γέροντες (s. γέρων).

Type 3f nouns

80. These are all neuter, and end in -υ:

ἄστυ, τό 'city' (3f)

	s.	*pl.*
Nom.	ἄστυ	ἄστη
Acc.	ἄστυ	ἄστη
Gen.	ἄστε-ως	ἄστε-ων
Dat.	ἄστε-ι	ἄστε-σι(ν)

■ *Form*

Note that the nom. and acc. pl. of this noun is a contraction of -εα.

EXERCISES

4A–B: 1. Add the correct form of the 3b-, c-, e- and f-type nouns listed on the vocabulary on p. 70 to agree with the following definite articles. (First, check by gender that they are able to agree.)

1. οἱ	6. ὁ
2. τήν	7. τό
3. τά	8. τόν
4. τούς	9. ἡ
5. τάς	10. αἱ

4A–B: 2. Add the correct form of the noun to agree with the article.

1. τῷ (πλῆθος)	6. τῷ (ἄστυ)
2. τοῖς (ἄστυ)	7. τοῦ (πρέσβυς)
3. τῇ (πόλις)	8. τοῦ (πλῆθος)
4. τοῦ (πρᾶγμα)	9. τῷ (πρᾶγμα)
5. τῶν (πρέσβυς)	10. ταῖς (πόλις)

TYPE 3 ADJECTIVES

81. There are a number of adjective types based on type 3 nouns.

> ▶ Just as the endings of καλός-type adjectives correspond to the endings
> of type 1 and 2 nouns, so the type 3 adjective endings correspond to the
> endings of type 3a and 3b nouns (and, like them, also have a *stem* which
> needs to be learned):

Adjectives in -ων -ον

82. Typical of this type 3 adjective is εὔφρων ον, 'well-disposed'. Note the *stem*
is εὐφρον-:

εὔφρων εὖφρον (εὐφρον-) **'well-disposed'**		
s.		
	m./f.	*n.*
Nom.	εὔφρων	εὖφρον
Acc.	εὔφρον-α	εὖφρον
Gen.	εὔφρον-ος	εὔφρον-ος
Dat.	εὔφρον-ι	εὔφρον-ι
Voc.	εὖφρον	
pl.		
	m./f.	*n.*
Nom.	εὔφρον-ες	εὔφρον-α
Acc.	εὔφρον-ας	εὔφρον-α
Gen.	εὐφρόν-ων	εὐφρόν-ων
Dat.	εὔφροσι(ν)	εὔφροσι(ν)

■ *Gender alert*

In these adjectives, the same form is used for both m. and f., e.g.

| εὔφρων ὁ ἀνήρ | 'The man is well-disposed' |
| εὔφρων ἡ θεά | 'The goddess is well-disposed' |

'A, A CERTAIN' τις τι; 'WHICH? WHO? WHAT?' τίς τί

83. The pronouns τις τι and τίς τί (which can be used adjectivally) follow a similar pattern to εὔφρων εὖφρον:

τις τι (τιν-), 'a, a certain, some'

s.

	m./f.	*n.*
Nom.	τις	τι
Acc.	τιν-ά	τι
Gen.	τιν-ός	τιν-ός
Dat.	τιν-ί	τιν-ί

pl.

	m./f.	*n.*
Nom.	τιν-ές	τιν-ά
Acc.	τιν-άς	τιν-ά
Gen.	τιν-ῶν	τιν-ῶν
Dat.	τισί(ν)	τισί(ν)

■ *Usage*

(a) When τις τι is used as an adjective (i.e. in conjunction with a noun) it means 'a' (pl. 'some') or 'a certain', e.g.

γεωργός τις	'A (certain) farmer'
πλοῖόν τι	'A (certain) ship'
ἄνδρες τινές	'Some men', 'Certain men'

(Note, though, that you do not always need to use τις when translating 'a(n)' into Greek: 'a farmer' can also be translated simply as γεωργός.)

(b) When τις τι is used on its own (i.e. as a *pronoun*) it means 'someone'/'anyone' or 'something'/'anything', e.g.

ἀλλά τις ἀφικνεῖται	'But someone is arriving'
ὁρᾷς τι;	'Can you see anything?' (lit. 'Do you see anything?')

(c) Remember that τις τι is enclitic (**42**) and cannot come first in a sentence or clause.

τίς τί (τίν-), 'which? who? what?'

s.

	m./f.	*n.*
Nom.	τίς	τί
Acc.	τίν-α	τί
Gen.	τίν-ος	τίν-ος
Dat.	τίν-ι	τίν-ι

τίς τί (τίν-), **'which? who? what?'** *(continued)*

pl.

	m./f.	*n.*
Nom.	τίν-ες	τίν-α
Acc.	τίν-ας	τίν-α
Gen.	τίν-ων	τίν-ων
Dat.	τίσι(ν)	τίσι(ν)

■ *Usage*

84. Note once more that the way in which τίς τί is used affects its translation into English:

    (a) When it is used as an adjective (i.e. in conjunction with a noun) it means 'which' or 'what', e.g.

        τίς γεωργός;   'What farmer?'

        τί πλοῖον;   'What ship?'

    (b) When τίς τί is used on its own (i.e. as a pronoun) it means 'who' or 'what', e.g.

        τίς ἀφικνεῖται;   'Who is arriving?'

        τί ὁρᾷς;   'What can you see?' (lit. 'What do you see?')

■ *Accent*

85. Note the difference in accent between τις τι and τίς τί. The accent on τίς τί ('who?', 'what?') *always* falls on the first ι and is *always* acute (i.e. ί).

'NO, NO-ONE, NOTHING': οὐδ-είς οὐδε-μία οὐδ-έν

86. οὐδείς 'no one' follows a different adjectival pattern:

	m.	*f.*	*n.*
Nom.	οὐδείς	οὐδε-μί-α	οὐδέν
Acc.	οὐδέν-α	οὐδε-μί-αν	οὐδέν
Gen.	οὐδεν-ός	οὐδε-μι-ᾶς	οὐδεν-ός
Dat.	οὐδεν-ί	οὐδε-μι-ᾷ	οὐδεν-ί

Form and use

■ *No + one*

(a) οὐδείς is simply οὐδέ, 'not, nor, not even', plus εἷς μία ἕν, 'one' (see **319**). Naturally, οὐδείς is very rare in the pl. It has a corresponding form μηδείς.

■ *The '3-1-3' pattern*

(b) Observe closely the declension patterns of the three genders of οὐδείς. You will see:

- That the f. form, -μία, declines exactly like a first declension noun (1b, such as ἀπορία with short α in nom. and acc.); but
- The m. and n. forms of the adjective decline like a third declension noun (types 3a and type 3b respectively).

▶ As you will discover, a number of Greek adjectives follow this '3-1-3' pattern, where the m. and n. forms follow the pattern of type 3 nouns and the f. follows that of a type 1 noun.

■ *Noun and adjective*

(c) Observe that οὐδείς and μηδείς are used as a pronoun and an adjective:

οὐδεὶς προσέρχεται	'No one [pronoun] is approaching'
οὐδὲν ὁρῶ	'I see nothing [pronoun]'
οὐδένα ναύτην ὁρῶ	'I see no [adjective] sailor' ('I don't see any sailor')

EXERCISES

4A–B: 3. Add the correct form or forms of εὔφρων, τις and οὐδείς to the following nouns (use οὐδείς only with s. nouns):

1. πλῆθος
2. πόλιν
3. πρέσβεις
4. ἄστυ
5. οἰκήσεις
6. τάξις
7. σκεύη

4A–B: 4. Add the correct form or forms of εὔφρων, τις and οὐδείς to the following nouns in the gen. and dat. (once more, use οὐδείς only with s. nouns):

1. πλήθει
2. πράγματος
3. πρέσβεων
4. τάξεως
5. πόλει
6. ἄστεσι

PRESENT PARTICIPLES

87. In the reading passages, you have met a number of forms of the present participle of the verb 'to be' (εἰμί). Here is the declension of ὤν, 'being', in full. It is a type 3 adjective, but note the difference from the type 3 adjectives you have met so far:

ὤν οὖσα ὄν (ὀντ-) **'being'**

s.

	m.	*f.*	*n.*
Nom.	ὤν	οὖσ-α	ὄν
Acc.	ὀντ-α	οὖσ-αν	ὄν
Gen.	ὀντ-ος	οὖσ-ης	ὀντ-ος
Dat.	ὀντ-ι	οὖσ-ῃ	ὀντ-ι

pl.

	m.	*f.*	*n.*
Nom.	ὀντ-ες	οὖσ-αι	ὀντ-α
Acc.	ὀντ-ας	οὖσ-ᾱς	ὀντ-α
Gen.	ὀντ-ων	οὐο-ῶν	ὀντ-ων
Dat.	οὖσι(ν)	οὖσ-αις	οὖσι(ν)

■ *Form*

Note that ὤν οὖσα ὄν (ὀντ-) follows a '3-1-3' pattern like οὐδείς:

- The m. and n. forms follow the pattern of type 3a and 3b nouns;
- The f. follows that of a type 1 noun (in this case a type 1c noun like θάλαττα, 'sea');
- Note, too, that the m./n. participle stem ends in τ- (ὀντ-), *unlike* the stem of adjectives like εὔφρων, in ν- (εὐφρον-).

■ *Usage*

88. Participles, of which you will meet more examples in 4C–D, occur frequently in Greek and are therefore important to master. Here are a few points to bear in mind:

- Participles are **adjectives**.
- Participles **derive from verbs**: ὤν, 'being', for example, derives from the verb εἰμί, 'I am'. In English, all present participles are formed by placing '-ing' on the end of a verb, e.g. 'be-ing', 'see-ing', 'go-ing', and so on.
- Like any other adjective, a participle has to **agree in gender, number and case** with the person or thing in the sentence it is describing, e.g.

　　οἱ ἄνδρες, μῶροι ὄντες,..　'The men, *being* stupid, ...' (m. nom. pl.)

　　τὴν θεάν, εὔφρονα οὖσαν...　'The goddess, *being* well-disposed, ...' (f. acc. s.)

- **Translation:** since Greek participles are often stilted when translated literally into English, you will need to think carefully about how you render them in English. Here are some of the ways participles may be translated:

οἱ ἄνδρες μῶροι ὄντες   'Since the men are stupid …'
'As the men are stupid …'
'While they are stupid, the men …'
'If the men are stupid …'
'Although the men are stupid …'
'The men, who are stupid, …'

So you see that the participle can be equivalent to a combination of conjunction ('although', 'since', 'if', 'when') and finite verb, or relative pronoun ('who', 'which') and finite verb.

▶ There is no one 'right way' of translating a participle. It is generally a good idea first to translate literally ('the men being stupid …', 'the goddess being well-disposed …', etc.) before deciding how best to render the participle in the given context.

EXERCISES

4A–B: 5. Add the correct form or forms of ὤν to agree with the following nouns:

1. ἄνθρωποι	6. λιμένες
2. γυνή	7. πλῆθος
3. πρέσβεις	8. πόλιν
4. ἄστη	9. θεαί
5. λόγον	10. θεός

4A–B: 6. Choose between the different versions of the Greek participles using the English translations beneath each sentence to guide you. (It will help to identify the gender, number and case of the noun which each participle is describing.)

1. βλέπουσι πρὸς τὴν γυναῖκα καλὴν <u>οὖσα/οὖσαν</u>.
   They are looking at the woman who is beautiful.

2. ὁ κυβερνήτης οὐκ εἰσβαίνει εἰς τὸ πλοῖον βεβαῖον <u>ὤν/ὄν</u>.
   The captain does not go on board the ship although it is secure.

3. οἱ ἄνθρωποι θνητοὶ <u>ὄντες/οὖσαι</u> τοὺς θεοὺς τιμῶσιν.
   Since men are mortal, they honour the gods.

4. μῶρος <u>ὤν/ὄντα</u> ὁ ναύτης καλός ἐστιν.
   While he is stupid, the sailor is handsome.

5. φοβούμεθα τὴν πόλιν μεγάλην <u>οὖσα/οὖσαν</u>.
   We are afraid of the city since it is big.

SUMMARY LEARNING VOCABULARY FOR SECTION 4A–B

ἄστυ, τό	city (of Athens) (3f)
ἀτῑμάζω	dishonour, hold in dishonour
γεωργός, ὁ	farmer (2a)
γυνή (γυναικ-), ἡ	woman, wife (3a)
δαίμων (δαιμον-), ὁ	god, (minor) deity, daimon (3a)
δεσπότης, ὁ	master (1d)
διαφθείρω (διαφθειρ-)	destroy, kill
ἔτι καὶ νῦν	even now, still now
εὔφρων, εὖφρον (εὐφρον-)	well-disposed
θεός, ὁ/ἡ	god(-dess) (2a)
θνητός ή όν	mortal
κακοδαίμων κακόδαιμον (κακόδαιμον-)	unlucky, dogged by an evil daimon
κρατέω	hold sway, power (over)
κωλύω	prevent, stop
μάλιστα	especially; particularly; yes
νεκρός, ὁ	corpse (2a)
νή	(+acc.) by …!
νόμος, ὁ	law, convention (2a)
νόσος, ἡ	plague, disease (2a)
οἴκησις, ἡ	dwelling (3e)
ὀλίγος η ον	small, few
οὐδείς οὐδεμία οὐδέν (οὐδεν-)	no; no one, nothing
πλῆθος, τό	number, crowd; the people (3c)
πόλις, ἡ	city (state) (3e)
πρᾶγμα (πρᾱγματ-), τό	thing; matter; affair; (pl.) troubles (3b)
πυρά, ἡ	funeral pyre (1b)
σκεύη, τά	gear, furniture (3c)
τάξις, ἡ	battle-array, order, rank (3e)
τῑμάω	honour
τίς τί (τίν-)	who? what?
τις τι (τιν-)	a, a certain; someone
τύπτω	strike, hit
φέρω (ἐνεγκ-)	carry, bear
φόβος, ὁ	fear (2a)

TAKING STOCK

1. Can you confidently recite the five new types of noun?
2. Do you understand the difference between third declension and 3-1-3 declension adjectives? Can you give an example of each?
3. Can you demonstrate the difference in meaning between τίς τί and τις τι?
4. Do you know what a participle is, and can you decline ὤν?
5. Of what verbs are the following the alternative stems: ἐνεγκ-, λαβ-, δραμ-?

REVISION EXERCISES FOR SECTION 4A–B

A VOCABULARY-BUILDING

1. Deduce the meaning of the words on the right from those on the left.

ἀπαίδευτος	ἡ παίδευσις, τὸ παίδευμα
ἀποθνῄσκω (ἀποθαν-) }	ἀθάνατος ον, ὁ θάνατος
θνητός	
γίγνομαι (γεν-)	ἡ γένεσις
δηλόω	ἡ δήλωσις
ἐμβαίνω (ἐμβα-)	ἡ ἔμβασις
ἐρωτάω	τὸ ἐρώτημα
ζητέω	ἡ ζήτησις
θεάομαι	τὸ θέαμα
καλέω	ἡ κλῆσις
καλός	τὸ κάλλος
κρατέω	τὸ κράτος
μανθάνω	ἡ μάθησις, τὸ μάθημα
ποιέω	τὸ ποίημα, ἡ ποίησις
στρατηγός	τὸ στρατήγημα
στρατιά	τὸ στράτευμα
ταχέως	τὸ τάχος
τιμάω	ἡ τιμή, ἄτιμος ον
τολμάω	ἡ τόλμησις, τὸ τόλμημα
ψευδῶς	τὸ ψεῦδος

B/C WORD SHAPE AND SYNTAX

1. Translate into Greek the italic phrases in the following sentences, including in each answer a part of ὤν οὖσα ὄν:

   a. *Since I am unhappy*, I shall leave the city.
   b. *We, who are few*, shall not defeat *you, who are many*.
   c. *As friends*, *ladies*, you do not quarrel.
   d. *I, an Athenian and fortunate*, hate *you, Spartan that you are and hated by the gods*.
   e. *Who are you* to threaten me?

D ENGLISH INTO GREEK

Translate these pairs of sentences:

1. ἐγὼ γὰρ θνητὸς ὢν οὐκ ἀτιμάζω τοὺς θεούς.
   Since you are a farmer you know the laws.

2. ἐκείνους οὖν, ἐμπείρους ὄντας κατὰ γῆν, Ἀθηναῖοι νικῶσι κατὰ θάλατταν.
   As sailors we hold sway on the sea.

3. τὸ δ’ ἄστυ καλὸν ὄν, οὐ τιμῶ.

I am not afraid of the number of corpses, large as it is.

4. ὁ δὲ στρατηγὸς οὗτος, ἄριστος ὤν, οὐ φοβεῖται τοὺς Λακεδαιμονίους πολεμίους ὄντας.

My wife, who is unlucky, is afraid of the plague, which is evil.

5. οἱ γὰρ ἄνθρωποι, κακοδαίμονες ὄντες, τιμῶσι τοὺς τῶν θεῶν νόμους, ἀρίστους ὄντας.

The people (use τὸ πλῆθος), since it is good, does not dishonour the gods, who are great.

E TEST EXERCISE FOUR A–B

Translate into English:

ΝΕΑΝΙΑΣ	δεῦρ’ ἐλθὲ καὶ εἰπέ. διὰ τί <u>ὀλοφύρῃ</u>, ὦ φίλε; ἆρα <u>υἱόν</u> τινα, κακοδαίμονα ὄντα, ὀλοφύρῃ, ἢ <u>θυγατέρα</u> ἢ γυναῖκα;
ΓΕΡΩΝ	κακοδαίμων δὴ ὢν ἔγωγε, ὦ φίλε, τοῦτο ποιῶ. ὀλοφύρομαι γὰρ τόν τε υἱὸν τὸν οὐκέτ’ ὄντα καὶ τὴν θυγατέρα τὴν ἤδη νεκρὸν οὖσαν.
5 ΝΕΑΝ.	κακοδαίμων δὴ φαίνῃ ὤν. ἀλλὰ τί αἴτιόν ἐστιν; πῶς ἀποθνῄσκουσιν οἱ ἄνθρωποι;
ΓΕΡ.	διὰ τὴν νόσον, ὦ φίλε, νεκροὶ <u>ἐπὶ νεκροῖς</u> πίπτουσι καὶ ἀποθνῄσκουσιν ἄνθρωποι κακοδαίμονες ὄντες.
ΝΕΑΝ.	πολλὰ δὴ <u>πράγματα</u> ἔχομεν διὰ τὴν νόσον. ὁρῶ γὰρ ἔγωγε τὸ
10	μὲν πλῆθος τῶν ἀνθρώπων κακόδαιμον ὄν, τὴν δὲ πόλιν <u>πολλῇ</u> ἐν <u>ἀπορίᾳ</u> οὖσαν, τοὺς δὲ ἀνθρώπους <u>ἐφημέρους</u> ὄντας καὶ κακοδαίμονας.
ΓΕΡ.	μὴ οὖν ἀτίμαζε τοὺς θεοὺς μηδὲ <u>ἀσέβει</u> εἰς τὴν πόλιν, ἀλλὰ τόλμα καὶ τίμα τοὺς θεούς.

Vocabulary

ὀλοφύρομαι lament	πράγματα, τά troubles
υἱός, ὁ son	πολλῇ … ἀπορίᾳ much perplexity
θυγάτηρ (θυγατ(ε)ρ-) ἡ daughter	ἐφήμερος ον short-lived
ἐπὶ νεκροῖς on top of corpses	ἀσεβέω commit irreverent acts (on)

EXERCISE

Answer the following questions using the passage above. Give the line numbers of each word you identify.

1. Find two examples of participles in the acc., giving their number and gender and say with which noun each agrees.
2. Find two examples of imperatives, and state whether each is s. or pl.
3. Find an example of an adjective which is (a) m. nom. pl., (b) m. acc. pl.
4. What case are (a) φίλε (line 1) and (b) ἀπορίᾳ (line 11)?

Grammar for Section 4C–D

> In this section you cover:
> - Present participles, active and middle: παύων, παυόμενος
> - Uses of participles; expressions using participles
> - 3g nouns: βασιλεύς
> - Elision and crasis

VOCABULARY CHECK

Ensure you know the meaning of:
ἀπάγω, ἀποφεύγω, δοῦλος, ξένος, ἀποκτείνω, μισέω, πάσχω, τυγχάνω, ὕβρις

MORE PRESENT PARTICIPLES

89. Just as the verb 'to be' gives us a participle form, 'being', so most verbs have a present participle in English: 'to run' gives 'running'; 'to stop', 'stopping', and so on. As you have already learnt, participles are adjectives (i.e. they change according to the gender, number and case of the noun they agree with or represent).

Present active participles

90. Present active participles are formed simply by adding -ων -ουσα –ον to the present stem.
They decline just like ὤν, 'being' and follow the '3-1-3' pattern (**86[b]**).

> ▶ Active participles are generally easy to spot: look for a verb stem plus -οντ- or -ουσ-:

παύ-ων παύ-ουσα παῦ-ον (παυοντ-) **'stopping'**

s.

	m.	*f.*	*n.*
Nom.	παύ-ων	παύ-ουσ-α	παῦ-ον
Acc.	παύ-οντ-α	παύ-ουσ-αν	παῦ-ον
Gen.	παύ-οντ-ος	παυ-ούσ-ης	παύ-οντ-ος
Dat.	παύ-οντ-ι	παυ-ούσ-ῃ	παύ-οντ-ι

παύ-ων παύ-ουσα παῦ-ον (παυοντ-) **'stopping'** *(continued)*

pl.

	m.	*f.*	*n.*
Nom.	παύ-οντ-ες	παύ-ουσ-αι	παύ-οντ-α
Acc.	παύ-οντ-ας	παυ-ούσ-ᾱς	παύ-οντ-α
Gen.	παυ-όντ-ων	παυ-ουσ-ῶν	παυ-όντ-ων
Dat.	παύ-ουσι(ν)	παυ-ούσ-αις	παύ-ουσι(ν)

Present active participles of contract verbs

91. Observe the endings which active contract verbs have in their participle forms:

- ποιέ-ων -ουσα -ον (-οντ-) contracts to: ποιῶν ποιοῦσα ποιοῦν (ποιουντ-), 'doing'
- τιμά-ων -ουσα -ον (-οντ-) contracts to: τιμῶν τιμῶσα τιμῶν (τιμωντ-), 'honouring'
- δηλό-ων -ουσα -ον (-οντ-) contracts to: δηλῶν δηλοῦσα δηλοῦν (δηλουντ-), 'showing, revealing'

■ Form

(a) These contractions follow the same principles as those in other verb forms you have met: e.g. τιμά-ομεν > τιμῶμεν (α + ο = ω); thus τιμά-ον > τιμῶν; ποιέ-ω > ποιῶ (ε + ω = ω); thus ποιέ-ων > ποιῶν, etc. (**25**).

(b) Note that the form τιμῶν could be the neuter s. nom. and acc. participle, or the masculine s. nom. participle.

(c) Once more, these contracted participles have exactly the same *case-endings* as ὤν, 'being', and παύων, 'stopping'. Only the contracted *stem* is different e.g.

ε-contract ποιῶν ποιοῦσα ποιοῦν (ποιουντ-) **'doing'**

s.

	m.	*f.*	*n.*
Nom.	ποιῶν	ποιοῦσ-α	ποιοῦν
Acc.	ποιοῦντ-α	ποιοῦσ-αν	ποιοῦν
Gen.	ποιοῦντ-ος	ποιούσ-ης	ποιοῦντ-ος
Dat.	ποιοῦντ-ι	ποιούσ-ῃ	ποιοῦντ-ι

ε-**contract** ποιῶν ποιοῦσα ποιοῦν (ποιουντ-) **'doing'** *(continued)*

pl.

	m.	*f.*	*n.*
Nom.	ποιοῦντ-ες	ποιοῦσ-αι	ποιοῦντ-α
Acc.	ποιοῦντ-ας	ποιούσ-ᾱς	ποιοῦντ-α
Gen.	ποιούντ-ων	ποιουσ-ῶν	ποιούντ-ων
Dat.	ποιοῦ-σι(ν)	ποιούσ-αις	ποιοῦ-σι(ν)

Present middle participles

92. (a) The present participles of middle verbs are formed by adding -ομεν-ος η ον to the present stem.

(b) They are '2-1-2' adjectives like καλός: that is, they decline like type 2 nouns in the m. (ἄνθρωπος) and n. (ἔργον) and type 1 nouns (like βοή) in the f.

▶ Middle participles are generally easy to spot. Look for a verb stem plus -ομεν-:

παυ-όμεν-ος η ον **'stopping oneself'**

s.

	m.	*f.*	*n.*
Nom.	παυ-όμεν-ος	παυ-ομέν-η	παυ-όμεν-ον
Acc.	παυ-όμεν-ον	παυ-ομέν-ην	παυ-όμεν-ον
Gen.	παυ-ομέν-ου	παυ-ομέν-ης	παυ-ομέν-ου
Dat.	παυ-ομέν-ῳ	παυ-ομέν-ῃ	παυ-ομέν-ῳ

pl.

	m.	*f.*	*n.*
Nom.	παυ-όμεν-οι	παυ-όμεν-αι	παυ-όμεν-α
Acc.	παυ-ομέν-ους	παυ-ομέν-ᾱς	παυ-όμεν-α
Gen.	παυ-ομέν-ων	παυ-ομέν-ων	παυ-ομέν-ων
Dat.	παυ-ομέν-οις	παυ-ομέν-αις	παυ-ομέν-οις

Present middle participles of contract verbs

93. Observe the the effect that contraction has on middle participle forms:

- φοβέ-ομεν-ος η ον contracts to: φοβούμεν-ος η ον 'fearing'
- θεά-ομενος η ον contracts to: θεώμεν-ος η ον 'watching
- δουλό-ομεν-ος η ον contracts to: δουλούμεν-ος η ον 'enslaving'

■ *Form*

(a) Since the contraction takes place *before* the endings -μεν-ος η ον are added, these participles have endings *identical* to παυ-όμεν-ος η ον.

(b) Note once more that the contractions in these participles follow the same principles as those in other verb forms you have met, e.g.

φοβέ-ομαι > φοβοῦμαι (ε + ο = ου)

φοβέ-ομενος > φοβούμενος (**25**).

EXERCISES

4C–D: 1. Add the correct form or forms of τρέχων and παυόμενος to the following nouns:

1. παῖδας	5. Ἀθηναῖοι
2. γυναῖκες	6. θεάν
3. πρέσβυς	7. θεός
4. Λακεδαιμόνιον	8. πλῆθος

4C–D: 2. Add the correct form or forms of τρέχων and παυόμενος to the following nouns (all of which are in the gen. or dat.):

1. παιδί	5. Ἀθηναίοις
2. γυναικός	6. θεᾷ
3. πρέσβεως	7. θεῷ
4. Λακεδαιμονίων	8. πλήθεσι

Use of participles

94. A very common Greek usage is to join a participle with a definite article and use it as a noun: e.g.

- ὁ τρέχων = lit. 'the [m. s.] running', 'he who runs, the man who is running, the runner'
- οἱ τρέχοντες = lit. 'the [m. pl.] running', 'those who run, the men who are running, the running men, the runners'; this form is used when referring to a group combining males and females
- αἱ τρέχουσαι = lit. 'the [f. pl.] running', 'the running women, the women who run, the runners'

EXERCISES

4C–D: 3. Add the correct form of the participle to the definite articles using the following verbs: δηλόω, θεάομαι, ὁράω, ποιέω, φοβέομαι. Then translate:

1. τόν (watching)	5. οἱ (fearing)
2. τάς (seeing)	6. ἡ (doing)
3. τούς (doing)	7. τήν (seeing)
4. αἱ (showing)	8. τό (showing)

4C–D: 4. Add the correct form of the participle to the definite articles (all of which are in the gen. or dat.) and translate:

1. τοῖς (watching)	5. τοῦ (fearing)
2. τῇ (seeing)	6. ταῖς (doing)
3. τῶν (doing)	7. τῷ (seeing)
4. ταῖς (showing)	8. τοῖς (showing)

Expressions using participles

95. Note the following expressions which tend to include a participle:

δῆλός εἰμι (φεύγων)	'I am obvious[ly] (fleeing)'
παύω (σε φεύγοντα)	'I stop (you fleeing)'
παύομαι (φεύγων)	'I stop [myself] (fleeing), I cease (fleeing)'
καίπερ (φεύγων)	'although/despite (fleeing)'
τυγχάνω (φεύγων)	'I happen, chance [to be], actually am (fleeing)'
*φαίνομαι (φεύγων)	'I appear [to be] (fleeing), I seem [to be] (fleeing)'
λανθάνω (σε φεύγων)	'I escape the notice of (you [in] fleeing)' (i.e. 'I flee without you seeing me')
φθάνω (σε φεύγων)	'I anticipate (you [in] fleeing), I flee before you (do)'

■ *Form and use*

▶ Remember that the participle must change to agree with the noun to which it refers, e.g. <u>αἱ γυναῖκες</u> τυγχάνουσι <u>φεύγουσαι</u> 'the women [f. nom. pl.] happen to be fleeing [f. nom. pl.]'.

*▶ Note that φαίνομαι φεύγων means 'I seem to be fleeing *and actually am*'.

EXERCISE

4C–D: 5. Choose the correct version of the Greek participles using the English translations beneath each sentence to guide you. (It will help to identify the gender, number and case of the noun which each participle is describing.)

1. <u>βαίνων/βαίνουσα</u> πρὸς τὰς Ἀθῆνας, ἡ γυνὴ βλέπει πρὸς τὸν Πειραιᾶ.
   Whilst going towards Athens, the woman looks towards the Piraeus.

2. δῆλός ἐστι <u>παίζων/παίζοντα</u> ὁ ῥαψῳδός.
   The rhapsode is clearly joking.

3. <u>φεύγων/φεύγοντα</u> ὁ κυβερνήτης λανθάνει τοὺς <u>βοῶντες/βοῶντας</u>.
   In fleeing, the captain escapes the notice of the men who are shouting.

4. ἆρα σὺ ὁρᾷς ἐκείνους τοὺς κακοὺς ἀνθρώπους <u>φεύγοντα/φεύγοντες/ φεύγοντας</u>;
   Can you see those wicked men running away?

5. ὁρῶ τὸν ναύτην <u>τρέχων/τρέχοντα</u> πρὸς τὴν ναῦν.
   I see the sailor running to the ship.

GREEK IDIOMS

96. You have already met one adjective in Greek (ἥσυχος, 'peaceful') which is best translated adverbially ('peacefully': **76[b]**). Another one is δῆλος, 'obvious, clear', when used in the phrase δῆλός ἐστι + participle, 'he is obviously …', e.g.

δῆλός ἐστι φεύγων   'He is obviously fleeing'

δήλη ἐστὶ θεωμένη   'She is obviously watching'

A FURTHER TYPE 3 NOUN: ὁ βασιλεύς, 'KING' (3G)

97. Here is a further type 3 noun to learn, classified as 3g.

▶ Type 3g nouns are typically m. and end in -εύς:

ὁ βασιλεύς, 'king' (3g)

	s.	pl.
Nom.	βασιλεύ-ς	βασιλῆς (or βασιλ-εῖς)
Acc.	βασιλέ-ᾱ	βασιλέ-ᾱς
Gen.	βασιλέ-ως	βασιλέ-ων
Dat.	βασιλε-ῖ	βασιλεῦ-σι(ν)
Voc.	ὦ βασιλεῦ	

ELISION AND CRASIS

Elision

■ *Dropping vowels*

98. Observe the following sentences and note the loss of vowels:

δεῦρ' ἐλθέ (= δεῦρο ἐλθέ)

βαρὺν δ' ὄντα φέρω (= βαρὺν δὲ ὄντα φέρω)

ἆρ' οὐ σέβῃ τοὺς θεούς (= ἆρα οὐ)

ἀποθνῄσκουσι δ' οἱ ἄνθρωποι (= ἀποθνῄσκουσι δὲ οἱ)

▶ To summarise, when a word ends in a short vowel, that vowel may be dropped if the next word begins with a vowel. This is called 'elision'.

■ *τ – θ and π – φ*

99. Observe what happens to the following words in elision:

ἀπὸ ἵππου → ἀφ' ἵππου

ἔστι ἡμέτερος → ἔσθ' ἡμέτερος

Prefixes to verbs beginning with vowels may be affected in the same way, e.g.

κατα-ὁράω → = κατ-ὁράω = καθοράω

ἀπο-ὁράω = ἀπ-ὁράω = ἀφοράω

So with μετά (μετ', μεθ') and ἐπί (ἐπ', ἐφ') when they prefix words beginning with vowels.

> ► To summarise, before a rough breathing, τ becomes θ and π becomes φ: that is, the aspiration 'spreads'.

Crasis

100. Observe the vowel-contraction in:

ὦνδρες (ὦ ἄνδρες) 'men'

This is called 'crasis'.

> ► Crasis occurs when a vowel or diphthong (i.e. vowel + ι or υ) at the end of a word coalesces with one at the beginning of the next word, making *one word* where you would expect two.

Consider further:

τἀγαθά* (τὰ ἀγαθά) 'good things'

οὑπί (ὁ ἐπί) 'the one on …'

ἁνήρ (ὁ ἀνήρ) 'the man'

*Observe that you can often spot crasis by the occurrence of what looks like a *breathing* where you would not usually expect it.

EXERCISES

4C–D: 6. Elide the following:

1. ὁ δὲ ἀνήρ
2. ἆρα ὁρᾷς;
3. ἀπὸ ἡμῶν
4. ἐπὶ ὑμᾶς
5. εἰμὶ Ὀδυσσεύς

4C–D: 7. De-elide the following:

1. νῦν δ' ἐπ' οἰκίαν
2. ἀλλ' ἐγώ
3. ἐν δ' ἀπορίᾳ
4. κακός ἐσθ' ὁ πόλεμος
5. ἆρ' εἴμ' ἔμπειρος;

SUMMARY LEARNING VOCABULARY FOR SECTION ꞁC–D

ἀνομίᾱ, ἡ	lawlessness (1b)
ἀπάγω (ἀπαγαγ-)	lead/take away
ἀποκτείνω (ἀποκτεινα-)	kill
ἀποφεύγω (ἀποφυγ-)	escape, run off
ἀσέβεια, ἡ	irreverence to the gods (1b)
αὐτόν ἥν ὁ	him, her, it, them
ἀφέλκω (ἀφελκυσα-)	drag off
βασιλεύς, ὁ	king (3g)
βωμός, ὁ	altar (2a)
δυῦλυς, ὁ	slave (2a)
ἐπικαλέομαι	call upon (to witness)
ἱερόν, τό	sanctuary (2b)
ἱκέτης, ὁ	suppliant (1d)
κῆρυξ (κηρῡκ-), ὁ	herald (3a)
λανθάνω (λαθ-)	escape notice of X (acc.) in –ing (part.)
μά	(+acc.) by …!
μισέω	hate
ξένος/ξεῖνος, ὁ	foreigner, guest, host (2a)
ὀλοφύρομαι	lament, mourn for
ὀρθός ή όν	straight, correct, right
πάσχω (παθ-)	suffer, experience, undergo
παύομαι	stop
πρεσβευτής, ὁ	ambassador (1d)
πρέσβεις, οἱ	ambassadors (3e)
τρέπομαι (τραπ-)	turn, turn in flight
τυγχάνω (τυχ-)	happen to be -ing, be actually –ing (+ nom. part.)
ὕβρις, ἡ	aggression, violence (3e)
ὑπηρέτης, ὁ	servant, slave (1d)
φαίνομαι (φαν-)	seem to be, appear to be, am clearly (+ part.)
φθάνω	anticipate X (acc.) in –ing (nom. part.)
ὤ	what ….! (+gen.)

TAKING STOCK
1. Can you describe accurately how φθάνω, λανθάνω, δῆλος, and καίπερ use the participle?
2. Can you describe how ὁ + participle works?
3. Can you decline βασιλεύς?

REVISION EXERCISES FOR SECTION 4C–D

A VOCABULARY-BUILDING

Deduce the meaning of the words on the right from those on the left:

ἀσέβεια	τὸ σέβας
ἱερόν	ὁ ἱερεύς
ἱκέτης	ἱκετεύω
μισέω	τὸ μῖσος
ξένος	ἡ ξενία, ξενίζω
τυγχάνω/δυστυχής	ἡ τύχη
ὕβρις	ὑβρίζω

B/C WORD SHAPE AND SYNTAX

Translate these sentences, completing the second sentence in each of the pairs by using a participle or combination of participle + definite article:

e.g. τίς ἐπικαλεῖται ἡμᾶς; οἱ δοῦλοι ἀφέλκουσι … <u>τὸν ἐπικαλούμενον</u>.

('Who is calling us to witness? The slaves are dragging away <u>the man who is calling us to witness</u>.')

a. τίς τρέχει; οὐχ ὁρῶ ἔγωγε …
b. τίνες ὀλοφύρονται; ποῦ εἰσιν …
c. οἶδα τίς ἀποφεύγει. οὐ γὰρ λανθάνει ἐμὲ …
d. τίνες φεύγουσιν; ἆρ' ὁρᾷς …
e. ὁ βασιλεὺς ἀποτρέχει καὶ οὐ παύεται …
f. αἱ γυναῖκες ἀεὶ φοβοῦνται. διὰ τί οὐ παύονται …

D ENGLISH INTO GREEK

Translate these pairs of sentences:

1. ἐγὼ δ' οὐχ ὁρῶ Λακεδαιμόνιον οὐδένα φεύγοντα.
   We see the men running.

2. ἆρα λανθάνει ὑμᾶς ὁ δεσπότης σκεύη ἔχων;
   Don't you (s.) see that the slave is dragging the suppliant away?

3. οἱ γὰρ πρέσβεις φθάνουσι τοὺς ὑπηρέτας ἀποφεύγοντες.
   For the Spartan runs into the sanctuary before his pursuers.

4. ὁ δὲ κῆρυξ οὐ παύεται μισῶν τοὺς ξένους καὶ φοβούμενος.
   The stranger does not stop calling on us and shouting.

5. ἀλλὰ δῆλος εἶ ἱκέτης ὢν καὶ τυγχάνεις ὀλοφυρόμενος τὸ πρᾶγμα.
   But the man is clearly an ambassador, and happens to be escaping.

E TEST EXERCISE FOUR C–D

Translate into English.

ξένος δέ τις τρέχων τυγχάνει εἰς τὸ Ἡράκλειον ἱερόν. καὶ δῆλός ἐστιν
ὁ ξένος δεινόν τι πάσχων, ἐπειδὴ ταχέως προσέρχονται ἄνδρες τινές,
διώκοντες αὐτόν. ὁ δὲ ξένος φθάνει τοὺς διώκοντας εἰς τὸ ἱερὸν φεύγων,
ἐγγὺς ὄν. ἀφικνοῦνται δὲ οἱ διώκοντες καὶ ἐρωτῶσι τὸν ῥαψῳδὸν ποῦ
5 τυγχάνει ὢν ὁ ξένος. δῆλον γάρ ἐστιν ὅτι ὁ ξένος οὐ λανθάνει τὸν
ῥαψῳδὸν ἀποφεύγων. ἐπειδὴ δὲ οἱ διώκοντες ὁρῶσιν αὐτὸν ἐν τῷ ἱερῷ
ὄντα, ἀπάγουσι, καίπερ βοῶντα καὶ τοὺς θεοὺς ἐπικαλούμενον. καὶ ὁ
μὲν ξένος οὐ παύεται ὀλοφυρόμενος καὶ δηλῶν τί πάσχει, ὁ δὲ ῥαψῳδὸς
καὶ ὁ Δικαιόπολις ἡσυχάζουσι, φοβούμενοι τοὺς ἕνδεκα. οὕτως οὖν ἥ τε
10 ἀνομία καὶ ἡ ἀσέβεια γίγνονται ἐν τῇ τῶν Ἀθηναίων πόλει.

Vocabulary

τῷ ἱερῷ	the sanctuary
τῇ πόλει	the city

EXERCISE

Answer the following questions based on the passage above.

1. Give the gender, number and case of the following participles: (a) τρέχων (line 1), (b) διώκοντες (line 3), (c) ὄν (line 4) and (d) φοβούμενοι (line 9).

2. Give the person and number (e.g. 3 pl.) of the following verbs: (a) προσέρχονται (line 2), (b) ἐρωτῶσι (line 4), (c) λανθάνει (line 5) and (d) ἡσυχάζουσι (line 9).

Grammar for Section 5A–B

In this section you cover:
● Imperfect indicative, active and middle: ἔπαυον, ἐπαυόμην
● Augments
● Position of adjectives

VOCABULARY CHECK

Ensure you know the meaning of:
αἴτιος, βίος, γάμος, δίκη, ἡδύς, ἵππος, ὀφείλω, πατήρ, κολάζω, νέος, πείθομαι

THE IMPERFECT TENSE

Imperfect indicative active

101. The forms of the imperfect active are as follows:

ἔ-παυ-ον 'I was stopping'

ἔ-παυ-ον	'I was stopping, I used to stop, I stopped'
ἔ-παυ-ες	'you (s.) were stopping, used to stop, stopped'
ἔ-παυ-ε(ν)	'he/she/it was stopping, used to stop, stopped'
ἐ-παύ-ομεν	'we were stopping, used to stop, stopped'
ἐ-παύ-ετε	'you (pl.) were stopping, used to stop, stopped'
ἔ-παυ-ον	'they were stopping, used to stop, stopped'

Imperfect indicative middle

102. The forms of the imperfect middle are as follows:

ἐ-παυ-όμην, 'I was stopping (myself)'

ἐ-παυ-όμην	'I was stopping, I used to stop, I stopped (myself)'
ἐ-παύ-ου	'you (s.) were stopping, used to stop, stopped (yourself)'
ἐ-παύ-ετο	'he/she/it was stopping, used to stop, stopped (him/her/itself)'
ἐ-παυ-όμεθα	'we were stopping, used to stop, stopped (ourselves)'
ἐ-παύ-εσθε	'you (pl.) were stopping, used to stop, stopped (yourselves)'
ἐ-παύ-οντο	'they were stopping, used to stop, stopped (themselves)'

Form

(a) Note the prefix of the stem, ἐ-. This is called the augment (**104–5**).
(b) Look back at **52**. There it was asserted that there were two forms of the middle ending, one being:

▶ -μαι -σαι -ται -μεθα -σθε -νται

Here, then, is the second:

> ▶ -μην -σο -το -μεθα -σθε -ντο

(c) Note the recurrence of the thematic vowels ο ε ε ο ε ο (**16b**).

(d) There were also wise words at **52** about the 2s. and intervocalic sigmas which you will well, ah, recall. So here: the 2s. was originally ἐπαύ-ε-σο, the intervocalic σ dropped out leaving ἐπαύ-ε-ο, which contracted into ἐπαύου.

Meaning

103. The new tense you meet in this section is called the imperfect. The word 'imperfect' comes from a Latin word meaning 'incomplete'.

- The imperfect is used to describe continuing, repeated or uncompleted actions in the past – something that *was* happening, *used to* happen, *began* to happen or *kept* happening.
- Depending on context, then, ἔπαυον (the imperfect of παύω) could be translated 'I was stopping', 'I used to stop' or simply 'I stopped'.
- Note, though, that in the last case, the use of the imperfect implies that 'I stopped' (i.e. 'used to stop' or 'kept stopping') on a continual basis or more than once, e.g. 'I stopped him going into the house every day.'

EXERCISE

5A–B: 1. Translate into English, then convert into the middle equivalent:

1. ἔπαυε
2. ἔφερον (two possibilitics)
3. ἐλάμβανες
4. ἐμανθάνομεν
5. ἐθύετε

Form

■ *The augment*

104. 'Augment' means 'growth' or 'increase' and is so named because the addition of an *augment* generally causes the verb to increase in size.

> ▶ The distinguishing mark of an indicative verb in the past is the presence of an augment at the front of the verb.

■ *Augments in ἐ-*

(a) When the verb begins with a consonant, the augment takes the form of ἐ-, e.g.

κελεύω   →   ἐ-κέλευ-ον, 'I was ordering, used to order, ordered'

βαίνω   →   ἔ-βαιν-ον, 'I was going, used to go, went'

■ *Augments as lengthened vowel*

(b) If the verb starts with a vowel, however, ἐ- is **NOT** added. Rather, this initial vowel will *lengthen* if it can, e.g.

ἀκούω	→ ἤκου-ον	'I was listening, used to listen, listened'
ἐλευθερόω	→ ἠλευθέρουν	'I was setting free, used to set free, set free'
οἰκέω	→ ᾤκουν	'I was living, used to live, lived'

(i) Note that, as in the last example, iota is traditionally written subscript after a long vowel (e.g. ῃ, ῳ).

(ii) A handful of verbs beginning in ἐ- has the augment εἰ- (rather than ἠ). Learn the most common example, which is ἔχω, 'I have', imperfect: εἶχον, 'I was having, used to have, had'.

(c) If a verb already begins with a long vowel, this vowel simply remains long in the imperfect too, e.g.

ἡσυχάζω	→ ἡσύχαζον	'I was keeping quiet, used to keep quiet, kept quiet'
ἥδομαι	→ ἡδόμην	'I was enjoying, used to enjoy, enjoyed'

Augment summary

105. The following chart summarises the rules of augmentation for verbs beginning with vowels:

unaugmented vowel	*augmented vowel*
α ε η	η
ᾳ αι ει	ῃ
ο ω	ω
αυ ευ	ηυ
ι	ῑ
υ	ῡ

EXERCISE

5A–B: 2. Translate and convert the following presents into the equivalent imperfect form:

1. ἀκούομεν
2. ἔχουσιν
3. ὀλοφύρεσθε
4. ὀφείλει
5. εὔχονται

Augment and prefix

There is an important rule applying to augment and prefixes:

> ► The augment is added to the *base* verb, NOT to any prefixes it may have acquired.

Thus διαβαίνω becomes δι-έ-βαινον in the imperfect and εἰσβαίνω becomes εἰσ-έ-βαινον. Observe how other prefixes react to the addition of an augment:

ἀποβαίνω	ἀπο⁺	+	ἔβαινον	→	ἀπέβαινον
εἰσβαίνω	εἰς	+	ἔβαινον	→	εἰσέβαινον
ἐκβαίνω	ἐκ**	+	ἔβαινον	›	ἐξέβαινον
ἐμβαίνω	ἐν***	+	ἔβαινον	→	ἐνέβαινον
ἐπιβαίνω	ἐπι*	+	ἔβαινον	→	ἐπέβαινον
καταβαίνω	κατα*	+	ἔβαινον	→	κατέβαινον
περιβαίνω	περι*	+	ἔβαινον	→	περιέβαινον
προβαίνω	προ*	+	ἔβαινον	→	προέβαινον
				or	προΰβαινον
μεταβαίνω	μετα⁺	+	ἔβαινον	→	μετέβαινον
ἐγκαλέω	ἐν***	+	ἐκάλουν	→	ἐνεκάλουν

* Note that all two-syllable prefixes ending in a vowel drop their final vowel before an augment. The exception to the above rule is περι-; προ- also can stay unchanged.
** Note that ἐκ- changes to ἐξ- before a vowel.
*** Note that with e.g. ἐμβαίνω and ἐγκαλέω, the prefix recovers its basic form ἐν.

EXERCISE

5A–B: 3. Translate and convert into the equivalent present forms:

1. κατέβαινε
2. ἀπέκτεινες
3. ἀπῆγον (two possibilities)
4. διεφθείρομεν
5. εἰσεφέρετε

THE IMPERFECT OF CONTRACT VERBS

106. As in the present, contract verbs (such as ποιέω, 'I make, do', τιμάω, 'I honour' and 'δηλόω', 'I show, reveal') also contract in the imperfect. Remember that these contractions follow predictable patterns (see **25**):

Active contract verbs

> ### ἐτίμων, 'I was honouring' (α-contract verb)
>
> | | | |
> |---|---|---|
> | ἐ-τίμα-ον | > ἐτίμων | 'I was honouring, used to honour, honoured' |
> | ἐ-τίμα-ες | > ἐτίμας | 'you (s.) were honouring, used to honour, honoured' |
> | ἐ-τίμα-ε | > ἐτίμα | 'he/she/it was honouring, used to honour, honoured' |
> | ἐ-τῑμά-ομεν | > ἐτῑμῶμεν | 'we were honouring, used to honour, honoured' |
> | ἐ-τῑμά-ετε | > ἐτῑμᾶτε | 'you (pl.) were honouring, used to honour, honoured' |
> | ἐ-τίμα-ον | > ἐτίμων | 'they were honouring, used to honour, honoured' |
>
> ### ἐποίουν 'I was making, doing' (ε-contract verb)
>
> | | | |
> |---|---|---|
> | ἐ-ποίε-ον | > ἐποίουν | 'I was making, used to make, made' |
> | ἐ-ποίε-ες | > ἐποίεις | 'you (s.) were making, used to make, made' |
> | ἐ-ποίε-ε | > ἐποίει | 'he/she/it was making, used to make, made' |
> | ἐ-ποιέ-ομεν | > ἐποιοῦμεν | 'we were making, used to make, made' |
> | ἐ-ποιέ-ετε | > ἐποιεῖτε | 'you (pl.) were making, used to make, made' |
> | ἐ-ποίε-ον | > ἐποίουν | 'they were making, used to make, made' |
>
> ### ἐδήλουν, 'I was showing, revealing' (o-contract verb)
>
> | | | |
> |---|---|---|
> | ἐ-δήλο-ον | > ἐδήλουν | 'I was showing, used to show, showed' |
> | ἐ- δήλο-ες | > ἐδήλους | 'you (s.) were showing, used to show, showed' |
> | ἐ-δήλο-ε | > ἐδήλου | 'he/she/it was showing, used to show, showed' |
> | ἐ-δηλό-ομεν | > ἐδηλοῦμεν | 'we were showing, used to show, showed' |
> | ἐ-δήλό-ετε | > ἐδηλοῦτε | 'you (pl.) were showing, used to show, showed' |
> | ἐ-δήλο-ον | > ἐδήλουν | 'they were showing, used to show, showed' |

Middle contract verbs

107. The forms of the imperfect middle contract verbs are as follows. Note once more that these verbs contract in the imperfect in the same way as in the present (**53**).

> ### ἐθεώμην, 'I was watching' (α-contract verb)
>
> | | |
> |---|---|
> | ἐ-θεα-όμην | > ἐθεώμην |
> | ἐ-θεά-ου | > ἐθεῶ |
> | ἐ-θεά-ετο | > ἐθεᾶτο |
> | ἐ-θεα-όμεθα | > ἐθεώμεθα |
> | ἐ-θεά-εσθε | > ἐθεᾶσθε |
> | ἐ-θεά-οντο | > ἐθεῶντο |

ἐφοβούμην, 'I was fearing (ε-contract verb)'

ἐ-φοβε-όμην   > ἐφοβούμην

ἐ-φοβέ-ου   > ἐφοβοῦ
ἐ-φοβέ-ετο   > ἐφοβεῖτο
ἐ-φοβε-όμεθα > ἐφοβούμεθα
ἐ-φοβέ-εσθε   > ἐφοβεῖσθε
ἐ-φοβέ-οντο   > ἐφοβοῦντο

ἐδουλούμην, 'I was enslaving' (o-contract verb)

ἐ-δουλο-όμην > ἐδουλούμην
ἐ-δουλό-ου   > ἐδουλοῦ
ἐ-δουλό-ετο   > ἐδουλοῦτο
ἐ-δουλο-όμεθα > ἐδουλούμεθα
ἐ-δουλό-εσθε > ἐδουλοῦσθε
ἐ-δουλό-οντο > ἐδουλοῦντο

Identifying imperfects: removing the augment

108. The imperfect is based on the *present* stem of the verb. As you have seen, to form the imperfect you add an augment to the beginning of the verb and the correct imperfect personal ending.

Now the dictionary form of any verb is the *present*. So if you meet an unfamiliar verb in the imperfect, you will need to be able to work out its present form in order to look it up in the dictionary. In other words, you will have to reverse the process of forming the imperfect from the present: you must learn to form the present from the imperfect.

■ *Verbs augmented with ἐ-*

ἐ- augments should generally be easy to deal with:

ἔλεγον = ἔ-λεγ-ον from λέγω, 'I/they say, speak'
Therefore ἔλεγον = 'I was/they were saying, speaking', etc.

διέβαινες = δι-έ-βαιν-ες from διαβαίνω, 'I go through'
Therefore διέβαινες = 'you were going through', etc.

■ *Verbs augmented with a long vowel*

If the imperfect form begins with a *long* vowel, the present stem of the verb may be more difficult to ascertain, e.g. ἠκούομεν has the ending -ομεν ('we'), but what of ἠ-κού-?

- The initial ἠ- must represent the augment, but what would it be in the present?
- The answer is that it could represent α, ε or η in the present (**105**).
- Therefore, the *present* stem of the verb could be ἀκου-, ἐκου- or ἠκου-.

● No doubt you recognise one of these stems as belonging to a verb with which you are familiar, namely ἀκούω, 'I hear, listen (to)', which allows you to work out that:

ἠκούομεν = 'we were hearing, listening to', etc.

You may find, of course, that, when you have removed the augment, you do not recognise any of the stems you are left with! In that case there is, unfortunately, no alternative but to hunt under all the possibilities in your dictionary (in the above case, e.g. ἀκου-, ἐκου- and ἠκου-) until you find a suitable candidate. The more you study the language, the more you will develop a good instinct for where to look first.

Different meanings of the imperfect

109. The imperfect tense can be translated in the following ways:

'I was ------ing'	'I kept on ------ing'
'I used to ------'	'I tried to ------'
'I continued ------ing'	'I began ------ing'

▶ Note that all these meanings denote an action which the speaker wishes to characterise as continuing or repeated in the past: a ***process*** rather than an ***event***, or put another way an ***incomplete*** rather than a ***completed*** action.

The past of 'to be'

110. Learn the irregular past of the verb 'to be':

ἦ *or* ἦν 'I was'

ἦ *or* ἦν	'I was'
ἦσθα	'you (s.) were'
ἦν	'he/she/it was'
ἦμεν	'we were'
ἦτε (ἦστε)	'you (pl.) were'
ἦσαν	'they were'

EXERCISES

5A–B: 4. Translate:

1. ἔπαυε	7. ἦν (two ways)
2. ἐτιμῶμεν	8. ἠλευθέρουν (two ways)
3. ἐποίουν (two ways)	9. ὤφειλες
4. ἐδήλους	10. ἀκούει
5. κολάζεις	11. ἐμένομεν
6. ἐγίγνωσκεν	12. ἐποίει

5A–B: 5. Translate into Greek using the following verbs: κελεύω, κωλύω, ὀφείλω, πάσχω, τιμάω.

1. They were honouring
2. He used to suffer
3. We were owing
4. I was preventing
5. You (pl.) were ordering

5A–B: 6. Translate:

1. ἐπαύετο
2. ἐπείθου
3. διελέγοντο
4 φοβούμεθα
5. ἦσαν
6. ἐδουλοῦντο
7. ἐφοβεῖτο
8. μάχονται
9. ἐπεκαλούμην
10. ἐτρεπόμεθα
11. ἐφαίνου
12. ὠλοφύρετο

5A–B: 7. Translate into Greek using the following verbs: διαλέγομαι, μάχομαι, πείθομαι, φαίνομαι, φοβέομαι.

1. They were obeying
2. He used to be afraid
3. We were fighting
4. I was seeming
5. You (pl.) were conversing

5A–B: 8. Translate into Greek using one word only:

1. He was preventing (κωλύω)
2. He used to stop (middle: παύομαι)
3. We were calling to witness (ἐπικαλέομαι)
4. You (s.) were owing (ὀφείλω)
5. I tried to hear (ἀκούω)
6. You (pl.) began to shout (βοάω)
7. They were enslaving (middle: δουλόομαι)
8. I kept on honouring (middle: τιμάομαι)
9. She continued making (middle: ποιέομαι)
10. They were conversing (διαλέγομαι)

'PREDICATIVE' ADJECTIVES

111. Observe the subtle Greek use of the position of the adjective in relation to its noun + definite article to indicate a slightly different meaning:

(a) ὁ σοφὸς ἀνήρ or ὁ ἀνὴρ ὁ σοφός 'the wise man'

BUT:(b) σοφὸς ὁ ἀνήρ or ὁ ἀνὴρ σοφός 'the man [is] wise'

The distinction applies to all cases of the noun, e.g.

πολλὴν τὴν δαπανὴν εἰσέφερεν lit. 'much the expense she caused', i.e. 'the expense she caused was great'

When the adjective stands outside the definite article + noun phrase, or is not linked with it by a preceding definite article (as in [b] above), it will carry this so-called 'predicative' meaning.

SUMMARY LEARNING VOCABULARY FOR SECTION 5A–B

αἴτιος ᾱ ον	responsible (for), guilty (of)
ἅπτω	light; fasten, fix
βαθύς	deep
βαρύς	heavy
βίος, ὁ	life, means, livelihood (2a)
γάμος, ὁ	marriage (2a)
διαλέγομαι	converse
δίκη, ἡ	lawsuit; penalty; justice (1a)
δίκην λαμβάνω (λαβ-)	exact one's due; punish (παρά + gen.)
διότι	because
δυστυχής	unlucky
εἰσφέρω (εἰσενεγκ-)	bring in, carry in
ἔνειμι	be in
ἡδύς	sweet, pleasant
ἵππος, ὁ	horse (2a)
κακὰ/κακῶς ποιέω	treat badly; do harm to
κολάζω	punish
νεᾱνίᾱς, ὁ	young man (1d)
νέος ᾱ ον	young
οἰκέτης, ὁ	house-slave (1d)
ὅλος η ον	whole of
οὐδέπω/οὔπω	not yet
ὀφείλω	owe
πατήρ (πατ(ε)ρ-), ὁ	father (3a)
παύω	stop
πείθομαι (πιθ-)	trust, obey (+dat.)
σχεδόν	near, nearly; almost
τότε	then
υἱός, ὁ	son (2a)
φής	you (s.) say
χρέα, τά	debts (3c uncontr.)
χρήματα, τά	money (3b)
χρηστός ή όν	good, fine, serviceable

TAKING STOCK

1. Do you understand the idea of the imperfect tense and know its endings? Can you therefore spot one at a hundred paces?
2. Can you confidently de-augment an imperfect verb to find its dictionary form? What, for example, could ὠ- de-augment to? What ἠ-?

REVISION EXERCISES FOR SECTION 5A–B

B/C WORD SHAPE AND SYNTAX

1. Translate each sentence, then change the verbs from the present to the imperfect tense:

   a. καθεύδω ἐγώ, ἀλλ' ἔτι διώκουσί με οἱ ἄνδρες οὗτοι.

   b. τίς αἴτιός ἐστιν; ἡ γυνή. ἀεὶ γὰρ λαμβάνει τὸν υἱὸν καὶ διαλέγεται περὶ τῶν ἵππων.

   c. ὁ γάμος ὡς πικρός ἐστιν. ἀεὶ γὰρ πικρὸν ποιεῖ τὸν γάμον ἡ γυνή.

   d. νέοι ἐσμὲν καὶ κολάζομεν τοὺς οἰκέτας. οὕτως γὰρ χρηστοὶ γίγνονται οἱ οἰκέται.

   e. οὐ φοβοῦνται τοὺς δεσπότας οἱ δοῦλοι, οὐδὲ πείθονται.

2. Translate each verb, then change to s. or pl. as appropriate (numbers in brackets indicate which person, where there is ambiguity):

   διελεγόμεθα, ἐθεώμεθα, εἰσέφερον (3), ὤφειλες, ἐνῆμεν, ἐθεᾶσθε, ἐπείθου, ἐφοβοῦντο, ἐπεκαλούμην, ἔπαυον (1), ἦν (3), ἐφοβοῦ, ἐθεᾶτο.

D ENGLISH INTO GREEK

Translate these pairs of sentences:

1. ὁ μὲν νεανίας ἐβόα, ὁ δὲ ναύτης οὐκ ἐπαύετο διώκων.
   I was sleeping deeply but my son did not stop shouting.

2. οἱ γεωργοὶ ἀεὶ τοὺς θεοὺς ἐτίμων.
   The father always punished his son.

3. οἱ υἱοὶ ὤφειλον πολλὰ χρήματα.
   Young men used to be good, and obey.

4. ηὐχόμεθα πρὸς τὴν θεάν, ἀλλὰ οὐκ ἐθύομεν θυσίας.
   We used to give orders, but the slaves mistreated us.

5. ἔπαυες τὴν γυναῖκα κολάζουσαν τοὺς οἰκέτας.
   We would shout and stop the slaves conversing.

Grammar for Section 5C–D

In this section you cover:
- Future indicative, active and middle: παύσω, παύσομαι
- Future of 'to be' and 'to go': ἔσομαι, εἶμι
- The meaning of the 'middle voice'
- Indefinite and interrogative words
- Type 3d nouns like τριήρης 'trireme'
- Nouns like πατήρ

VOCABULARY CHECK

Ensure you know the meaning of:
φιλέω, ἄδικος, δέχομαι, διδάσκω, δίκαιος, ἔνδον, πείθω, σοφός

THE FUTURE TENSE

112. In this section you meet another new tense: the future.

▶   As you will see, the big clue is the σ added to the present stem:

Future indicative active

παύσω, 'I shall stop'

παύσ-ω	'I shall stop'
παύσ-εις	'you (s.) will stop'
παύσ-ει	'he/she/it will stop'
παύσ-ομεν	'we shall stop'
παύσ-ετε	'you (pl.) will stop'
παύσ-ουσι(ν)	'they will stop'

Future indicative middle

παύσομαι 'I shall cease, stop myself'

παύσ-ομαι	'I shall cease'
παύσ-ῃ or παύσ-ει	'you (s.) will cease'
παύσ-εται	'he/she/it will cease'
παυσ-όμεθα	'we shall cease'
παύσ-εσθε	'you (pl.) will cease'
παύσ-ονται	'they will cease'

■ *Form*

Re-visit **102** and observe the -μαι -σαι -ται middle endings.

EXERCISE

5C–D: 1. Translate the following futures and turn them into the present:

1. κωλύσουσι   4. παύσῃ
2. κελεύσει   5. κωλύσεις
3. πορευσόμεθα

Forming the future

■ *Plain σ*

113. The future stem of a verb is typically formed by adding σ to the present stem:

παύ-ω 'I stop'   παυ + σ = παύσ-ω 'I shall stop'

■ *Consonant stems*

114. Note what happens to verbs with stems ending in consonants (but see **117** below):

(a) **β, π, πτ and φ** combine with σ to produce ψ:
πέμπ-ω   'I send'   πέμπ + σ = πέμψ-ω   'I shall send'

(b) **γ, κ, σκ, χ (and usually ττ)** combine with σ to produce ξ:
δέχ-ομαι   'I receive'   δέχ + σ = δέξ-ομαι   'I shall receive'

(c) **δ, ζ, θ and τ** are simply replaced by σ:
πείθ-ω   'I persuade'   πείθ + σ = πείσ-ω   'I shall persuade'

EXERCISE

5C–D: 2. Translate the following presents and turn them into the equivalent future:

1. εὔχονται   4. τρεπόμεθα
2. τύπτει   5. πείθεις
3. ἡσυχάζεις

■ *Contract verbs*

115. Contract verbs *lengthen* the contract vowel, then add σ:

- α and ε lengthen to η
- o lengthens to ω

Thus:

τιμ-ά-ω 'I honour'	(α > η + σ) = τιμ-ή-σω	'I shall honour'
ποιέω 'I make, do'	(ε > η + σ) = ποι-ή-σω	'I shall make, do'
δηλόω 'I show'	(ο > ω + σ) = δηλ-ώ-σω	'I shall show'

116. An exception to this rule affects verbs whose stems end in **-εα- and -ρα-**: the α of these verbs simply becomes *long* in the future:

δράω 'I do, act' (α > ᾱ) δρᾱ́-σω 'I shall do, act'

(This is an effect of the same phenomenon that you observed in the f. s. forms of adjectives like ἡμέτερος [**37**]: in Attic Greek long ᾱ remains after ε, ι and ρ and does not change to η.)

- Because the future stem of all contract verbs ends in -σ- (not a vowel), the *endings* in the future are not contracted: there is no vowel for them to contract with. So the endings are -σω, -σεις, -σει etc.

EXERCISE

5C–D: 3. Translate the following futures and turn them into the equivalent present:

1. νικήσομεν	4. ζητήσετε
2. φιλήσει	5. ἐλευθερώσουσιν
3. κρατήσω	

■ *Futures without σ*

117. Verbs with stems in λ, μ, ν or ρ do **NOT** form their future by the addition of σ. Instead, they characteristically become contract verbs in ε with a future stem similar to (but usually different from) that of the present:

- διαφθείρω 'I destroy' → διαφθερέω > διαφθερῶ 'I shall destroy'
- μένω 'I remain' → μενέω > μενῶ 'I shall remain'

These verbs conjugate as in **24** and in **118** below. Note the difference in accent between the present and future of μένω.

118. Verbs in -ίζω most commonly form the future in this way too, e.g. νομίζω 'I think' νομιέω > νομιῶ 'I shall think'.
The conjugation of such verbs in the future is as follows (a regular ε- contract just like the present tense of ποιέω):

νομιέ-ω	>	νομιῶ	'I shall think'
νομιέ-εις	>	νομιεῖς	'you (s.) will think'
νομιέ-ει	>	νομιεῖ	'he/she/it will think'

νομιέ-ομεν	>	νομιοῦμεν	'we shall think'
νομιέ-ετε	>	νομιεῖτε	'you (pl.) will think'
νομιέ-ουσι(ν)	>	νομιοῦσι(ν)	'they will think'

Verbs with a middle future

119. There is a handful of verbs which have *active* present forms and *middle* future forms: note that the meaning is not affected by the change. Examples include:

ἀκούω	→	ἀκού-σ-ομαι	'I shall hear'
βοάω	→	βο-ήσ-ομαι	'I shall shout'
σιωπάω	→	σιωπ-ήσ-ομαι	'I shall be silent'
φεύγω	→	φεύ-ξ-ομαι	'I shall flee'

Irregular future forms

120. Finally, the following common verbs have futures which are irregular. It is important to master these now, as you will find that familiarity with these irregular futures will later help you to recognise other tenses of the verbs listed:

βαίνω	→	βήσομαι	'I shall go'
γίγνομαι	→	γενήσομαι	'I shall become'
γιγνώσκω	→	γνώσομαι	'I shall get to know'
λαμβάνω	→	λήψομαι	'I shall take'
μανθάνω	→	μαθήσομαι	'I shall learn'
ὁράω	→	ὄψομαι	'I shall see'
πάσχω	→	πείσομαι	'I shall suffer, experience'

The future in English

121. In British English, the use of 'shall' in the 1 s. and 'will' in the 2 and 3 s. traditionally denotes simply that the event will take place in the future, whereas the inverse – 'I will have my revenge', 'you shall go to the ball' – serves to mark out the sentence as *emphatic*, in these examples expressing a threat and a promise respectively.

EXERCISES

5C–D: 4. Translate:

1. παύσει (two ways)
2. πείσονται (two ways)
3. πείσουσι
4. κόπτεις
5. εὐξόμεθα
6. ἐκέλευες

7. ποιήσετε
8. διαφθεροῦσι
9. κωλύομεν
10. διαλέξεται
11. νομιεῖ
12. δηλώσω

5C–D: 5. Translate into Greek using the following verbs: κελεύω, πείθομαι, πείθω, ποιέω, τιμάω.

1. They will order	4. I shall honour
2. She will persuade	5. You (pl.) will make
3. He will obey	

The future of the verb 'to be'

122. To form the future, the verb 'to be' adds middle endings to the stem ἐσ- :

ἔσ-ομαι 'I shall be'

ἔσ-ομαι	'I shall be'
ἔσει(η)	'you (s.) will be'
ἔσ-ται	'he/she/it will be'
ἐσ-όμεθα	'we shall be'
ἔσ-εσθε	'you (pl.) will be'
ἔσ-ονται	'they will be'

■ *Form*

The exception to the ἐσ- + middle endings 'rule' is the 3s. form: ἔσται.

The future of the verb 'to go'

123. This verb requires careful watching because of its similarity to εἰμί, 'I am':

εἶμι, 'I shall go' (used as the future of ἔρχομαι)

εἶμι	'I shall go'
εἶ	'you (s.) will go'
εἶσι	'he/she/it will go'
ἴμεν	'we shall go'
ἴτε	'you (pl.) will go'
ἴᾱσι(ν)	'they will go'

■ *Warning*

Be careful not to confuse:

- εἶμι, 'I shall go' with εἰμί, 'I am';
- εἶ, 'you will go', with εἶ, 'you are'; and
- εἶσι, 'he/she/it will go', with εἰσί, 'they are'.

For two of the forms, the difference in accents will help you, but with εἶ, only context will help.

- The participle with *present* meaning 'going', is ἰών ἰοῦσα ἰόν (ἰοντ-). Compare ὤν οὖσα ὄν (ὀντ-) 'being'.

EXERCISES

Translate:

5C–D: 6. Translate into English with reference to **120–3:**

1. λήψεται	7. ἴασιν
2. γενήσονται	8. ἔσονται
3. ἐσόμεθα	9. εἶμι
4. μαθήσεσθε	10. γνώσει
5. γνώσονται	11. γενήσεται
6. ἔσται	12. εἶσι

5C–D: 7. Translate into Greek with reference to **120–3:**

1. They will go	6. They will take
2. She will be	7. I shall learn
3. We will get to know	8. You (pl.) shall be
4. You (s.) will become	9. We shall go
5. He will go	10. You (pl.) will be

MIDDLES: MEANING AND USE

124. So far you have met verbs which have *active* forms, and verbs which have *middle* forms. But in this chapter you have met verbs which display both types of form, e.g.

παύω 'I stop x'   παύομαι 'I stop myself, I cease'
πείθω 'I persuade'   πείθομαι 'I persuade myself, I trust, I believe in'

■ *Acting in your own interests*

(a) Very crudely, the difference can be described as follows:

▶ In active verbs, the action moves out from the doer to affect someone or something else, but in middle verbs, the doer's own interest is somehow involved.

Let us consider how this works in practice:

■ *No object required*

(b) Often the difference between the active and middle forms of a verb is that the active requires a direct object to complete its sense (i.e the action is being done *to someone or something else*), whereas the middle does not (i.e. it is being done *to oneself*), e.g.

● παύω τὸν ἄνδρα τρέχοντα 'I stop the man running'
as against

- παύομαι τρέχων 'I stop (myself) running, I cease running'
- λούω τὸν παῖδα 'I am washing the child'
  as against
- λούομαι 'I am washing' (i.e. myself)

■ Doing unto each other

(c) Closely related is the 'reciprocal' use of the middle. For example, in the active the verb λοιδορέω can mean 'to insult someone', whereas in the middle it means 'to insult one another', i.e. 'to insult and be insulted', e.g.

- λοιδορῶ τοὺς γεωργούς 'I am insulting the farmers'
  as against
- ἐγὼ καὶ οἱ γεωργοὶ λοιδορούμεθα 'The farmers and I are insulting each other'

■ Winning out

(d) With some verbs, the middle is used to indicate an action from which the doer gains a certain benefit, e.g.

- φέρω, 'I bear, carry'
  as against
- φέρομαι 'I carry off for myself, I win'

■ Getting things done

(e) More rarely, the middle form of a verb has a so-called 'causative' sense, e.g.

- διδάσκω τὸν παῖδα 'I am teaching the boy'
  as against
- διδάσκομαι τὸν παῖδα 'I am having the boy taught'
- λύω 'I loose'
  as against
- λύομαι 'I get someone loosed, I ransom'

Remember that these 'rules' only apply to verbs which display **both** active **and** middle forms in any one tense. They do not apply, for example, to any of the verbs listed above (e.g. **119**) where the middle form of the future is the *only* form the verbs have.

The more Greek you read, the more you will get used to the way in which middle forms of active verbs are used.

INDEFINITES/INTERROGATIVES

125. You already know the distinction between τίς and τις. The accented form
means 'who?', the unaccented form means 'someone'. This distinction is
carried across a wide range of Greek words. Thus:

- You have recently met πῶς and πως: the accented form means 'how?',
  the unaccented form means 'somehow';
- Sometimes these words lose the initial π, whence ὡς 'how!';
- Sometimes they add ὁ- before the consonant, to give in this case ὅπως.

▶ Thus the complex of words πῶς; ὅπως, πως, ὡς all mean 'how' in
various ways, and Greek uses each in accordance with the context.

Learn the following chart:

Direct question	Indirect question	Indefinite*	Relative
?	'He asked where …'	'Some-'	'He finds where …'
ποῦ; where (at)?	ὅπου where … (at)	που somewhere	οὗ, ὅπου where …
ποῖ; where to?	ὅποι where … to	ποι to somewhere	οἷ, ὅποι to where …
πόθεν; where from?	ὁπόθεν where … from?	ποθεν from somewhere	ὅθεν, ὁπόθεν from where …
πότε; when?	ὅτε when …	ποτε at some time, ever	ὅτε, ὁπότε when …
πῶς; how?	ὅπως how …	πως somehow	ὡς, ὅπως as, in such a way …
τίς who?	ὅστις who …	τις someone	ὅς, ὅστις who …

* The indefinite forms are all enclitics (see **347(ii)**).

You will discover that Greek authors do not always follow the 'rules' in indirect questions, where they often use the direct question form (e.g. ποῦ instead
of ὅπου).

GREEK IDIOMS

126. Observe the way in which a Greek often repeats a question which he/she
has just been asked:

    a. πόθεν ἡ λαμπάς;   'Where is the torch (shining) from?'
    b. ὁπόθεν; …   'Where from? …'

As you can see, ὁ- is added as a prefix to the question word. Compare:

    a. τί ποιεῖς;   'What are you doing?'
    b. ὅ τι; οὐδὲν ποιῶ.   'What? I'm doing nothing.'

Once again, in such cases you will sometimes simply find the question word repeated, i.e. πόθεν and τί.

A FURTHER TYPE 3 NOUN
τριήρης, Σωκράτης; Περικλῆς 3(D)

127a. Here are two examples of a further type 3 noun, classified as 3d.
   Type 3d nouns end in -ης and are generally men's proper names and m.

ἡ τριήρης, 'trireme' (3d)			ὁ Σωκράτης, 'Socrates' (3d)	
	s.	*pl.*	*s.*	
Nom.	τριήρ-ης	τριήρ-εις	Σωκράτ-ης	*no pl.*
Acc.	τριήρ-η	τριήρ-εις	Σωκράτ-η	
Gen.	τριήρ-ους	τριηρ-ῶν	Σωκράτ-ους	
Dat.	τριήρ-ει	τριήρεσι(ν)	Σωκράτ-ει	
Voc.			ὦ Σώκρατες	

Form

(a) Be careful to distinguish 1d nouns like ναύτης (gen. ναύτου) from 3d nouns above, especially as a number of 1d nouns are also proper names, e.g. ὁ Ξέρξης (1d), 'Xerxes' (gen. Ξέρξου).

(b) A small number of type 3d nouns has a slightly different pattern of declension. This group consists only of proper names ending in -κλῆς, such as ὁ Περικλῆς, 'Perikles' and ὁ Ἡρακλῆς, 'Herakles'. Note that the difference in accentuation allows you to distinguish between the Περικλῆς type and Σωκράτης type:

ὁ Περικλῆς, 'Perikles' (3d)		
	s.	
Nom.	Περικλῆς	*no pl.*
Acc.	Περικλέᾱ	
Gen.	Περικλέους	
Dat.	Περικλεῖ	
Voc.	ὦ Περίκλεις	

FATHER, MOTHER, DAUGHTER

127b. Learn the declension of πατήρ 'father' (3a) and the way the stem alternates between πατρ- and πατερ-:

ὁ πατήρ, 'father' (3a)

	s.	pl.
Nom.	πατήρ	πατέρ-ες
Acc.	πατέρ-α	πατέρ-ας
Gen.	πατρ-ός	πατέρ-ων
Dat.	πατρ-ί	πατρ-άσι(ν)
Voc.	(ὦ) πάτερ	

ἡ μήτηρ 'mother' (3a) and ἡ θυγάτηρ 'daughter (3a) decline in the same way. (For full noun survey, see *Reference Grammar*, **353–9**.)

EXERCISE

5C–D: 8. Translate into Greek, adding the correct forms of ὤν and ἰών:

1. Towards the triremes being/going…
2. Of the mothers being/going…
3. From Perikles being/going…
4. Socrates being/going… (acc.)
5. The fathers being/going… (nom.)
6. The daughters being/going… (dat.)

TAKING STOCK

1. Can you distinguish clearly between the forms of present, imperfect and future tenses?
2. Do you know the future of irregular verbs like βαίνω, γίγνομαι, λαμβάνω? Not to mention the verbs 'to be' and 'to go'?
3. Do you understand the general idea behind middle verbs?
4. Can you decline 3d nouns?

REVISION EXERCISES FOR SECTION 5C–D

A VOCABULARY-BUILDING

1. Deduce the meaning of the words in the right-hand columns from those in the left:

αἴτιος/αἰτία	αἰτιάομαι		
διδάσκω	ὁ διδάσκαλος	ἡ δίδαξις	διδακτικός ἡ όν
δίκη	{ δίκαιος α ον	{ ὁ ἀντίδικος	ἄδικος ον
	{ ἀδικέω	{ ὁ δικαστής	δικάζω
δυστυχής	δυστυχέω		
μανθάνω	ὁ μαθητής	ἀμαθής	μαθηματικός ἡ όν
νοῦς	διανοέομαι	ἡ διάνοια	νοέω ἐννοέω
οἰκέτης	{ τὸ οἰκίδιον	{ ἡ οἰκία	ἐνοικέω
	{ ὁ οἶκος	{ οἰκεῖος α ον	
σοφός	ἡ σοφία	σοφιστής	ἡ φιλοσοφία φιλέω

B/C WORD SHAPE AND SYNTAX

Translate these sentences, then change the verb(s) from the present to the future tense:

a. ὁ πατὴρ κελεύει τὸν υἱόν.
b. τί λέγεις, ὦ τᾶν;
c. οὐ διδάσκομεν τοὺς διδασκάλους.
d. οἱ ἄνδρες πολλὰ χρήματα δέχονται.
e. οὐκ ἀκούομεν τοὺς λόγους.
f. ἐγώ εἰμι σοφός, οὗτος δ᾽ οὐ νικᾷ με.
g. ὁ υἱὸς οὐ φιλεῖ τὸν πατέρα.
h. ἡ διάνοια σῴζει ἡμᾶς.
[N.B. the iota of σῴζω is generally dropped outside the present and imperfect tense.]
i. κόπτω τὴν θύραν καὶ βοῶ.
j. τίς νικᾷ τὰς δίκας;
k. οὐ παύονται μανθάνοντες οἱ μαθηταί.
l. τίνες εἰσὶν οἱ σοφοί;

D ENGLISH INTO GREEK

Translate these pairs of sentences:

1. οἱ σοφισταὶ αὔριον σε διδάξουσιν.
   The young men will learn the unjust argument today.

2. οὐδέποτε τοὺς θεοὺς μισήσω.
   The good son will always love his father.

3. οἱ ναῦται οὐ παύσονται ζητοῦντες τὸν κυβερνήτην.
   This horse will not stop running.

4. ὁ δεσπότης κολάσει τὸν δοῦλον.
   The student will go into the house.

5. αἱ γυναῖκες ἀκούσονται τοὺς λόγους.
   The wise men will be just.

E TEST EXERCISE FIVE

Translate into English.

Dikaiopolis needs to borrow a costume from Euripides so that he can dress up to deliver a tragic-style speech. First, however, he must get past Euripides' slave. (From Aristophanes, Akharnians)

ΔΙΚΑΙΟΠΟΛΙΣ	ὦ παῖ, παῖ. ἐλθὲ δεῦρο.
ΔΟΥΛΟΣ	τίς οὗτος; τίς οὐ παύεται καλῶν με;
	(*Seeing Dikaiopolis*) οὗτος· τίς ἐβόα;
ΔΙΚ.	ὅστις; ὦ παῖ, ἐγὼ ἐβόων. ἀλλ᾽ εἰπέ <u>μοι</u>· ἔνδον ἐστ᾽
5	<u>Εὐριπίδης</u>;
ΔΟΥ.	οὐκ ἔνδον, καὶ ἔνδον, ἐστίν, εἰ <u>γνώμην ἔχεις</u>.
ΔΙΚ.	πῶς λέγεις, ὦ παῖ; πῶς ἄνθρωπος ἔνδον καὶ οὐκ ἔνδον ἐστί;
	δῆλον ὅτι οὐδὲν λέγεις.
ΔΟΥ.	ὀρθῶς ἔλεγον ἔγωγε. ὁ μὲν γὰρ νοῦς <u>ξυλλέγων</u> λόγους οὐκ
10	ἔνδον, ὁ δὲ ἄνθρωπος ἔνδον ἐστί, <u>τραγῳδίαν</u> ποιῶν.
ΔΙΚ.	ὦ <u>τρὶς</u> εὐδαίμον Εὐριδίπη, δοῦλον ἔχων οὕτως σοφὸν ὄντα.
	ὡς καλῶς λέγει. (*Addressing the slave again*) ἀλλὰ νῦν παῦε
	παίζων πρὸς ἐμὲ καὶ κάλει αὐτόν, ὦ παῖ.
ΔΟΥ.	ἀλλ᾽ <u>ἀδύνατόν</u> ἐστιν.
15 ΔΙΚ.	διὰ τί ἀδύνατον; Εὐριπίδην κάλει.

(*The slave shuts the door in his face*)
οὐκ ἄπειμι. οὐ μὰ Δία, ἀλλὰ κόψω τὴν θύραν καὶ Εὐριπίδην αὖθις <u>καλέσω</u>.
(*He knocks on the door*)
Εὐριπίδη, ὦ <u>Εὐριπίδιον</u>. οὐκ ἀκούεις; Δικαιόπολις καλεῖ σε Χολλήδης, ἐγώ.

Vocabulary

μοί to me	τρίς thrice, three times
Εὐριπίδης Euripides (1d) (voc.	ἀδύνατος ον impossible
Εὐριπίδη)	καλέσω I shall call (irreg. fut.
γνώμην ἔχω understand (lit.	of καλέω)
'have a mind')	Εὐριπίδιον dear Euripides
ξυλλέγω collect	Χολλήδης from (the deme of)
τραγῳδία, ἡ tragedy (1b)	Chollcidac (m. nom. s.)

EXERCISE

Answer the following questions based on the passage above.

1. Give the tense of the following verbs: (a) ἐβόων (line 4), (b) ἔλεγον (line 8), (c) κόψω (line 16) and (d) κάλει (line 15).

2. Give the gender, number and case of the following participles and adjectives: (a) ποιῶν (line 10), (b) εὐδαίμων (line 11), (c) ὄντα (line 11) and (d) ἀδυνάτον (line 14).

SUMMARY LEARNING VOCABULARY FOR SECTIONS 5C–D

ἄδικος ον	*unjust*
αἰτίᾱ, ἡ	*reason, cause, responsibility (1b)*
αὔριον	*tomorrow*
γε	*at least (denotes some sort of reservation)*
δέχομαι	*receive*
διανοέομαι	*intend, plan*
διάνοια, ἡ	*intention, plan (1b)*
διδάσκω	*teach*
δίκαιος α ον	*just*
εἰσέρχομαι (εἰσελθ-)	*enter*
ἔνδον	*inside*
καὶ δὴ καί	*moreover*
κόπτω	*knock (on), cut*
λόγος, ὁ	*argument; word, speech; story, tale; reason (2a)*
μαθητής, ὁ	*student (1d)*
νοῦς, ὁ (νόος contr.)	*mind, sense (2a)*
οὐδέποτε	*never*
οὔτε... οὔτε	*neither ... nor*
πείθω	*persuade*
Ποσειδῶν (Ποσειδων-), ὁ	*Poseidon (god of sea) (3a) (voc. Πόσειδον; acc. Πόσειδῶ)*
πως	*somehow*
σοφιστής, ὁ	*sophist, thinker (1d)*
σοφός ή όν	*wise, clever*
φιλέω	*love, kiss*

Grammar for Section 6A–B*

(* Formerly 5E–F)

> In this section you cover:
> - First aorist indicative, active and middle: ἔπαυσα, ἐπαυσάμην
> - Aspect
> - Type 3h nouns: ὀφρῦς

> VOCABULARY CHECK
>
> Ensure you know the meaning of:
> καίπερ, λύω, ὅτε, ῥᾴδιος, ἐν νῷ ἔχω, ἀδύνατος, δῆμος, θαυμάζω, ὅπου

THE AORIST

128. In this section you meet another new tense: the aorist. The aorist and the imperfect are the tenses most commonly used to denote past actions in Greek.

> ▶ Whereas the imperfect describes a continuous or repeated past action (a *process*), the aorist describes the action as a single past *event*. Usually, a verb in the aorist is best translated 'I –ed', 'you –ed', etc., e.g. ἔπαυσα, 'I stopped', ἔθυσας, 'you sacrificed', and so on.

First and second aorists: English and Greek

129. In **English** there are two ways in which verbs may be put into the 'past simple' (the tense which is the nearest equivalent in English to the Greek aorist):

> - The majority of verbs add '-ed' or '-d' to the present stem, e.g. 'I watch' → 'I watched', 'you like' → 'you liked'; but
> - some have a different stem in the past, e.g. 'I sing' → 'I sang', 'they go' → 'they went'.

The situation is similar in **Greek**:

> - The majority of verbs have a 'first' aorist – also called the 'weak aorist' – a form which is closely based on the present stem: it is this type of aorist you will meet here.
> - Some verbs have a less predictable 'second aorist' – also called 'strong aorist' – involving a strong change of stem: this type of aorist will be dealt with in section **6 C–D**.

First aorist

130. The aorist of a verb such as παύω, 'I stop', is formed by:

▶ adding σα to the present stem: παυ-σα;
▶ adding an 'augment' to this stem, ἐ-παυ-σα, to indicate that the action is past;
▶ adding the appropriate personal endings

■ *First aorist indicative active*

ἔ-παυσα 'I stopped'	
ἔ-παυσα	'I stopped'
ἔ-παυσα-ς	'you (s.) stopped'
ἔ-παυσε(ν)	'he/she/it stopped'
ἐ-παύσα-μεν	'we stopped'
ἐ-παύσα-τε	'you (pl.) stopped'
ἔ-παυσα-ν	'they stopped'

■ *First aorist indicative middle*

ἐ-παυσά-μην 'I ceased, stopped [myself]'	
ἐ-παυσά-μην	'I ceased'
ἐ-παύσω	'you (s.) ceased'
ἐ-παύσα-το	'he/she/it ceased'
ἐ-παυσά-μεθα	'we ceased'
ἐ-παύσα-σθε	'you (pl.) ceased'
ἐ-παύσα-ντο	'they ceased'

■ *Form*

(a) You can see why the first aorist is also known as the 'sigmatic' or 'alpha' aorist. Originally there was *no* α; ἔπαυσεν avoided confusion with ἔπαυσαν.

(b) Revisit **102** and observe that we have here the -μην -σο -το middle endings. With the loss of intervocalic sigma keenly in mind, you will understand how the original 2s. ἐπαύσα-σο became ἐπαύσα-ο and so ἐπαύσ-ω.

Forming the first aorist stem

■ *Simple verbs*

131. As you have seen above, the first aorist stem is typically formed by adding σα to the present stem: παύ-ω 'I stop' > παυ-σα. On to this is added the augment (ἔ + παυ-σα). The aorist stem is παυσα-.

EXERCISE

6A–B: 1. Form the aorist 3rd person s. and pl. of the following verbs, and translate:

1. θύω   3. κωλύω
2. κελεύω   4. λύομαι

■ *Consonant stems*

132. When σα is added to verbs with stems ending in consonants the following changes occur (note that these changes are, for the most part, *identical to those found in the future tense*: see **114**).

(a) β, π, πτ and φ combine with σ to produce ψ:

πέμπ-ω   'I send'   πέμπ + σ   →   ἔ-πεμψα   'I sent'

(b) γ, κ, χ (and usually ττ) combine with σ to produce ξ:

δέχ-ομαι   'I receive' δέχ + σ   →   ἐ-δεξά-μην 'I received'

(c) δ, ζ, θ and τ are simply replaced by σ:

πείθ-ω 'I persuade'   πείθ + σ   →   ἔ-πεισα   'I persuaded'

EXERCISE

6A–B: 2. Translate the following presents and turn them into the equivalent aorist. You may need to revise augments. See **104** or look ahead to **136**:

1. εὔχεσθε   4. τρεπόμεθα
2. τύπτουσιν   5. πείθω
3. ἡσυχάζει

■ *Contract verbs*

133. Contract verbs both active and middle lengthen the final vowel of their stem before σα is added (exactly as in the future, **115**):

* τιμάω 'I honour'   (α > η) ἐ-τίμησα 'I honoured'
* ποιέω 'I make, do' (ε > η) ἐ-ποίησα 'I made, did'
* δηλόω 'I show'   (ο > ω) ἐ-δήλωσα 'I showed'

Cf. δουλόομαι > ἐ-δουλωσά-μην, etc.

EXERCISE

6A–B: 3. Translate the following aorists and turn them into the equivalent present:

1. ἐνικήσαμεν   4. ἐζητήσατε
2. ἐφίλησε   5. ἠλευθέρωσαν
3. ἐκράτησα

■ *Contract verbs with stems ending in -εα- and -ρα-*

134. As in the future (**116**) an exception to this rule is verbs whose stems end in -εα- and -ρα-: the α of these verbs becomes long in the aorist.

δράω   'I do, act'   (α > ᾱ) →   ἔδρᾱσα 'I did, acted'

Verbs with stems ending in λ, μ, ν or ρ

135. Verbs whose stems end in λ, μ, ν or ρ do **not** form their aorist by the addition of σ. The general rule is that:

(a) the aorist stem of these verbs is the same as the present;
(b) but if the final vowel in the present stem is *short*, it lengthens, e.g.

- διαφθείρω 'I destroy' διαφθειρ- → διέφθειρα 'I destroyed'
- ἀμῡνω 'I ward off' ἀμῡν- → ἤμῡνα 'I warded off'
- μένω 'I remain' μειν- → ἔμεινα 'I remained'

(Note that verbs of this type usually have an aorist stem that is different from the future stem: see **117**.)

Augments

136. The principles of augmentation are exactly the same as for the imperfect (see **104–5**). Thus ἐ- is added to stems beginning in a consonant:

■ *Consonant stems*

διώκω   'I pursue'   διωξ-   → ἐ-δίωξα 'I pursued'
κολάζω   'I punish'   κολασ-   → ἐ-κόλασα 'I punished'

Vowel stems

137. When a stem begins in a vowel, this vowel lengthens where possible:

ἀκούω   'I hear'   ἀκουσ-   → ἤ-κουσα 'I heard'
ἐρωτάω   'I ask'   ἐρωτησ-   → ἠ-ρώτησα 'I asked'
εὔχομαι   'I pray'   εὐξ-   → η-ὐξά-μην 'I prayed'
ἡσυχάζω   'I keep quiet' ἡσυχασ-   → ἡ-σύχασα 'I became quiet'

■ *Compound verbs*

138. Remember that with compound verbs it is the *stem* which is augmented, not the prefix:

ἀνα-χωρέω 'I retreat' ἀνα-χωρησ- → ἀν-ε-χώρησα   'I retreated'
ἀπο-κτείνω 'I kill'   ἀπο-κτειν- → ἀπ-έ-κτεινα   'I killed'

EXERCISES

6A–B: 4. Form the aorist 3rd person s. and pl. of the following verbs, and translate:

1. ἀκούω	6. δέχομαι	11. νικάω
2. ἀναχωρέω	7. λύομαι	12. θεάομαι
3. ἀτιμάζω	8. διδάσκω	13. τρέπομαι
4. βλέπω	9. θαυμάζω	14. κόπτω
5. βοάω	10. θύω	15. χωρέω

6A–B: 5. Translate into Greek using the verbs in brackets:

1. We heard (ἀκούω)
2. They received (δέχομαι)
3. You (s.) retreated (ἀναχωρέω)
4. He pursued (διώκω)
5. They punished (κολάζω)
6. You (pl.) shouted (βοάω)
7. She considered (νομίζω)
8. I showed (δηλόω)
9. They waited (μένω)
10. He destroyed (διαφθείρω)

Recognising first aorist forms

139. When you encounter an aorist indicative form in a reading passage, you will at times be faced with a challenge. In order to look a verb up, you will have to ascertain its dictionary form (i.e. the first person s. present indicative).

■ *Simple stems*

Sometimes this process is simple, since it will require only the removal of the augment, σ and personal ending, e.g.

ἐκέλευσε:

(a) remove augment = κέλευσε
(b) Remove σε (3s. ending) = κελευ-
(c) κελευ- is the stem. Therefore the verb is κελεύω, 'I order'. Translation: 'he/she/it ordered'.

■ *Complex stems*

140. On other occasions, however, the process will be more complex. For example, it may not be immediately clear what the final consonant of the stem would be in the present, e.g.

ἔβλεψα:

(a) Remove augment = βλεψα
(b) Remove σα (1s. ending) = what stem?

- It might be ψ-, from the verb βλέψ-ω. Look it up – no such verb.
- But βλεψ- might have been produced by a combination of β or π or ππ or φ + σ.
- The stem could therefore be any of βλεβ-, βλεπ-, βλεπτ- or βλεφ- .
- If so, the verb could be βλέβω, βλέπω, βλέπτω or βλέφω.
- If you recognise βλέπω, 'I look (at)', you will translate ἔβλεψα 'I looked at'.

If you do not recognise any of them, there is no short cut: you must simply look up βλέβω, βλέπω, βλέπτω and βλέφω to see which of the verbs exists in Greek.

■ *Even more complex stems*

141. Here is a demanding example – and fortunately rare!

ἠτίμασαν:

- Remove the augment. But ἠ- could hide the original vowel α, ε or η (**137** above).
- Remove the ending -σαν (3rd pl. 'they').
- Stem therefore α/ε/ητίμα-
- The verb is therefore α/ε/ητιμάω. Look up vocabulary: no such verb. Infuriating, as there is a verb τιμάω.
- Think: what would the aorist of τιμάω be? ἐτίμησα. Ha! The contract vowel α has lengthened to η (see **133** above), as it does in contract verbs. But α did *not* lengthen to η with α/ε/ητίμα- (above). Therefore α/ε/ητίμα- is *not* a contract verb.
- The σ is therefore misleading us. *It must be part of the original verb.* So we were wrong to think (above) that it needed to be removed as the sign of the aorist. The verb is therefore α/ε/ητίμασ-ω. Look it up.
- No, it isn't. What *other* consonant might that σ hide, which would *turn into* a σ in the aorist? Answer: δ, θ, ζ or τ (see **132**).
- So the verb might therefore be any of ἀτιμάδω, ἀτιμάθω, ἀτιμάζω, ἀτιμάτω, ἐτιμάδω, ἐτιμάθω, ἐτιμάζω, ἐτιμάτω, ἠτιμάδω, ἠτιμάθω, ἠτιμάζω or ἠτιμάτω. If you recognise one of the items in this list, you can proceed to translate ἠτίμασαν. If you do not, however, you must hunt under ἀτιμα-, ἐτιμα- and ἠτιμα- in a dictionary or vocabulary list until you find a suitable candidate. The more you study the language, the more you will develop a good instinct for where to look first.

ἠτίμασαν is in fact the 3rd pl. aorist active indicative of ἀτιμάζω 'I dishonour', and may be translated 'they dishonoured'.

Aspect and the aorist

142. The most common meaning of the aorist is 'I -ed'. But:

- Because of the different ways in which Greek and English speakers use tenses, you may sometimes need to render an aorist as 'I have -ed' or 'I had -ed' to stop your translation sounding stilted.
- The essential point, however, is this: aorist indicatives are used to indicate something that happened in the past without reference to the

duration of time over which it occurred. The action is regarded as a single *complete event*, not as an *uncompleted process* (cf. the imperfect tense).

▶ The way in which a verb-form looks at an action – e.g. as an event (*complete*) or a process (*uncompleted*) – is known as *aspect*. You will learn more about aspect in future sections.

A FINAL TYPE 3 NOUN: ὀφρύς, ἡ 'EYEBROW' (3H)

143. Here is the final type 3 noun you are asked to learn, classified as 3h:

ὀφρῦς, ἡ **eyebrow (3h)**

	s.	*pl.*
Nom.	ὀφρῦ-ς	ὀφρῦ-ες
Acc.	ὀφρῦ-ν	ὀφρῦ-ς
Gen.	ὀφρῦ-ος	ὀφρῦ-ων
Dat.	ὀφρῦ-ι	ὀφρῦ-σι(ν)
Voc.	ὦ ὀφρῦ	

■ *Form*

(i) Be careful to distinguish 3h nouns like ὀφρύς from 3e nouns like πρέσβυς (**79**).

(ii) Some 3h nouns have acc. pl. in -ύας, e.g. ἰχθῦς → ἰχθύας 'fish'.

REVISION EXERCISES FOR SECTION 6A–B

B/C WORD SHAPE AND SYNTAX

1. Translate each sentence, then change the verb into the aorist:

   a. τίς κόπτει τὴν θύραν;
   b. τίς χωρεῖ εἰς τὸ φροντιστήριον;
   c. ἀλλ’ αὖθις κόπτω καὶ οὐ παύομαι κόπτων.
   d. λέξω σοί.
   e. τέλος δὲ τὰς ἐμβάδας λύσομεν.
   f. διὰ τί ἐκεῖνον τὸν Θαλῆν θαυμάζομεν;

2. Translate each sentence, then change the verb into the aorist:

   a. ἡ ψύλλα πηδᾷ ἐπὶ τὴν κεφαλὴν τὴν τοῦ Σωκράτους.
   b. ἀλλὰ πῶς μετρήσεις, ὦ Χαιρεφῶν (μετρέω ‘I measure’)
   c. τέλος δὲ μετροῦμεν τὸ χωρίον.
   d. ζητοῦσιν οὗτοι τὰ κατὰ γῆς καὶ οὐ παύονται ζητοῦντες.
   e. τί δηλοῖ τὸ πρᾶγμα, ὦ Σώκρατες;

3. Using the *Total Vocabulary* at the back of the book, find the dictionary forms of the following verb-forms, then translate:
   e.g. ἤκουσαν: ἀκούω, ‘they heard’

a. ηὔδησαν	f. ὤθησα
b. ἤλπισας	g. ἠρώτησαν
c. ὡμολογήσατε	h. ᾤκησα
d. ἡγησάμην	i. ἠσπάσαντο
e. ἤρξαντο	j. ἐξέπεμψε

4. Complete the following table with the 1st s. imperfect, future and aorist forms of the verbs:

present	imperfect	future	aorist
κελεύω	ἐκέλευον	κελεύσω	ἐκέλευσα
κωλύω			
παύομαι			
βλέπω	ἔβλεπον	βλέψω/ομαι	ἔβλεψα
κόπτω			
κρύπτω			
δέχομαι			
διώκω			
πράττω			
ἀτιμάζω			
κολάζω			

(continued)

present	imperfect	future	aorist
σπεύδω			
διαφθείρω			
μένω			
ἀπορέω			
δηλόω			
μισέω			
νικάω			

D ENGLISH INTO GREEK

Translate these pairs of sentences:

1. ἡ γυνὴ ἐζήτησε τὸν υἱόν.
   The farmer gave a shout and knocked on the door.

2. ἆρ᾽ οὐκ ἴσασιν ὅτι ἐποίησας τοῦτο τὸ ἔργον ῥᾳδίως;
   Don't they know that you received this idea with pleasure?

3. ὁ ἱκέτης οὐκ ἠτίμασε τὴν θεάν.
   The sophist did not persuade the clever young men.

4. οἱ γείτονες, καίπερ κακοὶ ὄντες, τὸν νεανίαν οὐκ ἐκόλασαν.
   The just man, though clever, was astounded at the unjust argument.

5. ἐπαύσατο βλέπουσα τὸν ξένον.
   They stopped looking at the horses.

Grammar for Section 6C–D*

(* Formerly 5G–H)

In this section you cover:
- Second aorist indicative, active and middle: ἔλαβον, ἐλαβόμην
- Interrogatives: τί
- Indirect speech
- Some particles

VOCABULARY CHECK

Ensure you know the meaning or significance of:

ἀπελθ-, ἐξευρ-, πρῶτος, θε-, γέρων, γνώμη, δράω, κλέπτω, κρείττων, σός

THE SECOND AORIST

144. As we earlier warned (**129**), a number of verbs do not form their aorists on the pattern of what we have called first aorist (basically, present stem + -σα) but on the pattern of what is called second aorist (or 'strong aorist'). Note carefully the following about second aorist forms:

▶ They have an aorist stem *different* from that of the present:
▶ For example, the aorist stem of λαμβάνω, 'I take', is λαβ-, and that of γίγνομαι, 'I become', is γεν- ;
▶ They form the strong aorist indicative by adding the augment to this stem in the usual way, ἐ-λαβ-, ἐ-γεν-, to indicate that the action is past.
▶ They have personal endings different from first aorist endings (no -σα).

Second aorist indicative active

ἔ-λαβ-ον 'I took'

ἔ-λαβ-ον	I took
ἔ-λαβ-ες	you (s.) took
ἔ-λαβ-ε(ν)	he/she/it took
ἐ-λάβ-ομεν	we took
ἐ-λάβ-ετε	you (pl.) took
ἔ-λαβ-ον	they took

Second aorist indicative middle

> **ἐ-γεν-όμην 'I became'**
>
> | | |
> |---|---|
> | ἐ-γεν-όμην | I became |
> | ἐ-γέν-ου | you (s.) became |
> | ἐ-γέν-ετο | he/she/it became |
> | ἐ-γεν-όμεθα | we became |
> | ἐ-γέν-εσθε | you (pl.) became |
> | ἐ-γέν-οντο | they became |

■ *Form and meaning*

145. (a) The meaning of the second aorist is the same as the first aorist: 'I -ed' (or sometimes 'I have -ed' or 'I had -ed': see **142**).

(b) Note the -μην -σο -το middle endings (**102**).

(c) The endings of the second aorist are *exactly the same as those of the imperfect*. The difference between the two tenses lies in the change of stem:

> ► Second aorists have a stem or a form of the stem which is *different* from that of the present whereas *the imperfect is based on the present stem.*

Observe the following:

Present	Imperfect	Aorist
λαμβάν-ω, 'I take'	ἐ-λάμβαν-ον, 'I was taking'	ἔ-λαβ-ον, 'I took'
γίγν-ομαι, 'I become'	ἐ-γιγν-όμην, 'I was becoming'	ἐ-γεν-όμην, 'I became'

Common verbs with second aorist forms

146. Verbs which take second aorist forms nearly always undergo a radical stem change. These stem changes have to be learnt. Some you should already recognise from earlier learning vocabularies. The most important and common verbs with second aorist forms are:

Present	Aorist stem	Aorist	Meaning in aorist
γίγνομαι	γεν-	ἐγενόμην	'I became'
εὑρίσκω	εὑρ-	ηὗρον	'I found'
ἔχω	σχ-	ἔσχον	'I had'
λαμβάνω	λαβ-	ἔλαβον	'I took'
μανθάνω	μαθ-	ἔμαθον	'I learned'
τυγχάνω	τυχ-	ἔτυχον	'I happened (to be)'

As you can see, present stems are generally longer versions of the aorist stem (e.g. μαθ- → μανθαν-) and/or different from, but nevertheless recognisably related to, the present stem (e.g. γιγν- → γεν- ; ἐχ- → σχ-). However, some verbs use a completely different stem for the present and aorist (cf. English, 'go' and 'went'):

ἔρχομαι	ἐλθ-	ἦλθον	'I came, went'
λέγω	εἰπ-	εἶπον	'I said, spoke'
ὁράω	ἰδ-	εἶδον	'I saw'
τρέχω	δραμ-	ἔδραμον	'I ran'

EXERCISES

6C–D: 1. Using the above information, form the aorist 3rd person s. and pl. of the following verbs, and translate:

1. λέγω
2. λαμβάνω
3. μανθάνω
4. ἔρχομαι
5. γίγνομαι
6. τρέχω
7. εὑρίσκω
8. ὁράω
9. τυγχάνω
10. ἔχω

6C–D: 2. Using the above information, translate into Greek:

1. They became
2. We saw
3. You (s.) found
4. He took
5. You (pl.) went
6. You (s.) said
7. I learnt
8. They ran

WHAT? WHY?

147. Observe that τί, which you have learnt to mean 'what?' can also, and very commonly, mean 'why?' When τί does mean 'why?', it is in the acc. case and being used adverbially. Its literal meaning is 'in relation to what?' or 'in respect of what?' – in other words, 'why?'

INDIRECT SPEECH

148. A common way of reporting what someone has said in Greek is by using a clause introduced by ὅτι, 'that', e.g.

λέγουσιν ὅτι ὁ Σωκράτης δεινός ἐστιν. 'They say that Socrates is clever.'

Observe, however, that in the ὅτι-clause Greek preserves the *original tense and mood* of the utterance. You must therefore pay special attention when the verb introducing the ὅτι-clause is in the past. Note the following examples:

(a) εἶπον ὅτι ὁ Σωκράτης δεινός ἐστιν. 'They said that Socrates *was* wise.'

The original utterance (i.e what 'they' originally 'said') was 'Socrates *is* wise'. In Greek the present tense is preserved (ἐστί = present), whereas English puts the verb into the past ('was').

(b) εἶπες ὅτι ὁ ναύτης ἔδραμεν εἰς τὴν ναῦν.   'You said that the sailor *had run/ran* onto the ship.'

The original utterance here (i.e. what 'you said') was 'the sailor *ran* onto the ship'. Greek preserves the aorist tense in the indirect speech, whereas in English there is a choice: a speaker can either put the verb into the 'pluperfect' tense ('had run') or use the past simple ('ran').

(c) The same rules apply to reported questions e.g.

ἠρώτησα διὰ τί Σωκράτης σοφός ἐστιν.   'I asked why Socrates was wise'.

GREEK IDIOMS: PARTICLES

149. As you are aware, Greek particles rarely have a single 'correct' translation in English. Note the range of meanings that the following particles can convey:

■ ἀλλά

The basic meaning of ἀλλά is 'but, alternatively'. It thus conveys the idea of 'but rather' or (especially in speech) 'oh, well', 'anyway', denoting a change in topic.

> οὐκ εἶδον τοὺς Ἀθηναίους, ἀλλὰ τοὺς Λακεδαιμονίους.
> 'I didn't see the Athenians, but rather the Spartans.'
> ἀλλ' εἰπέ μοι. 'Tell me, anyway', 'Now well, tell me.'

■ δέ

The basic meaning of δέ is 'and' or 'but'. Since it is such a common connective in Greek, however, it often requires no translation at all. Note, though, the use of def. art. with δέ (ὁ δέ, ἡ δέ, etc.) to denote a change of subject in Greek:

> ὁ ναύτης ἐδίωκε τὸν ξένον, ὁ δὲ οὐκ ἀπέφευγεν.
> 'The sailor was pursuing the foreigner, but he (i.e. the foreigner) wasn't running away.'

■ δή

δή has a range of uses which the meanings 'then', 'indeed' only begin to capture. It puts special stress on the preceding word or phrase and is often used to grab the listener's attention. It can even convey scepticism or sarcasm:

> οὐ διδάξω σ' οὐκέτι, ἀμαθῆ δὴ ὄντα.
> 'I shall not teach you any more as you are really ignorant.'
> εἰπὲ δή. 'Out with it!'

Note that in common with most particles, δέ and δή (unlike ἀλλά) never come as the first word in a sentence or clause (they are 'postpositives', whereas ἀλλά is a 'prepositive': *Reference Grammar*, **391**).

SUMMARY LEARNING VOCABULARY FOR SECTION 6A–D

ἄγροικος ον	from the country, boorish
ἀδύνατος ον	impossible
Ἀθῆναι, αἱ	Athens (1a)
ἀμαθής	ignorant
ἀπέρχομαι (ἀπελθ-)	depart, go away
ἄρα	then, in that case (inferring)
βάλλ᾽ εἰς κόρακας	go to hell!
βιάζομαι	use force
γέρων (γεροντ-), ὁ	old man (3a)
γνώμη, ἡ	mind, purpose, judgment, plan (1a)
δάκνω (δακ-)	bite, worry
δεξιός ᾱ́ όν	right
δεξιᾱ́, ἡ	right hand (1b)
δῆμος, ὁ	deme (2a)
δῆτα	then
δρᾱ́ω (δρᾱσα-)	do, act
εἰ	if
εἶτα	then, next
ἐκβάλλω (ἐκβαλ-)	throw out
ἐμαυτόν	myself
ἐν νῷ ἔχω	intend, have in mind
ἐξευρίσκω (ἐξευρ-)	find out
ἕτερος ᾱ ον	one (or the other) of two
ἥλιος, ὁ	sun (2a)
ἥττων ἧττον (ἡττον-)	lesser, weaker
θαυμάζω	wonder at, be amazed at
καίπερ	although (+part.)
κεφαλή, ἡ	head (1a)
κλέπτω	steal
κρείττων κρεῖττον (κρειττον-)	stronger, greater
λῡ́ω	release
ὁπόσος η ον, πόσος	how much, many
ὅπου	where
ὅτε	when
οὐρανός, ὁ	sky, heavens (2a)
οὗτος	hey there! hey you!
πάνυ	very (much); at all
πείθομαι (πιθ-)	believe, trust, obey
πηδάω	leap, jump
πόρρω	far, far off
πότερος ᾱ ον	which (of two)?

SUMMARY LEARNING VOCABULARY FOR SECTION 6A–D
(CONTINUED)

πούς (ποδ-), ὁ	foot (3a)
πρῶτον	first, at first
πρῶτος η ον	first
ῥᾴδιος ᾱ ον	easy
ῥᾳδίως	easily
σελήνη, ἡ	moon (1a)
σός σή σόν	your(s) (when 'you' is one person)
Σωκράτης, ὁ	Socrates (3d)
τήμερον	today
τί;	why?
(τίθημι) θε-	put, place
φροντίς (φροντιδ-), ἡ	thought, care, concern (3a)
χρήσιμος η ον	useful, profitable
χωρίον, τό	place, space, region (2b)
ὡς	as

REVISION EXERCISES FOR SECTION 6C–D

B/C WORD SHAPE AND SYNTAX

1. Form the aorist stem of these verbs and then give the aorist (1st s.):

   e.g. παύω παυσα ἔπαυσα
   βιάζομαι
   κλέπτω
   θαυμάζω
   διδάσκω
   δέχομαι
   φιλέω
   δηλόω

2. Give the aorist stem of these verbs and then the aorist (1st s.):

   e.g. τρέχω δραμ- ἔδραμον
   μανθάνω
   τυγχάνω
   ἐξευρίσκω
   διέρχομαι

3. Pair each aorist with the equivalent present from the list below (unaugmented stem in brackets). Then give the meaning of each verb:

   εἶδον (ἰδ-)   εἶπον (εἰπ-)   ἔλαθον (λαθ-)   ηὗρον (εὑρ-)
   ἔμαθον (μαθ-) ἦλθον (ἐλθ-)   ἐγενόμην (γεν-) ἔπαθον (παθ-)

   γίγνομαι, λέγω, πάσχω, λανθάνω, εὑρίσκω, ἔρχομαι, μανθάνω, ὁράω

D ENGLISH INTO GREEK

Translate these pairs of sentences:

1. οἱ ναῦται εἶπον ὅτι ὁ κυβερνήτης τέλος τἀληθῆ ἔμαθεν.
   The student said that he (had) discovered how big the space was.

2. οἱ νεανίαι τυγχάνουσι κακὰ πάσχοντες.
   The farmer happened to be a fool.

3. οἱ ἱκέται ἔδραμον εἰς τὸ ἱερόν.
   The old man departed to the city.

4. αἱ γυναῖκες εἶδον τὴν σελήνην.
   The father became unjust.

5. ἐλάβετε τὰ χρήματα διὰ τὰ χρέα.
   I noticed that you were a bumpkin.

SUMMARY EXERCISES FOR SECTION 6

A VOCABULARY BUILDING

1. Deduce the meaning of the words in the right-hand columns from those in the left:

ἀδύνατος	ἡ δύναμις	δύναμαι	
βιάζομαι	βίαιος α ον	ἡ βία	
δράω	τὸ δρᾶμα		
θαυμάζω	θαυμάσιος α ον	τὸ θαῦμα	θαυμαστός ἡ όν
ἱππομανής	μαίνομαι	ἡ μανία	
ἵππος	ἵππιος α ον	ἡ ἱππική	ὁ ἱππεύς
κλέπτω	ὁ κλέπτης	ἡ κλοπή	

2. Translate these pairs of words: what is the significance of the change from left to right?

γέρων	γερόντιον
παῖς	παιδίον
θύρα	θυρίδιον
οἰκία	οἰκίδιον
πατήρ	πατρίδιον
Σωκράτης	Σωκρατίδιον
Φειδιππίδης	Φειδιππίδιον

B/C WORD SHAPE AND SYNTAX

Translate this passage (if you did not do Test Exercise Two); then change the tense of the verbs to imperfect or aorist as indicated:

ἐπειδὴ οὖν προσέρχονται (aorist) ἡ τῶν Περσῶν στρατιὰ καὶ τὸ ναυτικόν, οἱ Ἀθηναῖοι ταχέως εἰσβαίνουσιν (imperfect) εἰς τὰς ναῦς καὶ πρὸς τὴν Σαλαμῖνα πλέουσιν (aorist). ἔπειτα δὲ οἵ τε Ἀθηναῖοι καὶ οἱ ἄλλοι Ἕλληνες ἡσυχάζουσι (imperfect). τέλος δὲ ἀφικνεῖται (aorist) τὸ τῶν Περσῶν ναυτικόν, καὶ ἐπειδὴ νὺξ γίγνεται (aorist), ἔνθα καὶ ἔνθα βραδέως πλέουσιν (aorist) αἱ νῆες. καὶ ἐπειδὴ γίγνεται (aorist) ἡ ἡμέρα, οἱ Ἕλληνες ἀποροῦσι (aorist) καὶ φοβοῦνται (imperfect). τέλος δὲ οὐκέτι φοβοῦνται (imperfect), ἀλλὰ τολμῶσι (imperfect) καὶ ἐπέρχονται (aorist) ἐπὶ τοὺς βαρβάρους. μάχονται (imperfect) οὖν εὐκόσμως καὶ νικῶσι (imperfect), φεύγει (aorist) δὲ καὶ ὁ Ξέρξης. οὕτως οὖν ἐλεύθεροι γίγνονται (aorist) οἱ Ἕλληνες διὰ τὴν ἀρετήν.

Vocabulary

ἔνθα καὶ ἔνθα up and down
ἡμέρα, ἡ day (1b)
εὐκόσμως in good order
ἀρετή, ἡ courage (1a)

πλέω aor. ἔπλευσα
ἀφικνέομαι aor. ἀφικόμην
φεύγω aor. ἔφυγον

D ENGLISH INTO GREEK

Below is the first passage of continuous prose you are asked to translate into Greek. Here are three tips to help you with this new kind of exercise.

- You will probably find it helpful at first – and less daunting – to consider each passage as a series of sentences. Simply attempt each of the twelve sentences in turn, looking up vocabulary and checking endings in the same way that you usually do when you translate from English to Greek.
- You will sometimes find that you have to think your way around problems when translating. For example, when you come to translate 'a great deal' in the fifth sentence of the passage, you won't find the word 'deal' in your English to Greek vocabulary. On such occasions you will have to ask yourself what Greek words and expressions you have met which can be of use to you.
- Once you have worked through the passage and checked your work, there will still be one job left to do: that is, to make sure that your passage of Greek contains the necessary *particles*. You will have noticed that most Greek sentences have a word near the beginning such as ἀλλά, γάρ, γε, δέ, δή, καί, μέν...δέ or οὖν. Sometimes words in the English passage like 'so', 'and' or 'but' will prompt you to use a particle, but to make your translation read well, you may need to add a word such as δέ (which usually comes as the second word, never the first) to join a sentence to a previous one.

Translate into Greek:

An old man and his son, a young man, were talking about money. The youngster, as it happened, owed a lot of money. And because of this, his creditors would not stop pursuing his father. The father did not punish the son (for his mother stopped him), but conceived a clever plan. So when the father managed to persuade his son, the boy went obediently to the sophists and learnt a great deal. The sophists always persuaded him, taught a lot of clever stuff and received a lot of money. So the son learnt quickly the just and unjust arguments, always winning his case. But when the youth came home, this plan did not put a stop to his father's debts. The young man did not like his father (who was a yokel), but hated him. So he never stopped mocking him. Finally, the old man threw him out.

E TEST EXERCISE SIX

Translate into English.

νεανίας δέ τις ἔτυχε πολλὰ χρήματα ὀφείλων διὰ τὴν ἱππικήν. οὕτως οὖν ὁ μὲν πατὴρ ἀεὶ τὰς δίκας τὰς τῶν χρηστῶν ἔφευγεν, οἱ δὲ χρῆσται ἐδίωκον αὐτὸν καὶ οὐκ ἐπαύοντο δίκην λαμβάνοντες. διαλέγονται οὖν ὅ τε πατὴρ καὶ ἡ μήτηρ.

5   ΠΑΤΗΡ   σὺ δή, ὦ γύναι, φαίνῃ αἰτία οὖσα τῶν ἐμῶν κακῶν. τίς γὰρ ἐλάμβανε τὸν υἱὸν καὶ περὶ ἵππων διελέγετο, εἰ μὴ σύ; τίς οὖν ἱππομανῆ ἐποίησε τὸν υἱόν, εἰ μὴ σύ; τί νῦν ποιήσω ἐγώ; πῶς παύσω τὰ χρέα;

ΜΗΤΗΡ   σὺ δὴ αἴτιος εἶ, ὦ ἄνερ. ἀμαθῆ μὲν γὰρ καὶ ἄγροικον ὄντα σὲ οὐ φιλεῖ ὁ
νεανίας οὐδὲ πείθεται, ἐμὲ δὲ ἀστικὴν οὖσαν μάλιστα φιλεῖ.
10   ἀλλὰ μὴ φρόντιζε. ἔχω γὰρ διάνοιάν τινα ἐγώ. πείσω καὶ διδάξω τὸν
υἱὸν ἔγωγε, πείθουσα δὲ παύσω ἐκ τῆς ἱππομανίας.

ἀλλὰ διδάσκουσα καὶ πείθουσα οὐκ ἐκώλυσε τὸν νεανίαν ἡ μήτηρ, οὐδὲ ἐπαύετο ὁ
υἱὸς ἱππομανὴς ὤν. τέλος δὲ ἦλθεν ὁ νεανίας εἰς τὸ τῶν σοφιστῶν φροντιστήριον
καὶ μαθητὴς ἐγένετο. πολλὰ δὲ καὶ σοφὰ εἶδέ τε καὶ ἤκουσε, πολλὰ δὲ ἐδίδαξαν οἱ
15   σοφισταί. ὅτε δὲ ἔμαθε τόν τε δίκαιον καὶ τὸν ἄδικον λόγον ὁ υἱός, εἶπεν ὁ πατήρ

ΠΑΤΗΡ   ἰοὺ ἰού. νῦν γὰρ οὐ λήψονται οὐκέτι οἱ χρῆσται τὰ χρήματα. ὁ μὲν γὰρ
υἱὸς νικήσει τὰς δίκας διὰ τὸν ἄδικον λόγον, τὸν κρείττονα ὄντα, ἡμεῖς
δὲ ἀποφευξόμεθα τοὺς χρήστας.

Vocabulary

ἱππική, ἡ horse-fever (1a)
χρήστης, ὁ creditor (1d)
μήτηρ (μητ(ε)ρ-), ἡ mother (3a)
ἱππομανῆ horse-mad (m. acc. s.)
ἀμαθῆ ignorant (m. acc. s.)

ἀστικός ή όν from the city
τῆς ἱππομανίας his horse-madness
ἱππομανής horse-mad (m. nom. s.)
ἰοὺ ἰού hurrah!

EXERCISE

Answer the following questions based on the passage above.

1. Give the tense of the following verbs: (a) ἔτυχε (line 1), (b) ἔφευγεν (line 2),
   (c) ἐδίωκον (line 2), (d) διαλέγονται (line 3), (e) ἐποίησε (line 6), (f) ποιήσω
   (line 7), (g) ἐγένετο (line 14)
2. Give the gender, number and case of the following participles: (a)
   λαμβάνοντες (line 3), (b) οὖσαν (line 9) and (c) ὄντα (line 17)
3. What is the case of (a) γύναι (line 5) and (b) σοφιστῶν (line 13)?

Grammar for Section 7A–C*

(* Formerly 6 A–C)

> In this section you cover:
> - Present infinitives, active and middle: παύειν, παύεσθαι
> - Irregular present infinitives: εἶναι, ἰέναι, εἰδέναι
> - Verbs taking infinitives (e.g. βούλομαι, δεῖ, δοκέω)
> - Comparative and superlative adjectives, regular and irregular
> - Past of εἶμι: ᾖα 'I went'

> VOCABULARY CHECK
>
> Ensure you know the meaning or significance of:
> ἀλήθεια, βούλομαι, δόξα, σοφίᾱ, ἀνάγκη, δεῖ, νοέω, πάρειμι, δοκέω, εἰδώς,
> εἶμι, πολλάκις

PRESENT INFINITIVE

150. In English the present infinitive is the form of the verb created by the addition of 'to': 'to go', 'to listen', 'to do', etc. This is how the infinitive is formed in Greek:

Non-contract verbs

Non-contract verbs form their infinitives as follows. Note the thematic vowel -ε-:

> **Active infinitive, -ειν**
>
> Add -ειν to the present stem, e.g.
> παύω, 'I stop'   > παύ-ειν, 'to stop'
>
> **Middle infinitive, -εσθαι**
>
> Add -εσθαι to the present stem, e.g.
> παύομαι, 'I stop (myself)' > παύ-εσθαι, 'to stop (oneself)', 'cease'

Contract verbs

151. Contract verbs form their infinitives in the following way:

> **α-contract verbs: α + -ειν/-εσθαι**
>
> Active infinitive in -ᾶν, e.g. τιμ-ᾶν, 'to honour'*
> Middle infinitive in -ᾶσθαι, e.g. θε-ᾶσθαι, 'to watch'
>
> *Rules of contraction would suggest the ending of τιμᾶν should be τιμᾷν; but the -ειν infinitive ending was originally -εν, and the form τιμᾶν reflects this lack of ι.

ε-contract verbs: ε + -ειν/-εσθαι

Active infinitive in -εῖν, e.g. ποιεῖν, 'to stop'
Middle infinitive in -εῖσθαι, e.g. φοβεῖσθαι, 'to be afraid'

o-contract verbs: ο + -ειν/-εσθαι

Active infinitive in -οῦν, e.g. δηλοῦν, 'to show' (not δηλοῖν: see on τιμᾶν above)
Middle infinitive in -οῦσθαι, e.g. δουλοῦσθαι, 'to enslave for oneself'

Irregular infinitives

152. Learn the following infinitives of irregular verbs:

εἰμί, 'I am'	→	εἶναι, 'to be'
εἶμι, 'I shall go'	→	ἰέναι, 'to go'
οἶδα, 'I know'	→	εἰδέναι, 'to know'

■ *Form and Usage*

(a) While εἶμι, 'I shall go', is used with reference to future time, its infinitive, ἰέναι, is *present* in meaning.
(b) The negative with the infinitive is usually μή.
(c) Note the -ναι ending. It will recur.

EXERCISE

7A–C: 1. Form in Greek the present infinitives of the following verbs and translate:

1. διαβάλλω	7. πάρειμι	13. θαυμάζω
2. εὑρίσκω	8. νομίζω	14. πείθομαι
3. πειράομαι	9. εἶμι	15. δέχομαι
4. οἶδα	10. κλέπτω	16. ποιέω
5. δηλόω	11. ἀπέρχομαι	17. μανθάνω
6. λογίζομαι	12. βιάζομαι	18. λαμβάνω

VERBS TAKING INFINITIVE CONSTRUCTIONS

153. Certain verbs take infinitive constructions, e.g.

βούλομαι	'I wish to' + inf.
δοκέω	'I seem (to myself)', 'I think that I' + inf.
δεῖ	'it is necessary to', 'X must' + inf.
ἀνάγκη ἐστί	'it is obligatory to, X is bound to' + inf.

Special cases

(a) With δεῖ, the person who 'must' goes into the acc. case, e.g.

> δεῖ με/σε/αὐτοὺς ἰέναι 'it is necessary for me/you/them/ to go', 'I/you/they must go'

(b) With ἀνάγκη ἐστί, the person for whom it is obligatory goes into the acc. case (or sometimes the dat.), e.g.

> ἀνάγκη ἐστὶ τὸν θεὸν/ὑμᾶς λέγειν   lit. 'It is obligatory for the god/you to speak' *or*
> ἀνάγκη ἐστὶ τῷ θεῷ/ὑμῖν λέγειν

> i.e. 'The god is/you are obliged to/bound to speak'

EXERCISE

7A–C: 2. Translate into Greek, using the infinitives of the verbs in brackets:

1. I wish to go (εἶμι)
2. They wish to believe (πιστεύω)
3. He seems to think (νομίζω)
4. They seem to slander (διαβάλλω)
5. I/we/you (pl.) ought to be present (πάρειμι)
6. Socrates ought to teach (διδάσκω)
7. It is obligatory to depart (ἄπειμι)
8. It is obligatory for you (s.) to learn (μανθάνω)

COMPARATIVE AND SUPERLATIVE ADJECTIVES

154. Comparative and superlative adjectives of the καλός type are formed as follows:

Positive	Comparative	Superlative
σοφ-ός	σοφ-ώτερ-ος ᾱ ον	σοφ-ώτατ-ος η ον
'wise'	'wiser'	'wisest, most/very wise'
δειν-ός	δειν-ότερ-ος ᾱ ον	δειν-ότατ-ος η ον
'clever'	'cleverer'	'cleverest, most/very clever'

Form

155. The big giveaway with comparatives and superlatives is the -τερος -τατος endings. But should that be -ωτερος or -οτερος, -ωτατος or -οτατος? Learn the usual rules for the formation of the comp. and sup. adjectives:

■ *(a) Short vowel stem: σοφ-*

Usually, when the last syllable of the adjective's *stem* is short (i.e. contains a single short vowel as in σο̆φ-ός), -ώτερος and -ώτατος are added to form the comparative and superlative adjectives, e.g. σοφώτερος and σοφώτατος.

■ *(b) Long vowel stem:* δηλ-

When the last syllable of the *stem* is long (i.e. contains a 'diphthong' [vowel + ι or υ] as in δειν-ός, or a long vowel as in δῆλ-ος), -ότερος, -ότατος are added, e.g. δηλότερος, δηλότατος.

Declension

156. All regular comparative adjectives decline in the same way as ἡμέτερος ᾱ ον (**36**), and all superlative adjectives decline like καλός ή όν (**10**).

Meanings of comp. and sup. adjectives

157. As well as '-er' and 'more –', comparatives can mean 'rather –', 'fairly –', 'quite –'; superlatives, on top of ' -est' and 'most –', also mean 'extremely –', 'very –'.

Comparison in Greek

158. When two things are being compared, Greek uses ἤ, 'than', e.g.

ὁ ἀνήρ ἐστι σοφώτερος ἢ ὁ παῖς. 'The man is wiser **than** the boy.'

Note that the two things being compared are in the *same* case.

Irregular comparative and superlative forms

159. There are some important irregular comparatives (like e.g. English 'good', 'better', 'best'):

Positive	Comparative	Superlative
ἀγαθός	ἀμείνων ἄμεινον (ἀμεινον-)	ἄριστος η ον
or	βελτῑ́ων βέλτῑον (βελτῑον-)	βέλτιστος η ον
'good'	'better'	'best'
κακός	κακῑ́ων κάκῑον (κακῑον-)	κάκιστος η ον
or	χείρων χεῖρον (χειρον-)	χείριστος η ον
'bad'	'worse'	'worst'
καλός	καλλῑ́ων κάλλῑον (καλλῑον-)	κάλλιστος η ον
'beautiful, fine'	'more beautiful, finer'	'most beautiful, finest'
μέγας	μείζων μεῖζον (μειζον-)	μέγιστος η ον
'big'	'bigger'	'biggest'
πολύς	πλείων πλεῖον (πλειον-)	πλεῖστος η ον
'much'	'more'	'most'

Declension

160. Irregular comparative adjectives in -(ι)ων decline like εὔφρων, 'well-disposed' (**82**), i.e.:

ἀμείνων ἄμεινον (ἀμεινον-) 'better' (comparative of ἀγαθός)

s.

	m./f.	*n.*
Nom.	ἀμείνων	ἄμεινον
Acc.	ἀμείνον-α or ἀμείνω	ἄμεινον
Gen.	ἀμείνον-ος	ἀμείνον-ος
Dat.	ἀμείνον-ι	ἀμείνον-ι

pl.

	m./f.	*n.*
Nom.	ἀμείνον-ες or ἀμείνους*	ἀμείνον-α or ἀμείνω
Acc.	ἀμείνον-ας or ἀμείνους*	ἀμείνον-α or ἀμείνω
Gen.	ἀμεινόν-ων	ἀμεινόν-ων
Dat.	ἀμείνοσι(ν)	ἀμείνοσι(ν)

---

* More will be said about these irregular, and other, forms at **181**.

EXERCISES

7A–C: 3. Add the correct comparative and superlative forms of the quoted adjectives to the following phrases, and translate:

1. τὸν (πολέμιος) ναύτην
2. τοὺς (βέβαιος) λιμένας
3. τὴν (ἀγαθός) θεάν
4. αἱ (πολύς) νῆες
5. οἱ (μέγας) βασιλῆς
6. τὰς (κακός) γυναῖκας
7. τὸ (καλός) ἄστυ
8. ἡ (δῆλος) ἀνομία

7A–C: 4. Add the correct comparative and superlative forms of the quoted adjectives to the following phrases, and translate:

1. τῷ (πολέμιος) ναύτῃ
2. τῶν (βέβαιος) λιμένων
3. τῆς (ἀγαθός) θεᾶς
5. τοῖς (μέγας) βασιλεῦσι
6. τῇ (κακός) γυναικί
7. τοῦ (καλός) ἄστεως

PAST OF εἶμι 'I SHALL GO'

161. εἶμι, 'I shall go', has an irregular imperfect:

ἦα 'I was going, went'

ἦα or ἤειν	'I was going, went'
ἤεισθα	'you (s.) were going, went'
ἤει(ν)	'he/she/it was going, went'
ἦμεν	'we were going, went'
ἦτε	'you (pl.) were going, went'
ἦσαν	'they were going, went'

EXERCISE

7A–C: 5. Revise the present and imperfect of εἰμί, 'I am/was' (**44**, **110**) and the future and imperfect of εἶμι, 'I shall go/was going', (**123**, **161**) and translate into Greek:

1. We were going	7. They are
2. We were	8. We were
3. They shall go	9. You (pl.) were going
4. She is	10. You (s.) were going
5. He was going	11. We are
6. She shall go	12. They were

SUMMARY LEARNING VOCABULARY FOR SECTION 7A–C

ἀλήθεια, ἡ	truth (1b)	εἶμι	I shall go; ἰέναι to go;
ἀνάγκη ἐστί	it is obligatory (for		ἦα I went
	X [acc. or dat].) to	ἐντεῦθεν	from then, from there
	– (inf.)	ἐξετάζω	question closely
ἀνάγκη, ἡ	necessity (1a)	εὑρίσκω (εὑρ-)	find, come upon
ἀποφαίνω	reveal, show	ἤ	than
βούλομαι	wish, want	ἴσως	perhaps
γὰρ δή	really; I assure you	λογίζομαι	reckon, calculate,
δεῖ	it is necessary for		consider
	X (acc.) to – (inf.)	νοέω	think, notice, mean,
διαβάλλω	slander		intend
(διαβαλ-)		μή	not; don't! (with imper.)
διαβολή, ἡ	slander (1a)	οἶμαι	think (impf. ᾤμην)
διαφθείρω	corrupt; kill; destroy	πάρειμι	be present, be at hand
(διαφθειρα-)		πειράομαι	try, test
δοκέω	seem; consider oneself	(πειρᾱυμ-)	
	to –	ποιήτης, ὁ	poet (1d)
δόξα, ἡ	reputation, opinion (1c)	πολλάκις	often
ἑαυτόν	himself	ποτε	once, ever
εἰδώς εἰδυῖα	knowing (part. of οἶδα)	σοφίᾱ, ἡ	wisdom (1b)
εἰδός (εἰδοτ-)		ὡς	that

REVISION EXERCISES FOR SECTION 7A–C

B/C WORD SHAPE AND SYNTAX

1a. Change the following verbs into the infinitive form:

1. λέγω	6. διαφθείρω
2. διαβάλλω	7. εὑρίσκω
3. δοκέω	8. εἶμι
4. ἀποφαίνω	9. εἰμί
5. διαλέγομαι	10. οἶδα

1b. Adding subjects where indicated, use the the ten infinitives you have created to complete the following sentences. Then translate the sentences:

a. δεῖ (you) (pl.) τὴν ἀλήθειαν (tell), καὶ μή (slander) Σωκράτη.
b. οὐ βουλόμεθα (to seem) ἄριστοι, ἀλλ’ (to be).
c. οἱ σοφοὶ δοκοῦσί τι (know), οὐκ εἰδότες.
d. ἀνάγκη ἦν (Socrates) (to go) πρὸς τοὺς σοφοὺς καὶ (to talk) περὶ σοφίας.
e. Σωκράτης, ὡς ἐγὼ οἶμαι, οὐ πειρᾶται (to corrupt) τοὺς νέους.
f. Σωκράτης ἐβούλετο (to discover) πότερον τὴν ἀλήθειαν λέγει ὁ ἐν
    Δελφοῖς θεὸς ἢ οὔ. καὶ πολλάκις ἐπειρᾶτο Σωκράτης (to show) τὸν θεὸν
    οὐ τἀληθῆ λέγοντα.

2. Pair up the positive forms on the left with the comparative forms on the right.
    Add the superlative in each case.

1. ἀγαθός	a. καλλίων
2. βέβαιος	b. μείζων
3. δεινός	c. φίλτερος/φιλαίτερος*
4. κακός	d. πολεμιώτερος
5. καλός	e. μωρότερος
6. μέγας	f. δεινότερος
7. μῶρος	g. βεβαιότερος
8. πολέμιος	h. ἀμείνων
9. πολύς	i. χρησιμώτερος
10. φίλος	j. πλείων
11. χρήσιμος	k. κακίων

* Note these unusual comparative forms. The superlative is based on φιλτ-

D ENGLISH INTO GREEK

Translate these pairs of sentences:

1. ἀνάγκη ἐστὶ τοὺς γεωργοὺς εἰς τὸ ἄστυ ἰέναι.
    I was obliged to go to the poets.

2. δεῖ ἡμᾶς θυσίας θύειν καὶ πρὸς τοὺς θεοὺς εὔχεσθαι.
    You (s.) must question me closely and consider carefully.

3. αἱ γυναῖκες πειρῶνται τὰ δράματα θεᾶσθαι.
   I am trying to discover how the poets show their wisdom.

4. ἴσμεν ὅτι ὁ βασιλεὺς ἐβούλετο τὸν κήρυκα κολάζειν.
   You know that you wanted to slander me.

5. δοκεῖς μῶρος εἶναι, καίπερ διδάσκαλος ὤν.
   From then on I appeared to be corrupting the young, although I knew nothing.

Grammar for Section 7D–F*

(*Formerly 6 D–F)

> In this section you cover:
> ● First aorist participles, active and middle: παύσας, παυσάμενος
> ● Aspect in participles
> ● Past of οἶδα: ᾔδη 'knew'
> ● Present and past of φημί 'say'
> ● More on the complement

> VOCABULARY CHECK
>
> Ensure you know the meaning or significance of:
> ἀποκριν-, ἀρετή, ἦν δ' ἐγώ, ὁμολογέω, ἐμπεσ-, γελάω, ἐπαινέω, φημί, ἦ δ'ὅς

AORIST PARTICIPLES

162. You have already met participles based on the present stem of verbs, e.g. βλέπων, 'looking', τρέχων, 'running'. Greek also has participles based on the aorist stem of verbs.

First aorist stems

The aorist participle is based on the aorist *stem*. To form the aorist stem:

> ● Take the aorist indicative;
> ● Remove the augment;
> ● Remove the personal endings, e.g.

> ἔ-παυσα > aorist stem: παυσα-
> ἤ-κουσα > aorist stem: ἀκουσα-
> ἀπ-ε-κρῑνά-μην > aorist stem: ἀποκρῑνα-

First aorist active participles: stem + endings

163. The first aorist active participle is formed by adding the following endings to the aorist stem: -(α)ς -(α)σ-α -(α)ν (-(α)ντ-), e.g.

> παύσα-ς παύσα-σ-α παύσα-ν (παυσα-ντ-) **'having stopped, on stopping, stopping'**
> *s.*
>
> | | *m.* | *f.* | *n.* |
> |---|---|---|---|
> | *Nom.* | παύσᾱ-ς | παύσᾱ-σ-α | παῦσα-ν |
> | *Acc.* | παύσα-ντ-α | παύσᾱ-σ-αν | παῦσα-ν |
> | *Gen.* | παύσα-ντ-ος | παυσᾱ́-σ-ης | παύσα-ντ-ος |
> | *Dat.* | παύσα-ντ-ι | παυσᾱ́-σ-ῃ | παύσα-ντ-ι |

παύσα-ς παύσᾱ-σ-α παύσα-ν (παυσα-ντ-) **'having stopped, on stopping, stopping'** *(continued)*

pl.

	m.	*f.*	*n.*
Nom.	παύσα-ντ-ες	παύσᾱ-σ-αι	παύσα-ντ-α
Acc.	παύσα-ντ-ας	παυσά-σ-ᾱς	παύσα-ντ-α
Gen.	παυσά-ντ-ων	παυσᾱ-σ-ῶν	παυσά-ντ-ων
Dat.	παύσᾱ-σι(ν)	παυσά-σ-αις	παύσᾱ-σι(ν)

■ *Forms*

Just like the present active participle (ὤν οὖσα ὄν, etc.), παύσας παύσασα παύσαν (παυσαντ-) follows a '3-1-3' pattern, i.e. the m. and n. forms follow the pattern of type 3a and 3b nouns and the f. follows that of a type 1c noun like θάλαττα. See **87**.

First aorist middle participles

164. The first aorist middle participle is formed by adding -μεν-ος -η -ον to the aorist stem:

παυσά-μεν-ος η ον **'having stopped / on stopping / stopping / onself / ceasing'**

s.

	m.	*f.*	*n.*
Nom.	παυσά-μεν-ος	παυσα-μέν-η	παυσά-μεν-ον
Acc.	παυσά-μεν-ον	παυσα-μέν-ην	παυσά-μεν-ον
Gen.	παυσα-μέν-ου	παυσα-μέν-ης	παυσα-μέν-ου
Dat.	παυσα-μέν-ῳ	παυσα-μέν-ῃ	παυσα-μέν-ῳ

pl.

	m.	*f.*	*n.*
Nom.	παυσά-μεν-οι	παυσά-μεν-αι	παυσά-μεν-α
Acc.	παυσα-μέν-ους	παυσα-μέν-ᾱς	παυσά-μεν-α
Gen.	παυσα-μέν-ων	παυσα-μέν-ων	παυσα-μέν-ων
Dat.	παυσα-μέν-οις	παυσα-μέν-αις	παυσα-μέν-οις

■ *Form*

Like all middle participles, first aorist middle participles are declined in the same way as καλ-ός -ή -όν.

PARTICIPLES AND ASPECT

165. What is the difference in meaning between, say, παύων and παύσας, or between βλέπων and βλέψας?

- One vital thing to say is that the difference is *not necessarily one of time*. παύσας or βλέψας need not be translated 'having stopped' or 'having looked'.
- The difference is one of what is called *aspect* and is the same difference that has already been shown to exist between the imperfect and aorist indicatives – i.e. the difference between regarding the action as an incomplete *process* (imperfect) and a complete *event* (aorist).
- A present participle regards the action as a *process* (and is therefore sometimes called 'imperfective', Latin *imperfectus* 'incomplete, unfinished').
- The aorist participle regards it as simply a single *event*.
- Thus it is possible to translate both βλέπων and βλέψας as 'looking'; in the former case, it would be understood that the look went on, in the latter that it simply took place.
- Another way of stating this difference is that the action described by a present ('imperfective') participle is capable of being broken off, whereas that of an aorist participle is not. Rather, the action of an aorist ('perfective') participle is conceived of as having a definite end point: it has been (Latin) *perfectus* 'completed'.

Consider the following pairs of sentences:

1. 'After boarding the ship, the sailors shouted.'
2. 'The sailors shouted while boarding the ship.'

In this case, the difference between the two acts of 'boarding' is one of time:

- In the first sentence, the sailors have finished 'boarding' before they shout: the action is *complete* and would therefore be translated by an *aorist* participle in Greek.
- In the second sentence, however, the 'boarding' is going on at the same time as the shouting – and as the action is *incomplete* it would therefore be translated into Greek by a *present* ('imperfective') participle.

It is important to note that *both* sentences could be rephrased as 'Boarding the ship, the sailors shouted.' That is to say, English practice differs from Greek, in that English speakers often use a present participle (such as 'entering') to describe a past, complete action. An implication of this is that when translating into Greek you will sometimes have to think carefully about what the English means, not just what it says.

1. 'With a laugh, the girl replied.'
2. 'The girl replied, laughing as she spoke.'

In this case, the difference between the sentences is not strictly one of time, since in both cases the girl's reply can be understood as being accompanied by laughter (i.e., in both cases the laughing and replying are simultaneous). However, in the first sentence, the laugh seems to be a single *event* with an identifiable start- and end-point, which suggests that 'with a laugh' should be translated into Greek with an *aorist* participle. In the second sentence, however, the laughter is ongoing: an *incomplete* action which would best be rendered in Greek by a *present* ('imperfective') participle.

Aspect in Greek is subtle, and is unlikely to be mastered overnight. Indeed, at times the distinction between the two aspects may seem quite arbitrary to an English speaker, but the more you read the more used you will get to the different ways in which Greek uses present and aorist participles.

> ▶ Whatever else you do, it is essential that you pay close attention to the actual Greek usage: ask yourself 'What does the aspect of this present or aorist participle here suggest about the way the *Greek* wants us to see the action (however much we may want to see it differently)?'

Translating aorist participles

166. What does all this mean in practical terms when you are translating from Greek into English? Perhaps the most important point to grasp is that there is rarely a single right way to translate an aorist participle. Depending on context:

- παύσας may be correctly translated as 'having stopped', 'on stopping', 'stopping'.
- On occasion you may find it best to translate an aorist participle as if it were an ordinary verb in the aorist, e.g. βλέψας πρὸς ἐμὲ ἠρυθρίασεν 'he glanced at me and blushed'.
- You may translate it as a noun e.g. βλέψας πρὸς ἐμὲ ἠρυθρίασεν 'with a glance at me, he blushed'.

Because aorist participles occur so regularly in Greek, you will find that you have plenty of opportunities to experiment with different ways of translating them.

EXERCISES

7D–F: 1. Give the gender, number and case of the following aorist participles (e.g. m. s. nom.) and the form in which you would find them if you looked them up in the dictionary:

1. παυσάμενοι
2. λύσαντας
3. ζητήσας
4. ζητησάσας
5. δεξαμένη
6. βλέψαντες
7. δηλώσασα
8. πείσαντα
9. βοήσας
10. τρεψαμένους

7D–F: 2. Turn the following present participles into their aorist equivalent:

1. βλέπουσαν
2. θαυμάζων
3. τρεπόμενον
4. διωκούσας
5. ποιοῦντες

6. βιαζόμενοι
7. κολάζοντας
8. μισοῦσα
9. δουλουμένους
10. δεχομένη

7D–F: 3. There is a famous vase-painting of Achilles killing the Amazon queen, Penthesileia. As she died, their eyes meet and (it was said) Achilles fell in love with her. Typical bloke. How would the following captions express that moment?

(a) Ἀχιλλεὺς βλέψας πρὸς Πενθεσιλείαν ἐφλέγετο*.
(b) Ἀχιλλεὺς βλέπων πρὸς Πενθεσιλείαν ἐφλέγετο.

* 'caught fire', 'burned with passion'.

TWO IRREGULAR VERBS
ᾔδη, 'I KNEW'; φημί, 'I SAY'

167. The past of οἶδα is as follows:

ᾔδη 'I knew'	
ᾔδη	'I knew'
ᾔδησθα	'you (s.) knew'
ᾔδει(ν)	'he/she/it knew'
ᾖσμεν	'we knew'
ᾖστε	'you (pl.) knew'
ᾖσαν or ᾔδεσαν	'they knew'

168a. φημί, 'I say', conjugates as follows:

Present: φημί 'I say'*	
φημί	'I say'
φής or φής	'you (s.) say'
φησί(ν)	'he/she/it says'
φαμέν	'we say'
φατέ	'you (pl.) say'
φᾱσί(ν)	'they say'
Infinitive	
φάναι	'to say'

* Note that the present indicative is enclitic (**347(ii)**) except for φής/φής.

Participle

φάσκων φάσκουσα φάσκον (φασκοντ-) or φάς φᾶσα φάν
(φαντ-), sometimes φάμεν-ος η ον 'saying'

Future

φήσ-ω 'I shall say'

Past: ἔφην 'I said'

ἔφην	'I said'
ἔφησθα or ἔφης	'you (s.) said'
ἔφη	'he/she/it said'
ἔφαμεν	'we said'
ἔφατε	'you (pl.) said'
ἔφασαν	'they said'

Form and use

(a) Do not use φημί if you are translating English 'say that…' into Greek. Use λέγω ὅτι for the moment. See further *Reference Grammar* **397**.

(b) You will find φάσκων (which is 'borrowed' from the verb φάσκω) used far more commonly than φάς as the present participle of φημί.

(c) In passages containing direct speech, you will often find ἦν δ' ἐγώ, 'said I', and ἦ δ' ὅς 'said he' used as alternatives to ἔφην and ἔφη.

EXERCISE

7D–F: 4. Revise the present and past of οἶδα, 'I know' (**44, 167**) and using φημί as 'say' translate into Greek:

1. We know	6. She said
2. They said	7. I knew
3. She knew	8. He says
4. We say	9. You (pl.) said
5. You (s.) know	10. They knew

MORE ON THE COMPLEMENT

168b. Usually, in sentences with two nouns either side of the verb 'to be', the complement lacks a definite article (**45–7**). But not always. In answer to the question 'Who are the learners, the clever or the stupid?', Greek will say οἱ σοφοί εἰσιν οἱ μανθάνοντες 'The learners are the (= those who are) clever', i.e. οἱ creates the *group*. What would it mean if it lacked οἱ? (As usual, the complement comes first.)

SUMMARY LEARNING VOCABULARY FOR SECTION 7D–F

ἀνδρεῖος ᾱ ον	brave, manly
ἀποκρῑ́νομαι (ἀποκρῑνα-)	answer
ἀρετή, ἡ	virtue, excellence (1a)
γελάω (γελασα-)	laugh
δήπου	of course, surely
διδάσκαλος, ὁ	teacher (2a)
ἐκδέχομαι	receive in turn
ἐμπῑ́πτω (ἐμπεσ-)	fall into, on (+ ἐν or εἰς)
ἐπαινέω (ἐπαινεσα-)	praise
εὐθύς	at once, straightaway
ἥδομαι	enjoy, be pleased
ἦν δ᾽ ἐγώ	I said
ἦ δ᾽ ὅς	he said
ὁμολογέω	agree
οὐκοῦν	therefore
οὔκουν	not … therefore
νεᾱνίσκος, ὁ	young man (2a)
προτρέπω	urge on, impel
φημί/ἔφην	I say/I said
φιλοσοφίᾱ, ἡ	philosophy (1b)

REVISION EXERCISES FOR SECTION 7D–F

B/C WORD SHAPE AND SYNTAX

1. Form the m. nom. s. aorist participles of these verbs:

1. βλέπω	6. δέχομαι
2. φροντίζω	7. βιάζομαι
3. ῥίπτω	8. λογίζομαι
4. σῴζω	9. μάχομαι (μαχεσα-)
5. παύομαι	10. ἀποκρίνομαι (ἀποκρινα-)

2. Form the m. nom. s. aorist participles of these contracted verbs:

1. ποιέω	4. ἐλευθερόω
2. βοηθέω	5. τολμάω
3. ἀπορέω	6. θεάομαι (θεασα-)

3. Translate into Greek the italicised phrases, using either aorist or present participles of the verb in brackets to suit the sense:

    a. We sat silently, *all the time perplexed* as to his meaning. (ἀπορέω)
    b. *With a glance* at me the teacher began to speak. (βλέπω)
    c. The spectators *heard* his arguments and applauded. (ἀκούω)
    d. Dionysodoros replied *with laughter constantly in his voice*. (γελάω: aor. stem γελασα-)
    e. The woman *picked up* the argument and replied. (ἐκδέχομαι)
    f. He happened to say *in answer*. (ἀποκρίνομαι: aor. stem ἀποκρινα-)

D ENGLISH INTO GREEK

Translate these pairs of sentences:

1. οἱ μαθηταὶ ἀποκρινάμενοι εἶπον ὅτι ἡ ἀνομία οὐκ ἔστι δικαία.
   The teacher answered and said that the love of wisdom was a virtue.

2. ὁ Σωκράτης ἀκούσας τὸν λόγον ἐγέλασεν.
   Dionysodorus laughed and took up the argument.

3. οἱ ἱκέται σπεύσαντες πρὸς τὸ ἱερὸν ηὔξαντο πρὸς τοὺς θεούς.
   The sophist, with a glance at me, agreed.

4. βλέψασα πρὸς ἐμὲ ἡ γυνὴ ἐσιώπησεν.
   I praised them and said, 'Urge them on at once.'

5. κλέψας τὰ χρήματα ὁ νεανίας μέγα ἐβόησεν.
   Once in a state of perplexity, the student tried to escape.

E TEST EXERCISE SEVEN D–F

Translate into English:

    Kriton reports how he and Socrates discussed the nature of expertise and

decided that an expert's opinion is more valuable than another man's.
(From Plato, *Kriton*)

'σὺ μέν, ὦ Σώκρατες,' ἔφην ἐγώ, 'ἐξέταζε, ἐγὼ δ' ἀποκρινοῦμαι.'
'σκόπει οὖν,' ἦ δ' ὃς ὁ Σωκράτης, 'καὶ εἴ τι ἔχεις <u>ἀντιλέγειν</u>, ἀντίλεγε, καὶ
πείσομαι ἔγωγε.'
'καλῶς δοκεῖς λέγειν,' ἦν δ' ἐγώ, 'ὡς ἐγὼ οἶμαι.'
5   '<u>εἶεν</u>,' ἔφη, 'ἆρα ἀληθῆ λέγει ὁ φιλόσοφος ὁ λέγων ὅτι οὐ δεῖ ἡμᾶς
ἐπαινεῖν <u>πάσας</u> τὰς δόξας τῶν ἀνθρώπων; τί φής; ἆρα ἀληθῆ δοκεῖ
λέγειν, ταῦτα λέγων, ἢ οὔ; ἀποκρίνου.'
'ἀληθῆ,' ἔφην.
'οὐκοῦν δεῖ ἡμᾶς τὰς μὲν ἀγαθὰς δόξας ἐπαινεῖν καὶ τιμᾶν, τὰς δὲ κακὰς
10 μή;'
ὡμολόγουν.
'<u>φέρε</u> δή,' ἔφη ὁ Σωκράτης, 'ἐπειδὴ ἡ νόσος ἀνέπιπτε καὶ διέφθειρε τὴν
πόλιν, ποῖ ᾔεισθα σύ, πότερον πρὸς τοὺς φίλους, ἢ πρὸς τὸν <u>ἰατρόν</u>;'
'πρὸς τὸν ἰατρὸν ᾖα,' ἦν δ' ἐγώ, 'ᾖσαν δὲ <u>ἐνταῦθα</u> καὶ οἱ φίλοι. ᾔδει γὰρ ὁ
15 ἰατρὸς τὰ περὶ τῆς νόσου, ἐμπειρότερος ὢν ἢ οἱ ἄλλοι.'
'ἐμπειρότατος δὴ ἐφαίνετο ὢν ὁ ἰατρός,' ἦ δ' ὃς ὁ Σωκράτης. 'ἔδει οὖν σὲ
πρὸς τὸν ἰατρὸν ἰέναι, καὶ πρὸς οὐδένα ἄλλον;'
'ἔδει,' ἔφην ἐγώ.
'περὶ τῆς νόσου ἆρα οὐ δεῖ ἡμᾶς ἐπαινεῖν καὶ <u>φοβεῖσθαι</u> τὰς τῶν πολλῶν
20 δόξας, ἀλλὰ τὴν τῶν ἰατρῶν, εἴ τις ἐμπειρότατος τυγχάνει ὤν; οὕτω
φαμὲν ἢ οὔ;'
'φάμεν νὴ τὸν Δία,' ἔφην.

Vocabulary

ἀντιλέγειν object   ἰατρός, ὁ doctor (2a)
εἶεν well then   ἐνταῦθα here
πάσας all (f. acc. pl.)   φοβεῖσθαι respect
φέρε come!

EXERCISE

Answer the following questions based on the passage above:

1. Give the tense of the following verbs: (a) ἔχεις (line 2), (b) πείσομαι (line 3),
    (c) ὡμολόγουν (line 11), (d) ἀνέπιπτε (line 12)
2. What is the case of (a) ἡμᾶς (b) ταῦτα (c) πόλιν (d) ἄλλοι (e) οὐδένα and
    (f) Δία?

Grammar for Section 7G–H*

(*Formerly 6 G–H)

> In this section you cover:
> - Second aorist participles, active and middle: λαβών, γενόμενος
> - Pronouns: αὐτός, ὁ αὐτός, αὐτόν; ἐμαυτόν, σεαυτόν, ἑαυτόν/αὑτόν
> - δύναμαι

VOCABULARY CHECK

Ensure you know the meaning or significance of:

ἀνελ-, ἕπομαι, μάχη, μέντοι, νομίζω, ἀγαγ-, δύναμαι, καταλαβ-, μετά + acc., οἰκέω, ὑμέτερος

SECOND AORIST PARTICIPLES

169. You have aready learnt how verbs with a first aorist form their aorist participle on the first aorist stem. Verbs with a second aorist form it (hard to believe though it is) on the second aorist stem.

Second aorist stems

You are already familiar with how to form the first aorist stem (**131ff.**): take the aorist indicative, and remove (i) the augment and (ii) the personal endings. As you have seen, it works for second aorists as follows (**144ff.**):

ἔ-λαβ-ον	aorist stem: λαβ-
ἦλθ-ον	aorist stem: ἐλθ-
ἐ-γεν-όμην	aorist stem: γεν-
ἀπ-έ-φυγ-ον	aorist stem: ἀποφυγ-

Second aorist active participles: stem + endings

170. The second aorist active participle is formed by adding the endings -ών -οῦσ-α -όν to the aorist stem:

> **λαβ-ών λαβ-οῦσα λαβ-όν (λαβ-οντ-), 'taking', 'on taking', 'having taken'**
> **(λαμβάνω)**
>
> *s.*
>
> | | *m.* | *f.* | *n.* |
> |---|---|---|---|
> | *Nom.* | λαβ-ών | λαβ-οῦσ-α | λαβ-όν |
> | *Acc.* | λαβ-όντ-α | λαβ-οῦσ-αν | λαβ-όν |
> | *Gen.* | λαβ-όντ-ος | λαβ-ούσ-ης | λαβ-όντ-ος |
> | *Dat.* | λαβ-όντ-ι | λαβ-ούσ-ῃ | λαβ-όντ-ι |

λαβ-ών λαβ-οῦσα λαβ-όν (λαβ-οντ-), 'taking', 'on taking', 'having taken'
(λαμβάνω) *(continued)*

pl.

	m.	*f.*	*n.*
Nom.	λαβ-όντ-ες	λαβ-οῦσ-αι	λαβ-όντ-α
Acc.	λαβ-όντ-ας	λαβ-ούσ-ᾱς	λαβ-όντ-α
Gen.	λαβ-όντ-ων	λαβ-ουσ-ῶν	λαβ-όντ-ων
Dat.	λαβ-οῦσι(ν)	λαβ-ούσ-αις	λαβ-οῦσι(ν)

■ *Form*

The endings for these participles (-ών -οῦσ-α -όν) are exactly the same as for
present participles (**87**).

Second aorist middle participles

171. The second aorist middle participle is formed by adding the familiar -ομεν-
ος -η -ον endings to the aorist stem:

γεν-όμεν-ος γεν-ομέν-η γεν-όμεν-ον '**becoming**', '**on becoming**', '**having
become**' (γίγνομαι)

s.

	m.	*f.*	*n.*
Nom.	γεν-όμεν-ος	γεν-ομέν-η	γεν-όμεν-ον
Acc.	γεν-όμεν-ον	γεν-ομέν-ην	γεν-όμεν-ον
Gen.	γεν-ομέν-ου	γεν-ομέν-ης	γεν-ομέν-ου
Dat.	γεν-ομέν-ῳ	γεν-ομέν-ῃ	γεν-ομέν-ῳ

pl.

	m.	*f.*	*n.*
Nom.	γεν-όμεν-οι	γεν-όμεν-αι	γεν-όμεν-α
Acc.	γεν-ομέν-ους	γεν-ομέν-ᾱς	γεν-όμεν-α
Gen.	γεν-ομέν-ων	γεν-ομέν-ων	γεν-ομέν-ων
Dat.	γεν-ομέν-οις	γεν-ομέν-αις	γεν-ομέν-οις

EXERCISES

7G–H: 1. Attach the appropriate form of the aorist participle to the given form of
the definite article:

1. τὸν (λαμβάνω)   5. οἱ (γίγνομαι)
2. τοὺς (ἔρχομαι)   6. τὰς (ἀφικνέομαι)
3. τὴν (μανθάνω)   7. τὸ (πίπτω)
4. αἱ (ὁράω)   8. ἡ (αἱρέω)

7G–H: 2. Attach the appropriate form of the aorist participle to the given form of the definite article:

1. τῷ (μανθάνω)   5. τῇ (λέγω)
2. τῆς (τυγχάνω)   6. τοῖς (γίγνομαι)
3. ταῖς (τρέχω)   7. τῷ (εὑρίσκω)
4. τοῦ (ἀφικνέομαι)   8. τοῦ (λαμβάνω)

PRONOUN/ADJECTIVE: αὐτ-ός -ή -ό

172. The declension of αὐτ-ός -ή -ό ('self, same'); αὐτ-όν -ήν -ό ('him, her, it') is as follows:

αὐτός αὐτή αὐτό

s.

	m.	*f.*	*n.*
Nom.	αὐτ-ός	αὐτ-ή	αὐτ-ό
Acc.	αὐτ-όν	αὐτ-ήν	αὐτ-ό
Gen.	αὐτ-οῦ	αὐτ-ῆς	αὐτ-οῦ
Dat.	αὐτ-ῷ	αὐτ-ῇ	αὐτ-ῷ

pl.

	m.	*f.*	*n.*
Nom.	αὐτ-οί	αὐτ-αί	αὐτ-ά
Acc.	αὐτ-ούς	αὐτ-άς	αὐτ-ά
Gen.	αὐτ-ῶν	αὐτ-ῶν	αὐτ-ῶν
Dat.	αὐτ-οῖς	αὐτ-αῖς	αὐτ-οῖς

■ *Form*

173. αὐτός is one of very few pronouns in Greek which (like the def. art.) end in -ο in the n. s. nom./acc. You have already met others: e.g. οὗτος and ἐκεῖνος (**69**).

Meanings of αὐτός

174. αὐτός has a variety of meanings:

■ *'Him', 'her', 'it', 'them'*

Used as an *unstressed* pronoun, but never in the nom. (nor as the first word of a clause, when it will always mean 'self') αὐτός means 'him', 'her', 'it', 'them', e.g.

εἶδεν αὐτοὺς τρέχοντας   'he saw them running'
ἔλαβον αὐτήν   'I caught her'

Note that οὗτος and ἐκεῖνος are used when the pronoun is *stressed*.

■ *'Self'*

Agreeing with the noun it picks out, it means 'self', e.g.

Σωκράτης αὐτός   'Socrates himself'
τὸν ἄνδρα αὐτόν   'the man himself'

■ *'Myself', 'yourself', etc.*

Combined with the appropriate pronoun, it serves as a reflexive pronoun:

'Myself'

	m.	*f.*
Acc.	ἐμαυτ-όν	ἐμαυτ-ήν
Gen.	ἐμαυτ-οῦ	ἐμαυτ-ῆς
Dat.	ἐμαυτ-ῷ	ἐμαυτ-ῇ

'Ourselves'

	m.	*f.*
Acc.	ἡμᾶς αὐτ-ούς	ἡμᾶς αὐτ-άς
Gen.	ἡμῶν αὐτ-ῶν	ἡμῶν αὐτ-ῶν
Dat.	ἡμῖν αὐτ-οῖς	ἡμῖν αὐτ-αῖς

'Yourself'

	m.	*f.*
Acc.	σ(ε)αυτ-όν	σ(ε)αυτ-ήν
Gen.	σ(ε)αυτ-οῦ	σ(ε)αυτ-ῆς
Dat.	σ(ε)αυτ-ῷ	σ(ε)αυτ-ῇ

'Yourselves'

	m.	*f.*
Acc.	ὑμᾶς αὐτ-ούς	ὑμᾶς αὐτ-άς
Gen.	ὑμῶν αὐτ-ῶν	ὑμῶν αὐτ-ῶν
Dat.	ὑμῖν αὐτ-οῖς	ὑμῖν αὐτ-αῖς

'Himself', 'herself', 'itself'

	m.	*f.*	*n.*
Acc.	ἑαυτ-όν* (αὐτ-όν)	ἑαυτ-ήν (αὐτ-ήν)	ἑαυτ-ό (αὐτ-ό)
Gen.	ἑαυτ-οῦ (αὐτ-οῦ)	ἑαυτ-ῆς (αὐτ-ῆς)	ἑαυτ-οῦ (αὐτοῦ)
Dat.	ἑαυτ-ῷ (αὐτ-ῷ)	ἑαυτ-ῇ (αὐτῇ)	ἑαυτ-ῷ (αὐτ-ῷ)

'Themselves'

	m.	*f.*	*n.*
Acc.	ἑαυτ-ούς* (αὐτ-ούς)	ἑαυτ-άς (αὐτ-άς)	ἑαυτ-ά (αὐτ-ά)
Gen.	ἑαυτ-ῶν (αὐτ-ῶν)	ἑαυτ-ῶν (αὐτ-ῶν)	ἑαυτ-ῶν (αὐτ-ῶν)
Dat.	ἑαυτ-οῖς (αὐτ-οῖς)	ἑαυτ-αῖς (αὐτ-αῖς)	ἑαυτ-οῖς (αὐτ-οῖς)

* Note that the ἑ- is a 3rd person pronoun found mostly in Homer. Watch the breathing where ἑ- is contracted out!

Meaning

175. Reflexive forms are used when 'me', 'you', 'him', etc. refer to the same person as the subject of the clause e.g. μὴ ἀπόκτεινε σεαυτόν 'don't kill yourself/commit suicide!'. In further clauses, they can refer to the subject of the main verb of the sentence, e.g.

ἡ Ἀμαζὼν ἔπεισε τὸν ἄνδρα ἑαυτὴν/αὑτὴν λύειν.

'The Amazon persuaded the man to release her' (i.e. the Amazon).

ἡ Ἀμαζὼν ἔπεισε τὸν ἄνδρα αὐτὴν λύειν.

'The Amazon persuaded the man to release her' (i.e. another woman).

■ *'Same'*

176. αὐτός preceded by the definite article is an adjective meaning 'same', e.g.

ὁ αὐτὸς νεανίας   'the same youth'

EXERCISES

7G–H: 3. Translate into English:

1. τὸν ἄνδρα εἶδον
2. αὐτὸν εἶδον
3. τὸν ἄνδρα αὐτὸν εἶδον
4. αὐτὸς τὸν ἄνδρα αὐτὸν εἶδον

5. αὐτὸς τὸν αὐτὸν ἄνδρα εἶδον
6. αὐτὸς τὸν αὐτὸν εἶδον
7. αὐτὸς αὐτὸν εἶδεν
8. αὐτὸς ἐποίησε τὸ αὐτὸ πρᾶγμα

7G–H: 4. Translate each of the words in brackets into Greek using a version of αὐτός ἡ ὁ:

1. τὸν ἄνδρα (same)
2. ἆρ' εἶδες (them, f.)
3. ἦλθε (herself)
4. ἔλαβεν (him)

5. ἀφίκοντο (themselves, m.)
6. τὴν γυναῖκα (herself)
7. οἱ νόμοι (same)
8. εἶδεν (it)

δύναμαι 'I AM ABLE, CAN'

177. Note the -α- dominated δύναμαι, 'I am able, can'. The stem is δυνα-. Instead of taking the thematic vowel and being a contract verb, it is *athematic*: the endings are simply added to the stem. You should learn this verb now as you will meet other verbs that conjugate in the same way (such as ἀνίσταμαι, 'I get up, emigrate': **187**):

δύναμαι **'I am able, can'**

δύναμαι	'I am able, can'
δύνασαι	'you (s.) are able, can'
δύναται	'he/she/it is able, can'
δυνάμεθα	'we are able, can'
δύνασθε	'you (pl.) are able, can'
δύνανται	'they are able, can'

Infinitive

δύνασθαι	'to be able'

Participle

δυνάμεν-ος -η -ον	'being able'

SUMMARY LEARNING VOCABULARY FOR SECTION 7G–H

ἄγω (ἀγαγ-)	lead, bring	κτῆμα (κτηματ-), τό	possession,
ἀναιρέω (ἀνελ-)	pick up		acquisition (3b)
ἀποβαίνω (ἀποβα-)	leave, depart	μάχη, ἡ	fight, battle (1a)
αὐτός ἡ ό	self	μέντοι	however, but
διαβαίνω (διαβα-)	cross	μετά	(+acc.) after
δύναμαι	be able	νομίζω	think,
δύο	two		acknowledge
ἑαυτ-όν (αὐτ-όν),	him/her/itself	ὁ αὐτός	the same
ἑαυτ-ήν (αὐτ-ήν),	(pronoun)	οἰκέω	dwell (in), live
ἑαυτ-ό (αὐτ-ό)		πάλιν	back, again
ἑαυτ-ούς (αὐτ-ούς),	themselves	ποταμός, ὁ	river (2a)
ἑαυτ-ᾱς		σ(ε)αυτ-όν, -ήν	yourself (s.)
(αὐτ-ᾱς), ἑαυτ-ά	(pronoun)		(pronoun)
(αὐτ-ά)		σημεῖον, τό	sign, signal (2b)
ἐμαυτ-όν, -ήν	myself (pronoun)	ὑμᾶς αὐτ-ούς, -ᾱς	yourselves
ἐπανέρχομαι	return		(pronoun)
(ἐπανελθ-)		ὑμέτερος ᾱ ον	your(s)
ἕπομαι (ἑσπ-)	follow	φυλάττω	guard
ἡμᾶς αὐτ-ούς,	ourselves	φωνέω	speak, utter
-ᾱς	(pronoun)	φωνή, ἡ	voice, language,
καταλαμβάνω	come across,		speech (1a)
(καταλαβ-)	overtake		

REVISION EXERCISES FOR SECTION 7G–H

B/C WORD SHAPE AND SYNTAX

1. Form the 1st person s. aorist indicative of these verbs, then construct the m. nom. s. aorist participle:

   1. γίγνομαι
   2. μανθάνω
   3. ὁράω
   4. ἀφικνέομαι
   5. ἔρχομαι
   6. λαμβάνω
   7. εὑρίσκω
   8. αἱρέω
   9. πίπτω

2. Translate the following sentences, completing them with the aorist participle of the verbs indicated:

   a. οἱ νεανίσκοι (ἀπέρχομαι) εἶπον ταῦτα πρὸς τοὺς λοιπούς ('the rest').
   b. αἱ Ἀμαζόνες, (καταλαμβάνω) ιυὺς νεανίας, διελέγοντο πρὸς αὐτούς.
   c. ὁ νεανίας, (ὁράω) τὴν Ἀμαζόνα, προσῆλθεν πρὸς αὐτήν.
   d. οἱ Σκύθαι, (εὑρίσκω) τὰς Ἀμαζόνας, πλησίον ἀφικνοῦνται.
   e. οἱ νεανίσκοι, πλησίον (ἀφικνέομαι), ἐστρατοπεδεύσαντο ('pitched camp').
   f. οἱ Σκύθαι, (ἀν-αιρέω) τοὺς νεκροὺς καὶ (μανθάνω) γυναῖκας οὔσας, ἐθαύμαζον.

3. In the following sentences, translate only the words in italics by the correct forms of αὐτός, αὐτόν, ὁ αὐτός:

   a. We saw *them* approaching.
   b. *The same man* did this same thing.
   c. She *herself* brought another Amazon with her.
   d. Did you see *the same* woman as I?
   e. What does *he himself* think of it?
   f. They all speak about (περί + acc.) *the same things*.
   g. I *myself* do not enjoy sentences.
   h. I saw the *young men themselves* behaving like this.
   i. Women? We love *them*! Men? We hate *them*.

D ENGLISH INTO GREEK

Translate these pairs of sentences:

1. αἱ γυναῖκες τὸν γέροντα ἰδοῦσαι ἀπῆλθον.
   The men picked up the bodies of the women and went away.

2. ταῦτα εἰπὼν ὁ ναύτης ἐγέλασεν.
   Coming upon these women, the young men were amazed.

3. μαθηταὶ γενόμενοι, οἱ νεανίσκοι ἐβούλοντο μανθάνειν.
   Once friends, the young men are able to converse with those women.

4. τοὺς ἄνδρας εὑροῦσαι, αἱ γυναῖκες ἐπαύσαντο φροντίζουσαι.
   The women said these things and persuaded the young men.

5. μετὰ δὲ ταῦτα ὁ παῖς δραμὼν εἰς τὴν οἰκίαν τὸν πατέρα ἐζήτει.
   Because of this the young men returned to their houses and took their possessions.

SUMMARY EXERCISES FOR SECTION 7

A VOCABULARY-BUILDING

1. Deduce the meaning of the words in the right-hand columns from those in the left:

ἀνάγκη	ἀναγκαῖος ᾱ ον	ἀναγκάζω	
γελάω	ὁ γέλως	γέλοιος	
διαβαίνω	ἡ διάβασις		
διαφθείρω	ἡ διαφθορά		
δύναμαι	δυνατός ή όν	ἡ δύναμις	
ἐπαινέω	ὁ ἔπαινος		
κτῆμα	κτάομαι	ἡ κτῆσις	
λογίζομαι	ὁ λογισμός		
ὁμολογέω	ἡ ὁμολογία		
πειράομαι	ἡ πεῖρα		
φυλάττω	ὁ φύλαξ	ἡ φυλακή	ἀφύλακτος ον

2. Group this pool of words into sets of cognate words (i.e. words which share common roots). Give the meaning of each word:

μάχη	ἀληθής	διαβάλλω	σοφία	ἀποφαίνω	λόγος
ἡδέως	νέος	οἰκέω	φάσμα	δοκέω	νεανίας
διαβολή	μάχομαι	λογίζομαι	φαίνομαι	ἥδομαι	δόξα
σοφός	οἰκία	ἀλήθεια			

D ENGLISH INTO GREEK

Translate into Greek (and don't forget connecting particles!):

When the Amazons had killed the Athenians, they came to the land of the Scythians. On arrival, they found horses and fought with the Scythians. The Scythians, defeating them and learning about them, wished to become friends. The young men therefore followed closely, but did not fight; and the Amazons, seeing this, kept quiet themselves. At last they became friends and lived together*; but it was necessary for the young men and their wives to cross the river and inhabit another place. 'For', said the Amazons, 'we do not want to live in your land, since on arrival we fought you.'

    * Use συνοικέω

E TEST EXERCISE SEVEN

Translate into English:

        Ἀμαζόνες τινές, εἰς τὴν τῶν Σκυθῶν γῆν ἀφικόμεναι καὶ ἀπὸ τῶν πλοίων ἀποβᾶσαι, εἰσπεσοῦσαι τὴν γῆν <u>διήρπασαν</u>. οἱ δὲ Σκύθαι, ἐν
5   μάχῃ νικήσαντες αὐτάς, τοὺς νεκροὺς ἀνεῖλον καὶ μαθόντες γυναῖκας οὔσας, ἐβούλοντο ἐκ τῶν Ἀμαζόνων παιδοποιεῖσθαι. κελεύοντες οὖν τοὺς νεανίσκους μάχεσθαι μὲν <u>μηδέποτε</u>, πλησίον δὲ ἐλθόντας φίλους γίγνεσθαι, ἀπέπεμψαν αὐτοὺς πρὸς τὰς Ἀμαζόνας. αἱ δὲ Ἀμαζόνες, ἰδοῦσαι αὐτοὺς πλησίον μὲν ἑπομένους, μαχομένους δὲ οὐδέποτε, οὐκέτι

ἐφρόντιζον αὐτῶν. ἔπειτα δὲ Σκύθης τις, καταλαβὼν Ἀμαζόνα τινὰ
μόνην οὖσαν, καὶ φίλος γενόμενος, ἐκέλευε τοὺς ἄλλους ποιεῖν τὸ αὐτό,
10   καὶ Ἀμαζόνας τινὰς εὑρόντας, φίλους γίγνεσθαι. ἐπείθοντο οὖν οἱ ἄλλοι,
τέλος δὲ συνῴκουν οἵ τε Σκύθαι καὶ αἱ Ἀμαζόνες. ἀλλ' αἱ Ἀμαζόνες οὐκ
ἐβούλοντο ἐπανιέναι εἰς τὸ τῶν Σκυθῶν πλῆθος. 'οὐ γὰρ δυνάμεθα,'
ἔφασαν, 'συνοικεῖν μετὰ τῶν γυναικῶν τῶν ὑμετέρων. οὐ γὰρ οἱ αὐτοὶ
οἱ ἡμέτεροι νόμοι καὶ οἱ τῶν Σκυθῶν.' λαβόντες οὖν τὰ κτήματα καὶ
15   διαβάντες τὸν ποταμόν, ηὗρον χωρίον τι πλησίον ὂν καὶ ᾤκησαν αὐτό.

Vocabulary

διαρπάζω lay waste   μετά + gen. with
μηδέποτε never

EXERCISE

Answer the following questions based on the passage above:

1. Give the aspect (i.e. present or aorist) of the following participles: (a) εἰσπεσοῦσαι (line 2), (b) μαθόντες (line 3), (c) κελεύοντες (line 4), (d) ἰδοῦσαι (line 7), (e) μαχομένους (line 7), (f) καταλαβών (line 8)
2. Give the tense of the following verbs: (a) ἐβούλοντο (line 4), (b) ἀπέπεμψαν (line 6), (c) ἐφρόντιζον (line 8), (d) ηὗρον (line 15)

Grammmar for Section 8A–C*

(*Formerly 7 A–C)

> In this section you cover:
> - The genitive case and its uses
> - Further comparative and superlative adjectives
> - Mood
> - Present optative, active and middle: παύοιμι, παυοίμην
> - ἄν + optative
> - ἀνίσταμαι 'I get up and go'

GENITIVE CASE

178. The forms of the gen. s. and pl. across the range of noun and adjective types you have met are as follows:

	s. nom.	acc.	gen.	dat.	pl. nom.	acc.	gen.	dat.
1a	βο-ή, ἡ	βο-ήν	βο-ῆς	βο-ῇ	βο-αί	βο-άς	βο-ῶν	βο-αῖς
1b	ἀπορί-α, ἡ	ἀπορί-αν	ἀπορί-ας	ἀπορί-ᾳ	ἀπορί-αι	ἀπορί-ας	ἀπορι-ῶν	ἀπορί-αις
1c	θάλαττα, ἡ	θάλαττ-αν	θαλάττ-ης	θαλάττ-ῃ	θάλαττ-αι	θαλάττ-ᾱς	θαλαττ-ῶν	θαλάττ-αις
1d	ναύτ-ης, ὁ	ναύτ-ην	ναύτ-ου	ναύτ-ῃ	ναῦτ-αι	ναύτ-ᾱς	ναυτ-ῶν	ναύτ-αις
	νεανί-ας, ὁ	νεανί-αν	νεανί-ου	νεανί-ᾳ				
2a	ἄνθρωπ-ος, ὁ	ἄνθρωπ-ον	ἀνθρώπ-ου	ἀνθρώπ-ῳ	ἄνθρωπ-οι	ἀνθρώπ-ους	ἀνθρώπ-ων	ἀνθρώπ-οις
2b	ἔργ-ον, τό	ἔργ-ον	ἔργ-ου	ἔργ-ῳ	ἔργ-α	ἔργ-α	ἔργ-ων	ἔργ-οις
3a	λιμήν, ὁ	λιμέν-α	λιμέν-ος	λιμέν-ι	λιμέν-ες	λιμέν-ας	λιμέν-ων	λιμέ-σι(ν)
3b	πρᾶγμα, τό	πρᾶγμα	πράγματ-ος	πράγματ-ι	πράγματ-α	πράγματ-α	πραγμάτ-ων	πράγμα-σι(ν)
3c	πλῆθ-ος, τό	πλῆθ-ος	πλήθ-ους	πλήθ-ει	πλήθ-η	πλήθ-η	πληθ-ῶν	πλήθ-εσι(ν)
3d	τριήρ-ης, ἡ	τριήρ-η	τριήρ-ους	τριήρ-ει	τριήρ-εις	τριήρ-εις	τριηρ-ῶν	τριήρ-εσι(ν)
3e	πόλ-ις, ἡ	πόλ-ιν	πόλ-εως	πόλ-ει	πόλ-εις	πόλ-εις	πόλ-εων	πόλ-εσι(ν)
	πρέσβ-υς, ὁ	πρέσβ-υν						
3f	ἄστ-υ, τό	ἄστ-υ	ἄστ-εως	ἄστ-ει	ἄστ-η	ἄστ-η	ἄστ-εων	ἄστ-εσι(ν)
3g	βασιλ-εύς, ὁ	βασιλ-έα	βασιλ-έως	βασιλ-εῖ	βασιλ-ῆς			
					βασιλ-εῖς	βασιλ-έας	βασιλ-έων	βασιλ-εῦσι(ν)
3h	ὀφρύ-ς, ἡ	ὀφρύ-ν	ὀφρύ-ος	ὀφρύ-ι	ὀφρύ-ες	ὀφρῦ-ς	ὀφρύ-ων	ὀφρύ-σι(ν)
Irregular nouns								
	ναῦς, ἡ	ναῦν	νεώς	νηί	νῆες	ναῦς	νεῶν	ναυσί(ν)
	γραῦς, ἡ	γραῦν	γραός	γραί	γρᾶες	γραῦς	γραῶν	γραυσί(ν)
	Ζεύς, ὁ	Δία	Διός	Διί				

	s.				*pl.*			
	nom.	*acc.*	*gen.*	*dat.*	*nom.*	*acc.*	*gen.*	*dat.*

Personal pronouns

	nom.	*acc.*	*gen.*	*dat.*	*nom.*	*acc.*	*gen.*	*dat.*
	ἐγώ	(ἐ)μέ	(ἐ)μοῦ	(ἐ)μοί	ἡμεῖς	ἡμᾶς	ἡμῶν	ἡμῖν
	σύ	σέ	σοῦ	σοί	ὑμεῖς	ὑμᾶς	ὑμῶν	ὑμῖν

Adjectives

	nom.	*acc.*	*gen.*	*dat.*	*nom.*	*acc.*	*gen.*	*dat.*
m.	καλ-ός	καλ-όν	καλ-οῦ	καλ-ῷ	καλ-οί	καλ-ούς	καλ-ῶν	καλ-οῖς
f.	καλ-ή	καλ-ήν	καλ-ῆς	καλ-ῇ	καλ-αί	καλ-άς	καλ-ῶν	καλ-αῖς
n.	καλ-όν	καλ-όν	καλ-οῦ	καλ-ῷ	καλ-ά	καλ-ά	καλ-ῶν	καλ-οῖς
m.	ἡμέτερ-ος	ἡμέτερ-ον	ἡμέτερ-ου	ἡμέτερ-ῳ	ἡμέτερ-οι	ἡμέτερ-ους	ἡμέτερ-ων	ἡμέτερ-οις
f.	ἡμετέρ-α	ἡμετέρ-αν	ἡμετέρ-ας	ἡμετέρ-ᾳ	ἡμέτερ-αι	ἡμέτερ-ας	ἡμετέρ-ων	ἡμετέρ-αις
n.	ἡμέτερ-ον	ἡμέτερ-ον	ἡμετέρ-ου	ἡμέτερ-ῳ	ἡμέτερ-α	ἡμέτερ-α	ἡμετέρ-ων	ἡμέτερ-οις
m.	οὗτ-ος	τοῦτ-ον	τούτ-ου	τούτ-ῳ	οὗτ-οι	τούτ-ους	τούτ-ων	τούτ-οις
f.	αὕτ-η	ταύτ-ην	ταύτ-ης	ταύτ-ῃ	αὗτ-αι	ταύτ-ας	τούτ-ων	ταύτ-αις
n.	τοῦτ-ο	τοῦτ-ο	τούτ-ου	τούτ-ῳ	ταῦτ-α	ταῦτ-α	τούτ-ων	τούτ-οις
m.	ἐκεῖν-ος	ἐκεῖν-ον	ἐκείν-ου	ἐκείν-ῳ	ἐκεῖν-οι	ἐκείν-ους	ἐκείν-ων	ἐκείν-οις
f.	ἐκείν-η	ἐκείν-ην	ἐκείν-ης	ἐκείν-η	ἐκεῖν-αι	ἐκείν-ας	ἐκείν-ων	ἐκείν-αις
n.	ἐκεῖν-ο	ἐκεῖν-ο	ἐκείν-ου	ἐκείν-ῳ	ἐκεῖν-α	ἐκεῖν-α	ἐκείν-ων	ἐκείν-οις
m.	αὐτ-ός	αὐτ-όν	αὐτ-οῦ	αὐτ-ῷ	αὐτ-οί	αὐτ-ούς	αὐτ-ῶν	αὐτ-οῖς
f.	αὐτ-ή	αὐτ-ήν	αὐτ-ῆς	αὐτ-ῇ	αὐτ-αί	αὐτ-άς	αὐτ-ῶν	αὐτ-αῖς
n.	αὐτ-ό	αὐτ-ό	αὐτ-οῦ	αὐτ-ῷ	αὐτ-ά	αὐτ-ά	αὐτ-ῶν	αὐτ-οῖς
m.	πολ-ύς	πολ-ύν	πολλ-οῦ	πολλ-ῷ	πολλ-οί	πολλ-ούς	πολλ-ῶν	πολλ-οῖς
f.	πολλ-ή	πολλ-ήν	πολλ-ῆς	πολλ-ῇ	πολλ-αί	πολλ-άς	πολλ-ῶν	πολλ-αῖς
n.	πολ-ύ	πολύ	πολλ-οῦ	πολλ-ῷ	πολλ-ά	πολλ-ά	πολλ-ῶν	πολλ-οῖς
m./f.	εὔφρων	εὔφρον-α	εὔφρον-ος	εὔφρον-ι	εὔφρον-ες	εὔφρον-ας	εὐφρόν-ων	εὔφρο-σι(ν)
n.	εὔφρον	εὔφρον	εὔφρον-ος	εὔφρον-ι	εὔφρον-α	εὔφρον-α	εὐφρόν-ων	εὔφρο-σι(ν)
m./f.	τις	τιν-α	τιν-ος	τιν-ι	τιν-ες	τιν-ας	τιν-ων	τι-σι(ν)
n.	τι	τι	τιν-ος	τιν-ι	τιν-α	τιν-α	τιν-ων	τι-σι(ν)
m.	οὐδ-είς	οὐδ-ένα	οὐδ-ενός	οὐδ-ενί				
f.	οὐδε-μία	οὐδε-μίαν	οὐδε-μιᾶς	οὐδε-μιᾷ				
n.	οὐδ-έν	οὐδ-έν	οὐδ-ενός	οὐδ-ενί				
m.	ὤν	ὄντ-α	ὄντ-ος	ὄντ-ι	ὄντ-ες	ὄντ-ας	ὄντ-ων	οὖ-σι(ν)
f.	οὖσ-α	οὖσ-αν	οὔσ-ης	οὔσ-ῃ	οὖσ-αι	οὔσ-ας	οὐσ-ῶν	οὔσ-αις
n.	ὄν	ὄν	ὄντ-ος	ὄντ-ι	ὄντ-α	ὄντ-α	ὄντ-ων	οὖ-σι(ν)
m.	παύσα-ς	παύσα-ντα	παύσα-ντος	παύσα-ντι	παύσα-ντες	παύσα-ντας	παυσά-ντων	παύσα-σι(ν)
f.	παύσα-σα	παύσα-σαν	παυσά-σης	παυσά-σῃ	παυσά-σαι	παυσά-σας	παυσα-σῶν	παυσά-σαις
n.	παῦσα-ν	παῦσα-ν	παύσα-ντος	παύσα-ντι	παύσα-ντα	παύσα-ντα	παυσά-ντων	παύσα-σι(ν)

179. Form

> ▸ (a) **All gen. plurals** end in -ων.
> ▸ (b) **Gen. singulars of type 3** nouns/adjectives all originally ended in -ος. Later contractions and other changes gave rise to forms in -ους and -εως.
> ▸ (c) **Gen. singulars in types 1 and 2** nouns/adjectives end (masculine) in -ου and (feminine) in -ης (1a, 1c) or -ας (1b). Remind yourself of the rules for these nouns (especially the ι ρ ε rule) at **56–57**.
> ▸ (d) **1d nouns** like ναύτης, νεανίας are tricky: ναύτης, νεανίας is their nom. form (not feminine gen. s.!) and their gen. s. is ναύτου, νεανίου.

EXERCISES

Select from this list according to need.

8A–C: 1. Give the meaning and gen. s. and pl. (with def. art.) of the following 1a–c type nouns:

1. ἀνομία   5. μάχη
2. εἰρήνη   6. φωνή
3. ἀγορά   7. ἀρετή
4. ἐκκλησία

8A–C: 2. Give the meaning and gen. s. and pl. (with def. art.) of the following 1d type nouns:

1. πολίτης   3. ποιητής
2. δικαστής   4. σοφιστής

8A–C: 3. Give the meaning and (where possible) gen. s. and pl. (with def. art.) of the following 3d type nouns:

1. τριήρης   3. συγγενής
2. Σωκράτης   4. Περικλῆς

8A–C: 4. Give the meaning and gen. s. and pl. (with def. art.) of the following 2a–b type nouns:

1. σῖτος   5. χρόνος
2. φιλόσοφος   6. ποταμός
3. δῆμος   7. νεανίσκος
4. δικαστήριον   8. οὐρανός

8A–C: 5. Give the meaning and gen. s. and pl. in all genders (with def. art.) of the following type '2-1-2' adjectives:

1. ἄξιος   5. αὐτός
2. ἐκεῖνος*   6. χαλεπός
3. δεξιός   7. ὑμέτερος
4. ἕτοιμος   8. μέγιστος

     9. βέλτιστος   11. πολύς (N.B. irregular stem)

    10. σός   12. οὗτος* (N.B. irregular stem)

* Position def. art. correctly with these words.

8A–C: 6. Give the meaning and gen. s. and pl. (with def. art.) of the following type 3c nouns:

     1. πάθος   3. τεῖχος

     2. πλῆθος

8A–C: 7. Give the meaning and gen. s. and pl. of the following 3a–b type nouns:

     1. πρᾶγμα   6. πούς

     2. κῆρυξ   7. φροντίς

     3. κτῆμα   8. χρῆμα

     4. ῥήτωρ   9. δαίμων

     5. γέρων   10. γυνή

8A–C: 8. Give the meaning and gen. s. and pl. in all genders of the following type 3rd declension and '3-1-3' adjectives/participles:

     1. κακοδαίμων   5. λύσας

     2. ἰών   6. χείρων

     3. ὤν   7. τις

     4. βελτίων

8A–C: 9. Give the meaning and gen. s. and pl. (with def. art. [where meaningful]) of the following:

     1. Ζεύς   5. σύ

     2. ἐγώ   6. ὀφρῦς

     3. ναῦς   7. γραῦς

     4. βασιλεύς

8A–C: 10. Give the meaning and gen. s. and pl. (with def. art.) of the following:

     1. δικαστής   5. κτῆμα

     2. παῖς   6. διάνοια

     3. ἥλιος   7. ἱερόν

     4. οἴκησις   8. ἄστυ

USES OF THE GENITIVE

180. The most common uses of the genitive are as follows:

(a) To correspond to English phrases introduced by 'of' in such senses as:

■ *(i) possession, e.g.*

     ἡ τοῦ Δικαιοπόλεως οἰκία 'the house of [belonging to] Dikaiopolis'

■ *(ii) a part, e.g.*

ὀλίγοι τῶν ἀνθρώπων   'few of ['out of the whole number of'] the men'

■ *(iii) source or origin, e.g.*

οἱ λόγοι οἱ τοῦ ἀνθρώπου 'the words of ['that come from'] the fellow'
ἡ τῶν Ἕνδεκα ἀνομία   'the lawlessness of the Eleven'

■ *(iv) content or material, e.g.*

τὸ τῶν πολιτῶν πλῆθος 'the crowd of ['made up of'] citizens, the citizen crowd'

(b) With certain adjectives, e.g.

ἄξιος 'worthy of'
πλέως 'full of'
αἴτιος 'responsible for'

(c) With certain prepositions, e.g.

ἀπό   'away from'
παρά   'from' (esp. a person)
ἐκ   'out of, from'
μετά   '(in company) with'
ἐπί   'on', 'on part of', 'in the time of'
διά   'through'
ἕνεκα 'for the sake of' (comes *after* the noun)
περί   'concerning, about' (also with acc.)

> ► Note that διά and μετά have quite different meanings depending on the case they take:
> ► διά + acc. 'because of'; διά + gen. 'through'
> ► μετά + acc. 'after'; μετά + gen. 'with'

(d) With certain verbs, e.g.

ἀκούω   'I hear' (a person)*
καταδικάζω 'I condemn'
λαμβάνομαι 'I seize, take hold of' (see (a)[ii] above)

* ἀκούω normally takes the acc. of the thing heard (e.g. words) but the gen. of the source of sound (e.g. the person who is speaking):

ἀκούω τοὺς λόγους   'I hear the words'
ἀκούω σοῦ λέγοντος   'I hear you speaking'

Cf. [a](iii) above. You will find that other verbs of perception behave in a similar way.

(e) To express comparison

So far you have met comparisons of the type described at **158** i.e. constructed with ἤ = 'than'. Greek can also express comparison *without* ἤ by putting the thing compared in the gen., e.g.

Σωκράτης σοφώτερός ἐστι <u>τούτου τοῦ ἀνθρώπου</u>.
'Socrates is wiser <u>than this fellow</u>.'

(This can also be expressed as Σωκράτης σοφώτερός ἐστιν ἢ οὗτος ὁ ἄνθρωπος.)

EXERCISE

8A–C: 11. Translate into Greek using the prepositions and adjectives listed at (c) above:

1. in company with (the) Socrates
2. away from the assembly
3. through the crowd
4. out of the ship
5. I condemn the man
6. I hear the women
7. I seize the citizen
8. worthy of (the) excellence
9. responsible for (the) lawlessness
10. in company with the herald
11. through the river
12. concerning the law
13. away from (the) Athens
14. out of the house

ALTERNATIVE COMPARATIVE FORMS

181. Revise the alternative comparative and superlative forms of ἀγαθός and κακός:

Positive		Comparative	Superlative
ἀγαθός		ἀμείνων ἄμεινον (ἀμεινον-)	ἄριστος η ον
	or	βελτίων βέλτιον (βελτιον-)	βέλτιστος η ον
'good'		'better'	'best'
κακός		κακίων κάκιον (κακιον-)	κάκιστος η ον
	or	χείρων χεῖρον (χειρον-)	χείριστος η ον
'bad'		'worse'	'worst'

Meaning

The alternative comparative and superlative forms of ἀγαθός carry slightly different nuances:

- ἀμείνων and ἄριστος imply superiority in terms of physical or mental *ability*
- βελτίων and βέλτιστος imply *moral* superiority

Form

The full declension of comparative adjectives is as follows:

βελτίων βέλτιον (βελτιον-) **'better' (comparative of** ἀγαθός**)**

s.

	m./f.	*n.*
Nom.	βελτίων	βέλτῑον
Acc.	βελτίον-α or βελτίω	βέλτῑον
Gen.	βελτίον-ος	βελτίον-ος
Dat.	βελτίον-ι	βελτίον-ι

pl.

	m./f.	*n.*
Nom.	βελτίον-ες or βελτίους	βελτίον-α or βελτίω
Acc.	βελτίον-ας or βελτίους*	βελτίον-α or βελτίω
Gen.	βελτῑόν-ων	βελτῑόν-ων
Dat.	βελτίοσι(ν)	βελτίοσι(ν)

Note the alternative forms in the m./f. acc. s. and the m./f./n. nom. and acc. pl. These are old forms, arising from a stem ending not in -ιον- but in -ιο-:

βελτίο(ν)α > βελτίω (m./f. acc. s.; n. nom./acc. pl.)
βελτίο(ν)ες > βελτίους (m./f. nom. pl.)

* This form, which should by contraction be βελτίως, has not in fact been contracted but simply taken over from the nom. pl.
You will find that these old forms are used far more often by Greek authors than their new -ν- stem equivalents.

EXERCISE

8A–C: 12. Add the correct forms of the βελτίων to the following phrases, giving alternatives where appropriate, and translate:

1. τὸν ναύτην
2. τοὺς λιμένες
3. τὴν θεάν
4. αἱ νῆες
5. οἱ γεωργοί
6. τὰς γυναῖκας
7. τὸ ἄστυ
8. τὰ πλοῖα

COMPARING ADJECTIVES LIKE εὔφρων

182. Observe also that adjectives ending in -ων like εὔφρων form their comparatives and superlatives as follows:

Positive	Comparative	Superlative
εὔφρων ον 'lucky'	εὐφρονέστερος α ον 'luckier'	εὐφρονέστατος η ον 'luckiest, very lucky'

The regular suffixes -τερος and -τατος are still there waving like mad, but on a stem extended by -εσ-.

EXERCISE

8A–C: 13. Add the correct comparative and superlative forms of the quoted adjectives to the following phrases, and translate:

1. ὁ (εὐδαίμων) ναύτης   4. τὰς (κακοδαίμων) γυναῖκας
2. τὸ (κακοδαίμων) ἄστυ   5. ἡ (εὐδαίμων) νῆσος
3. τὴν (εὔφρων) θεάν   6. τοὺς (κακοδαίμων) διδασκάλους

MOOD: THE OPTATIVES

183. Most of the verbs you have met so far have been in one of two 'moods': the indicative or the imperative. The 'mood' of a verb gives important clues as to its function in a sentence:

● The indicative mood, for example, is generally used to make statements or ask questions.
● The imperative mood is used to give orders.

▶ There are two further moods in Greek: the *optative* and the *subjunctive*.

Here you encounter the optative (and you can fight over whether to stress the 'o' or the 'a'). You will meet a number of uses of this mood in future sections, but as you will discover, most examples of the optative in Greek require the use of words like 'would', 'could' and 'might' when translating in English.

Present optative active and middle

184. The forms of the present optative active and middle for non-contract verbs are as follows:

Present optative active: παύοιμι

παύ-οιμι
παύ-οις
παύ-οι
παύ-οιμεν
παύ-οιτε
παύ-οιεν

Present optative middle: παυοίμην

παυ-οίμην
παύ-οιο
παύ-οιτο
παυ-οίμεθα
παύ-οισθε
παύ-οιντο

■ *Form*

- Note the -μην -σο -το middle endings (**102**). The 2s. was originally παυ-οι-σο, with the intervocalic sigma dropping out to give παύ-οι-ο.
- The thematic vowel is -ο- throughout; the optative mood is marked by the immediately following -ι-.

EXERCISE

8A–C: 14. Translate the following present indicatives and turn them into the equivalent optative forms:

1. εὑρίσκουσιν   4. γίγνεται
2. ἐξετάζει   5. θαυμάζεις
3. λογιζόμεθα

Present optative of contract verbs

185. The forms for contract verbs in the active are as follows. Note that in the s. active the forms arise from contracting the vowel with the endings -οίην, -οίης, -οίη:

Active contract optative

τιμάω, 'I honour'		ποιέω, 'I make, do'		δηλόω, 'I show, reveal'	
(α-contract verb)		(ε-contract verb)		(ο-contract verb)	
τιμα-οίην	> τιμῴην	ποιε-οίην	> ποιοίην	δηλο-οίην	> δηλοίην
τιμα-οίης	> τιμῴης	ποιε-οίης	> ποιοίης	δηλο-οίης	> δηλοίης
τιμα-οίη	> τιμῴη	ποιε- οίη	> ποιοίη	δηλο-οίη	> δηλοίη
τιμά-οιμεν	> τιμῷμεν	ποιέ-οιμεν	> ποιοῖμεν	δηλό-οιμεν	> δηλοῖμεν
τιμά-οιτε	> τιμῷτε	ποιέ-οιτε	> ποιοῖτε	δηλό-οιτε	> δηλοῖτε
τιμά-οιεν	> τιμῷεν	ποιέ-οιεν	> ποιοῖεν	δηλό-οιεν	> δηλοῖεν

Middle contract optative

θεάομαι, 'I watch'			ποιέομαι, 'I make, do'			δουλόομαι, 'I enslave for myself'		
(α-contract verb)			(ε-contract verb)			(o-contract verb)		
θεα-οίμην	>	θεῴμην	ποιε-οίμην	>	ποιοίμην	δουλο-οίμην	>	δουλοίμην
θεά-οιο	>	θεῷο	ποιέ-οιο	>	ποιοῖο	δουλό-οιο	>	δουλοῖο
θεά-οιτο	>	θεῷτο	ποιέ-οιτο	>	ποιοῖτο	δουλό-οιτο	>	δουλοῖτο
θεα-οίμεθα	>	θεῴμεθα	ποιε-οίμεθα	>	ποιοίμεθα	δουλο-οίμεθα	>	δουλοίμεθα
θεά-οισθε	>	θεῷσθε	ποιέ-οισθε	>	ποιοῖσθε	δουλό-οισθε	>	δουλοῖσθε
θεά-οιντο	>	θεῷντο	ποιέ-οιντο	>	ποιοῖντο	δουλό-οιντο	>	δουλοῖντο

■ *Form*

You can recognise present optatives from the combination of a present stem and -οι- (or ῳ).

EXERCISE

8A–C: 15. Translate the following present indicatives and turn them into the equivalent optatives:

1. φιλεῖς
2. διανοοῦνται
3. νικᾷ
4. πειρᾶται
5. τολμῶσιν

ἄν + OPTATIVE

186. The optative forms are used with the particle ἄν to express a 'polite' request or agreement, or the potential 'would' usage. Sometimes 'polite' requests are difficult to distinguish from straightforward requests. The best translations involve using the English forms 'would', 'would like to', 'can', or the simple future 'will', e.g.

- λέγοις ἄν μοι; 'Would you tell me? Would you like to/could you/will you tell me?'
- λέγοιμι ἄν 'I would/would like to/can/will tell you.'

Note that ἄν cannot come as first word.

EXERCISE

8A–C: 16. Translate into the 'polite' or 'would' form, using the verbs in brackets:

1. They would bring (φέρω)
2. We would converse (διαλέγομαι)
3. She would consider (σκοπέω)
4. I would send (πέμπω)
5. You (s.) would receive (δέχομαι)
6. They would do wrong (ἀδικέω)
7. He would see (ὁράω)
8. You (pl.) would persuade (πείθω)
9. We would guard (φυλάττω)
10. They would obey (πείθομαι)

187. The verb ἀνίσταμαι, 'I get up and go, leave, emigrate' (stem ἀνιστα-), conjugates in the same way as δύναμαι, 'I am able, can' (**177**):

ἀνίσταμαι 'I leave'

ἀνίσταμαι	'I leave'
ἀνίστασαι	'you (s.) leave'
ἀνίσταται	'he/she/it leaves'
ἀνιστάμεθα	'we leave'
ἀνίστασθε	'you (pl.) leave'
ἀνίστανται	'they leave'

Infinitive

ἀνίστασθαι	'to leave'

Participle

ἀνιστάμενος η ον	'leaving'

As with δύνα-μαι, there is no thematic vowel between stem and ending.

EXERCISE

8A–C: 17. Revise δύναμαι (**177**) and translate:

1. ἀνίστασαι	6. δύνανται
2. δύναται	7. δυνάμενος
3. ἀνιστάμενος	8. ἀνίσταται
4. δύνασθαι	9. δυνάμεθα
5. ἀνίστασθε	10. ἀνιστάσθαι

GREEK IDIOMS

τί + participle

188. Note the Greek love of τί + participle and the variety of possible translations it takes:

τί βουλόμενος τοῦτο ποιεῖς;
lit. 'Wanting what do you do this?'
i.e. 'What is your motive/purpose/intention in doing this?'
τί παθὼν τοῦτο λέγεις;
lit. 'On suffering what do you say this?'
i.e. 'What did you suffer to make you say this?'

> ► Note also that, since πάσχω basically means 'I have something done
> to me', a perfectly good translation of this last sentence would also be
> 'What made you say this?'

SUMMARY LEARNING VOCABULARY FOR SECTION 8A–C

ἀγορά, ἡ	market-place, agora (1b)
ἄγω (ἀγαγ-)	live in, be at; lead, bring
ἀδικέω	be unjust, commit a crime, do wrong
ᾄδω/ἀείδω	sing
ἀνίσταμαι (ἀναστα-)	get up, emigrate
ἄξιος ᾱ ον	worth, worthy of (+gen.)
ἀπολέω	I shall kill, destroy
βέλτιστος η ον	best
βελτῑ́ων βέλτῑον (βελτῑον-)	better
δεξιός ᾱ́ όν	clever; right-hand
δῆμος, ὁ	people; deme (2a)
διά	(+gen.) through
δικαστήριον, τό	law-court (2b)
δικαστής, ὁ	juror, dikast (1d)
ἐγγύς	(+gen.) near
εἰρήνη, ἡ	peace (1a)
εἰρήνην ἄγω	live in/be at peace
ἐκεῖσε	(to) there
ἐκκλησίᾱ, ἡ	assembly, ekklesia (1b)
ἐναντίον	(+gen.) opposite, in front of
ἐν τούτῳ	meanwhile
ἐπεί	since
ἐπί	(+g en.) on
ἕτοιμος η ον	ready (to) (+inf.)
εὐδαίμων εὔδαιμον (εὐδαιμον-) (comp. εὐδαιμονέστερος ᾱ ον; sup. εὐδαιμονέστατος η ον)	happy, rich, blessed by the gods
ἡγεμών (ἡγεμον-), ὁ	leader (3a)
ἡγέομαι	think, consider; lead (+ dat.)
ἡδονή, ἡ	pleasure (1a)
Ἡρακλῆς, ὁ	Herakles (3d uncontr.)
καθοράω (κατιδ-)	see, look down on
λαμβάνομαι	take hold of (+gen.)
μετά	(+ gen.) with
μέγιστος η ον	greatest (sup. of μέγας)
μείζων μεῖζον (μειζον-)	greater (comp. of μέγας)

SUMMARY LEARNING VOCABULARY FOR SECTION 8A–C
CONTINUED

μόνος η ον	alone
μῶν;	surely not?
νυν	so, then (cf. νῦν now)
οἰκτίρω (οἰκτῑρα-)	pity
ὁ μέν … ὁ δέ	one … another
πάθος, τό	experience, suffering (3C)
πανταχοῦ	everywhere
πέμπω	send
περί	(+gen.) about
πλέως ᾱ ων	full of (+ gen.) (as if α-ος α-α α-ον contr.)
ποιέομαι	make
πολῑτης, ὁ	citizen (1d)
προστρέχω (προσδραμ-)	run towards
ῥήτωρ (ῥήτορ-) ὁ	orator, politician (3a)
σῖτος, ὁ	food (2a) (pl. σῖτα, τά 2b)
σπονδαί, αἱ	treaty, truce (1a)
συγγενής, ὁ	relation (3d)
τᾶν	my dear chap (condescendingly)
ὑπέρ	(+gen.) for, on behalf of
ὑπό	(+gen.) by, at the hands of
φιλόσοφος, ὁ	philosopher (2a)
χαῖρε	hello! farewell!
χαλεπός ή όν	difficult, hard
χείρ (χειρ-), ἡ	hand (3a)
χείρων χεῖρον (χειρον-)	worse
χρόνος, ὁ	time (2a)

SUMMARY EXERCISES FOR SECTION 8

A VOCABULARY-BUILDING

1. Deduce the meaning of the words in the right-hand columns from those in the left:

ἀδικέω	τὸ ἀδίκημα		
ἀνίσταμαι	ἡ ἀνάστασις		
ἄξιος	ἀξιόλογος ον		
δῆμος/κρατέω	ἡ δημοκρατία		
ἡγεμών	ἡ ἡγεμονία		
κρατέω	κράτιστος		
πέμπω	ἡ πομπή		
πολίτης	ἡ πολιτεία	πολιτεύω	πολιτικός ή όν
χαλεπός	χαλεπαίνω		
χείρ	ἐπιχειρέω		

B/C WORD SHAPE AND SYNTAX

1. Translate the whole passage into English, putting the bracketed words into the gen. case:

A. ἀλλὰ τίς αἴτιός ἐστι (οὗτος ὁ πόλεμος) καὶ (αὕτη ἡ ἀπορία);

B. οἱ ῥήτορες, εὖ οἶδ᾽ ὅτι, αἴτιοι (τοῦτο τὸ πρᾶγμα). ἡ γὰρ πόλις πλέα (θόρυβος) καὶ (βοή) διὰ τόν τε πόλεμον καὶ τὴν (οἱ ῥήτορες) τόλμαν. τίς γὰρ οὐκ οἶδε περὶ (ἡ τόλμα) (αὐτούς);

A. ἀλλ᾽ οὐκ αἰτίους (ταῦτα τὰ πράγματα) ἡγοῦμαι τοὺς ῥήτορας ἔγωγε, ἀλλὰ βελτίστους (ἄνθρωποι). ἀεὶ γὰρ μάχονται ὑπὲρ (τὸ πλῆθος) καὶ (ἡ πόλις), ὡς φασὶν αὐτοί.

B. ναί. ἀλλὰ ψευδῆ λέγουσι. κακὸν γὰρ τὸ (οὗτοι οἱ ἄνδρες) πλῆθος καὶ οὐδεὶς χείρων (ῥήτωρ). οἱ γὰρ ῥήτορες λαμβάνονται (ἡ ἐκκλησία) καὶ (τὸ δικαστήριον).

2. Convert these verb-forms into the corresponding polite or 'would' form (optative + ἄν) and translate:

1. μένεις   5. ἀποκρίνῃ
2. λέγω   6. κελεύεις
3. βουλόμεθα   7. παύομαι
4. πείθεσθε   8. φέρομεν

3. Translate these sentences and contrast the use and construction of the preposition in each pair.

a. (i) ὁ ξένος ἐπὶ τοῦ βωμοῦ καθίζεται.
(ii) ἡ ναῦς ἐπὶ τοὺς πολεμίους ἐπέρχεται.

b. (i) εἶμι αὔριον εἰς τὴν ἀγορὰν μετὰ τῶν φίλων.
(ii) μετὰ δὲ ταῦτα ἐπάνειμι εἰς τὴν οἰκίαν.

c. (i) τὸ πλοῖον πλεῖ παρὰ τὴν νῆσον.
   (ii) ὁ σοφιστὴς πολλὰ χρήματα δέχεται παρὰ τῶν μαθητῶν.

d. (i) ὁ παῖς προσέδραμε πρὸς ἡμᾶς, βιαζόμενος διὰ τοῦ πλήθους.
   (ii) ἡ ἐμὴ γυνὴ φοβεῖται τὸ ἄστυ διὰ τὴν νόσον.

4. Compare Dionysodorus with Euthydemos using the adjectives listed below and these formulae:

Διονυσόδωρος κακίων ⎫ ἐστί(ν) ⎧ Εὐθυδήμου
                χείρων ⎭   ⎨ ἢ Εὐθύδημος

   1. καλός   5. ἀγαθός
   2. μέγας   6. μῶρος
   3. κακοδαίμων   7. σοφός
   4. εὔφρων

D ENGLISH INTO GREEK

1. Translate these pairs of sentences:

1. ὁ υἱὸς ὁ τοῦ κήρυκος ἀκούει τοῦ ῥήτορος.
   The man's slave grabs the rhapsode's hand.

2. τίς αἴτιός ἐστι ταύτης τῆς ἀνομίας, δεινοτάτης οὔσης;
   Who is responsible for those shouts, which are very loud?

3. Ἀθηναῖοι ὄντες, πολλοῦ ἄξιοί ἐσμεν.
   You are a sophist and worth nothing.

4. διὰ τί λέγεις ὅτι οὐδεὶς σοφώτερος τοῦ Σωκράτους;
   Why are the politicians richer than the people of the city? Tell me!

5. ἐπορευόμεθα διὰ τῆς πόλεως τῆς τῶν Λακεδαιμονίων.
   We suffered many bad experiences, but fought against the Persians for freedom.

2. Translate into Greek using the hints below to guide you:

Dikaiopolis	Look! I see a slave running towards us. Whose slave are you?
Slave	As it happens I am the slave of Euelpides, your friend.
Dik.	Would you please say what you want, and for what reason you ran to me?
Slave	I will. For I must, as Euelpides ordered, ask you to wait.
Dik.	Then I shall wait. Hello, Euelpides and Peisetairos. What is your purpose in leaving the city? Where are you off to?
Peisetairos	We have to go away to a new and more useful city.

Hints

'As it happens': i.e. 'I happen to be ...'

'your friend': this must be in the same case as the noun it is in apposition to (i.e. further describing), i.e. Euelpides.

'Would you please say?': use optative + ἄν.

'I will': i.e. 'I will say'. Remember, too, that in a reply to a question Greek often repeats the question word prefixed with ὁ- (**126**).

When 'ask'= 'request', use κελεύω

'Hello': s. χαῖρε, pl. χαίρετε.

E TEST EXERCISE EIGHT

Translate into English:

παῖς τις, διὰ τοῦ τῶν πολιτῶν πλήθους ἰών, προσέδραμε πρὸς τὸν
Δικαιόπολιν καί, λαβόμενος τῆς χειρός, μένειν ἐκέλευεν. ἔπειτα οἱ τὸν
παῖδα πέμψαντες, ὅ τε Εὐελπίδης καὶ ὁ Πεισέταιρος, φίλοι ὄντες τοῦ
5   Δικαιοπόλεως προσελθόντες ἠσπάζοντο Δικαιόπολιν. ὁ δέ, οὐκ εἰδὼς τί
βουλόμενοι ἐκ τοῦ ἄστεως ἀπέρχονται, ἤρετο ποῖ ἀπιέναι διανοοῦνται
καὶ τίνος ἕνεκα. ἐκεῖνοι δὲ ἀπεκρίναντο ὅτι δεῖ αὐτοὺς <u>Νεφελοκοκκυγίαν</u>
ζητεῖν, εὑρόντας δὲ οἰκεῖν. Δικαιόπολις δὲ εὐδαιμονεστάτας ἡγεῖτο
τὰς Ἀθήνας καὶ βελτίω τῶν Ἀθηνῶν οὐδεμίαν πόλιν. πρῶτον μὲν οὖν
10   μανθάνειν οὐκ ἐδύνατο τίνος ἕνεκα ἀνίστανται, ἔπειτα ἀκούσας τὰ περὶ
τῶν δικαστῶν καὶ τοῦ δικαστηρίου καὶ τῶν ῥητόρων, ὡμολόγησεν. οἱ
μὲν γὰρ δικασταὶ ἐφαίνοντο ἀδικοῦντες τοὺς ἀγαθούς, οἱ δὲ ῥήτορες (ὡς
ἔδοξαν) ἔτυχον διαφθείροντες τὸν δῆμον καὶ οὐκ οἰκτίροντες. οἱ μὲν
οὖν φίλοι οἱ Δικαιοπόλεως ἀπῆσαν. αὐτὸς δέ, βαρέως φέρων τὰ τῆς τε
15   πόλεως καὶ τοῦ δήμου καὶ βελτίστην ἡγούμενος τὴν εἰρήνην, διενοεῖτο
σπονδὰς ποιεῖσθαι ἐν τῇ ἐκκλησίᾳ. ἀλλ' ὁ ῥαψῳδός, <u>ἀμαθεῖς</u> ἡγούμενος
τοὺς ἄνδρας καὶ μώρους, αὐτὸς οὐκ ἐβούλετο <u>μετιέναι</u> μετ' αὐτοῦ, ἀλλ'
ἀπῆλθε μόνος.

Vocabulary

Νεφελοκοκκυγία, ἡ Cloud-cuckooland (1b)
ἀμαθεῖς ignorant (m. acc. pl.)
μετιέναι inf. of μετέρχομαι accompany

EXERCISE

Answer the following questions based on the passage above.

1. Give the aspect (i.e. present or aorist) of the following participles: (a) λαβόμενος (line 2), (b) προσελθόντες (line 4), (c) βουλόμενοι (line 5), (d) εὑρόντας (line 7), (e) ἀκούσας (line 9), (f) διαφθείροντες (line 12), (g) φέρων (line 13), (h) ἡγούμενος (line 15)
2. Give the case of the following: (a) πλήθους (line 1), (b) τίνος (line 6), (c) βελτίω (line 8), (d) ῥήτορες (line 11), (e) πόλεως (line 14), (f) ἄνδρας (line 16)

Grammar for Section 9A–E*

(*Formerly 8 A–E)

> In this section you cover:
> - The dat. case and its uses
> - Time phrases
> - More optatives: δυναίμην, ἀνισταίμην
> - Principal parts: ἐρωτάω, λέγω, λανθάνω

THE DATIVE CASE

189. The forms of the dat. s. and pl. across the range of noun and adjective types you have met are as follows:

	s. nom.	acc.	gen.	dat.	*pl.* nom.	acc.	gen.	dat.
1a	βο-ή, ἡ	βο-ήν	βο-ῆς	βο-ῇ	βο-αί	βο-άς	βο-ῶν	βο-αῖς
1b	ἀπορί-α, ἡ	ἀπορί-αν	ἀπορί-ας	ἀπορί-ᾳ	ἀπορί-αι	ἀπορί-ας	ἀπορι-ῶν	ἀπορί-αις
1c	θάλαττα, ἡ	θάλαττ-αν	θαλάττ-ης	θαλάττ-ῃ	θάλαττ-αι	θαλάττ-ᾱς	θαλαττ-ῶν	θαλάττ-αις
1d	ναύτ-ης, ὁ	ναύτ-ην	ναύτ-ου	ναύτ-ῃ	ναῦτ-αι	ναύτ-ας	ναυτ-ῶν	ναύτ-αις
	νεανί-ας, ὁ	νεανί-αν	νεανί-ου	νεανί-ᾳ				
2a	ἄνθρωπ-ος, ὁ	ἄνθρωπ-ον	ἀνθρώπ-ου	ἀνθρώπ-ῳ	ἄνθρωπ-οι	ἀνθρώπ-ους	ἀνθρώπ-ων	ἀνθρώπ-οις
2b	ἔργ-ον, τό	ἔργ-ον	ἔργ-ου	ἔργ-ῳ	ἔργ-α	ἔργ-α	ἔργ-ων	ἔργ-οις
3a	λιμήν, ὁ	λιμέν-α	λιμέν-ος	λιμέν-ι	λιμέν-ες	λιμέν-ας	λιμέν-ων	λιμέ-σι(ν)
3b	πρᾶγμα, τό	πρᾶγμα	πράγματ-ος	πράγματ-ι	πράγματ-α	πράγματ-α	πραγμάτ-ων	πράγμα-σι(ν)
3c	πλῆθ-ος, τό	πλῆθ-ος	πλήθ-ους	πλήθ-ει	πλήθ-η	πλήθ-η	πληθ-ῶν	πλήθ-εσι(ν)
3d	τριήρ-ης, ἡ	τριήρ-η	τριήρ- ους	τριήρ-ει	τριήρ-εις	τριήρ-εις	τριηρ-ῶν	τριήρ-εσι(ν)
3e	πόλ-ις, ἡ	πόλ-ιν	πόλ-εως	πόλ-ει	πόλ-εις	πόλ-εις	πόλ-εων	πόλ-εσι(ν)
	πρέσβ-υς, ὁ	πρέσβ-υν						
3f	ἄστ-υ, τό	ἄστ-υ	ἄστ-εως	ἄστ-ει	ἄστ-η	ἄστ-η	ἄστ-εων	ἄστ-εσι(ν)
3g	βασιλ-εύς, ὁ	βασιλ-έα	βασιλ-έως	βασιλ-εῖ	βασιλ-ῆς			
					βασιλ-εῖς	βασιλ-έας	βασιλ-έων	βασιλ-εῦσι(ν)
3h	ὀφρύ-ς, ἡ	ὀφρύ-ν	ὀφρύ-ος	ὀφρύ-ι	ὀφρύ-ες	ὀφρῦ-ς	ὀφρύ-ων	ὀφρύ-σι(ν)
Irregular nouns								
	ναῦς, ἡ	ναῦν	νεώς	νηί	νῆες	ναῦς	νεῶν	ναυσί(ν)
	γραῦς, ἡ	γραῦν	γραός	γραί	γρᾶες	γραῦς	γραῶν	γραυσί(ν)
	Ζεύς, ὁ	Δία	Διός	Διί				

	s.				pl.			
	nom.	*acc.*	*gen.*	*dat.*	*nom.*	*acc.*	*gen.*	*dat.*

Personal pronouns

	nom.	*acc.*	*gen.*	*dat.*	*nom.*	*acc.*	*gen.*	*dat.*
	ἐγώ	(ἐ)μέ	(ἐ)μοῦ	(ἐ)μοί	ἡμεῖς	ἡμᾶς	ἡμῶν	ἡμῖν
	σύ	σέ	σοῦ	σοί	ὑμεῖς	ὑμᾶς	ὑμῶν	ὑμῖν

Adjectives

	nom.	*acc.*	*gen.*	*dat.*	*nom.*	*acc.*	*gen.*	*dat.*
m.	καλ-ός	καλ-όν	καλ-οῦ	καλ-ῷ	καλ-οί	καλ-ούς	καλ-ῶν	καλ-οῖς
f.	καλ-ή	καλ-ήν	καλ-ῆς	καλ-ῇ	καλ-αί	καλ-άς	καλ-ῶν	καλ-αῖς
n.	καλ-όν	καλ-όν	καλ-οῦ	καλ-ῷ	καλ-ά	καλ-ά	καλ-ῶν	καλ-οῖς
m.	ἡμέτερ-ος	ἡμέτερ-ον	ἡμετέρ-ου	ἡμετέρ-ῳ	ἡμέτερ-οι	ἡμετέρ-ους	ἡμετέρ-ων	ἡμετέρ-οις
f.	ἡμετέρ-α	ἡμετέρ-αν	ἡμετέρ-ας	ἡμετέρ-ᾳ	ἡμέτερ-αι	ἡμετέρ-ας	ἡμετέρ-ων	ἡμετέρ-αις
n.	ἡμέτερ-ον	ἡμέτερ-ον	ἡμετέρ-ου	ἡμετέρ-ῳ	ἡμέτερ-α	ἡμέτερ-α	ἡμετέρ-ων	ἡμετέρ-οις
m.	οὗτ-ος	τοῦτ-ον	τούτ-ου	τούτ-ῳ	οὗτ-οι	τούτ-ους	τούτ-ων	τούτ-οις
f.	αὕτ-η	ταύτ-ην	ταύτ-ης	ταύτ-ῃ	αὗτ-αι	ταύτ-ας	τούτ-ων	ταύτ-αις
n.	τοῦτ-ο	τοῦτ-ο	τούτ-ου	τούτ-ῳ	ταῦτ-α	ταῦτ-α	τούτ-ων	τούτ-οις
m.	ἐκεῖν-ος	ἐκεῖν-ον	ἐκείν-ου	ἐκείν-ῳ	ἐκεῖν-οι	ἐκείν-ους	ἐκείν-ων	ἐκείν-οις
f.	ἐκείν-η	ἐκείν-ην	ἐκείν-ης	ἐκείν-ῃ	ἐκεῖν-αι	ἐκείν-ας	ἐκείν-ων	ἐκείν-αις
n.	ἐκεῖν-ο	ἐκεῖν-ο	ἐκείν-ου	ἐκείν-ῳ	ἐκεῖν-α	ἐκεῖν-α	ἐκείν-ων	ἐκείν-οις
m.	αὐτ-ός	αὐτ-όν	αὐτ-οῦ	αὐτ-ῷ	αὐτ-οί	αὐτ-ούς	αὐτ-ῶν	αὐτ-οῖς
f.	αὐτ-ή	αὐτ-ήν	αὐτ-ῆς	αὐτ-ῇ	αὐτ-αί	αὐτ-άς	αὐτ-ῶν	αὐτ-αῖς
n.	αὐτ-ό	αὐτ-ό	αὐτ-οῦ	αὐτ-ῷ	αὐτ-ά	αὐτ-ά	αὐτ-ῶν	αὐτ-οῖς
m.	πολ-ύς	πολ-ύν	πολλ-οῦ	πολλ-ῷ	πολλ-οί	πολλ-ούς	πολλ-ῶν	πολλ-οῖς
f.	πολλ-ή	πολλ-ήν	πολλ-ῆς	πολλ-ῇ	πολλ-αί	πολλ-άς	πολλ-ῶν	πολλ-αῖς
n.	πολ-ύ	πολύ	πολλ-οῦ	πολλ-ῷ	πολλ-ά	πολλ-ά	πολλ-ῶν	πολλ-οῖς
m./f.	εὔφρων	εὔφρον-α	εὔφρον-ος	εὔφρον-ι	εὔφρον-ες	εὔφρον-ας	εὐφρόν-ων	εὔφρο-σι(ν)
n.	εὖφρον	εὖφρον	εὔφρον-ος	εὔφρον-ι	εὔφρον-α	εὔφρον-α	εὐφρόν-ων	εὔφρο-σι(ν)
m./f.	τις	τιν-α	τιν-ος	τιν-ι	τιν-ες	τιν-ας	τιν ων	τι-σι(ν)
n.	τι	τι	τιν-ος	τιν-ι	τιν-α	τιν-α	τιν-ων	τι-σι(ν)
m.	οὐδ-είς	οὐδ-ένα	οὐδ-ενός	οὐδ-ενί				
f.	οὐδε-μία	οὐδε-μίαν	οὐδε-μιᾶς	οὐδε-μιᾷ				
n.	οὐδ-έν	οὐδ-έν	οὐδ-ενός	οὐδ-ενί				
m.	ὤν	ὄντ-α	ὄντ-ος	ὄντ-ι	ὄντ-ες	ὄντ-ας	ὄντ-ων	οὖ-σι(ν)
f.	οὖσ-α	οὖσ-αν	οὖσ-ης	οὖσ-ῃ	οὖσ-αι	οὖσ-ας	οὐσ-ῶν	οὖσ-αις
n.	ὄν	ὄν	ὄντ-ος	ὄντ-ι	ὄντ-α	ὄντ-α	ὄντ-ων	οὖ-σι(ν)
m.	παύσα-ς	παύσα-ντα	παύσα-ντος	παύσα-ντι	παύσα-ντες	παύσα-ντας	παυσά-ντων	παύσα-σι(ν)
f.	παύσα-σα	παύσα-σαν	παυσά-σης	παυσά-σῃ	παύσα-σαι	παύσα-σας	παυσα-σῶν	παυσά-σαις
n.	παῦσα-ν	παῦσα-ν	παύσα-ντος	παύσα-ντι	παύσα-ντα	παύσα-ντα	παυσά-ντων	παύσα-σι(ν)

Form

(a) Dat. s. all end in -ι (whether subscript or not).

(b) Dat. pls. all end in -ις or -σι(ν) (but note the exceptions: ἡμῖν, ὑμῖν.)

(c) Type 3 nouns:

  (i)   those with stems ending in -οντ- have dat. pl. in -ουσι(ν), e.g. participles like παύ-ων with stem παυοντ- produce the dat. pl. παύουσι(ν).*

  (ii) those in -σαντ- have dat. pl. in -σᾱσι(ν).

  (iii) those with a single consonant at the end of the stem either drop it in the dat. pl. (λιμήν, stem λιμεν-, dat. pl. λιμέσι) or let it coalesce with the σ of the ending (φύλαξ, stem φυλακ-, dat. pl. φύλαξι [= φύλακ-σι]). See also **359**.

(d) Note

ἀνήρ → ἀνδράσι

γραῦς → γραυσί

πατήρ → πατράσι

χείρ   → χέρσι

* Ouch! For the form παύουσι(ν) can be **either** 3rd pl. pres. indic. 'they stop' **or** a m./n. dat. pl. of the pres. participle! Only context will tell you which.

EXERCISES

Select from the list according to need.

9A–E: 1. Give the meaning and dat. s. and pl. (with def. art.) of the following 1a–c type nouns:

1. θάλαττα   5. θεά
2. ἀπορία   6. νίκη
3. ἐλευθερία   7. ὁμόνοια
4. σωτηρία   8. τόλμα

9A–E: 2. Give the meaning and dat. s. and pl. (with def. art.) of the following 1d type nouns:

1. θεατής   3. ποιητής
2. κυβερνήτης 4. σοφιστής

9A–E: 3. Give the meaning and (where possible) dat. s. and pl. (with def. art.) of the following 3d type nouns:

1. τριήρης   3. συγγενής
2. Σωκράτης

9A–E: 4. Give the meaning and dat. s. and pl. (with def. art.) of the following 2a–b type nouns:

1. ἡμίονος   5. χρόνος
2. πλοῖον   6. φίλος
3. ἄνθρωπος   7. λόγος
4. δικαστήριον 8. θεός

9A–E: 5. Give the meaning and dat. s. and pl. in all genders (with def. art. for 1–11) of the following type '2-1-2' adjectives:

5. κακός	9. σός
6. σῶος	10. πολύς (N.B. irregular stem)
7. μέγιστος	11. οὗτος (N.B. irregular stem)
8. δῆλος	12. τοιοῦτος

9A–E: 6. Give the meaning and dat. s. and pl. (with def. art.) of the following type 3c nouns:

1. πάθος	3. τεῖχος
2. πλῆθος	

9A–E: 7. Give the meaning and dat. s. and pl. (with def. art.) of the following 3a–b type nouns:

1. δρᾶμα	6. λαμπάς
2. ἄναξ	7. νύξ
3. ὄνομα	8. πατρίς
4. χρῆμα	9. ἡγεμών
5. γείτων	10. γυνή

9A–E: 8. Give the meaning and dat. s. and pl. in all genders of the following 3rd declension and '3-1-3' adjectives/participles:

1. ἀμείνων	4. θύσας
2. ἰών	5. εὐδαίμων
3. ὤν	6. τις

9A–E: 9. Give the meaning and (where possible) dat. s. and pl. (with def. art.) of the following:

1. Ζεύς	5. σύ
2. ἐγώ	6. ὀφρύς
3. ναῦς	7. γραῦς
4. βασιλεύς	

9A–E: 10. Give the meaning and dat. s. and pl. (with def. art.) of the following:

1. δικαστής	5. κτῆμα
2. παῖς	6. μάχη
3. ποταμός	7. ἱερόν
4. οἴκησις	8. ἄστυ

Usage

190. The most common uses of the dat. are as follows:

(a) **To express an 'indirect object'**. Indirect objects are most often found after verbs of giving or saying: they are the person or thing *to whom* something is given or said (or *for whom* something is done). In English, indirect objects are regularly introduced by 'to', e.g.

| λέγε τοῖς θεαταῖς | 'speak *to the spectators*' |
| παρέχει μοι τοῦτο | 'he offers this *to me*' |

[N.B. In English if the indirect object is sandwiched between the verb and direct object the word 'to' is omitted: for example, the last sentence could also be translated 'he offers me this'.]

(b) To express **the idea of possession with the verb 'to be'**, e.g.

| ἔστι μοι πατήρ | (lit.) 'there is to me a father', i.e. 'I have a father' |

(c) To show the **means by which or instrument with which** something is achieved, usually expressed in English with 'by', 'by means of' or 'with', e.g.

φυλάττομεν τὸν γέροντα τοῖς δικτύοις   'we guard the old man *with the nets*'

(d) To show **the way in which something is done** (rather like an adverb), again usually expressed by the English 'with', e.g.

| πολλῇ σπουδῇ | 'with much enthusiasm, enthusiastically' |

(e) **Certain verbs take the dat.**, e.g.

χράομαι	'I use, have to do with, treat'
πείθομαι	'I obey, trust in'
ἐμπίπτω	'I fall on, attack'
ἐντυγχάνω	'I meet with'
ἕπομαι	'I follow'
δοκεῖ (μοι)	'it seems a good idea (to me)'

(f) **Certain adjectives take the dat.**, e.g.

| ὅμοιος | 'resembling, like, the same as' |

(g) **With prepositions**, e.g.

ἐν	'in'
ἐπί	'on, for the purpose of'
παρά	'with, near'
πρός	'near, in addition to'
σύν	'with (the help of)'

Note that ἐπί, παρά and πρός have different meanings depending on the case they take. See **390**.

(h) **Note the two expressions:**

| (a) αὐτοῖς τοῖς κανθηλίοις | 'baggage and all' |
| (b) λόγῳ μέν … ἔργῳ δέ … | 'in theory/ostensibly… but in fact …', i.e. outwardly something appears to be the case, but the reality is very different. |

EXERCISE

9A–E: 11. Translate into Greek:

1. It seems to Socrates	7. With our help (with the help of us)
2. I follow you (pl.)	8. I use you (s.)
3. I meet with the king	9. I follow them
4. In the ships	10. In the crowd
5. It seems to us	11. For the purpose of victory
6. In addition to the spectators	12. In word/theory … but in fact

TIME PHRASES

191. Greek can express the idea of time by the use of case *alone*:

Accusative ('throughout')

The acc. case expresses a length of time, the time *throughout* which something happens (often expressed in English by 'for'), e.g.

ἔμενεν ἐν τῇ οἰκίᾳ δέκα ἡμέρας 'he stayed in the house *for 10 days*'
καθεύδει ὅλην τὴν νύκτα 'he sleeps *(for) the whole night*'

Genitive ('within')

The gen. case expresses time *within which* something happens (generally expressed in English by 'during', 'in the course of', 'within' or simply 'in'), e.g.

τῆς νυκτὸς κρίνει 'he judges *during the night/in (the course of) the night*'
ἐπάνειμι δέκα ἡμερῶν 'I shall return *within/in ten days*'

Dative ('on')

The dat. case expresses the point of time *at which* something happens (English 'at, on'), e.g.

τῇ ὑστεραίᾳ ἀπῆλθεν 'he left *on the following day*'
ἐπανῆλθε τῇ τρίτῃ ἡμέρᾳ 'he returned *on the third day*', i.e. two days later

A visual representation may help:

The **acc.** case (length of time) may be considered	as a line _____
The **gen.** case	as a circle ○ (the action is taking place somewhere within the circle but one doesn't know where.)
The **dat.** case ('point at which')	as a dot ·

EXERCISE

9A–E: 12. Translate into English:

> 1. ἀπήλθομεν τῆς νυκτός.
> 2. ὁ ἱκέτης ἔμενεν ἐν τῷ ἱερῷ δύο ἡμέρας.
> 3. χωρήσω δύο ἡμερῶν.
> 4. ἐνέτυχεν τῷ ἀνδρὶ τῇ πρώτῃ ἡμέρᾳ.
> 5. ἐβόα ὅλην τὴν νύκτα.

MORE OPTATIVES

192. You have already seen how -α- characterises the stem of certain verbs in the indicative, e.g. δύναμαι 'I can' and ἀνίσταμαι 'I emigrate' (**177, 187**). It continues to do so in the optative:

Present optative δυναίμην	**Present optative** ἀνισταίμην
δυναίμην	ἀνισταίμην
δύναιο	ἀνισταῖο
δύναιτο	ἀνισταῖτο
δυναίμεθα	ἀνισταίμεθα
δύναισθε	ἀνισταῖσθε
δύναιντο	ἀνισταῖντο

PRINCIPAL PARTS

193. In order to be able to form all parts of a verb you need to be familiar with its principal parts:

- Knowledge of the first person s. present form of a verb, e.g. παύω, λαμβάνω, allows you to conjugate the verb in the present and – with the addition of an augment – the imperfect as well.
- But it does not *necessarily* allow you to predict the future or aorist forms.
- If the verb is regular, like, παύω you *can* predict παύσω, ἔπαυσα, but in the case of λαμβάνω, for instance, there is no way of predicting the forms λήψομαι, 'I shall take', and ἔλαβον, 'I took'.
- Once you *know* all these forms, however, you are able to use the future and aorist stems to form other parts of the verbs, e.g. the whole of the future indicative, the aorist indicative, the aorist participle and so on.

Greek verbs have up to six principal parts in all, three of which you have yet to meet (perfect active, perfect middle/passive and aorist passive: these will be covered in future sections). Much the most important are the three you are currently meeting: present, future, and aorist.

> ▶ From now on, when you meet a new irregular verb, you should get into the habit of learning its first three principal parts – 1st s. present, future and aorist indicative forms. In this way you will be able to recognize all forms of the verb that occur in your reading passages.

Three verbs

194. Note the principal parts of the verbs ἐρωτάω, 'I ask', λέγω, 'I say', and λανθάνω, 'I escape the notice of'.

Present	Future	Aorist
ἐρωτάω	ἐρωτήσω	ἠρόμην (stem ἐρ-) (or ἠρώτησα)
'I ask'	'I shall ask'	'I asked'
λέγω	ἐρέω > ἐρῶ (or λέξω)	εἶπον (stem εἰπ-) (or ἔλεξα)
'I say'	'I shall say'	'I said'
λανθάνω	λήσω	ἔλαθον (stem λαθ-)
'I escape the notice of'	'I shall escape the notice of'	'I escaped the notice of'

■ *Form*

Like a number of verbs, ἐρωτάω and λέγω have both first *and* second aorist forms.

EXERCISE

9A–E: 13. Translate into Greek:

1. He shall escape the notice of
2. They asked
3. He would be able (opt. + ἄν)
4. We shall say
5. He escaped the notice of
6. He would get up and go
7. He asked
8. They shall say
9. They would be able
10. We asked

SUMMARY LEARNING VOCABULARY FOR SECTION 9A–E

ἀμείνων ἄμεινον (ἀμεινον-)	better
ἄναξ (ἀνακτ-), ὁ	prince, lord, king (3a)
ἀναπείθω	persuade over to one's side
ἄνω	up, above
ἀποτρέχω (ἀποδραμ-)	run away
βαρέως φέρω	take badly, find hard to bear
δικάζω	be a juror; make a judgment
δοκεῖ	it seems a good idea to X (dat.) to Y (inf.); X (dat.) decides to Y (inf.)
δρᾶμα (δρᾱμat-), τό	play, drama (3b)
ἐγκλείω	shut in, lock in
ἐκφεύγω (ἐκφυγ-)	escape
ἐνταῦθα	here, at this point
ἐντυγχάνω	I meet with (+ dat.)
ἐξάγω (ἐξαγαγ-)	lead/bring out
ἐξέρχομαι (ἐξελθ-)	go out; come out
ἐπεί	when; since
ἡμέρᾱ, ἡ	day (1b)
ἡμίονος, ὁ	mule (2a)
ἥσυχος ον	quiet, peaceful
θεᾱτ-ής, ὁ	spectator, member of audience (1d)
καθίζομαι	sit down
καθίζω	sit down
μέλᾱς μέλαινα μέλαν (μελαν-)	black
μηκέτι	no longer
μιαρός ᾱ́ όν	foul, polluted
ὅμοιος ᾱ ον	like, similar to (+dat.)
ὄνομα (ὀνοματ-), τό	name (3b)
παρέχω (παρασχ-)	give to, provide
πλησίον	nearby, (+gen.) near
πονηρός ᾱ́ όν	wicked, wretched
πρᾱ́γματα παρέχω	cause trouble
πρός	near, in addition to (+ dat.)
πωλέω	sell
στένω	groan
σύν	with (the help of) (+ dat.)
τάλᾱς τάλαινα τάλαν (ταλαν-)	wretched, unhappy

SUMMARY LEARNING VOCABULARY FOR SECTION 9A–E
CONTINUED

τοιοῦτος τοιαύτη τοιοῦτο(ν)	of this kind, of such a kind
φέρε	come!
χράομαι	use, employ (+ dat.)

REVISION EXERCISES FOR 9A–E

B/C WORD SHAPE AND SYNTAX

1. Translate the sentences, then change underlined dat. s. into pl. or vice versa, as appropriate:

   1. ἔστι πατήρ <u>μοι</u>, πάνυ πονηρὸς ὤν.
   2. μέγα κακόν <u>σοι</u> ἐμπεσεῖται, <u>κακοδαίμονι ὄντι</u>.
   3. λόγῳ μὲν ἐν <u>τῇ πόλει</u> οὐδεὶς ἀμείνων ἐστὶ τοῦ πατρός, ἔργῳ δὲ οὐδεὶς χείρων.
   4. λέγε <u>τῷ θεατῇ</u> τὸν τοῦ δράματος λόγον πάσῃ προθυμίᾳ ('enthusiasm').
   5. <u>βοαῖς</u> χρώμεθα <u>μεγάλαις</u>.
   6. ἐν <u>τοῖς πλοίοις</u> ἔτυχον ὄντες οἱ ναῦται.
   7. <u>τοῖς κελεύουσι</u> δεῖ ἡμᾶς πείθεσθαι.
   8. τί τὸ ὄνομα <u>τῷ βασιλεῖ</u>;
   9. διὰ τί πειρᾶσθε ἀναπείθειν ἐμὲ <u>τούτῳ τῷ λόγῳ</u>;
   10. τῇ δ' ὑστεραίᾳ ὁ υἱὸς ἐδίωξε τὸν πατέρα πάλιν εἰς τὴν οἰκίαν <u>τοῖς μεγάλοις δικτύοις</u>.

D ENGLISH INTO GREEK

Translate these pairs of sentences:

1. ἡ διάνοια ταύτῃ τῇ γυναικὶ δεινή ἐστι.
   This spectator's name is Philoxenos.

2. λέγουσιν ἡμῖν καὶ τοῖς παισίν.
   He is speaking to you and the spectators.

3. εἰσέφερε τὸν ἄνδρα εἰς τὸ πλοῖον σὺν τοῖς ναύταις.
   They will find sitting in the court hard to bear.

4. ἔκλεψα τὰ χρήματα τῇ δεξιᾷ χρώμενος.
   I shut my father in by using many slaves.

5. τὸν Σωκράτη διαφθείρει κακῇ διαβολῇ.
   The politicians persuaded the people with fine words.

Grammar for Section 9F–G*

(* Formerly 8 F–G)

> In this section you cover:
> - Aorist infinitives, first and second, active and middle
> - Aspect in the infinitive
> - Aorist imperatives, first and second, active and middle
> - Present imperatives: εἰμί, εἶμι, οἶδα, δύναμαι, ἀνίσταμαι
> - ἔξεστι, δεινός
> - Vocatives
> - Adjectives: πᾶς

AORIST INFINITIVES

195. You have already met present infinitives ('to – ') formed by adding -ειν -εσθαι to the present stem (**150**). Greek also has aorist infinitives, formed by adding the appropriate endings to the aorist stem (first and second). Their forms are as follows:

First aorist infinitive active

> **παῦσα-ι, 'to stop'**
>
> To form the first aorist infinitive active, add -αι to the aorist stem, e.g
>
> ἔ-παυσα, 'I stopped' > stem: παυσα- > παῦσα-ι, 'to stop'

First aorist infinitive middle

> **παύσα-σθαι, 'to stop (oneself), cease'**
>
> To form the first aorist infinitive middle, add -[α]σθαι to the aorist stem, e.g.
>
> ἐ-παυσά-μην, 'I stopped (myself)' > stem: παυσα- > παύσα-σθαι, 'to stop (oneself), cease'

■ *Forms*

- Observe once again the familiar first aorist stem in -σα- (cf. aorist indicatives **131**).
- The first aorist active infinitive ending in -[σ]αι may look odd, but you have already met -αι as an infinitive ending in e.g. εἶν-αι, 'to be', ἰέν-αι, 'to go', and εἰδέν-αι, 'to know'.
- In the middle infinitive, the ending -σθαι is the same as in the present infinitive (παύ-ε-σθαι).

Second aorist infinitive active

196. Second aorist infinitives are, to no one's amazement, based on second aorist stems (**146**):

λαβ-εῖν, **'to take'**

To form the second aorist infinitive active, add -εῖν to the second aorist stem, e.g

ἔ-λαβ-ον, 'I took' > stem: λαβ- > λαβ-εῖν, 'to take'

Second aorist infinitive middle

λαβ-έσθαι, **'to take hold of'**

To form the second aorist infinitive middle, add -εσθαι to the aorist stem, e.g.

ἐ-λαβ-όμην, 'I took hold of' > stem: λαβ- > λαβ-έσθαι, 'to take hold of'

■ *Forms*

Observe that the endings of second aorist infinitives (except for accent) are just the same as the endings for the present infinitives active and middle (παύ-ειν, παύ-εσθαι), *but the stem is the second aorist stem.* (Cf. present infinitives **150** and second aorist participles **169–70**.)

EXERCISE

9F–G: 1. Translate the following present infinitives and form the equivalent aorist infinitive from them:

1. μανθάνειν	6. ἀδικεῖν
2. ἐκτρέχειν	7. νομίζειν
3. ἄρχεσθαι	8. φυλάττειν
4. ἐξάγειν	9. προτρέπειν
5. ποιεῖσθαι	10. θύειν

ASPECT IN THE INFINITIVE

197. The difference between present and aorist infinitives is *not* one of time, but one of aspect (cf. on aorist participles **165**):

● Both παύειν and παῦσαι mean 'to stop (someone else)', but the present infinitive carries the idea of process with it ('keep on stopping', 'be in the process of stopping'), the aorist looks at the action as a simple, one-off event ('bring to a halt').

- But this distinction is often a very fine one and 'rules' as such are very difficult to make. It is far better to observe closely actual Greek usage and ask, 'What is the Greek suggesting about the way we should understand this infinitive by using this particular aspect?'

EXERCISE

9F–G: 2. Give the meaning and aspect (pres./aor.) of the following infinitives:

1. ποιῆσαι	5. μανθάνειν	9. ἄρχεσθαι
2. νικᾶν	6. δραμεῖν	10. γενέσθαι
3. λέγειν	7. δικάσαι	11. ἐλθεῖν
4. ἐλευθερῶσαι	8. ἰδεῖν	12. ἄγειν

AORIST IMPERATIVES

198. You have already met present imperatives (active -ε -ετε, middle -ου -εσθε). These are based on the present stem (**18**). There are also imperatives based (do *you* ever get that *déjà vu* feeling?) on the aorist stem, first and second. Their forms are as follows:

First aorist imperatives active and middle

> **Active (-[σ]ον, -[σ]α-τε)**
>
> 2s.   παῦσ-ον 'stop!'
> 2pl.   παύσα-τε 'stop!'
>
> **Middle (-[σ]-αι, –[σ]-ασθε)**
>
> 2s.   παῦσα-ι 'cease!'
> 2pl.   παύσα-σθε 'cease!'

■ *Forms*

Observe once again the familiar first aorist stem in -(σ)α-. Note particularly carefully:

- The s. active imperative form in -(σ)ον (cf. from the Mass, Κύριε, ἐλέησον, Χριστέ, ἐλέησον 'Lord, have mercy, Christ, have mercy!') – the absence of α makes this look strange as a first aorist form cf. **130(a)**;
- The ambiguity of παυσαι, which is (1) aor. act. inf. 'to stop (someone else)' (**195**) and (ii) 2s. middle imperative, 'cease!'

Second aorist imperatives active and middle

199. Like many other forms in the second aorist, the imperative endings are like the present:

Active (-ε, -ετε)

2s.   λαβ-έ 'take!'
2pl.   λάβ-ετε 'take!'

Middle (-ου, -εσθε)

2s.   λαβ-οῦ 'take!'
2pl.   λάβ-εσθε 'take!'

■ *Forms*

As with second aorist participles (**169–70**) and second aorist infinitives (**196**):

- The endings of the second aorist imperatives are identical to those of *present* imperatives, but based on the *aorist* stem.
- Observe too that you have already been meeting second aorist imperatives

ἐλθέ	'come!'	(ἦλθον, 'I came', from ἔρχομαι)
εἰπέ	'say!'	(εἶπον, 'I said', from λέγω)
ἰδού	'look!'	(εἶδον, 'I saw', from ὁράω: unusually, the aorist imperative is middle)

ASPECT IN THE IMPERATIVE

200. Again, the distinction between present and aorist imperatives is one not of time but of aspect (**197**); and again, it is sometimes very difficult indeed to tell the precise difference in nuance between the two, or to decide exactly why a writer used this, rather than that, imperative at any one time. Aristophanes, for example, seems to use φέρε and ἔνεγκε, 'bring!', quite indiscriminately.

- The distinction, when it can be made, is between an instruction to do something and keep on doing it (present imperative), and one to do something, but just once (aorist imperative).
- Key to this distinction, you will remember, is that the action of a present ('imperfective') imperative is capable of being broken off, whereas an aorist action is not.
- So when I use the present imperative ἄκουε, 'listen!', I am telling you to listen to me and to keep listening: I do not envisage the activity having any specific end-point.
- When I use the aorist, ἄκουσον, on the other hand, I am telling you to listen until I have said what I have to say – I am envisaging the action as an indivisible unit of activity with a specific end-point.
- It is natural that certain verbs have, by their very nature, a tendency to lean towards one aspect or the other. Thus, for example, λαμβάνω, 'I

take', tends to use the aorist forms of participle, infinitive and imperative, because 'taking' is the sort of thing that occurs once or at once and
does not involve a long-drawn-out process. On the other hand, a verb
like ζητέω, 'I seek', which naturally implies a process, tends to appear
in the present forms of participle, infinitive and imperative.

MORE PRESENT IMPERATIVES

201. Note the following imperative forms:

εἰμί, 'I am'

2s.   ἴσθι 'be!'
2pl.   ἔστε 'be!'

εἶμι, 'I shall go'

2s.   ἴθι 'go!'*
2pl.   ἴτε 'go!'

οἶδα, 'I know'

2s.   ἴσθι 'know!'
2pl.   ἴστε 'know!'

δύναμαι, 'I am able'

2s.   δύνασο 'be able!'
2pl.   δύνασθε 'be able!'

ἀνίσταμαι, 'I get up, emigrate'

2s.   ἀνίστασο 'get up!'
2pl.   ἀνίστασθε 'get up!'

---

* These function as *present* forms (like the participle ἰών ἰοῦσα ἰόν).

EXERCISE

9F–G: 3. Translate these imperatives. Give in brackets the number and aspect
(i.e. s./pl., pres./aor.):

1. μάθετε	5. ζήτει	9 πιθοῦ
2. λέγε	6. μείνατε	10. εὕρετε
3. εἰπέ	7. γενοῦ	11. παύσατε
4. παῦσον	8. δέξαι	12. λῦσον

TWO INFINITIVE USAGES

ἔξεστι (+ infinitive) 'it is permitted to/for X to Y'

202. You have already met δεῖ (and χρή), which mean 'must, ought' and take an accusative and infinitive (**153**):

> δεῖ με πρὸς τὰς Ἀθήνας πλεῖν   'I must/ought to sail to Athens'

ἔξεστι 'it is permitted, it is possible' works in the same way, except that it takes a dat. (not acc.) of the person, e.g.

> ἔξεστι τῷ ἀνθρώπῳ ἐξελθεῖν   'it is permitted/possible for the man to go out', i.e. 'the man is permitted/allowed to go out', 'the man may go out'

(Cf. ἀνάγκη ἐστί which can take either acc. or dat. and infinitive: **153[b]**.)

δεινός (+ infinitive) 'clever at'

203. δεινός means 'clever *at –ing*' when followed by the infinitive, e.g. δεινή ἐστι λέγειν 'she is clever *at speaking*'

VOCATIVES: REVISION

204. As you learnt at **22**, the vocative is the case used when a person or thing is directly addressed (such as 'rhapsode' in 'O rhapsode, come here and look!'). The vocative form of nouns is often the same as the nom. in the s. and **always** the same as the nom. in the pl. Those noun types which have vocative s. forms different from the nom. s. are as follows:

1d	ὦ ναῦτα	3d	ὦ τριῆρες	3g	ὦ βασιλεῦ
	ὦ νεανία		ὦ Περίκλεις	3h	ὦ ὀφρύ
2a	ὦ ἄνθρωπε	3e	ὦ πόλι		

The vocatives of type 3a nouns are less easy to predict, although they are easily recognisable. Here are some examples:

Short vowel

ὁ ἀνήρ (ἀνδρ-) ὦ ἄνερ 'O man'
ὁ δαίμων (δαιμον-) ὦ δαῖμον 'O god'; cf. ὦ γέρον
ὁ σωτήρ (σωτηρ-) ὦ σῶτερ 'O saviour'
ὁ πατήρ (πατ(ε)ρ-) ὦ πάτερ 'O father'

Ones to watch

ἡ γυνή (γυναικ-) ὦ γύναι 'O woman'
ὁ παῖς (παιδ-) ὦ παῖ 'O son'

> **No change**
>
> ἡ νύξ (νυκτ-) ὦ νύξ 'O night'
> ὁ Ἕλλην (Ἕλλην-) ὦ Ἕλλην 'O Greek'

EXERCISE

9F–G: 4. Say whether the following forms are nom., voc., or both:

1. δοῦλε	5. Σώκρατες	9. γέρον
2. γυναῖκες	6. βασιλῆς	10. φίλε
3. πρέσβυς	7. ναύτης	11. δέσποτα
4. θεά	8. βάρβαροι	12. παῖ

πᾶς παντ- 'ALL, WHOLE, EVERY'

205. The adjective πᾶς declines like an aorist active participle of the παύσας type (**163**):

> **πᾶς, πᾶσα, πᾶν (παντ-) 'all, whole, every'**
>
> *s.*
>
> | | *m.* | *f.* | *n.* |
> |---|---|---|---|
> | *Nom.* | πᾶς | πᾶσ-α | πᾶν |
> | *Acc.* | πάντ-α | πᾶσ-αν | πᾶν |
> | *Gen.* | παντ-ός | πάσ-ης | παντ-ός |
> | *Dat.* | παντ-ί | πάσ-ῃ | παντ-ί |
>
> *pl.*
>
> | | *m.* | *f.* | *n.* |
> |---|---|---|---|
> | *Nom.* | πάντ-ες | πᾶσ-αι | πάντ-α |
> | *Acc.* | πάντ-ας | πάσ-ᾱς | πάντ-α |
> | *Gen.* | πάντ-ων | πασ-ῶν | πάντ-ων |
> | *Dat.* | πᾶσι(ν) | πάσ-αις | πᾶσι(ν) |

Usage

(a) When used with the definite article, πᾶς means 'all' or 'whole':

πᾶσα ἡ πόλις	'All the city'
διῆλθέ μοι τὸν πάντα λόγον	'He related the whole story to me'
πάντες οἱ πολῖται	'All the citizens'

(b) Without the article, πᾶς means 'every':

πᾶς πολίτης	'Every citizen'
πᾶς τις	'Everyone'

(c) πᾶς is often used on its own in the m. pl. to mean 'everyone' and in the n. pl. to mean 'everything':

ὁμολογοῦσι πάντες	'Everyone agrees'
ὁ ῥήτωρ πάντας ἐξηπάτησεν	'The speaker deceived everyone'
ἡ γυνὴ πάντα εἶδεν	'The woman saw everything'

Cf. **49–50** on adjectives used as nouns.

EXERCISE

9F–G: 5. Translate into English:

1. ἴσθι (two ways)
2. ἴτε πᾶσαι (two ways)
3. ἐξῆν ὑμῖν πᾶσιν πάντα φέρειν.
4. πάντες δεινοὶ ἔστε πωλεῖν.
5. ἀνίστασθε πάντες καὶ μὴ μένετε ἀλλ' ἴτε.
6. πᾶσιν ἐξέσται ἀνίστασθαι.
7. ἴθι πᾶς τις καὶ ἔνεγκε πάντα.
8. οὐκ ἔξεστί μοι ταῦτα πάντα ἐνέγκαι.
9. ἀνίστασο καὶ ἴθι.
10. ἴτε καὶ ἐνέγκατε πάντα τὰ σκεύη.

SUMMARY LEARNING VOCABULARY FOR SECTION 9F–G

ἀγορά, ἡ	market-place, agora (1b)
ἀναμένω (ἀναμεινα-)	wait, hold on
ἄρχομαι	begin (+inf. or part.)
ἀτάρ	but
δεινός ή όν	clever at (+inf.); dire, terrible
ἐάω (ἐᾶσα-)	allow
ἐκτρέχω (ἐκδραμ-)	run out
ἐκφέρω (ἐξενεγκ-)	carry out; (often: carry out for burial)
ἕνεκα	(+gen.) because, for the sake of (usually placed after the noun)
ἐνθάδε	here
ἔξεστι	it is possible (for X [dat.] to – [inf.])
ἐσθίω (φαγ -)	eat (fut. ἔδομαι)
ὅμως	nevertheless, however
ὅ τι;	what? (in reply to τί;)
πᾶς πᾶσα πᾶν (παντ-)	all, every
ὁ πᾶς	the whole of
πλήν	(+gen.) except
πῦρ (πυρ-), τό	fire (3b)
χρή	it is necessary, right (for X [acc.] to – [inf.])

REVISION EXERCISES FOR 9F–G

B/C WORD SHAPE AND SYNTAX

1. Write down the 1s. aorist of these verbs. Then construct the aorist infinitive:

   1. παύομαι   6. φέρω   11. ὁράω
   2. ἀκούω   7. γίγνομαι   12. πείθομαι
   3. ποιέω   8. μανθάνω   13. πίπτω
   4. ἀδικέω   9. λαμβάνω
   5. λέγω   10. ἀφικνέομαι

2. Translate these imperatives. Give in brackets the number and aspect (i.e. s./pl., pres./aor.):

   1. φεύγετε   5. ἀφίκεσθε   9. ἰδού
   2. ἴσθι   6. ἔνεγκε   10. παῦσαι
   3. ὅρα   7. ἴτε
   4. δήλωσον   8. φοβεῖσθε

3. Put the verbs in brackets into the present or aorist infinitive as indicated, and translate the sentences:

   1. βούλομαι (δικάζω) (aorist) ἐν τῇ οἰκίᾳ, ἀλλ' ὁ υἱὸς οὐκ ἐᾷ με (δικάζω) (present) ἐνθάδε.
   2. δεῖ ἡμᾶς πάντας (ἔξειμι) (present) εἰς τὴν ἀγοράν.
   3. τί χρή σε (ποιέω) (aorist);
   4. ἔξεστι Φιλοκλέωνι (κατηγορέω) (present).
   5. ὁ υἱὸς οὐκ εἴασε τὸν πατέρα (εἶμι/ἔρχομαι) (aorist) εἰς τὸ δικαστήριον.
   6. πῶς πείσω σε, ὦ πάτερ, (ἀκούω) (aorist) πάντας τοὺς λόγους;
   7. διὰ τί οὐ βούλῃ (ἐκφέρω) (aorist) Φιλοκλέωνα, ὦ ἡμίονε;
   8. δεῖ σε δικαστὴν (γίγνομαι) (aorist) ἐν τῇ οἰκίᾳ.
   9. χρὴ αὐτοὺς (μανθάνω) (aorist) τοὺς τοῦ δράματος λόγους.
   10. βούλεται αὐτὸς (λαμβάνω) (present) πάντα τὸν μισθὸν παρὰ τοῦ υἱοῦ.
   11. οὐκ ἐάσω αὐτὸν (ἀφικνέομαι) (present) εἰς τὸ δικαστήριον.
   12. ἔξεστί μοι ἐνθάδε καὶ (λαμβάνω) (aorist) πάντα τὸν μισθὸν καὶ (ἐσθίω) (aorist).

D ENGLISH INTO GREEK

Translate:

1. ὦ στρατηγέ, δεῖ ἡμᾶς ἐνθάδε μένειν καὶ μάχεσθαι.
   Father, you must stay here and give judgements.

2. ἔξεστί μοι ἀκούειν τῶν ῥητόρων.
   It will be possible for you all to sell your mules.

3. μανθάνω πολλὰ ἀλλ' οὐκ ἐπίσταμαι πάντα.
   Everything is here except the fire.

4. βλέψατε τὰς ναῦς, ὦ παῖδες.
   Bring out the torches, slaves!

5. 'εἴπετε μοι, τί βουλόμενοι τὴν θύραν ἐκόψατε;' 'ὅ τι; τὸν δεσπότην.'
   'Out with it, what were you looking for when you ran out?' 'What? Everything.'

Grammar for Section 9H–J*

(*Formerly 8 H–J)

> In this section you cover:
> - Third person imperatives, present and aorist, active and middle, incl. εἰμί, εἶμι, οἶδα
> - Future infinitive and its uses
> - Root aorists: ἔβην, ἔγνων
> - ἐπίσταμαι 'I know'
> - Principal parts: αἱρέω, αἱρέομαι, πάσχω, φέρω, πείθω, πείθομαι

THIRD PERSON IMPERATIVES: 'LET HIM/HER/THEM'

206. As well as having second person imperatives, which you have already met, Greek has third person imperative forms. Third person imperatives do not exist in English, but their nearest equivalent is 'let him/her –', 'let them –', etc.

Here are the imperative forms of παύω in full, with the third person imperatives taking their place beside the second persons:

Present 3rd person imperatives

Active παυ-έτω, -όντων			**Middle** παυ-έσθω, -έσθων	
2s.	παῦ-ε		*2s.*	παύ-ου
3s.	παυ-έτω	'let him stop'	*3s.*	παυ-έσθω
2pl.	παύ-ετε		*2pl.*	παύ-εσθε
3pl.	παυ-όντων	'let them stop'	*3pl.*	παυ-έσθων

■ *Contract verbs*

These will contract in accordance with the normal rules:

Active		**Middle**	
2s.	τίμα	*2s.*	τιμῶ
3s.	τιμάτω	*3s.*	τιμάσθω
2pl.	τιμᾶτε	*2pl.*	τιμᾶσθε
3pl.	τιμώντων	*3pl.*	τιμάσθων
2s.	ποίει	*2s.*	ποιοῦ
3s.	ποιείτω	*3s.*	ποιείσθω
2pl.	ποιεῖτε	*2pl.*	ποιεῖσθε
3pl.	ποιούντων	*3pl.*	ποιείσθων
2s.	δήλου	*2s.*	δουλοῦ
3s.	δηλούτω	*3s.*	δουλούσθω
2pl.	δηλοῦτε	*2pl.*	δουλοῦσθε
3pl.	δηλούντων	*3pl.*	δουλούσθων

First aorist 3rd person imperatives

Active παυσά-τω, (ά)-ντων		Middle παυσά-σθω, (ά)-σθων	
2s.	παῦσον	2s.	παῦσα-ι
3s.	παυσά-τω 'let him stop'	3s.	παυσά-σθω
2pl.	παύσα-τε	2pl.	παύσα-σθε
3pl.	παυσά-ντων 'let them stop'	3pl.	παυσά-σθων

Second aorist 3rd person imperatives

Active λαβ-έτω, -όντων		Middle λαβ-έσθω, -έσθων	
2s.	λαβ-έ	2s.	λαβ-οῦ
3s.	λαβ-έτω 'let him take'	3s.	λαβ-έσθω
2pl.	λάβ-ετε	2pl.	λάβ-εσθε
3pl.	λαβ-όντων 'let them take'	3pl.	λαβ-έσθων

■ *Form and usage*

(a) Note once again the similarity between the endings of the second aorist and present forms of the imperative.

(b) Third person imperatives *are fairly rare*, but note that:

- The present/second aorist pl. form (in -όντων) and the first aorist pl. form (in -[σ]άντων) could be mistaken for present and aorist participles in the gen. pl.!

The presence of a stated subject in the nom. and/or lack of any other possible finite verb-form will tell you that the third person imperative is being used, e.g.

| ἀπελθόντων οἱ Ἀθηναῖοι | 'let the Athenians depart!' |
| διωκόντων τὸν ἄνδρα | 'let them pursue the man!' |

Contrast:

| ἀκούω τῶν λεγόντων | 'I hear the men talking' |

Irregular imperatives

207. Note the full imperatives of εἰμί, εἶμι, and οἶδα:

	εἰμί, 'I am'		εἶμι, 'I shall go'		οἶδα, 'I know'	
2s.	ἴσθι	'be!'	ἴθι	'go!'	ἴσθι	'know!'
3s.	ἔστω	'let him be!'	ἴτω	'let him go!'	ἴστω	'let him know!'
2pl.	ἔστε	'be!'	ἴτε	'go!'	ἴστε	'know!'
3pl.	ἔστων	'let them be!'	ἰόντων	'let them go!'	ἴστων	'let them know!'

■ *Form*

Note that you will also find ὄντων used as well as ἔστων as the 3pl. imperative of εἰμί.

EXERCISES

9H–J: 1. Translate into English:

1. ἀκουέτω	6. νικήσασθε
2. ἀναχωρησάντων	7. ἐνεγκάτω
3. διαλεγέσθω	8. λυόντων
4. μαθέτω	9. ἀρχέσθω
5. σιωπώντων	10. τρεψάσθων

9H–J: 2. Translate into English:

1. ἔστω.	6. ἴτω.
2. πάντα ἔξεστιν ἰδεῖν ἐν τῇ οἰκίᾳ.	7. ἐξενεγκάντων πάντες τὸν ἄνδρα.
3. πάντα μαθέτω.	8. μὴ ἐξέστω ταῦτα εὑρεῖν ἐν τῷ λιμένι.
4. πᾶς τις ἀφικέσθω.	9. ἴστω.
5. ἀνιστάσθων καὶ μὴ μενόντων.	10. θὲς ταῦτα πάντα ἐνθάδε.

FUTURE INFINITIVES: 'TO BE ABOUT TO'

208. Future infinitives are formed as follows, based inevitably on the future stem (**114**):

Future active infinitives

> παύσ-ειν, 'to be about to stop (someone else)'
>
> To form the future active infinitive, add -ειν to the *future* stem, e.g.
>   παύσω, 'I shall stop' > παύσ-ειν, 'to be about to stop'
>   ποιήσω, 'I shall do' > ποιήσ-ειν, 'to be about to do'

Future middle infinitives

> παύσ-εσθαι, 'to be about to stop (oneself), cease'
>
> To form the future middle infinitive, add -εσθαι to the *future* stem, e.g.
>   παύσομαι, 'I shall stop (myself)' > παύσ-εσθαι, 'to be about to stop (oneself), cease'
>   δέξομαι, 'I shall receive' > δέξ-εσθαι, 'to be about to receive'

■ *Form and meaning*

(a) The endings of the future infinitives are the same as those of the present (and second aorist) infinitives: the difference lies solely in the *stem*.

(b) The meaning of the future infinitive is 'to be about to –', 'to be going to –'.

(c) One common use of the future infinitive is with verbs that offer some future hope, intention or promise, for example:

- ἐλπίζω, 'I hope/expect (to …)', e.g. ἐλπίζω νικήσειν 'I hope/expect to win'
- μέλλω, 'I am about to, intend (to …)', e.g. ἔμελλε παύσεσθαι 'she was about to stop'
- ὑπισχνέομαι, 'I promise (to …)', e.g. ὑπισχνεῖται λήψεσθαι 'he promises to take'

EXERCISE

9H–J: 3. Form the future infinitive of the following verbs and then translate into English:

1. κελεύω	6. ἐξαπατάω
2. κωλύω	7. ἀπολογέομαι
3. ζητέω	8. κατηγορέω
4. πείθομαι	9. γράφομαι
5. δέχομαι	10. βιάζομαι

ROOT AORISTS

209. A small number of verbs such as βαίνω, 'I go' and γιγνώσκω, 'I get to know' have a distinct kind of aorist called a 'root aorist'. The augment and personal endings are added to the absolutely basic aorist stem, or 'root', ending in a vowel – in these cases βη/βα- and γνω/γνο-:

ἔβην, 'I went'

ἔ-βη-ν	'I went'
ἔ-βη-ς	'you (s.) 'went'
ἔ-βη	'he/she went'
ἔ-βη-μεν	'we went'
ἔ-βη-τε	'you (pl.) went'
ἔ-βη-σαν	'they went'

Infinitive

βῆναι	'to go'

Participle

βάς βᾶσα βάν (βαντ-)   'having gone, on going, going'

ἔγνων, 'I knew'

ἔ-γνω-ν   'I knew'
ἔ-γνω-ς   'you (s.) knew'
ἔ-γνω   'he/she/it knew'
ἔ-γνω-μεν   'we went'
ἔ-γνω-τε   'you (pl.) knew'
ἔ-γνω -σαν   'they knew'

Infinitive

γνῶναι   'to know'

Participle

γνούς γνοῦσα γνόν (γνοντ-)   'having known, on knowing, knowing'

■ *Forms*

Note the infinitive in -ναι and the participles βάς and γνούς.

ἐπίσταμαι, 'I KNOW (HOW TO), UNDERSTAND'

210. The verb ἐπίσταμαι conjugates in the same way as δύναμαι, 'I am able', and ἀνίσταμαι, 'I get up and go, emigrate' (**177, 187**), ἐπιστα- + endings:

ἐπίσταμαι, 'I know'   **Imperative**

ἐπίσταμαι   'I know'
ἐπίστασαι   'you (s.) know'   ἐπίστασο   'know! (s.)'
ἐπίσταται   'he/she/it knows'   ἐπιστάσθω   'let him know!'
ἐπιστάμεθα   'we know'
ἐπίστασθε   'you (pl.) know'   ἐπίστασθε   'know! (pl.)'
ἐπίστανται   'they know'   ἐπιστάσθων   'let them know!'

Infinitive

ἐπίστασθαι   'to know'

Participle

ἐπιστάμενος η ον   'knowing'

Optative

ἐπισταίμην etc. (**192**)

■ *Usage*

When ἐπίσταμαι is followed by an infinitive it means 'know how to', e.g.

ἐπίσταμαι κιθαρίζειν   'I know how to play the kithara'

IRREGULAR PRINCIPAL PARTS

211. Note the first three principal parts of the following verbs:

αἱρέω, 'I take, capture, condemn', and its middle, αἱρέομαι, 'I take for myself, choose';
πάσχω, 'I suffer, experience, have something happen to me';
φέρω, 'I carry, bear, put up with';
πείθω, 'I persuade', and its middle, πείθομαι, 'I trust, obey'.

Present	Future	Aorist
αἱρέω	αἱρήσω	εἷλον (ἑλ-)
'I take'	'I shall take'	'I took'
αἱρέομαι	αἱρήσομαι	εἱλόμην
'I choose'	'I shall choose'	'I chose'
πάσχω	πείσομαι	ἔπαθον (παθ-)
'I suffer'	'I shall suffer'	'I suffered'
φέρω	οἴσω	ἤνεγκον or ἤνεγκα (ἐνεγκ-)
'I carry'	'I shall carry'	'I carried'
πείθω	πείσω	ἔπεισα
'I persuade'	'I shall persuade'	'I persuaded'
πείθομαι	πείσομαι	ἐπιθόμην (πιθ-)
'I trust, obey'	'I shall trust'	'I trusted'

■ *Form and meaning*

Note that the future of πάσχω, 'I suffer', is πείσομαι – exactly the same as the future of πείθομαι, 'I trust, obey'. Only the context will tell you whether πείσομαι means, 'I shall suffer' or 'I shall trust, obey'.

EXERCISE

9H–J: 4. Translate into Greek:

1. I shall take
2. They know how to persuade
3. He hopes to choose
4. They took
5. He went (use βαίνω)
6. They are about to suffer

7. She promises to go (βαίνω)
8. They suffered
9. They persuaded
10. He chose
11. He took
12. You (s.) went (use βαίνω)

SUMMARY LEARNING VOCABULARY FOR SECTION 9H–J

αἱρέω (ἑλ-)	take, capture, convict
αἰτέω	ask (for)
ἀκούω	hear, listen to (+ gen. of person/thing)
ἀμφότεροι αι α	both
ἀπολογέομαι	defend oneself, make a speech in one's own defence
ἀπολογίᾱ, ἡ	speech in one's own defence (1b)
ἀπολύω	acquit, release
ἄρχομαι	begin (+gen.); begin to (+part. or inf.)
αὖ	again, moreover
γραφή, ἡ	indictment, charge, case (1a)
γράφομαι	indict, charge
γραφὴν γράφομαι	indict X (acc.) on a charge of Y (gen.)
διώκω	prosecute, pursue
ἐθέλω	wish, want (to)
ἐλπίζω	hope, expect (+fut. inf.)
ἐξαπατάω	deceive, trick
ἐπίσταμαι	know how to (+inf.); understand
θάνατος, ὁ	death (2a)
καταδικάζω	condemn, convict (X [gen.] on a charge of Y [acc.])
κατηγορέω	prosecute X (gen.) on a charge of Y (acc.)
κατηγορίᾱ, ἡ	speech for the prosecution (1b)
κλέπτης, ὁ	thief (1d)
κύων (κυν-), ὁ	dog (3a)
μάρτυς (μαρτυρ-), ὁ	witness (3a)
μέλλω	be about to (+fut. inf.); intend; hesitate (+pres. inf.)
μέρος, τό	share, part (3c)
ὅδε ἥδε τόδε	this here
ὅτι	because
παιδίον, τό	child; young slave (2b)
παρά	(+gen.) from
πολύ	(adv.) much
πρός	(+gen.) in the name of, under the protection of
συγγνώμην ἔχω	forgive, pardon (+dat.)
τυγχάνω (τυχ-)	hit, chance on, happen on, be subject to (+gen.); happen (to), be actually (+part.)
ὑπισχνέομαι	(+ fut. inf.) I promise
ὕστερος ᾱ ον	later, last (of two)

SUMMARY LEARNING VOCABULARY FOR SECTION 9H–J
CONTINUED

ὕστερον	later, further (adverb)
ὑφαιρέομαι (ὑφελ-)	steal, take for oneself by stealth
φεύγω (φυγ-)	be a defendant, be on trial; flee
ψῆφος, ἡ	vote, voting-pebble (2a)

REVISION EXERCISES FOR 9H–J

B/C WORD SHAPE AND SYNTAX

1. Sort this list into present, aorist and future infinitives:

πλεῖν	φροντιεῖν	βοηθῆσαι	διώξειν
ἀποχωρεῖν	ἔσεσθαι	μαχέσασθαι	μαθήσεσθαι
ἀφικέσθαι	σπεύδειν	ὀλοφυρεῖσθαι	κρατῆσαι
ποιήσειν	ὀφείλειν	παύσεσθαι	δέξεσθαι
βιάσασθαι	λήψεσθαι		

2. Give the aorist imperative, infinitive and participle (m./f./n.) of these verbs:

1. δέχομαι
2. δράω
3. ἔρχομαι
4. γίγνομαι
5. κωλύω
6. ἐπαινέω
7. βάλλω
8. παύω

3. Give meaning of verb and analyse part shown in right-hand box. Then connect the forms in the right-hand box with the dictionary forms in the left-hand box:

αἱρέω	λήσειν
ἀποθνῄσκω	λάβετε
βάλλω	ἑλεῖν
γίγνομαι	ἰδών
εἰμί	λαθών
εἶμι	ἐλθέ
ἔρχομαι	λήψεσθαι
ἐρωτάω	ἀπέθανε
εὑρίσκω	γενήσεσθαι
ἔχω	ἐρόμενος
λαμβάνω	μαθόντες
λανθάνω	γένεσθε
μανθάνω	δραμεῖν
οἶδα	οἴσει
ὁράω	τυχούσῃ
πίπτω	ἐνέγκατε
τρέχω	εἶναι
τυγχάνω	ἰόντος
φέρω	ᾔδεσαν
	ᾔεισθα
	βαλεῖν
	εἰδότες
	εὑρήσειν
	πεσόντι
	σχές
	πεσούμεν
	ἕξειν

D ENGLISH INTO GREEK

Translate:

1. οἱ παῖδες παιζόντων.
   Let the dogs come in!

2. ὁ κῆρυξ εἰσελθέτω εἰς τὴν πόλιν.
   Let the thief steal this dog's share!

3. ἐλπίζει τὸν κακὸν πολίτην διώξειν.
   I expect the defendants will make a good defence speech.

4. αὕτη ἡ γυνὴ μέλλει τοῦ ξένου ἀκούσεσθαι.
   This juror is going to condemn the dog to death.

5. οἱ ἱκέται εὐχέσθων πρὸς τοὺς θεούς.
   Let the prosecutor begin the prosecution!

SUMMARY EXERCISES FOR SECTION 9

A WORDS

Deduce the meaning of the words on the right from those on the left:

αἱρέω	καθαιρέω
γράφομαι	τὸ γράμμα
ἐλπίζω	ἡ ἐλπίς
ἐπίσταμαι	ἡ ἐπιστήμη
μάρτυς	ἡ μαρτυρία, μαρτυρέω
ὄνομα	ὀνομάζω
πονηρός	ἡ πονηρία

D ENGLISH INTO GREEK

1. Translate into Greek using the hints below to guide you:

   A young man had an old man for a father. The young man's name was Bdelykleon, the old man's Philokleon. The old man, it happened, had a terrible disease – he never stopped wanting to judge in the law-courts. The young man tried to persuade him not to judge, but the old man would not obey him, for all his persuasion. Finally, the young man locked him in the house. The old man was in despair and tried to escape, using all sorts of arguments. But he was not able to escape without being seen by the slaves, who guarded the house.

   Hints

   'A young man …': lit. 'To a young man there was a father who was old.'
   'tried to persuade': use imperfect of 'persuade'.
   'would not obey': use imperfect.
   'for all his persuasion': use καίπερ + participle, 'although persuading'.
   'all sorts of': use the appropriate form of πολύς.

2. Translate into Greek using the hints below to guide you:

BDELYKLEON	Once and for all, father, listen and obey me. I shall not allow you to leave the house and judge in the courtroom.
PHILOKLEON	Why aren't I allowed to? I expect you to tell me everything.
BDEL.	Because you are the wickedest man in the city.
PHIL.	Well, what am I allowed to do? What do you intend to do?
BDEL.	I shall allow you to pass judgement here in the house. Would you like that?
PHIL.	Yes, I would. Tell me quickly, what must I do?
BDEL.	Wait here. I shall fetch out the legal equipment. (Fetches gear; sets up the court.) Let the advocate come forward! Let the trial begin! Where is the prosecutor? Come here, dog, and prosecute. Go up

and speak. Tell us who has made the charge and for what
reason. Father, I hope you will pay attention.

PHIL.   Don't worry. Come on, dog, speak up!

Hints

'Once and for all': no need to translate this phrase – though it does affect the
aspect of the imperatives that follow.
'Why aren't I allowed to?': translate 'Won't you allow me?' (ἔξεστι + dat.).
'Would you like that?': lit. 'Would you want to do these things?'
'Yes, I would.': i.e. 'I would want to'.
Voc. of 'dog': κύον.
'Get up': use root aorist imperative of ἀναβαίνω: ἀναβῆθι.
'I hope you will pay attention': use ἐλπίζω followed by acc. ('you') + fut. inf.
('will pay attention').

E TEST EXERCISE NINE

Translate into English:

Philokleon laments his luck to the passing jurors, and prays to Zeus and Lykos to
change his appearance, so that he will be able to escape; the jurors send for help
to rescue him. (From Aristophanes, *Wasps*)

ΦΙΛΟΚΛΕΩΝ		ἴτε, πάντες φίλοι, ἴτε. ἀκούω γὰρ ὑμῶν ᾀδόντων, ἀλλ' οὐχ
		οἷός τ' εἰμὶ ᾄδειν ἐγώ. τί ποιήσω; οὗτοι γάρ με φυλάττουσιν,
		καίπερ βουλόμενον μεθ' ὑμῶν ἐλθεῖν πρὸς τὸ δικαστήριον καὶ
		κακόν τι ποιῆσαι. ἀλλ' ὦ Ζεῦ, παῦσαι πράγματά μοι παρέχων
	5	καὶ φίλος γενοῦ καὶ οἴκτιρον τὸ πάθος. σῶσόν με, ὦ Ζεῦ. ἤ με
		ποίησον <u>καπνὸν</u> ἐξαίφνης, ἢ δῆτα <u>λίθον</u> με ποίησον, <u>ἐφ' οὗ</u>
		τὰς ψήφους <u>ἀριθμοῦσιν</u>. τόλμησον, ἄναξ, σῶσαί με.
ΔΙΚΑΣΤΑΙ		τίς γάρ ἐστιν ὁ ἐγκλείων σε; λέξον, αἰτοῦμέν σε.
ΦΙΛ.		ὁ ἐμὸς υἱός, εὖ ἴστε. ἀλλὰ μὴ βοᾶτε. καὶ γὰρ τυγχάνει
	10	οὑτοσὶ <u>πρόσθεν</u> καθεύδων.
ΔΙΚ.		τίνος ἕνεκα οὐκ ἔξεστί σοι μεθ' ἡμῶν συνελθόντι ἀκοῦσαι
		τῶν τε κατηγορούντων καὶ τῶν ἀπολογουμένων;
ΦΙΛ.		ὁ υἱὸς οὐκ ἐᾷ με, ὦνδρες, δικάζειν οὐδὲ δρᾶν οὐδὲν
		κακόν. ἀλλὰ ζητεῖτε <u>μηχανήν</u> τινα, αἰτῶ ὑμᾶς. μέλλω
	15	γὰρ ἐγὼ τήμερον ἀκούσεσθαι τῶν τε διωκόντων καὶ τῶν
		φευγόντων.
ΔΙΚ.		οὐκ ἂν δυναίμεθα, ὦ φίλε, σῶσαί σε. φυλάττουσι γάρ σε
		οἱ <u>οἰκεῖοι</u> πάντες, καὶ οὐκ ἔξεστί σοι φυγεῖν.
ΦΙΛ.		χρὴ οὖν με εὔξασθαι τοῖς θεοῖς, ἐλπίζοντα φεύξεσθαι.
	20	ἀκουόντων οὖν οἱ θεοί, καὶ βοηθούντων. ὦ Λύκε
		δέσποτα, γείτων <u>ἥρως</u> – σὺ γὰρ φιλεῖς τὸ δικαστήριον
		– οἴκτιρον καὶ σῶσόν με ἐν ἀπορίᾳ ὄντα.
ΔΙΚ.		(addressing slaves who are leading them)

25   καὶ ὑμεῖς, ὦ παῖδες, τρέχετε καὶ βοᾶτε καὶ Κλέωνι ταῦτ' <u>ἀγγέλλετε</u> καὶ
κελεύετε αὐτὸν <u>ἥκειν</u>. ὁ γὰρ Βδελυκλέων λέγει ὅτι χρὴ μὴ δικάζειν
δίκας. ἴτω οὖν Κλέων καὶ σωτὴρ γενέσθω τῷ γέροντι.

Vocabulary

καπνός, ὁ smoke (2a)   μηχανή, ἡ device (1a)
λίθος, ὁ stone (2a)   οἰκεῖος, ὁ family member (2a)
ἐφ' οὗ on which   ἥρως, ὁ hero (his shrine was next to the lawcourts)
ἀριθμέω count   ἀγγέλλω tell
πρόσθεν in front   ἥκω have come, be present

EXERCISE

Answer the following questions based on the passage above.

1. Give the number, person and aspect of the following imperatives (e.g. 2 s. pres.): (a) παῦσαι (line 4), (b) γενοῦ (line 5), (c) λέξον (line 8), (d) βοᾶτε (line 9), (e) ζητεῖτε (line 14), (f) βοηθούντων (line 20), (g) οἴκτιρον (line 22), (h) γενέσθω (line 26)
2. Give the case of the following words and phrases: (a) φίλοι (line 1), (b) κακόν τι (line 4), (c) Ζεῦ (line 4), (d) πάντες (line 18), (e) δέσποτα (line 21), (f) τῷ γέροντι (line 26)

Grammar for Section 10

In this section you cover:
- Aorist optative, active and middle
- Verbs: δίδωμι, γιγνώσκω
- Adjectives: ἀμελής, γλυκύς
- Relatives: 'who/which/what/that'

THE AORIST OPTATIVE

212. You have already met the present optative active (-οιμι -οις -οι, etc., **184**). Here is the aorist optative active:

- It features, as you will see, σ and α, just like the aorist indicative active (**129–31**). This would lead you to expect the active aorist optative endings to be -σαιμι -σαις -σαι, and these do occur.
- However, Greek prefers the alternatives using -ει- given in the conjugation below:

First aorist optative active

παύσαιμι

παύσα-ι-μι
παύσ-ειας (α-ις)
παύσ-ειε(ν) (-αι)
παύσα-ι-μεν
παύσα-ι-τε
παύσ-ειαν (α-ι-εν)

■ *Forms*

(a) You know that the 'sign' of the optative is ι, and first aorist stem is σα. So there is nothing very difficult here. Look for σ-αι σ-ει.
(b) Note the absence of augment.
(c) Take care with the alternative forms of the 2s. and 3s. and 3pl.

First aorist optative middle

παυσαίμην

παυσα-ί-μην
παύσα-ι-ο
παύσα-ι-το
παυσα-ί-μεθα
παύσα-ι-σθε
παύσα-ι-ντο

■ *Forms*

(d) The aorist stem with optative 'signature' (ι) here takes regular past middle endings (-μην -[σ]ο -το, **102**).

Second aorist optative active

Active	Middle
λάβοιμι	λαβοίμην
λάβ-οι-μι	λαβ οί-μην
λάβ-οι-ς	λάβ-οι-ο
λάβ-οι	λάβ-οι-το
λάβ-οι-μεν	λαβ-οί-μεθα
λάβ-οι-τε	λάβ-οι-σθε
λάβ-οι-εν	λάβ-οι-ντο

■ *Form and meaning*

(e) Observe yet again that the second aorist takes endings identical to those for the present, i.e. aorist stem + οι (cf. **144–5**). The formal difference between e.g. λάβ-οι and λαμβάν-οι is purely one of *stem*.

(f) Again, there is no difference of *time* between present and aorist optative. The difference is one of aspect (**165**), if there is a difference at all which is really noticeable in translation.

EXERCISE

10: 1. Translate the following forms and turn them into the equivalent form in the present and aorist optative:

1. ἔσωσε
2. ποιοῦσιν
3. ἀπέσχοντο
4. καταλύει
5. συνῳκήσαμεν
6. ἐψηφισάμην
7. παυόμεθα
8. ἠνάγκασας
9. ἐμέμψατο
10. φεύγω

EXPRESSING A WISH

213. ἀπολοίμην (sometimes just ὀλοίμην) means 'May I die! Damn me!' (cf. the stem ἀπολ- learned at vocabulary 8C). This use of the optative on its own to express a wish for the future is very common. It will be fully introduced later on.

MORE VERBS IN -μι

214. You have already met some verbs ending in -μι, e.g. εἰ-μί, 'I am', εἶ-μι 'I shall go' and φη-μί 'I say' (see **386–8**). You will have noticed that they are quite different from verbs in -ω.

There are a number of such verbs in Greek, of which the most common are:

- δίδωμι 'I give'
- τίθημι 'I place'
- ἵημι 'I let go, shoot'
- ἵστημι 'I set up'
- δείκνυμι 'I show'

Here now, in full, is the conjugation of δίδωμι. It will give you the key to *all* -μι verbs. Know δίδωμι, and the rest will be relatively straightforward:

δίδωμι **'I give': stem** διδο-

Present active **'I give'**

Indicative	Participle	Infinitive	Imperative	Optative
δίδω-μι	διδούς	διδό-ναι		διδο-ίην
δίδω-ς	διδοῦσα		δίδου	διδο-ίης
δίδω-σι(ν)	διδό-ν		διδό-τω	διδο-ίη
δίδο-μεν	(διδο-ντ-)			διδο-ῖμεν
δίδο-τε			δίδο-τε	διδο-ῖτε
διδό-ασι(ν)			διδό-ντων	διδο-ῖεν

Present middle **'I give'**

Indicative	Participle	Infinitive	Imperative	Optative
δίδο-μαι	διδό-μεν-ος	δίδο-σθαι		διδο-ίμην
δίδο-σαι	-η		δίδο-σο	διδο-ῖο
δίδο-ται	-ον		διδό-σθω	διδο-ῖτο
διδό-μεθα				διδο-ίμεθα
δίδο-σθε			δίδο-σθε	διδο-ῖσθε
δίδο-νται			διδό-σθων	διδο-ῖντο

ἐδίδουν **'I was giving'**: stem διδο-

Imperfect indicative active **'I was giving'**

ἐ-δίδουν
ἐ-δίδους
ἐ-δίδου
ἐ-δίδο-μεν
ἐ-δίδο-τε
ἐ-δίδο-σαν

Imperfect indicative middle **'I was giving'**

ἐ-διδό-μην
ἐ-δίδο-σο
ἐ-δίδο-το
ἐ-διδό-μεθα
ἐ-δίδο-σθε
ἐ-δίδο-ντο

ἔδωκα **'I gave'**: stem δο-

Aorist active **'I gave'**

Indicative	Participle	Infinitive	Imperative	Optative
ἔ-δω-κα	δούς	δοῦναι		δο-ίην
ἔ-δω-κας	δοῦσα		δό-ς	δο-ίης
ἔ-δω-κε	δό-ν		δό-τω	δο-ίη
ἔ-δο-μεν	(δο-ντ-)			δο-ῖμεν
ἔ-δο-τε			δό-τε	δο-ῖτε
ἔ-δο-σαν			δό-ντων	δο-ῖεν
(ἔ-δω-καν)				

Aorist middle **'I gave'**

Indicative	Participle	Infinitive	Imperative	Optative
ἐ-δό-μην	δό-μεν-ος	δό-σθαι		δο-ίμην
ἔ-δου	-η		δοῦ	δο-ῖο
ἔ-δο-το	-ον		δό-σθω	δο-ῖτο
ἐ-δό-μεθα				δο-ίμεθα
ἔ-δο-σθε			δό-σθε	δο-ῖσθε
ἔ-δο-ντο			δό-σθων	δο-ῖντο

Future active and middle: stem δωσ- 'I will give'

δώ-σω, δώ-σομαι (etc., like παύσ-ω, παύσ-ομαι)

■ *Form*

(a) -ω/ομαι verbs are called 'thematic', because they have a stem, e.g. παυ-, to which they add a 'thematic' vowel -ο- or -ε-, and an ending, e.g. -μεν, to give e.g. παύομεν 'we stop' (see **16(b)**, **52(b)**, **102(c)**).

- But δίδωμι has no thematic vowel: it is therefore 'athematic'.
- What this means is that the endings go *straight onto the stem* without any intervening vowel.
- In other words, the stem is διδο- in the present and δο- in the past.
- The same is true for -μι verbs in general. Simply add endings and enjoy.

(b) Note how the 2s. middle endings (-μαι) -σαι (-ται) and (-μην) -σο (-το) appear in full for the first time (but cf. **177**).

(c) Given that one keeps a firm grip on these stems (διδο-, δο-), there is very little here that is difficult to recognise. The most remarkable feature is the aorist inflection with its change from ἔ-δω-κα, -κας, -κε to ἔ-δο-μεν, -τε, -σαν in the plural. For the full conjugation, see **376**, and cf. **426–7**.

EXERCISES

10: 2. Translate into English:

1. ἐδίδους	6. δός
2. δίδωσιν	7. δοῦσα
3. ἔδωκε	8. δώσεις
4. δοῦναι	9. διδόναι
5. διδόμενος	10. ἐδίδοσαν

10: 3. Change presents into equivalent forms of the aorist and likewise aorists into futures:

1. δίδοται	6. ἐδόμην
2. ἔδοτο	7. διδούς
3. διδοίη	8. ἔδοτε
4. ἔδοσαν	9. διδοῖτο
5. δίδοτε	10. δόσθαι

ADJECTIVES

215. Here are two more adjective-types illustrated by ἀμελής 'uncaring' and γλυκύς 'sweet':

ἀμελ-ής -ές 'uncaring'

s.	m. and f.	n.
Nom.	ἀμελ-ής	ἀμελ-ές
Acc.	ἀμελ-ῆ	ἀμελ-ές
Gen.	ἀμελ-οῦς	ἀμελ-οῦς
Dat.	ἀμελ-εῖ	ἀμελ-εῖ

pl.		
Nom.	ἀμελ-εῖς	ἀμελ-ῆ
Acc.	ἀμελ-εῖς	ἀμελ-ῆ
Gen.	ἀμελ-ῶν	ἀμελ-ῶν
Dat.	ἀμελ-έσι(ν)	ἀμελ-έσι(ν)

γλυκ-ύς -εῖα -ύ 'sweet'

s.	m.	f.	n.
Nom.	γλυκ-ύς	γλυκ-εῖ-α	γλυκ-ύ
Acc.	γλυκ-ύν	γλυκ-εῖ-αν	γλυκ-ύ
Gen.	γλυκ-έος	γλυκ-εί-ᾱς	γλυκ-έος
Dat.	γλυκ-εῖ	γλυκ-εί-ᾳ	γλυκ-εῖ

pl.			
Nom.	γλυκ-εῖς	γλυκ-εῖ-αι	γλυκ-έα
Acc.	γλυκ-εῖς	γλυκ-εί-ᾱς	γλυκ-έα
Gen.	γλυκ-έων	γλυκ-ει-ῶν	γλυκ-έων
Dat.	γλυκ-έσι(ν)	γλυκ-εί-αις	γλυκ-έσι(ν)

■ *Forms*

(a) ἀμελής has the same forms for the m. and f. (cf. εὔφρων, **82**).

(b) γλυκύς types are of mixed declension 3-1-3 – the m. and n. declining like type 3 nouns, the f. declining like a 1st declension noun ἀπορία, but with short -α. (Cf. **90**)

(c) The dominant vowel in the stem of both of these types of adjective is -ε-. Compare their declension with noun-types 3c, d, e and f (see **78**, **79**, **80**, **127a**).

(d) υἱός 'son' can decline like 2a nouns, but it can also decline like the m. form of γλυκύς (except for the acc. s.):

υἱός, ὁ 'son' (2a, and mixed)

s.
Nom. υἱός
Acc. υἱόν
Gen. υἱέος
Dat. υἱεῖ

pl.
Nom. υἱεῖς
Acc. υἱεῖς
Gen. υἱέων
Dat. υἱέσι(ν)

EXERCISE

10: 4. Add the correct forms of the def. art. with both ἀμελής and γλυκύς to the following nouns, e.g. γυναικί = τῇ ἀμελεῖ/γλυκείᾳ γυναικί:

1. φύλακας
2. μητρός
3. παιδία
4. ἀμφοτέροις
5. μάρτυρες
6. υἱέων
7. Now add the correct forms of ἀληθής ('true') and βραχύς ('short').

THE RELATIVE PRONOUN

216a. The relative pronoun, 'who, which, what' in English, declines as follows:

ὅς ἥ ὅ 'who, which, what'

	m.	*f.*	*n.*
s.			
Nom.	ὅς	ἥ*	ὅ
Acc.	ὅν	ἥν	ὅ
Gen.	οὗ	ἧς	οὗ
Dat.	ᾧ	ᾗ	ᾧ
pl.			
Nom.	οἵ*	αἵ*	ἅ
Acc.	οὕς	ἅς	ἅ
Gen.	ὧν	ὧν	ὧν
Dat.	οἷς	αἷς	οἷς

■ *Form*

- Except for ὅς, the relative declines exactly like the definite article without the τ-.

* In the three places where the forms of the relative are *exactly the same as* the definite article, the relative is distinguished by its accent, i.e. ἥ οἵ αἵ.

Meaning and usage of the relative

216b. The relative pronoun means:

     nom.:   'who, which, what, that'
     acc: 'who, whom, which, what, that'
     gen.:   'of whom, of which, whose'
     dat.:   'to, for, by, with which/whom'

Consider the following utterances:

1. ἡ γυνὴ ἣ οὐ φιλεῖ τὸν ἄνδρα 'the woman *who does not love her husband*'
   Comment: ἣ refers to ἡ γυνή, and is therefore f. and s. Another way of putting it is to say that ἡ γυνή is the *antecedent* of ἣ (Latin, 'that which comes before'). The case of ἣ is nom., because ἣ is the person who does not love her husband, i.e. is subject of the 'who' clause.

2. ὁ παῖς ὃν φιλῶ 'the boy *whom I like*'
   Comment: ὃν refers to ὁ παῖς, and is therefore m. and s. (ὁ παῖς is the antecedent of ὃν). Its case, however, is acc., because ὃν is the object of φιλῶ 'I like' (I like the boy, represented by 'whom').

3. ἡ γυνὴ ἧς τὸν ἄνδρα μισῶ 'the woman *whose husband I hate*'
   Comment: ἧς refers to ἡ γυνή, so is f. and s. So ἡ γυνή is the antecedent … . But its case is gen. because 'whose' = 'of whom'. Put another way, the relative clause means 'I hate the husband *of the woman*', gen.

4. οἱ παῖδες οἷς δίδωμι τὰ μῆλα 'the boys *to whom I give the apples*'
   Comment: οἷς is pl. and m. because its antecedent is οἱ παῖδες. It is dat. because 'I am giving the apples *to the boys*'.

5. ἡ οἰκία εἰς ἣν ἔρχομαι 'the house *into which I go*'
   Comment: ἣν refers to its antecedent ἡ οἰκία, so is f. and s. But it is acc. because εἰς works with the acc.

6. αἱ γυναῖκες μεθ' ὧν πορεύομαι 'the women *with whom I travel*'
   Comment: ὧν is f. and pl. because its antecedent is αἱ γυναῖκες. It is gen. because μεθ' (μετά) takes the gen. – 'I am travelling *with the women*'.

7. ἡ οἰκία ἐν ᾗ οἰκῶ 'the house *in which I live*'
   Comment: ᾗ, antecedent ἡ οἰκία, is f. s.; and dat. because ἐν works with the dat.

RULE

> ▶ **217.** The relative takes the *gender* and *number* of its *antecedent*. It does *not* take the antecedent's case. The relative's *case* is entirely determined by the function it fulfils *within the relative clause* – as you can see from the examples given, in all of which the antecedent is in the nom., but only one of the relatives is in the nom. (the first one). Here come the exceptions:

Some wrinkles (1): suppressing your antecedents

218. (a) Consider the English 'whom the gods love, dies young'. Who, *exactly*, is the subject of 'dies'?

> ● The answer is an *understood* 'he' or 'she': '(s)he whom the gods love dies young'.
> ● In other words, the antecedent of 'whom' has been *suppressed*.

This is common in Greek: ὃν οἱ θεοὶ φιλοῦσιν ἀποθνῄσκει νέος.*

> ▶ When you find a suppressed antecedent, check the gender of the relative:

If m., it will mean 'the man/he who', e.g. ὃν φιλεῖς ἄπεστιν '[He] whom you love is absent'.
If f., 'the woman/she who', e.g. ἣν φιλεῖς ἄπεστιν '[She] whom you love is absent'.
If n., 'the thing which/what', e.g. ἃ ἐθέλεις, ἔχεις 'what [things, n.pl.] you want, you have' (i.e. 'the things which you want …').

* The Roman comic poet Plautus translates this: *quem di diligunt adolescens moritur*. Byron mistranslated this line as 'Whom the gods love die young': why is that wrong? What would it be in Greek?

Some wrinkles (2): attracting your relatives

(b) If the antecedent is in the genitive or dative case, the Greek relative is sometimes changed ('attracted') into that case, irrespective of the function it should have in the relative clause, e.g.

> ● περὶ τῶν ἀνδρῶν ὧν γιγνώσκω 'concerning the men whom I recognise'. (We would expect: περὶ τῶν ἀνδρῶν οὓς γιγνώσκω, since 'whom' is the object of 'recognise'; but the relative is attracted into the case of its antecedent ἀνδρῶν and becomes ὧν instead of οὕς.)
> ● τοῖς ἀνδράσιν οἷς γιγνώσκω 'to the men whom I recognise'. (We would, again, expect οὓς γιγνώσκω; but the relative is attracted into the case of its antecedent ἀνδράσιν and becomes οἷς instead.)

● This feature is known as 'relative attraction'.

ὅσπερ (ὅσ-περ) and ὅστις (ὅσ-τις)

219. The relative pronoun does have a number of other forms, though its meaning is only slightly altered thereby:

ὅσπερ (ὅσ-περ) 'the very one who'
ὅστις (ὅσ-τις) 'anyone who'. Observe that this declines like the separate parts of ὅς and τις combined.

ὅστις ἥτις ὅτι '[anyone] who, which, what'

	m.	*f.*	*n.*
s.			
Nom.	ὅστις	ἥτις	ὅτι (or ὅ τι)
Acc.	ὅντινα	ἥντινα	ὅτι (or ὅ τι)
Gen.	οὗτινος	ἧστινος	οὗτινος
	(ὅτου)		(ὅτου)
Dat.	ᾧτινι	ᾗτινι	ᾧτινι
	(ὅτῳ)		(ὅτῳ)
pl.			
Nom.	οἵτινες	αἵτινες	ἅτινα
			(ἅττα)
Acc.	οὕστινας	ἅστινας	ἅτινα
			(ἅττα)
Gen.	ὧντινων	ὧντινων	ὧντινων
	(ὅτων)	(ὅτων)	(ὅτων)
Dat.	οἷστισι(ν)	αἷστισι(ν)	οἷστισι(ν)
	(ὅτοις)		(ὅτοις)

Form and use

(a) Sometimes the two words appear as one (e.g. as declined above), at other times they are kept separate, e.g. ὅς τις, ὅ τι etc.

(b) Note the variant forms:

gen.:   ὅτου for οὗτινος; ὅτων for ὧντινων
dat.:   ὅτῳ for ᾧτινι; ὅτοις for οἷστισι
nom./acc. pl. ἅττα for ἅτινα

(c) ὅστις can be used to introduce indirect questions (cf. **125** and check the list of relative usages there).

EXERCISES

10: 5. Supply a form of the relative in English and Greek (ὅς and ὅστις) that makes sense of the following utterances:

1. Where is the soldier — is forcing me to hide?
2. They could not see the men — they were commanding.
3. The woman — sons he will teach comes from Miletos.
4. I cannot find the women — I was going to give the apples.
5. The girls — he was intending to pursue gave him the slip.
6. They gave the arms to the men — had survived.
7. — you hold dear, I hold dear too. [*Many possibilities here*]
8. Three cheers for the boys — fathers come from Athens!
9. — [*neuter*] I know, he does not know.
10. Do you see — [*neuter*] I see?

10: 6. Following the pattern noted at **218 (b)** above, supply the appropriate relative in Greek (ὅς and ὅστις) for the following:

1. I shall give an apple to the women — I prefer.
2. Which of the men — you saw were foreigners?
3. He arrived with [*what case does* μετά *take?*] the slaves — he had captured.
4. I shall give nothing to the slave — once I loved.
5. We are not worthy — you have given us.

SUMMARY LEARNING VOCABULARY FOR SECTION 10

ἀναγκάζω	force, compel
ἀμελής ές	uncaring
ἅπᾱς ἅπᾱσα ἅπαν (ἁπαντ-)	all, the whole
ἀπέχομαι	refrain, keep away (from) (+gen.)
ἄρτι	just now, recently
βαδίζ-ω	walk, go (fut. βαδιέομαι)
γλυκύς εῖα ύ	sweet
γοῦν	at any rate
γραῦς (γρα-), ἡ	old woman (3 irr.) (acc. s. γραῦν; acc. pl. γραῦς). See **357**.
δέομαι	need, ask, beg (+gen.)
δίδωμι (δο-)	give, grant
δοκεῖ	it seems a good idea to X (dat.) to do Y (inf.); X (dat.) decides to do Y (inf.)
δῶρον, τό	gift, bribe (2b)
ἐκδύομαι	undress
ἐξαίφνης	suddenly

SUMMARY LEARNING VOCABULARY FOR SECTION 10 *(continued)*

καίτοι	and yet
κατακλίνομαι	lie down
καταλύω	bring to an end; finish
μέμφομαι	blame, criticise, find fault with (+acc. or dat.)
μηδαμῶς	not at all, in no way
μηδείς μηδεμία μηδέν (μηδεν-)	no, no one
μήτηρ (μητ(ε)ρ-), ἡ	mother (3a)
μηχανή, ἡ	device, plan (1a)
οἷος ᾱ ον	what a! what sort of a!
ὅς ἥ ὅ	who, what, which
ὅσπερ ἥπερ ὅπερ	who/which indeed
ὅστις ἥτις ὅτι	who(ever), what(ever)
οὐδαμῶς	in no way, not at all
παρά	(+dat.) with, beside, in the presence of
παύομαι	cease from (+gen.)
ποῖος ᾱ ον	what sort of?
προσαγορεύω	address, speak to
σπουδή, ἡ	haste, zeal, seriousness (1a)
συνοικέω	live with, live together
τεῖχος, τό	wall (of a city) (3c)
τοι	then (inference)
φίλτατος η ον	most dear (φίλος)
φύλαξ (φυλακ-), ὁ, ἡ	guard (3a)
ψηφίζομαι	vote (fut. ψηφιέομαι)

REVISION EXERCISES FOR SECTION 10

(A) WORDS

1. Deduce the meaning of the words in the right-hand columns from those in the left:

ἀμελής	μέλει		
δίδωμι	ἀποδίδωμι	ἡ δόσις	ἡ ἀντίδοσις
δῶρον	ἡ δωρεά	δωρέω	
μηχανή	μηχανάομαι		
σπουδή	σπουδάζω	σπουδαῖος α ον	
συνοικέω	ἡ συνοίκησις		
τεῖχος	τειχίζω		

(B/C) MORPHOLOGY AND SYNTAX

1. Translate each sentence, then convert present optatives to aorist:

   a. προσαγορεύοις ἂν ἐμέ.
   b. ἡδέως ἂν παυοίμην τοῦ πολέμου.
   c. ἐθέλοιμεν ἂν σπονδὰς ποιεῖσθαι πολλῇ σπουδῇ.
   d. οὐκ ἂν ποιοίην ταῦτα, ὦ μῆτερ.
   e. ὁρῴην ἂν ἐγὼ τὴν πόλιν.

2. Translate each sentence, then substitute the correct part of δίδωμι for παρέχω:

   a. ἆρα παρέξεις μοι ὃ ἔχεις;
   b. παρεῖχε τὰ χρήματα τῇ γυναικί.
   c. τί οὐκ ἐθέλεις παρέχειν μοι ὧν δέομαι;
   d. τί παρέχεις μοι τοῦτο τὸ μῆλον, ὦ Μυρρίνη;
   e. ἐξαίφνης παρασχὼν τὰ χρήματα ὧν ἐδεῖτο ἡ γυνή, ἀπῆλθεν ὁ ἄνθρωπος.

3. Translate each of the following pairs of sentences. Then join them together into one sentence, following these patterns:

   (a) Λυσιστράτη γυνὴ Ἀθηναία ἐστί· Λυσιστράτη λέγει.
       = Λυσιστράτη, ἣ γυνὴ Ἀθηναία ἐστί, λέγει.
   (b) τίνες εἰσὶν οὗτοι; τίνες διώκουσι τὸν ἄνδρα;
       = τίνες εἰσὶν οὗτοι, οἳ διώκουσι τὸν ἄνδρα;

   a. Κινησίας ἐστὶν ἀνὴρ Μυρρίνης. Κινησίας βαδίζει πρὸς τὴν ἀκρόπολιν.
   b. αἱ γυναῖκές εἰσιν ἐν τῇ ἀκροπόλει. αἱ γυναῖκες βοῶσιν.
   c. οἱ ἄνδρες τὰς μάχας μάχονται. οἱ ἄνδρες οὐκ ἐθέλουσιν οὐδαμῶς τὸν πόλεμον καταλῦσαι.
   d. τί ἐστι τοῦτο; τί ἐθέλεις λέγειν;
   e. αἱ γυναῖκες ἐθέλουσιν ἀκούειν τοὺς λόγους. τοὺς λόγους λέγει Λυσιστράτη.
   f. αἱ γρᾶες ἔχουσι τὴν ἀκρόπολιν. ἐγὼ τὰς γραῦς ἰδεῖν δύναμαι.

g. ποῦ ἐστι Κινησίας; Μυρρίνη ἐστὶν ἡ γυνὴ αὐτοῦ.
h. ποῦ αἱ γρᾶες; τὸ ἔργον ἐστὶν αὐτῶν φυλάττειν τὰ χρήματα.
i. ἆρα γιγνώσκεις τὸν ἄνδρα; ὁ ἀνὴρ προσέρχεται.
j. δεῖ ἡμᾶς εἰρήνην ἄγειν. ἡ εἰρήνη αἰτία ἐστὶ πολλῶν καλῶν.

(D) ENGLISH INTO GREEK

1. Translate into Greek:

1. Will the women refrain from the bribes which the men will give them?
2. These guards are uncaring and guard with no zeal.
3. The old women are making a plan by which they will capture the walls.
4. It seems a good idea to us women to bring the war to an end.
5. Won't anyone force the men to stop fighting?

2. Translate into Greek (words in italics are given in the vocabulary):

LYSISTRATA We must stop the war and make a truce. We will persuade the men, whose duty it is to fight, to do what we want.

WOMAN I should like to. But how is it possible for us, who are women, to do this? Say what you have in mind.

LYS. Would you do what I order?

WOMEN We would, by Zeus.

LYS. The plan I have in mind happens to be difficult. Listen then to the words I speak, and obey. We must all refrain from *sex*!

MYRRHINE I will not do it!

KLEONIKE Neither will I!

LYS. Is there anyone who will do what I order?

LAMPITO We must bring peace and stop the men who fight the wars. I will *vote with* you.

LYS. Dear Lampito! Give me your hand.

LAMP. Here, I give it.

LYS. Go then to *Sparta* and persuade the Spartans.

LAMP. I will go at once.

Vocabulary

sex ἀφροδίσια, τά (2b)
vote with συμψηφίζομαι (+ dat.)
Sparta Λακεδαίμων (Λακεδαιμον-), ἡ (3a)

TEST EXERCISE TEN
Translate into English:

A Spartan envoy arrives. After he has explained how things stand in Sparta, he and his Athenian counterpart agree to come to terms with Lysistrata. Lysistrata states the conditions on which a return to peace might be agreed.

(From Aristophanes, *Lysistrata*)

ΛΑΚΕΔΑΙΜΟΝΙΟΣ   ποῦ ἡ τῶν Ἀθηναίων <u>βουλή</u>; ἐθελήσαιμι ἂν <u>ἀγγεῖλαι</u> νέον τι.

ΑΘΗΝΑΙΟΣ   σὺ δὲ τίς εἶ ὃς δεῦρο βαίνεις πρὸς τὸ τεῖχος, πολλῇ σπουδῇ βαδίζων;

5 ΛΑΚ.   κῆρυξ ἐγώ, <u>ναὶ τὼ σιώ</u>, καὶ ἔβην ἄρτι ἀπὸ Σπάρτης περὶ εἰρήνης.

ΑΘ.   τί δ' ἐστί σοι τόδε, ὃ ἔχεις ἐν ταῖς χερσίν;

ΛΑΚ.   <u>σκυτάλα Λακαινικά</u>.

ΑΘ.   εὖ οἶδ' ὃ λέγεις. ἀλλὰ τί γίγνεται ἐν Λακεδαιμόνι; εἴποις

10 ἄν.

ΛΑΚ.   εἴποιμι ἂν ἡδέως. κακὸν γάρ τι μέγα ἐνέπεσεν ἡμῖν· αἰτία δὲ Λαμπιτώ, ἣ ἐξ Ἀθηνῶν ἀναβᾶσα ἔπεισε τὰς γυναῖκας ἀπέχεσθαι <u>τῶν ἀφροδισίων</u>.

ΑΘ.   καὶ πῶς ἔχετε; κακῶς πάσχετε, ἐξ ὧν λέγεις.

15 ΛΑΚ.   κακῶς παθὼν τυγχάνω, ναὶ τὼ σιώ. δεῖ οὖν ἡμᾶς, πειθομένους ταῖς γυναιξί, σπονδὰς ποιήσασθαι, ἃς κελεύσουσιν αὐταί, καὶ καταλῦσαι τὸν πόλεμον.

ΑΘ.   τί οὐ καλοῦμεν δῆτα τὴν Λυσιστράτην, ἣ ποιήσαιτ' ἂν ἡμῖν σπονδὰς μόνη; ἐπάθομεν γὰρ καὶ ἡμεῖς τοῦτο τὸ

20 κακόν.

ΛΑΚ.   ναὶ τὼ σιώ. τίς ἂν εἴποι ποῦ ἐστιν ἡ Λυσιστράτη;

ΑΘ.   ἀλλ' ἡμᾶς οὐ δεῖ καλεῖν αὐτήν· αὐτὴ γάρ, ἀκούσασα ἃ ἐλέγομεν, ἥδε βᾶσα τυγχάνει.

ΛΥΣΙΣΤΡΑΤΗ   ἴτε, ἄνδρες. τῶν λόγων ἀκούετε ὧν λέγω. ἐγὼ γυνὴ μέν

25 εἰμι, νοῦς δ' ἔνεστί μοι. τί νῦν οὕτως μάχεσθε καὶ οὐ παύεσθε <u>τῆς μοχθηρίας</u> ὑμεῖς, οἷς οἱ αὐτοί εἰσι βωμοὶ καὶ αἱ αὐταὶ θυσίαι; τί νῦν Ἕλληνας ἄνδρας καὶ πόλεις <u>ἀπόλλυτε</u>, οἷς ἀντὶ τούτων ἔξεστιν εἰρήνην ἰδεῖν, φίλοις τ' οὖσι καὶ <u>συμμάχοις</u>;

30 ΛΑΚ. ΚΑΙ ΑΘ.   καίτοι οὐδὲν ἄλλο δῶρον δεόμεθα ἢ <u>βινεῖν</u> δύνασθαι.

ΛΥΣ.   ἅπαντες οὖν σπονδὰς ποιησάμενοι καταλύσατε τὸν πόλεμον. κἄπειτα τὴν αὐτοῦ γυναῖκα λαβὼν ἀπίτω <u>ἕκαστος</u>.

Vocabulary

βουλή, ἡ Council of Five Hundred (1a)
ἀγγέλλω announce (aor. ἤγγειλα)
ναὶ τὼ σιώ by the Two Gods*
σκυτάλα Λακαινικά a Spartan code-staff**
ἀφροδίσια, τά sex (2b)
μοχθηρία, ἡ nastiness (1b)
ἀπόλλυμι destroy

ἀντί (+gen.) instead of
σύμμαχος, ὁ ally (2a)
βινέω make love (*colloquial*)
ἕκαστος η ον each

* The two gods – Castor and Pollux.
** The message was written on a leather strip wrapped round the pole and when removed was unintelligible; the recipient would have a similar staff for use in decoding. There is a *double entendre* at work here.

Grammar for Section 11

In this section you cover:
- Present and imperfect passive
- Genitive absolute
- Comparative adverbs and two-termination adjectives
- Optative of φημί 'I say'

THE PASSIVE

220. So far you have met and learnt verbs which are *active* in voice and verbs which are *middle* in voice. The distinction has usually been one of form (active verbs in -ω or -μι, middle verbs in -μαι, etc.), though occasionally the meaning has been radically altered by the conversion of an active verb into a middle, e.g.

> πείθω 'I persuade'
> πείθομαι 'I believe in, trust, obey'

We now come to the third and final voice – the PASSIVE (see **412**).

▶ The passive has a specific meaning, which cannot be ignored. It signifies that the subject of the sentence is *having something done to it*, e.g. 'the slave is being beaten', 'the soldiers were cut down', 'I shall be defeated.'

▶ the forms of the passive in the present and imperfect are identical to the forms for the *MIDDLE*. So YOU HAVE NO NEW LEARNING TO DO FOR THESE TENSES.

▶ BUT YOU MUST NOW BE ALERT TO THE POSSIBILITY THAT WHAT YOU ARE USED TO AS A *MIDDLE* FORM MIGHT BE *PASSIVE* – AND THEREFORE CARRY *A QUITE DIFFERENT MEANING*.

Here is a summary of the forms and their new meanings:

Passive forms and meaning

Present passive				
Indicative	**Participle**	**Infinitive**	**Imperative**	**Optative**
παύομαι	παυόμεν-ος -η -ον	παύεσθαι	παύου	παυοίμην
'I am being stopped'	'being stopped'	'to be stopped'	'be stopped!'	'I would be stopped'

Imperfect indicative passive

ἐπαυόμην

'I was being stopped'

To take an extreme example, πείθομαι could mean:

- 'I trust, obey' (middle); or
- 'I am being persuaded' (the *passive* form of πείθω).

Likewise, παύεται could mean:

- 'He stops himself' (middle); or
- 'He is being stopped' (passive).

In practice, of course, the context will make it clear which meaning is required.

Now revise the present and imperfect middle (**52**, **102**, **107**, δίδωμι **214**) before attempting the exercise.

EXERCISE

11: 1. Turn the following present active forms into their equivalent passive forms in the present and imperfect, and translate:

1. κηρύττει
2. φιλεῖς
3. ἄρχουσιν
4. ἐλευθεροῦμεν
5. τιμᾶτε
6. δίδωσι
7. ἀναγκάζω
8. καταλύει
9. διώκουσιν
10. ἐξάγομεν

'BY' A PERSON OR THING

221. A verb with a passive meaning will always (by definition) indicate to whom the action is being done. It will be the subject of the sentence:

'*We* are being ruled' ἀρχόμεθα;
'*It* was being announced' ἐκηρύττετο,
'*She* is being kissed' φιλεῖται.

Such an utterance will also frequently tell you *by whom* or *by/with what* the action was being carried out. Look at the following:

πείθεται ὑπ' ἐμοῦ 'he is being persuaded *by me*'
ἐπαύοντο ὑπὸ τῶν ἀνδρῶν 'they were being stopped *by the men*'

φυλαττόμεθα <u>τοῖς</u> <u>δικτύοις</u> 'we are being guarded *by the nets*'
ἐβαλλόμην <u>τοῖς</u> <u>λίθοις</u> 'I was being pelted *with the stones*'

You can now work out the rule:

▶   'By' a *person* = ὑπό + genitive;
▶   'By' a thing or 'with' a thing = plain dative.

So to help you get used to the new meaning, passive forms in extended sentences will for the moment be accompanied by one of these two 'markers': ὑπό, or the plain dative.

Note the technical terms:

●   'By a person' = the *agent* (Latin *agens* lit. 'the one doing, acting');
●   'By/with a thing' = the *instrument*.

EXERCISE

11: 2. Construct two intelligible sentences for each of the verbs in (a) by combining each with *either* an agent *or* instrument:

(a) ἐφιλοῦντο κηρύττεται ἐφυλαττόμην ἐκωλυόμεθα ἐξεφέρετο πείθονται
(b) ὑπό
(c) τοῦ κήρυκος τῇ ἀληθείᾳ τῶν φυλάκων τῷ τείχει τοῖς λόγοις τῶν ἀνδρείων τῶν ἀνδρῶν τοῦ διδασκάλου τῇ φιλοσοφίᾳ

GENITIVE ABSOLUTE

222. We know that a participle, being an adjective, describes, and therefore agrees with, its noun. But what case is 'the men' in the following sentence? 'The men being pelted with the stones, Brasidas retreated.'

●   'Being pelted' is the participle agreeing with 'the men'.
●   Being a participle, its case will depend on the case of 'the men'.
●   So what case *is* 'the men'?
●   It is certainly not the subject: that is 'Brasidas', subject of the main verb 'retreated'. Well?

The difficulty is caused by the clause 'The men … stones' *standing free* of any obvious grammatical link with the subject and main verb. 'Released, freed' in Latin is *absolutus*.

▶   This therefore is an 'absolute' phrase – and absolute phrases in Greek go into the *genitive*, thus: τῶν ἀνδρῶν βαλλομένων τοῖς λίθοις, ἀνεχώρησεν ὁ Βρασίδας.

Translating genitive absolutes

223. When you come across a genitive absolute:

- Translate literally, starting with the word 'with': 'with X doing/having done something' or 'with X being/having been done'.
- Then re-translate into good English.

For example:

- κελεύοντος τοῦ κήρυκος, τί μένεις;

lit. 'With the herald giving orders (present participle), why do you wait?'
i.e. 'Why do you wait when the herald is giving his orders?' 'The herald is giving his orders – why wait?'

- τῶν ἀνδρῶν φυγόντων, ἐπανῆλθον.

lit. 'with the men having fled (aorist participle), I returned'
i.e. 'The men fled but/and I returned'; 'Because/as/since/when the men fled, I returned'; 'After the men fled, I returned'; 'Although the men fled, I returned'.

■ *Participle tense*

224. As you can see from the above examples, in these participle constructions, the *temporal* force of the participle sometimes comes to the fore. In other words, a present participle can show that the action is going on *at the same time as* the main verb, the aorist participle that it occurred *before* the action of the main verb. But see on aspect, **417**.

EXERCISE

11: 3. Turn the following clauses into genitive absolutes, assigning the tense of the verb to that of the participle:

1. ἐφύγομεν εἰς τὴν ἀκρόπολιν
2. οἱ ῥήτορες ἤκουσαν τῶν λόγων
3. ἔδωκας ἡμῖν τὰ σῖτα
4. οἱ δοῦλοι ἐλευθεροῦνται
5. οἱ σοφισταὶ τοὺς νεανίσκους ἐδίδαξαν
6. ἔλαβον οἱ Πέρσαι τὰς ναῦς
7. ἦλθον ἐγὼ πρὸς τὴν πόλιν
8. τὸ δῶρον δίδοται τῇ γυναικί

COMPARATIVE AND SUPERLATIVE ADVERBS

225. Adverbs, indeclinable adjectives usually ending '-ly' in English ('foolishly', 'hopefully': see **28–9**) also have comparative and superlative forms:

σοφώτερον **'more wisely'**

The comparative adverb is formally identical with the *accusative singular neuter* of the comparative adjective, e.g.

> σοφώτερος (adj.) 'more wise' → σοφώτερον lit. 'a wiser thing', i.e. 'more wisely'
>
> κακίων (adj.) 'worse' → κάκιον lit. 'a worse thing', i.e. 'in a worse way, worse'

σοφώτατα **'most, very wisely'**

The superlative adverb is formally identical with the *accusative neuter plural* of the superlative adjective, e.g.

> σοφώτατος (adj.) 'most, very wise' → σοφώτατα 'most, very wisely'

The full sequence, therefore, is:

> ▶ σοφῶς 'wisely' – σοφώτερον 'more wisely' – σοφώτατα 'most, very wisely'.

Irregular adverbs include:

> μάλα 'very', μᾶλλον 'more, rather (more)' μάλιστα 'much, very much, a great deal'. See **366**.

TWO-TERMINATION ADJECTIVES

226. You have already met 3rd declension adjectives that decline the same in the m. and f. (e.g. εὔφρων, see **82**). Some adjectives which *look like* the 2-1-2 καλός type decline like this as well: in other words, their feminine, as well as masculine, forms end -ος -ον, etc.

> ▶ These καλός-type adjectives with identical m. and f. forms are called 'two-termination' adjectives because they have only two sets of endings – one for m./f., one for n.

You have already met one of these, ἐρῆμος 'deserted', which has occurred in the sentence ἐρῆμος ἡ Πνύξ 'the Pnyx is deserted'. One might have expected *ἐρήμη, but the adjective is two-termination, using the same form for m. and f. Most two-termination adjectives are *compounds*, and pretty well *all* compounds are two-termination adjectives, e.g.

> ἄ-δικ-ος -ον 'unjust'
> ἀ-θάνατ-ος -ον 'immortal'
> εὐ-δόκιμ-ος -ον 'of good reputation'
> ἀ-δύνατ-ος -ον 'impossible'

But there are a number of other adjectives which are two-termination without being compounds, e.g.

βάρβαρ-ος -ον 'barbarian, foreign'

OPTATIVE OF φημί

227. Revise the indicative of φημί 'I say' (**168**) and now learn the optative:

φα-ίην 'I would say'

φα-ίην
φα-ίης
φα-ίη
φα-ῖμεν
φα-ίητε
φα-ῖεν

SUMMARY LEARNING VOCABULARY FOR SECTION 11

ἀγορεύω	speak (in assembly), proclaim
ἀγρός, ὁ	field, country(side) (2a)
ἀθάνατος ον	immortal
αἱρέομαι (ἑλ-)	choose
αἰσθάνομαι (αἰσθ-)	perceive, notice
ἄκων ἄκουσα ἄκον (ἀκοντ-)	unwilling(ly)
ἄνευ	(+gen.) without
ἀποβλέπω	look steadfastly at (and away from everything else)
ἀπόλλῡμι (ἀπολεσα-, ἀπολ-)	kill, ruin, destroy; (in pass.) be killed etc. (aor. ἀπωλόμην)
ἀρέσκω	please (+dat.)
ἄρχομαι	be ruled
ἄρχω	rule (+gen.)
γεῦμα (γευματ-), τό	taste, sample (3b)
γεύομαι	taste
δραχμή, ἡ	drachma (1a) (coin; pay for two days' attendance at the ekklesia)
εἶεν	very well then!
εὔνους ουν	well-disposed
ἥδιστος η ον	most pleasant (sup. of ἡδύς)
ἥκω	come, have come
θορυβέω	make a disturbance, din

SUMMARY LEARNING VOCABULARY FOR SECTION 11 *(continued)*

κάτω	below
κηρΰττω	announce, proclaim
λίθος, ὁ	stone (2a)
μήτε . . . μήτε	neither . . . nor
ὁ δέ	and/but he
ὁδοιπόρος, ὁ	traveller (2a)
ὁδός, ἡ	road, way (2a)
οἱ δέ	and/but they
ὄλλῡμι (ὀλεσα-, ὀλ-)	destroy, kill; (in pass.) be killed, die, perish (aor. ὠλόμην)
ὀξύς εῖα ύ	sharp; bitter; shrill
ὅπως	how? (answer to πῶς;), how (indir. q.)
ὅσος η ον	as much as (pl. as many as)
παρασκευή, ἡ	preparation, equipping; force (1a)
παρέρχομαι (παρελθ-)	come forward, pass by, go by
πολεμέω	make war
πρύτανις, ὁ	prytanis (3e) (member of the βουλή committee currently in charge of public affairs)
σῑγάω	be quiet
τρεῖς τρία	three
τριήρης, ἡ	trireme (3d)
φιλέω	be used to; love; kiss
χρηματίζω	do business

REVISION EXERCISES FOR SECTION 11

(A) WORDS

1. Deduce the meaning of the words on the right from those on the left:

αἰσθάνομαι	ἡ αἴσθησις
ἄκων	ἑκών
πρύτανις	τὸ πρυτανεῖον

(B/C) MORPHOLOGY AND SYNTAX

1. Translate each sentence, then, making the necessary changes in nouns and verbs, change from active to passive:

     a. τιμᾷ τοὺς χρηστούς ὁ δῆμος.
     b. ἀναγκάζει ἡμᾶς σπονδὰς ποιεῖσθαι ἡ Λυσιστράτη.
     c. ἀδικοῦσιν οἱ ῥήτορες τὴν πόλιν.
     d. ἐξαπατᾷ ὁ ῥήτωρ τὸν δῆμον.
     e. θωπεύομεν τὴν ἐκκλησίαν τοῖς λόγοις.
     f. πείθετε τοὺς πολίτας εἰρήνην ἄγειν.
     g. τὰ δῶρα ἔπειθε τὸν δῆμον.
     h. οἱ τῶν ῥητόρων λόγοι ἠδίκουν τὴν ἐκκλησίαν.
     i. τὰ τείχη ἐφύλαττε τὴν πόλιν.
     j. αἱ μηχαναὶ αἱ τῶν γυναικῶν ἠνάγκαζον τοὺς ἄνδρας σπονδὰς ποιεῖσθαι.

2. Translate each pair of sentences, then join them into one, using the genitive absolute construction. Remember to eliminate particles which connect clauses of equal grammatical structure, e.g. μέν and δέ – because, when one of the clauses is a participial clause and the other a main verb, they will no longer be syntactically equivalent.

     a. ἀπῆλθον οἱ ἄνδρες. ἡμεῖς δὲ πρὸς τὴν πόλιν ἐπορευόμεθα.
     b. ἔδωκέ μοι τὸ ἀργύριον ἡ γυνή. ἐγὼ δ' ἀπῆλθον.
     c ὁ θεὸς μένει. οἱ δ' Ἀθηναῖοι οὐ βούλονται ἀκούειν.
     d. οἱ ἄλλοι πολεμοῦσιν. ἐγὼ δ' οὐ πολεμήσω.
     e. ἡ πόλις ἀδικεῖται ὑπὸ τῶν ῥητόρων, οἱ δ' Ἀθηναῖοι οὐδὲν φροντίζουσιν.
     f. ἡ ἐκκλησία περὶ τοῦ πολέμου ἐχρημάτιζεν. ὁ δὲ Δικαιόπολις οὐδὲν ἐφρόντιζεν.
     g. ἡ ἐκκλησία ὑπ' οὐδενὸς ἄρχεται, ὁ δὲ δῆμος ποιεῖ ἃ ἐθέλει.
     h. οἱ Ἀχαρνεῖς λίθους ἔλαβον. ἐγὼ δ' ἔφευγον.
     i. ὁ μὲν Ἀμφίθεος ἔδωκε τὰς σπονδάς. Δικαιόπολις δ' ἐδέξατο.
     j. ὁ μὲν κῆρυξ ἐκήρυξεν, ὁ δὲ θεὸς ἐσίγησεν.

(D) ENGLISH INTO GREEK

1. Translate into Greek:

1. The herald was making his announcement while the prytanes came into the assembly.
2. The people were being persuaded to make war by the politicians, while the farmers gazed out into the countryside.
3. The politicians are said to be well-disposed towards the city.
4. The Spartans are destroying our land while we are being deceived by the politicians.
5. The assembly is ruled by no one.

2. Translate into Greek:

Here are the prytanes! Now they have come, you can be sure that the politicians will come forward, wishing to speak. We farmers will keep quiet, looking out into the country, forced against our will to hear the words spoken by them. But they will not tell the truth. They always say that the city is ruled by itself and is beloved of all the politicians. But they are well-disposed only to themselves. The city is being destroyed by them; but no one will move business about that, or about peace. The whole thing is not at all to my liking.

TEST EXERCISE II
Translate into English:

Dikaiopolis defends his action in getting a peace treaty for himself with the Spartans. He gives his own version of the causes of the Peloponnesian War. (From Aristophanes, Akharnians)

ΔΙΚΑΙΟΠΟΛΙΣ   μὴ θορυβεῖτε, ὦνδρες οἱ θεώμενοι, εἰ <u>πτωχὸς</u> ὢν ἥκω
ἐγὼ καὶ ἐν Ἀθηναίοις λέγων ἄρχομαι περὶ τῆς πόλεως,
κωμῳδίαν ποιῶν. τὸ γὰρ δίκαιον οἶδε καὶ <u>κωμῳδία</u>. ἐγὼ
δὲ λέξω δεινὰ μέν, δίκαια δέ. οὐ γάρ με νῦν γε διαβαλεῖ
5   Κλέων ὅτι, ξένων παρόντων, ὑπ' ἐμοῦ κακῶς λέγεται ἡ
πόλις. <u>αὐτοὶ</u> γάρ ἐσμεν, κοὔπω ξένοι πάρεισιν. ἐγὼ δὲ μισῶ
μὲν Λακεδαιμονίους <u>σφόδρα</u>. ἀπόλοιντο αὐτοὶ καὶ οἱ παῖδες
καὶ αἱ γυναῖκες. ὑπ' αὐτῶν γὰρ ἡ <u>ἀμπελία</u> μου κόπτεται,
ἡμεῖς δ' ἐν τῇ πόλει ἐγκλειόμεθα ἄκοντες, τῇ δὲ νόσῳ
10   ἀπολλύμεθα, εἰς δὲ τοὺς ἀγροὺς ἀεὶ ἀποβλέπομεν. <u>ἀτάρ</u>
(ὑμεῖς γὰρ οἱ παρόντες φίλοι), πῶς αἴτιοι Λακεδαιμόνιοι
τούτων τῶν κακῶν; ἡμῶν γὰρ ἄνδρες (οὐχὶ τὴν πόλιν
λέγω, <u>μέμνησθε</u> τοῦθ', ὅτι οὐχὶ τὴν πόλιν λέγω) αἴτιοι,
μάλιστα δὲ Περικλῆς <u>Οὐλύμπιος</u>, ὃς ἐτίθει νόμον ὡς χρὴ
15   Μεγαρέας μήτ' ἐν γῇ μήτ' ἐν ἀγορᾷ, μήτ' ἐν θαλάττῃ μήτ' ἐν
<u>ἠπείρῳ</u> μένειν. τῶν δὲ Μεγαρέων καὶ τῶν Λακεδαιμονίων
δεομένων πολλάκις καὶ αἰτούντων ἡμᾶς <u>ἀφέλεσθαι</u> τὸ
<u>ψήφισμα</u>, οὐκ ἠθέλομεν· οὐ γὰρ ἤρεσκε τῷ Περικλεῖ.
αὕτη ἡ <u>ἀρχὴ</u> τοῦ πολέμου.

Vocabulary

πτωχός, ὁ beggar (2a)
   (*Dikaiopolis has borrowed some rags from Euripides to gain sympathy*)
κωμῳδία, ἡ comedy (1b)
αὐτοί alone, by ourselves
σφόδρα very much
ἀμπελία, ἡ vineyard (1b)
ἀτάρ but
μέμνησθε remember!
Οὐλύμπιος the Olympian
τίθημι pass (of a law)
ἤπειρος, ἡ mainland (2a)
ἀφαιρέομαι (ἀφελ-) withdraw
ψήφισμα, τό decree (3b)
ἀρχή, ἡ cause (1a)

Grammar for Section 12A–D

> In this section you cover:
> - Aorist passive
> - Verbs: ἵστημι, καθίστημι

THE AORIST PASSIVE

228. In the last section, you met the passive forms of the present and imperfect indicative and discovered they were the same as the middle forms (παύομαι, ἐπαυόμην). The aorist middle is ἐπαυσάμην. Regrettably, the same is not true of the aorist passive:

> ἐπαύθην **'I was stopped'**
>
> **Indicative**
>
> ἐ-παύθ-ην   'I was stopped'
> ἐ-παύθ-ης   'you were stopped'
> ἐ-παύθ-η   'he was stopped'
> ἐ-παύθ-ημεν   'we were stopped'
> ἐ-παύθ-ητε   'you were stopped'
> ἐ-παύθ-ησαν   'they were stopped'
>
> **Participle**
>
> παυθ-είς -εῖσα -έν (εντ-)   '[having been] stopped'

Form and meaning

■ *Indicative*

(a) The aorist passive means 'I was -ed', regarded simply as an *event*, not a process (cf. the imperfect passive, which regards the action as a *process* – 'I was being -ed'). See **142** on aspect.

(b) Note the augment ἐ-, to show the finite past tense in the indicative.

(c) The big sign of the aorist passive is the stem/endings in θ-η.

(d) Note that the *regular* form of the aorist passive is θ-η added to the aorist stem without the σ, e.g. ἔλυσα 'I released' ἐλύθην 'I was released'; ἐποίησα 'I made', ἐποιήθην 'I was made', etc.

(e) But though the aorist passive forms are usually easy to recognise (the θ-η gives the clue), they are not always wholly predictable. Thus:

> - ἐκώλυσα–ἐκωλύθην 'I was prevented' is regular; but compare e.g.
> - ἔπαυσα→–ἐπαύθην *or* ἐπαύσθην;

- ἐκέλευσα–ἐκελεύσθην 'I was ordered';
- ἔπεισα–ἐπείσθην 'I was persuaded'.

(f) Note the change of the final consonant of the stem before -θ in (and cf. **359(x)**):

- πέμπ-ω (ἐπέμπ-θην) > ἐπέμφ-θην
- διώκω (ἐδιώκ-θην) > ἐδιώχ-θην
- φυλάττω (uncontr. aor. ἐφυλακ-σα) > ἐφυλάχ-θην

(g) Not all verbs have the θ in the aorist passive, but the augment and -η- will give the clue, e.g. γράφει 'he describes', ἐγράφ-η 'he was described'.

(h) Some verbs adopt the aorist passive *form*, but are active in *meaning*: see **324**.

(i) The aorist pass of δίδωμι is what one would expect, given the aorist stem δο-: ἐ-δόθ-ην.

■ *Participle*

229. The aorist participle passive, '[having been] -ed', declines on the same 3-1-3 pattern as the active present and aorist participles, but on the aorist *passive* stem (παυθ-):

m.	*f.*	*n.*
παυθ-είς	παυθ-εῖσ-α	παυθ-έν
παυθ-έντ-α	παυθ-εῖσ-αν	παυθ-έν
παυθ-έντ-ος	παυθ-είσ-ης	παυθ-έντ-ος
παυθ-έντ-ι	παυθ-είσ-η	παυθ-έντ-ι
παυθ-έντ-ες	παυθ-εῖσ-αι	παυθ-έντ-α
παυθ-έντ-ας	παυθ-είσ-ᾱς	παυθ-έντ-α
παυθ-έντ-ων	παυθ-εισ-ῶν	παυθ-έντ-ων
παυθ-εῖσι(ν)	παυθ-είσ-αις	παυθ-εῖσι(ν)

▶ Remember, therefore, παυθείς παυθεῖσα παυθέν (παυθεντ-).

EXERCISES

12A–D: 1. Convert the following verbs from aorist active to the equivalent aorist passive form, and translate:

1. ἐκώλυσαν
2. ἐπέμψαμεν
3. ἔλυσε
4. ἐπείσατε
5. ἔδωκα
6. ἐφύλαξε
7. ἐδίωξας
8. ἔγραψαν
9. ἐτίμησας
10. ἐποιήσατε

12A–D: 2. Turn the given verbs into the aorist passive participle to agree with the nouns:

1. τοὺς πολεμίους (πείθω)
2. τῷ δούλῳ (λύω)
3. τῶν χρημάτων (δίδωμι)
4. αἱ γυναῖκες (κελεύω)
5. τοῦ ἀνδρός (ἀδικέω)

ANOTHER VERB IN -μι: ἵστημι

230. You have already met ἀνίσταμαι 'I get (myself) up and go' (ἀνά + ἵσταμαι **187**). Here are the details of ἵστημι (middle/passive ἵσταμαι), the verb of which it is a compound:
Remember three things:

(a) the *active* form of ἵστημι means 'I am in the act of setting something up';

(b) the *passive* form ἵσταμαι means 'I am in the act of being set up'.

So far, so normal. Now a complexity looms:

(c) the *middle* form ἵσταμαι is used in two senses:

(i) 'I am in the act of setting *myself* up', i.e. it has a reflexive meaning. This is usually best translated 'I am (in the act of) standing'.

(ii) 'I am in the act of setting something up for myself', i.e. it takes a direct object ('transitive' is the term for a verb taking a direct object).

So when you see e.g. ἵσταται, you must be ready for it to mean:

(Passive) '(s)he/it is being set up';
(Middle and reflexive) '(s)he/it is setting him/her/itself up'; '(s)he/it is (in the act of) standing';
(Middle and transitive) '(s)he/it is setting something up for him/her/itself'.

▶ To put it crudely, if you see any form of ἵστημι with a direct object, translate '(s)he/it is setting up X' and add 'for him/her/itself' if the verb is middle in form.

Here are the principal forms and meanings of ἵστημι, set out by *meaning*:

Active (taking a direct object)

231. The active forms of ἵστημι will always be accompanied by an object in the accusative:

Present active ἵστη-μι **'I am setting X up': stem** ἱστα-

Indicative	Participle	Infinitive	Imperative	Optative
ἵστη-μι	ἱστά-ς	ἱστά-ναι		ἱστα-ίην
ἵστη-ς	ἱστᾶ-σα		ἵστη	ἱστα-ίης
ἵστη-σι(ν)	ἱστά-ν		ἱστά-τω	ἱστα-ίη
ἵστα-μεν	(ἱστα-ντ-)			ἱστα-ῖμεν
ἵστα-τε			ἵστα-τε	ἱστα-ῖτε
ἱστᾶ-σι(ν)			ἱστά-ντων	ἱστα-ῖεν

Imperfect indicative active 'I was setting X up' (augmented with long ῑ)

ῑ̔́στη-ν
ῑ̔́στη-ς
ῑ̔́στη
ῑ̔́στα-μεν
ῑ̔́στα-τε
ῑ̔́στα-σαν

Aorist active ἔ-στησ-α **'I (did) set X up' : stem** στησα- **(exactly like** ἔ-παυσα **in all forms)**

Indicative	Participle	Infinitive	Imperative	Optative
ἔ-στησα-, etc.	στήσᾱ-ς	στῆσα-ι	στῆσ-ον	στήσα-ιμι
	-ᾱσα -αν			
	(στησα-ντ-)			

Future active στήσ-ω **'I will set X up': stem** στησ- **(exactly like** παύσ-ω **in all forms)**

στήσ-ω, etc.

Form and meaning

- These forms are *active*, and take a direct object. The subject, in another words, is setting something up.
- The present stem is ἱστα-, ἱστη-, and that controls the shape of all *present* and *imperfect* forms. If you know δίδωμι (**214**), replace διδο-/διδω- with ἱστα-/ἱστη- (watch out for a few exceptions).
- The future and aorist stem (+α) is στησ-, and gives absolutely regular first aorist (ἔστησα) and future (στήσω) forms.

EXERCISE

12A–D: 3. Create the equivalent forms of ἵστημι from the given forms of δίδωμι, and translate:

1. δίδομεν
2. δίδοναι
3. ἐδίδους
4. διδοῦσα
5. διδοίη

Intransitive middle/passive (taking no direct object)

232. ἵστημι in the middle will not take an object in the accusative when it is intransitive /reflexive and means 'X is setting up himself/standing'. In the passive it will mean 'X is being set up'. The big surprise here is the (second/ root) aorist:

Present middle/passive 'I am setting myself up, standing/being set up': present stem ἱστα-

Indicative	Participle	Infinitive	Imperative	Optative
ἵστα-μαι	ἱστά-μεν-ος	ἵστα-σθαι		ἱστα-ίμην
ἵστα-σαι	-η		ἵστα-σο	ἱστα-ῖο
ἵστα-ται	-ον		ἱστά-σθω	ἱστα-ῖτο
ἱστά-μεθα				ἱστα-ίμεθα
ἵστα-σθε			ἵστα-σθε	ἱστα-ῖσθε
ἵστα-νται			ἱστά-σθων	ἱστα-ῖντο

Imperfect indicative middle/passive

'I was setting myself up, standing/was being set up' (augmented with long ι)

ἱστά-μην
ἵστα-σο
ἵστα-το
ἱστά-μεθα
ἵστα-σθε
ἵστα-ντο

Second/root aorist active ἔστην 'I did set myself up, I stood up': aorist stem στη-/στα

Indicative	Participle	Infinitive	Imperative	Optative
ἔ-στη-ν	στά̄-ς	στῆ-ναι		στα-ίην
ἔ-στη-ς	στᾶ-σα		στῆ-θι	στα-ίης
ἔ-στη	στά-ν		στή-τω	στα-ίη
ἔ-στη-μεν	(στα-ντ-)			στα-ῖμεν
ἔ-στη-τε			στῆ-τε	στα-ῖτε
ἔ-στη-σαν			στά-ντων	στα-ῖεν

> **Aorist passive: stem** σταθ-
>
> ἐ-στάθ-ην 'I was set up'
> (etc., like ἐ-παύ-θην)
>
> **Future indicative: stem** στησ-
>
> 'I shall set myself up/stand up'
> στήσ-ομαι
> (etc., like παύσ-ομαι)

Form and meaning

(a) When these forms are passive or represent the *reflexive* middle, they do *not* take a direct object (they are 'intransitive'). They denote the subject as *setting itself* up/standing (middle) or *being* set up (passive).

(b) The present stem is ἱστα-, ἱστη-, and (again) works like δίδωμι but in the *middle* (see **214**): where διδο-/διδω- occur, observe now ἱστα-/ἱστη-.

(c) The future stem is στησ-, and gives absolutely regular future middle forms, like παύσομαι.

(d) The aorist ἔστην is a root aorist, like ἔβη-ν, ἔγνω-ν (see **209**) and does not conform to the usual pattern. It means 'I stood up'.

(e) The aorist passive ἐστάθην 'I was set up' is wholly regular, like ἐπαύθην.

EXERCISE

12A–D: 4.Create the *passive* forms of ἵστημι from the given active forms, and translate:

    1. ἱστάναι
    2. ἵστασαν
    3. ἱστάντες
    4. ἔστησε
    5. ἵστησι

Transitive middle (taking a direct object)

233. All the middle forms listed above in the present (ἵσταμαι) and imperfect (ἱστάμην) (but NOT the second aorist) can *also* be transitive and mean 'I am setting up x for myself'. The *aorist* forms with this transitive meaning are quite regular, based on the regular first aorist ἔστησα and conjugating like the first aorist middle ἐπαυσάμην:

> **Aorist middle:** ἐστησάμην 'I did set up X for myself'
>
> | Indicative | Participle | Infinitive | Imperative | Optative |
> |---|---|---|---|---|
> | ἐ-στησά-μην | στησάμεν-ος | στήσα-σθαι | | στησα-ίμην |
> | ἐ-στήσω | | | στῆσα-ι | στήσα-ιο |
> | ἐ-στήσα-το | | | στησά-σθω | στήσα-ιτο |
> | ἐ-στησά-μεθα | | | | στησα-ίμεθα |
> | ἐ-στήσα-σθε | | | στήσα-σθε | στήσα-ισθε |
> | ἐ-στήσα-ντο | | | στησά-σθων | στήσα-ιντο |
>
> Cf. the aorist indicative active.

EXERCISE

12A–D: 5. Translate the following forms in all ways possible:

1. ἔστη	6. στῆτε
2. ἵσταντο	7. στήσονται
3. ἱστάμενος	8. ἐστήσατο
4. στῆσον	9. ἔστην
5. ἵσταμεν	10. στῆσαι

Summary form and meaning

> ► With all forms of ἵστημι, look for a *direct object* first of all. If you find one, translate 'set X up'.
>
> ► Since you will tend to meet aorists most frequently in reading, hold on to the vital difference in form and meaning between the aorists:
>
> ἔστησα (στησ-) 'I did set (someone) up' (needing an object)
> ἔστην (στα-, στη-) 'I stood' (no object possible) cf. **378–81**

The compound καθίστημι

234. The most important compound of ἵστημι is καθίστημι. In its active forms (καθίστημι, καθίστην, καταστήσω, κατέστησα) it means 'I put someone in (usually εἰς) a certain position'; in its middle forms (καθίσταμαι, καθῑστάμην, καταστήσομαι, κατέστην), it means 'I find myself/become/get myself/am put into a certain position', or 'I am elected, I am made/become', e.g.

κατέστην εἰς πενίαν 'I was placed/found myself in poverty, I became poor'
κατέστησεν ἡμᾶς εἰς ἀπορίαν 'he placed us in despair, he made us despair, he reduced us to despair'

SUMMARY LEARNING VOCABULARY FOR SECTION 12A-D

ἀγών (ἀγων-), ὁ	contest, trial (3a)
ἀγωνίζομαι	contest, go to law
ἄλλος ... ἄλλον	one ... another
ἀλλότριος ᾱ ον	someone else's, alien
ἀντίδικος, ὁ	contestant in a lawsuit (2a)
ἀρχή, ἡ	beginning, start (1a)
ἀσεβέω εἰς	commit sacrilege upon
ἀσπάζομαι	greet, welcome
ἄτῑμος ον	deprived of citizen rights
ἀφαιρέομαι (ἀφελ-)	take X (acc.) from Y (acc.), claim
διαφέρ-ω	make a difference; differ from (+gen.); be superior to (+gen.)
δικανικός ή όν	judicial
εἰσάγω (εἰσαγαγ-)	introduce
εἴτε ... εἴτε	whether ... or
ἑκάτερος ᾱ ον	each/both (of two)
ἐντυγχάνω (ἐντυχ-)	meet with, come upon (dat.)
ἔσχατος η ον	worst, furthest, last
ἕτερος ... ἕτερον	one ... another (of two)
εὔνοια, ἡ	good will (1b)
εὖ ποιέω	treat well, do good to
ἔχθρᾱ, ἡ	enmity, hostility (1b)
ἐχθρός, ὁ	enemy (2a)
ἐχθρός ᾱ́ όν	hostile, enemy
θυγάτηρ (θυγατ(ε)ρ-), ἡ	daughter (3a)
θωπεύω	flatter
ἱμάτιον, τό	cloak (2b)
καθίστημι (καταστησ-)	set up, make, place, put X (acc.) in (εἰς) Y
καθίσταμαι (καταστα-)	be placed, be put, be made
καὶ γάρ	in fact; yes, certainly
καὶ μήν	what's more; look!
κατά	(+ acc.) according to; down; throughout; in relation to
κατήγορος, ὁ	prosecutor (2a)
μηδέ ... μηδέ	neither ... nor
οἷός τ᾽ εἰμί	be able to (+inf.)
ὅρκος, ὁ	oath (2a)
οὐ μόνον ... ἀλλὰ καί	not only ... but also
παρά	(+acc.) against; to; compared with; except; along, beside
πενίᾱ, ἡ	poverty (1b)

SUMMARY LEARNING VOCABULARY FOR SECTION 12A–D

(continued)

πιστεύω	trust (+dat.)
προσέχω τὸν νοῦν	pay attention to (+ dat.)
πρότερος ᾱ ον	first (of two), previous
πρότερον	(adv.) previously
τῑμάω	fine (+dat.)
τῑμημα (τῑμηματ-), τό	a fine (3b)
τῑμωρέομαι	take revenge on
τῑμωρίᾱ, ἡ	revenge, vengeance (1b)
τοσοῦτος αὕτη οὗτο(ν)	so great
τύχη, ἡ	chance, fortune (good or bad) (1a)
ὑπάρχω	begin (+gen.)
ψευδής ές	false, lying
ψήφισμα (ψηφισματ-), τό	decree (3b)
ὠθέω	push, shove

REVISION EXERCISES FOR SECTION 12A–D

(B/C) MORPHOLOGY AND SYNTAX

1. Translate the passage, choosing the form of the verb which fits the context:

> Ἀπολλόδωρος ἐμὲ ἠδίκησε μεγάλα καὶ (κατέστη/κατέστησεν) ἡμᾶς πάντας εἰς πολλὴν ἀπορίαν. μάρτυρας γὰρ ψευδεῖς (ἀναστὰς/ἀναστήσας) ἐν τῷ δικαστηρίῳ εἷλεν ἐμὲ καὶ τίμημα ᾔτησε μέγα. ἐγὼ οὖν ὀφείλων τὸ τίμημα τῇ πόλει καὶ εἰς ἀτιμίαν (καταστὰς/καταστήσας), ἐκ τῆς πόλεως (ἐξανέστησα/ἐξανέστην). ἔπειτα δέ, ἐκ τῆς πατρίδος (ἀναστὰς/ ἀναστήσας), εἰς Μέγαρα ἀπῆλθον, οὗ εἰς πενίαν (καταστὰς/καταστήσας) ἔμενον δύο ἔτη.

2. Translate each sentence, then change present tense to aorist:

   a. ἡ γὰρ ἐμὴ θυγάτηρ εἰς πενίαν καθίσταται διὰ ταύτην τὴν δίκην.
   b. Ἀθηναῖοι οὖν ἀνίστασιν ἐκ τῆς Αἰγίνης τοὺς Αἰγινήτας.
   c. ὑμεῖς δέ, ὦ ἄνδρες δικασταί, καθίστατε εἰς πολλὴν ἀπορίαν τὰς ἐμὰς θυγατέρας, καταδικάσαντες ἐμοῦ.
   d. ὁ δὲ κατήγορος οὑτοσὶ ἀνίσταται ἐν τῷ δικαστηρίῳ καὶ τὸν φεύγοντα εἰς φόβον καθίστησιν.

3. Translate these aorist passives, then pair with their present forms:

   > ἐκλήθησαν, ἐλήφθη, ἠπορήθην, κατεδικάσθητε, ἐξηλέγχθης (convict), ἐξεδόθημεν (give in marriage), ὑβρίσθη (do violence to), διηλλάχθησαν (be reconciled to), ἐγράφην, ὠργίσθητε (be made angry), ἐλέχθη, ἐβιάσθημεν, κατηγορήθη, ἀπελύθης, ἀπεπέμφθησαν (send away), ἐξηπατήθης, ἐπείσθην

   > πείθω, λέγω, καλέω, λαμβάνω, βιάζομαι, ἐκδίδωμι, ὀργίζομαι, ὑβρίζω, ἐξαπατάω, ἀποπέμπω, ἐξελέγχω, διαλλάττομαι, γράφομαι, κατηγορέω, ἀπορέω, ἀπολύω, καταδικάζω

4. Translate these sentences, then change the aorist passive verbs, with their subjects if necessary, to singular or plural as appropriate:

   a. οἱ μὲν γὰρ δικασταὶ ὑπὸ τῆς ἀπολογίας οὐκ ἐπείσθησαν, ἐγὼ δὲ κατεδικάσθην.
   b. ἀλλὰ μὴν οὐ διαφέρει μοι εἰ μὴ ἀπελύθης, ἀλλὰ κατεδικάσθης.
   c. καὶ γὰρ οὗτος ὁ λόγος ἐλέχθη ὑπὸ τοῦ ἀντιδίκου.
   d. ὑμεῖς δὲ ἠδικήθητε ὑπὸ τούτου μεγάλα.

5. Translate these sentences, filling in the correct form of the *aorist passive participle*:

   a. ἐγὼ εὔνοιαν ἔχω εἰς τὸν ἄνδρα τὸν ὑπὸ Στεφάνου ἀδικηθ– .
   b. ἡμεῖς δὲ πεισθ– ὑπὸ τοῦ ἀντιδίκου δίκην ἐλάβομεν.

   c. τῆς δὲ γυναικὸς ἐξαπατηθ– ὑπὸ τοῦ ἀτίμου κατεφρόνησεν ὁ ἀνήρ.

   d. βιασθ– δ' ἐμοῦ εἰσάγειν τὸ παιδίον εἰς τοὺς φράτερας, ἡ θυγάτηρ εἰς ἔχθραν κατέστη.

   e. ἐμοὶ δὲ ἀτίμῳ ὄντι καὶ ἀπορηθ– οἱ φίλοι ἐβοήθησαν.

   f. τοῖς δὲ γεροῦσι τοῖς ὑπὸ Κλέωνος ἐξαπατηθ- πολλὰς δραχμὰς ἔδομεν.

(D) ENGLISH INTO GREEK

Translate into Greek:

1. Apollodoros was grievously wronged by Stephanos and Neaira.
2. A big fine was asked for by Stephanos.
3. Apollodoros faced the prospect of getting into terrible trouble.
4. Stephanos put Apollodoros in great danger.
5. Apollodoros was persuaded to take vengeance against Stephanos.

Grammar for Section 12E

> In this section you cover:
> ● Infinitives in indirect/reported speech

INDIRECT SPEECH USING THE INFINITIVE

235. You have already met indirect, or reported, speech, using the ὅτι 'that' construction: λέγω ὅτι σὺ μῶρος εἶ 'I say that you are stupid'. We now examine reported speech constructions using not ὅτι 'that' but the *infinitive*.

We have already already met constructions using the infinitive, so the principle is not a new one e.g.

βούλομαι ἰέναι 'I want to go' (**153**);
or, using an accusative and infinitive,
βούλομαί σε ἰέναι 'I want you to go'

(Compare e.g. δεῖ με ἰέναι 'It is necessary for me to go' **153**).
Note the *change of subject*:

> ● In the first sentence, it is the subject of the main verb βούλομαι ('I') who wishes to do the going;
> ● In the second, the subject 'I' wishes *someone else* – σε – to go, and σε appears in the *accusative*.

Here, then, is a list of verbs that introduce indirect/reported speech (which includes anything said, thought, felt etc. but not directly quoted), using the *infinitive* construction (*not* ὅτι):

οἴομαι	'I think …' (but not necessarily very strongly)
φημί	'I say …'
νομίζω	'I consider …'
ἡγοῦμαι	'I think …' (of a firmly held opinion)
φάσκω	'I allege, claim …'

The infinitive construction

Look closely at the following sentences and their *literal* translation:

a. νομίζω σε μῶρον οὐκ εἶναι 'I consider you not to be foolish'
b. ἔφη Νέαιραν καταφρονεῖν τῶν θεῶν 'he said Neaira to despise the gods'
c. ᾤοντο τὸν ἄνδρα τὴν γυναῖκα οὐ πείσειν 'they thought the man not to be about to persuade the woman'

d.   ἡγοῦμαι σοφὸς εἶναι 'I think wise [note nom.] to be' = 'I think [myself] to be wise'

e.   φάσκομεν ἐλθεῖν εἰς τὴν οἰκίαν 'we claim to have gone into the house' = 'we claim [that we] have gone/went into the house'

■ *Comment*

a.   Should be translated in good English 'I consider that you are not foolish'. Note that:

   (i)   'I' is the subject of the main verb 'consider'
   (ii)   'you' is the subject of the verb in the 'that' clause, in the accusative
   (iii) the negative is οὐ
   (iv) there is no Greek word for 'that'.

b.   Should be translated 'He said that Neaira despised the gods'. Note that:

   (i)   'He' is the subject of the main verb 'said'
   (ii)   'Neaira' is the subject of the verb in the 'that' clause, in the accusative
   (iii) καταφρονεῖν is present infinitive, indicating that the man actually said 'Neaira despises (present) the gods'
   (iv) there is no Greek word for 'that'

c.   Should be translated 'They thought that the man would not persuade the woman'. Note that:

   (i)   'They' is the subject of the main verb 'thought'
   (ii)   'the man' is the subject of the verb in the 'that' clause, in the accusative, and 'the woman' is the object of 'would persuade', also in the accusative. This means that the sentence *could* mean 'they thought that the woman would persuade the man'. Only the context will tell you which is right.
   (iii) the negative with πείσειν is οὐ.
   (iv) πείσειν is future infinitive, indicating that they actually said 'The man will not persuade (future) the woman/the woman will not persuade the man'.
   (v)   there is no Greek word for 'that'.

d.   Should be translated 'I think that I am wise'. Note that:

   (i)   'I' is the subject of both the main verb *and* of the 'that' clause
   (ii)   No word for 'I' appears in the 'that' clause in Greek
   (iii) σοφός is in the *nominative*, not the accusative. This indicates that it refers to the subject of the main verb, 'I'.
   (iv) there is no Greek word for 'that'.

e.   Should be translated 'We claim that we went into the house'. Note that:

   (i)   'We' is the subject of both the main verb *and* of the 'that' clause

(ii) No word in the nominative or accusative appears in the 'that' clause in Greek. This indicates that the subject of the 'that' clause is the same as the subject of the main verb, 'we'.

(iii) ἐλθεῖν is aorist infinitive, indicating that we actually said 'we went into the house'

(iv) there is no Greek word for 'that'.

■ *Rules*

236. From the above, you can deduce the following rules:

- The tense of the infinitive tells you what was actually said. In other words, the tense of verb in the original utterance is duplicated in the infinitive;
- If the subject of the 'that' clause is the same as that of the main verb, it will normally not appear; but if the speaker wants to emphasise it, it will appear as a *nominative*;
- If the subject of the 'that' clause is different from that of the main verb, it will appear in the accusative;
- If there are two accusatives in the 'that' clause, only the context will tell you which is the subject, which the object, of the verb in the infinitive.
- In general, it is best to translate literally to start with, however awkward, and then re-translate into ordinary English.
- The negative is οὐ or μή, depending on what was *originally* said.

There is a general set of rules here:

- ▶ In infinitive constructions, a change of subject goes into the accusative;
- ▶ If there is no change of subject, normally the subject is not repeated;
- ▶ But if it is repeated, it goes into the nominative.
- ▶ With infinitive constructions, therefore, *watch for the change of subject in the accusative*. See **397**.

EXERCISE

12E: 1. Translate literally, and then turn into correct English:

1. ἔφην ἀφίξεσθαι.
2. ἔφην ἐκεῖνον ἀφίξεσθαι.
3. ἡγεῖτο σοφὸς εἶναι αὐτός.
4. ἡγεῖτο σοφὸν εἶναι αὐτόν.
5. οἰόμεθα οὐ δύνασθαι ἰδεῖν.
6. ἐνόμισαν Στέφανον τὴν γυναῖκα οὐκ ἐξαπατῆσαι.

In each of the above, what was *originally* said in English?

REVISION EXERCISES FOR SECTION 12E

(B/C) MORPHOLOGY AND SYNTAX

1. Translate each statement, then, using the verbs given, turn them into indirect statements. How is the translation altered if you use the past form of the verb?

   1. ὁ κατήγορος σπουδαιότατός ἐστιν ἀνθρώπων. (φημί/ἔφην)
   2. ἐγὼ εἰς μέγαν κίνδυνον κατέστην. (φησί/ἔφη)
   3. ἀεὶ λέγουσί τι δεινὸν οἱ ἀντίδικοι. (ἡγοῦμαι/ἡγούμην)
   4. ὁ Στέφανος εἰσήγαγεν εἰς τοὺς φράτερας τοὺς ἀλλοτρίους παῖδας. (φασί/ἔφασαν)
   5. ἡ Νέαιρα οὐκ αἰσχύνεται καταφρονοῦσα τῶν νόμων. (τίς οὐκ ἂν οἴοιτο;/ τίς οὐκ οἴεται;)
   6. ἐβουλόμεθα τότε τιμωρεῖσθαι τοὺς ἐχθρούς. (φαμέν/ἔφαμεν)

Grammar for Section 12F

In this section you cover:
- τίθημι 'I place, put' δείκνυμι 'I show, reveal'

THE -μι VERB τίθημι

237. τίθημι 'I place, put' follows exactly the same pattern as the other -μι verbs you have already met (δίδωμι **214** and ἵστημι **230–3**). Here are the forms in full (cf. **377**):

τίθημι **'I put, place'**

Present: stem τιθε-

Active

Indicative	Participle	Infinitive	Imperative	Optative
τίθη-μι	τιθείς	τιθέ-ναι		τιθε-ίην
τίθη-ς	τιθεῖσα		τίθει	τιθε-ίης
τίθη-σι(ν)	τιθέ-ν		τιθέ-τω	τιθε-ίη
τίθε-μεν	(τιθε-ντ-)			τιθε-ῖμεν
τίθε-τε			τίθε-τε	τιθε-ῖτε
τιθέ-ασι(ν)			τιθέ-ντων	τιθε-ῖεν

Middle/passive

Indicative	Participle	Infinitive	Imperative	Optative
τίθε-μαι	τιθέ-μεν-ος	τίθε-σθαι		τιθε-ίμην
τίθε-σαι	-η		τίθε-σο	τιθε-ῖο
τίθε-ται	-ον		τιθέ-σθω	τιθε-ῖτο
τιθέ-μεθα				τιθε-ίμεθα
τίθε-σθε			τίθε-σθε	τιθε-ῖσθε
τίθε-νται			τιθέ-σθων	τιθε-ῖντο

ἐτίθην **'I was placing': stem** τιθε-

Imperfect indicative active

ἐ-τίθη-ν
ἐ-τίθη-ς (ἐ-τίθει-ς)
ἐ-τίθ-η (ἐ-τίθει)
ἐ-τίθε-μεν
ἐ-τίθε-τε
ἐ-τίθε-σαν

Imperfect indicative middle/passive

ἐ-τιθέ-μην
ἐ-τίθε-σο
ἐ-τίθε-το
ἐ-τιθέ-μεθα
ἐ-τίθε-σθε
ἐ-τίθε-ντο

ἔθηκα 'I put, placed'

Aorist: stem θε-

Active

Indicative	Participle	Infinitive	Imperative	Optative
ἔ-θη-κα	θείς	θε-ῖναι		θε-ίην
ἔ-θη-κας	θεῖσα		θέ-ς	θε-ίης
ἔ-θη-κε (ν)	θέ-ν		θέ-τω	θε-ίη
ἔ-θε-μεν	(θέ-ντ-)			θε-ῖμεν
ἔ-θε-τε			θέ-τε	θε-ῖτε
ἔ-θε-σαν			θέ-ντων	θε-ῖεν
(ἔ-θη-καν)				

Middle

Indicative	Participle	Infinitive	Imperative	Optative
ἐ-θέ-μην	θέ-μεν-ος	θέ-σθαι		θε-ίμην
ἔ-θου	-η		θοῦ	θε-ῖο
ἔ-θε-το	-ον		θέ-σθω	θε-ῖτο
ἐ-θέ-μεθα				θε-ίμεθα
ἔ-θε-σθε			θέ-σθε	θε-ῖσθε
ἔ-θε-ντο			θέ-σθων	θε-ῖντο

Passive: stem τεθ-

Indicative	Participle	Infinitive	Imperative	Optative
ἐ-τέθ-ην	τεθ-είς	τεθ-ῆναι		τεθ-είην
ἐ-τέθ-ης	τεθ-εῖσα		τέθ-ητι	τεθ-είης
ἐ-τέθ-η	τεθ-έν		τεθ-ήτω	τεθ-είη
ἐ-τέθ-ημεν	(τεθ-εντ-)			τεθ-εῖμεν
ἐ-τέθ-ητε			τέθ-ητε	τεθ-εῖτε
ἐ-τέθ-ησαν			τεθ-έντων	τεθ-εῖεν

(The aorist passive regular, like ἐ-παύθ-ην)

Future active and middle: stem θήσ-

θή-σω, θή-σομαι (etc., all regular like παύσ-ω, παύσ-ομαι)

■ *Forms*

238. You can see that τίθημι 'I place, put' follows exactly the same pattern as δίδωμι 'I give' :

▶ For διδο-, δο- write τιθε-, θε- (but τε- in aorist passive)
▶ For διδω-, δω- write τιθη- θη-
▶ διδου-, δου- corresponds to τιθει- θει- (but note the impf. ἐτίθην)

The two can be instantly compared as follows:

		Indicative	Participle	Infinitive	Imperative	Optative
Present	⎧	τίθη-μι	τιθείς	τιθέ-ναι	τίθει	τιθε-ίην
(stem τιθε/	⎩	δίδω-μι	διδούς	διδό-ναι	δίδου	διδο-ίην
η-, διδο/ω-)	⎧	τίθε-μαι	τιθέ-μενος	τίθε-σθαι	τίθε-σο	τιθε-ίμην
	⎩	δίδο-μαι	διδό-μενος	δίδο-σθαι	δίδο-σο	διδο-ίμην
Imperfect	⎧	ἐ-τίθη-ν				
	⎩	ἐ-δίδουν				
	⎧	ἐ-τιθέ-μην				
	⎩	ἐ-διδό-μην				
Aorist	⎧	ἔ-θη-κα	θείς	θεῖναι	θέ-ς	θε-ίην
(stem θε-,	⎩	ἔ-δω-κα	δούς	δοῦναι	δό-ς	δο-ίην
δο-):	⎧	ἐ-θέ-μην	θέ-μενος	θέ-σθαι	θοῦ	θε-ίμην
	⎩	ἐ-δό-μην	δό-μενος	δό-σθαι	δοῦ	δο-ίμην
Future	⎧	θή-σω *(regular)*				
(stem θη-,	⎩	δώ-σω				
δω-):	⎧	θή-σομαι				
	⎩	δώ-σομαι				

■ *Meaning*

Note that κεῖμαι 'I lie' can also mean 'be placed, be made' and as such is often used as the *perfect passive* of τίθημι (see **313**).

EXERCISE

12F: 1. Translate the following forms of δίδωμι and τίθημι and then turn them into the equivalent forms of τίθημι and δίδωμι and translate, e.g. ἔδωκα 'I gave', ἔθηκα 'I placed':

1. δίδωσι	6. ἔθηκε
2. ἐτίθετε	7. δόντες
3. ἔδομεν	8. θές
4. ἐτέθη	9. διδόναι
5. δοῦναι	10. θήσετε

THE -μι VERB δείκνυ-μι

239. There are some verbs ending in -νῡ-μι, e.g. δείκ-νῡ-μι 'I show'.

- They mostly follow the δίδω-μι/τίθη-μι pattern in the present and imperfect;
- But note that the optative is formed like παύω, i.e. παύοιμι = δεικνύοιμι; contrast διδο-ίην (**214**)
- They tend to have fut. and aor. stems in -ξ-, and in these forms conjugate exactly like παύω (i.e. fut. δείξω, aor. ἔδειξα, aor. pass. ἐδείχθην) (see **383**):

δείκνῡμι **'I show, reveal'**

Present: stem δεικνυ-

Active

Indicative	Participle	Infinitive	Imperative	Optative
δείκνῡ-μι	δεικνΰ-ς -ῦσα -ύν	δεικνύ-ναι		δεικνύ-οιμι
δείκνῡ-ς	(δεικνυντ-)		δείκνυ	(like παύ-οιμι)
δείκνῡ-σι(ν)			δεικνύ-τω	
δείκνυ-μεν				
δείκνυ-τε			δείκνυ-τε	
δείκνυ-(ᾱ)σιν			δεικνύ-ντων	

Middle/passive

Indicative	Participle	Infinitive	Imperative	Optative
δείκνυ-μαι	δεικνύ-μενος	δείκνυ-σθαι		δεικνυ-οίμην
δείκνυ-σαι	-η -ον		δείκνυ-σο	(like παυ-οίμην
δείκνυ-ται			δεικνύ-σθω	
δεικνύ-μεθα				
δείκνυ-σθε			δείκνυ-σθε	
δείκνυ-νται			δεικνύ-σθων	

ἔδεικνῡν 'I was showing': stem δεικνυ-

Imperfect indicative active

ἐδείκνῡ-ν
ἐδείκνῡ-ς
ἐδείκνῡ
ἐδείκνυ-μεν
ἐδείκνυ-τε
ἐδείκνυ-σαν

Imperfect indicative middle/passive

ἐδεικνύ-μην
ἐδείκνυ-σο
ἐδείκνυ-το
ἐδεικνύ-μεθα
ἐδείκνυ-σθε
ἐδείκνυ-ντο

Aorist active and middle: stem δειξα-

ἔδειξα, ἐδειξά-μην (like ἔπαυσα, ἐπαυσά-μην in all forms)

Aorist passive: stem δείχθ-

ἐδείχθ-ην (like ἐπαύθ-ην in all forms)

Future active and middle: stem δείξ-

δείξ-ω, δείξ-ομαι (like παύσ-ω, παύσ-ομαι in all forms)

EXERCISES

12F: 2. Translate the following forms of τίθημι and δείκνυμι, then turn them into the equivalent forms of the other verb and translate:

1. τίθετε
2. δείξομεν
3. ἔθεσαν
4. ἐδείκνυ
5. τιθεῖσαι

12F: 3. Identify the forms which are passive, and translate:

ἐδείχθημεν, ἐθέμην, ἐτέθησαν, ἐδεικνυμεθα, ἔθεσθε, δειχθέντες, τίθεμεν

REVISION EXERCISES FOR SECTION 12F

(B/C) MORPHOLOGY AND SYNTAX

1. Translate the following sentences, then change the tense or aspect of the verbs as indicated:

   a. ὑπὲρ δὲ τῆς Μετανείρας ὁ σοφιστὴς πολλὰς δραχμὰς τίθησιν (aor.).

   b. τιθέντος (aor.) δὲ τοῦ σοφιστοῦ τὰ χρήματα ὑπὲρ Μετανείρας, ἡ Νικαρέτη οὐκ ἐδίδου (pres.) αὐτῇ οὐδέν, ἀλλὰ καθίστη (aor.) εἰς ἀπορίαν τὴν παῖδα.

   c. ἔπειτα δέ, τῆς παιδὸς εἰς ἀπορίαν καταστάσης (pres.), ἔδοξε τῷ σοφιστῇ τιθέναι (aor.) πολλὰς δραχμὰς εἰς τὰ μυστήρια.

   d. 'ἐγὼ δέ', ἔφη, 'οὕτω ποιῶν τὰ χρήματα ταῦτα ὑπὲρ Μετανείρας θήσω (aor.) αὐτῆς.'

   e. ἐλθὼν δ' Ἀθήναζε ὁ Λυσίας καὶ πολλὰς δραχμὰς θείς (pres.), καθίστησι (aor.) τὴν Νικαρέτην καὶ Μετάνειραν ὡς Φιλόστρατον.

(D) ENGLISH INTO GREEK

Translate into Greek:

1. Stephanos will say that Apollodoros began their enmity.
2. Apollodoros said that he wanted to avenge himself on Stephanos.
3. Apollodoros will say that he did not wrong Stephanos.
4. Many men put down a lot of money on Neaira's account.
5. Apollodoros says that Stephanos is living with a slave as his wife.

Grammar for Section 12G

> In this section you cover:
> - 'Would-should' conditions: future 'remote' and present 'contrary to fact'
> - Wishes: 'Would that/O that …'
> - ὅπως + future indicative 'see to it that'
> - Optative forms of εἰμί 'I am', εἶμι 'I shall go', οἶδα 'I know'

CONDITIONAL SENTENCES (WITH ἄν)

240. So far, you have met ἄν + optative in the 'potential/polite' sense 'would you …', 'would you like to …', 'please …', expressing a polite request or agreement, e.g. δοίης ἄν μοι ταῦτα 'Please would you give me this' (cf. **186, 401**).

But in some 'conditional clauses', ἄν + optative is used in a related, but slightly different sense. By way of example, such clauses are introduced by the word 'if', and take a number of forms, e.g. 'If X were the case, Y would be the case.'

Technical terms

> - The Greek for 'if' is εἰ; the 'if' clause is technically called the 'protasis' (Greek πρότασις 'proposition, premiss')
> - The main clause is called the 'apodosis' (Greek ἀπόδοσις 'pay-off')

e.g. 'If you do not hand over the money (protasis), the dog gets it' (apodosis)

Future 'remote' conditions

241. The 'future remote' conditional usage takes the following form in English:

> - 'If x *were to happen*, Y *would result*.'

'Future remote' is a good term: the future, after all, is hypothetical enough, but in these conditions, even more so.

Examine the following sentences:

a. εἴ με πείθοις/πείσειας, λέγοιμι ἄν/εἴποιμι ἄν σοι.
   'If you were to persuade me, I would tell you'.
b. εἰ φεύγοιεν/φύγοιεν, διώκοιμεν ἄν/διώξαιμεν ἄν.
   'If they were to flee, we would pursue'.

You will notice a number of vital features of this 'potential > conditional' construction:

- the verbs in both the 'if' clause (protasis) and the main clause (apodosis) are in the *optative*;
- the optatives can be either *present or aorist*. We are used to this: the difference, as usual, is one of aspect, not time (see **142**, **165**), and will affect the translation very little;
- ἄν appears in the *main clause* (but NOT in the 'if' clause).

Present 'contrary to fact' conditions

242. Now examine these sentences, in the present 'contrary to fact' form:

- 'If X were [now] happening, Y would [now] be resulting'

a. εἴ με ἔπειθες, ἔλεγον ἄν.
    'If you were [now] persuading me, I would [now] be telling'.
b. εἰ ἔφευγον, ἐδιώκομεν ἄν.
    'If they were [now] fleeing, we would [now] be pursuing'.

You will see at once that:

- the verbs in both the protasis and the apodosis are IMPERFECT INDICATIVE;
- The meaning has changed to the PRESENT time: 'If x *were the case NOW, Y would NOW be resulting*';
- ἄν appears in the *main clause* (but NOT in the 'if' clause);
- 'contrary to fact' is again an accurate description, since the subject is obviously *not* doing what is being merely put forward as a hypothetical possibility.

■ Negatives

243. Look closely at the negatives in this sentence:

εἰ μὴ ἔφευγον, οὐκ ἄν ἐδιώκομεν.

'If they were not [now] fleeing, we would not [now] be pursuing'.

- ▶ In other words, the negative in the 'if' clause is μή, in the main clause οὐ. This applies across *all* conditional clauses.

This can be very helpful if the protasis is not expressed by an εἰ clause, but some other way. Take, for example, the following sentence:

πῶς ἄν τιθεῖτό τις τὴν ψῆφον, μὴ μνημονεύσας τοὺς λόγους;

'How would one vote, not remembering the speeches?'

The μή in the participial phrase strongly suggests the phrase is the equivalent of a conditional clause, i.e. '*if* one were not to remember the speeches'.

- Watch out for μή with this 'conditional' force where one might otherwise expect οὐ. See further **393(vi)** and **430**.

EXERCISE

12G: 1. Convert these conditionals into 'future remote' or 'present contrary to fact' conditionals, in accordance with the tense of the verbs:

1. εἰ μὴ ἀκούσει, οὐ μενῶ.
2. εἰ ὑμεῖς κελεύετε, πείθομαι ἐγώ.
3. εἰ μὴ φιλήσει, φιλήσω ἐγώ.
4. εἰ μὴ τρέχομεν, οὐ φεύγομεν.
5. εἰ μὴ ζητήσεις, οὐχ εὑρήσεις.

WISHES 'IF ONLY...!'

Wishes for the future

244. You have already met ἀπολοίμην 'may I be killed', expressing a wish for the future (cf. **213**). The plain optative *is* found in this sense, but such wishes are usually expressed by:

- εἴθε or εἰ γάρ + optative, e.g.

εἰ γάρ/εἴθε γενοίμην/γιγνοίμην σοφώτερος

'Would that I were to become wiser!' 'O that/If only I could become wiser!' Be aware that:

- the tense of the optative is aspectual, not temporal
- the negative is μή
- ἄν is NOT used in wishes

Wishes for the present and past

Wishes for the *present* are expressed by:

- εἰ γάρ/εἴθε + imperfect indicative, e.g.

εἰ γὰρ σοφὸς ἦ 'Would that I were [now] wise!'

Wishes for the *past* are expressed by:

- εἰ γάρ/εἴθε + aorist indicative, e.g.

εἴθε ἀπῆλθον 'Would that I had departed!'

or

- ὤφελον ('I ought to have') + infinitive

Put ὤφελον in the appropriate person e.g. ὠφέλομεν ἐλθεῖν lit. 'We ought to have gone!' = 'Would that we had gone!'
εἰ γάρ/εἴθε can be added to the above, if so desired, i.e. the same sentiment could have been expressed εἰ γάρ/εἴθε ὠφέλομεν ἐλθεῖν (ὤφελον is the past of ὀφείλω, 'I owe').

■ *Form*

▶ You will notice how these wishes conform to the pattern of conditionals: future wishes in the optative and present in the imperfect indicative. You will also have observed that wishes for the past take the *aorist indicative*: a useful preparation for what is to come in 'would-should' conditions that refer to the past. See further **403**.

EXERCISE

12G: 2. Express these sentiments as wishes:

1. ἐκφεύγομεν
2. ἔδωκε
3. ἔστη
4. τιθέασι(ν)
5. ἀποθνήσκω

ὅπως + FUTURE INDICATIVE 'SEE TO IT THAT. . .'

245. Serious warnings/exhortations in Greek are issued by ὅπως:

- ὅπως σώφρων ἔσει 'See to it/Mind that you are sensible'
- ὅπως μὴ παύσῃ 'See to it/Mind that you do not stop'

Nothing difficult here: ὅπως in such constructions is followed by a *future indicative* (negative μή).
This construction is also used with verbs expressing effort, where ὅπως reverts to its more normal meaning 'how' and is best translated 'to, that, so that', e.g.

οἱ μαθηταὶ πράττουσιν ὅπως μαθήσονται τὴν Ἑλληνικήν 'The students are taking action to learn Greek' (lit. '... how they will learn').

OPTATIVES OF εἰμί **'I AM',** οἶδα **'I KNOW',** εἶμι **'I SHALL GO'**

246. See to it that you do not forget the following optatives:

εἴην ('I would be')	εἰδείην ('I would know')	ἴοιμι ('I would go')
εἴην	εἰδείην	ἴοιμι
εἴης	εἰδείης	ἴοις
εἴη	εἰδείη	ἴοι
εἶμεν	εἰδεῖμεν	ἴοιμεν
εἶτε	εἰδεῖτε	ἴοιτε
εἶεν	εἰδεῖεν	ἴοιεν

EXERCISE

12G: 3. Translate these commands into the ὅπως construction, and translate:

     1. μὴ ἴθι
     2. ἀκούετε
     3. κόλασον
     4. μὴ γίγνου
     5. ἴσθι

12G: 4. Using εἰμι, εἶμι and οἶδα as your 'pool', convert the forms given into the identical forms of the other two:

     1. εἴης
     2. εἰδεῖεν
     3. ἴοιμεν
     4. εἴη
     5. ἴοιμι

SUMMARY LEARNING VOCABULARY FOR SECTION 12E–G

Ἀθήνᾱζε	to Athens
αἰσχῡ́νομαι	be ashamed, feel shame
ἄν	(use of, in conditionals, see Grammar **240–2**)
ἄρχω	begin (+gen.); rule (+gen.)
ἀστή, ἡ	female citizen (1a)
ἀστός, ὁ	male citizen (2a)
ἀτῑμίᾱ, ἡ	loss of citizen rights (1b)
εἴθε	(+ opt.) I wish that! would that!

SUMMARY LEARNING VOCABULARY FOR SECTION 12E–G

(continued)

εἰκός	likely, probable, reasonable, fair
ἐπιλανθάνομαι (ἐπιλαθ-)	forget (+gen.)
ἑταίρᾱ, ἡ	whore, prostitute (1b)
ἑταῖρος, ὁ	(male) companion (2a)
καταλέγω (κατειπ-)	recite, list
καταφρονέω	despise, look down on (+gen.)
μαρτυρίᾱ, ἡ	evidence, witness (1b)
μνείᾱ, ἡ	mention (1b)
μνημονεύω	remember
ὅπως	(+fut. ind.) see to it that
παιδοποιέομαι	have children
πένης (πενητ-), ὁ	poor man (3a) (or adj., poor)
πλούσιος ᾱ ον	rich, wealthy
(σ)μῑκρός ᾱ́ όν	small, short, little
σπουδάζω	be concerned, serious; do seriously
σπουδαῖος ᾱ ον	important, serious
συγγίγνομαι (συγγεν-)	be with, have intercourse with (+ dat.)
συνέρχομαι (συνελθ-)	come together
τεκμήριον, τό	evidence, proof (2b)
τίθημι (θε-)	put, place, make
φανερός ᾱ́ όν	clear, obvious
ὡς	(+ acc.) towards, to the house of

REVISION EXERCISES FOR SECTION 12G

(B/C) MORPHOLOGY AND SYNTAX

1. Translate the following statements; then change them into wishes for the future (vary your construction and aspect of the verb). Remember that the negative is μή.

   a. βούλομαι δικαστὴς καθίστασθαι καὶ τίθεσθαι τὴν ψῆφον.
   b. ἐθέλεις σοφιστὴς γενέσθαι.
   c. βούλομαι σὲ εἰς ἐμὲ χρήματα θεῖναι.
   d. οὐκ ἐθέλω ἀπολέσθαι.
   e. οὐ βούλομαι ὑμᾶς εἰδέναι ταῦτα.
   f. ἐθέλει σοφιστὴν ποιεῖν τὸν παῖδα.
   g. βούλομαι αὐτὸν μνημονεῦσαι τὴν μαρτυρίαν.
   h. ἐθέλω αὐτοὺς ἐπιλαθέσθαι τούτων τῶν λόγων.
   i. βούλεσθε πλούσιοι εἶναι.
   j. οὐκ ἐθέλω τοὺς οἰκείους εἶναι πλουσίους.

2. Translate each pair of statements (omitting εἰ), then link them by making them future remote conditions AND present 'contrary to fact' conditions (see **240–2**).

   a. (εἰ) τιμῶ τίμημα μέγα/δίκην λαμβάνει ὁ ἀντίδικος.
   b. (εἰ) οἱ δικασταὶ πείθονται ὑπὸ τοῦ κατηγόρου/τοῦ φεύγοντος καταδικάζουσιν.
   c. (εἰ) ὑπάρχετε τῆς ἔχθρας/τὰ τεκμήριά ἐστι φανερά.
   d. (εἰ) μνείαν ποιεῖς τῶν ἀστῶν/οὐκ ἐπιλανθάνεται ὁ κατήγορος.
   e. (εἰ) οἱ ἀστοὶ ἐξ ἑταιρῶν παιδοποιοῦνται/ἴσμεν σαφῶς.
   f. (εἰ μὴ) οἱ πλούσιοι ταῖς ἑταίραις συγγίγνονται/τοὺς πένητας ἀσπάζονται ἐκεῖναι.

3. Translate these commands. Turn each into a warning/exhortation using ὅπως or ὅπως μή + fut. ind.

   a. πρόσεχε τὸν νοῦν καὶ ἄκουε.
   b. μὴ θωπεύετε τοὺς δικαστάς.
   c. μὴ ἐπιλανθάνου τῶν λόγων.
   d. κάτειπε τὸν τοῦ δράματος λόγον.
   e. μνημόνευε τοὺς λόγους.
   f. μὴ παιδοποιεῖσθε ἐκ τῶν ἑταιρῶν.
   g. εὖ τίθει τὸ πρᾶγμα.
   h. μὴ καταφρόνει τοῦ ἑταίρου.

Grammar for Section 12H–I

> In this section you cover:
> - Participial constructions in reported speech
> - The future passive

THE PARTICIPLE IN INDIRECT/REPORTED SPEECH

247. You have already met verbs which take an infinitive construction in reported speech (see **235**). Some verbs, however – verbs of knowing, perceiving, recognising – prefer a *participle* to express their 'that' clauses, e.g.

οἶδα	'I know that …'
πυνθάνομαι	'I learn by inquiry/hear that …'
μανθάνω	'I learn that …'
γιγνώσκω	'I recognise that …'

Examine the following sentences:

a. οἶδα σοφὸς ὤν   'I know being wise (nom., present participle)'

b. οἶδα σε μῶρον οὐκ ὄντα   'I know you not being foolish' (present participle)

c. ἐμάθομεν φεύγοντας αὐτούς   'We learnt them fleeing' (present participle)

d. ἐπύθοντο ἡμᾶς ἐλθόντας   'They heard us having gone' (aorist participle)

Precisely the same principles apply to these clauses as to those already described in **235**:

> - If the 'that' clause has a subject *different* from the main verb, the subject and its participle will go into the *accusative*;
> - If subjects are the same, there will be no accusative and the participle will go into the *nominative*;
> - No Greek word for 'that' appears.

Observe one point of interest: the meaning of the tense of the participle. Participles in general have an aspectual sense ('process' or 'event') rather than temporal. But in this construction, the temporal sense comes to the fore:

> ▶ In other words, in this construction the tense of the participle will point to the *tense of what was originally known/recognised/perceived.*

So:

γιγνώσκει τὸν ἄνδρα οὐ παυσάμενον/παυόμενον/παυσόμενον

'He recognises the man not having stopped' ('that the man did not stop')/ 'the man not stopping' ('that the man is not stopping')/ 'the man not being about to stop' ('that the man will not stop').

- Note that the negative is that of the *original* direct usage. See further **397**.

EXERCISES

12H–I: 1. Translate sentences a–d above into the normal English form. Remember 'that', and pay attention to the tense of the participle.

12H–I: 2. Translate the following sentences and explain the nature of the reported speech construction, whether ὅτι, nom. or acc., inf. or part.:

1. λέγομεν ὅτι οἱ ῥήτορες τὰ ἀληθῆ οὐκ ἀγορεύουσιν.
2. ἔφη παρέσεσθαι.
3. ἐπύθετο τοὺς πολεμίους φυγόντας.
4. ἤλπισαν ταχέως ἀφίξεσθαι.
5. ᾔδει αὐτὰς πεισαμένας.

THE FUTURE PASSIVE, 'I SHALL BE -ED'

248. We have met the future active and middle ('I shall – '), all based on the future stem (παύσ-ω, παύσ-ομαι). The forms of the future passive, however, are based on a different stem:

παυθήσομαι **'I shall be stopped'**

παυθή-σ-ομαι
παυθή-σ-ῃ (-ει)
παυθή-σ-εται
παυθη-σ-όμεθα
παυθή-σ-εσθε
παυθή-σ-ονται

Infinitive

παυθή σ εσθαι ('to be about to be stopped')

■ *Form*

▶ The -θη- gives the game away: somewhat surprisingly, the forms of the future passive are based on the *AORIST PASSIVE* (see **228**).

- Take the aorist passive *stem* (remember to remove the augment); and
- Add σ-ομαι, σ-ει, σ-εται etc. (the σ- is, of course, the usual give-away clue to the future):

Aorist passive	Stem	Future passive
ἐ-παύθη-ν →	παύθη-	παυθή-σ-ομαι 'I shall be stopped'
ἠδικήθη-ν →	ἀδικήθη-	ἀδικηθή-σ-ομαι 'I shall be wronged'
εἰσήχθη-ν →	εἰσάχθη-	εἰσαχθή-σ-ομαι 'I shall be introduced'

EXERCISE

12H–I: 3. Convert the following forms into their future passive equivalent and translate:

1. ἤκουσα
2. δουλώσει
3. ἐδίδοσαν
4. τίθησιν
5. ἔστησεν

SUMMARY LEARNING VOCABULARY FOR SECTION 12H–I

Ἀθήνησι(ν)	at Athens
ἀργύριον, τό	silver, money (2b)
διατρίβω	pass time, waste time
ἐλπίς (ἐλπιδ-), ἡ	hope, expectation (3a)
ἐπιδημέω	come to town, be in town
ἐργάζομαι	work, perform
κατατίθημι (καταθε-)	put down, pay, perform
οἰκίδιον, τό	small house (2b)
ὀργίζομαι	grow angry with (+ dat.)
παραλαμβάνω (παραλαβ-)	take, receive from
τοίνυν	well then (resuming and pushing argument on further)
τρόπος, ὁ	way, manner (2a)

REVISION EXERCISES FOR SECTION 12H–I

(B/C) MORPHOLOGY AND SYNTAX

1. Translate these future passives. Then pair each with its present form:

   εἰσαχθήσομαι, ἐξελεγχθησόμεθα (convict), ἀναγκασθήσει, ὀργισθήσεται, ζημιωθήσεσθαι (fine), ἀδικηθήσονται
   ἀναγκάζω, εἰσάγω, ἀδικέω, ἐξελέγχω, ὀργίζομαι, ζημιόω

2. Translate each statement, then, using the present tense verbs given, turn them into indirect statements. What difference does the use of the past introductory verb make to your translation?

   a. ἡ γυνὴ ἀδικηθήσεται ὑπ᾽ οὐδενός. (φαμέν/ἔφαμεν)
   b. οἱ τῆς ἑταίρας παῖδες πολῖται γενήσονται. (οἴεται/ᾤετο)
   c. ἀφίξονται Στέφανος καὶ Νέαιρα ἐκ τῶν Μεγάρων Ἀθήναζε. (ἡγεῖται/ ἡγήσατο)
   d. ἀναγκασθήσομαι παρὰ Φρυνίωνος τὴν Νέαιραν ἀφαιρεῖσθαι. (φησίν/ ἔφη)

3. Translate each statement, then, using the present tense verbs given, turn them into indirect statements. What difference does the use of the past introductory verb make to your translation?

   a. ὁ Φρυνίων ἠδικήθη ὑπ᾽ ἐμοῦ καὶ ὠργίσθη ἐμοί. (οἶδα/ᾔδη)
   b. ἡ Νέαιρα ἐπεδήμει καὶ ἦλθεν ὡς Στέφανον. (ὁρᾷ/εἶδεν)
   c. ἠδικήθημεν ὑπὸ τοῦ κατηγόρου καὶ κατεδικάσθημεν ὑπὸ τῶν δικαστῶν. (αἰσθάνονται/ᾔσθοντο)
   d. ἠδικήσατε τὴν πόλιν καὶ τῶν νόμων κατεφρονεῖτε καὶ ἠσεβεῖτε εἰς τοὺς θεούς. (γιγνώσκετε/ἔγνωτε)
   e. ἑταίρα εἶ καὶ παιδοποιεῖ ἐξ ἀστῶν. (οἶσθα/ᾔδεισθα)

(D) ENGLISH INTO GREEK

1. Sentences
   Translate into Greek:

   1. If only I could remember the arguments of the prosecutor!
   2. If I were a sophist, I would be remembering these arguments.
   3. If I could remember the evidence, I would cast my vote justly.
   4. Phrynion knew that Neaira was in town and had the money.
   5. Stephanos says that Neaira will be wronged by nobody.

2. Prose
   Translate into Greek:

   Apollodoros, wronged and put into a dangerous position by Stephanos, is contesting this suit. For the laws do not allow a citizen to live with a prostitute as his wife. Apollodoros says that he will give clear evidence that Stephanos is doing this very thing. If Stephanos were doing this, it would clearly be a

very serious matter. Consequently, I hope that Apollodoros will win the suit.
If he were to win it, it would be a good thing for the city.

TEST EXERCISE 12
Translate into English:

The prosecutor describes how the man Timarkhos, on trial for immoral behaviour, left Antikles to live with the slave Pittalakos. Timarkhos soon deserted Pittalakos to live with Hegesandros.
(From Aiskhines *Timarkhos*, 53–62)

ἀλλὰ τὰ μετὰ ταῦτα ἐρῶ. ὅπως ἀκούσεσθε, ὦ ἄνδρες δικασταί. ὡς γὰρ ἀπηλλάγη παρὰ τοῦ Ἀντικλέους Τίμαρχος οὑτοσί, διημέρευεν ἐν τῷ κυβείῳ. τῶν δὲ κυβευτῶν ἐστί τις Πιττάλακος, οἰκέτης τῆς πόλεως. οὗτος, ἰδὼν Τίμαρχον ἐν τῷ κυβείῳ, ἀνέλαβεν αὐτὸν καὶ ἔσχε παρ᾽
5   ἑαυτῷ.

κaὶ τὰς ὕβρεις ἃς ἐγὼ οἶδα σαφῶς γενομένας ὑπὸ τοῦ ἀνθρώπου τούτου εἰς Τίμαρχον, ἐγὼ μὰ τὸν Δία τὸν Ὀλύμπιον οὐκ ἂν τολμήσαιμι πρὸς ὑμᾶς εἰπεῖν. νὴ Δία, κάκιστ᾽ ἀπολοίμην εἰ μνείαν ποιοῦμαι τῶν τοιούτων. ἐγὼ γάρ, εἰ ἐν ὑμῖν εἴποιμι ἃ οὑτοσὶ ἔπραξεν, οὐκ ἂν
10   δυναίμην ἔτι ζῆν.

ἐν δὲ τούτῳ καταπλεῖ δεῦρο ἐξ Ἑλλησπόντου Ἡγήσανδρος, οὗ τὸν τρόπον ἄδικον ὄντα καὶ ὀλίγωρον ὑμεῖς ἴστε κάλλιον ἢ ἐγώ. εἰσφοιτῶν δ᾽ οὗτος ὡς τὸν Πιττάλακον συγκυβευτὴν ὄντα, καὶ Τίμαρχον ἐκεῖ πρῶτον ἰδών, ἐβούλετο ὡς αὐτὸν ἀναλαβεῖν. καὶ γὰρ ἡγήσατο αὐτὸν
15   ἐγγὺς εἶναι τῆς αὑτοῦ φύσεως.

The jilted Pittalakos, trying to get Timarkhos back, is beaten up for his pains and next day takes refuge at an altar, where Timarkhos appeases him.

ὡς δ᾽ ἀπηλλάγη μὲν παρὰ τοῦ Πιτταλάκου, ἀνελήφθη δὲ ὑπὸ Ἡγησάνδρου, ὠργίσθη ὁ Πιττάλακος, γνοὺς τοσοῦτον ἀργύριον μάτην ὑπὲρ Τιμάρχου καταθείς, καὶ ἐφοίτα ἐπὶ τὴν οἰκίαν τὴν Ἡγησάνδρου πολλάκις. ὅτε δ᾽ αὐτῷ ὠργίζοντο φοιτῶντι Ἡγήσανδρος καὶ Τίμαρχος, εἰσπηδήσαντες
20   νύκτωρ εἰς τὴν οἰκίαν οὗ ᾤκει ὁ Πιττάλακος, πρῶτον μὲν συνέτριβον τὰ σκεύη, τέλος δὲ αὐτὸν τὸν Πιττάλακον ἔτυπτον πολὺν χρόνον. τῇ δ᾽ ὑστεραίᾳ, ὀργισθεὶς τῷ πράγματι ὁ Πιττάλακος ἔρχεται γυμνὸς εἰς τὴν ἀγορὰν καὶ καθίζει ἐπὶ τὸν βωμὸν τὸν τῆς μητρὸς τῶν θεῶν. ὄχλου δὲ συνδραμόντος, ὅ τε Ἡγήσανδρος καὶ ὁ Τίμαρχος τρέχουσι πρὸς τὸν
25   βωμὸν καὶ περιστάντες ἐδέοντο τοῦ Πιτταλάκου ἀναστῆναι, φάσκοντες τὸ ὅλον πρᾶγμα παροινίαν γενέσθαι. καὶ αὐτὸς ὁ Τίμαρχος ἔφασκε πάντα πραχθήσεσθαι ὑφ᾽ αὑτοῦ, τοῦ Πιτταλάκου ἀναστάντος. τέλος δὲ πείθουσιν αὐτὸν ἀναστῆναι ἀπὸ τοῦ βωμοῦ.

Vocabulary

ἀπηλλάγη aor. pass. of ἀπαλλάττω release

διημερεύω spend one's days

κυβεῖον, τό casino, gambling-den (2b)

κυβευτής, ὁ gambler (1d)

ζῆν inf. of ζάω live

ὀλίγωρος ον disdainful

εἰσφοιτάω go into

συγκυβευτής *cf.* κυβευτής

φύσις, ἡ nature (3e)

μάτην to no purpose

φοιτάω *cf.* εἰσφοιτάω

νύκτωρ at night

συντρίβω smash up

ὑστεραία, ἡ next day (1b)

γυμνός ή όν naked

ὄχλος, ὁ crowd (2a)

φάσκω assert

παροινία, ἡ drunken behaviour (1b)

Grammar for Section 13A–B

In this section you cover:
- Aorist infinitive passive
- Future participles active, middle and passive
- ὡς + future participle
- πρίν + infinitive

AORIST INFINITIVE PASSIVE, 'TO BE/TO HAVE BEEN -ED'

249. The aorist infinitive passive:

- Is based (as you would expect) on the aorist passive stem (minus the augment);
- Uses -ναι as the infinitive ending (cf. εἶναι 'to be', ἰέναι 'to go', etc. cf. **385–7**).
- Means 'to be -ed' or 'to have been -ed', depending on context.

Thus:

> παυθῆ-ναι 'to be/have been stopped'.

Remember that:

- The aorist passive stem is -[θ]η-;
- The stem must be de-augmented, e.g.

> ἠδικήθην > ἀδικηθη- >ἀδικηθῆ-ναι,   'to be/have been wronged'
> ἐγράφην > γραφη-   >γραφῆ-ναι   'to be/have been written'.

EXERCISE

13A–B: 1. Give the aorist passive infinitive of:

> δίδωμι, πείθω, φέρω, λύω, τίθημι

FUTURE PARTICIPLES ACTIVE, MIDDLE, PASSIVE, 'ABOUT TO –'

250. By now it will come as no surprise to learn that future participles are based on the stems of the future indicative forms:

Future active indic.	Future participle	Meaning
παύσ-ω	παύσ-ων -ουσα -ον (-οντ-)	'about to stop'
Future middle indic.		
παύσ-ομαι	παυσ-όμεν-ος -η –ον	'about to stop [oneself], cease'
Future passive indic.		
παυθήσ-ομαι	παυθησ-όμεν-ος -η –ον	'about to be stopped'

Form and meaning

- The future participles mean 'about to – ', 'on the point of -ing';
- The endings attached to the appropriate stem are the regular endings for:

    present participles active, i.e. -ων -ουσα -ον (-οντ-) (see **90**); and middle/passive, i.e. -ομεν-ος -η -ον (see **92**);

- Remember that many verbs have irregular or unpredictable future stems, e.g. the future of βάλλω is βαλέω (βαλῶ), etc. Revise **117–20**.

EXERCISE

13A–B: 2. Give the future active, middle and passive participles, with meanings, of the following verbs:

λύω, πείθω, φέρω, ἵστημι, λαμβάνω

ὡς + FUTURE PARTICIPLE, 'IN ORDER TO'

251. The future participle in Greek often carries with it a sense of *intention*. This is entirely understandable. If you are about to do something, presumably (a Greek would argue) you intend to do it and have some purpose in doing it – otherwise you wouldn't bother.

- In order clearly to mark this intentional/purposive usage, Greek often prefaces the future participle with ὡς (literally '*as* [one] on the point of -ing'), giving it the meaning 'with the intention of -ing', 'in order to –', e.g.

ἦλθον ὡς ἄξων Νέαιραν means 'I came as (one) on the point of taking Neaira/with the intention of taking Neaira/in order to take Neaira'.
The participle must agree with the person to whom it refers, e.g. if the 'I' above were feminine, it would be ἄξουσα (etc.). See **393**.

EXERCISE

13A–B: 3. Translate the italicised words with ὡς + future participle. If it helps, turn them into the 'as one[s] about to' form first. Then decide who the 'one' is, enabling you to put the participle in the right gender, case and number:

1. The woman came *to take her*.
2. I saw the men fleeing *with the intention of saving* themselves.
3. The man gave money to the woman *in order to persuade her*.
4. Where shall we go *to give* the food to the poor?

πρίν + INFIN., 'BEFORE'

252. The infinitive has a wide range of uses in Greek, one of which is with the conjunction πρίν. This means 'before', and controls a subordinate clause, i.e. a clause with a verb.

- In English, such a clause can take a verb in the indicative, e.g. 'before he departed' or some other form e.g. 'before departing'.
- In Greek, such a 'before' clause constructs with an *infinitive*, e.g. πρὶν ἀπελθεῖν 'before [X] departed'.

Distinguish πρίν + infin. 'before X happened' from 'before' as a preposition which controls not a verb but a noun e.g. 'before dawn', πρό + gen.

Usage

252a. In the subordinate clause πρὶν ἀπελθεῖν 'before [X] departed', how do you know *who* departed? Who is the subject of 'depart'? Examine these two sentences:

εὔξαντο πρὶν ἀπελθεῖν '*they* prayed before [*they*] departed'
ἀφικόμην πρὶν Νέαιραν Ἀθήναζε ἐλθεῖν '*I* arrived before *Neaira* went to Athens'

Nothing new here! As we saw with the infinitive and participle in reported speech (**235–6, 247**), it all depends on who the subject of the main verb is:

- If the subject of the πρίν clause is the *same person* as the subject of the main verb, no new subject will appear (or if it does, it will be in the *nominative*);
- If the subject of the πρίν clause is *not the same person* as the subject of the main verb, the new subject of the πρίν clause will appear in the *accusative* case. See **398**(i).

As usual, beware of the 'double accusative' problem: if there are *two* accusatives in the πρίν clause, only the context will tell you who is the subject, who the object.

Again as usual, the tense of the infinitive has no temporal, only aspectual, force.

Change of subject in the accusative

253. So far we have learned that subordinate clauses taking the infinitive (and participles clauses in reported speech):

- Put the subject of the subordinate clause into the accusative if the subject is *different* from the subject of the main verb;
- Do not refer to the subject at all, or only in the nominative, if the subject is the *same* as the subject of the main verb.

▶ In future, we shall refer to this practice as 'change of subject in the accusative'.

EXERCISE

13A–B: 4. Translate the italicised words into Greek, using both the present and aorist infinitive:

1. They thought for a long time *before they were persuaded*.
2. The women prayed *before their husbands departed*.
3. *Before eating*, he always drank.
4. He consulted his friends *before he divorced the woman*.

SUMMARY LEARNING VOCABULARY FOR SECTION 13A–B

ἀναλαμβάνω (ἀναλαβ-)	take back, take up
ἄπαις (ἀπαιδ-)	childless
ἀποδίδωμι (ἀποδο-)	give back, return
ἀποπέμπω	send away, divorce
ἀφίσταμαι (ἀποστα-)	relinquish claim to; revolt from
ἐγγυάω	engage, promise
ἐκβάλλω (ἐκβαλ-)	throw out; divorce
ἐκδίδωμι (ἐκδο-)	give in marriage
ἐκπέμπω	send out, divorce
ἐκπίπτω (ἐκπεσ-)	be thrown out, divorced
ἐξελέγχω	convict, refute, expose
ἐπιμελέομαι	care for (+ gen.)
ἔρημος ον	empty, deserted; devoid of (+ gen.)
ζημίᾱ, ἡ	fine (1b)

SUMMARY LEARNING VOCABULARY FOR SECTION 13A–B
(continued)

ἠπιστάμην	impf. of ἐπίσταμαι know how to (+inf.)
καὶ δή	and really; as a matter of fact; let us suppose; there! look!
κατεγγυάω	demand securities from (+acc.)
κόρη, ἡ	maiden, girl (1a)
λογισμός, ὁ	calculation (2a)
μῖσος, τό	hatred (3c)
μνᾶ, ἡ	mina (100 drachmas) (1b)
οἰκεῖος, ὁ	relative (2a)
οἰκεῖος ᾱ ον	related, domestic, family
ὀργή, ἡ	anger (1a)
παλαιός ᾱ́ όν	ancient, old, of old
πρίν	(+ inf.) before
πρόθῡμος -ον	ready, eager, willing, active
προίξ (προικ-), ἡ	dowry (3a)
ὑβρίζω	treat violently, disgracefully
φρᾱ́τηρ (φρᾱτερ-), ὁ	member of a phratry (a group of families with certain religious and social functions) (3a)
φύσις, ἡ	nature, temperament, character (3e)
ὡς	(+fut. part.) in order to

REVISION EXERCISES FOR SECTION 13A–B

(B/C) MORPHOLOGY AND SYNTAX

1. Pick out from the following list the future participles. Give their dictionary form and its meaning:

   ἐκβαλοῦντι, λαβούσης, ἐντευξομένη, εἰσαχθησόμενος, θωπεύσαντος, ὑπαρξάσας, καταστήσοντι, παρέξοντες, τιμῶσα, ἐκδώσοντα, ἀδικηθεῖσι, ἐρῶν, θησόντων, καταφρονοῦντες, ἀφαιρησόμενος, ἀγωνισαμέναις, γνωσομένην, ὀλέσασι, λήσουσαν, ἑλόν, ἐσόμενον, ἀναγκασθησομένῳ, ἐπιδειξουσῶν, πευσομένων, γραψαμένῳ, ἀποθανουμένη, παραληψομένη, ἐργασαμένους, ἐκπεσούμενοι, ἐκπέμποντι

2. Pick out from this list aorist passive infinitives. Give their dictionary form. What verbs do the other infinitives in the list belong to?

   εἶναι, πεισθῆναι, ἐκπεμφθῆναι, εἰδέναι, ἀποδιδόναι, ἐξαπατηθῆναι, θεῖναι, ἐξελεγχθῆναι, δεικνύναι, ἀπολλύναι, ὑβρισθῆναι, ἐκβληθῆναι, ἀποδοῦναι, ἀφιστάναι, διατεθῆναι, τιθέναι

3. Translate these sentences, changing the form of the bracketed word to future participle, to complete the sense:

   a. ἦλθον ἐκεῖνοι ἐπὶ τὴν οἰκίαν τὴν Στεφάνου ὡς (ἄγω) τὴν Νέαιραν.
   b. ἀπῆλθον αἱ γυναῖκες Ἀθήναζε ὡς (διατρίβω) ἐν τῇ Στεφάνου οἰκίᾳ καὶ (ἐργάζομαι).
   c. βαδίζω οὖν πρὸς αὐτὸν ὡς (λέγω) ἀληθῆ καὶ (ἀκούω) ψευδῆ.
   d. εἰσῆλθεν εἰς τὸ δικαστήριον ὁ ἀνὴρ ὡς (ἀπολογέομαι) καὶ (ἀπολύομαι).

4. Translate the introductory statements (a) and (b) and each of the bracketed sentences; then change the bracketed sentences into πρίν+inf. clauses, dependent upon the introductory statement. Translate your answers:

   a. ὁ Στέφανος εἰσήγαγεν εἰς τὸ δικαστήριον τὸν Φράστορα.

      (i) (ὁ Φράστωρ ἐγράψατο γραφήν)
      (ii) (τὸ τῆς Φανοῦς παιδίον ἐγένετο)
      (iii) (τὸ παιδίον ἀνελήφθη ὑπὸ Φράστορος)
      (iv) (ἔγνω ὅτι ἐξελεγχθήσεται ἀδικῶν)

   b. ὁ Φράστωρ ἀνείλετο τὴν γραφήν.

      (i) (εἰσῆλθεν εἰς τὸ δικαστήριον)
      (ii) (ἐξέπεμπε τὴν Φανώ)
      (iii) (ὑπισχνεῖται ἀναλήψεσθαι τὸ παιδίον)
      (iv) (ἐλέχθησαν οὗτοι οἱ λόγοι ὑπὸ τῆς Νεαίρας)

Grammar for 13C

> In this section you cover:
> • Conditional clauses: past 'unfulfilled'; 'mixed'; and 'open/simple' (no ἄν)

CONDITIONAL SENTENCES WITH ἄν (PAST, 'UNFULFILLED')

254. You have already met:

'Future remote conditions', indicated by an optative in both clauses (**241**); and 'Present contrary-to-fact conditions' (**242**), indicated by an imperfect indicative in both clauses. Both were marked with ἄν in the apodosis/main clause, and both were translated with 'were/would/ should' in English.

Now examine the following (to which you were alerted at **244**):

εἰ ἡμᾶς ἔπεισας, ἠκούσαμεν ἄν 'If you *had* persuaded us, we *would have* listened'

As you can see, this conditional features:

> • The marker ἄν in the apodosis;
> • Verbs in both clauses in the aorist INDICATIVE.

This is a *past* 'unfulfilled condition', which takes the English form:

'If x *had* –, Y WOULD HAVE RESULTED'.
It is clear from the form of words that X did not happen, so Y did not result. Hence 'unfulfilled'. See **402**, **425**.

'Mixed' conditional sentences with ἄν

255. Consider the English 'If I *had* done this, I would *now* be happy.' This is undoubtedly a 'would/should' 'unfulfilled' condition, but the protasis refers to the past, the apodosis to the present. It is therefore a temporally 'mixed' condition.
Greek plays the same game, e.g.

εἰ τοῦτο ἔπραξα [aorist], οὐκ ἄν ἡμάρτανον [imperfect], i.e. 'If I had done this, I would not [now] be making a mistake.'

As you can see, Greek (like English) follows the individual rules for each clause separately – in this case:

> • the verb in the protasis, referring to the past, is aorist indicative; and
> • the verb in the apodosis, referring to the present, is imperfect indicative (with, of course, ἄν).

'Open' conditional sentences (no ἄν)

256. Neither in Greek nor in English do conditional sentences *have* to be 'remote' or 'unfulfilled', using 'were/would/should' etc. They can be 'open' or 'simple':

'If he ran, I walked', εἰ ἐκεῖνος ἔδραμε, ἐβάδισα ἐγώ

'If she is happy, I too am happy' εἰ ἐκείνη εὐδαίμων ἐστίν, εὐδαίμων καὶ ἐγώ.

In these cases, in which no ἄν appears, translate them perfectly normally, e.g.

εἰ σοφός εἰμι ἐγώ, σὺ μῶρος εἶ 'If I am wise, you are foolish.'

CONDITIONAL SUMMARY

256a.

▶ Future 'remote': 'If X *were to* happen (optative), Y ἄν *would* happen (optative)'.

▶ Present 'contrary to fact': 'If X *were now* happening (imperfect indicative), Y ἄν *would now* be happening (imperfect indicative)'.

▶ Past 'unfulfilled': 'If X *had* happened (aorist indicative), Y ἄν *would have* happened (aorist indicative)'.

▶ 'Mixed': e.g. 'If X *had* happened (aorist indicative), Y ἄν *would now* happen (imperfect indicative)', etc.

▶ 'Open/simple' conditions (no 'would/should'): 'If you chased me, I ran away' (plain indicative in both clauses).

REVISION EXERCISES FOR SECTION 13C

1. Link the two statements by making them into past 'unfufilled' conditions with ἄν and translate:

   a. (εἰ) ἄπαις ἀποθνῄσκει Φράστωρ/οἱ οἰκεῖοι λαμβάνουσι τὰ αὐτοῦ
   b. (εἰ) ἀστῆς θυγάτηρ ἐστὶ* Φανώ/οὐκ ὀργίζεται Στέφανος
   c. (εἰ) οἶδε* Φανὼ Νεαίρας οὖσαν θυγατέρα ὁ Φράστωρ/ἐκβάλλει ὡς τάχιστα αὐτήν
   d. (εἰ) Φανὼ ξένης θυγάτηρ καλεῖται/Φράστωρ οὐκ ἐξαπατᾶται
   e. (εἰ) μὴ λαγχάνει Στέφανος τὴν δίκην ταύτην/οὐ γράφεται Φράστωρ αὐτὸν γραφήν

   *Use the past forms of these verbs.

Grammar for 13D

> In this section you cover:
> - Gerunds (verbs used as nouns): τό + infinitive

VERBS IN THE INFINITIVE USED AS NOUNS

257. Verbs can be construed finitely, in conjugations ('I go', 'you come', 'he deceives'), and also act as adjectives ('I see the women *running, jumping, shouting*') i.e. as participles. They can also act as *nouns*, sometimes called 'gerunds'. Consider the English 'I like *to run*' and 'I like *running*'. In both cases, 'to run' and 'running' are nouns – the object of 'like'.

Form and usage

Observe how Greek turns a verb into a noun:

τὸ φιλεῖν, or τὸ φιλῆσαι	'the [act of] loving/kissing, love/a kiss'
τὸ μισεῖν, or τὸ μισῆσαι	'the [act of] hating, hatred'
τὸ μὴ τρέχειν, or τὸ μὴ δραμεῖν	'the [act of] not running'

In other words, verbs are turned into (neuter) nouns/gerunds in Greek by:

- Prefacing the *infinitive* with the neuter definite article τό;
- Changing the case of τό to show what case the noun is in.

E.g.

διὰ τὸ μισεῖν	'because of the hatred'
τῷ μὴ ἀδικεῖν	'by not wronging'
τοῦ ἀπολογεῖσθαι ἕνεκα	'for the sake of defending'

Observe how, by using this construction, Greek can 'work round' nouns if it needs to. For example:

- 'childlessness' could be expressed as 'the to-be childless', τὸ εἶναι ἄπαις (and ἄπαις, being an adjective, would agree with whoever was 'childless');
- 'introduction into a clan' could 'the to-be-introduced into a clan', τὸ εἰς γένος εἰσάγεσθαι (passive), and so on.

> ▶ In summary, a gerund like τὸ φιλῆσαι '[the act of] kissing' acts exactly like any neuter noun, e.g. τὸ ἔργον, except that τό alone changes to indicate the case of the noun: φιλῆσαι does not change. See **394**(vi).
> ▶ The negative is μή.

EXERCISE

13D. 1. Express the following English and Greek phrases with τό + the indicated infinitive:

1. on account of flight (aorist)
2. after time-wasting (present)
3. instead of ceasing (aorist)
4. by means of fighting (present)
5. for the sake of guarding (aorist)

6. ἄνευ τοῦ μίσους (present)
7. διὰ τὴν διάνοιαν (present)
8. τοῦ θορύβου ἕνεκα (aorist)
9. τῇ ἀπορίᾳ (present)
10. διὰ τὴν βοήν (present)

Changes of subject

258. The infinitive, being a *verb*-form, can take a subject and an object; and the 'change of subject in the accusative' rule applies (**253**), e.g.

- Νέαιρα ἀπῆλθε διὰ τὸ κακοδαίμων εἶναι 'Neaira left because of the to-be unlucky', i.e. 'because of being/because she was unlucky': κακοδαίμων (nom.) agrees with Νέαιρα (nom.), no change of subject.
- Νέαιρα ἀπῆλθε διὰ τὸ Φράστορα μισεῖν αὐτήν 'Neaira left because of the Phrastor to-hate her', i.e. 'because Phrastor (acc.: change of subject) hated her'.

Note αὐτήν: this is the reflexive form 'herself' because it refers to Neaira, subject of the main verb.

Aspect

259. Pay attention, as far as is possible, to the aspectual sense of the verb. Thus τὸ φιλεῖν means 'the process of loving', while τὸ φιλῆσαι means demonstrating φιλία by an act, e.g. 'kissing'. By using the article with the infinitive, it is possible to indicate differences of *aspect*, which nouns cannot indicate.

REVISION EXERCISES FOR SECTION 13D

(B/C) MORPHOLOGY AND SYNTAX

1. Translate each sentence, then convert the underlined words or clauses into expressions using τό, τοῦ, τῷ + inf.:

    a. κακόν ἐστιν ἡ ἀσθένεια

    b. Φράστωρ ἀνέλαβε τὸ παιδίον διὰ τὴν νόσον καὶ τὸ μῖσος τὸ πρὸς τοὺς οἰκείους καὶ τὴν ἀπαιδίαν.

    c. Στέφανος δῆλος ἦν ἀδικῶν, διότι οὐκ ὤμοσεν.

    d. φάνερόν ἐστι τὸ παιδίον ξένης ὄν, διότι οἱ γεννῆται ἀπεψηφίσαντο αὐτοῦ καὶ οὐκ ἐνέγραψαν εἰς τὸ γένος.

    e. οἱ δὲ γεννῆται ἐβιάσθησαν ἀποψηφίσασθαι τοῦ παιδίου, διότι ᾔδεσαν αὐτὸν οὐ γνήσιον ὄντα.

    f. ἀγαθόν ἐστιν ἡ θεράπεια.

    g. καὶ μνείαν ἐποιήσατο τούτων, ὅτι ἠσθένει καὶ εἰς ἀπορίαν κατέστη καὶ ὅτι ὑπὸ Νεαίρας ἐθεραπεύετο.

    h. μέγα γὰρ κακόν ἐστιν ἡ ἀσέβεια.

    i. ἠναγκάσθην εἰσελθεῖν βιαζόμενος.

(D) ENGLISH INTO GREEK

Translate into Greek:

1. Stephanos went to Phrastor, intending to promise him Phano in marriage.
2. Phrastor married Phano before he knew she was Neaira's daughter.
3. If Phano had not looked after Phrastor, he would not have taken back the child.
4. Phrastor took back Phano's child because of his being ill and because of Phano's looking after him.
5. If the child had been legitimate, Phrastor would have sworn the oath.

Grammar for 13E

In this section you cover:
- The perfect indicative active, 'have -ed'

THE PERFECT INDICATIVE ACTIVE, 'I HAVE –ED'

260. We have already learned the aorist. Why, then, do we need a perfect tense? Do not 'I wrote' and 'I have written' mean, effectively, the same thing? No, actually. But first examine the forms of the perfect indicative active:

πέπαυκ-α **'I have stopped'**

πέπαυκ-α
πέπαυκ-ας
πέπαυκ-ε(ν)
πεπαύκ-αμεν
πεπαύκ-ατε
πεπαύκ-ᾱσι(ν)

■ *Forms*

261. The two marks of the perfect are:

- **The -κ- addition to the stem:** -κα is the usual ending for the perfect tense, though κ sometime does not feature, e.g. γράφω – γέγραφ-α 'I have written'.
- **Reduplication:** The 'reduplicated stem' is e.g. the πέ- of πέπαυκ-α. This 'reduplication' is a feature of *all the forms* of the perfect (participle, infinitive, etc.) and is not dropped in some forms (as the augment is).
- Note that perfects reduplicate *after* any prefixes. Thus the perfect of ἀπο-λύω is ἀπο-λέλυκα.

■ *Patterns of reduplication*

Observe the following patterns:

(a) Normal

παύω – πέπαυκα   'I have stopped'
λύω – λέλυκα   'I have released'

(b) θ, φ, χ reduplicate with τ, π, κ, e.g.

θύω – τέθυκα   'I have sacrificed'
φαίνω – πέφηνα   'I have revealed'
χαίρω – κεχάρηκα 'I have rejoiced'

■ *-μι perfects*

Note the following perfects:

> δίδωμι – δέδωκα 'I have given'
> τίθημι – τέθηκα 'I have placed'
> δείκνυμι – δέδειχα 'I have shown'.

Their conjugation in the perfect is entirely regular.

■ *Contract verbs*

Note that contract verbs lengthen the contract vowel before the ending, e.g. τιμάω > τετίμηκα, ποιέω > πεποίηκα, δηλόω > δεδήλωκα.

Meaning

262. (a) At an early stage of the language, the perfect meant 'I am in the position of having -ed', i.e. there is a strong *present* force to it. So, for example:

- The perfect of θνῄσκω 'I am dying' is τέθνηκα 'I am in the position of having died', i.e. 'I am dead';
- The perfect of ὄλλυμαι 'I am being ruined' is ὄλωλα, meaning 'I am in the position of having been ruined', i.e. 'I am ruined/done for';
- The perfect of ἵσταμαι 'I am setting myself up' is ἕστηκα 'I am in the position of having set myself up', i.e. 'I am standing'.

(b) In Classical Greek, the perfect also acquired the meaning 'I have -ed'. Sometimes the same perfect form can have both forces. It is important to bear the early meaning in mind. See **418–19**.

REVISION EXERCISES FOR SECTION 13E

(B/C) MORPHOLOGY AND SYNTAX

1. Write down the perfect reduplication of the following verbs, going no further than the first three letters (e.g. for θύω, write τεθ-: do *not* count prefixes):

    τιμάω, θωπεύω, μαρτυρέω, γίγνομαι, φαίνομαι, πυνθάνομαι, ἐπιδημέω, ἐπιδείκνυμι, καλέω, τίθημι, πείθω, ἐκβάλλω, γράφω, ἐκπέμπω, πράττω, βιάζομαι, λείπω, λύω, νικάω, χράομαι, φύω, γαμέω

2. Translate and give the dictionary form of each of these regular perfects (consulting the Greek–English vocabulary where necessary). Change singulars to plural and vice-versa:

    λελύκασι, μεμαρτυρήκατε, νενίκηκε, τετιμήκαμεν, ἐπιδεδήμηκας, γέγραφα, βεβοήκατε, κεκέλευκε, πεπράχαμεν, πεφίληκα, κεχώρηκας, πεφροντίκασι

Grammar for 13F

> In this section you cover:
> - the aorist optative passive
> - the use of the optative in indirect speech
> - sequence of tenses
> - the future optative

THE AORIST OPTATIVE PASSIVE

263. By now you will not be surprised to learn that the aorist optative passive is based on the aorist indicative passive, i.e. –θ- is a key marker:

> παυθείην
>
> παυθ-είην
> παυθ-είης
> παυθ-είη
> παυθ-εῖμεν
> παυθ-εῖτε
> παυθ-εῖεν

Form

The optative mood has been predominantly characterised by -οι- (present) and -αι- (aorist) so far (**212**). Here –ει- comes into its own:

- Watch out for the aorist passive stem, usually θ, + ει.
- We have met the -ει- marker before in e.g. εἰδείην, the optative of οἶδα (**246**).

EXERCISE

13F: 1. Give the first person singular of the aorist passive optative of the following. Remember to check the aorist passive indicative first and remove the augment:

βάλλω, τιμάω, πέμπω, εὑρίσκω, δουλόω, διαφθείρω, δίδωμι, λαμβάνω, τίθημι, κελεύω, πείθω, ποιέω

USE OF THE OPTATIVE IN INDIRECT SPEECH

264. We already know that indirect speech using ὅτι 'that' or e.g. διὰ τί 'why', ὅπου 'where' (etc., **148**) reports what was *originally* said in the same tense and mood as the *original*. So:

- If the speaker originally *said* 'I am intelligent', σοφός εἰμι, this would be *reported* in the present tense, e.g. ἔλεξεν ὅτι σοφός ἐστιν, whereas we would say in English 'he said that he *was* (Greek 'is') intelligent';
- If the speaker said 'Where am I?', ποῦ εἰμι; it would be reported ἤρετο ὅπου ἐστίν, in English 'he asked where he *was* (Greek 'is').'

Now consider:

(a) ἔλεξεν ὅτι ἐπαύσατο 'He said that he had ceased' (originally 'I ceased'), and its legitimate alternative ἔλεξεν ὅτι παύσαιτο

(b) ᾔδη διὰ τί παύεται, 'I knew why he was ceasing' (original 'why is he ceasing?'), and its legitimate alternative ᾔδη διὰ τί παύοιτο.

Reflection on the alternatives will have led you to the following conclusions:

- The *optative* has been used in place of the indicative;
- The optative has taken on *the same tense* as the indicative – aorist in (a), present in (b); and
- The use of the optative has *not changed the meaning* in the slightest.

What is going on? It is all to do with *tense of the main verb*.

SEQUENCE OF TENSES

265. 'Sequence of tenses' in Greek relates to the tense of the *main verb* in the sentence:

- The main verb is a finite verb that is not subordinated, i.e. not introduced by subordinating conjunctions like 'if, when, because, since, although, that', or a relative clause, and so on. In the sentences you have just been examining above, for example, the main verb is 'he said' (past).

The rule of the 'sequence of tenses' is as follows:

- ▶ If the main verb is past (imperfect or aorist, i.e. with an *augment*), the sequence is 'secondary' (or 'historic');
- ▶ If the main verb is any other tense (present, future or perfect), the sequence is 'primary'.

To apply it to the use of the optative in reported speech:

- ▶ In *secondary* sequence, verbs in reported speech are allowed to be optative, of the same tense as what was originally said, but *without affecting the original meaning*.

THE FUTURE OPTATIVE

266. On what stem will the future optative be based? The future indicative stem, of course:

Future optative active παύσοιμι

παύσ-οιμι
παύσ-οις
παύσ-οι
παύσ-οιμεν
παύσ-οιτε
παύσ-οιεν

Future optative middle παυσοίμην

παυσ-οίμην
παύσ-οιο
παύσ-οιτο
παυσ-οίμεθα
παύσ-οισθε
παύσ-οιντο

Future optative passive παυθησοίμην

παυθησ-οίμην
παυθήσ-οιο
παυθήσ-οιτο
παυθησ-οίμεθα
παυθήσ-οισθε
παυθήσ-οιντο

EXERCISE

13F: 2. Translate the following, and then turn them into the optative:

ψηφίσομαι, φυλαχθήσεται, σωθήσεσθε, δοθήσονται, μέμψεσθε, προσκαλοῦμεν, δραμοῦμαι, οἰσόμεθα

Use of the future optative

The future optative is used *only* in indirect speech, in *secondary* sequence, as an alternative to the indicative. For example:

ἔλεξεν ὅτι παύσεται ʽHe said that he would cease' (originally ʽI will cease'), and its legitimate alternative ἔλεξεν ὅτι παύσοιτο (future optative).

You will not find the future optative used in any other way.

> • Where the optative appears in place of the indicative in indirect speech, be careful to distinguish between the present, future, and aorist optatives in order to translate correctly. In this case alone, the optative refers to *tense*, not *aspect*. See **397**(i) and **421**(iii).

EXERCISE

13F: 3. Translate the following sentences, check the sequence, and *where possible* turn the indicative into the optative:

1. ἀπεκρίνατο ὅτι ὁ βασιλεὺς ἀπέθανεν.
2. εἶπεν ὅτι οἱ πολῖται οὐ παρέσονται.
3. αἰσθήσεσθε διὰ τί ὀργίζονται.
4. ᾗστε ὅπου οἱ πολέμιοι συνέρχονται.
5. οἶδα διὰ τί οὐ πείθεται.
6. ἤδη διὰ τί τὸν δοῦλον κολάσει.

SUMMARY LEARNING VOCABULARY FOR SECTION 13C–F

ἄνθρωπος, ἡ	woman (2a)
ἄπειρος ον	inexperienced in (+gen.)
ἀποψηφίζομαι	reject (+gen.)
ἀρχή, ἡ	position, office; start; rule (1a)
ἄρχων (ἀρχοντ-), ὁ	archon (3a)
ἀσεβής ές	unholy
ἀσθένεια, ἡ	illness, weakness (1b)
ἀσθενέω	be ill, fall ill
βασιλεύς, ὁ	king, king archon (3g)
βασιλεύω	be king, be king archon
βουλή, ἡ	council (1a)
γαμέω (γημα-)	marry
γεννήτης, ὁ	member of genos (1d)
γένος, τό	genos (smaller groupings of families within the phratry) (3c)
γνήσιος ᾱ ον	legitimate, genuine
δέδειχα	I have shown, revealed
δέδωκα	I have given
διοικέω	administer, run
ἐγγράφω	enrol, enlist, register
ἔθος, τό	manner, habit (3c)
ἑκών οὖσα όν	willing(ly)
ἐμφανής ές	open, obvious
ἐπιδείκνῡμι (ἐπιδειξα-)	prove, show, demonstrate
ἕστηκα	I stand
θεραπεύω	look after, tend

SUMMARY LEARNING VOCABULARY FOR SECTION 13C–F

(continued)

ἱερά, τά	rites, sacrifices (2b)
ἱκετεύω	beg, supplicate
καταμαρτυρέω	give evidence against (+gen.)
κρῑ́νω (κρῑνα-)	judge, decide
λαγχάνω (δίκην) (λαχ-)	bring (suit) against, obtain by lot, run as candidate for office
λείπω (λιπ-)	leave, abandon
μαρτυρέω	give evidence, bear witness
νοσέω	be sick
οἷ	(to) where
ὄλωλα	I am ruined, done for
ὄμνῡμι (ὀμοσα-)	swear
ὁποῖος ᾱ ον	of what kind
περιφανής ές	very clear
πρᾶξις, ἡ	fact, action (3e)
πρᾱ́ττω (πρᾱξα-)	do, perform, fare
πυνθάνομαι (πυθ-)	learn, hear by inquiry
τέθηκα	I have placed/put
τέθνηκα	I am dead
φαίνομαι	(+inf.) seem to – (but not in fact to –)
χαλεπῶς φέρω	be angry at, displeased with
ψεύδομαι	lie, tell lies

REVISION EXERCISES FOR SECTION 13F

(B/C) MORPHOLOGY AND SYNTAX

1. Translate these sentences, then change the subordinate verbs from indicative to optative:

   a. οἱ δικασταὶ ἤροντο ὅ τι ἔπραξεν ὁ Στέφανος καὶ ὁποία ἦν ἡ ἀσέβεια ἡ τῆς Νεαίρας καὶ ὅπως τὴν πόλιν ἠδίκησεν.

   b. οὐ γὰρ ᾔδει ὁ Θεογένης ὅτου θυγάτηρ ἐστὶν οὐδὲ ὅτι ἠργάζετο τῷ σώματι.

   c. Θεογένης εἶπεν ὅτι οὐκ ᾔδει ὁποῖοι ἦσαν οἱ τῆς Φανοῦς τρόποι καὶ ὅτι ἐπείσθη ὑπὸ Στεφάνου ποιεῖν τοῦτο.

   d. ἡ βουλὴ χαλεπῶς ἔφερεν τὸ πρᾶγμα, ὅτι Φανὼ ἐξεδόθη τῷ Φράστορι καὶ ὡς τὰ ἱερὰ ὑπὲρ τῆς πόλεως ἐπράχθη ὑπὸ ξένης.

   e. ἆρ' οὐκ ἤκουες ὡς εἰς τὸ δικαστήριον εἰσήλθομεν καὶ ὡς ἐκεῖνοι οἱ ἄνδρες κατεδικάσθησαν καὶ ἅττα ἐλέχθη ἐν τῇ κατηγορίᾳ;

   Vocabulary

   ἅττα = ἅτινα

2. Translate the following questions, then turn them into indirect questions, using ἠρόμην as the introductory verb. Remember to alter direct question words to indirect (see **125** and **219[c]**), and indicative verbs to optative e.g.

   τί ἔπραξεν ὁ Στέφανος; = ἠρόμην ὅ τι πράξειεν ὁ Στέφανος.

   a. τίς ταῦτα ἐποίησεν;
   b. πῶς ἔπραξεν οἱ ἄρχοντες;
   c. τίς ἦν ἡ γυνὴ ἡ Θεογένους;
   d. ποία γυνὴ ἦν ἡ Φανώ;
   e. πόθεν ἐξέβαλε τὴν γυναῖκα ὁ Θεογένης;

Grammar for 13G–I

In this section you cover:
- More forms of the perfect:
  - perfect indicative middle and passive
  - perfect infinitive
  - perfect participle
- Some irregular perfects

PERFECT INDICATIVE MIDDLE AND PASSIVE

267. As with the present and imperfect, the middle and passive forms of the perfect are identical.

- Perfect middle/passives also show reduplication – the constant feature of the perfect;
- But the -κ, so characteristic of perfect active forms, is never there.

Examine the endings. You will find that they are familiar:

πέπαυμαι **'I have ceased (middle), been stopped (passive)'**

πέπαυ-μαι
πέπαυ-σαι
πέπαυ-ται
πεπαύ-μεθα
πέπαυ-σθε
πέπαυ-νται (or πεπαυμέν-οι -αι εἰσίν)

■ *Form*

You will have noticed our old middle friends -μαι -σαι -ται.

Consonantal endings

268. Here the stem of the perfect ends in a *consonant*:

γέγραμμαι (γέγραφ-μαι) **'I have been described'**

γέγραμμαι
γέγραψαι
γέγραπται
γεγράμμεθα
γέγραφθε
γεγραμμέν-οι –αι εἰσί(ν)

πέπρᾱγ-μαι **'I have been acted upon'**

πέπρᾱγμαι
πέπρᾱξαι
πέπρᾱκται
πεπρᾱ́γμεθα
πέπρᾱχθε
πεπρᾱγμέν-οι –αι εἰσι(ν)

Note how the final consonant changes to accommodate the middle/passive endings. See **359**(x).

Form and use

269. (a) In the third person plural form –μέν-οι –αι εἰσί(ν) (i.e. perfect participle + εἰμί), the participle changes according to the gender of the subject, e.g. γεγραμμέναι εἰσί 'they [women] have been described'.

   (b) Note that, after a perfect, 'by a person' is usually expressed by the PLAIN DATIVE rather than by ὑπό + genitive, e.g. πάνθ' ἡμῖν πεποίηται 'everything has been done by us'.

EXERCISE

13G-I: 1. Turn the following perfects active into perfects passive and translate:

κεκώλυκε, τεθύκαμεν, γεγάμηκα, τετιμήκασιν, δεδηλώκατε

PERFECT INFINITIVES AND PARTICIPLES

270. The forms of the perfect infinitives and participles are, as you would expect, based on the reduplicated perfect stem:

Perfect infinitives

Perfect active infinitive

πεπαυκ-έναι 'to have stopped'

■ *Form*

Note the common infinitive ending in -έναι.

> **Perfect middle/passive infinitive**
>
> πεπαῦ-σθαι 'to have ceased/been stopped'
> γεγρά-φ-θαι 'to have been described'
> πεπρᾶ-χ-θαι 'to have been acted on'

■ *Form*

(a) The infinitive ending in -(σ)θαι is a well-known acquaintance (cf. e.g. παύ-ε-σθαι).

(b) Observe what happens to *consonant* endings before -σθαι:

- The -σ- of -σθαι drops out;
- The consonant blends with -θαι;
- Producing e.g. γέγραφα > γεγράφ-θαι, πέπραγ(χ)α > πεπράχ-θαι, etc.

EXERCISE

13G-I: 2.Turn the perfects in the first exercise (above) into perfect infinitives middle and passive.

Perfect participles

271. Here are the forms of the perfect participle 'having –ed', 'having been -ed':

πεπαυκ-ὼς υῖα ός (-οτ-) **'having stopped'**		
	m.	*f.*	*n.*
s.			
Nom.	πεπαυκώς	πεπαυκυῖ-α	πεπαυκός
Acc.	πεπαυκότ-α	πεπαυκυῖ-αν	πεπαυκός
Gen.	πεπαυκότ-ος	πεπαυκυί-ᾶς	πεπαυκότ-ος
Dat.	πεπαυκότ-ι	πεπαυκυί-ᾳ	πεπαυκότ-ι
	m.	*f.*	*n.*
pl.			
Nom.	πεπαυκότ-ες	πεπαυκυῖ αι	πεπαυκότ α
Acc.	πεπαυκότ-ας	πεπαυκυί-ᾶς	πεπαυκότ-α
Gen.	πεπαυκότ-ων	πεπαυκυι-ῶν	πεπαυκότ-ων
Dat.	πεπαυκό-σι(ν)	πεπαυκυί-αις	πεπαυκό-σι(ν)

■ *Form*

The perfect active participle is of mixed 3-1-3 declension, with the m. and n. declining like 3a nouns on the stem -οτ-, and the f. declining like 1c nouns (short -α).

Perfect participle middle/passive

πεπαυ-μέν-ος -η -ον (n.b. accent) 'having ceased/having been stopped'

s.

	m.	*f.*	*n.*
Nom.	πεπαυμέν-ος	πεπαυμέν-η	πεπαυμέν-ον
Acc.	πεπαυμέν-ον	πεπαυμέν-ην	πεπαυμέν-ον
Gen.	πεπαυμέν-ου	πεπαυμέν-ης	πεπαυμέν-ου
Dat.	πεπαυμέν-ῳ	πεπαυμέν-ῃ	πεπαυμέν-ῳ

pl.

	m.	*f.*	*n.*
Nom.	πεπαυμέν-οι	πεπαυμέν-αι	πεπαυμέν-α
Acc.	πεπαυμέν-ους	πεπαυμέν-ᾱς	πεπαυμέν-α
Gen.	πεπαυμέν-ων	πεπαυμέν-ων	πεπαυμέν-ων
Dat.	πεπαυμέν-οις	πεπαυμέν-αις	πεπαυμέν-οις

(a) The middle/passive participle declines like καλός. Note the -μέν-ος -η -ον endings, which you have already met with middle/passive participle forms (**92**).

(b) You can often spot a perfect participle middle/passive instantly because the accent *always* falls on the -μέν-ος -η -ον; with other -μενος participles, the accent falls on the -μέν- only when the final syllable is long, e.g. παυομένων.

EXERCISE

13G–I: 3. Turn the perfects of exercise 1 (p. 292) into gen. s. and nom. pl. perfect participles (all genders).

NON-REDUPLICATING PERFECT FORMS

272. We have already seen that perfects reduplicate the opening consonant, e.g. παύω → πέπαυκα. But verbs beginning with *double* consonants are different. Observe:

ζητέω→ἐζήτηκα	'I have sought'
στερέω→ἐστέρηκα	'I have deprived'
ῥίπτω→ἔρριφα	'I have hurled'

So:

> ▶ If a verb begins with a *double* consonant e.g. ζ, ψ, ξ, στ, reduplicate with ἐ- .
>
> ▶ If a verb begins with ρ, reduplicate with ἐ- and double ρ to ρρ.

But what if the verb does not start with a consonant? Observe the behaviour of the following perfect forms:

ἀσεβέω→ἠσέβηκα	'I have acted impiously'
ἀδικέω→ἠδίκηκα	'I have done wrong'
ἀγγέλλω→ἤγγελκα	'I have announced'
ὑβρίζω →ὕβρικα	'I have acted aggressively'

So:

> ▶ If a verb begins with a vowel, 'reduplicate' by lengthening the vowel.

IRREGULAR PERFECTS

273. Inevitably, there are some irregular perfects that just have to be learned. Among the most common are:

ἔρχομαι	→ ἐλήλυθα	'I have come'
λαμβάνω	→ εἴληφα	'I have taken'
λέγω	→ εἴρηκα	'I have said' (from stem ἐρ – cf. **194**)
φέρω	→ ἐνήνοχα	'I have carried, endured' (cf. aorist stem ἐνεγκ-)
πάσχω	→ πέπονθα	'I have suffered'
ἵσταμαι	→ ἕστηκα	'I stand' (participle ἑστ-ώς, ἑστωτ- 'standing, established')

■ *Warning*

Do not confuse the aorists of τίθημι and δίδωμι (ἔθηκα, ἔδωκα) with their perfects (τέθηκα, δέδωκα).

EXERCISES

13G–I: 4. Translate into English:

ἤγγελται, ἑστήκασιν, ἐλήλυθε, ἐρρίφατε, πέπονθας, ἠδίκηται

13G–I: 5. Translate into Greek:

They have said, we have endured, I stand, you (s.) have sought, she has been deprived, I have been wronged.

SUMMARY LEARNING VOCABULARY FOR SECTION 13G–I

αἰσχρός ᾱ́ όν	base, shameful; ugly (of people) (comp. αἰσχῑ́ων; sup. αἴσχιστος)
ἁμαρτάνω (ἁμαρτ-)	err; do wrong, make a mistake
ἀπόλωλα	(perf. of ἀπόλλυμαι) I am lost
γεγένημαι	(perf. of γίγνομαι) I have been
διαπρᾱ́ττομαι (διαπρᾱξα-)	do, act, perform
εἰκότως	reasonably, rightly
εἴληφα	I have taken (perf. of λαμβάνω)
εἴρηκα	I have spoken/said (perf. of λέγω)
εἴρημαι	I have been said (perf. pass. of λέγω)
ἐλήλυθα	I have gone (perf. of ἔρχομαι)
ἐνήνοχα	I have carried, borne, endured (perf. of φέρω)
ἕστηκα	I stand (perf. of ἵστημι)
ἑστώς (ἑστωτ-)	standing, established
ἰσχυρός ᾱ́ όν	strong, powerful
καθέστηκα	I have been made, put (perf. pass. of καθίσταμαι)
πέπονθα	I have suffered (perf. of πάσχω)
πολῑτείᾱ, ἡ	state, constitution (1b)
πολῑτεύομαι	be a citizen
πρόγονος, ὁ	forebear, ancestor (2a)
φαίνω	reveal, declare, indict
φάσκω	allege, claim, assert
φύω	bear; mid., grow; aor. mid. ἔφῡν, perf. πέφῡκα be naturally

REVISION EXERCISES FOR SECTION 13G–I

(B/C) MORPHOLOGY AND SYNTAX

1. Translate the sentences, then change singular verbs to plural and vice-versa:

   a. εὖ πεπολίτευσαι.
   b. ἠδικήμεθα μεγάλα ὑπὸ Στεφάνου.
   c. οὗτοι οἱ λόγοι ὑπὸ τῆς Νεαίρας εἴρηνται.
   d. τεκμηρίῳ φανερῷ κέχρησθε, ὦ ἄνδρες.
   e. ἐγὼ αὐτὸς καταμεμαρτύρημαι ὑπ' ἐμαυτοῦ.
   f. ἐκεῖνοι δὲ οἱ ἄνδρες ταῦτα διαπεπραγμένοι εἰσίν.
   g. ὁ Φανοῦς παῖς εἰσῆκται ὑπὸ Στεφάνου εἰς τοὺς φράτερας.
   h. οὗτοι αἴτιοι γεγενημένοι εἰσὶ πολλῶν κακῶν ἐν τῇ πόλει.
   i. μεγάλα, ὦνδρες, ὕβρισθε καὶ ἠδίκησθε.
   j. τοῦτο δ' εἴργασται ὁ κατήγορος.

2. Using the first person singular of (a) οἶδα and (b) φάσκω, change the above sentences into indirect statements using nom./acc. + part. with οἶδα and nom./acc.+ inf. with φάσκω.

3. Do the same as in 2 with the following sentences:

   a. (ἴσμεν/φαμέν) Στέφανος οὐδέποτε δίκην δέδωκεν.
   b. (εὖ οἶδα/φημί) Φανὼ ξένη πέφυκεν.
   c. (ᾔδεισθα/ἔφασκες) ἡ Νέαιρα ἠσέβηκεν εἰς τοὺς θεούς.
   d. (ἴστε/φατέ) δικασταὶ καθεστήκατε.
   e. (οἶσθα/φής) ὡς τὴν αὑτοῦ θυγατέρα τὴν Φανὼ ἐκδέδωκεν ὁ Στέφανος.

(D) ENGLISH INTO GREEK

1. Sentences

Translate into Greek:

1. I have shown that Phano has made sacrifices on behalf of the city.
2. The council asked what sort of wife the king archon had married.
3. Theogenes said that he had been deceived by Stephanos.
4. Stephanos has governed well and performed many noble deeds.
5. We all know that nothing noble has ever been said or done by Stephanos.

2. Prose

Translate into Greek:

Once Phano was proved to be Neaira's daughter, Phrastor divorced her. She, divorced, waited for a short time, intending that Phrastor should take back her child. And, not long afterwards, Phrastor fell ill. And, because he hated his family and did not want them to get his property, he took back the child before he recovered, not wishing to die childless. Clearly, Phrastor would never have taken back the child had he not fallen ill; for when he recovered, he married a legitimate wife, according to the laws.

TEST EXERCISE 13
Translate into English:

Menekles put away his wife, since he could not give her children. But, being childless and aging, he wished to adopt a son. He opted for one of his ex-wife's two brothers. The adopted brother here describes how Menekles made this choice.
(From Isaios, *Menekles,* 10–13, 46–7)

μετὰ δὲ ταῦτα ἐσκόπει ὁ Μενεκλῆς ὅπως μὴ ἔσοιτο ἄπαις, ἀλλ' ἔσοιτο αὐτῷ παῖς, ὅς τις θεραπεύσοι αὐτὸν πρὶν ἀποθανεῖν καὶ <u>τελευτήσαντα</u> <u>θάψοι</u> καὶ εἰς τὸν ἔπειτα χρόνον <u>τὰ</u> <u>νομιζόμενα</u> αὐτῷ ποιήσοι.
ἐπειδὴ οὖν ηὕρισκεν οὐδένα ἄλλον οἰκειότερον ἡμῶν ὄνθ' ἑαυτῷ,
5 λόγους πρὸς ἡμᾶς ἐποιεῖτο, καὶ 'ἡ τύχη', ἔφη, 'οὐκ εἴασε ἐκ τῆς <u>ἀδελφῆς</u> τῆς ὑμετέρας παῖδας ἐμαυτῷ γενέσθαι. οὐ μὴν ἀλλ' ἐκ ταύτης τῆς οἰκίας ἐπαιδοποιησάμην ἄν, εἰ οἷός τ' ἦ. ὑμῶν οὖν βούλομαι τὸν ἕτερον ποιήσασθαι υἱόν.' καὶ <u>ὁ</u> ἐμὸς <u>ἀδελφὸς</u> ἀκούσας ταῦτα ἐπῄνεσέ τε τοὺς λόγους αὐτοῦ καὶ εἶπεν ὅτι ὁ Μενεκλῆς διὰ τό τε γέρων εἶναι καὶ τὸ
10 ἔρημος εἶναι δέοιτο ἐμοῦ ὡς θεραπεύσοντος αὐτόν. 'ἐγὼ μὲν γάρ', ἔφη, 'ἀεὶ <u>ἀποδημῶ</u>, ὡς σὺ οἶσθα· ὁ δὲ ἀδελφὸς οὑτοσί', ἐμὲ λέγων, 'ὃς ἀεὶ ἐπιδημεῖ, τῶν τε σῶν ἐπιμελήσεται καὶ τῶν ἐμῶν. τοῦτον οὖν ποιῆσαι υἱόν.' καὶ ὁ Μενεκλῆς καλῶς ἔφη αὐτὸν λέγειν, καὶ οὕτως ἐποιεῖτό με.

The brother, who claims to have looked after Menekles from then until his death, ends his case with a plea to the jurors not to allow his opponent, who is challenging his right to Menekles' property, to take away his estate and leave Menekles without heirs.

ὁ δ' ἀντίδικος οὗτος νυνὶ <u>ἄκληρον</u> μὲν ἐμὲ ποιεῖν, ἄπαιδα δὲ τὸν
15 τελευτήσαντα καὶ <u>ἀνώνυμον</u> βούλεται καταστῆσαι. μὴ οὖν, ὦ ἄνδρες, πεισθέντες ὑπὸ τούτου ἀφαιρεῖσθέ μου τὸ ὄνομα. ἀλλ' ἐπειδὴ τὸ πρᾶγμα εἰς ὑμᾶς ἀφῖκται καὶ ὑμεῖς <u>κύριοι</u> γεγένησθε, βοηθήσατε καὶ ἡμῖν καὶ ἐκείνῳ τῷ <u>ἐν</u> <u>Ἅιδου</u> ὄντι, καὶ <u>μεμνημένοι</u> τοῦ νόμου καὶ τοῦ ὅρκου ὃν <u>ὀμωμόκατε</u> καὶ τῶν εἰρημένων ὑπὲρ τοῦ πράγματος, τὰ δίκαια κατὰ
20 τοὺς νόμους ψηφίσασθε.

Vocabulary

τελευτάω die
θάπτω bury
νομιζόμενα, τά customary rites (2b)
ἀδελφή, ἡ sister (1a)
ἀδελφός, ὁ brother (2a)

ἀποδημέω go abroad
ἄκληρος ον disinherited
ἀνώνυμος ον nameless
κύριος α ον responsible (for making the decision)
ἐν Ἅιδου in Hades
μεμνημένος perf. part. of μιμνήσκομαι
ὀμώμοκα perf. of ὄμνυμι

Grammar for Section 14

> In this section you cover:
> - The subjunctive mood: present, aorist and perfect
> - Indefinite constructions with ἄν

THE SUBJUNCTIVE

274. It is rare in this life for anything to come easy. The Greek subjunctive is the exception that proves the rule.

The subjunctive endings

The good news is:

> - The subjunctive mood occurs only in the present, aorist and perfect;
> - The endings for *all* subjunctives – present, aorist and perfect – are as follows:

All active subjunctives (and the aorist passive)	All middle/passive subjunctives
Stem + -ω	Stem + -ωμαι
-ῃς	-ῃ
-ῃ	-ηται
-ωμεν	-ωμεθα
-ητε	-ησθε
-ωσι(ν)	-ωνται

Present subjunctive

275. Here, then, is the present subjunctive: present stem + the above endings:

Present subjunctive active
παύ-ω
παύ-ῃς
παύ-ῃ
παύ-ωμεν
παύ-ητε
παύ-ωσι(ν)

Present subjunctive middle/passive

παύ-ωμαι
παύ-ῃ
παύ-ηται
παυ-ώμεθα
παύ-ησθε
παύ-ωνται

Aorist subjunctive

276. Here is the aorist subjunctive (first and second), formed by taking the aorist stem and adding the subjunctive endings (no augment):

First and second aorist subjunctive active

παύσ-ω	λάβ-ω
παύσ-ῃς	λάβ-ῃς
παύσ-ῃ	λάβ-ῃ
παύσ-ωμεν	λάβ-ωμεν
παύσ-ητε	λάβ-ητε
παύσ-ωσι(ν)	λάβ-ωσι(ν)

Aorist subjunctive middle

παύσ-ωμαι	λάβ-ωμαι
παύσ-ῃ	λάβ-ῃ
παύσ-ηται	λάβ-ηται
παυσ-ώμεθα	λαβ-ώμεθα
παύσ-ησθε	λάβ-ησθε
παύσ-ωνται	λάβ-ωνται

Aorist subjunctive passive

παυθ-ῶ	ληφθ-ῶ
παυθ-ῇς	ληφθ-ῇς
παυθ-ῇ	ληφθ-ῇ
παυθ-ῶμεν	ληφθ-ῶμεν
παυθ-ῆτε	ληφθ-ῆτε
παυθ-ῶσι(ν)	ληφθ-ῶσι(ν)

EXERCISE

14: 1. Translate and turn the following forms into their equivalent subjunctive form (but check carefully that they do in fact *have* a subjunctive form):

ἥμαρτε, ἔπαυε, πείσει, ἐξέπεσε, ἔσχον (pl.)

Perfect subjunctive

277. Same again for the perfect: perfect stem + endings (remember to *keep* the reduplication):

Perfect subjunctive active

πεπαύκ-ω
πεπαύκ-ῃς
πεπαύκ-ῃ
πεπαύκ-ωμεν
πεπαύκ-ητε
πεπαύκ-ωσι(ν)

Alternatively:

πεπαυκώς υἷα ός ὦ
πεπαυκώς υἷα ός ᾖς
πεπαυκώς υἷα ός ᾖ
πεπαυκότες υἷαι ότα ὦμεν
πεπαυκότες υἷαι ότα ἦτε
πεπαυκότες υἷαι ότα ὦσι(ν)

Perfect subjunctive middle/passive

πεπαυμένος η ον ὦ
πεπαυμένος η ον ᾖς
πεπαυμένος η ον ᾖ
πεπαυμένοι αι α ὦμεν
πεπαυμένοι αι α ἦτε
πεπαυμένοι αι α ὦσι(ν)

■ *Forms*

The alternative forms of the perfect active, and the regular forms of the perfects middle and passive, are nothing but the perfect participle + the subjunctive of the verb 'to be' – as you will shortly see. The participle changes (s. or pl., m. f. or n.) to agree with the subject. Thus πεπαυκυῖα ᾖ 'she has stopped'.

Subjunctives of contract verbs

278. Inevitably, contract verbs loom. But they follow exactly the same rules of vowel-contraction as they have always done:

Present active subjunctive

ποιέ-ω		τῑμά-ω		δουλό-ω	
ποι-ῶ	(έ-ω)	τῑμ-ῶ	(ά-ω)	δουλ-ῶ	(ό-ω)
ποι-ῇς	(έ-ης)	τῑμ-ᾷς	(ά-ης)	δουλ-οῖς	(ό-ῇς)
ποι-ῇ	(έ-η)	τῑμ-ᾷ	(ά-η)	δουλ-οῖ	(ό-η)
ποι-ῶμεν	(έ-ωμεν)	τῑμ-ῶμεν	(ά-ωμεν)	δουλ-ῶμεν	(ό-ωμεν)
ποι-ῆτε	(έ-ητε)	τῑμ-ᾶτε	(ά-ητε)	δουλ-ῶτε	(ό-ητε)
ποι-ῶσι(ν)	(έ-ωσι)	τῑμ-ῶσι(ν)	(ά-ωσι)	δουλ-ῶσι(ν)	(ό-ωσι)

Present middle/passive subjunctive

ποιέ-ομαι		τῑμά-ομαι		δουλό-ομαι	
ποι-ῶμαι	(έ-ωμαι)	τῑμ-ῶμαι	(ά-ωμαι)	δουλ-ῶμαι	(ό-ωμαι)
ποι-ῇ	(έ-η)	τῑμ-ᾷ	(ά-η)	δουλ-οῖ	(ό-η)
ποι-ῆται	(έ-ηται)	τῑμ-ᾶται	(ά-ηται)	δουλ-ῶται	(ό-ηται)
ποι-ώμεθα	(ε-ώμεθα)	τῑμ-ώμεθα	(α-ώμεθα)	δουλ-ώμεθα	(ο-ώμεθα)
ποι-ῆσθε	(έ-ησθε)	τῑμ-ᾶσθε	(ά-ησθε)	δουλ-ῶσθε	(ό-ησθε)
ποι-ῶνται	(έ-ωνται)	τῑμ-ῶνται	(ά-ωνται)	δουλ-ῶνται	(ό-ωνται)

Subjunctives of εἰμί, εἶμι and οἶδα

279. Even irregular verbs take on regularity (of a sort) in the subjunctive mood:

εἰμί 'I am'	εἶμι 'I shall go'*	οἶδα 'I know'
ὦ	ἴω	εἰδῶ
ᾖς	ἴῃς	εἰδῇς
ᾖ	ἴῃ	εἰδῇ
ὦμεν	ἴωμεν	εἰδῶμεν
ᾖτε	ἴητε	εἰδῆτε
ὦσι(ν)	ἴωσι(ν)	εἰδῶσι(ν)

* In the subjunctive, of course, it means 'I go'.

Subjunctive of δίδωμι

280. There is a very small exception to the rule of the subjunctive. A very few verbs – very few indeed – keep the -ω- *all the way through* the conjugation, e.g. δίδωμι:

Present active	Present middle/passive
διδῶ	διδῶμαι
διδῷς	διδῷ
διδῷ	διδῶται
διδῶμεν	διδώμεθα
διδῶτε	διδῶσθε
διδῶσι(ν)	διδῶνται

Aorist active	Aorist middle
δῶ	δῶμαι
δῷς	δῷ
δῷ *etc.*	δῶται *etc.*

Cf. So too ἔγνων (**209**): aorist subjunctive γνῶ, γνῷς, γνῷ etc.

EXERCISE

14: 2. Translate and turn the following into their equivalent subjunctive forms (if they have them). Remember to de-augment where appropriate:

γεγάμηκα, εἶσι, εἰσί, γεγενήμεθα, ἔθηκαν, ποιούμεθα, ὁρῶσιν, ἔγνωσαν, ἐδίδοσαν, ἤνεγκε

Meaning of the subjunctive

281. (a) The difference between present and aorist subjunctives is aspectual, not temporal (**142, 165**).

(b) While the subjunctive does have a special meaning when used on its own, you will not be meeting this usage for some time. For the moment, you will learn that the subjunctive is used in certain contexts where a special translation into English is not required. Register that the verb is subjunctive, therefore, but translate it into the most natural English.

ἄν with the subjunctive

282. So far, ἄν has been found only in *main* 'potential > conditional' clauses:

- In 'polite' requests with the optative (**186**), and
- As the (apodosis) of various would-should conditional sentences, with the verb in the optative or indicative (see **256[a]**).

But ἄν is also found in *subordinate* clauses, beginning e.g. 'when ...', 'who ...', 'if ...', etc. Its purpose is to give the clause an 'indefinite' feel to it, e.g.

- '*Whoever* does this [but we don't know precisely who it will be] ...';
- '*When* it rains [but we are not saying whether it will rain or won't]...;

- '*If* I go to town tomorrow [but I may not] …'.

In other words, Greeks liked to distinguish between the definite and the vague or indefinite, especially when referring to future time. Look at the following and deduce the rules:

ὅστις ἂν τοῦτο ποιῇ/ποιήσῃ …   'Whoever does this …'
τρόπῳ ᾧ ἂν βούλωνται …   'In a way in which [ever] they want …'
ὅταν ἔλθωσι/ἴωσι …   'When they go (whenever *that* is) …'
ἐὰν ποιῶμεν/ποιήσωμεν τοῦτο, παύσομεν τοὺς πολεμίους 'If we do this, we shall stop the enemy' [but we don't know if we will do it].
ἐὰν οἰκάδε ἐπανίῃ/ἐπανέλθῃ, ὄψεται τὴν γυναῖκα 'If he returns home, he will see his wife' [but we don't know if he will return home].

Note in particular the last two sentences. They are both 'open' conditions (**256**, i.e. no 'would-should', so no ἄν in the *main* clause). It would be possible to translate them into Greek in the usual 'open' form, i.e. εἰ ποιήσομεν τοῦτο 'If we [shall] do this …', but Greek much prefers the 'indefinite' usage here, ἐὰν + subjunctive.

So, we find ἄν:

(a) Attached to a subordinating conjunction like 'if', when', 'where', or relative 'who', 'which', 'what';
(b) Sometimes combined with the conjunction in question, e.g. εἰ ('if') + ἄν = ἐὰν or ἤν; ὅτε ('when') + ἄν = ὅταν; ἐπειδή ('since') + ἄν = ἐπειδάν;
(c) Sometimes standing free of it e.g. ὅς ('who') ἄν, ὅπου ('where') ἄν;
(d) With the verb of that sub-clause in the *subjunctive* (aspectual, not temporal);
(e) And creating a sense of indefiniteness about the clause. See **398(ii)**, **422(ii)**.

Two uses of ἄν

283. To summarise:

> ► ἄν in a *main clause* (with optative) will indicate a polite request or (with a protasis beginning with εἰ and optative/indicative) a 'would-should' condition;
>
> ► ἄν in a *subordinate clause* (typically beginning e.g. 'if…', 'when…', 'who/which…' etc.) will take the subjunctive and will indicate an indefiniteness or lack of certainty/precision about what is happening or may happen. This might be expressed in English by 'ever' or an understood 'but we don't know if this will happen or not'. 'Would-should' will NOT feature in such clauses. Cf. **407(iii)**, **(v)**, **(vi)**.

EXERCISE

14: 3.Translate into indefinite Greek, using both present and aorist subjunctives (remember to run together the subordinating conjunction and ἄν, if it is possible):

> If they see, when I hear, whoever goes, wherever she is, when they depart, if we enslave, whoever they are, when I know.

SUMMARY LEARNING VOCABULARY FOR SECTION 14

ἀδίκημα (ἀδικηματ-), τό	crime (3b)
ἄκῡρος ον	invalid
ἀποψηφίζομαι	acquit (+gen.); reject (+gen.)
διακρῑνω	decide, judge between
διηγέομαι	explain, relate, go through
ἐᾱν	if (ever)
ἕκαστος η ον	each
ἔλεγχος, ὁ	examination, refutation (2a)
ἐλέγχω	refute, argue against
ἐλήλυθα	perf. of ἔρχομαι I have come
Ἑλλάς (Ἑλλαδ-), ἡ	Greece (3a)
ἔοικε	it seems, it is reasonable, it resembles (+ dat.)
ἐπειδάν	when(ever)
ἐπί	(+dat.) for the purpose of, at, near
ἐπιμέλεια, ἡ	care, concern (1b)
ἐπιμελής ές	careful
ἡμέρᾱ, ἡ	day (1b)
ἱκανός ή όν	sufficient, able
καταλείπω (καταλιπ-)	leave behind, bequeath
κῡριος ᾱ ον	able, with power, by right, sovereign
μέλει	X (dat.) is concerned about Y (gen.)
μετέχω	share in (+gen.)
μισθός, ὁ	pay (2a)
ὀλίγωρος ον	contemptuous
ὅταν	whenever
παντελῶς	completely, outright
πολῖτις (πολῑτιδ-), ἡ	female citizen (3a: but acc. s. πολῖτιν)
πόρνη, ἡ	prostitute (1a)
σῶμα (σωματ-), τό	body, person (3b)
τῑμή, ἡ	honour, privilege, right (1a)
τρέφω (θρεψα-)	rear, raise, feed, nourish

REVISION EXERCISES FOR SECTION 14

(B/C) MORPHOLOGY AND SYNTAX

1. Translate these sentences, changing the verbs underlined into the subjunctive requested to make the Greek grammatical:

a. ὅ τι ἂν μαρτυροῦσι (pres.) καὶ λέγουσιν (pres.) οἱ μάρτυρες, ἀεὶ ἐπιμελῶς διακρίνομεν.

b. ἐπειδὰν λέγει (pres.) καὶ πείθει (pres.) ἡμᾶς ὁ κατήγορος, καταδικάζομεν.

c. ἐπειδὰν ἢ ἀστός τις ἀγωνίζεται (aor.) ἢ οἱ γεννηται ἀποψηφίζονται (aor.) παιδίου ἐκ ξένης τινὸς γενομένου, οἱ νόμοι σῴζονται.

d. ὃς ἂν μὴ καταδικάζεται (aor.), ἀλλ' ἀπολύεται (aor.) ὑπὸ τῶν δικαστῶν, τοῦτον ἀναίτιον εἶναι οἰόμεθα.

e. ἐὰν εἰς ἀτιμίαν καθίσταται (aor.) πονηρός τις, πάντες οἱ πολῖται ἥδονται.

f. ὅταν βούλει (pres.) λέγειν τι δεινὸν καὶ δηλοῖς (pres.) τἀληθῆ, ἀεὶ τιμωρήσονται σὲ οἱ ἐχθροί.

g. ὅπερ ἂν δίκαιον ἡγεῖσθε (pres.) καὶ τιμᾶτε (pres.), τοῦτο τὸ τίμημα, ὦ δικασταί, ὁ καταδικασθεὶς ὀφείλει τῇ πόλει.

h. ᾗτινι ἂν ὁ πατὴρ προῖκα μὴ δίδωσι (aor.), ταύτῃ ἱκανὴν τὴν προῖκα παρέχει ὁ νόμος.

i. ἐὰν ἐπιμελῶς προσέχετε (aor.) τὸν νοῦν πρὸς τὴν κατηγορίαν καὶ προθυμεῖσθε (pres.), καταψηφιεῖσθε τῆς Νεαίρας.

j. ἐπειδὰν εἰσέρχῃ (pres.) εἰς τὴν οἰκίαν καὶ ἐντυγχάνει (aor.) σοι ἡ γυνή, ὅπως θωπεύσεις αὐτήν.

(D) ENGLISH INTO GREEK

1. Sentences

Translate into Greek:

1. When the dikasts go home, their wives greet them.
2. When a woman gets hold of money, she becomes difficult.
3. If you pay attention to the defence speech, you will acquit the defendant.
4. When prosecutors speak, they always say the same thing.
5. If you are loved by your daughters, they will give you whatever you want.

2. Prose

Translate into Greek:

When Stephanos makes his defence speech, what will he say? Obviously he will claim that he has been a good governor and has performed many noble deeds. And yet we all know that nothing noble or good has ever been done by him. Or have you ever heard of any such thing at all? You have not; for neither he nor his forefathers are naturally inclined to piety, but to impiety.

TEST EXERCISE 14
Translate into English:

In Lokris, because of a singular method of treating the legislator, only one new law has been passed in a very long time. The story involves a one-eyed man's search for justice.
(From Demosthenes, *Timokrates*, 139–41)

βούλομαι δ' ὑμῖν διηγήσασθαι ὡς ἐν Λοκροῖς <u>νομοθετοῦσιν</u>. ἐκεῖ γὰρ
οἴονται τοὺς πολίτας δεῖν τοῖς <u>πάλαι</u> <u>κειμένοις</u> νόμοις χρῆσθαι καὶ
τὰ πάτρια φυλάττειν. <u>ὥστε</u> ἐάν τις βούληται νόμον <u>καινὸν</u> τιθέναι,
ἐν <u>βρόχῳ</u> τὸν <u>τράχηλον</u> ἔχων νομοθετεῖ. καὶ ἐὰν μὲν δόξῃ καλὸς καὶ
χρήσιμος εἶναι ὁ νόμος, <u>ζῇ</u> ὁ τιθεὶς καὶ ἀπέρχεται. εἰ δὲ μή, τέθνηκεν
<u>ἐπισπασθέντος</u> τοῦ βρόχου. καὶ γάρ τοι καινοὺς μὲν οὐ τολμῶσι τιθέναι
νόμους, τοῖς δὲ πάλαι κειμένοις ἀκριβῶς χρῶνται. ἐν πολλοῖς δὲ πάνυ
<u>ἔτεσιν</u> εἷς λέγεται νόμος καινὸς τεθῆναι. νόμος μὲν γὰρ ἐν Λοκροῖς
κεῖται ὅτι, ἐάν τις <u>ὀφθαλμὸν</u> ἐκκόψῃ, δεῖ τὸν ἐκκόψαντα παρασχεῖν τὸν
ἑαυτοῦ ὀφθαλμὸν <u>ἀντεκκόψαι</u>. ἐχθρὸς δέ τις λέγεται <u>ἀπειλῆσαι</u> ἐχθρῷ
ὃς <u>ἕνα</u> ὀφθαλμὸν ἔτυχεν ἔχων, ὅτι ἐκκόψοι τοῦτον τὸν ἕνα ὀφθαλμόν.
γενομένης δὲ ταύτης τῆς ἀπειλῆς, χαλεπῶς ἐνεγκὼν ὁ <u>ἑτερόφθαλμος</u>,
καὶ ἡγούμενος <u>ἀβίωτον</u> εἶναι τὸν βίον ἑαυτῷ τοῦτο παθόντι, λέγεται
τολμῆσαι νόμον τοιόνδε εἰσενεγκεῖν· ἐάν τις ἑτεροφθάλμου τινὸς τὸν
ὀφθαλμὸν ἐκκόψῃ, δεήσει αὐτὸν <u>ἀμφὼ</u> τοὺς ὀφθαλμοὺς ἀντεκκόψαι
παρασχεῖν. οὕτω γὰρ τὸ αὐτὸ πάθος ἀμφότεροι πάθοιεν ἄν. καὶ τοῦτον
μόνον λέγονται Λοκροὶ θέσθαι τὸν νόμον ἐν πλέον ἢ <u>διακοσίοις</u> ἔτεσιν.

5

10

15

Vocabulary

νομοθετέω frame laws
πάλαι long ago
κεῖμαι be established
ὥστε and so
καινός ή όν new
βρόχος, ὁ noose (2a)
τράχηλος, ὁ neck (2a)
ζάω live
ἐπισπασθέντος aor. part. pass. of ἐπισπάω draw tight
ἔτος, τό year (3c)
ὀφθαλμός, ὁ eye (2a)
ἀντεκκόπτω knock out in return
ἀπειλέω threaten (+dat.)
εἷς (ἑν-) one
ἑτερόφθαλμος, ὁ one-eyed man (2a)
ἀβίωτος ον unlivable
ἄμφω both
διακόσιοι αι α two hundred

Grammar for Section 15

> **In this section you cover:**
> - The future perfect
> - Tragic usages
> - Scanning Greek verse
> - Iambic trimeters

284. There is only one form of the future perfect. This is the middle/passive form, as follows:

πεπαύ-σομαι **'I shall have ceased/been stopped'**

πεπαύ-σομαι
πεπαύ-σῃ (-σει)
πεπαύ-σεται
πεπαυ-σόμεθα
πεπαύ-σεσθε
πεπαύ-σονται

Infinitive
πεπαύ-σεσθαι

Participle
πεπαυ-σόμενος

Optative
πεπαυ-σοίμην

Form and meaning

285. (a) Look for a perfect middle/passive stem (no -κ-, but reduplication), with future middle endings i.e. -σομαι -σῃ -σεται etc., e.g.

λελύσομαι	(λύω) 'I shall have been released'
	(λύομαι) 'I shall have ransomed'
πεπράξεται	(πράσσω) 'it will have been done'
πεπαύσομαι	(παύομαι) 'I shall have ceased'

As usual, the middle verbs will carry an active meaning:

κεκτήσομαι	(κτάομαι) 'I shall have obtained'

(b) In meaning, particularly in poetry, it can be used as an *emphatic* future, e.g.

κεκτήσεται   'she *will* possess'
φράζε καὶ πεπράξεται   'speak, and it *shall* be done'

(c) The active 'I shall have -ed' is supplied by the perfect active participle and the future of the verb 'to be' e.g.

λελυκότες ἐσόμεθα   'we shall have released'

The passive may also be formed with the passive participle:

λελυμένος ἔσομαι (=λελύσομαι)   'I shall have been released'

Tragic usages

286. Note the following usages common in Greek tragedy:

(a) Observe the elision or crasis displayed by the following phrases in the *Text*:

l.25 κᾆπειτα (καὶ ἔπειτα)
l.16 τἀμά (τὰ ἐμά)
l.38 κἄρριψεν (καὶ ἔρριψεν)
l.47 τἄν (τοι ἄν)
l.9   ᾔσθεθ' ἡμέραν (ᾔσθετο ἡμέραν)

Verse displays far more features of this type than prose, though doubtless crasis and elision occurred in spoken language, even if they were not indicated in writing.

(b) Note the prefixes to:

l.1   καταθνῄσκω
l.13 κατεύχομαι
l.22 προσεύχομαι
l.45 προσλέγω

The basic meaning of the word is retained, but the prefix shades its meaning differently. This subtlety is one you should try to take into account when translating.

(c) Note particularly the splitting of preposition from its verb ('tmesis'):

l.11 ἐκ⌈ δ' ⌉ἑλοῦσα κεδρίνων δόμων 'taking from the cedar box'

(d) Observe the use of the poetic forms (e.g. τοῖσι for τοῖς in τοισίδε κακοῖς, l.49), and the figurative use of words, e. g. l. 11 δόμων, usually 'house', here = 'chest, box'.

(e) Word order in verse can be far more flexible than in prose; again, utterances can be far more oblique and tightly packed with meaning. Since this is a matter of the individual author's style, only wide reading in an author will accustom you to his particular quirks.

Tragic verse metre

■ *English verse*

287. English verse can be described in terms of the number of 'beats' to a line, and sometimes in terms of rhyme as well, e.g.

> 'As I was going up the stair
> I met a man who wasn't there.
> He wasn't there again today.
> I wish, I wish he'd stay away.'

There are four 'beats' to each line, and the lines rhyme AA, BB.

■ *Greek verse*

Greek verse does *not* rhyme; nor is it to be described in terms of 'beats'. It is made up of *regular* sequences of syllables, *each* of which counts as long or short for the purpose of the metre.

> ▶ EVERY SYLLABLE COUNTS IN GREEK VERSE. To scan Greek verse, therefore, requires you to work out the *value (long or short) of each and every syllable that makes up the line.*

■ *Long and short syllables*

288. The 'quantity' of the syllable (i.e. whether it is long or short) is determined by the vowel(s) and consonant(s) which make it up. Here are the basic rules:

Long syllables
(a) Syllables containing η, ω, and diphthongs, and long ᾱ, ῑ, ῡ (these last three have to be *known* to be long, or adduced from context) are pronounced long and *always* count as LONG in verse.

Short syllables
(b) Syllables containing ε, ο and ᾰ, ῐ, ῠ are pronounced short and count as SHORT in verse – with exceptions:

Two-consonant law
(c) If a 'short' vowel is followed by *two consonants* – these include ζ (= σδ), ξ (= κς) and ψ (= πς) – it will still be *pronounced* short, but the syllable will *count as* long for the purposes of scansion.

Consider the vowels of ἔρχονται 'they go':

(i)   ε would be pronounced short, but ἔρχ would *count as* a long syllable in metre, because it is followed by two consonants, ρχ;
(ii)   Likewise, ο, pronounced short, but οντ would *count as* a long syllable because it is followed by two consonants ντ;
(iii)   αι, a diphthong, would be pronounced, and count as, long. Thus ἔρχονται would scan long-long-long.

(iv) Word division makes *no* difference here. Thus, the ο of ἄνθρωπός τις would scan as a LONG syllable, because it is followed by two consonants, ς τ.

The two-consonant law exception

(d) There is one major exception to this 'two-consonant' law. It all depends on *which* two consonants. Any combination of short vowel followed by πτκφθχβδγ ('mute' consonants) + λμνρ ('liquid' consonants) need not necessarily make the syllable long for scansion purposes. For example, the α of πατρός is short; it is followed by two consonants τ+ρ; but the syllable can scan long *or* short because the consonants are a mute+liquid combination.

■ *The iambic trimeter*

289. The commonest metre of Greek tragedy is the IAMBIC TRIMETER (nearly all the *dialogue* of Greek tragedy is written in iambic trimeters). A trimeter is composed of three 'metra'.

An iambic 'metron' is ⏓ – ⏑ – i.e.

(i) doubtful syllable, called 'anceps', which can be either long or short, followed by:

(ii) long—short—long syllables.

(Note that an iambic 'foot' is ⏑ – or – –. An iambic 'metron' consists of *two* such feet.)

Thus, in terms of long and short syllables, an iambic trimeter looks like:

⏓ – ⏑ – / ⏓ – ⏑ – / ⏓ – ⏑ ⏓

One might express it 'blank tum-ti-tum, blank tum-ti-tum, blank tum-ti-tum'. Note that the *last* syllable can be long *or* short.

■ *Resolving a long into shorts*

290. In some Greek metres (and the iambic trimeter is among them), one *long* syllable can be replaced by *two short* syllables. This 'resolution' of one long into two shorts is more common in some authors than others, and in some parts of the line than others.

Here are five lines of the passage from *Alkestis* scanned, i.e. with the longs and shorts marked and the line split up into metra:

πῶς δ' οὐκ ἄρισ/τη; τις δ' ἐναν/τιωσεται;

τι χρη λεγεσ/θαι τηνδ' ὑπερ/βεβλημενην

γυναικα; πῶς / δ' ἀν μαλλον ἐν/δειξαιτο τις

ποσιν προτι/μωσ' ἠ θελου/σ' ὑπερθανειν;

καὶ ταῦτᾰ μὲν / δὴ πᾶσ’ ἐπισ/τᾰται πόλις.

(a) You will have noticed (future perfect) that the last syllable counts LONG for the purpose of scansion, whatever its actual composition.

(b) There are no ‘resolutions’ in these five lines. Contrast l. 18:

ἤκουσᾰν ὑδᾰ / σι ποταμίοις / λευκὸν χρόᾰ

SUMMARY LEARNING VOCABULARY FOR SECTION 15

ἄθλιος ᾱ ον	pathetic, miserable, wretched
βάρος, τό	weight, burden (3c)
γενναῖος ᾱ ον	noble, fine
δάκρυον, τό	tear (2b)
δακρῡ́ω	weep
δέσποινα, ἡ	mistress (1c)
δόμοι, οἱ	house, home (2a)
εἰσπῑ́πτω (εἰσπεσ-)	fall into, on
ἔνθα	there
ἐσθλός ἡ όν	noble, fine, good
εὐπρεπής ές	seemly, proper, becoming
εὐτυχής ές	fortunate, lucky
θάλαμος, ὁ	bedchamber (2a)
θνήσκω (θαν-)	die
ἵστημι/ἵσταμαι	set up, stand, raise
κατά	(+gen.) below
καταθνήσκω (καταθαν-)	die away
κλαίω	weep
κλύω	hear
κόσμος, ὁ	decoration, ornament; order; universe (2a)
κτάομαι	acquire, get, gain
μακρός ᾱ́ όν	large, big, long
οἶκος, ὁ	household, house (2a)
οὔποτε	never
οὔτις	no one
πανύστατος η ον	for the very last time
πατρῷος ᾱ ον	of one’s father, ancestral
προδίδωμι (προδο-)	betray
πόσις, ὁ	husband, spouse (3e)
προσλέγω	address
προσπίτνω	fall upon, embrace
στείχω	go, come

SUMMARY LEARNING VOCABULARY FOR SECTION 15

(continued)

σώφρων ον (σωφρον-)	modest, chaste, discreet, sensible, law-abiding, prudent, disciplined, temperate
τέκνον, τό	child (2b)
τίκτω (τεκ-)	bear, give birth to
ὕδωρ (ὑδατ-), τό	water (3b)
ὑπό	(+dat.) under, beneath
χρώς (χρωτ-), ὁ	flesh, skin (acc. χρόα) (3a)

Grammar for Section 16A–B

> In this section you cover:
> - The pluperfect 'I had -ed'
> - Imperatives using μή + the aorist subjunctive
> - Verbs of 'fearing': φοβοῦμαι μή + subjunctive
> - Verb-forms in -τέος, expressing necessity

THE PLUPERFECT

291. The pluperfect tense is 'more than perfect': not 'I have -ed', but 'I *had* -ed':

Pluperfect active ἐπεπαύκη, 'I had stopped'	Pluperfect middle/passive, ἐπεπαύμην, 'I had ceased/been stopped'
ἐ-πεπαύκ-η	ἐ-πεπαύ-μην
ἐ-πεπαύκ-ης	ἐ-πέπαυ-σο
ἐ-πεπαύκ-ει	ἐ-πέπαυ-το
ἐ-πεπαύκ-εμεν	ἐ-πεπαύ-μεθα
ἐ-πεπαύκ-ετε	ἐ-πέπαυ-σθε
ἐ-πεπαύκ-εσαν	ἐ-πέπαυ-ντο

■ *Form*

The pluperfect is formed by additions and changes to the perfect stem:

- The stem is given an augment ἐ-;
- The pluperfect active has new endings dominated by κ-η, κ-ε;
- The pluperfect middle/passive takes the familiar -μην -σο -το imperfect middle/passive endings (**102**).

EXERCISE

16A–B: 1. Turn the following perfects into their pluperfect form and translate:

τετίμηκας, τέθηκε, τεθνήκαμεν, βεβλήκασιν, βέβηκα, πεφιλήμεθα, δεδουλῶνται, κεκρατήκατε

LAST ORDERS: μή + SUBJUNCTIVE

292. You have already met μή + present imperative meaning 'don't', e.g. μὴ ἄκουε 'don't listen' (**21**).

Greek has another way of expressing this. Look at the following:

μὴ ἀκούσῃς   'don't listen' (s.)
μὴ ἔλθητε   'don't go' (pl.)

What verb-forms are these?

Nothing but our new best friend, the subjunctive – and the *aorist* subjunctive at that.

So μή + 2s. or 2pl. aorist subjunctive = 'don't'. The idiom has an aoristic aspect, and it may imply 'don't do it just this once'. See **404, 406(iii)**.

EXERCISE

16A–B: 2. Translate the following μή commands, and turn present imperatives into aorist subjunctives, and vice versa:

1. μὴ ποιήσῃς τοῦτο.
2. μὴ τρέχετε.
3. μὴ μείνητε.
4. μὴ πίπτε.
5. μὴ εἴπητε ταῦτα.

VERBS OF FEARING

293. φοβοῦμαι 'I fear' means:

- 'I fear, am afraid of'. Here it takes an object in the accusative, e.g. φοβοῦμαι τοὺς Πέρσας 'I fear/am afraid of the Persians.'
- 'I am afraid to do X'. Here it takes the infinitive, e.g. φοβοῦμαι φυγεῖν 'I am afraid to run away.'
- 'I am afraid that/lest X is the case':

In this last sense it takes:

(i) μή + subjunctive if the fear refers to the *future* e.g. 'I am afraid that the allies will not come' φοβοῦμαι μὴ οὐκ ἐλθῶσιν οἱ σύμμαχοι (note: the negative is οὐ);

(ii) otherwise, it takes μή + the natural tense of the indicative, e.g. 'I am afraid that he came' φοβοῦμαι μὴ ἦλθεν. See **400, 407(ii), 422(ii)(d)**.

EXERCISE

16A–B: 3. Translate these fears for the past, re-configure as fears for the future, and re-translate:

1. φοβοῦνται μὴ ἀφίκετο.
2. φοβούμεθα μὴ ἔφυγον.

3. φοβεῖται μὴ ἐμείναμεν.

4. φοβεῖσθε μὴ ἐδουλώθη.

5. φοβοῦμαι μὴ οὐκ ἐμάχοντο.

VERB-FORMS IN -τέος EXPRESSING NECESSITY

294. Forms like πεμπτέος (πέμπω) 'to be sent' and τιμητέος (τιμάω) 'to be honoured' are based upon the verb-stem, act as *adjectives*, and can be used in two ways, personally and impersonally.

Personal use of -τέος forms

In the personal sense, -τέ-ος -ᾱ -ον forms are used as straight adjectives, meaning 'needing to be -ed', 'to be -ed'. Consider:

> ἡ γυνὴ τιμητέα ἐστίν ὑμῖν 'the woman is to be honoured/must be honoured by you';
> ἔφη τὰς ναῦς πεμπτέας εἶναι 'he said the ships were to be sent/had to be sent';
> πειστέοι οἱ ἄνθρωποί εἰσιν ἡμῖν 'the men are to be persuaded/must be persuaded by us'.

- In these usages, the agent ('by you' and 'by us' above) is expressed by the plain dative.
- Note particularly οἰστέος (φέρω) 'to be carried', πρακτέος (πράττω) 'to be done'.

Impersonal use of -τέος forms

295. We are already familiar with δεῖ 'it is necessary for X (accusative) to Y (infinitive)', e.g.

> δεῖ ἐκείνους ποιεῖν τοῦτο 'it is necessary for them (acc.) to do (inf.) this', 'they must do this' (**153**).

That sentiment can also be expressed by:

- Replacing δεῖ ποιεῖν with the verb 'to be' + the fixed NEUTER -τέος form (s. or pl.). So δεῖ ποιεῖν becomes either ποιητέον (n.s.) or ποιητέα ἐστίν (n. pl.).
- Putting the people who 'must' into the accusative or dative, ἐκείνους/ ἐκείνοις.
- So δεῖ ἐκείνους ποιεῖν τοῦτο becomes ποιητέον/ποιητέα ἐστὶν ἐκείνους/ἐκείνοις τοῦτο.

Compare e.g.

(i) ἔδει με τὴν ἐπιστολὴν γράψαι 'it was necessary for me to write the letter'
= γραπτέον/γραπτέα ἦν με/μοι τὴν ἐπιστολήν

(ii) δεῖ ἡμᾶς ἀθυμεῖν 'we must be down-hearted' = ἀθυμητέον/ἀθυμητέα ἐστὶν ἡμᾶς/ἡμῖν

Observe two points:

- As in (i) and (ii) above, the agent of -τέον/τέα constructions can go into the accusative (as with δεῖ) *or* the dative;
- The verb 'to be' can be omitted, e.g.

ἰτέον/ἰτέα [ἐστὶν] τοὺς ἄνδρας/τοῖς ἀνδράσιν 'the men must go' (ἰτέος is the adjectival form of εἶμι 'I will go') – the equivalent of δεῖ τοὺς ἄνδρας ἰέναι.

SUMMARY LEARNING VOCABULARY FOR SECTION 16A–B

ἀπελευθέρᾱ, ἡ	freedwoman (1b)
ἀπελεύθερος, ὁ	freedman (2a)
διεξέρχομαι (διεξελθ-)	go through, relate
ἔξω	(+gen.) outside
ἔοικα	seem, resemble
εὐθύς	(+gen.) straight towards
ἰτέ-ος ᾱ ον	to be gone
οἰστέ-ος ᾱ ον	to be carried, borne, endured
πρᾱκτέ-ος ᾱ ον	to be done
πύλη, ἡ	gate (1a)
συμφορᾱ́, ἡ	disaster, mishap, occurrence (1b)
συντυγχάνω (συντυχ-)	meet with (+dat.)
ὑβριστής, ὁ	violent, criminal person (1d)
ὑπό	(+ acc.) under, along under, up under
χωρίον, τό	farm; place, space, region (2b)

REVISION EXERCISES FOR SECTION 16A–B

(B/C) MORPHOLOGY AND SYNTAX

1. Translate these commands, then change into negative commands using μή + aorist subjunctive:

   a. κωλύσατε τὸν ἄνδρα.
   b. τιμωρήσασθε τοὺς φίλους.
   c. καταφρόνησον τῶν θεῶν.
   d. θοῦ τὴν ψῆφον.
   e. ἐπιλάθεσθε τούτου τοῦ πράγματος.
   f. κάτειπε τὸν τῆς ἀπολογίας λόγον.
   g. μνημονεύσατε πάντας τοὺς λόγους.
   h. παράλαβε τοὺς νεανίσκους.
   i. ἐπίσχες.
   j. ἐπιθυμήσατε.
   k. ἀθύμησον.

2. Translate the following sentences:

   a. φοβούμεθα μὴ ταῦτ' ἀκούσας ἀθυμήσῃ ὁ ἀνήρ.
   b. δεινῶς ἀθυμῶ μὴ οὐ ποιῇ τοῦτο ὁ ἑταῖρος.
   c. ὅρα μὴ ψευδῆ λέγῃς πρὸς τοὺς δικαστὰς περὶ τῶν γεγενημένων.
   d. φοβοῦμαι μὴ τοὺς ἄνδρας οὐκ ἔσωσεν ὁ Δημοσθένης.

3. Translate these statements, then using the pool of -τέος verb-forms below, convert them as follows:

   e.g. δεῖ ἐμὲ ποιεῖν ταῦτα→ἐμοὶ/ἐμὲ ποιητέον/ποιητέα ταῦτα

   a. δεῖ ἡμᾶς ἀκριβῶς σκοπεῖσθαι περὶ ταῦτα.
   b. δεῖ σὲ ἰέναι οἴκαδε.
   c. δεῖ αὐτοὺς βοηθεῖν.
   d. δεῖ τὸν ἄνδρα φέρειν τὴν συμφοράν.
   e. δεῖ ὑμᾶς πολεμεῖν.
   f. δεῖ οἴκαδε πέμπειν σέ.
   σκεπτέος, οἰστέος, ἰτέος, πολεμητέος, βοηθητέος, πεμπτέος

Grammar for Section 16C

In this section you cover:
- The accusative absolute
- ὡς + the superlative

THE ACCUSATIVE ABSOLUTE

296. We are familiar with the genitive absolute, that is, participle phrases in the genitive which have no obvious grammatical connection with the rest of the sentence, e.g.

ἀπόντος ἐμοῦ, ἔπαιζον οἱ παῖδες 'me being absent/in my absence, the children began to play' (**222-3**).

▶ Impersonal verbs, however, put their absolute forms into the *neuter accusative participle*:

- δεῖ 'it is necessary for X (acc.)' > δέον 'it being necessary'
- ἔξεστι 'it is permitted to X (dat.)' > ἐξόν 'it being permitted'
- δοκεῖ 'it seems best to X (dat.)' > δόξαν 'it seeming best' (aorist aspect).

So:

δέον ἡμᾶς ἐλθεῖν, ἵμεν 'it being necessary for us to go, we shall go' (or 'since we must go …')
ἐξὸν ἡμῖν ἐλθεῖν, ἐμείναμεν 'it being permitted for us to go, we stayed put' (or 'although we could go …')
δόξαν μοι μένειν, ἔμεινα 'it seeming good to me to wait, I waited'.

EXERCISE

16C: 1. Turn the following clauses with finite verbs into subordinate clauses with accusative absolutes, and translate:

1. ἔξεστιν ἡμῖν ἀπιέναι
2. δεῖ ὑμᾶς θεραπεύειν τὰς γυναῖκας
3. δοκεῖ μοι ποιῆσαι τοῦτο
4. τοῖς παισὶν ἔξεστι παίζειν
5. δεῖ τοὺς ἄνδρας ἐκδοῦναι τὰς θυγατέρας

ὡς + SUPERLATIVE

297. Superlative adjectives and adverbs mean 'very – ', 'most – ', 'the -est' (**154,** **225**). Put ὡς before those superlatives, however, and they will mean 'as – as possible', e.g.

- ὡς τάχιστα 'as quickly as possible'
- ὡς μάλιστα 'as much as can be'
- ὡς πλεῖστοι 'as many as possible'

EXERCISE

16C: 2. Turn these adjectives into superlatives with ὡς and translate:

ἀγαθός (two possibilities), ὀλίγος, σαφής, σώφρων, φοβερός, ἄδικος, μέγας, κακός (two possibilities)

REVISION EXERCISE FOR SECTION 16C

(B/C) MORPHOLOGY AND SYNTAX

Translate the following pairs of statements, then join into one sentence by the use of acc. absolute:

a. δεῖ τὸν ὀφείλοντα τῇ πόλει τὰ σκεύη παραδιδόναι τῷ τριηραρχήσοντι/ ἐγὼ ὡς τὸν Θεόφημον προσῆλθον.

b. εἶτα οὐκ ἔξεστί μοι τὴν τριήρη παρασκευάζειν/προσῆλθον πρὸς τὴν βουλήν.

c. ἔδει ἡμᾶς παρασκευάζειν ὡς τάχιστα τὰς ναῦς/γράφει Χαιρέδημος ψήφισμα.

d. οὐκ ἐξῆν ἐν τῷ Πειραιεῖ οὐδὲν πρίασθαι ὧν ἔδει/οἱ τριήραρχοι οὐκ ἐδύναντο παρασκευάζειν τὰς ναῦς.

Grammar for Section 16D

> **In this section you cover:**
> ● ἵνα or ὅπως + subjunctive or optative

PURPOSE CLAUSES

298. We have already encountered one way of expressing 'purpose' in a sentence: ὡς + future participle (**251**). Greek has another way of doing it: by the subordinating conjunction ἵνα or ὅπως, 'in order that, in order to, to'. See what is going on in the following sentences:

(i) ἀφικνεῖται ἵνα πείθῃ/πείσῃ τοὺς ἄνδρας 'he is coming in order that he may persuade the men/in order to persuade the men/to persuade the men';

(ii) ἀφίκετο ἵνα πείθοι/πείσειε τοὺς ἄνδρας 'he came in order that he might persuade the men/in order to persuade the men/to persuade the men'.

> ● In (i), the ἵνα (or ὅπως) subordinate clause has its verb in the *subjunctive* (present or aorist);
> ● In (ii) in the *optative* (present or aorist). See **399, 407(1), 422(ll)(e)**.

299. This illustrates an extremely important principle, which we shall meet again and again:

> ▶ Subordinate clauses which take the *subjunctive* in primary sequence (see **265**) may take the *optative* in secondary sequence. See **306**.

So here:

in (i), the main verb is present (primary sequence) – therefore the subordinate clause is in the subjunctive;
in (ii) the main verb is past (secondary sequence) – therefore the subordinate clause is in the optative.

Note the way in which English too (in theory at any rate) acknowledges sequence, using 'may' in primary and 'might' in secondary.

> ▶ A second principle is one with which we are already familiar: the subjunctive and optative moods are aspectual, not temporal (**142, 165**).

EXERCISE

16D: 1. Go back to the exercise at **13A–B: 3** and turn the purpose clauses there into ἵνα or ὅπως + subjunctive or optative.

REVISION EXERCISE FOR SECTION 16D

(D) ENGLISH INTO GREEK

Translate into Greek:

1. Don't be downhearted, my friend.
2. Are you afraid that you will suffer again at the hands of these rogues?
3. Although Theophemos is obliged to hand over the gear, I cannot force him to do this.
4. I shall go to the council, so that they may draft a decree.
5. I went to a friend's house, to find out where Theophemos lived.

Grammar for Section 16E

In this section you cover:
● Indefinite clauses in secondary sequence

'INDEFINITES' IN SECONDARY SEQUENCE

300. We have already met subordinate clauses that use ἄν + subjunctive to give an uncertainty or lack of precision to the clause, e.g. ὁπόταν 'when(ever)', ἐάν 'if (ever)', ὅστις ἄν 'who(ever)' (cf. **282**).

But these clauses were all in primary sequence. What if they were in secondary sequence? Examine the following:

> ὁπότε ἔλθοι/ἴοι, ἀπῆλθον　　　　'whenever he came, I left'
> ὅστις τοῦτο ποιοίη/ποιήσειεν, ἥμαρτεν 'whoever made this got it wrong'

In other words, indefinite subordinate clauses in secondary sequence:

● Omit ἄν
● Put the verb in the *optative* (but see **306**)

> ▶ **RULE:** if you meet a subordinate clause controlled by ὁπότε, ἐπειδή, ἐπεί, ὅς(τις) etc., and the verb is in the *optative*, treat it as indefinite (no 'would/should'). See **407(iii)**, **(v)**.

There are two subordinate clauses where this rule does not apply:
(a) εἰ, 'if'
When εἰ is followed by an optative, check the main clause for signs of ἄν:

● If the verb of the *main clause* is in the optative with ἄν, you are dealing with a remote future condition ('if X were to be the case, Y would happen' **241**) cf. **407(vi)**;
● If not, you are dealing with an indefinite conditional. Therefore translate the εἰ clause indefinitely (e.g. 'if ever X happened, …'), without any 'would/should' cf. **407(v)**.

(b) ὅτι in reported speech

If you find the main verb of a reported-speech ὅτι-clause in the optative, translate it as a normal indicative. The optative will be being used *in place of the indicative* to report what was originally said e.g. ἔλεξεν ὅτι πείσοιτο/πείσεται 'he said that he would obey' (**265, 407(iv)**).

EXERCISE

16E: 1. Translate the following indefinite clauses in primary sequence and turn them into indefinites in secondary sequence (remember to remove ἄν). Keep the same aspect of verb in the secondary sequence as there is in the primary sequence:

      1. ἐὰν μὴ ποιῇ τοῦτο …

      2. ὁπόταν ἴδω αὐτόν…

      3. ὅντινα ἂν κελεύωσι…

      4. ἐπειδὰν μάθω…

      5. ἐάν μοι διδῷς ταῦτα…

SUMMARY LEARNING VOCABULARY FOR SECTION 16C–E

ἀδελφός, ὁ	brother (2a)
ἀπαιτέω	demand X (acc.) from Y (acc.)
ἄπειμι	be absent
βοήθεια, ἡ	help, rescue operation (1b)
γράφω	propose (a decree); write
δείκνῡμι (δειξα-)	show
δέον	it being necessary
διαλείπω (διαλιπ-)	leave
ἐξόν	it being permitted, possible
ἵνα	(+subj., opt.) in order to, that
κοινός ή όν	common, shared
κομίζομαι	collect
ὅθεν	from where
ὁπόταν	whenever
ὁπότε	when (+opt.=whenever)
οὗ	where (at)
οὐσίᾱ, ἡ	property, wealth (1b)
παραδίδωμι (παραδο-)	hand over
παρασκευάζω	prepare, equip
πλεῖστος η ον	very much, most (sup. of πολύς)
πρός	(+dat.) in addition to, near
σκεύη, τά	ship's gear; gear, furniture (3c)
σύμμαχος, ὁ	ally (2a)
τριηραρχέω	serve as trierarch
ὑπακούω	reply, answer; obey (+dat.)
φράζω	utter, mention, talk
χωρίς	apart; separately; (prep.) apart/separately from (+gen.)
ὠνέομαι (πρια-)	buy
ὡς	(+sup.) as - as possible
ὥστε	so that, with the result that, consequently

REVISION EXERCISE FOR SECTION 16E

(B/C) MORPHOLOGY AND SYNTAX

1. Translate the following sentences, then change from primary to secondary sequence or vice-versa (remember to change both introductory and subordinate verbs):

   a. ἐβούλετο κομίζεσθαι τὰ σκεύη, ἵνα τὴν τριήρη παρασκευάζοι.

   b. φοβοῦμαι μὴ Εὔεργος οὐ δείξῃ τὸ πρᾶγμα τῷ Θεοφήμῳ.

   c. ἐκέλευον τὸν παῖδα καλέσαι τοὺς πολίτας, ἵνα μάρτυρές μοι εἶεν τῶν λεχθέντων.

   d. οὐ παύονται ἑπόμενοι, ἵνα τὰ γεγενημένα μάθωσιν.

2. Translate the following pairs of sentences:

   a. (i) ὅτε εἰσέλθοι, ἑώρα καθιζομένην τὴν γυναῖκα.
      (ii) ὅτε εἰσῆλθεν, εἶδε τὴν γυναῖκα ἐπὶ τοῦ βωμοῦ καθιζομένην.

   b. (i) ἠρόμην τὸν παῖδα ὅπου εἴη ὁ δεσπότης.
      (ii) ἐκέλευον τὴν ἄνθρωπον μετελθεῖν τὸν δεσπότην, ὅπου εἴη.

   c. (i) ἤδη ἐπεπύσμην ἐγὼ ὅτι τύχοι γεγαμηκώς.
      (ii) ὁ δεσπότης ἐκέλευεν αὐτὸν ἀποδιδόναι τῇ πόλει, ὅ τι τύχοι ἔχων.

   d. (i) ὁ παῖς ἐκάλεσεν ἐκ τῆς ὁδοῦ πάντας τοὺς πολίτας, οὓς εἶδεν, ὡς μαρτυρήσοντας.
      (ii) ἐκελεύσθη ὁ παῖς καλέσαι ἐκ τῆς ὁδοῦ πολίτας ὡς μαρτυρήσοντας, εἴ τινας ἴδοι.

   e. (i) ἡμῖν ἔδοξεν χρῆναι ἕκαστον λόγον περὶ Ἔρωτος εἰπεῖν ὡς δύναιτο κάλλιστον. (Plato, abridged)
      (ii) Λύσανδρος δὲ ἀφικόμενος εἰς Αἴγιναν ἀπέδωκε τὴν πόλιν Αἰγινήταις, ὅσους ἐδύνατο πλείστους αὐτῶν ἀθροίσας. (Xenophon)

Vocabulary

χρῆναι inf. of χρή
ἀθροίζω collect, gather

Grammar for Section 16F

In this section you cover:
- The perfect optative
- ἁλίσκομαι 'I am being captured'

PERFECT OPTATIVE, ACTIVE AND MIDDLE/PASSIVE

301. You should by now consider it a routine task to construct the optative of the perfect. One applies optative endings to a perfect stem:

Perfect optative active, πεπαύκοιμι

πεπαύκ-οιμι
πεπαύκ-οις
πεπαύκ-οι
πεπαύκ-οιμεν
πεπαύκ-οιτε
πεπαύκ-οιεν

Alternatively:

πεπαυκὼς υἷα ός εἴην
πεπαυκὼς υἷα ός εἴης
πεπαυκὼς υἷα ός εἴη
πεπαυκότες υἷαι ότα εἶμεν
πεπαυκότες υἷαι ότα εἶτε
πεπαυκότες υἷαι ότα εἶεν

Perfect optative middle/passive, πεπαυμένος η ον εἴην

πεπαυμένος η ον εἴην
πεπαυμένος η ον εἴης
πεπαυμένος η ον εἴη
πεπαυμένοι αι α εἶμεν
πεπαυμένοι αι α εἶτε
πεπαυμένοι αι α εἶεν

Usage

The perfect optative is just another optative which writers will use when they feel like it, in contexts where optatives are used, e.g. indefinite clauses, reported speech, etc. It has to be said it is not very common. If you have an interest in rare grammatical features, you may therefore like to watch out for an example in order to add it to your collection.

ἁλίσκομαι

302. ἁλίσκομαι has the passive meaning 'be captured, found guilty' and is rather irregular. It needs careful learning:

> ἁλίσκομαι 'I am being captured'
> ἁλώσομαι (fut.) 'I will be captured'
> ἑάλω-ν (ἁλ-) (aor.) 'I was captured'
> ἑάλωκα (perf.) 'I have been captured'

The aorist ἑάλων is a 'root' aorist (cf. ἔβην **209**) and keeps its ω all the way through the indicative and subjunctive, like ἔγνων (γιγνώσκω 'I get to know', **209**). Here are its other aorist forms, all compared with ἔγνων:

Participle

ἁλούς, stem ἁλοντ- (cf. γνούς, γνοντ-)

Infinitive

ἁλῶναι (cf. γνῶναι)

Optative

ἁλοίην (cf. γνοίην)

Subjunctive

ἁλῶ, ἁλῷς, ἁλῷ etc. (cf. γνῶ, cf. **280**)

EXERCISE

16F: 1. Using γιγνώσκω, βαίνω and ἁλίσκομαι as your 'pool', transform each of the following forms into the equivalent form of the other two:

1. ἔγνω
2. βάντες
3. ἁλοίη
4. βῆναι
5. γνῶ

Grammar for Section 16G

> In this section you cover:
> - 'Jussive'/'Hortatory' subjunctive
> - ἕως ἄν 'until'

'LET US …' (SUBJUNCTIVE)

303. So far we have met the subjunctive only in subordinate clauses. But it can be used as a main verb in its own right, when it has its own specific meaning. Look at the following:

μένωμεν	'let us wait'
πυθώμεθα	'let us inquire'
μὴ φοβώμεθα	'let us not be afraid'
ἴωμεν	'let's go'

Usage

- As you can see, its use is restricted to the first person, and virtually always plural too;
- The subjunctive can be either present or aorist (its force is aspectual, not temporal);
- It is called the 'jussive' (Latin *iubeo* 'I order') or 'hortatory' (Latin *hortor* 'I urge, exhort') subjunctive. See **406(i)**, **422(i)(a)**.

EXERCISE

16G: 1. Turn the following plural imperatives into 1pl. jussive subjunctives, and translate. Keep the same aspect of subjunctive as the imperative:

1. ἀκούσατε
2. μὴ ἄπιτε
3. λάβεσθε
4. στῆτε
5. μὴ δῶτε

ἕως ἄν 'UNTIL'

304. Here is another use of the subjunctive + ἄν in a subordinate clause with an indefinite or imprecise outcome to it: ἕως ἄν, meaning 'until [such time as]'. Observe:

μένωμεν ἕως ἂν ἐπανέλθῃ ὁ δεσπότης 'let us wait till [such time as] the master returns' (whenever *that* may be).

The implication behind this sense of 'until' is that the time of the event awaited in the 'until' clause is viewed as being not entirely certain, or as lying in the indefinite future (on indefinite use of ἄν, see **283** cf. **398(ii)**).

EXERCISE

16G: 2. Turn the following clauses into indefinite clauses with ἕως ἄν, and translate indefinitely (in the grammatical, not temporal, sense):

1. ὁρῶμεν τοὺς ἄνδρας
2. ὑπισχνεῖται ἀκούσεσθαι
3. διδόασι τὰ χρήματα
4. παραλαμβάνετε τοὺς μάρτυρας
5. εὑρίσκω τὴν ναῦν

Grammar for Section 16H

> In this section you cover:
> • φοβοῦμαι μή + optative

φοβοῦμαι AGAIN

305. You have already met φοβοῦμαι μή + subjunctive, meaning 'I fear that something will/may happen' (**293**). It should come as no surprise to see what happens to the construction here:

> ἐφοβεῖτο μὴ οὐκ ἀφίκοιτο ἡ στρατιά 'he was afraid the army might not come'

Of course!

> • The sequence is secondary, ἐφοβεῖτο being past; and
> • The verb in the subordinate μή clause therefore goes into the optative, ἀφίκοιτο.

> ▶ You have now met three constructions in which the verbs in subordinate clauses are in the subjunctive in primary sequence, and optative in secondary sequence – ἵνα expressing purpose (**298–9**), indefinite clauses (**282, 300**) and now with verbs of fearing. Cf. **400, 407(ii)**.

Warning

306. Be aware, however, that Greek usage in this respect is very flexible. It is not at all uncommon to find Greek using the *subjunctive* instead of the more normal optative in subordinate clauses in secondary sequence – the so-called 'vivid' use of the subjunctive.

EXERCISE

16H: 1. Turn these sentences from primary sequence into secondary, and vice versa, and translate:

> 1. ἐφοβοῦντο μὴ αὐτοὺς ζημιώσειεν.
> 2. εἶμι ἵνα εἰσαγγείλω τὸν μάρτυρα.
> 3. ἐάν σοι πείθωμαι, πείσῃ μοι σύ.
> 4. φοβεῖται μή τις ἐκφύγῃ.
> 5. εἰ εἴποι, ἤκουον.

SUMMARY LEARNING VOCABULARY FOR SECTION 16F–H

ἀθῡμίᾱ, ἡ	lack of spirit, depression (1b)
ἁλίσκομαι (ἁλ-)	be caught, convicted (aor. ἑάλων)
ἀναίτιος ον	innocent
ἀντί	(+gen.) instead of, for
ἀπολαμβάνω (ἀπολαβ-)	take
βουλευτής, ὁ	member of council (1d)
διάκειμαι	be in X (adv.) state, mood
διακωλύω	prevent
εἴκοσι	twenty
εἰσαγγελίᾱ, ἡ	impeachment (1b)
εἰσαγγέλλω (εἰσαγγειλα-)	impeach
ἐκεῖ	there
ἐνέχυρον, τό	security, pledge (2b)
ἐνθῡμέομαι	take to heart, be angry at
ἐπί	(+ dat.) at, on; for the purpose of
ἐπιεικής ές	fair, reasonable, moderate
ἕως ἄν	(+ subj.) until
ζημιόω	fine, penalise, punish
ἥκιστα	least of all, no, not
καταδίκη, ἡ	fine (1a)
κρίσις, ἡ	judgment, dispute, trial, decision (3e)
μάλα	very, quite, virtually (cf. μᾶλλον, μάλιστα)
μετέρχομαι (μετελθ-)	send for, chase after
μέτριος ᾱ ον	fair, moderate, reasonable
πλέον	more (adv.)
προάγω	lead on
συλλέγω	collect, gather
στόμα (στοματ-), τό	mouth (3b)
συγχωρέω	agree with, to (+ dat.); yield to
τεκμαίρομαι	conclude, infer
ὑπισχνέομαι (ὑποσχ-)	promise (to) (+ fut. inf.)
φοβέομαι μή	fear that/lest (+ subj./opt.)

REVISION EXERCISES FOR SECTION 16F–H

ENGLISH INTO GREEK

1. Sentences
Translate into Greek:

1. The decree demanded that the trierarchs get back the gear in whatever
    way was most easy for them.
2. Whenever the trierarchs came across someone not handing over the gear,
    they went back to the council.
3. Let us stop travelling and sit down.
4. We shall stay here until we feel better.
5. Before returning home, let us sit down over there until the sun becomes
    more tolerable.

2. Prose
Translate into Greek:

Since it was impossible to get the gear, the city was in great danger. So the
council had to do something, in order that we might equip a rescue-force of
triremes as soon as possible. I had gone to Theophemos' house, but he was
not in. I was afraid that he would not hand over the gear. So Khairedemos
drafted a decree. And the trierarchs, whenever they came across someone
who would not give back the gear, showed him the decree.

TEST EXERCISE 16
Translate into English:

*Apollodoros claims that the defendant Polykles refused to take over from him
as trierach of a trireme, even though Polykles had been appointed as its joint-
trierarch for the next year. The result was that he himself had to serve several
months overtime with the boat. Apollodoros relates what happened when he
first tackled Polykles about the matter, in Thasos.*
(From Demosthenes, *Polykles*, 29–37)

ἐπειδὴ οὗτος ἀφίκετο εἰς Θάσον, παραλαβὼν ἐγὼ μάρτυρας τῶν τε
πολιτῶν ὡς ἐδυνάμην πλείστους καὶ τοὺς ἐπιβάτας, προσέρχομαι αὐτῷ
ἐν Θάσῳ ἐν τῇ ἀγορᾷ, καὶ ἐκέλευον αὐτὸν τήν τε ναῦν παραλαμβάνειν
παρ' ἐμοῦ ὡς διάδοχον ὄντα, καὶ τοῦ ἐπιτετριηραρχημένου χρόνου
5   ἀποδιδόναι μοι τὰ ἀναλώματα. λογίσασθαι δ' ἤθελον αὐτῷ καθ'
ἕκαστον, ἕως μοι μάρτυρες παρῆσαν τῶν ἀνηλωμένων, ἵνα, εἴ τι
ἀντιλέγοι, εὐθὺς ἐξελέγχοιμι. ἐγέγραπτο γὰρ ὑπ' ἐμοῦ ἀκριβῶς τὰ
ἀναλώματα. προκαλουμένου δέ μου ταῦτα, ἀπεκρίνατό μοι Πολυκλῆς
ὅτι οὐδὲν αὐτῷ μέλοι ὧν λέγοιμι.

*Apollodoros gets no further on the next occasion either. Returning from
a voyage ordered by the general Timomakhos to Thasos, he decides to go*

straight to the top and ensure the general himself is in attendance when he
tries to hand over the vessel formally to Polykles for the second time.

10 καταλαμβάνω οὖν καὶ Πολυκλέα ἐκεῖ καὶ τοὺς τριηράρχους καὶ τοὺς
διαδόχους καὶ ἄλλους τινὰς τῶν πολιτῶν, καὶ εἰσελθὼν εὐθὺς ἐναντίον
τοῦ στρατηγοῦ λόγους πρὸς αὐτὸν ἐποιούμην, καὶ ἐκέλευον αὐτὸν τήν
τε ναῦν παραλαμβάνειν παρ' ἐμοῦ, καὶ τοῦ ἐπιτετριηραρχημένου χρόνου
ἀποδιδόναι μοι τὰ ἀναλώματα. ταῦτα δέ μου προκαλουμένου αὐτόν,
15 'τίς ἂν δύναιτ'', ἔφη, 'τὴν σὴν <u>μανίαν</u> καὶ <u>πολυτέλειαν</u> <u>ὑπομεῖναι</u>, ὃς
σκεύη <u>ἴδια</u> μόνος ἔχεις τῶν τριηράρχων, καὶ ἀργύριον πολὺ δίδως τοῖς
ναύταις; κακῶν γὰρ διδάσκαλος γέγονας ἐν τῷ <u>στρατεύματι</u>, διαφθείρας
τοὺς ναύτας καὶ τοὺς ἐπιβάτας, δέον σε <u>τὰ</u> <u>αὐτὰ</u> ποιεῖν τοῖς ἄλλοις
τριηράρχοις.' λέγοντος δὲ αὐτοῦ ταῦτα, ἀπεκρινάμην αὐτῷ, 'περὶ μὲν
20 τῶν ναυτῶν καὶ τῶν ἐπιβατῶν, εἰ φὴς ὑπ' ἐμοῦ αὐτοὺς διεφθάρθαι,
παραλαβὼν τὴν τριήρη αὐτὸς σαυτῷ <u>κατασκεύασαι</u> καὶ ναύτας καὶ
ἐπιβάτας, οἵτινές σοι μηδὲν ἀργύριον λαβόντες <u>συμπλεύσονται</u>. τὴν
δὲ ναῦν παράλαβε· οὐ γὰρ ἔτι μοι <u>προσήκει</u> τριηραρχεῖν.' λέγοντος δέ
μου ταῦτα, ἀποκρίνεταί μοι ὅτι ὁ <u>συντριήραρχος</u> αὐτῷ οὐχ ἥκοι ἐπὶ τὴν
25 ναῦν· 'οὔκουν παραλήψομαι μόνος τὴν τριήρη.'

Vocabulary

ἐπιβάτης, ὁ marine (1d)
διάδοχος, ὁ successor (2a)
ἐπιτριηραρχέω serve overtime as trierarch
ἀνάλωμα (ἀναλωματ-), τό expense (3b)
ἕως (+ indic.) while
ἀνηλωμένος perf. part. pass. of ἀναλίσκω spend
ἀντιλέγω object
προκαλέομαι challenge
μανία, ἡ madness (1b)
πολυτέλεια, ἡ extravagance (1b)
ὑπομένω (ὑπομεινα-) endure
ἴδιος α ον private
στράτευμα (στρατευματ-), τό army (3b)
ὁ αὐτός (+ dat.) the same as
κατασκευάζομαι provide
συμπλέω (fut. συμπλεύσομαι) sail with
προσήκει it is the business of (dat.)
συντριήραρχος, ὁ joint-trierarch (2a)

Grammar for Section 17A

In this section you cover:
- ἕως + optative 'until such time as'
- (ἀφ)ἵημι

---

307. You will not be surprised to learn that ἕως 'until such time as', which took ἄν + subjunctive in primary sequence (see **304**), should react differently in secondary sequence:

ἐμένομεν ἕως ἔλθοι 'we waited until he should come/for him to come'

- In other words, ἕως 'until such time as' joins a growing number of constructions in subordinate clauses that take ἄν + subjunctive in primary sequence, and may take plain optative in secondary. Cf. **300**, **398(ii)**, **407(iii)**.

EXERCISE

17A: 1. Transform sentences in primary sequence into secondary, and vice versa, and translate. Maintain the aspect of the original verb:

1. ἐμένομεν ἕως ἔλθοι.
2. μάχονται ἕως ἄν νικῶσιν.
3. δραμεῖν ἐβούλοντο ἕως στῆναι μὴ οἷοί τ' εἶεν.
4. δεῖ σε εὔχεσθαι ἕως ἄν σωθῇς.
5. ἐβουλεύοντο ἕως συγχωρήσειεν.

THE FINAL –μι VERB: (ἀφ)ἵημι 'RELEASE, LET GO, SHOOT'

308. We have already met the -μι verbs:

- δίδωμι 'I give' (**214**)
- τίθημι 'I put/place' (**237**)
- ἵστημι 'I set X up' (**230–3**)

We have also seen how their closely forms are related.
ἵημι is no exception, and basically follows the pattern of τίθημι. ἀφίημι, the common compound, is used here. See **382**, **426**.

ἀφίημι 'I release, let go'

Present: stem ἀφ-ιε-

Active

Indicative	Imperative	Optative	Subjunctive
ἀφίη-μι		ἀφιε-ίην	ἀφῑ-ῶ
ἀφίη-ς	ἀφίε-ι	ἀφιε-ίης	ἀφῑ-ῇς
ἀφίη-σι(ν)	ἀφιέ-τω	ἀφιε-ίη	ἀφῑ-ῇ
ἀφίε-μεν		ἀφιε-ῖμεν	ἀφῑ-ῶμεν
ἀφίε-τε	ἀφίε-τε	ἀφιε-ῖτε	ἀφῑ-ῆτε
ἀφῑ-ᾶσι(ν)	ἀφιέ-ντων	ἀφιε-ῖεν	ἀφῑ-ῶσι(ν)

Infinitive	Participle
ἀφιέ-ναι	ἀφιε-ίς ἀφιεῖ-σα ἀφιέ-ν (ἀφιε-ντ-)

Middle/passive

Indicative	Imperative	Optative	Subjunctive
ἀφίε-μαι		ἀφιε-ίμην	ἀφῑ-ῶμαι
ἀφίε-σαι	ἀφίε-σο	ἀφιε-ῖο	ἀφῑ-ῇ
ἀφίε-ται	ἀφιέ-σθω	ἀφιε-ῖτο	ἀφῑ-ῆται
ἀφιέ-μεθα		ἀφιε-ίμεθα	ἀφῑ-ώμεθα
ἀφίε-σθε	ἀφίε-σθε	ἀφιε-ῖσθε	ἀφῑ-ῆσθε
ἀφίε-νται	ἀφιέ-σθων	ἀφιε-ῖντο	ἀφῑ-ῶνται

Infinitive	Participle
ἀφίε-σθαι	ἀφῑέ-μεν-ος -η -ον

Imperfect indicative active

ἀφίη-ν
ἀφίε-ις
ἀφίε-ι
ἀφίε-μεν
ἀφίε-τε
ἀφίε-σαν

Imperfect indicative middle/passive

ἀφῑέ-μην
ἀφίε-σο
ἀφίε-το
ἀφῑέ-μεθα
ἀφίε-σθε
ἀφίε-ντο

ἀφῑ́ημι **'I release, let go'** *(continued)*

Aorist: stem ἀφε- (note: the augmented form is ἀφ-η- or ἀφ-ει-)
Active

Indicative	Imperative	Optative	Subjunctive
ἀφῆ-κα		ἀφε-ίην	ἀφ-ῶ
ἀφῆ-κας	ἄφε-ς	ἀφε-ίης	ἀφ-ῇς
ἀφῆ-κε	ἀφέ-τω	ἀφε-ίη	ἀφ-ῇ
ἀφεῖ-μεν		ἀφε-ῖμεν	ἀφ-ῶμεν
ἀφεῖ-τε	ἄφε-τε	ἀφε-ῖτε	ἀφ-ῆτε
ἀφεῖ-σαν	ἀφέ-ντων	ἀφε-ῖεν	ἀφ-ῶσι(ν)
(ἀφῆ-καν)			

Infinitive	Participle
ἀφε-ῖναι	ἀφε-ίς ἀφεῖσα ἀφέ-ν (ἀφεντ-)

Aorist: stem ἀφε- (note: the augmented form is ἀφ-η- or ἀφ-ει-)
Middle

Indicative	Imperative	Optative	Subjunctive
ἀφε-ίμην		ἀφε-ίμην	ἀφ-ῶμαι
ἀφε-ῖσο	ἀφ-οῦ	ἀφε-ῖο	ἀφ-ῇ
ἀφε-ῖτο	ἀφέ-σθω	ἀφε-ῖτο	ἀφ-ῆται
ἀφε-ίμεθα		ἀφε-ίμεθα	ἀφ-ώμεθα
ἀφε-ῖσθε	ἄφε-σθε	ἀφε-ῖσθε	ἀφ-ῆσθε
ἀφε-ῖντο	ἀφέ-σθων	ἀφε-ῖντο	ἀφ-ῶνται

Infinitive	Participle
ἀφέ-σθαι	ἀφέ-μεν-ος -η -ον

Passive: stem ἀφ-εθ-

Indicative	Imperative	Optative	Subjunctive
ἀφείθ-ην		ἀφεθ-είην	ἀφεθ-ῶ
ἀφείθ-ης	ἀφέθ-ητι	ἀφεθ-είης	ἀφεθ-ῇς
ἀφείθ-η	ἀφεθ-ήτω	ἀφεθ-είη	ἀφεθ-ῇ
ἀφείθ-ημεν		ἀφέθ-ειμεν	ἀφεθ-ῶμεν
ἀφείθ-ητε	ἀφέθ-ητε	ἀφέθ-ειτε	ἀφεθ-ῆτε
ἀφείθ-ησαν	ἀφεθ-έντων	ἀφέθ-ειεν	ἀφεθ-ῶσι(ν)

Infinitive	Participle
ἀφεθ-ῆναι	ἀφεθ-είς ἀφεθ-εῖσα ἀφεθ-έν (ἀφεθ-εντ-)

Future indicative active

ἀφήσ-ω (regular, like παύσ-ω)

Future indicative middle

ἀφήσ-ομαι (regular, like παύσ-ομαι)

> **ἀφίημι 'I release, let go'** *(continued)*
>
> **Future indicative passive**
>
> ἀφεθ-ήσ-ομαι (regular, like παυθ-ήσ-ομαι)
>
> **Perfect indicative active**
>
> ἀφεῖκ-α (regular, like πέπαυκ-α)
>
> **Perfect indicative middle/passive**
>
> ἀφεῖ-μαι (regular, like πέπαυ-μαι)

Form and compounds

(i) The main stems of ἵημι are ἱε- and ἑ- (εἱ- is the augmented/reduplicated form).

- For τιθε- in the present and imperfect forms of τίθημι, you will find ἱε- in ἵημι.
- For θε- in the *unaugmented* aorist forms of τίθημι, you will find ἑ- in ἵημι;

BUT

- For augmented forms, you will find the ἐθε- of τίθημι replaced by ἡ- or εἱ-, e.g. ἔθηκα —> ἧκα, ἐθέμην —> εἵμην.

(ii) Common compounds of ἵημι are συνίημι 'I understand' and μεθίημι 'I let go of'.

(iii) On -μι verbs in general, see Language Survey **426–7**.

EXERCISE

17A: 2. Replace the forms of δίδωμι, τίθημι and ἵστημι with the same form of ἀφίημι and (except for the optative and subjunctive) translate them both:

1. ἔδωκε	11. ἔθεντο
2. θές	12. ἐστάθη
3. στήσουσιν	13. δεδώκασιν
4. διδοίη	14. θείη
5. τιθέναι	15. ἱστάμενοι
6. ἵσταται	16. δοῦναι
7. δόντας	17. τεθήσεται
8. θῇ	18. σταθῆναι
9. στήσασθαι	19. δοῦ
10. δώσεις	20. θεῖσαι

EXERCISE FOR SECTION 17A

(B/C) MORPHOLOGY AND SYNTAX

1. Translate these sentences. Say what each of the other choices of verb would mean:

   a. ἡ θεράπαινα ὑπὸ τοῦ πατρὸς τοῦ ἐμοῦ ἀφεῖται ἐλευθέρα.
      (ἀφείθη/ἀφεθήσεται/ἀφίεται/ἀφίετο)

   b. ὁ δὲ πατὴρ ὁ ἐμὸς ἀφῆκε τὴν θεράπαιναν.
      (ἀφίησι/ἀφεῖκε/ἀφίει/ἀφήσει)

   c. ἡ γὰρ θεράπαινα, ἀφειμένη ἐλευθέρα ὑπὸ τοῦ πατρός, συνῴκησεν ἀνδρὶ
      ἀφειμένῳ καὶ ἐκείνῳ ὑπὸ τοῦ δεσπότου.
      (ἀφεθεῖσα/ἀφεθέντι : ἀφιεμένη/ἀφιεμένῳ : ἀφεθησομένη/
      ἀφεθησομένῳ)

   d. τοὺς γὰρ δούλους τοὺς ἐν ἐκείνῃ τῇ ναυμαχίᾳ ναυμαχήσαντας ἀφεῖσαν
      οἱ Ἀθηναῖοι.
      (ἀφείκασι/ἀφίασιν/ἀφήσουσιν/ἀφίεσαν)

Grammar for Section 17B

> In this section you cover:
> - ἕως + indicative 'while, until'
> - πρὶν ἄν + subjunctive and πρίν + optative 'until'
> - διατίθημι, διάκειμαι

ἕως 'UNTIL, WHILE'

309. We have already met ἕως meaning 'until such time as' (**304**, **307**). In those cases, it took:

- Subjunctive + ἄν in primary sequence;
- Plain optative in secondary sequence (optionally).

It did so because there was a degree of uncertainty or indefiniteness about when the action of the 'until' clause would be completed – presumably some time, but possibly never: we just did not know.
But when ἕως takes the *indicative*, it means:

- 'until' (and the action of the 'until' is *known* to be completed); *or*
- 'while'.

Only the context will tell you which is correct, though it is usual that (in past time) the 'until' meaning will be conveyed by ἕως + aorist indicative, the 'while' meaning by ἕως + imperfect indicative (a useful lesson in aspect), e.g.

ἐβόα ἕως ἐκέλευσα παύσασθαι 'he shouted until I told him to stop'
ἐβόα ἕως ἐσίγων 'he shouted while I stayed silent'
μένωμεν ἕως ἔξεστιν 'let us wait while it is possible'

Meaning and use

310. We now have a 'full hand' with ἕως 'until, while' and very instructive it is:

- ► When it is used indefinitely, it means 'until such time as [but we don't know when, if ever]' and takes subjunctive + ἄν in primary sequence and may take plain optative in secondary;
- ► When it is used definitely, i.e. we *know* the action of the ἕως subordinate clause is completed, it means 'until' and takes the indicative;
- ► It can *also* mean 'while', when it takes the indicative.

Now prepare for a similar phenomenon with πρίν.

πρίν 'UNTIL'

311. We have already met πρίν. As a subordinating conjunction it took the infin.,
and meant 'before' (**252**).

But with a different construction, it has a different meaning:

when πρίν is followed by ἄν + subjunctive (primary sequence) or optative
(secondary sequence – cf. **300**), it means 'until'. In this sense it is used
indefinitely. Thus:

οὐ χρή με ἀπελθεῖν πρὶν ἂν ἴδω τὴν γυναῖκα 'I must not leave till I see
my wife [but I do not know whether I will or not]'.

- When πρίν is followed by the indicative, it also means 'until', but in
  that case we know that the action of the 'until' clause *will have been
  completed*, e.g.
- οὐκ ἀπῆλθον πρὶν ἔδειξα τὴν ὁδόν 'they did not leave till I showed them
  the road [and they did leave because I did actually show them the road]'.

Usage

312. (i) It is noticeable that when πρίν means 'until', it is very often preceded by
a negative clause (as in the two examples above).
(ii) It is worth noting now that, especially in poetry, ἄν sometimes drops
out of indefinite constructions in primary sequence with the subjunctive.
But you still have the subjunctive to cling on to, telling you that this is an
indefinite usage. (In general, see **421(iii)**, **422(ii)**, **423** and cf. **407**.)

EXERCISE

17B: 1. What meaning, or meanings, would you assign to the following πρίν and
ἕως clauses, and why?

1. πρὶν πέσοι
2. ἕως ἔπεσε
3. ἕως ἂν πέσῃ
4. πρὶν πεσεῖν
5. πρὶν ἂν πίπτωμεν

Which of these clauses might change in poetry, and how?

διατίθημι/διάκειμαι 'TREAT, BE TREATED'

313. διατίθημι means 'I dispose, I treat' someone in a certain way; to express its
passive form Greek normally uses διάκειμαι 'I am treated, disposed' in a
certain way (cf. **238**). Here, then, is κεῖμαι in the (thankfully) limited forms
that are found:

κεῖμαι 'I lie, am placed'

Present

Indicative	Participle	Infinitive	Imperative	Optative
κεῖ-μαι	κείμεν-ος	κεῖσθαι		κε-οίμην
κεῖ-σαι	-η		κεῖ-σο	κέ-οιο
κεῖ-ται	-ον		κεί-σθω	κέ-οιτο
κεί-μεθα				κε-οίμεθα
κεῖ-σθε			κεῖ-σθε	κέ-οισθε
κεῖ-νται			κεί-σθων	κέ-οιντο

Imperfect indicative

ἐ-κεί-μην
ἔ-κει-σο
ἔ-κει-το
ἐ-κεί-μεθα
ἔ-κει-σθε
ἔ-κει-ντο

Future

κείσ-ομαι (like παύσ-ομαι)

EXERCISE

17B: 2. Give the forms of διάκειμαι parallel to those of διατίθημι and translate both (where possible):

     1. διετίθετο
     2. διατιθέμενοι
     3. διατιθεῖτο
     4. διατίθεσθε (two meanings)
     5. διατίθενται

EXERCISE FOR SECTION 17B

(B/C) MORPHOLOGY AND SYNTAX

1. Translate the following sentences:

   a. αἱ μὲν θεράπαιναι ἔμειναν ἐν τῷ πυργῷ ἕως ἀπῆλθον οἱ ἄνδρες.
   b. ἡ δὲ γυνὴ ᾔτει τὸν Θεόφημον μὴ λαβεῖν τὰ σκεύη πρὶν ἐπανίοι ὁ ἀνήρ.
   c. ʻἀλλὰ μὴ αἴτει μηδὲ τοῦτοʼ, ἦ δʼ ὃς ὁ γείτων. ʻὑβρισταὶ γὰρ ὄντες οἱ ἄνδρες οὗτοι οὐ παύσονται ἁρπάζοντες τὴν οἰκίαν πρὶν ἂν ἀφαιρῶνται πάντα.ʼ
   d. ἐγὼ δʼ ἦν ἐν Πειραιεῖ, ἕως ἡ οἰκία ἡ ἐμὴ ἐπορθεῖτο, καὶ οὐκ ἀπῇα οἴκαδε πρὶν ἀπηγγέλθη μοι ἐκεῖσε τὰ γεγενημένα.
   e. πρὶν ἐξελθεῖν ἐκ τῆς οἰκίας, εἰρήκη τῇ γυναικὶ ὡς τὸ ἀργύριον κέοιτο ἐπὶ τῇ τραπέζῃ.

2. Complete these sentences by inserting the correct word from the brackets. Then translate:

   a. ἡ γραῦς κακῶς (ἔκειτο/διέκειτο) διὰ τὸ συγκοπῆναι.
   b. Θεόφημος καὶ Εὔεργος οὕτω (ἔθεσαν/διέθεσαν) τὴν γραῦν ὥστε ὕφαιμοι ἐγένοντο οἱ βραχίονες.
   c. ἡ γυνὴ εἶπε τῷ Θεοφήμῳ ὅτι τὸ ἀργύριον (διάκειται/κεῖται) ἐπὶ τῇ τραπέζῃ.
   d. ἡ γραῦς (ἐνέθηκεν/διέθηκεν) εἰς τὸν κόλπον τὸ κυμβίον ὃ (παρέκειτο/διέκειτο) αὐτῇ.

Grammar for Section 17C

> In this section you cover:
> - ὥστε clauses 'so as to, so that' + indicative and infinitive
> - Numerals

'RESULT' CLAUSES

314. Subordinate clauses of purpose (ἵνα and ὅπως, 'in order to', + subjunctive or optative) state what people's *intentions* are in carrying out any activity (**298–9**). ὥστε-based subordinate clauses focus on the *consequences* or *results* of an action.

ὥστε 'consequently'

We have already met ὥστε used as a co-ordinating conjunction (a conjunction that links clauses together, like 'and', 'but', 'however', and so on): in this usage, it appears at the start of sentence, meaning 'consequently, as a result'. But it can also introduce a subordinate clause:

ὥστε 'so as to'

315. In this usage, ὥστε takes the infinitive, e.g.

- μηχανὴν εὑρίσκουσιν ὥστε ἐκφυγεῖν 'they are finding a plan so as [*for themselves*] to escape' (or 'an escape-plan');
- οἱ φίλοι μηχανὴν ηὗρον ὥστε τὸν Σωκράτη ἐκφυγεῖν 'His friends found a plan [so as] for Socrates [*change of subject*] to escape'.

In both cases it is not clear what the result actually *was*, only that it was one that could be expected to happen. Note the change of subject in the accusative rule (**253**).

ὥστε 'so that'

316. In this usage, ὥστε takes the indicative, e.g.

- μηχανὴν ηὗρον ὥστε ἐξέφυγον 'they found a plan so that they escaped'.

This produces an *actual result*: they actually did escape, and the end result was achieved.

οὕτως ...ὥστε 'so ... that'

317. Frequently, ὥστε is preceded by οὕτω(ς) 'so' (or by words such as τοσοῦτος 'so great', τοιοῦτος 'of such a sort', τόσος 'so many'). This construction forms what is called a 'result' or 'consecutive' clause:

- οὕτως ἀνόητός ἐστιν ὥστε ἐλπίζει ἐκφεύξεσθαι 'he is so foolish that he hopes to escape';
- οὕτως ἀνόητός ἐστιν ὥστε ἐλπίζειν ἐκφεύξεσθαι 'he is so foolish as to hope to escape';
- τοιοῦτός ἐστι Σωκράτης ὥστε μὴ βούλεσθαι ἐκφυγεῖν 'Socrates is of such a sort that he does not wish to/so as not to wish to escape' 'Socrates is the sort of person not to wish to escape' (note the negative μή).

There is sometimes a very fine distinction between the force of the clauses taking the infinitive and those taking the indicative, and it is often not possible to make as clear a distinction as we have done. See **396**.

NUMERALS

318. Here is a summary of the basic information required to work out Greek numerals:

	Cardinals	**Ordinals**	**Adverbs**
	('one, two' *etc.*)	('first, second' *etc.*)	('once, twice' *etc.*)
1	εἷς μία ἕν	πρῶτ-ος -η -ον	ἅπαξ
2	δύο	δεύτερ-ος -ᾱ -ον	δίς
3	τρεῖς τρία	τρίτ-ος -η -ον	τρίς
4	τέτταρες τέτταρα	τέταρτ-ος (etc.)	τετράκις
5	πέντε	πέμπτος	πεντάκις
6	ἕξ	ἕκτος	ἑξάκις
7	ἑπτά	ἕβδομος	ἑπτάκις
8	ὀκτώ	ὄγδοος	ὀκτάκις
9	ἐννέα	ἔνατος	ἐνάκις
10	δέκα	δέκατος	δεκάκις
11	ἕνδεκα	ἑνδέκατος	ἑνδεκάκις
12	δώδεκα	δωδέκατος	δωδεκάκις
13	τρεῖς καὶ δέκα	τρίτος καὶ δέκατος	τρισκαιδεκάκις
14	τέτταρες καὶ δέκα	τέταρτος καὶ δέκατος	τετταρακαιδεκάκις
15	πεντεκαίδεκα	πέμπτος καὶ δέκατος	πεντεκαιδεκάκις
16	ἑκκαίδεκα	ἕκτος καὶ δέκατος	ἑκκαιδεκάκις
17	ἑπτακαίδεκα	ἕβδομος καὶ δέκατος	ἑπτακαιδεκάκις
18	ὀκτωκαίδεκα	ὄγδοος καὶ δέκατος	ὀκτωκαιδεκάκις
19	ἐννεακαίδεκα	ἔνατος καὶ δέκατος	ἐννεακαιδεκάκις
20	εἴκοσι(ν)	εἰκοστός	εἰκοσάκις
30–90	-κοντα	-κοστός	-κοντάκις
100	ἑκατόν	ἑκατοστός	ἑκατοντάκις
200–900	-κόσιοι -αι -α	-κοσιοστός	-κοσιάκις
1,000	χῑλιοι -αι -α	χῑλιοστός	χῑλιάκις
10,000	μῡριοι -αι -α	μῡριοστός	μῡριάκις

■ *Form*

All ordinals, and cardinals in the 100s and above, decline in full like καλ-ός -ή
-όν, or ἡμέτερ-ος -α -ον.

One, two, three, four

319. The declension of 'one', 'two', 'three', 'four' is as follows:

εἷς μία ἕν 'one'

	m.	*f.*	*n.*
s.			
Nom.	εἷς	μί-α	ἕν
Acc.	ἕν-α	μί-αν	ἕν
Gen.	ἑν-ός	μι-ᾶς	ἑν-ός
Dat.	ἑν-ί	μι-ᾷ	ἑν-ί

δύο 'two'

	m./f./n.
Nom.	δύο
Acc.	δύο
Gen.	δυοῖν
Dat.	δυοῖν

τρεῖς 'three'

	m./f.	*n.*
Nom.	τρεῖς	τρία
Acc.	τρεῖς	τρία
Gen.	τριῶν	τριῶν
Dat.	τρισί(ν)	τρισί(ν)

τέτταρες 'four'

	m./f.	*n.*
Nom.	τέτταρες	τέτταρα
Acc.	τέτταρας	τέτταρα
Gen.	τεττάρων	τεττάρων
Dat.	τέτταρσι(ν)	τέτταροι(ν)

Duals

320. Note the genitive and dative plural of δύο – δυοῖν. This –οιν ending is a
special form known as the 'dual', used when nouns feature in *pairs*. We
shall meet it fully in Section 18.

EXERCISE FOR 17C

1. Translate these sentences, then convert indicative to infinitive in the ὥστε clauses and translate the new versions:

   a. οὕτω πονηροὶ ἦσαν οἱ ἄνδρες ἐκεῖνοι ὥστε ἔτυπτον τὴν γυναῖκα καὶ ἀφείλοντο ἀπ' αὐτῆς τὸ κυμβίον.

   b. ἀλλ' οὕτω αἰσχροὶ ἦσαν ἐκεῖνοι ὥστε οὐκ ᾐσχύνοντο εἰς τὴν γυναῖκα εἰσιόντες.

   c. πᾶν ποιοῦσιν ὥστε δίκην οὐ διδόασιν.

   d. εἰς τοῦτο ἀσεβείας ἦλθεν ὁ ἄνθρωπος ὥστε εἰσελθὼν εἰς τὸ ἱερὸν τὸν ἱκέτην ἀφείλκυσεν ἀπὸ τοῦ βωμοῦ.

Grammar for Section 17D

In this section you cover:
- Aorist passive imperatives
- Root aorist imperatives
- Middle verbs which take passive forms in the aorist

AORIST PASSIVE IMPERATIVES παύθητι 'BE STOPPED!'

321. The forms of the aorist passive imperative depend on the aorist passive stems (**228**) and are as follows:

2s.	παύθ-ητι	'be stopped!'
3s.	παυθ-ήτω	'let him be stopped!'
2pl.	παύθ-ητε	'be stopped!'
3pl.	παυθ-έντων	'let them be stopped!'

■ *Alternatively …*

Note that the base 2s. form is -ηθι, e.g. κατακλίν-ηθι 'lie down!'. But two aspirates so close together (θηθι) are dissimilated into <u>θ</u>ητι.

ROOT AORIST IMPERATIVES

322. Observe the similarities between the forms of the aorist passive imperatives and the imperatives of the 'root' aorists (**209**, **232[d]**):

	ἔγνων **'I got to know'**	ἔβην **'I went'**	ἔστην **'I stood'**
2s.	γνῶ-θι 'know!'	βῆ-θι 'go!'	στῆ-θι 'stand!'
3s.	γνώ-τω	βή-τω	στή-τω
2pl.	γνῶ-τε	βῆ-τε	στῆ-τε
3pl.	γνό-ντων	βά-ντων	στά-ντων

THE IMPERATIVE OF φημί 'I SAY'

323. Learn the imperative of φημί 'I say':

2s.	φα-θί 'say!'	
3s.	φά-τω	
2pl.	φά-τε	
3pl.	φά-ντων	

Now revise aorist imperatives as a whole (**198–9**).

EXERCISE

17D: 1. Turn these active into passive imperatives, and translate:

1. λυσάτω
2. κολασάντων
3. λάβετε
4. τίμησον
5. γράψατε

17D: 2. Turn s. into pl. and vice-versa

1. γνῶθι
2. βῆτε
3. στάντων
4. φάτε
5. γνόντων

MIDDLES WHICH ADOPT AORIST PASSIVE FORMS

324. Many middles become passive in FORM (but NOT in meaning) in the aorist. Learn the following list (and cf. **413[v]**):

βούλομαι → ἐβουλήθην	'I wished'
δύναμαι → ἐδυνήθην	'I was able'
δέομαι → ἐδεήθην	'I begged'
ἐπίσταμαι → ἠπιστήθην	'I knew'
ἥδομαι → ἥσθην	'I found pleasure in'
μιμνήσκομαι → ἐμνήσθην	'I remembered'
διαλέγομαι → διελέχθην	'I conversed'
οἴομαι → ᾠήθην	'I thought'
φοβέομαι* → ἐφοβήθην	'I feared'
χαίρω → ἐχάρην	'I rejoiced'
ὀργίζομαι* → ὠργίσθην	'I grew angry'

* These forms, which we translate as 'middle' in English are in fact *passive* in Greek, 'I am being frightened…', 'I am being angered…'.

Grammar for Section 17E

In this section you cover:
- Deliberative subjunctives
- χράομαι
- Correlatives

DELIBERATIVE QUESTIONS 'WHAT AM I TO?'

325. When a person deliberates with himself on a topic, it tends to take the form in English 'What *am I to* say/think/do' etc. Look carefully at the following:

> ποῖ τράπωμαι;   'Where am I to turn?'
> τί γένωμαι;   'What is to become of me?' (lit. 'am I to become')?'
> τί τις λέγῃ;   'What is [any]one to say?' (where 'one' really = 'I')

- As you can see, the question-word is followed by a *subjunctive*, called the 'deliberative' subjunctive. It appears most commonly in the first person singular or plural.

Deliberatives with βούλομαι

326. This deliberative construction with the subjunctive sometimes appears after βούλομαι, e.g.

- βούλῃ εἴπω τοῦτο;   'Do you wish me to say this?' (lit. '[that] I should say this?')
- βούλῃ ποιήσω τοῦτο; 'Do you wish me to do this?' (lit. '[that] I should do this?')

(N.B. ποιήσω is 1st person aor. subj., NOT future!)
(Cf. in general **405**, **406(ii)**, **422(i)(b)**)

χράομαι as deliberative

327. χράομαι means basically 'I use, treat' or 'I have to do with' (+ dat.). It is used quite often as a deliberative (in the subjunctive) to mean 'what am I to do with …?' e.g.

- τί χρῶμαι ἐμαυτῷ; 'What am I to do with myself?'

CORRELATIVES

328. You have already met the sentence: οὐ γὰρ τούτους οὕτως μισῶ ὡς ἐμαυτὸν φιλῶ 'For I do not hate these as (so) much as I like myself'.

Note the parallel of οὕτως 'as/so much' with ὡς 'as'. In the same way, Greek pairs such words as τοιοῦτος 'of such a sort' with οἷος 'of what sort', 'as'; τοσοῦτος 'so great/many' with ὅσος 'how great/many, as', e.g.

- οὐκ ἔστι μοι τοιαύτη ἐπιστολὴ οἵα (ἐστί) σοι 'There is not to me a letter of such a sort of what sort there is to you', i.e. 'I do not have a letter of the sort that you have';
- οὐκ ἔλεγε τοσούτους λόγους ὅσους σὺ (ἔλεγες) 'he did not speak as many words [as] how many you [spoke]' 'as many words as you'.

SUMMARY LEARNING VOCABULARY FOR SECTION 17

ἄγγελος, ὁ	messenger (2a)
ἀκολουθέω + dat.	follow, accompany
ἄλλως	otherwise; in vain
ἀναγκαῖος ᾱ ον	necessary
ἀνόητος ον	foolish
ἀπαγγέλλω (ἀπαγγειλα-)	announce, report
ἀπαγορεύω (ἀπειπ-)	forbid
ἀπόκρισις, ἡ	reply, answer (3e)
ἀποφέρω (ἀπενεγκ-)	carry back
ἁρπάζω	seize, plunder, snatch
αὐλή, ἡ	courtyard (1a)
αὐτίκα	at once
ἀφῑημι (ἀφε-)	release, let go
βουλεύομαι	discuss, take advice
δέκα	ten
διατίθημι (διαθε-)	dispose, put X in Y (adv.) state
διατριβή, ἡ	delay; pastime; discussion; way of life (1a)
διαφεύγω (διαφυγ-)	get away, flee
δίκη, ἡ	fine; case; justice (1a)
ἐκβάλλω (ἐκβαλ-)	break open; throw out
ἐκτίνω (ἐκτεισα-)	pay
ἐκφορέω	carry off
ἐντίθημι (ἐνθε-)	place in, put in
ἐπαγγέλλω (ἐπαγγειλα-)	order
ἐπεισέρχομαι (ἐπεισελθ-)	attack
ἔτος, τό	year (3c)
ἕως	(+opt.) until
θεράπων (θεραποντ-), ὁ	servant (3a)
θεράπαινα, ἡ	maidservant (1c)
ἰᾱτρός, ὁ	doctor (2a)
καταφέρω (κατενεγκ-)	carry down

(continued)

κεῖμαι	lie, be placed, be made
κινδῡνεύω	be in danger, run risk, be likely to
κλείω	close, shut
λοιπός ή όν	left, remaining
μιμνήσκομαι (μνησθ-)	remember, mention
οἴχομαι	be off, depart
οὗπερ	where
ὁρμάομαι	charge, set off, make a move
παραγίγνομαι (παραγεν-)	be present, turn up at (+dat.)
παράκειμαι	lie beside, be placed beside (+dat.)
πεντήκοντα	fifty
πῑ́νω (πι-)	drink
πιστός ή όν	faithful, trustworthy, reliable
πλησίος ᾱ ον	nearby
ποιμήν (ποιμεν-), ὁ	shepherd (3a)
πρεσβύτερος ᾱ ον	older, rather old
πρίν	(+opt.) until
πρίν ἄν	(+subj.) until
πρόβατον, τό	sheep (2b)
προσκαλέω	summon, call (aor. part. pass. προσκληθείς)
προτεραῖος ᾱ ον	previous, of previous day
πρός	(+dat.) near; in addition to
πύργος, ὁ	tower (2a)
ῥᾷστος η ον	very easy
συγκόπτω	beat up, strike (aor. pass., συνεκόπην)
συμβουλεύομαι	discuss with (+dat.)
συμπροθῡμέομαι	share enthusiasm of (+dat.)
σφόδρα	very much, exceedingly
τελευτάω	die, end, finish
τῑμάω	value, reckon; honour
τίτθη, ἡ	nurse (1a)
τράπεζα, ἡ	bank; table (1c)
ὑπόλοιπος ον	remaining
ὑστεραῖος ᾱ ον	next day
φέρω (ἐνεγκ-)	carry; bear, endure; lead
φόνος, ὁ	murder (2a)
χαλκοῦς ῆ οῦν	bronze
χθές	yesterday
χῑ́λιοι αι α	thousand
ψῡχή, ἡ	soul, life (1a)

REVISION EXERCISES FOR SECTION 17

(D) ENGLISH INTO GREEK

1. Sentences

Translate into Greek:

1. The maidservants did not wait until they were caught.
2. They didn't stop carrying furniture out of the house until they had grabbed everything.
3. They were taking off my son, until a neighbour told them that he was the child of a citizen, and not a slave.
4. I was angry that the rogues had put my nurse into such poor condition that she was actually in danger of her life.
5. They were disdainful enough to enter my house and carry out my furniture.

2. Prose

Translate into Greek:

My wife got angry and said, 'Do not seize this furniture. Have you not already got fifty sheep? Wait for a while; you must not go off till my husband returns.' They took no notice of my wife's words, but took everything and left. A messenger came to the Piraeus to tell me what had happened. When I heard the news, I risked being angry enough to strike Theophemos myself. But I went to him the next day and ordered him to follow me to the bank, to collect the money which was deposited.

TEXT EXERCISE 17

Translate into English:

Socrates and Phaidros are taking a walk at midday, when most people take a nap. Socrates tells the story of the cicadas and their close connection with the Muses to explain his reasons for feeling that philosophic discussion should be the order of the day.
(From Plato, *Phaidros* 258e–259d)

ΣΩΚΡΑΤΗΣ   διαλεγώμεθα οὖν, ὦ φίλε Φαῖδρε· σχολὴ μὲν δή, ὡς ἔοικε. καὶ ἅμα μοι δοκοῦσιν οἱ τέττιγες ἡμᾶς καθορᾶν, ᾄδοντες καὶ ἀλλήλοις διαλεγόμενοι. εἰ οὖν ἴδοιεν καὶ ἡμᾶς ὥσπερ τοὺς πολλοὺς ἐν μεσημβρίᾳ μὴ διαλεγομένους, ἀλλὰ καθεύδοντας
5   καὶ κηλουμένους ὑφ' αὑτῶν δι' ἀργίαν τῆς διανοίας, δικαίως ἂν καταγελῷεν, ἡγούμενοι δούλους τινὰς ὥσπερ πρόβατα περὶ τὴν κρήνην εὕδειν. ἐὰν δὲ ὁρῶσιν ἡμᾶς διαλεγομένους καὶ ἀκηλήτους παραπλέοντάς σφας ὥσπερ Σειρῆνας, τάχ' ἂν δοῖεν ἡμῖν ἡσθέντες ἐκεῖνο τὸ δῶρον, ὃ παρὰ θεῶν ἔχουσιν ἀνθρώποις διδόναι.
10   ΦΑΙΔΡΟΣ   τί τὸ δῶρον; μὴ ἀποκρύψῃς. ἀνήκοος γάρ, ὡς ἔοικε, τυγχάνω ὤν.

ΣΩΚ.   τί δρῶ; δῆλον ὅτι ἐμὲ δεῖ σοι λέγειν· <u>πρέπον</u> γὰρ φιλόμουσον
         καλεῖσθαι σέ, φοβοῦμαι μὴ ἄμουσος εἶναι δοκῇς, τῶν τοιούτων
         ἀνήκοος ὤν. λέγεται δ᾽ ὥς ποτ᾽ ἦσαν οἱ τέττιγες ἄνθρωποι, πρὶν

15   τὰς Μούσας <u>γεγονέναι</u>. γενομένων δὲ Μουσῶν καὶ φανείσης
         <u>ᾠδῆς</u>, οὕτως ἄρα τινὲς τῶν τότε ἀνθρώπων <u>ἐξεπλάγησαν</u>
         ὑφ᾽ ἡδονῆς ἀκούοντες, ὥστε ᾄδοντες <u>ἠμέλησαν</u> σίτων τε καὶ
         <u>ποτῶν</u>, καὶ ἔλαθον αὑτοὺς τελευτήσαντες. καὶ ἐκ τούτων τῶν
         ἀνθρώπων τὸ τῶν τεττίγων γένος μετ᾽ ἐκεῖνο φύεται, δῶρον

20   τοῦτο παρὰ Μουσῶν λαβόν, μηδὲν <u>τροφῆς</u> δεῖσθαι, ἀλλ᾽
         ἄσιτόν τε καὶ ἄποτον ὂν ᾄδειν, ἕως ἂν τελευτήσῃ, καὶ μετὰ
         ταῦτα ἐλθὸν παρὰ Μούσας ἀπαγγέλλειν, τίς τῶν ἀνθρώπων
         τὰς Μούσας τιμᾷ. πολλῶν δὴ οὖν ἕνεκα λεκτέον τι καὶ οὐ
         καθευδητέον ἐν τῇ μεσημβρίᾳ.

25 ΦΑΙΔ.   λεκτέον γὰρ οὖν.

Vocabulary

τέττιξ (τεττιγ-), ὁ cicada (3a)
μεσημβρία, ἡ midday (1a)
κηλέω bewitch
ἀργία, ἡ laziness (1b)
κρήνη, ἡ fountain (1a)
ἀκήλητος ον uncharmed
παραπλέω cf. πλέω
σφας them
ἀποκρύπτω conceal
ἀνήκοος ον unaware (of) (+gen.)
πρέπει it is fitting
γεγονέναι perf. inf. of γίγνομαι
ᾠδή, ἡ song, singing (1a)
ἐξεπλάγησαν aor. pass. of ἐκπλήττω astound
ἀμελέω neglect (+gen.)
ποτά, τά drink (2b)
τροφή, ἡ nourishment (1a)

Grammar for Section 18

In this section you cover:
- Deliberatives in secondary sequence
- ἅτε + participle 'as one who'
- Duals

DELIBERATIVES AGAIN

329. When a deliberative question is reported in indirect speech (e.g. 'he won-dered what he was to do') the question may be followed by the *optative* in secondary sequence, e.g.

(direct) τίνα μηχανὴν εὕρω; 'What device am I to find?'
(indirect) ἠπόρει ἥντινα μηχανὴν εὕροι 'He did not know what device [he was] to find' (cf. **405**).

ἅτε + PARTICIPLE 'BECAUSE, AS'

330. ἅτε (fixed form) means 'as [one who]' or 'because' and is followed by a participle, e.g.

ἅτε οὐ πάνυ τι σοφὸς ὤν . . . lit. 'because (as) not being too smart'.

Translate literally at first, and then turn the participle into an indicative, e.g.

'because he was not too smart'

(On participles in general, see **393**.)

DUALS

331. When a verb has two people or things as its subject, or when a noun or adjective represents two people or things, the words can adopt a special form known as the dual.

Verbs

Verbs are restricted to duals in 2pl. 'you two, you both', 'the two of you' and 3pl. 'they both', 'the two/both of them' only.

■ *Regular endings*

The dual endings are as follows:

		Active	**Middle/passive**
2pl.	'you two'	-τον	-σθον
3pl.	'they both'	-τον (primary sequence)	-σθον (primary sequence)
		-την (secondary)	-σθην (secondary)

You will find these endings replacing whatever the non-dual form of the appropriate tense and mood would be. So:

παύσε-τε 'you (pl.) will stop'	>	παύσε-τον 'you two will stop'
παύονται 'they cease'	>	παύε-σθον 'they both cease'
ἔπαυσα-ν 'they stopped'	>	ἐπαυσά-την 'they both stopped'
ἐπαύσα-σθε 'you ceased'	>	ἐπαυσά-σθον 'you both ceased'
παύσαι-ντο 'they cease' (aor. opt. mid.)	>	παυσαί-σθην 'they both cease'

Dual forms of εἰμί

Indicative:	ἔστον 'you/they two are'
	ἦστον 'you two were'
	ἤστην 'they two were'
Subjunctive:	ἦτον
Optative:	εἶτον, εἴτην

Nouns/adjectives

332. Nouns and adjectives too have dual forms, referring to two people or things. They are as follows:

1st and 2nd declension nouns and adjectives

pl.

	m.	*f.*	*n.*
Nom./acc.	-ω	-ᾱ	-ω
Gen./dat.	-οιν	-αιν	-οιν

Definite article

pl.

	m.	*f.*	*n.*
Nom./acc.	τώ	τώ, τά	τώ
Gen./dat.	τοῖν	τοῖν/ταῖν	τοῖν

For example:

- οἱ σοφοὶ ἄνθρωποι 'the wise men' (nom.) becomes τὼ σοφὼ ἀνθρώπω 'the two wise men' (nom.)

- τοὺς σοφοὺς ἀνθρώπους 'the wise men' (acc.) becomes τὼ σοφὼ ἀνθρώπω 'the two wise men' (acc.)
- τῶν σοφῶν ἀνθρώπων 'of the wise men' (gen.) becomes τοῖν σοφοῖν ἀνθρώποιν 'of the two wise men' (gen.)

<table>
<tr><td colspan="4">3rd declension nouns and adjectives</td></tr>
</table>

3rd declension nouns and adjectives			
pl.	*m.*	*f.*	*n.*
Nom./acc.	-ε	-ε	-ε
Gen./dat.	-οιν	-οιν	-οιν

For example:

- αἱ σοφαὶ γυναῖκες 'the wise women' (nom.) becomes τὼ σοφὼ γυναῖκε 'the two wise women' (nom.)

Grammar for Section 19

In this section you cover:
- Herodotus' dialect
- Accusative of respect
- οὐ φημί 'I say that ... not', 'I deny'

THE DIALECT OF HERODOTUS

333. The Greek world was not politically unified, but consisted of about 1500 autonomous city-states like Athens, Sparta, Thebes and so on. Up till the 4thC BC, each city-state tended to have its own dialect and alphabet. Here are the main features of the dialect of Herodotus, who came from the Greek-speaking city of Halikarnassos (modern Bodrum) on the west coast of Turkey. Since the region was called Ionia, the dialect is called 'Ionic':

(a) Herodotus may have η where Attic has ᾱ (especially after ρ, ε, ι), e.g. πρῆγμα (Attic πρᾶγμα). This phenomenon is called 'ētacism'.
Give the Attic form for: νεηνίης, συμφορή.

(b) Herodotus uses σσ for Attic ττ, e.g. θάλασσα (Attic θάλαττα).
Give the Attic form for: πρήσσω, φυλάσσω.

(c) Herodotus can have:
ει for ε e.g. ξεῖνος (Attic ξένος);
ου for ο e.g. οὔνομα (Attic ὄνομα);
ηι for ει e.g. ἑταιρήϊος (Attic ἑταιρεῖος);
Give the Attic form for: μοῦνος, εἵνεκα.

(d) Herodotus may not contract ε verbs, nor nouns with ε in the stem, e.g.
φιλέω   (Attic φιλῶ)
ποιέειν   (Attic ποιεῖν)
ἐδέετο   (Attic ἐδεῖτο)
ὄρεος   (Attic ὄρους)
σεο   (Attic σου)

(e) εο can change to ευ, giving e.g.
σευ (for σεο, Attic σου)
μευ (for Attic μου)
ποιεύμενα (for ποιεόμενα, Attic ποιούμενα)
Give the Attic form for: ἐγένεο, καλεόμενος, ἀπολέει, ποιεῦμεν.

(f) Herodotus uses -εω for the gen. s. of 1d nouns (e.g. νεηνίεω, not νεηνίου), and -έων for the gen. pl. of all type 1 nouns, e.g. θυρέων, not θυρῶν.
Give the Attic form for: Περσέων.

(g) Herodotus uses -σι in the dat. pl. of type 1/2 adjectives and nouns, e.g.
τούτοισι (Attic τούτοις)
τοῖσι (Attic τοῖς)
Give the Attic form for: ταύταισι, χρηστοῖσι.

(h) Except for ὅς, Herodotus uses the form of the definite article in place of the relative, e.g. παῖς τὸν φυλάσσεις (Attic παῖς ὃν φυλάττεις).

(i) Herodotus often omits aspiration in composition (i.e. words with prefixes, etc.), e.g.
ἀπικνέομαι (Attic ἀφικνέομαι)
μετίημι   (Attic μεθίημι)

Some important Herodotean forms

334. Here are some forms you will meet regularly:

Herodotus		**Attic**
ὦν	'therefore'	οὖν
ἐών	'being'	ὤν
ἑωυτόν	'himself'	ἑαυτόν
ἐμεωυτόν	'myself'	ἐμαυτόν
κοῖος (ὁκοῖος)	'of what sort'	ποῖος
κότε (ὁκότε)	'when'	πότε
κῶς (ὁκῶς)	'how'	πῶς
μιν	'him, her' (acc.)	no comparable Attic form
οἱ	'to him, to her' (dat.)	rare in Attic

■ *Warning*

It should be stressed that these are general rules, applying to most instances; that some of them illustrate simply alternative forms; and that the 'rules' are in fact far more complex than they are made to seem here (which is why you will be able to spot what look like inconsistencies).

ACCUSATIVE OF RESPECT

335. You have already met τί in the sense 'why?', when it was explained that the literal meaning in this context was 'in respect of what?' (**147**). This use of the accusative to mean 'in respect of' is very common, especially after adjectives, and should be carefully looked for, e.g.

οὐ καθαρὸς χεῖρας 'not pure in respect of his hands' (i.e. 'with impure hands');

διεφθαρμένος τὴν ἀκοήν 'disabled in respect of his hearing' (i.e. 'deaf').
This construction is very common in poetry, and Homer is full of examples, e.g.

πόδας ὠκὺς Ἀχιλλεύς 'Achilles, swift in respect of his feet' (i.e. 'swift-footed').

οὐ φημί

336. Observe that οὐ φημί means 'I say that x is NOT the case' (cf. Latin *nego*), e.g.

Κροῖσος οὐκ ἔφη τὸν παῖδα συμπέμψειν 'Croesus *said* that he would *not* send his son' 'Croesus denied that he would send his son'.

- In other words, οὐ φημί does NOT mean 'I do not say that …'.

Grammar for Section 20

> In this section you cover:
> - Homeric dialect
> - Homeric hexameters

HOMERIC DIALECT AND SYNTAX

337. Homer, who lived somewhere on or off the west coast of Turkey, used a uniquely mixed dialect, developed over hundreds of years by oral poets who handed it down from generation to generation of poets; so it was never used in everyday speech. Its main purpose was to enable the poet to compose hexameter poetry orally, without the use of writing. This explains why so many different variations are available to the poet (see e.g. [e]!). Note the following highly characteristic features:

(a) lack of augment – βάλον = ἔβαλον; ἔμβαλε = ἐνέβαλε;

(b) dative plurals in -σι, -εσσι e.g. δώροισι, πόδεσσι;

(c) dative plural ταῖς appears as τῆς, τῆσι; so all type 1(a) (b) and (c) nouns (e.g. θύρῃσι);

(d) genitive singular in -οιο e.g. δώροιο; and in -αο, -εω, in place of -ου of 1d types;

(e) infinitives in -μεν, -μεναι, -εναι (e.g. ἀκουέμεναι = ἀκούειν). Note ἔμεν, ἔμμεν, ἔμεναι, ἔμμεναι = εἶναι; ἴμεν(αι) = ἰέναι;

(f) use of οἱ to mean 'to him, her', and τοι meaning 'to you' (2s.);

(g) definite articles οἱ, αἱ appear also as τοί, ταί;

(h) presence of η where Attic has α or ε, e.g. χώρη = χώρα; βασιλῆας = βασιλέας;

(i) use of definite article to mean 'he', 'she', 'it', 'they';

(j) 'tmesis', i.e. the splitting of the prefix of a verb from the verb with which it is (in Attic) normally joined, e.g. πρὸς μῦθον ἔειπεν = μῦθον προσέειπεν 'he addressed a word';

(k) κεν (κε, κ') is used in place of ἄν.

(l) forms identical with the definite article being used as relative pronouns.

■ *Warning*

It should be stressed that the above list does not represent a series of hard-and-fast rules, which will always apply; the examples given are the most important alternative forms that Homer uses. **349–52** contains a fuller list of features of Homeric dialect.

THE HOMERIC HEXAMETER

338. Like the iambic trimeter of tragedy (see **287–8**), the Homeric hexameter is made up of long and short syllables according to the fixed hexameter pattern:

(a) Number of feet

There are six feet in a hexameter

(b) Dactyls and spondees

Each foot consists of either a *dactyl* or *a spondee*

Dactyl

A dactyl scans: - ⌣ ⌣ (long-short-short, 'tum-ti-ti')

Spondee

A spondee scans: - - (long-long, 'tum-tum').

(c) The hexameter pattern

(i)   the FIRST FOUR FEET can be either dactyl or spondee;

(ii) the FIFTH FOOT is usually a DACTYL;

(iii) the SIXTH FOOT is always a SPONDEE if we assume a final syllable is always treated as long.

Thus a Homeric hexameter can be visually expressed as follows:

1		2	3	4	5	6
- ⌣ ⌣	- ⌣ ⌣	- ⌣ ⌣	- ⌣ ⌣	- ⌣ ⌣	- ⌣ ⌣	
or		or	or	or	or	or
- -		- -	- -	- -	- -	(- -)

Special features of Homeric scansion

339. The 'rules' for identifying long and short feet metrically are largely the same as for the iambic trimeter (see **288–90**). But there are some peculiar features of Homeric scansion, of which the three most important are as follows:

(a) Correption

'Correption' occurs when a naturally long vowel/diphthong at the *end* of a word becomes short because the next word begins with a vowel, e.g.

⌣   - -
καὶ ἡμῖν

(b) The influence of 'digamma' (F)

Digamma is a consonant pronounced like English 'w'. By classical times the letter 364

(c) Effects of metre on the language

The pattern of the dactyl–spondee rhythm of the Homeric hexameter imposes certain limitations and makes some words unusable. Homer gets round this by a number of devices:

(i) words which are naturally long-short-long are scanned long-long-long, e.g.

ἱστίη is scanned ἱστιη.

(ii) words which are naturally short-short-short have the first element lengthened, e.g.

ἀκάματος – ἀκάματος 'unwearied'

ἀνέρα – ἀνέρα 'man' (acc.)

(iii) the use of alternative forms, e.g. dative in -εσσι (long-short) rather than -εσι (short-short) e.g. ἔπεσσι or ἔπεσι, etc.

(iv) in some cases one is given a choice whether to scan dactyl or spondee, e.g.

Ἀργει/φόντης or Ἀργεϊ/φόντης 'slayer of Argos' (epithet for Hermes)

Here are the first five lines of the Homer extract scanned:

ὣς ὃ μὲ/ν ἔνθα κα/θεῦδε πο/λύτλας / δῖος Ὀ/δυσσεύς,

ὕπνῳ / καὶ καμά/τῳ ἀ/ρημένο/ς. αὐτὰρ Ἀ/θήνη

βῆ ῥ' ἐς / Φαιή/κων ἀν/δρῶν δῆ/μόν τε πό/λιν τε

ἡ δ' ἀνέ/μου ὡς / πνοιὴ ἐ/πέσσυτο / δέμνια / κούρης

στῆ δ' ἄρ' ὑ/πὲρ κεφα/λῆς, καὶ / μιν πρὸς / μῦθον ἔ/ειπεν

Introduction to writing in Greek

In the ENGLISH INTO GREEK Exercises you will practise translating English sentences into Greek. To get you started on this, bear in mind the following tips:

- Do not rush into translating – look carefully at the WHOLE sentence in English.
- First translate the 'guide'-sentence in Greek which precedes the one you have to translate from English into Greek. This has the same general shape as the sentence you will be writing. Use it to guide the shape of your sentence.
- Remember that Greek will often use just one word where English will use several, e.g. 'you are going' is translated by one word, βαίνεις.
- Think about the English sentence in terms of SUBJECT, VERB, and OBJECT.
- Remember, when turning the English SUBJECT and OBJECT into Greek, that it is vital to get the endings right in Greek – simply putting the Greek in the same order as the English will not get the meaning across. SUBJECTS will go into the NOM. case, OBJECTS into the ACC.
- You will have to check carefully on the NUMBER of the subject (s. or pl.), and make sure the verb corresponds to it (but remember that n. pl. subjects take s. verbs: see **35**).
- Check also the number and gender (m., f., or n.) of nouns and make certain that any def. art. or adjective going with a noun agrees with it in CASE, NUMBER, and GENDER.

So, work through these points for the following sentence:

'Guide'-sentence: οἱ ἄνθρωποι ὁρῶσι τὸν Ἡγέστρατον.
Translate: 'The men see [the] Hegestratos.'
Your sentence for translation into Greek: 'The friends pursue the man.'

What is the SUBJECT? (It is 'the friends')
    What is Greek for 'friend'? (It is φίλος)
    What gender is φίλος? (M.)
    So what form of 'the' will you need? (Some form of ὁ)
    What CASE does this need to be in your sentence?
    How many friends? (More than one – you need the pl.)
    So how do you translate 'the friends' here?
What is the VERB? (It is 'pursue')
    What is the Greek for 'I pursue'? (It is διώκω)
    What form do you need? (It is the third person pl.)
    So what is 'pursue' here?
Does this VERB have an OBJECT (remember, not all verbs have objects)?
What is the OBJECT? (It is 'the man')
    What is Greek for 'the man'?
    Make sure that 'the' agrees with 'man'.
    What CASE does this need to be in your sentence?
    How many men?
    So what is 'the man' here?

Putting it all together – look at the guide-sentence to structure your sentence.

The sentence should be:

οἱ φίλοι διώκουσι τὸν ἄνθρωπον.

Introduction to Greek to English Test Exercises

In the TEST EXERCISES you will translate passages of continuous Greek without the help from vocabulary or grammar. Here are some tips to get you started:

- Do not rush into translating – look carefully at the WHOLE of a sentence before you start writing.
- Remember that you need to look at the ENDINGS of words to find out their role in the sentence – you can't simply read the meaning of the sentence from the left-to-right order of the words.
- Pay attention to the def. arts. in a sentence (they tell you the GENDER, CASE, and NUMBER of their nouns).
- Analyse Greek sentences into SUBJECT, VERB, and OBJECT.

Now apply these lessons to a sentence:

τοὺς οὖν ἀνθρώπους διώκουσιν ὁ κυβερνήτης καὶ ὁ Ζηνόθεμις.

- Read through the whole sentence first.
- Read through the sentence again carefully:
- τοὺς – what is this? (def. art. – there should be a noun it AGREES with nearby)
  - □ What gender, case, number? (m., acc., pl.)
  - □ Hold this information in your head. So far our sentence goes 'The [objects, m.]'
- οὖν – what is this? (particle)
  - □ What does it mean? ('so': it will probably be the *first* word in English)
  - □ Hold this in your head too. So far our sentence goes 'So the [objects, m.]'
- ἀνθρώπους – what is this? (noun)
  - □ What gender, case, number? (m., acc., pl.)
  - □ Where have you seen this combination of gender, case, and number? (in the article τούς just now – so τούς probably goes with ἀνθρώπους)
  - □ What does it mean? ('men')
  - □ Is it likely to be SUBJECT or OBJECT? (Object, because it is ACC.) So far our sentence goes 'So the men [object]'
- διώκουσιν – what is this? (verb)
  - □ What person and number? (third person pl.)
  - □ What does it mean? ('they [or people later specified in the sentence] pursue')
  - □ Hold this too. So far our sentence goes 'So the men [obj.] they pursue'. Is it 'the men' who are pursuing? No. 'The men' are the OBJECT, not the subject. So in English, at the moment, the sentence means 'So they are pursuing the men'.

- ὁ κυβερνήτης – what is this (def. art. plus noun)
  - ☐ What gender, case, number? (m., nom., s.)
  - ☐ What does it mean? ('the captain')
  - ☐ Is it likely to be SUBJECT or OBJECT? (Subject, because it is NOM., but it is also S., while the verb, διώκουσιν, is PL. But remember there could be a further person specified in the sentence who, together with ὁ κυβερνήτης, makes up the subject.) So far our sentence goes 'So the men [obj.] they pursue the captain [subj.]'
- καί – what is this? ('and')
  - ☐ 'And' what? So far our sentence goes 'So the men [obj.] they pursue the captain [subj.] and'
- ὁ Ζηνόθεμις – what is this? (def. art. plus noun)
  - ☐ What gender, case, number? (m., nom., s.)
  - ☐ What does it mean? ('[the] Sdenothemis')
  - ☐ Is it likely to be SUBJECT or OBJECT? (Subject, because it is NOM., but it is also S., when the verb, διώκουσιν is PL. But we have just seen καί, 'and', connecting ὁ κυβερνήτης and ὁ Ζηνόθεμις)
- So, what is the SUBJECT? (ὁ κυβερνήτης καὶ ὁ Ζηνόθεμις)
- What is the OBJECT? (τοὺς ἀνθρώπους)
- What is the VERB? (διώκουσιν)
- Putting all of this together, the sentence means, 'the captain and [the] Sdenothemis [SUBJECTS] chase [VERB] the men [OBJECT].'
- Are there any words you have left out? (yes, οὖν)
- It is a particle meaning 'so'.
- With οὖν the whole sentence means:
- 'So the helmsman and [the] Sdenothemis chase the men.'

You can now see why ancient Greek is so good for the brain and for the understanding of the workings of language. You have to pay close attention to every word. The rewards of this way of thinking about what you are saying and how you are saying it will be immense.

B   Reference Grammar

Some definitions

(i) *Aspect*

340. This refers to the way in which a *verb* form suggests that the reader should look at the action. The clearest example of aspect can perhaps be best seen in Greek's use of the imperfect and aorist to refer to action in the past: the imperfect suggests that the action should be viewed as continuing, as a process, the aorist suggests that it simply took place as an event. Participles, infinitives, imperatives, optatives and subjunctives are virtually always differentiated in their present and aorist forms by *aspect*, not by time. Their present forms suggest that the action should be viewed as continuing, a process; their aorist forms suggest that the action should be viewed as simply happening, an event.

(ii) *Change of subject in the accusative*

In clauses which take a verb in the infinitive or participle, the subject is placed in the *accusative* if it is different from that of the main verb, e.g.

> οἶδά σε μῶρον ὄντα 'I know that *you* are foolish'
> ἐνομίζομεν τοὺς Ἕλληνας παῖδας εἶναι '*we* used to consider *the Greeks* to be/that *the Greeks* were children'

(iii) *Sequence*

'Primary sequence' means that the main verb is present, future or perfect; 'secondary (or historic) sequence' means that the main verb is aorist, imperfect or pluperfect. Sequence plays an important part in determining whether the subjunctive or optative is available for use in certain constructions.

(iv) *Voice and mood*

'Voice' is the term used to indicate the relationship between the subject of a verb and the action, i.e. active, middle or passive; while 'mood' indicates the function in which the verb is used, i.e. whether it is indicative, imperative, subjunctive or optative, to which are added the infinitive and participle.

369

THE GREEK ALPHABET

341. Before the fourth century there were many forms of the Greek alphabet in use in different cities. After 403 Athens and eventually most other cities adopted the so-called Ionic form of the alphabet, which is the one in use today.

One important letter which does not appear in the Ionic alphabet is the digamma (Ϝ). This was originally the sixth letter of the alphabet (cf. English fϜ), and had the value of English 'w'. The Attic and Ionic dialects lost the sound at prehistoric date, and consequently the letter was not used in their alphabets. Other dialects maintained the sound, and the letter continued in use in these dialects down to the adoption of the Ionic alphabet in the fourth century. After this, traces of digamma are found, sometimes represented by Greek β, e.g. a Hellenistic text writes ῥίζα 'root' in Sapphic dialect as βρίσδα, using the β to represent the digamma which Sappho used (Ϝρισδα). The importance of the digamma lies in the fact that Homeric scansion may react to it *as if it were still there.* Thus one would expect, for example, ἐνὶ οἴκῳ in Homer to elide into ἐν οἴκῳ; but no, for it was originally Ϝοῖκος, starting with a consonant. (See further notes on Homeric metre in the Running Grammar **338–9**.)

ALPHABET AND PRONUNCIATION

342. Here is a more detailed guide to the sound of ancient Greek on the assumption of a standard English pronunciation of the examples:

Greek capital	Greek minuscule	English transcription used in this course[1]	Pronunciation (recommended)	Phonetic transcription[2]
A (when long)	α (*alpha*)	a	English 'c*u*p' (Italian 'amare')	[a]
	ᾱ		English 'c*a*lm' (Italian 'amare')	[a:]
	ᾳ		as ᾱ (more correctly, with ι at the end)	[a:i]
	αι		English 'h*i*gh'	[ai]
	αυ		English 'h*ow*'	[au]
	ᾱυ		as αυ (with first element long)	[a:u]
B	β (*beta*)	b	as English 'b'	[b]
Γ	γ (*gamma*)	g	English 'g*o*t'; before κ, χ, γ, as 'i*n*k' or 'so*ng*'	[gn;ŋ]
Δ	δ (*delta*)	d	French 'd' (with tongue on teeth, not gums)	[d]
E	ε (*epsilon*)	e	English 'p*e*t'	[e]
	ει		English 'fianc*ée*' (German 'B*ee*t')	[e:]
	ευ		Cockney 'b*e*lt' (Italian '*eu*logia')	[eu]
Z	ζ (*zeta*)	sd	English 'wi*sd*om'	[zd]

Greek capital	Greek minuscule	English transcription used in this course[1]	Pronunciation (recommended)	Phonetic transcription[2]
H	η (*eta*)	e	English 'h*ai*ry' (French 't*ê*te')	[ɛ:]
	η		as η (more correctly, with ι at the end)	[ɛ:i]
	ηυ		as ευ (with first element long)	[ɛ:u]
Θ	θ (*theta*)	th	English '*t*op' (emphatically pronounced; later, as in '*th*in')	[th]
I	ι (*iota*)	i	English 'b*i*t' (French V*i*tesse')	[i]
(long)	ῑ		English 'b*ea*d'	[i:]
K	κ (*kappa*)	k	English 's*k*in'	[k]
Λ	λ (*lambda*)	l	English '*l*eft'	[l]
M	μ (*mu*)	m	English '*m*an'	[m]
N	ν (*nu*)	n	English '*n*et'	[n]
Ξ	ξ (*xi*)	x	English 'bo*x*'	[ks]
O	ο (*omicron*)	o	English 'p*o*t' (or German 'G*o*tt')	[o]
	οι		English 'b*o*y'	[oi]
	ου		English 't*oo*'	[u:]
Π	π (*pi*)	p	English 's*p*in'	[p]
P	ρ (*rho*)	r	Scottish 'rolled' r	[r]
Σ	σ, ς (*sigma*)[3]	s	English 's*ing*', 'le*ss*on'	[s]
T	τ (*tau*)	t	t (with tongue on teeth, not gums)	[t]
Y	υ (*upsilon*)	u, y	u, as in French 'l*u*ne' (German 'M*ü*ller')	[y]
(long)	ῡ		u, as in French 'r*u*se' (German M*ü*hle')	[y:]
	υι		close to French 'huit'	[yi]
Φ	φ (*phi*)	ph	English '*p*ot' (emphatically pronounced; later, as in '*f*ear')	[ph]
X	χ (*khi*)	kh	English '*c*at' (emphatically pronounced; later, as in 'lo*ch*')	[kh]
Ψ	ψ (*psi*)	ps	English 'la*ps*e'	[ps]
Ω	ω (*omega*)	o	English 's*aw*'	[ɔ:]
	ῳ		As ω (more correctly, with ι at the end)	[ɔ:i]

1 See also notes at **454**.
2 IPA system, in which : adds length; th, ph, kh mean aspirated t, p, k.
3 Most Greek texts use two forms of minuscule sigma: ς at the end of the word, σ elsewhere (e.g. ὅσος).
   Some Greek texts print a 'lunate' sigma, c, which is used in all positions (e.g. ὅcoc).

Double consonants

343. (i) ζ, ξ, and ψ indicate a double consonant:

> ζ is written for σδ
> ξ is written for κς
> ψ is written for πς

Double consonants are given their full value in pronunciation, e.g.

> ππ is pronounced as in 'hip-pocket'
> ττ is pronounced as in 'rat-trap'
> σσ is pronounced as in 'disservice'
> λλ is pronounced as in 'wholly' (cf. 'holy').

The exception is γγ, which is pronounced as in 'fi*n*ger'; and so too γκ [as in 'i*n*k'], γξ [as in 'ly*n*x'] and γχ [as in 'i*n*khorn']. It is debated whether γμ was pronounced 'ha*ngm*an'.

Vowel length

(ii) Vowels do not always indicate a distinction of length (or quantity):

> ε, o always indicate a short vowel
> η, ω always indicate a long vowel
> α, ι, υ are used for both long and short vowels. In this Course the main vocabularies and tables indicates long vowels thus: ᾱ ῑ ῡ

Breathing marks

(iii) Words beginning with a vowel show a 'breathing' mark over the first (sometimes the second) letter, either ' or ' e.g.

> ὄρος ('oros')
> ὅρος ('horos')

The 'rough' breathing, ', denotes the presence of 'h'.
The 'smooth' breathing, ', is merely a convention to denote the absence of 'h'.
Note that all words beginning with ρ take a rough breathing, e.g. ῥήτωρ ('rhetor'). This may have indicated a special pronunciation.

Accents

(iv) You will already have noticed that Greek words have accent marks, i.e.' (acute), '(grave), ˜ (circumflex). These denote the *musical pitch* at which the accented syllable was pronounced high pitch ('), low pitch ('), high pitch falling to low (˜: originally written as a combination of acute + grave, ⌃. This accent is found only on long vowels, and diphthongs).
There is no reason why you should not attempt to 'pitch' the accent, but you will find it fairly difficult to do without constant care and attention. English speakers naturally 'stress' syllables. If you cannot 'pitch', then you must 'stress' the accented

syllable, even though this may obscure the accent which is being used (whether ΄, ὶ or ˜). Learn the word with its accent as part of its pronunciation. That is why the accent is there.

For a fuller, though by no means complete, account of Greek methods of accentuation, see **344–8**.

Punctuation

(v) There are four punctuation marks in Greek, though we have used some English ones in places to ease reading. The four Greek marks are:

> . full stop, as in English
> , comma, as in English
> • colon or semicolon (note that · is placed slightly above the line)
> ; question-mark

Ancient conventions

(vi) Now the truth must be told that a fifth-century Greek would hardly have recognised a single one of all these conventions you have just learnt. Fifth-century Greeks wrote in CAPITAL LETTERS, with NOGAPSBETWEENWORDS, with NO ACCENTS, with NO SMOOTH BREATHINGS and virtually NO PUNCTUATION.[4] All these conventions sprang up later, some very much later indeed. Modern Greek continues to use most of them.

Smoothing the gaps

(vii) Greeks generally liked their language to run smoothly, and to achieve this they regularly ran words together, or modified their endings (as we do too, e.g. 'isn't' for 'is not', 'we're' for 'we are', 'Tom 'n' Jerry' for 'Tom and Jerry'):
> (a) οὐ, οὐκ, οὐχ; ἐκ, ἐξ

---

4 *Consequently the act of reading for an ancient Greek must have required a high level of intelligence and concentration, especially since the* endings *of the words are so crucial for meaning. It is bad enough in English: here is a translated extract from Plato's* Republic:

FARLESSIAGREESOWECANTHAVEHOMERSAYINGOFTHEGODSANDAFITOFHELPLE
SSLAUGHTERSEIZEDTHEHAPPYGODSASTHEYWATCHEDHEPHAESTUSBUSTLINGU
PANDDOWNTHEHALLYOURARGUMENTWOULDNTALLOWTHATCALLITMYARGUM
ENTIFYOULIKEHEREPLIEDINANYEVENTWECANTALLOWITANDSURELYWEMUSTV
ALUETRUTHFULNESSHIGHLY,

and so on.
The Greek looked roughly as follows:

ΠΟΛΥΜΕΝΤΟΙΗΔΟΣΟΥΚΟΥΝΗΟΜΗΡΟΥΟΥΔΕΤΑΤΟΙΑΥΤΑΑΠΟΔΕΞΜΕΘΑΠΕΡΙΘΕΩΝΑΣΒΕΣΤΟΣ
ΔΑΡΕΝΩΡΤΟΓΕΛΩΣΜΑΚΑΡΕΣΣΙΘΕΟΙΣΙΝΗΩΣΙΔΟΝΗΦΑΙΣΤΟΝΔΙΑΔΩΜΑΤΑΠΟΙΠΝΥΟΝΤΑΟΥΚ
ΑΠΟΔΕΚΤΕΟΝΚΑΤΑΤΟΝΣΟΝΛΟΓΟΝΕΙΣΥΕΦΗΒΟΥΛΕΙΕΜΟΝΤΙΘΕΝΑΙΟΥΓΑΡΟΥΝΑΠΟΔΕΚΤΕΟΝ
ΑΛΛΑΜΗΝΚΑΙΑΛΗΘΕΙΑΝ ΓΕΠΕΡΙΠΟΛΛΟΥΠΟΙΗΤΕΟΝ …

Notice the changes that the Greek for 'no(t)' undergoes in response to its environment:

Δικαιόπολις οὐ βαίνει πρός ...　'Dikaiopolis does not go to ...'
Δικαιόπολις οὐκ ἔστιν ἐν ...　'Dikaiopolis is not in . . .'
Δικαιόπολις οὐχ ὁρᾷ τόν ...　'Dikaiopolis does not see the ...'

▶ **RULES:** οὐ before a consonant
　　　οὐκ before a vowel with no 'h' sound ('unaspirated')
　　　οὐχ before a vowel with an 'h' sound ('aspirated').

On the same principle, ἐκ 'out of' changes to ἐξ before a vowel, e.g.

ἐκ τοῦ πλοίου 'out of the boat'
ἐξ Ἀθηνῶν 'out of Athens'

(b) νυ-moveable
The letter -ν is used at the end of some words to smooth over 'hiatus', i.e. the awkward transition between two vowels, one ending a word and the next beginning a word, or at the end of sentences. It is found in:

● Most words ending in –σι, including -ξι and -ψι, e.g. πόλεσι(ν), νύξι(ν), βαίνουσι(ν)
● All third person verbs ending in –ε, e.g. ἐκέλευσε(ν)
● ἐστί(ν)

e.g. βαίνουσι πρός ... 'they go towards ...'; βαίνουσιν εἰς ... ; 'they go into ...'; βαίνουσιν 'they go [full stop]'. For other consonantal changes, see **359**.

Transcribing Greek

(viii) For the principles of transcription of names from Greek into English, see **342** above and, for the traditional Latinate method, see **454**.

Alphabet poem

(ix) The following poem was composed by the fifth-century poet Kallias:

　　　α　β　γ　δ　　ε
ἔστ' ἄλφα, βῆτα, γάμμα, δέλτα καὶ τὸ εἶ,

　　ζ　η　θ　ι　κ　λ　μ
ζῆτα, ἦτα, θῆτα, ἰῶτα, κάππα, λάβδα, μῦ,

　ν　ξ　ο　　π　ρ　σ,ς　τ　υ
νῦ, ξεῖ, τὸ οὖ, πεῖ, ῥῶ, τὸ σῖγμα, ταῦ, τὸ ὒ

　φ　χ　　ψ　　　　ω
φεῖ, χεῖ τε καὶ ψεῖ καὶ τελευταῖον τὸ ὦ.

ACCENTUATION

General remarks[5]

344. Accent-marks were invented about the third century. Their purpose was to indicate the musical pitch of the syllable on which the accent was placed.

There are three accents:

▶ the acute   ΄ (high pitch)
▶ the grave   ` (low pitch, or perhaps a *falling* of the voice)
▶ the circumflex   ῀ (high pitch falling to low)

Most Greek words have their own accent, which has to be learnt with the word. Observe the differing accents on:

ἄνθρωπος, πλοῖον, βοή, οἰκία.

▶ In NOUNS and ADJECTIVES, the accent is persistent – that is, it nearly always stays where it occurs in its dictionary form unless forced to move or change by the rules of accent which follow. You must *learn* where the accent falls *when you learn the word.*

▶ In VERBS, accentuation is almost entirely predictable: a basic grasp of the rules of accentuation will give you almost complete mastery over all verb accents.

The position of the accent

345. If a word has an accent, it will fall on one of the last three syllables. The following diagram shows you where it is *possible* for accents to fall:

	Third syllable back (antepenultimate)	Second Syllable back (penultimate)	Last syllable (ultimate)
Acute ΄	yes	yes	yes
Circumflex ῀	no	yes	yes
Grave `	no	no	yes

Each of these accents has a technical name, by which you may find it denoted:

	Third-last	Second-last	Last
Acute:	΄proparoxytone	΄paroxytone	΄oxytone
	ἄνθρωπος	ὀλίγος	ἀγαθός
Circumflex:		῀ properispomenon	῀ perispomenon
		Παρθενῶνα	ὁρῶ
Grave:			` barytone
			ἀγαθὸς

5 This is a basic introduction to a big topic. Readers wishing to take it further are strongly advised to buy Philomen Probert, *A New Short Guide to the Accentuation of Ancient Greek* (Bristol Classical Press, 2003), a brilliant introduction, complete with exercises and discussion of difficult issues.

(i) The acute ´

346. Observe the following principles:

> ▶ The acute can fall on any of the *last three* syllables.

(i) If the last syllable has a long vowel or diphthong, the accent can fall only on the last two, e.g.

   ἄνθρωπος, ἀνθρώπου.

(ii) If the acute falls on the last syllable, it will become grave when followed by another word in the same sentence (unless a comma, full-stop or question-mark intervene, or the following word is an enclitic, q.v.), e.g.

   πόθεν ἡ βοή; ἡ βοὴ τοῦ ἀνθρώπου …

(ii) The circumflex ˜

> ▶ The circumflex can fall only on the *last two* syllables; it can stand only on a long vowel or a diphthong.

If the last syllable is LONG, a circumflex cannot stand on the second last but will be replaced by an acute, e.g.

   οὗτος, αὕτη.

(iii) The grave `

> ▶ The grave can stand only on the *last* syllable, and will do so only when the word is followed directly by another word in the same sentence which is not an enclitic (see 'The acute' (ii) above).

Observe the change of accent on the last syllable in:

   καλὴ ἡ γυνή. ἡ γυνὴ βαίνει. ἡ γυνὴ καλή.

Proclitics and Enclitics

347. Not all words have an accent of their own. Those which do not are distinguished into two types:

(i) Proclitics

These words have no accent of their own, because they are accentually linked to the word which *follows* them. The commonest proclitics are ὁ, ἡ, οἱ, αἱ, ἐν, εἰς, οὐ(κ/χ), εἰ. They show an accent only when the word which follows is an *enclitic*, e.g. εἴ γε (see next).

(ii) Enclitics

These are accentually linked to the preceding word, and often change the accentuation of the preceding word. The principal enclitics are: τε, τις ('a certain', and all indefinite words, e.g. που 'somewhere'), unemphatic με, μου, μοι, σε, σου, σοι, εἰμί ('I am') and φημί ('I say') in the PRESENT INDICATIVE (though not the 2s.), γε.

Note:
An enclitic cannot stand first in a clause.

(a) Acute on the last remains acute if the following word is enclitic, e.g.

ἀνὴρ βαίνει, ἀνήρ τις βαίνει.

(b) If the preceding word has an acute on the third last syllable, or a circumflex on the second last, that word will take *as well as its normal accent* an acute on its last syllable, e.g.

ἄνθρωπός τις
πλοῖόν τι

(c) If the preceding word has a circumflex on the last syllable, the enclitic simply loses any accent, e.g. οὖν ἐστι

(d) Strings of enclitics will throw accents back onto each other, e.g.

ἄνθρωπός τίς ποτέ μοι ἔλεγε … 'a certain man once said to me …'

(do not confuse τίς *here* with τίς; = 'who, what?')

(e) Forms of τις with two syllables will accent the *last* if they follow a paroxytone word, e.g.

πρὸς οἰκίαν τινά 'to a certain house'

(τινά cannot throw its accent back onto οἰκίαν because οἰκίαν does not have an acute on the third-last or a circumflex on the second-last. Note that the accent on τίς; falls on the *first* syllable in all its forms, e.g.

πρὸς τίνα οἰκίαν βαίνεις; 'to what house are you going?')

Some general hints

348. Here are some of the more general rules of accentuation:

(a) Nouns, pronouns, adjectives

(i) For the purposes of accentuation (NOT METRE), -οι and -αι of nom. pl. count SHORT at the end of these words. Thus ἄνθρωποι, διάνοιαι.

(ii) Words of 1st and 2nd declension with an acute on the last syllable of nom. s. take circumflex in the genitives and datives, e.g. ἀγαθός: ἀγαθοῦ ἀγαθῷ / ἀγαθῆς ἀγαθῇ / ἀγαθῶν / ἀγαθοῖς ἀγαθαῖς.

(iii) ALL 1st declension nouns have a circumflex on the -ῶν of the genitive plural *(no matter where* the accent was originally), e.g. νίκη gen. pl. νικῶν; so with 3rd declension nouns in -ος *(σκευῶν),* if contracted (cf. σκευέων).

(iv) Note especially πόλεως, πόλεων, breaking the rule of **346(a)**.

(v) Monosyllables of the 3rd declension are accented on the final syllable of the genitive and dative; e.g. πούς; gen. s. ποδός; dat. s. ποδί; gen. pl. ποδῶν; dat. pl. ποσί.

(vi) Noms. and accs. accented on the final syllable are acute, unless contracted; e.g.

ὁ Παρθενών but ὁ Περικλῆς *(Περικλέης).*

(b) Verbs

(vii) The accent normally goes back as far as it can, and is nearly always acute (but see under contracted verbs [xi] below).

(viii) For the purposes of accentuation (NOT METRE), αι counts SHORT (except in the optative, in which both αι and οι count long), e.g.

ἀποκρίνεται, λύεσθαι but νομίζοι

(ix) If the infinitive ends in -ναι, the infinitive will be accented on the second last (acute or circumflex), and its nom. s. m. participle on the last syllable:

λελυκέναι – λελυκώς (gen. m./n. λελυκότος)
διδόναι – διδούς (f. διδοῦσα; gen. m./n. διδόντος)
λυθῆναι – λυθείς (f. λυθεῖσα; gen. m./n. λυθέντος)

(x) Strong aorists accent on the last syllable in infinitive and participle active, e.g.

φυγεῖν, φυγών (contrast φεύγειν, φεύγων of the present)

(xi) For contracted verbs, examine the *uncontracted* form and determine where the accent would come on that. If an accented syllable is involved in the contraction, the accent will be circumflex on the resulting contraction, if the rule under **346(ii)** does not apply. If **346(ii)** does apply, the accent will be acute, e.g.

ποιέει > ποιεῖ
ἐποίεε > ἐποίει
ὁραοίην > ὁρῷην

HOMERIC DIALECT: THE MAIN FEATURES

349. Homer's Greek differs in important ways from Attic Greek, as follows:

Nouns

First declension	Second declension	Third declension

Nominative s.
Types 1a b c (f.)
Ends in -η, even
after ρ, ε, ι e.g.
χώρη, not χώρᾱ.

Accusative s.
Ends in -ιν as well as
-ιδα, e.g. γλαυκῶπιν and
γλαυκώπιδα.

Type 1d (m.) may
end in -ᾰ, not - ης,
e.g. ἱππότᾰ, not
ἱππότης

Endings in -ηα
correspond to εᾱ, e.g.
βασιλῆα =βασιλέᾱ.

Genitive s.
Type 1d (m.) ends
in -αο, -εω, not -ου,
e.g. Ἀτρείδαο, not
Ἀτρείδου.

Genitive s.
Ends in -οιο
as well as -ου, e.g.
πεδίοιο
and πεδίου.

Genitive s.
Endings in -ηος and
-ιος correspond to -εως,
e.g. βασιλῆος =
βασιλέως;
πόλιος = πόλεως.

Accusative pl.
Endings in -ηας
correspond to -εᾱς, e.g.
βασιλῆας = βασιλέᾱς.

Genitive pl.
Usually ends in
-άων, -έων, e.g.
νυμφάων,
not νυμφῶν.

Genitive pl.
Dual ends in
-οιϊν, so ἵπποιϊν, not
ἵπποιν (dat. pl. too)

Genitive pl.
Endings in -ηων
correspond to -εων, e.g.
βασιλήων = βασιλέων.

Dative pl.
Nearly always ends
in -ῃσι(ν), or -ῃς, e.g.
πύλῃσιν = πύλαις.

Dative pl.
Ends in -οισι and -οις,
e.g. φύλλοισι,
φύλλοις.

Dative pl.
Ends in -εσσι and -σι, e.g.
πόδεσσι, ἔπεσσι.

Note:

(i) Observe the Homeric alternation between σ and σσ (which can be metrically useful), e.g. τόσος > τόσσος, μέσος > μέσσος, ποσί > ποσσί.

(ii) The termination -φι (-οφι) may be used for the dat. s. and pl. of nouns and adjectives (and sometimes the gen. s. and pl. too), e.g. βιῆφι 'by force', δακρύοφιν 'with tears', ὀρέσφιν 'in the mountains'.

350. Pronouns

ἐγώ
Gen. s – ἐμεῖο, ἐμέο, ἐμεῦ, μευ, ἐμέθεν

σύ 'I', 'you'
Gen. s. – σεῖο, σέο, σεῦ, σέθεν

ἡμεῖς 'we'
Acc. – ἡμέας, ἄμμε
Gen. – ἡμείων, ἡμέων
Dat. – ἄμμι(ν)

ὑμεῖς 'you'
Acc. – ὑμέας, ὔμμε.
Gen. – ὑμείων, ὑμέων
Dat. – ὔμμι(ν).

ἕ 'him'
Gen. – εἷο, ἕο, εὗ, ἕθεν
Dat. – ἑοῖ, οἱ

σφε 'them'
Acc. – σφε, σφέας, σφας.
Gen. – σφείων, σφέων.
Dat. – σφι, σφισί.

τίς 'who, what, which'
Nom. – τίς
Acc. – τίνα
Gen. – τέο/τεῦ
Dat. – τέῳ
Gen. pl. – τέων.

ὁ ἡ τό 'he, she, it'
Nom. pl. – οἱ, αἱ, *or* τοί, ταί.
Dat. pl. – τοῖς, τοῖσι, τῆς,
τῆσι as well as ταῖς.

351. Verbs

(i) Person endings
-σαν can become –ν in 3pl. act., e.g. ἔστησαν becomes ἔσταν

-ανται, –αντο in 3pl. mid./pass. often becomes -αται, -ατο, e.g. ἥατο instead of ἥντο

(ii) Tenses

Future: generally uncontracted, e.g. ἐρέω (ἐρῶ), τελέω (τελέσω).

Present/Imperfect: sometimes reinforced by a form in –σκ- implying repetition, e.g.

φύγεσκον 'they kept on running away'.

Aorist/Imperfect: in both the augment may be missing e.g. βάλον (ἔβαλον). Observe the necessary adjustments in compounds, e.g. ἔμβαλε (ἐνέβαλε).

(iii) Moods

Subjunctive:
  (a) appears with a short vowel, e.g. ἴομεν= ἴωμεν
  (b) has 2s. mid. in -ηαι, -εαι
  (c) has 3s. act. in -σι, e.g. φορεῆσι=φορῇ
  (d) is used in place of the future; and can be used in general remarks.

(iv) Infinitive

It appears with the endings -μεν, -μεναι, -ναι for -ειν, -ναι e.g. δόμεναι = δοῦναι; ἴμεν =ἰέναι; ἔμεν, ἔμμεν, ἔμμεναι = εἶναι; ἀκουέμεν(αι) = ἀκούειν.

Contracted verbs

In contracted verbs, we can find:

  –οω-, -ωω- in place of –αο- (Attic –ω-) e.g. ὁρόωντες for Attic ὁρῶντες;
  - αα-, -αᾳ where Attic would contract αε to α, and αει to ᾳ.

352. Adverbs

Note the way the following suffixes are used to create adverbs:

  -δε 'whither', as in πόλεμόνδε 'to the war' (Note that -δε here is attached to the acc.; in all the rest, the suffix is attached to the stem.)
  -δον 'how', as in κλαγγηδόν 'with cries'
  -θεν 'whence', as in ὑψόθεν 'from above'
  -θι 'where', as in ὑψόθι 'on high'
Cf. **451**.

Particles

Note particularly the use and force of the following particles:

ἄρα (ἄρ, ῥά)	'so, next' (showing transition)
δή	'indeed' (emphasising)
ἦ	'surely' (emphasising)
περ	'just, even' (emphasising)

τε   'and' (or to show a general remark)
τοι   'I tell you' (assertion) (But it may also=σοι, 'to you, for you'.)

THE DEFINITE ARTICLE, NOUNS AND PRONOUNS

353. The definite article ὁ, ἡ, τό, 'the'

Singular			
	M	*F*	*N*
Nominative	ὁ	ἡ	τό
Accusative	τόν	τήν	τό
Genitive	τοῦ	τῆς	τοῦ
Dative	τῷ	τῇ	τῷ
Plural			
	M	*F*	*N*
Nominative	οἱ	αἱ	τά
Accusative	τούς	τάς	τά
Genitive	τῶν	τῶν	τῶν
Dative	τοῖς	ταῖς	τοῖς

354. First declension nouns

βοή, ἡ, **'shout'** **(1a)**

	s.	*pl.*
Nom.	βοή	βοαί
Acc.	βοήν	βοάς
Gen.	βοῆς	βοῶν
Dat.	βοῇ	βοαῖς

ἀπορία, ἡ, **'perplexity'** **(1b)**

	s.	*pl.*
Nom.	ἀπορίᾱ	ἀπορίαι
Acc.	ἀπορίᾱν	ἀπορίᾱς
Gen.	ἀπορίᾱς	ἀποριῶν
Dat.	ἀπορίᾳ	ἀπορίαις

θάλαττᾰ, ἡ, **'sea'** **(1c)**

	s.	*pl.*
Nom.	θάλαττᾰ	θάλατται
Acc.	θάλαττᾰν	θαλάττᾱς
Gen.	θαλάττης	θαλαττῶν
Dat.	θαλάττῃ	θαλάτταις

ναύτης, ὁ 'sailor' (1d)

	s.	pl.
Nom.	ναύτης	ναῦται
Acc.	ναύτην	ναύτᾱς
Gen.	ναύτου	ναυτῶν
Dat.	ναύτῃ	ναύταις
Voc.	ὦ ναῦτᾰ	

νεανίας, ὁ 'young man' (1d)

	s.	pl.
Nom.	νεᾱνίᾱς	νεᾱνίαι
Acc.	νεᾱνίᾱν	νεᾱνίᾱς
Gen.	νεᾱνίου	νεᾱνιῶν
Dat.	νεᾱνίᾳ	νεᾱνίαις
Voc.	ὦ νεᾱνίᾱ	

355. Second declension nouns

ἄνθρωπος, ὁ 'man/fellow' 2(a)

	s.	pl.
Nom.	ἄνθρωπος	ἄνθρωποι
Acc.	ἄνθρωπον	ἀνθρώπους
Gen.	ἀνθρώπου	ἀνθρώπων
Dat.	ἀνθρώπῳ	ἀνθρώποις
Voc.	ὦ ἄνθρωπε	

ἔργον, τό 'task/duty/job/work' 2(b)

	s.	pl.
Nom.	ἔργον	ἔργα
Acc.	ἔργον	ἔργα
Gen.	ἔργου	ἔργων
Dat.	ἔργῳ	ἔργοις

356. Third declension nouns

ὁ λιμήν (λιμεν-), 'harbour' (3a)

	s.	pl.
Nom.	λιμήν	λιμένες
Acc.	λιμένα	λιμένας
Gen.	λιμένος	λιμένων
Dat.	λιμένι	λιμέσι(ν) [< λιμένσι(ν)]

ἡ νύξ (νυκτ-), 'night' (3a)

	s.	pl.
Nom.	νύξ	νύκτες
Acc.	νύκτα	νύκτας
Gen.	νυκτός	νυκτῶν
Dat.	νυκτί	νυξί(ν) [< νυκτσί(ν)]

πρᾶγμα (πρᾱγματ-), τό 'thing, matter' (3b)

	s.	pl.
Nom.	πρᾶγμα	πράγματα
Acc.	πρᾶγμα	πράγματα
Gen.	πράγματος	πραγμάτων
Dat.	πράγματι	πράγμασι(ν)

πλῆθος, τό 'number, crowd, the people' (3c)

	s.	pl.
Nom.	πλῆθος	πλήθη
Acc.	πλῆθος	πλήθη
Gen.	πλήθους	πληθῶν
Dat.	πλήθει	πλήθεσι(ν)

ὁ τριήρης, 'trireme' (3d)

	s.	pl.
Nom.	τριήρης	τριήρεις
Acc.	τριήρη	τριήρεις
Gen.	τριήρους	τριήρων
Dat.	τριήρει	τριήρεσι(ν)

ὁ Σωκράτης, 'Socrates' (3d)

	s.	
Nom.	Σωκράτης	no pl.
Acc.	Σωκράτη	
Gen.	Σωκράτους	
Dat.	Σωκράτει	
Voc.	ὦ Σώκρατες	

ὁ Περικλῆς, 'Pericles' (3d)

	s.	
Nom.	Περικλῆς	no pl.
Acc.	Περικλέᾱ	
Gen.	Περικλέους	
Dat.	Περικλεῖ	
Voc.	ὦ Περίκλεις	

πόλις, ἡ 'city-state' (3e)

	s.	pl.
Nom.	πόλις	πόλεις
Acc.	πόλιν	πόλεις
Gen.	πόλεως	πόλεων
Dat.	πόλει	πόλεσι(ν)
Voc.	ὦ πόλι	

πρέσβυς, ὁ 'old man' ; *pl.* 'ambassadors' (3e)

	s.	*pl.*
Nom.	πρέσβυς	πρέσβεις
Acc.	πρέσβυν	πρέσβεις
Gen.	πρέσβεως	πρέσβεων
Dat.	πρέσβει	πρέσβεσι(ν)
Voc.	ὦ πρέσβυ	

ἄστυ, τό 'city' (3f)

	s.	*pl.*
Nom.	ἄστυ	ἄστη
Acc.	ἄστυ	ἄστη
Gen.	ἄστεως	ἄστεων
Dat.	ἄστει	ἄστεσι(ν)

ὁ βασιλεύς, 'king' (3g)

	s.	*pl.*
Nom.	βασιλεύς	βασιλῆς (*or* βασιλεῖς)
Acc.	βασιλέᾱ	βασιλέᾱς
Gen.	βασιλέως	βασιλέων
Dat.	βασιλεῖ	βασιλεῦσι(ν)
Voc.	ὦ βασιλεῦ	

ὀφρύς, ἡ **eyebrow** (3h)

	s.	*pl.*
Nom.	ὀφρύς	ὀφρύες
Acc.	ὀφρύν	ὀφρῦς
Gen.	ὀφρύος	ὀφρύων
Dat.	ὀφρύι	ὀφρύσι(ν)
Voc.	ὦ ὀφρύ	

357. Some irregular nouns

ὁ Ζεύς, 'Zeus'			ἡ ναῦς, 'ship'[6]	
			s.	*pl.*
Nom.	Ζεύς		ναῦς	νῆες
Acc.	Δία	(Ζῆνα)	ναῦν	ναῦς
Gen.	Διός	(Ζηνός)	νεώς	νεῶν
Dat.	Διί	(Ζηνί)	νηί	ναυσί(ν)
Voc.	ὦ Ζεῦ		ὦ ναῦ	

6 So too γραῦς 'old woman', gen.s γραός with -α- replacing -ε- in the stem and -η- throughout.

υἱός, ὁ 'son' (2a, and mixed)

s.

nom.	υἱός
acc.	υἱόν
gen.	υἱέος
dat.	υἱεῖ

pl.

nom.	υἱεῖς
acc.	υἱεῖς
gen.	υἱέων
dat.	υἱέσι(ν)

πατήρ, ὁ 'father' (so too μήτηρ, ἡ 'mother' and θυγάτηρ, ἡ 'daughter')

s.

nom.	πατήρ
acc.	πατέρα
gen.	πατρός
dat.	πατρί
voc.	ὦ πάτερ

pl.

nom.	πατέρες
acc.	πατέρας
gen.	πατέρων
dat.	πατρᾶσι(ν)

358. Vocatives

The vocatives of type 3a nouns are less easy to predict, although they are easily recognizable. Here are some examples:

Short vowel

ὁ ἀνήρ (ἀνδρ-) ὦ ἄνερ 'O man'
ὁ δαίμων (δαιμον-) ὦ δαῖμον 'O god'; cf. ὦ γέρον
ὁ σωτήρ (σωτηρ-) ὦ σῶτερ 'O saviour'
ὁ πατήρ (πατ(ε)ρ-) ὦ πάτερ 'O father'

Ones to watch

ἡ γυνή (γυναικ-) ὦ γύναι 'O woman'
ὁ παῖς (παιδ-) ὦ παῖ 'O son'

No change

ἡ νύξ (νυκτ-) ὦ νύξ 'O night'
ὁ Ἕλλην (Ἕλλην-) ὦ Ἕλλην 'O Greek'

359. Consonant change: dative plurals of 3a nouns

In the interests of euphony, certain consonants in Greek combine with each other to produce a different consonant. Among the most common combinations are:

- π, β, φ + σ   > ψ   e.g. πέμπω   >   future πέμψω
- κ, γ, κτ, χ + σ > ξ   e.g. ἄγω   >   future ἄξω
- τ, δ, ζ, θ + σ   > σ   e.g. πείθω   >   future πείσω

These combinations are especially common in forming the future and aorist tenses and the dat. pl. of 3a nouns.

▶ The dat. pl. of type 3a nouns is formed by adding the ending -σι or -σιν to the **stem** of the noun.

▶ The sigma of the -σι(ν) ending combines with the last consonant of the noun's **stem** in the predictable ways set out below:

(i) stems ending in γ-, κ-, κτ- or χ- (guttural or velar consonants, pronounced in the throat) combine with -σι(ν) to produce -ξι(ν):

e.g.   γυνή (γυναικ-)   γυναικ+σι(ν)   >   γυναιξί(ν)
         κῆρυξ (κηρυκ-)   κηρυκ+σι(ν)   >   κήρυξι(ν)
         νύξ (νυκτ)-   νυκτ+σι(ν)   >   νυξί(ν)

(ii) stems ending in β, π or φ (labial consonants, pronounced on the lips) combine with the -σι(ν) ending to produce -ψι(ν):

e.g.   φλέψ (φλεβ-)   φλεβ+σι(ν)   >   φλέψι(ν)

(iii) stems ending in ρ (or λ) (liquid consonants, pronounced by allowing the air to flow around the tongue) simply add the -σι(ν) ending to the noun's stem:

e.g.   ῥήτωρ (ῥητορ-)   ῥητορ+σι(ν)   >   ῥήτορσι

(iv) with stems ending in a dental consonant, δ, ζ, τ or θ (dental consonants, pronounced on the teeth) the final consonant drops out and is replaced by the sigma (note below, though, different rules when the stem ends in -κτ- or -ντ-):

e.g.   παῖς (παιδ-)   >   παιδ+σι(ν)   >   παισί(ν)
         πατρίς (πατριδ-) >   πατριδ+σι(ν)   >   πατρίσι(ν)
         πούς (ποδ-)   >   ποδ+σι(ν)   >   ποσί(ν)

(v) the same happens with stems ending in a nasal consonant, ν or μ (nasal consonants, pronounced through the nose): the final consonant drops out and is replaced by the sigma:

e.g.   γείτων (γειτον-) >   γειτον+σι(ν)   >   γείτοσι(ν)

$$\delta\alpha\acute{\iota}\mu\omega\nu\ (\delta\alpha\iota\mu o\nu\text{-}) > \quad \delta\alpha\iota\mu o\nu\text{+}\sigma\iota(\nu) \quad > \quad \delta\alpha\acute{\iota}\mu o\sigma\iota(\nu)$$
$$\H{E}\lambda\lambda\eta\nu\ (\H{}E\lambda\lambda\eta\nu\text{-}) > \quad \H{}E\lambda\lambda\eta\nu\text{+}\sigma\iota(\nu) \quad > \quad \H{E}\lambda\lambda\eta\sigma\iota(\nu)$$

(vi) with stems ending in –αντ-, the two final consonants are also replaced by the sigma:

    e.g.   γίγας (γιγαντ-) > γιγαντ+σι > γίγασι(ν)

(vii) the stem ending –οντ- combines with -σι(ν) to produce -ουσι(ν):

    e.g.   γέρων (γεροντ) > γεροντ+σι(ν) > γεροῦσι(ν)

Exceptions

(viii) Two exceptions to these rules come in the form of the slightly irregular nouns πατήρ (πατ(ε)ρ-) and ἀνήρ (ἀνδρ-) both of which form their dat. pl.s by adding —ασι(ν) to their (syncopated) stems:

$$\pi\alpha\tau\acute{\eta}\rho\ (\pi\alpha\tau(\varepsilon)\rho\text{-}) \quad > \quad \pi\alpha\tau\rho\acute{\alpha}\sigma\iota(\nu)$$
$$\dot{\alpha}\nu\acute{\eta}\rho\ (\dot{\alpha}\nu\delta\rho\text{-}) \quad\quad > \quad \dot{\alpha}\nu\delta\rho\acute{\alpha}\sigma\iota(\nu)$$

(ix) The noun χείρ, 'hand', has a slightly irregular dat. pl. too:

$$\chi\varepsilon\acute{\iota}\rho\ (\chi\varepsilon\iota\rho\text{-}) \quad\quad\quad > \quad \chi\varepsilon\rho\sigma\acute{\iota}(\nu)$$

Stem + ending consonant chart

(x) The following chart tracks the consonant changes that occur when a stem *ending* in a consonant (e.g. λιμεν-) meets an ending *beginning* with a consonant e.g. -σ(ι) in the dat. pl. (as you have seen above).

Endings most usually begin with -σ(ι) in nouns (see dat. pls. above); in verbs, -σ too, but also e.g. -μαι -σαι -ται etc., participles –μενος, aor. pass. –θην, perfects –κα, and noun-forms whose endings begin with e.g. –μα and –σις.

Stems can end in almost anything (λιμεν-, πατριδ-, νυκτ-, etc.) The following chart deals with most of the common combinations:

	+ μ *gives*	+ σ *gives*	+ τ *gives*	+ θ *gives*	+ κ *gives*
κ, γ, χ (velars)	γμ e.g. πεφυλακ-μαι > πεφύλαγμαι	ξ e.g. διωρυχ-σι > διώρυξι πρᾱγ-σις> πρᾶξις	κτ e.g. ἠγ-ται > ἦκται ἀπρᾱγ-τος ἄπρᾱκτος	χθ e.g. ἐφυλακ-θην > ἐφυλάχθην πεπραγ-θαι > πέπρᾱχθαι	χ e.g. ἠγ-κα > ἦχα

	+ μ *gives*	+ σ *gives*	+ τ *gives*	+ θ *gives*	+ κ *gives*
π, β, φ (labials)	μμ e.g. βεβλαβ-μαι > βέβλαμμαι γραφ-μα > γράμμα	ψ e.g. Ἀραβ-σι > Ἄραψι	πτ e.g. βεβλαβ-ται > βέβλαπται γεγραφ-ται > γέγραπται	φθ e.g. ἐλειπ-θην > ἐλείφθην	
τ, δ, θ (dentals)	σμ e.g. ἐσκευαδ-μαι > ἐσκεύασμαι	σ e.g. χαριτ-σι > χάρισι	στ e.g. ἐσκευαδ-ται > ἐσκεύασται	σθ e.g. ἐπειθ-θην > ἐπείσθην	κ e.g. ἐσκευαδ-κα > ἐσκεύακα
ν	σμ e.g. πεφαν-μαι > πέφασμαι	σ e.g. λιμεν-σι > λιμέσι			γκ e.g. πεφαν-κα > πέφαγκα
ντ		σ e.g. -αντσι > -ᾱσι -οντσι > -ουσι			

360. Pronouns

s.

	ἐγώ **'I/me'**	σύ **'you'** (*s.*)
Nom.	ἐγώ	σύ
Acc.	με *or* ἐμέ	σέ
Gen.	μου *or* ἐμοῦ	σοῦ
Dat.	μοι *or* ἐμοί	σοί

pl.

	ἡμεῖς **'we/us'**	ὑμεῖς **'you'** (*pl.*)
Nom.	ἡμεῖς	ὑμεῖς
Acc.	ἡμᾶς	ὑμᾶς
Gen.	ἡμῶν	ὑμῶν
Dat.	ἡμῖν	ὑμῖν

οὗτος αὕτη τοῦτο **'this'**, **'he, she, it'**

s.

	m.	*f.*	*n.*
Nom.	οὗτος	αὕτη	τοῦτο
Acc.	τοῦτον	ταύτην	τοῦτο
Gen.	τούτου	ταύτης	τούτου
Dat.	τούτῳ	ταύτῃ	τούτῳ

οὗτος αὕτη τοῦτο 'this', 'he, she, it' (continued)
pl.

	m.	*f.*	*n.*
Nom.	οὗτοι	αὗται	ταῦτα
Acc.	τούτους	ταύτᾱς	ταῦτα
Gen.	τούτων	τούτων	τούτων
Dat.	τούτοις	ταύταις	τούτοις

ἐκεῖνος ἐκείνη ἐκεῖνο 'that', 'he, she, it'
s.

	m.	*f.*	*n.*
Nom.	ἐκεῖνος	ἐκείνη	ἐκεῖνο
Acc.	ἐκεῖνον	ἐκείνην	ἐκεῖνο
Gen.	ἐκείνου	ἐκείνης	ἐκείνου
Dat.	ἐκείνῳ	ἐκείνῃ	ἐκείνῳ

pl.

	m.	*f.*	*n.*
Nom.	ἐκεῖνοι	ἐκεῖναι	ἐκεῖνα
Acc.	ἐκείνους	ἐκείνᾱς	ἐκεῖνα
Gen.	ἐκείνων	ἐκείνων	ἐκείνων
Dat.	ἐκείνοις	ἐκείναις	ἐκείνοις

αὐτός αὐτή αὐτό 'self', 'him/her/it'
s.

	m.	*f.*	*n.*
Nom.	αὐτός	αὐτή	αὐτό
Acc.	αὐτόν	αὐτήν	αὐτό
Gen.	αὐτοῦ	αὐτῆς	αὐτοῦ
Dat.	αὐτῷ	αὐτῇ	αὐτῷ

pl.

	m.	*f.*	*n.*
Nom.	αὐτοί	αὐταί	αὐτά
Acc.	αὐτούς	αὐτᾱς	αὐτά
Gen.	αὐτῶν	αὐτῶν	αὐτῶν
Dat.	αὐτοῖς	αὐταῖς	αὐτοῖς

αὐτός αὐτή αὐτό 'self', 'him/her/it' (continued)
pl.

	m.	f.
Acc.	ἐμαυτόν	ἐμαυτήν
Gen.	ἐμαυτοῦ	ἐμαυτῆς
Dat.	ἐμαυτῷ	ἐμαυτῇ

	m.	f.
Acc.	ἡμᾶς αὐτούς	ἡμᾶς αὐτάς
Gen.	ἡμῶν αὐτῶν	ἡμῶν αὐτῶν
Dat.	ἡμῖν αὐτοῖς	ἡμῖν αὐταῖς

	m.	f.
Acc.	σ(ε)αυτόν	σ(ε)αυτήν
Gen.	σ(ε)αυτοῦ	σ(ε)αυτῆς
Dat.	σ(ε)αυτῷ	σ(ε)αυτῇ

	m.	f.
Acc.	ὑμᾶς αὐτούς	ὑμᾶς αὐτάς
Gen.	ἡμῶν αὐτῶν	ὑμῶν αὐτῶν
Dat.	ὑμῖν αὐτοῖς	ὑμῖν αὐταῖς

	m.	f.	n.
Acc.	ἑαυτόν (αὐτόν)	ἑαυτήν (αὐτήν)	ἑαυτό (αὐτό)
Gen.	ἑαυτοῦ (αὐτοῦ)	ἑαυτῆς (αὐτῆς)	ἑαυτοῦ (αὐτοῦ)
Dat.	ἑαυτῷ (αὐτῷ)	ἑαυτῇ (αὐτῇ)	ἑαυτῷ (αὐτῷ)

	m.	f.	n.
Acc.	ἑαυτούς (αὐτούς)	ἑαυτάς (αὐτάς)	ἑαυτά (αὐτά)
Gen.	ἑαυτῶν (αὐτῶν)	ἑαυτῶν (αὐτῶν)	ἑαυτῶν (αὐτῶν)
Dat.	ἑαυτοῖς (αὐτοῖς)	ἑαυταῖς (αὐταῖς)	ἑαυτοῖς (αὐτοῖς)

361. τίς τί (τίν-), 'which? who? what?'

s.

	m./f.	n.
Nom.	τίς	τί
Acc.	τίνα	τί
Gen.	τίνος	τίνος
Dat.	τίνι	τίνι

pl.

	m./f.	n.
Nom.	τίνες	τίνα
Acc.	τίνας	τίνα
Gen.	τίνων	τίνων
Dat.	τίσι(ν)	τίσι(ν)

οὐδείς οὐδεμία οὐδέν 'no, no one'

	m.	f.	n.
Nom.	οὐδείς	οὐδεμία	οὐδέν
Acc.	οὐδένα	οὐδεμίαν	οὐδέν
Gen.	οὐδενός	οὐδεμιᾶς	οὐδενός
Dat.	οὐδενί	οὐδεμιᾷ	οὐδενί

ὅς ἥ ὅ 'who, which, what'

	m.	f.	n.
s.			
nom.	ὅς	ἥ	ὅ
acc.	ὅν	ἥν	ὅ
gen.	οὗ	ἧς	οὗ
dat.	ᾧ	ᾗ	ᾧ
pl.			
nom.	οἵ	αἵ	ἅ
acc.	οὕς	ἅς	ἅ
gen.	ὧν	ὧν	ὧν
dat.	οἷς	αἷς	οἷς

ὅστις ἥτις ὅτι '[anyone] who, which, what'

	m.	f.	n.
s.			
nom.	ὅστις	ἥτις	ὅτι
acc.	ὅντινα	ἥντινα	ὅτι
gen.	οὗτινος	ἧστινος	οὗτινος
	(ὅτου)		(ὅτου)
dat.	ᾧτινι	ᾗτινι	ᾧτινι
	(ὅτῳ)		(ὅτῳ)

ὅστις ἥτις ὅτι '[anyone] who, which, what' (continued)

	m.	f.	n.
pl.			
nom.	οἵτινες	αἵτινες	ἅτινα (ἅττα)
acc.	οὕστινας	ἅστινας	ἅτινα (ἅττα)
gen.	ὧντινων (ὅτων)	ὧντινων (ὅτων)	ὧντινων (ὅτων)
dat.	οἷστισι(ν) (ὅτοις)	αἷστισι(ν)	οἷστισι(ν) (ὅτοις)

ADJECTIVES

362. Here is a summary of all the adjective/pronoun types you have met, including participles:

'212' adjectives

κᾱλός ἥ όν, 'fine, beautiful'

Singular

	m.	f.	n.
Nom.	καλός	καλή	καλόν
Acc.	καλόν	καλήν	καλόν
Gen.	καλοῦ	καλῆς	καλοῦ
Dat.	καλῷ	καλῇ	καλῷ
Vocative	καλέ		

Plural

	m.	f.	n.
Nom.	καλοί	καλαί	καλά
Acc.	καλούς	καλᾱ́ς	καλά
Gen.	καλῶν	καλῶν	καλῶν
Dat.	καλοῖς	καλαῖς	καλοῖς

ἡμέτερος, ᾱ, ον, 'our(s)'

s.

	m.	*f.*	*n.*
Nom.	ἡμέτερος	ἡμετέρᾱ	ἡμέτερον
Acc.	ἡμέτερον	ἡμετέρᾱν	ἡμέτερον
Gen.	ἡμετέρου	ἡμετέρᾱς	ἡμετέρου
Dat.	ἡμετέρῳ	ἡμετέρᾳ	ἡμετέρῳ
Voc.	ἡμέτερε		

pl.

	m.	*f.*	*n.*
Nom.	ἡμέτεροι	ἡμέτεραι	ἡμέτερα
Acc.	ἡμετέρους	ἡμετέρᾱς	ἡμέτερα
Gen.	ἡμετέρων	ἡμετέρων	ἡμετέρων
Dat.	ἡμετέροις	ἡμετέραις	ἡμετέροις

πολύς πολλή πολύ (πολλ-), 'many, much'

s.

	m.	*f.*	*n.*
Nom.	πολύς	πολλή	πολύ
Acc.	πολύν	πολλήν	πολύ
Gen.	πολλοῦ	πολλῆς	πολλοῦ
Dat.	πολλῷ	πολλῇ	πολλῷ

pl.

	m.	*f.*	*n.*
Nom.	πολλοί	πολλαί	πολλά
Acc.	πολλούς	πολλᾱς	πολλά
Gen.	πολλῶν	πολλῶν	πολλῶν
Dat.	πολλοῖς	πολλαῖς	πολλοῖς

μέγας μεγάλη μέγα (μεγαλ-), 'big, great'

s.

	m.	*f.*	*n.*
Nom.	μέγας	μεγάλη	μέγα
Acc.	μέγαν	μεγάλην	μέγα
Gen.	μεγάλου	μεγάλης	μεγάλου
Dat.	μεγάλῳ	μεγάλη	μεγάλῳ

μέγας μεγάλη μέγα (μεγαλ-), **'big, great'** (continued)
pl.

	m.	*f.*	*n.*
Nom.	μεγάλοι	μεγάλαι	μεγάλα
Acc.	μεγάλους	μεγάλᾱς	μεγάλα
Gen.	μεγάλων	μεγάλων	μεγάλων
Dat.	μεγάλοις	μεγάλαις	μεγάλοις

363. '333' adjectives

τις τι (τιν-), **'a, a certain, some'**
s.

	m./f.	*n.*
Nom.	τις	τι
Acc.	τινά	τι
Gen.	τινός	τινός
Dat.	τινί	τινί

pl.

	m./f.	*n.*
Nom.	τινές	τινά
Acc.	τινάς	τινά
Gen.	τινῶν	τινῶν
Dat.	τισί(ν)	τισί(ν)

εὔφρων εὖφρον (εὐφρον-) **'well-disposed'**
s.

	m./f.	*n.*
Nom.	εὔφρων	εὖφρον
Acc.	εὔφρονα	εὖφρον
Gen.	εὔφρονος	εὔφρονος
Dat.	εὔφρονι	εὔφρονι
Voc.	εὖφρον	

pl.

	m./f.	*n.*
Nom.	εὔφρονες	εὔφρονα
Acc.	εὔφρονας	εὔφρονα
Gen.	εὐφρόνων	εὐφρόνων
Dat.	εὔφροσι(ν)	εὔφροσι(ν)

ἀμελής -ές 'uncaring'

	m. /f.	n.
s.		
nom.	ἀμελής	ἀμελές
acc.	ἀμελῆ	ἀμελές
gen.	ἀμελοῦς	ἀμελοῦς
dat.	ἀμελεῖ	ἀμελεῖ
voc.	ἀμελές	
pl.		
nom.	ἀμελεῖς	ἀμελῆ
acc.	ἀμελεῖς	ἀμελῆ
gen.	ἀμελῶν	ἀμελῶν
dat.	ἀμελέσι(ν)	ἀμελέσι(ν)

364. '313' adjectives

ὤν οὖσα ὄν (ὀντ) 'being'

s.

	m.	f.	n.
Nom.	ὤν	οὖσα	ὄν
Acc.	ὄντα	οὖσαν	ὄν
Gen.	ὄντος	οὔσης	ὄντος
Dat.	ὄντι	οὔσῃ	ὄντι

pl.

	m.	f.	n.
Nom.	ὄντες	οὖσαι	ὄντα
Acc.	ὄντας	οὔσᾱς	ὄντα
Gen.	ὄντων	οὐσῶν	ὄντων
Dat.	οὖσι(ν)	οὔσαις	οὖσι(ν)

πᾶς, πᾶσα, πᾶν (παντ) 'all, whole, every'

s.

	m.	f.	n.
Nom.	πᾶς	πᾶσα	πᾶν
Acc.	πάντα	πᾶσαν	πᾶν
Gen.	παντός	πάσης	παντός
Dat.	παντί	πάσῃ	παντί

πᾶς, πᾶσα, πᾶν (παντ) **'all, whole, every'** (continued)
pl.

	m.	*f.*	*n.*
Nom.	πάντες	πᾶσαι	πάντα
Acc.	πάντας	πάσᾱς	πάντα
Gen.	πάντων	πᾱσῶν	πάντων
Dat.	πᾶσι(ν)	πάσαις	πᾶσι(ν)

γλυκύς εῖα ύ **'sweet'**

	m.	*f.*	*n.*
s.			
nom.	γλυκύς	γλυκεῖα	γλυκύ
acc.	γλυκύν	γλυκεῖαν	γλυκύ
gen.	γλυκέος	γλυκείᾱς	γλυκέος
dat.	γλυκεῖ	γλυκείᾳ	γλυκεῖ
pl.			
nom.	γλυκεῖς	γλυκεῖαι	γλυκέα
acc.	γλυκεῖς	γλυκείᾱς	γλυκέα
gen.	γλυκέων	γλυκειῶν	γλυκέων
dat.	γλυκέσι(ν)	γλυκείαις	γλυκέσι(ν)

Note
A number of adjectives are contracted e.g. χρυσοῦς χρυσῆ χρυσοῦν 'of gold' are the contracted forms of χρυσέος χρυσέα χρυσέον. Cf. χαλκοῦς 'of bronze', ἀργυροῦς 'of silver'.

Among o-contract adjectives is διπλοῦς διπλῆ διπλοῦν 'double', contracted from διπλόος διπλόη διπλόον.

For contract rules see **373**.

365. Comparison of adjectives

▶ Most comparatives end in -τερος -α -ον (some irregulars end in -(ι)ων). Comparatives basically mean 'more , -er', but can also mean 'quite -, fairly -, rather -'.

▶ Most superlatives end in -τατος -η -ον (some irregulars end in -(ι)στος). Superlatives basically mean '-est, most -, very -, extremely –'.

Regular comparative forms

δεινός	'clever'	δεινότερος	δεινότατος
σοφός	'wise'	σοφώτερος	σοφώτατος
γλυκύς	'sweet'	γλυκύτερος	γλυκύτατος
ἀμελής	'careless'	ἀμελέστερος	ἀμελέστατος
εὔφρων	'pleasant'	εὐφρονέστερος	εὐφρονέστατος

Irregular comparative forms

ἀγαθός	'good'	ἀμείνων	ἄριστος
		βελτίων	βέλτιστος
αἰσχρός	'disgraceful'	αἰσχίων	αἴσχιστος
ἡδύς	'sweet'	ἡδίων	ἥδιστος
κακός	'bad'	κακίων	κάκιστος
		χείρων	χείριστος
καλός	'fine'	καλλίων	κάλλιστος
μέγας	'great'	μείζων	μέγιστος
ὀλίγος	'little, few'	ἐλάττων	ἐλάχιστος
πολύς	'much'	πλείων	πλεῖστος
ῥᾴδιος	'easy'	ῥᾴων	ῥᾷστος
ταχύς	'swift'	θάττων	τάχιστος

βελτίων βέλτιον (βελτῑον-) 'better' (comparative of ἀγαθός)

s.

	m./f.	n.
Nom.	βελτίων	βέλτιον
Acc.	βελτίονα or βελτίω	βέλτιον
Gen.	βελτίονος	βελτίονος
Dat.	βελτίονι	βελτίονι

pl.

	m./f.	n.
Nom.	βελτίονες or βελτίους	βελτίονα or βελτίω
Acc.	βελτίονας or βελτίους	βελτίονα or βελτίω
Gen.	βελτιόνων	βελτιόνων
Dat.	βελτίοσι(ν)	βελτίοσι(ν)

ἀμείνων ἄμεινον (ἄμεινον) 'better' (comparative of ἀγαθός)

s.

	m./f.	n.
Nom.	ἀμείνων	ἄμεινον
Acc.	ἀμείνονα or ἀμείνω	ἄμεινον
Gen.	ἀμείνονος	ἀμείνονος
Dat.	ἀμείνονι	ἀμείνονι

pl.

	m./f.	n.
Nom.	ἀμείνονες or ἀμείνους	ἀμείνονα or ἀμείνω
Acc.	ἀμείνονας or ἀμείνους	ἀμείνονα or ἀμείνω
Gen.	ἀμεινόνων	ἀμεινόνων
Dat.	ἀμείνοσι(ν)	ἀμείνοσι(ν)

Construction with comparatives

When two things are being compared (using English 'than'), Greek either:

(i) uses ἤ='than', and puts the two things being compared in the same case, e.g. Σωκράτης σοφώτερός ἐστιν ἢ Κρίτων 'Socrates is wiser than Kriton'; or

(ii) puts the thing compared into the genitive (no ἤ), e.g. Σωκράτης σοφώτερός ἐστι Κρίτωνος 'Socrates is wiser than Kriton'.

Notes

(i) Comparatives in -ων decline like εὔφρων.

(ii) Comparatives declining like εὔφρων can drop the final ν and contract in the nominative and accusative, e.g.

βελτίο(ν)α   }   > βελτίω
βελτίο(ν)-ες/ας   }   > βελτίους

366. Adverbs

Most adverbs are formed by the addition of -ως to the stem of the adjective, e.g.

σοφός	'wise'	σοφ-ῶς	'wisely'
βαθύς (βαθc)	'deep'	βαθέ ως	'deeply'
σώφρων (σωφρον-)	'sensible'	σωφρόν-ως	'sensibly'

Comparative and superlative adverbs are formed by using the neuter singular comparative of the adjective (for comparative adverbs) and the neuter plural superlative of the adjective (for superlative adverbs), e.g.

σοφῶς	'wisely'	σοφώτερον	'more wisely'	σοφώτατα	'most wisely'
κακῶς	'badly'	κάκῑον	'worse, more evilly'	κάκιστα	'very evilly'
ταχέως	'quickly'	θᾶττον	'more quickly'	τάχιστα	'very quickly'

Note:

εὖ	'well'	ἄμεινον	'more well, better'	ἄριστα	'best'
μάλα	'much'	μᾶλλον	'rather, more'	μάλιστα	'very much'

Cf. **451**.

VERBS IN –ω

The verb παύω with second aorist λαμβάνω in full

Here is a complete synopsis of παύω/παύομαι with λαμβάνω representing second aorist forms:

367. 'Imperfective' system

Present active (stem παυ-), 'I am stopping'

	Indicative	*Imperative*	*Optative*	*Subjunctive*
1s.	παύω		παύοιμι	παύω
2s.	παύεις	παῦε	παύοις	παύῃς
3s.	παύει	παυέτω	παύοι	παύῃ
1pl.	παύομεν		παύοιμεν	παύωμεν
2pl.	παύετε	παύετε	παύοιτε	παύητε
3pl.	παύουσι(ν)	παυόντων	παύοιεν	παύωσι(ν)

	Infinitive	*Participle*
	παύειν	παύων παύουσα παῦον (παυοντ-)

παύων παύουσα παῦον (παυοντ-) 'stopping'

s.

	m.	*f.*	*n.*
Nom.	παύων	παύουσα	παῦον
Acc.	παύοντα	παύουσαν	παῦον
Gen.	παύοντος	παυούσης	παύοντος
Dat.	παύοντι	παυούσῃ	παύοντι

pl.

	m.	*f.*	*n.*
Nom.	παύοντες	παύουσαι	παύοντα
Acc.	παύοντας	παυούσᾱς	παύοντα
Gen.	παυόντων	παυουσῶν	παυόντων
Dat.	παύουσι(ν)	παυούσαις	παύουσι(ν)

Present middle and passive (stem παυ-), 'I cease, am stopped'

	Indicative	Imperative	Optative	Subjunctive
1s.	παύομαι		παυοίμην	παύωμαι
2s.	παύῃ (-ει)	παύου	παύοιο	παύῃ
3s.	παύεται	παυέσθω	παύοιτο	παύηται
1pl.	παυόμεθα		παυοίμεθα	παυώμεθα
2pl.	παύεσθε	παύεσθε	παύοισθε	παύησθε
3pl.	παύονται	παυέσθων	παύοιντο	παύωνται

Infinitive	Participle
παύεσθαι	παυόμενος η ον

παυόμενος η ον 'ceasing, being stopped'

s.

	m.	*f.*	*n.*
Nom.	παυόμενος	παυομένη	παυόμενον
Acc.	παυόμενον	παυομένην	παυόμενον
Gen.	παυομένου	παυομένης	παυομένου
Dat.	παυομένῳ	παυομένῃ	παυομένῳ

pl.

	m.	*f.*	*n.*
Nom.	παυόμενοι	παυόμεναι	παυόμενα
Acc.	παυομένους	παυομένᾱς	παυόμενα
Gen.	παυομένων	παυομένων	παυομένων
Dat.	παυομένοις	παυομέναις	παυομένοις

Imperfect indicative active (stem παυ-), 'I was stopping'

1s.	ἔπαυον
2s.	ἔπαυες
3s.	ἔπαυε(ν)
1pl.	ἐπαύομεν
2pl.	ἐπαύετε
3pl.	ἔπαυον

Imperfect indicative middle and passive (stem παυ-), 'I was ceasing, was being stopped'

1s.	ἐπαυόμην
2s.	ἐπαύου
3s.	ἐπαύετο
1pl.	ἐπαυόμεθα
2pl.	ἐπαύεσθε
3pl.	ἐπαύοντο

'Aorist' system

368.

First aorist active (stem παυσα-), 'I stopped'

1s.	ἔπαυσα		παύσαιμι	παύσω
2s.	ἔπαυσας	παῦσον	παύσειας (αις)	παύσῃς
3s.	ἔπαυσε(ν)	παυσάτω	παύσειε(ν) (αι)	παύσῃ
1pl.	ἐπαύσαμεν		παύσαιμεν	παύσωμεν
2pl.	ἐπαύσατε	παύσατε	παύσαιτε	παύσητε
3pl.	ἔπαυσαν	παυσάντων	παύσειαν (αιεν)	παύσωσι(ν)

Infinitive	*Participle*
παῦσαι	παύσᾱς παύσᾱσα παῦσαν (παυσαντ-)

παύσᾱς παύσᾱσα παῦσαν (παυσαντ-) 'having stopped, stopping'

s.

	m.	*f.*	*n.*
Nom.	παύσᾱς	παύσᾱσα	παῦσαν
Acc.	παύσαντα	παύσᾱσαν	παῦσαν
Gen.	παύσαντος	παυσάσης	παύσαντος
Dat.	παύσαντι	παυσάσῃ	παύσαντι

pl.

	m.	*f.*	*n.*
Nom.	παύσαντες	παύσᾱσαι	παύσαντα
Acc.	παύσαντας	παυσάσᾱς	παύσαντα
Gen.	παυσάντων	παυσᾱσῶν	παυσάντων
Dat.	παύσᾱσι(ν)	παυσάσαις	παύσᾱσι(ν)

First Aorist middle (stem παυσα-), 'I ceased, stopped myself'

1s.	ἐπαυσάμην		παυσαίμην	παύσωμαι
2s.	ἐπαύσω	παῦσαι	παύσαιο	παύσῃ
3s.	ἐπαύσατο	παυσάσθω	παύσαιτο	παύσηται
1pl.	ἐπαυσάμεθα		παυσαίμεθα	παυσώμεθα
2pl.	ἐπαύσασθε	παύσασθε	παύσαισθε	παύσησθε
3pl.	ἐπαύσαντο	παυσάσθων	παύσαιντο	παύσωνται

Infinitive	*Participle*
παύσασθαι	παυσάμενος η ον

παυσάμενος η ον 'having ceased, on ceasing, ceasing'

s.

	m.	*f.*	*n.*
Nom.	παυσάμενος	παυσαμένη	παυσάμενον
Acc.	παυσάμενον	παυσαμένην	παυσάμενον
Gen.	παυσαμένου	παυσαμένης	παυσαμένου
Dat.	παυσαμένῳ	παυσαμένῃ	παυσαμένῳ

pl.

	m.	*f.*	*n.*
Nom.	παυσάμενοι	παυσάμεναι	παυσάμενα
Acc.	παυσαμένους	παυσαμένᾱς	παυσάμενα
Gen.	παυσαμένων	παυσαμένων	παυσαμένων
Dat.	παυσαμένοις	παυσαμέναις	παυσαμένοις

369.

First (and Second) Aorist passive (stem παυθ-) 'I was stopped'

	Indicative	*Imperative*	*Optative*	*Subjunctive*
1s.	ἐπαύθην		παυθείην	παυθῶ
2s.	ἐπαύθης	παύθητι*	παυθείης	παυθῇς
3s.	ἐπαύθη	παυθήτω	παυθείη	παυθῇ
1pl.	ἐπαύθημεν		παυθεῖμεν	παυθῶμεν
2pl.	ἐπαύθητε	παύθητε	παυθεῖτε	παυθῆτε
3pl.	ἐπαύθησαν	παυθέντων	παυθεῖεν	παυθῶσι(ν)

* at end of stem -ηθι where no θ for stem

Infinitive	*Participle*
παυθῆναι	παυθείς παυθεῖσα παυθέν (παυθεντ-)

παυθείς παυθεῖσα παυθέν (παυθεντ-) 'having been / being stopped'

s.	m.	f.	n.
nom.	παυθείς	παυθεῖσα	παυθέν
acc.	παυθέντα	παυθεῖσαν	παυθέν
gen.	παυθέντος	παυθείσης	παυθέντος
dat.	παυθέντι	παυθείσῃ	παυθέντι

pl.	m.	f.	n.
nom.	παυθέντες	παυθεῖσαι	παυθέντα
acc.	παυθέντας	παυθείσᾱς	παυθέντα
gen.	παυθέντων	παυθεισῶν	παυθέντων
dat.	παυθεῖσι(ν)	παυθείσαις	παυθεῖσι(ν)

370.

Second aorist active ἔλαβον 'I took' (stem λαβ-)

	Indicative	Imperative	Optative	Subjunctive
1s.	ἔλαβον		λάβοιμι	λάβω
2s.	ἔλαβες	λαβέ	λάβοις	λάβῃς
3s.	ἔλαβε(ν)	λαβέτω	λάβοι	λάβῃ
1pl.	ἐλάβομεν		λάβοιμεν	λάβωμεν
2pl.	ἐλάβετε	λάβετε	λάβοιτε	λάβητε
3pl.	ἔλαβον	λαβόντων	λάβοιεν	λάβωσι(ν)

	Infinitive	Participle
	λαβεῖν	λαβών λαβοῦσα λαβόν (λαβοντ-)

λαβών λαβοῦσα λαβόν (λαβοντ-) 'having taken, taking'

s.	m.	f.	n.
Nom.	λαβών	λαβοῦσα	λαβόν
Acc.	λαβόντα	λαβοῦσαν	λαβόν
Gen.	λαβόντος	λαβούσης	λαβόντος
Dat.	λαβόντι	λαβούσῃ	λαβόντι

pl.	m.	f.	n.
Nom.	λαβόντες	λαβοῦσαι	λαβόντα
Acc.	λαβόντας	λαβούσᾱς	λαβόντα
Gen.	λαβόντων	λαβουσῶν	λαβόντων
Dat.	λαβοῦσι(ν)	λαβούσαις	λαβοῦσι(ν)

Second aorist middle ἐλαβόμην **'I took for myself'** (stem λαβ-)

	Indicative	Imperative	Optative	Subjunctive
1s.	ἐλαβόμην		λαβοίμην	λάβωμαι
2s.	ἐλάβου	λαβοῦ	λάβοιο	λάβῃ
3s.	ἐλάβετο	λαβέσθω	λάβοιτο	λάβηται
1pl.	ἐλαβόμεθα		λαβοίμεθα	λαβώμεθα
2pl.	ἐλάβεσθε	λάβεσθε	λάβοισθε	λάβησθε
3pl.	ἐλάβοντο	λαβέσθων	λάβοιντο	λάβωνται

	Infinitive	Participle
	λαβέσθαι	λαβόμενος λαβομένη λαβόμενον

λαβόμενος η ον **'having taken/taking for myself'**

s.

	m.	f.	n.
Nom.	λαβόμενος	λαβομένη	λαβόμενον
Acc.	λαβόμενον	λαβομένην	λαβόμενον
Gen.	λαβομένου	λαβομένης	λαβομένου
Dat.	λαβομένῳ	λαβομένῃ	λαβομένῳ

pl.

	m.	f.	n.
Nom.	λαβόμενοι	λαβόμεναι	λαβόμενα
Acc.	λαβομένους	λαβομένᾱς	λαβόμενα
Gen.	λαβομένων	λαβομένων	λαβομένων
Dat.	λαβομένοις	λαβομέναις	λαβομένοις

'Future' system

371.

Future active (stem παυσ-) **'I shall stop'**

	Indicative	Infinitive	Participle	Optative
1s.	παύσω	παύσειν	παύσων ουσα ον	παύσοιμι
2s.	παύσεις			

etc., exactly like the present active, on the stem παυσ-

Future middle (stem παυσ-) 'I shall cease'

	Indicative	*Infinitive*	*Participle*	*Optative*
1s.	παύσομαι	παύσεσθαι	παυσόμενος	παυσοίμην
2s.	παύσει (*or* η)			

etc., *exactly like the present middle, on the stem* παυσ-

**Future passive (stem παυθησ-, based on aorist passive),
'I shall be stopped'**

	Indicative	*Infinitive*	*Participle*	*Optative*
1s.	παυθήσομαι	παυθήσεσθαι	παυθησόμενος η ον	παυθησοίμην
2s.	παυθήση (-ει)			

etc., *exactly like the present middle/passive on the stem* παυθησ-

'Perfect' system

372.

Perfect active (stem πεπαυκ-) 'I have stopped'

	Indicative	*Imperative*	*Optative*	*Subjunctive*
1s.	πέπαυκα		πεπαύκοιμι	πεπαύκω
2s.	πέπαυκας	πέπαυκε*	πεπαύκοις	πεπαύκῃς
3s.	πέπαυκε(ν)	πεπαυκέτω	πεπαύκοι	πεπαύκῃ
1pl.	πεπαύκαμεν		πεπαύκοιμεν	πεπαύκωμεν
2pl.	πεπαύκατε	πεπαύκετε	πεπαύκοιτε	πεπαύκητε
3pl.	πεπαύκᾱσι(ν)	πεπαυκέτωσαν	πεπαύκοιεν	πεπαύκωσι(ν)

*Only in verbs where the perfect has a present meaning (very rare).

Infinitive	*Participle*
πεπαυκέναι	πεπαυκώς πεπαυκυῖα πεπαυκός (πεπαυκοτ-)

πεπαυκώς πεπαυκυῖα πεπαυκός 'having stopped'

	m.	f.	n.
s.			
nom.	πεπαυκώς	πεπαυκυῖα	πεπαυκός
acc.	πεπαυκότα	πεπαυκυῖαν	πεπαυκός
gen.	πεπαυκότος	πεπαυκυίᾱς	πεπαυκότος
dat.	πεπαυκότι	πεπαυκυίᾳ	πεπαυκότι
pl.			
nom.	πεπαυκότες	πεπαυκυῖαι	πεπαυκότα
acc.	πεπαυκότας	πεπαυκυίᾱς	πεπαυκότα
gen.	πεπαυκότων	πεπαυκυιῶν	πεπαυκότων
dat.	πεπαυκόσι(ν)	πεπαυκυίαις	πεπαυκόσι(ν)

Perfect middle/passive (stem πεπαυ-) 'I have ceased, have been stopped'

	Indicative	Imperative	Optative	Subjunctive
1s.	πέπαυμαι		πεπαυμένος εἴην	πεπαυμένος ὦ
2s.	πέπαυσαι	πέπαυσο	πεπαυμένος εἴης	πεπαυμένος ᾖς
3s.	πέπαυται	πεπαύσθω	πεπαυμένος εἴη	πεπαυμένος ᾖ
1pl.	πεπαύμεθα		πεπαυμένοι εἶμεν	πεπαυμένοι ὦμεν
2pl.	πέπαυσθε	πέπαυσθε	πεπαυμένοι εἶτε	πεπαυμένοι ἦτε
3pl.	πέπαυνται	πεπαύσθων	πεπαυμένοι εἶεν	πεπαυμένοι ὦσι(ν)
	(πεπαυμένοι εἰσί(ν))			

Infinitive	Participle
πεπαῦσθαι	πεπαυμένος η ον

πεπαυμένος η ον 'having ceased, been stopped'

Singular

	m.	f.	n.
Nom.	πεπαυμένος	πεπαυμένη	πεπαυμένον
Acc.	πεπαυμένον	πεπαυμένην	πεπαυμένον
Gen.	πεπαυμένου	πεπαυμένης	πεπαυμένου
Dat.	πεπαυμένῳ	πεπαυμένῃ	πεπαυμένῳ

πεπαυμένος η ον **'having ceased, been stopped'** (continued)
Plural

	m.	*f.*	*n.*
Nom.	πεπαυμένοι	πεπαυμέναι	πεπαυμένα
Acc.	πεπαυμένους	πεπαυμένᾱς	πεπαυμένα
Gen.	πεπαυμένων	πεπαυμένων	πεπαυμένων
Dat.	πεπαυμένοις	πεπαυμέναις	πεπαυμένοις

Future perfect middle/passive (stem πεπαυ-),
'I shall have ceased, been stopped'

	Indicative	*Optative*
1s.	πεπαύσομαι	πεπαυσοίμην
2s.	πεπαύσει (or η)	πεπαύσοιο
3s.	πεπαύσεται	πεπαύσοιτο
1pl.	πεπαυσόμεθα	πεπαυσοίμεθα
2pl.	πεπαύσεσθε	πεπαύσοισθε
3pl.	πεπαύσονται	πεπαύσοιντο
	Infinitive	*Participle*
	πεπαύσεσθαι	πεπαυσόμενος η ον

Pluperfect active (stem ἐπεπαυκ-) 'I had stopped'

1s.	ἐπεπαύκη (ειν)
2s.	ἐπεπαύκης (εις)
3s.	ἐπεπαύκει(ν)
1pl.	ἐπεπαύκεμεν
2pl.	ἐπεπαύκετε
3pl.	ἐπεπαύκεσαν

Pluperfect middle/passive (stem ἐπεπαυ-)
'I had ceased, had been stopped'

1s.	ἐπεπαύμην
2s.	ἐπέπαυσο
3s.	ἐπέπαυτο

Pluperfect middle/passive (stem ἐπεπαυ-)
'I had ceased, had been stopped' (continued)

1pl.	ἐπεπαύμεθα
2pl.	ἐπέπαυσθε
3pl.	ἐπέπαυντο

CONTRACT VERBS

373. Contracted verbs form different endings, owing to the contraction of their final vowel with the ending. Rules of contraction are, in summary form:

	α	ε	ει	ι	η	ῃ	ο	ου	οι	ω	ῳ
α	α	α	ᾳ	αι	α	ᾳ	ω	ω	ῳ	ω	ῳ
ε	η	ει	ει	ει	η	ῃ	ου	ου	οι	ω	ῳ
ο	ω	ου	οι	οι	ω	οι	ου	ου	οι	ω	ῳ

The first vowel is in the LEFT-HAND column, the second in the TOP ROW: read off the resultant contraction where they intersect, e.g. α + ει = ᾳ. Remember that this grid refers to contract verbs *only*: do not use it to e.g. change the ἐ- *augment*.

Present active α-contract τῑμάω 'I honour'

	Indicative	*Imperative*	*Optative*	*Subjunctive*
1s.	τῑμῶ		τῑμῴην	τῑμῶ
2s.	τῑμᾷς	τίμα	τῑμῴης	τῑμᾷς
3s.	τῑμᾷ	τῑμάτω	τῑμῴη	τῑμᾷ
1pl.	τῑμῶμεν		τῑμῷμεν	τῑμῶμεν
2pl.	τῑμᾶτε	τῑμᾶτε	τῑμῷτε	τῑμᾶτε
3pl.	τιμῶσι(ν)	τῑμώντων	τῑμῷμεν	τῑμῶσι(ν)

	Infinitive	*Participle*
	τῑμᾶν*	τῑμῶν τῑμῶσα τῑμῶν (τῑμωντ-)

*One might expect τῑμάειν to contract into τῑμᾷν, but the original infinitive ending was in fact –εν > –αεν, > -ᾶν. So too δούλο-εν > δουλοῦν (below).

τῑμῶν τῑμῶσα τῑμῶν (τῑμωντ-) **'honouring'**

s.

	m.	*f.*	*n.*
Nom.	τῑμῶν	τῑμῶσα	τῑμῶν
Acc.	τῑμῶντα	τῑμῶσαν	τῑμῶν
Gen.	τῑμῶντος	τῑμώσης	τῑμῶντος
Dat.	τῑμῶντι	τῑμώσῃ	τῑμῶντι

pl.

	m.	*f.*	*n.*
Nom.	τῑμῶντες	τῑμῶσαι	τῑμῶντα
Acc.	τῑμῶντας	τῑμώσᾱς	τῑμῶντα
Gen.	τῑμώντων	τῑμωσῶν	τῑμώντων
Dat.	τῑμῶσι(ν)	τῑμώσαις	τῑμῶσι(ν)

Present active ε-contract ποιέω **'I make, do'**

	Indicative	*Imperative*	*Optative*	*Subjunctive*
1s.	ποιῶ		ποιοίην	ποιῶ
2s.	ποιεῖς	ποίει	ποιοίης	ποιῇς
3s.	ποιεῖ	ποιείτω	ποιοίη	ποιῇ
1pl.	ποιοῦμεν		ποιοῖμεν	ποιῶμεν
2pl.	ποιεῖτε	ποιεῖτε	ποιοῖτε	ποιῆτε
3pl.	ποιοῦσι	ποιούντων	ποιοῖεν	ποιῶσι(ν)

Infinitive	*Participle*
ποιεῖν	ποιῶν ποιοῦσα ποιοῦν (ποιουντ-)

ποιῶν ποιοῦσα ποιοῦν (ποιουντ-) **'making, doing'**

s.

	m.	*f.*	*n.*
Nom.	ποιῶν	ποιοῦσα	ποιοῦν
Acc.	ποιοῦντα	ποιοῦσαν	ποιοῦν
Gen.	ποιοῦντος	ποιούσης	ποιοῦντος
Dat.	ποιοῦντι	ποιούσῃ	ποιοῦντι

ποιῶν ποιοῦσα ποιοῦν (ποιουντ-) **'making, doing'** (continued)
pl.

	m.	*f.*	*n.*
Nom.	ποιοῦντες	ποιοῦσαι	ποιοῦντα
Acc.	ποιοῦντας	ποιούσᾱς	ποιοῦντα
Gen.	ποιούντων	ποιουσῶν	ποιούντων
Dat.	ποιοῦσι(ν)	ποιούσαις	ποιοῦσι(ν)

Present active o-contract δουλόω 'I enslave'

	Indicative	*Imperative*	*Optative*	*Subjunctive*
1s.	δουλῶ		δουλοίην	δουλῶ
2s.	δουλοῖς	δούλου	δουλοίης	δουλοῖς
3s.	δουλοῖ	δουλούτω	δουλοίη	δουλοῖ
1pl.	δουλοῦμεν		δουλοῖμεν	δουλῶμεν
2pl.	δουλοῦτε	δουλοῦτε	δουλοῖτε	δουλῶτε
3pl.	δουλοῦσι	δουλούντων	δουλοῖεν	δουλῶσι(ν)

	Infinitive	*Participle*
	δουλοῦν	δουλῶν οὖσα οὖν (δουλουντ-)

δουλῶν οὖσα οὖν (δουλουντ-) **'enslaving'**
s.

	m.	*f.*	*n.*
Nom.	δουλῶν	δουλοῦσα	δουλοῦν
Acc.	δουλοῦντα	δουλοῦσαν	δουλοῦν
Gen.	δουλοῦντος	δουλούσης	δουλοῦντος
Dat.	δουλοῦντι	δουλούσῃ	δουλοῦντι

pl.

	m.	*f.*	*n.*
Nom.	δουλοῦντες	δουλοῦσαι	δουλοῦντα
Acc.	δουλοῦντας	δουλοῦσᾱς	δουλοῦντα
Gen.	δουλούντων	δουλουσῶν	δουλούντων
Dat.	δουλοῦσι(ν)	δουλούσαις	δουλοῦσι(ν)

374.

Present middle α-contract τῑμάομαι 'honour, estimate'

	Indicative	Imperative	Optative	Subjunctive
1s.	τῑμῶμαι		τῑμῴμην	τῑμῶμαι
2s.	τῑμᾷ	τῑμῶ	τῑμῷο	τῑμᾷ
3s.	τῑμᾶται	τῑμάσθω	τῑμῷτο	τῑμᾶται
1pl.	τῑμώμεθα		τῑμῴμεθα	τῑμώμεθα
2pl.	τῑμᾶσθε	τῑμᾶσθε	τῑμῷσθε	τῑμᾶσθε
3pl.	τῑμῶνται	τῑμάσθων	τῑμῷντο	τῑμῶνται

	Infinitive	Participle
	τῑμᾶσθαι	τῑμώμενος η ον

τῑμώμενος η ον 'honouring, estimating'

s.

	m.	f.	n.
Nom.	τῑμώμενος	τῑμωμένη	τῑμώμενον
Acc.	τῑμώμενον	τῑμωμένην	τῑμώμενον
Gen.	τῑμωμένου	τῑμωμένης	τῑμωμένου
Dat.	τῑμωμένῳ	τῑμωμένῃ	τῑμωμένῳ

pl.

	m.	f.	n.
Nom.	τῑμώμενοι	τῑμώμεναι	τῑμώμενα
Acc.	τῑμωμένους	τῑμωμένᾱς	τῑμώμενα
Gen.	τῑμωμένων	τῑμωμένων	τῑμωμένων
Dat.	τῑμωμένοις	τῑμωμέναις	τῑμωμένοις

Present middle ε-contract ποιέομαι 'create, consider'

	Indicative	Imperative	Optative	Subjunctive
1s.	ποιοῦμαι		ποιοίμην	ποιῶμαι
2s.	ποιῇ (ποιεῖ)	ποιοῦ	ποιοῖο	ποιῇ
3s.	ποιεῖται	ποιείσθω	ποιοῖτο	ποιῆται

Present middle ε-contract ποιέομαι 'create, consider' (continued)

	Indicative	Imperative	Optative	Subjunctive
1pl.	ποιούμεθα		ποιοίμεθα	ποιώμεθα
2pl.	ποιεῖσθε	ποιεῖσθε	ποιοῖσθε	ποιῆσθε
3pl.	ποιοῦνται	ποιείσθων	ποιοῖντο	ποιῶνται

Infinitive	Participle
ποιεῖσθαι	ποιούμενος η ον

ποιούμενος η ον 'creating, considering'

s.

	m.	f.	n.
Nom.	ποιούμενος	ποιουμένη	ποιούμενον
Acc.	ποιούμενον	ποιουμένην	ποιούμενον
Gen.	ποιουμένου	ποιουμένης	ποιουμένου
Dat.	ποιουμένῳ	ποιουμένῃ	ποιουμένῳ

pl.

	m.	f.	n.
Nom.	ποιούμενοι	ποιούμεναι	ποιούμενα
Acc.	ποιουμένους	ποιουμένᾱς	ποιούμενα
Gen.	ποιουμένων	ποιουμένων	ποιουμένων
Dat.	ποιουμένοις	ποιουμέναις	ποιουμένοις

Present middle ο-contract δουλόομαι 'make subject (to oneself)'

	Indicative	Imperative	Optative	Subjunctive
1s.	δουλοῦμαι		δουλοίμην	δουλῶμαι
2s.	δουλοῖ	δουλοῦ	δουλοῖο	δουλοῖ
3s.	δουλοῦται	δουλούσθω	δουλοῖτο	δουλῶται
1pl.	δουλούμεθα		δουλοίμεθα	δουλώμεθα
2pl.	δουλοῦσθε	δουλοῦσθε	δουλοῖσθε	δουλῶσθε
3pl.	δουλοῦνται	δουλούσθων	δουλοῖντο	δουλῶνται

Infinitive	Participle
δουλοῦσθαι	δουλούμενος η ον

δουλούμενος η ον 'making subject'

s.

	m.	*f.*	*n.*
Nom.	δουλούμενος	δουλουμένη	δουλούμενον
Acc.	δουλούμενον	δουλουμένην	δουλούμενον
Gen.	δουλουμένου	δουλουμένης	δουλουμένου
Dat.	δουλουμένῳ	δουλουμένη	δουλουμένῳ

pl.

	m.	*f.*	*n.*
Nom.	δουλούμενοι	δουλούμεναι	δουλούμενα
Acc.	δουλουμένους	δουλουμένᾱς	δουλούμενα
Gen.	δουλουμένων	δουλουμένων	δουλουμένων
Dat.	δουλουμένοις	δουλουμέναις	δουλουμένοις

375.

Imperfect indicative active α-contract 'I was honouring'

1s.	ἐτίμων
2s.	ἐτίμᾱς
3s.	ἐτίμᾱ
1pl.	ἐτῑμῶμεν
2pl.	ἐτῑμᾶτε
3pl.	ἐτίμων

Imperfect indicative active ε-contract 'I was making, doing'

1s.	ἐποίουν
2s.	ἐποίεις
3s.	ἐποίει
1pl.	ἐποιοῦμεν
2pl.	ἐποιεῖτε
3pl.	ἐποίουν

Imperfect indicative active o-contract 'I was enslaving'

1s.	ἐδούλουν
2s.	ἐδούλους
3s.	ἐδούλου
1pl.	ἐδουλοῦμεν
2pl.	ἐδουλοῦτε
3pl.	ἐδούλουν

**Imperfect indicative middle/passive α-contract
'I was honouring, estimating'**

1s.	ἐτῑμώμην
2s.	ἐτῑμῶ
3s.	ἐτῑμᾶτο
1pl.	ἐτῑμώμεθα
2pl.	ἐτῑμᾶσθε
3pl.	ἐτῑμῶντο

**Imperfect indicative middle/passive ε-contract
'I was creating, considering'**

1s.	ἐποιούμην
2s.	ἐποιοῦ
3s.	ἐποιεῖτο
1pl.	ἐποιούμεθα
2pl.	ἐποιεῖσθε
3pl.	ἐποιοῦντο

Imperfect indicative middle/passive o-contract 'I was making subject'

1s.	ἐδουλούμην
2s.	ἐδουλοῦ
3s.	ἐδουλοῦτο
1pl.	ἐδουλούμεθα
2pl.	ἐδουλοῦσθε
3pl.	ἐδουλοῦντο

VERBS IN −μι IN FULL

376. δίδωμι 'I give'

Present active 'I give' (stem διδο-)

Indicative	Imperative	Optative	Subjunctive
δίδωμι		διδοίην	διδῶ
δίδως	δίδου	διδοίης	διδῷς
δίδωσι(ν)	διδότω	διδοίη	διδῷ
δίδομεν		διδοῖμεν	διδῶμεν
δίδοτε	δίδοτε	διδοῖτε	διδῶτε
διδόᾱσι(ν)	διδόντων	διδοῖεν	διδῶσι(ν)

Infinitive	Participle
διδόναι	διδούς διδοῦσα διδόν (διδοντ-)

Present middle/passive 'I give, am given' (stem διδο-)

Indicative	Imperative	Optative	Subjunctive
δίδομαι		διδοίμην	διδῶμαι
δίδοσαι	δίδοσο	διδοῖο	διδῷ
δίδοται	διδόσθω	διδοῖτο	διδῶται
διδόμεθα		διδοίμεθα	διδώμεθα
δίδοσθε	δίδοσθε	διδοῖσθε	διδῶσθε
δίδονται	διδόσθων	διδοῖντο	διδῶνται

Infinitive	Participle
δίδοσθαι	διδόμενος η ον

Imperfect indicative active 'I was giving' (stem διδο-)

ἐδίδουν
ἐδίδους
ἐδίδου
ἐδίδομεν
ἐδίδοτε
ἐδίδοσαν

Imperfect indicative middle/passive 'I was giving/was given' (stem διδο-)

ἐδιδόμην
ἐδίδοσο
ἐδίδοτο
ἐδιδόμεθα
ἐδίδοσθε
ἐδίδοντο

Aorist active ἔδωκα 'I gave' (stem δο-)

Indicative	Imperative	Optative	Subjunctive
ἔδωκα		δοίην	δῶ
ἔδωκας	δός	δοίης	δῷς
ἔδωκε	δότω	δοίη	δῷ
ἔδομεν		δοῖμεν	δῶμεν
ἔδοτε	δότε	δοῖτε	δῶτε
ἔδοσαν (ἔδωκαν)	δόντων	δυῖεν	δῶυι(ν)

Infinitive	Participle
δοῦναι	δούς δοῦσα δόν (δοντ-)

Aorist middle ἐδόμην 'I gave' (stem δο-)

Aorist indicative middle	Imperative	Optative	Subjunctive
ἐδόμην		δοίμην	δῶμαι
ἔδου	δοῦ	δοῖο	δῷ
ἔδοτο	δόσθω	δοῖτο	δῶται
ἐδόμεθα		δοίμεθα	δώμεθα
ἔδοσθε	δόσθε	δοῖσθε	δῶσθε
ἔδοντο	δόσθων	δοῖντο	δῶνται

Infinitive	Participle
δόσθαι	δόμενος η ον

Aorist passive ἐδόθην 'I was given' (stem δοθ-)

Indicative	Imperative	Optative	Subjunctive
ἐδόθην		δοθείην	δοθῶ
ἐδόθης	δόθητι	δοθείης	δοθῇς
ἐδόθη	δοθήτω	δοθείη	δοθῇ
ἐδόθημεν		δοθεῖμεν	δοθῶμεν
ἐδόθητε	δόθητε	δοθεῖτε	δοθῆτε
ἐδόθησαν	δοθέντων	δοθεῖεν	δοθ(σι)ν

Infinitive	Participle
δοθῆναι	δοθείς δοθεῖσα δοθέν (δοθεντ-)

Future active
δώσω
(etc., like παύσω)

Future middle 'I shall give'
δώσομαι
(etc., like παύσομαι)

Future passive 'I shall be given'
δοθήσομαι
(etc., like παυθήσομαι)

Perfect forms (all regular, as for παύω) 'I have given', etc.

Perfect active
δέδωκα

Perfect middle/passive
δέδομαι

Pluperfect active
ἐδεδώκη

Pluperfect middle/passive
ἐδεδόμην

377. τίθημι 'I put, place'

Present active 'I put, place', stem τιθε-

Indicative	Imperative	Optative	Subjunctive
τίθημι		τιθείην	τιθῶ
τίθης	τίθει	τιθείης	τιθῇς
τίθησι(ν)	τιθέτω	τιθείη	τιθῇ
τίθεμεν		τιθεῖμεν	τιθῶμεν
τίθετε	τίθετε	τιθεῖτε	τιθῆτε
τιθέᾱσι(ν)	τιθέντων	τιθεῖεν	τιθῶσι(ν)

Infinitive	Participle
τιθέναι	τιθείς τιθεῖσα τιθέν (τιθεντ-)

Present middle/passive 'I place for myself/am placed', stem τιθε-

Indicative	Imperative	Optative	Subjunctive
τίθεμαι		τιθείμην	τιθῶμαι
τίθεσαι	τίθεσο	τιθεῖο	τιθῇ
τίθεται	τιθέσθω	τιθεῖτο	τιθῆται
τιθέμεθα		τιθείμεθα	τιθώμεθα
τίθεσθε	τίθεσθε	τιθεῖσθε	τιθῆσθε
τίθενται	τιθέσθων	τιθεῖντο	τιθῶνται

Infinitive	Participle
τίθεσθαι	τιθέμενος η ον

Imperfect indicative active, stem τιθε- 'I was placing'

ἐτίθην
ἐτίθεις
ἐτίθει
ἐτίθεμεν
ἐτίθετε
ἐτίθεσαν

**Imperfect indicative middle/passive, stem τιθε-
'I was placing for myself/being placed'**

ἐτιθέμην
ἐτίθεσο
ἐτίθετο
ἐτιθέμεθα
ἐτίθεσθε
ἐτίθεντο

Aorist active, stem θε- 'I placed'

Indicative	*Imperative*	*Optative*	*Subjunctive*
ἔθηκα		θείην	θῶ
ἔθηκας	θές	θείης	θῇς
ἔθηκε(ν)	θέτω	θείη	θῇ
ἔθεμεν		θεῖμεν	θῶμεν
ἔθετε	θέτε	θεῖτε	θῆτε
ἔθεσαν (ἔθηκαν)	θέντων	θεῖσεν	θῶσι(ν)

Infinitive	*Participle*
θεῖναι	θείς θεῖσα θέν (θέντ-)

Aorist middle, stem θε- 'I placed for myself'

Indicative	*Imperative*	*Optative*	*Subjunctive*
ἐθέμην		θείμην	θῶμαι
ἔθου	θοῦ	θεῖο	θῇ
ἔθετο	θέσθω	θεῖτο	θῆται
ἐθέμεθα		θείμεθα	θώμεθα
ἔθεσθε	θέσθε	θεῖσθε	θῆσθε
ἔθεντο	θέσθων	θεῖντο	θῶνται

Infinitive	*Participle*
θέσθαι	θέμενος η ον

Aorist passive, stem τεθ- 'I was placed'

Indicative	Imperative	Optative	Subjunctive
ἐτέθην		τεθείην	τεθῶ
ἐτέθης	τέθητι	τεθείης	τεθῇς
ἐτέθη	τεθήτω	τεθείη	τεθῇ
ἐτέθημεν		τεθεῖμεν	τεθῶμεν
ἐτέθητε	τέθητε	τεθεῖτε	τεθῆτε
ἐτέθησαν	τεθέντων	τεθεῖεν	τεθῶσι(ν)

Infinitive	Participle
τεθῆναι	τεθείς τεθεῖσα τεθέν (τεθεντ-)

Future active
θήσω (etc., like παύσω)

Future middle
θήσομαι (etc., like παύσομαι)

Future passive
τεθήσομαι (etc., like παυθήσομαι)

Perfect forms (all regular, as for παύω)

Perfect active
τέθηκα

Perfect passive
κεῖμαι (see **313**)

Pluperfect active
ἐτεθήκη

ἵστημι 'I set up, make x stand'

ACTIVE (TRANSITIVE)

378.

Present active ἵστημι, 'I am setting x up': stem ἱστα-

Indicative	Imperative	Optative	Subjunctive
ἵστημι		ἱσταίην	ἱστῶ
ἵστης	ἵστη	ἱσταίης	ἱστῇς
ἵστησι(ν)	ἱστάτω	ἱσταίη	ἱστῇ
ἵσταμεν		ἱσταῖμεν	ἱστῶμεν
ἵστατε	ἵστατε	ἱσταῖτε	ἱστῆτε
ἱστᾶσι(ν)	ἱστάντων	ἱσταῖεν	ἱστῶσι(ν)

Infinitive	Participle
ἱστάναι	ἱστάς ἱστᾶσα ἱστάν (ἱσταντ-)

Imperfect indicative active ἵστην, 'I was setting X up'

ἵστην
ἵστης
ἵστη
ἵσταμεν
ἵστατε
ἵστασαν

Aorist active ἔστησα, 'I (did) set x up' : stem στησ-

Indicative	Imperative	Optative	Subjunctive
ἔστησα		στήσαιμι	στήσω
ἔστησας	στῆσον	στήσ-ειας (-αις)	στήσῃς
ἔστησε(ν)	στησάτω	στήσειε (-αι)	στήσῃ
ἐστήσαμεν		στήσαιμεν	στήσωμεν
ἐστήσατε	στήσατε	στήσαιτε	στήσητε
ἔστησαν	στησάντων	στήσαιεν	στήσωσι(ν)

Infinitive	Participle
στῆσαι	στήσᾱς στήσᾱσα στῆσαν (στησαντ-)

Future active στήσω, 'I will set x up': stem στησ-
(exactly like παύσω in all forms)

Indicative	στήσω, etc.
Optative	στήσοιμι, etc.
Infinitive	στήσειν
Participle	στήσων στήσουσα στῆσον (στησοντ-)

PASSIVE (INTRANSITIVE)

379.

Present passive ἵσταμαι, **'I am being set up': stem** ἱστα-

Indicative	*Imperative*	*Optative*	*Subjunctive*
ἵσταμαι		ἱσταίμην	ἱστῶμαι
ἵστασαι	ἵστασο	ἱσταῖο	ἱστῇ
ἵσταται	ἱστάσθω	ἱσταῖτο	ἱστῆται
ἱστάμεθα		ἱσταίμεθα	ἱστώμεθα
ἵστασθε	ἵστασθε	ἱσταῖσθε	ἱστῆσθε
ἵστανται	ἱστάσθων	ἱσταῖντο	ἱστῶντο

Infinitive	*Participle*
ἵστασθαι	ἱστάμενος η ον

Imperfect indicative passive, ἱστάμην **'I was being setting up'**

ἱστάμην
ἵστασο
ἵστατο
ἱστάμεθα
ἵστασθε
ἵσταντο

Aorist 'I was set up', ἐστάθην **(regular, like** ἐπαύθην**)**

Future 'I shall be set up', σταθήσομαι **(regular, like** παυθήσομαι**)**

Indicative	σταθήσομαι, etc.
Optative	σταθησοίμην, etc.
Infinitive	σταθήσεσθαι
Participle	σταθησόμενος η ον

MIDDLE (TRANSITIVE OR INTRANSITIVE)

380.

Present middle ἵσταμαι, **'I set X up for myself' or
'I am setting myself up'** : stem ἱστα-

Indicative	Imperative	Optative	Subjunctive
ἵσταμαι		ἱσταίμην	ἱστῶμαι
ἵστασαι	ἵστασο	ἱσταῖο	ἱστῇ
ἵσταται	ἱστάσθω	ἱσταῖτο	ἱστῆται
ἱστάμεθα		ἱσταίμεθα	ἱστώμεθα
ἵστασθε	ἵστασθε	ἱσταῖσθε	ἱστῆσθε
ἵστανται	ἱστάσθων	ἱσταῖντο	ἱστῶντο

Infinitive	Participle
ἵστασθαι	ἱστάμενος η ον

Imperfect indicative middle: **'I was setting X up for myself' or
'I was setting myself up'**
ἱστάμην
ἵστασο
ἵστατο
ἱστάμεθα
ἵστασθε
ἵσταντο

Aorist middle (transitive) ἐστησάμην, **'I did set up X for myself'**:
stem στησα-

Indicative	Imperative	Optative	Subjunctive
ἐστησάμην		στησαίμην	στήσωμαι
ἐστήσω	στῆσαι	στήσαιο	στήσῃ
ἐστήσατο	στησάσθω	στήσαιτο	στήσηται
ἐστησάμεθα		στησαίμεθα	στησώμεθα
ἐστήσασθε	στήσασθε	στήσαισθε	στήσησθε
ἐστήσαντο	στησάσθων	στήσαιντο	στήσωνται

Infinitive	Participle
στήσασθαι	στησάμενος η ον

Future στήσομαι, 'I shall set up for myself, stand up'
(regular, like παύσομαι)

Indicative	στήσομαι, etc.
Optative	στησοίμην, etc.
Infinitive	στήσεσθαι
Participle	στησόμενος η ον

INTRANSITIVE USAGES, 'I STAND/WAS STANDING/STOOD'

381.

Perfect intransitive ἕστηκα, '[Here] I stand': stem ἑστ-

Indicative	*Imperative*	*Optative*	*Subjunctive*
ἕστηκα		ἑσταίην	ἑστῶ
ἕστηκας	ἕσταθι	ἑσταίης	ἑστῇς
ἕστηκε(ν)	ἑστάτω	ἑσταίη	ἑστῇ
ἕσταμεν		ἑσταῖμεν (αίημεν)	ἑστῶμεν
ἕστατε	ἕστατε	ἑσταῖτε (αίητε)	ἑστῆτε
ἑστᾶσι(ν)	ἑστάντων	ἑσταῖεν (αίησαν)	ἑστῶσι(ν)

Infinitive	*Participle*
ἑστάναι	ἑστώς ῶσα ός (ἑστοτ-)

Pluperfect intransitive εἱστήκη, '[Here] I was standing':
stem ἑιστ-, ἑστ-

εἱστήκη
εἱστήκης
εἱστήκει
ἕσταμεν
ἕστατε
ἕστασαν

SECOND AORIST

Second/root aorist intransitive ἔστην, 'I stood': stem στη-/στα-

Indicative	Imperative	Optative	Subjunctive
ἔστην		σταίην	στῶ
ἔστης	στῆθι	σταίης	στῇς
ἔστη	στήτω	σταίη	στῇ
ἔστημεν		σταῖμεν	στῶμεν
ἔστητε	στῆτε	σταῖτε	στῆτε
ἔστησαν	στάντων	σταῖεν	στῶσι(ν)

Infinitive	Participle
στῆναι	στάς στᾶσα στάν (σταντ-)

ἀφίημι 'I RELEASE, LET GO'

382.

Present active 'I release, let go': stem ἀφῑε-

Indicative	Imperative	Optative	Subjunctive
ἀφίημι		ἀφῑείην	ἀφῑῶ
ἀφίης	ἀφίει	ἀφῑείης	ἀφῑῇς
ἀφίησι(ν)	ἀφῑέτω	ἀφῑείη	ἀφῑῇ
ἀφίεμεν		ἀφῑεῖμεν	ἀφῑῶμεν
ἀφίετε	ἀφίετε	ἀφῑεῖτε	ἀφῑῆτε
ἀφῑᾶσι(ν)	ἀφῑέντων	ἀφῑεῖεν	ἀφῑῶσι(ν)

Infinitive	Participle
ἀφῑέναι	ἀφῑείς ἀφῑεῖσα ἀφῑέν (ἀφῑεντ-)

Present middle/passive 'I aim at/am released': stem ἀφῑε-

Indicative	Imperative	Optative	Subjunctive
ἀφίεμαι		ἀφῑείμην	ἀφῑῶμαι
ἀφίεσαι	ἀφίεσο	ἀφῑεῖο	ἀφῑῇ
ἀφίεται	ἀφῑέσθω	ἀφῑεῖτο	ἀφῑῆται
ἀφῑέμεθα		ἀφῑείμεθα	ἀφῑώμεθα
ἀφῑεσθε	ἀφίεσθε	ἀφῑεῖσθε	ἀφῑῆσθε
ἀφίενται	ἀφῑέσθων	ἀφῑεῖντο	ἀφῑῶνται

Infinitive	Participle
ἀφίεσθαι	ἀφῑέμενος η ον

Imperfect indicative active 'I was letting go/releasing'
ἀφῑην
ἀφῑεις
ἀφῑει
ἀφῑεμεν
ἀφῑετε
ἀφῑεσαν

Imperfect indicative middle/passive 'I was aiming at/being let go'
ἀφῑέμην
ἀφῑεσο
ἀφῑετο
ἀφῑέμεθα
ἀφῑεσθε
ἀφῑεντο

Aorist active: stem ἀφε- (note: the augmented form is ἀφη- or ἀφει-) 'I released, let go'

Indicative	Imperative	Optative	Subjunctive
ἀφῆκα		ἀφείην	ἀφῶ
ἀφῆκας	ἄφες	ἀφείης	ἀφῇς
ἀφῆκε(ν)	ἀφέτω	ἀφείη	ἀφῇ
ἀφεῖμεν		ἀφεῖμεν	ἀφῶμεν
ἀφεῖτε	ἄφετε	ἀφεῖτε	ἀφῆτε
ἀφεῖσαν (ἀφῆκαν)	ἀφέντων	ἀφεῖεν	ἀφῶσι(ν)

Infinitive	Participle
ἀφεῖναι	ἀφείς ἀφεῖσα ἀφέν (ἀφεντ-)

Aorist middle: stem ἀφε- 'I was aiming at'

Indicative	Imperative	Optative	Subjunctive
ἀφείμην		ἀφείμην	ἀφῶμαι
ἀφεῖσο	ἀφοῦ	ἀφεῖο	ἀφῇ
ἀφεῖτο	ἀφέσθω	ἀφεῖτο	ἀφῆται
ἀφείμεθα		ἀφείμεθα	ἀφώμεθα
ἀφεῖσθε	ἄφεσθε	ἀφεῖσθε	ἀφῆσθε
ἀφεῖντο	ἀφέσθων	ἀφεῖντο	ἀφῶνται

Infinitive	Participle
ἀφέσθαι	ἀφέμενος η ον

Aorist passive: stem ἀφεθ- 'I was released, let go'

Indicative	Imperative	Optative	Subjunctive
ἀφείθην		ἀφεθείην	ἀφεθῶ
ἀφείθης	ἀφέθητι	ἀφεθείης	ἀφεθῇς
ἀφείθη	ἀφεθήτω	ἀφεθείη	ἀφεθῇ
ἀφείθημεν		ἀφέθειμεν	ἀφεθῶμεν
ἀφείθητε	ἀφέθητε	ἀφέθειτε	ἀφεθῆτε
ἀφείθησαν	ἀφεθέντων	ἀφέθειεν	ἀφεθῶσι(ν)

Infinitive	Participle
ἀφεθῆναι	ἀφεθείς ἀφεθεῖσα ἀφεθέν (ἀφεθεντ-)

Future indicative active
ἀφήσω (regular, like παύσω)

Future indicative middle
ἀφήσομαι (regular, like παύσομαι)

Future indicative passive
ἀφεθήσομαι (regular, like παυθήσομαι)

Perfect indicative active
ἀφεῖκα (regular, like πέπαυκα)

Perfect indicative middle/passive
ἀφεῖμαι (regular, like πέπαυμαι)

Pluperfect indicative middle/passive
ἀφείμην (regular, like ἐπεπαύμην)

δείκνῡμι **'I SHOW'**

383.

δείκνῡμι 'I SHOW'

383.

Present active, stem δεικνυ-

Indicative	*Imperative*	*Optative*	*Subjunctive*
δείκνῡμι		δεικνύοιμι	δεικνύω
δείκνῡς	δείκνῡ	δεικνύοις	δεικνύῃς
δείκνῡσι(ν)	δεικνύτω	δεικνύοι	δεικνύῃ
δείκνυμεν		δεικνύοιμεν	δεικνύωμεν
δείκνυτε	δείκνυτε	δεικνύοιτε	δεικνύητε
δείκνυ(ᾶ)σιν	δεικνύντων	δεικνύοιεν	δεικνύωσι(ν)

Infinitive	*Participle*
δεικνύναι	δεικνῡς δεικνῦσα δεικνύν (δεικνυντ-)

Present middle/passive, stem δεικνυ-

Indicative	*Imperative*	*Optative*	*Subjunctive*
δείκνυμαι		δεικνυοίμην	δεικνύωμαι
δείκνυσαι	δείκνυσο	δεικνύοιο	δεικνύῃ
δείκνυται	δεικνύσθω	δεικνύοιτο	δεικνύηται
δεικνύμεθα		δεικνυοίμεθα	δεικνυώμεθα
δείκνυσθε	δείκνυσθε	δεικνύοισθε	δεικνύησθε
δείκνυνται	δεικνύσθων	δεικνύοιντο	δεικνύωνται

Infinitive	*Participle*
δείκνυσθαι	δεικνύμενος η ον

Imperfect indicative active

ἐδείκνῡν
ἐδείκνῡς
ἐδείκνῡ
ἐδείκνυμεν
ἐδείκνυτε
ἐδείκνυσαν

Imperfect indicative middle/passive

ἐδεικνύμην
ἐδείκνυσο
ἐδείκνυτο
ἐδεικνύμεθα
ἐδείκνυσθε
ἐδείκνυντο

Aorist active
ἔδειξα (like ἔπαυσα)

Aorist passive
ἐδείχθην (like ἐπαύθην)

Future active
δείξω (like παύσω)

Future middle
δείξομαι (like παύσομαι)

Perfect forms (all regular, as for παύω)

Perfect active
δέδειχα

Perfect middle/passive
δέδειγμαι

Pluperfect active
ἐδεδείχη

Pluperfect middle/passive
ἐδεδείγμην

THE ENDINGS OF NON-INDICATIVE FORMS (ASPECTUAL)

384. In general, these forms point to the *aspect* of the action (**340[i]**). The endings are added to the appropriate *unaugmented* stem of the verb.

Infinitive

Present, Future
active   -ειν
middle/passive   -εσθαι

First Aorist
active   -σαι
middle   -σασθαι
passive   -(θ)ῆναι

Second Aorist
active   -εῖν
middle   -έσθαι
passive   -(θ)ῆναι

Perfect
active   -έναι
middle/passive   -σθαι

Participle

Present, Future
active   -ων -ουσα -ον (οντ-)
middle/passive   -όμεν-ος -η -ον

First Aorist
active   -(σ)ᾱς -(σ)ᾱσα- (σ)αν ([σ]αντ-)
middle   -(σ)άμεν-ος -η -ον
passive   -(θ)είς -εῖσα -έν ([θ]εντ-)

Second Aorist
active   -ων -ουσα -ον (οντ-)
middle   -όμεν-ος -η -ον
passive   -είς -εῖσα -έν (εντ-)

Perfect
active   -ώς -υῖα -ός (οτ-)
middle/passive   -μέν-ος -η -ον

Imperative

Present
active   -ε -έτω -ετε -όντων
middle/passive   -ου- έσθω -εσθε -έσθων

First Aorist
active   -ον -άτω -ατε -άντων
middle   -αι -άσθω -ασθε -άσθων
passive   -ητι -ήτω -ητε -έντων

Second Aorist
active   -ε -έτω -ετε -όντων
middle   -ου- έσθω -εσθε -έσθων
passive   -ητι *or* -ηθι -ήτω -ητε -έντων

Optative

Present, Future, Perfect active

- οιμι   -οις   -οι
or   *or*   *or*   } -οιμεν -οιτε -οιεν
-οίην   -οίης   -οίη

Present, Future, Second Aorist
-οίμην -οιο -οιτο -οίμεθα -οισθε -οιντο

First Aorist active
-αιμι -ειας (-αις) -ειε-(αι) -αιμεν -αιτε -ειαν (-αιεν)

First Aorist middle
-αίμην -αιο -αιτο -αίμεθα -αισθε -αιντο

First and Second Aorist passive
-είην- είης -είη -εῖμεν -εῖτε -εῖεν

Subjunctive

Active (and Aorists passive)
-ω -ῃς -ῃ -ωμεν -ητε -ωσι(ν)

Middle/passive
-ωμαι -ῃ -ηται -ώμεθα -ησθε -ωνται

Note that it is only in indirect speech that participles, infinitives and optatives can take on a specifically temporal function. In all other cases, their function is aspectual i.e. they give a particular view about the way in which the action is taking place, not when it is taking place. In general, see **415–417**.

IRREGULAR VERBS

385.

εἰμί **'I am'**

Present

	Indicative	Imperative	Optative	Subjunctive
1s.	εἰμί		εἴην	ὦ
2s.	εἶ	ἴσθι	εἴης	ἦς
3s.	ἐστί(ν)	ἔστω	εἴη	ἦ
1pl.	ἐσμέν		εἶμεν	ὦμεν
2pl.	ἐστέ	ἔστε	εἶτε	ἦτε
3pl.	εἰσί(ν)	ὄντων	εἶεν	ὦσι(ν)

Infinitive	Participle
εἶναι	ὤν οὖσα ὄν (ὀντ-)

Past 'I was'

1s.	ἦ(ν)
2s.	ἦσθα
3s.	ἦν
1pl.	ἦμεν
2pl.	ἦτε
3pl.	ἦσαν

Future 'I shall be'

1s.	ἔσομαι	ἐσοίμην
2s.	ἔσει	ἔσοιο
3s.	ἔσται	ἔσοιτο
1pl.	ἐσόμεθα	ἐσοίμεθα
2pl.	ἔσεσθε	ἔσοισθε
3pl.	ἔσονται	ἔσοιντο

Infinitive	Participle
ἔσεσθαι	ἐσόμεν-ος η ον

386.

εἶμι **'I shall go' (present in non-indicative forms)**

Future

	Indicative	Imperative	Optative	Subjunctive
1s.	εἶμι		ἴοιμι/ἰοίην	ἴω
2s.	εἶ	ἴθι	ἴοις	ἴῃς
3s.	εἶσι(ν)	ἴτω	ἴοι	ἴῃ
1pl.	ἴμεν		ἴοιμεν	ἴωμεν
2pl.	ἴτε	ἴτε	ἴοιτε	ἴητε
3pl.	ἴᾱσι(ν)	ἰόντων	ἴοιεν	ἴωσι(ν)

Infinitive	Participle
ἰέναι 'to go'	ἰών 'going' ἰοῦσα ἰόν (ἰοντ-)

εἶμι 'I shall go' (present in non-indicative forms) (continued)

Past 'I went'
1s. ᾖα (ᾔειν)
2s. ᾔεισθα (ᾔεις)
3s. ᾔει(ν)
1pl. ᾖμεν
2pl. ᾖτε
3pl. ᾖσαν (ᾔεσαν)

387.

οἶδα 'I know'

Present

	Indicative	*Imperative*	*Optative*	*Subjunctive*
1s.	οἶδα		εἰδείην	εἰδῶ
2s.	οἶσθα	ἴσθι	εἰδείης	εἰδῇς
3s.	οἶδε	ἴστω	εἰδείη	εἰδῇ
1pl.	ἴσμεν		εἰδεῖμεν	εἰδῶμεν
2pl.	ἴστε	ἴστε	εἰδεῖτε	εἰδῆτε
3pl.	ἴσᾱσι(ν)	ἴστων	εἰδεῖεν	εἰδῶ(σι)ν

	Infinitive	*Participle*
	εἰδέναι	εἰδ-ώς υῖα ός (εἰδοτ-)

Past 'I knew'
1s. ᾔδη (ᾔδειν)
2s. ᾔδησθα (ᾔδεις)
3s. ᾔδει(ν)
1pl. ᾖσμεν (ᾔδεμεν)
2pl. ᾖστε (ᾔδετε)
3pl. ᾖσαν (ᾔδεσαν)

Future 'I shall know'
1s. εἴσομαι *or* εἰδήσω
2s. εἴσει *etc.* εἰδήσεις *etc.*

388.

φημί 'I say'

Present

	Indicative	Imperative	Optative	Subjunctive
1s.	φημί		φαίην	φῶ
2s.	φής	φαθί	φαίης	φῇς
3s.	φησί(ν)	φάτω	φαίη	φῇ
1pl.	φαμέν		φαῖμεν	φῶμεν
2pl.	φατέ	φάτε	φαίητε	φῆτε
3pl.	φᾱσί(ν)	φάντων	φαῖεν	φῶσι(ν)

Infinitive	Participle
φάναι	φάσκων ουσα ον (φασκοντ-)

Note
The form φᾱ́ς, φᾶσα, φάν (φαντ-) for participle is found: also φάμεν-
ος η ον often in Homer. Both have the same meaning as φάσκων.

Imperfect 'I said'

1s.	ἔφην
2s.	ἔφησθα *or* ἔφης
3s.	ἔφη
1pl.	ἔφαμεν
2pl.	ἔφατε
3pl.	ἔφασαν

Note
In Homer middle forms often occur, e.g. ἔφατο for ἔφη.

Aorist 'I said'

1s.	ἔφησα
2s.	ἔφησας *etc. (regular)*

Future 'I shall say'

1s.	φήσω
2s.	φήσεις *etc. (regular)*

IMPORTANT PRINCIPAL PARTS

389. The following list gives the main principal parts of verbs learnt in the first
half of the Course, which may be said to be difficult. A few other verbs are
also included for reference, and should be learnt as well.

Verb	Main stem (no aug.)	Future	Aorist	Perfect	Aorist passive
ἀγγέλλω 'announce'	ἀγγειλ-	ἀγγελέω	ἤγγειλα	ἤγγελκα	ἠγγέλθην
ἄγω 'lead'	ἀγαγ-	ἄξω	ἤγαγον	ἦχα	ἤχθην
ᾄδω (ἀείδω) 'sing'	ᾀσ-/ἀεισ-	ᾄσομαι	ᾖσα		ᾔσθην
αἰνέω 'praise'	αἰνεσ-	αἰνέσω	ᾔνεσα	ᾔνεκα	ᾐνέθην
αἱρέω 'take' (mid. 'choose')	ἑλ-	αἱρήσω	εἷλον	ᾕρηκα	ᾑρέθην
αἴρω (ἀείρω) 'lift, remove'	ἀρ-/ἀειρ-	ἀρέω	ἦρα	ἦρκα	ἤρθην
αἰσθάνομαι 'perceive'	αἰσθ-	αἰσθήσομαι	ᾐσθόμην	ᾔσθημαι	
αἰσχύνω 'disgrace' (pass. 'be ashamed')	αἰσχυν(θ)-	αἰσχυνέω αἰσχυνέομαι (pass.)	ᾔσχῡνα		ᾐσχύνθην
ἀκούω 'hear'	ἀκουσ-	ἀκούσομαι	ἤκουσα	ἀκήκοα	ἠκούσθην
ἁλίσκομαι 'be caught'	ἁλ-	ἁλώσομαι	ἑάλων	ἑάλωκα	
ἀλλάττω 'change, exchange'	ἀλλαξ-	ἀλλάξω	ἤλλαξα	ἤλλαχα	ἠλλάχθην ἠλλάγην }
ἁμαρτάνω 'err, miss'	ἁμαρτ-	ἁμαρτήσομαι	ἥμαρτον	ἡμάρτηκα	ἡμαρτήθην
ἀμῡ́νω 'ward off' (mid. 'defend oneself)	ἀμυν-	ἀμυνέω	ἤμῡνα		
ἀνᾱλίσκω 'spend'	ἀνᾱλωσ-	ἀνᾱλώσω	ἀνᾱ́λωσα ἀνήλωσα }	ἀνᾱ́λωκα ἀνήλωκα }	ἀνᾱλώθην ἀνηλώθην }
ἀνέχομαι 'put up with'	ἀνασχ-	ἀνέξομαι	ἠνεσχόμην		
ἀνοίγνυμι 'open'	ἀνοιξ-	ἀνοίξω	ἀνέῳξα	ἀνέῳγμαι (pass.)	ἀνεῴχθην
ἅπτω 'fasten, light' (mid. 'touch')	ἁψ-/ἁφθ-	ἅψω	ἧψα	ἧμμαι (mid., pass.)	ἥφθην
ἀρέσκω 'please'	ἀρεσ(θ)-	ἀρέσω	ἤρεσα		ἠρέσθην
ἁρπάζω 'seize'	ἁρπασ-	ἁρπάσω	ἥρπασα	ἥρπηκα	ἡρπάσθην

Verb	Main stem (no aug.)	Future	Aorist	Perfect	Aorist passive
ἄρχω 'rule', 'begin' (usu. mid.)	ἀρχ-/ἀρξ-	ἄρξω	ἦρξα	ἦργμαι (mid.)	ἤρχθην
ἀφικνέομαι 'arrive'	ἀφικ-	ἀφίξομαι	ἀφικόμην	ἀφῖγμαι	
βαίνω 'go'	βη-/βα-	βήσομαι	ἔβην	βέβηκα	
βάλλω 'throw, pelt'	βαλ-/βληθ-	βαλέω	ἔβαλον	βέβληκα	ἐβλήθην
βλάπτω 'harm'	βλάψ-/βλαβ-	βλάψω	ἔβλυψα	βέβλαφα	ἐβλάβην / ἐβλάφθην
βούλομαι 'wish'	βουλ-/βουληθ-	βουλήσομαι		βεβούλημαι	ἐβουλήθην 'I wished'
γαμέω 'marry'	γημ-	γαμέω	ἔγημα	γεγάμηκα	
γελάω 'laugh'	γελασ-	γελάσομαι	ἐγέλασα		ἐγελάσθην
γίγνομαι 'become'	γεν-	γενήσομαι	ἐγενόμην	γεγένημαι / γέγονα	
γιγνώσκω 'recognise'	γνο-/γνω	γνώσομαι	ἔγνων	ἔγνωκα	ἐγνώσθην
γράφω 'write'	γραψ-	γράψω	ἔγραψα	γέγραφα	ἐγράφην
δάκνω 'bite'	δακ-/δηχθ-	δήξομαι	ἔδακον	δέδηγμαι (pass.)	ἐδήχθην
δέδοικα 'fear'	δεισ-/δεδοικ-/δειδ-	δείσομαι	ἔδεισα		
δείκνῡμι 'show'	δειξ-	δείξω	ἔδειξα	δέδειχα	ἐδείχθην
δέχομαι 'receive'	δεξ-/δεγ-	δέξομαι	ἐδεξάμην	δέδεγμαι	ἐδέχθην
δέω 'want, need' (mid. 'ask'; δεῖ 'it is necessary')	δεησ-	δεήσω	ἐδέησα	δεδέηκα	ἐδεήθην (mid.)
διδάσκω 'teach'	διδαξ-	διδάξω	ἐδίδαξα	δεδίδαχα	ἐδιδάχθην
δίδωμι 'give'	διδο-/δο-	δώσω	ἔδωκα, ἐδόμην (mid.)	δέδωκα	ἐδόθην
δράω 'do, act'	δρασ-	δράσω	ἔδρᾱσα	δέδρᾱκα	ἐδράσθην
δύναμαι 'be able'	δυνα-/δυνηθ-	δυνήσομαι		δεδύνημαι	ἐδυνήθην 'I was able'

Verb	Main stem (no aug.)	Future	Aorist	Perfect	Aorist passive
ἐάω 'allow'	ἐᾱσ-	ἐᾱσω	εἴᾱσα	εἴᾱκα	εἰᾱθην
ἐγείρω 'arouse'	ἐγειρ-	ἐγερέω	ἤγειρα	ἐγρήγορα 'I am a wake'	ἠγέρθην
ἐθέλω 'wish'	ἐθελησ-	ἐθελήσω	ἠθέλησα	ἠθέληκα	
εἰμί 'be'	ὀντ-/εἰ-	ἔσομαι	ἦ(ν) (impf.)		
εἶμι 'shall go'	ἰ-	εἶμι	ᾖα (impf.)		
ἐκπλήττω 'terrify'	ἐκπληξ-	ἐκπλήξω	ἐξέπληξα	ἐκπέπληγμαι (pass.)	ἐξεπλάγην
ἐλαύνω 'drive'	ἐλασ-/ἐλα-	ἐλάω	ἤλασα	ἐλήλακα	ἠλάθην
ἕλκω 'drag'	ἑλκυσ-	ἕλξω ἑλκύσω }	εἵλκυσα	εἵλκυκα	εἱλκύσθην
ἐλπίζω 'hope, expect'	ἐλπισ-	ἐλπιέω	ἤλπισα		
ἐπίσταμαι 'know, understand'	ἐπιστα-/η-	ἐπιστήσομαι			ἠπιστήθην 'I knew'
ἕπομαι 'follow'	σπ-	ἕψομαι	ἑσπόμην (εἱπόμην impf.)		
ἐργάζομαι 'work' (pass, 'be made')	ἐργασ-	ἐργάσομαι	εἰργασάμην	εἴργασμαι	εἰργάσθην
ἔρχομαι 'go'	ἐλθ-	ἐλεύσομαι εἶμι }	ἦλθον	ἐλήλυθα	
ἐρωτάω 'ask'	ἐρ-/ἐρωτησ-	ἐρήσομαι ἐρωτήσω }	ἠρόμην ἠρώτησα	ἠρώτηκα	ἠρωτήθην
ἐσθίω 'eat'	ἐδ-/φαγ	ἔδομαι	ἔφαγον	ἐδήδοκα	ἠδέσθην
εὑρίσκω 'find'	εὑρ-	εὑρήσω	ηὗρον	ηὕρηκα	ηὑρέθην
ἔχω 'have, hold'	σχ-	ἕξω σχήσω }	ἔσχον (εἶχον impf.)	ἔσχηκα	ἐσχέθην
ζάω 'live'	ζήσ-/ζω-	ζήσω	ἔζων ἔζην } (impf.)		
ἥδομαι 'be pleased, enjoy'	ἡσθ-	ἡσθήσομαι			ἥσθην "I enjoyed'
ἧμαι (καθ-) 'be seated'	ἡμ-		ἥμην/ἐκαθήμην (impf.)		

Verb	Main stem (no aug.)	Future	Aorist	Perfect	Aorist passive
ἠμί 'say'			ἦν δ᾿ ἐγώ, ἦ δ᾿ ὅς, ἦ 'I said' 'he said'		
θάπτω 'bury'	θαψ-	θάψω	ἔθαψα	τέθαμμαι (pass.)	ἐτάφην
θνήσκω (ἀπο-) 'die'	θαν-	θανέομαι	ἔθανον	τέθνηκα	
ἵημι 'shoot, let go, send'	ἱε-/ἑ-/εἱ-	ἥσω	ἧκα	εἷκα	εἵθην
ἵστημι 'set up' (intrans. 'stand')	στησ-/στα-/ στη	στήσω	ἔστησα ἔστην (intrans.)	ἔστηκα (intrans.)	ἐστάθην
καίω 'burn'	καυσ-	καύσω	ἔκαυσα	κέκαυκα	ἐκαύθην
καλέω 'call'	καλεσ-/κληθ-	καλέω	ἐκάλεσα	κέκληκα	ἐκλήθην
κάμνω 'toil'	καμ-	καμέομαι	ἔκαμον	κέκμηκα	
κεῖμαι 'lie, be placed'	κει-	κείσομαι	ἐκείμην (impf.)		
κλαίω 'weep'	κλαυσ-	κλαύσομαι	ἔκλαυσα	κέκλαυ(σ)μαι (pass.)	ἐκλαύσθην
κλέπτω 'steal'	κλεψ-	κλέψω	ἔκλεψα	κέκλοφα	ἐκλάπην
κλῑ́νω 'cause to lean' (pass. 'lean, lie')	κλῑν-/κλιθ-	κλινέω	ἔκλῑνα	κέκλιμαι	ἐκλίθην ⎫ ἐκλίνην ⎭
κόπτω 'hit'	κοψ-/κοπ-	κόψω	ἔκοψα	κέκοφα	ἐκόπην
κρῑ́νω 'judge'	κρῑν(α)-/κριθ-	κρινέω	ἔκρῑνα	κέκρικα	ἐκρίθην
κτάομαι 'gain'	κτη-	κτήσομαι	ἐκτησάμην	κέκτημαι	ἐκτήθην
κτείνω (ἀπο-) 'kill'	(ἀπο)κτειν-/ κταν-	(ἀπο)κτενέω	(ἀπ)έκτεινα (ἀπ)έκτανον	(ἀπ)έκτονα	
λαγχάνω 'obtain by lot'	λαχ-	λήξομαι	ἔλαχον	εἴληχα	ἐλήχθην
λαμβάνω 'take'	λαβ-	λήψομαι	ἔλαβον	εἴληφα	ἐλήφθην
λανθάνω 'escape notice of' (mid. 'forget')	λαθ-	λήσω	ἔλαθον	λέληθα	

Verb	Main stem (no aug.)	Future	Aorist	Perfect	Aorist passive
λέγω 'say'	λεξ-/εἰπ-/ἐρ-	λέξω ἐρέω }	ἔλεξα εἶπον }	εἴρηκα	ἐλέχθην
λείπω 'leave'	λιπ-	λείψω	ἔλιπον	λέλοιπα 'I have left/have failed'	ἐλείφθην
μανθάνω 'learn'	μαθ-	μαθήσομαι	ἔμαθον	μεμάθηκα	
μάχομαι 'fight'	μαχεσ-	μαχέ(σ) ομαι	ἐμαχεσάμην	μεμάχημαι	
μέλλω 'intend'	μελλ(ησ)-	μελλήσω	ἐμέλλησα		
μέλει 'it concerns'	μελησ-	μελήσει	ἐμέλησε	μεμέληκε	
μένω 'remain'	μειν-	μενέω	ἔμεινα	μεμένηκα	
μιμνήσκω 'remind' (*mid.* 'remember')	μνησ(θ)-	μνήσομαι	ἔμνησα	μέμνημαι (*mid.*)	ἐμνήσθην (*mid.*)
νέμω 'distribute'	νειμ-	νεμέω	ἔνειμα	νενέμηκα	ἐνεμήθην
νομίζω 'think, consider'	νομισ-	νομιέω	ἐνόμισα	νενόμικα	ἐνομίσθην
οἶδα 'know'	εἰδ-	εἴσομαι	ᾔδη (*impf.*)		
οἴομαι 'think'	οἰη-	οἰήσομαι	ᾤμην (*impf.*)		ᾠήθην 'I thought'
ὄλλῡμι (ἀπ-) 'destroy' (*mid.* 'perish')	ὀλεσ-/ὀλο-	ὀλέω	ὤλεσα ὠλόμην (*mid.*)	ὀλώλεκα ὄλωλα (*mid.*)	
ὄμνῡμι 'swear'	ὀμοσ-	ὀμέομαι	ὤμοσα	ὀμώμοκα	ὠμό(σ)θην
ὁράω 'see'	ἰδ-	ὄψομαι	εἶδον	ἑώρακα	ὤφθην
ὄρνῡμι 'raise' (*mid.* 'rise, rush')	ὀρσ-/ὀρμ-	ὄρσω	ὦρσα ὠρόμην (*mid.*)	ὄρωρα (*mid.*)	
ὀφείλω 'owe'	ὀφε(ι)λ-	ὀφειλήσω	ὠφείλησα ὤφελον ('would that')		
ὀφλισκάνω 'incur charge of	ὀφλ-	ὀφλήσω	ὦφλον	ὤφληκα	
πάσχω 'experience, suffer'	παθ-	πείσομαι	ἔπαθον	πέπονθα	

Verb	Main stem (no aug.)	Future	Aorist	Perfect	Aorist passive
πέμπω 'send'	πεμψ-	πέμψω	ἔπεμψα	πέπομφα	ἐπέμφθην
πίνω 'drink'	πι-	πίομαι	ἔπιον	πέπωκα	ἐπόθην
πίπτω 'fall'	πεσ-	πεσέομαι	ἔπεσον	πέπτωκα	
πίμπλημι 'fill'	πλησ-	πλήσω	ἔπλησα	πέπληκα	ἐπλήσθην
πίμπρημι 'burn up'	πρησ-	πρήσω	ἔπρησα	πέπρημαι (*pass.*)	ἐπρήσθην
πλέω 'sail'	πλευσ-	πλεύσομαι	ἔπλευσα	πέπλευκα	ἐπλεύσθην
πρᾱ́ττω 'act, fare'	πρᾱξ-/πρᾱγ-	πρᾱ́ξω	ἔπρᾱξα	πέπρᾱχα πέπρᾱγα ('I have fared')	ἐπρᾱ́χθην
πυνθάνομαι 'hear, inquire'	πυθ-	πεύσομαι	ἐπυθόμην	πέπυσμαι	
πωλέω 'sell'		πωλήσω	ἀπεδόμην	πέπρακα	ἐπράθην
ῥήγνῡμι 'break'	ῥηξ-	ῥήξω	ἔρρηξα	ἔρρωγα 'I am broken'	ἐρράγην
ῥῑ́πτω 'throw'	ῥιψ-/ῥιφ-	ῥίψω	ἔρριψα	ἔρριφα	ἐρρίφ(θ)ην
σκοπέω (σκέπτομαι) 'view'	σκεψ-	σκέψομαι	ἐσκεψάμην	ἔσκεμμαι	
σπένδω 'pour a libation'	σπεισ-	σπείσω	ἔσπεισα	ἔσπεισμαι	
στέλλω 'send'	στειλ-	στελέω	ἔστειλα	ἔσταλκα	ἐστάλην
σῴζω 'save'	σωσ-	σώσω	ἔσωσα	σέσωκα	ἐσώθην
τέμνω 'cut'	τεμ-	τεμέω	ἔτεμον	τέτμηκα	ἐτμήθην
τίθημι 'place, put, make'	τιθε-/θε-	θήσω	ἔθηκα ἐθέμην (*mid.*)	τέθηκα	ἐτέθην
τίκτω 'bear'	τεκ-	τέξω-/ομαι	ἔτεκον	τέτοκα	
τίνω 'pay'	τισ-/τεισ-	τ(ε)ίσω	ἔτ(ε)ισα	τέτ(ε)ικα	ἐτ(ε)ίσθην
τιτρώσκω 'wound'	τρωσ-	τρώσω	ἔτρωσα	τέτρωμαι (*pass.*)	ἐτρώθην

Verb	Main stem (no aug.)	Future	Aorist	Perfect	Aorist passive
τρέπω 'turn'	τρεψ-/τραπ-	τρέψω	ἔτρεψα ἐτραπόμην ('I was turned')	τέτροφα	ἐτρέφθην ἐτράπην }
τρέφω 'rear, nourish'	θρεψ-	θρέψω	ἔθρεψα	τέτροφα	ἐθρέφθην
τρέχω 'run'	δραμ-	δραμέομαι	ἔδραμον	δεδράμηκα	
τυγχάνω 'happen, chance'	τυχ-	τεύξομαι	ἔτυχον	τετύχηκα τέτευχα }	
τύπτω 'strike'	τυπ-	τυπτήσω	ἐτύπτησα		ἐτύπην
ὑπισχνέομαι 'promise'	ὑποσχ-	ὑποσχήσομαι	ὑπεσχόμην	ὑπέσχημαι	
φαίνω 'reveal' (*mid.* 'appear, seem')	φαν-	φανέω	ἔφηνα	πέφαγκα πέφηνα (*intrans.*) }	ἐφάν(θ)ην
φέρω 'bear, carry'	ἐνεγκ-	οἴσω	ἤνεγκον ἤνεγκα }	ἐνήνοχα	ἠνέχθην
φεύγω 'flee, run off'	φυγ-	φεύξομαι	ἔφυγον	πέφευγα	
φημί 'say'	φα-/η-	φήσω	ἔφησα ἔφην (*impf.*)		
φθάνω 'anticipate'	φθα(σ)-	φθήσομαι	ἔφθασα ἔφθην }		
φθείρω(δια) 'destroy, corrupt'	φθειρ-/φθαρ-	φθερέω	ἔφθειρα	ἔφθαρκα	ἐφθάρην
φύ̄ω 'produce' (*mid.* 'be, be naturally')	φῡ-/πεφῡ(κ)	φύ̄σω	ἔφῡσα ἔφῡν (*mid.*)	πέφῡκα (*mid.*)	
χαίρω 'rejoice, bid farewell'	χαρ-	χαιρήσω		κεχάρηκα	ἐχάρην 'I rejoiced'
χράομαι 'use; consult oracle' (*act.* 'give oracle')	χρησ(θ)-	χρήσομαι	ἐχρησάμην (ἐ)χρῆν (*impf.*)	κέχρημαι	ἐχρήσθην
ὠνέομαι 'buy'	ὠνε-/πρια-	ὠνήσομαι	ἐπριάμην	ἐώνημαι 'I have bought-/I have been bought'	ἐωνήθην

PREPOSITIONS

390. It is worth noting that prepositions were originally adverbs and so used just in conjunction with verbs. So, in Homer, one frequently finds what looks like a preposition but is in fact an adverb, modifying the verb. The original meaning of the adverb (where it is possible to determine it) is indicated in the first column. Observe how the original adverbial meaning is modified according to the case the preposition takes.

	Accusative	Genitive	Dative
ἀμφί ('around')	*'about, near'* ἀμφὶ δείλην 'about evening' οἱ ἀμφὶ Πλάτωνα 'those around Plato', 'followers of Plato'		
ἀνά ('up')	*'up, through, by'* ἀνὰ τὸν πόταμον 'up the river' ἀνὰ τὸν πόλεμον 'through the war' ἀνὰ ἑκατόν 'by hundreds'		
ἀντί ('against')		*'instead of, for the sake of'* ἀντὶ πολέμου 'instead of war' ἀντὶ ἀδελφοῦ 'for the sake of a brother'	
ἀπό ('from')		*'from'* ἀπὸ τῆς πόλεως 'from the city'	
διά ('through')	*'because of, through'* διὰ τοῦτο 'because of this'	*'through'* (time, place) διὰ νυκτός 'through the night' διὰ τῆς τραπέζης 'through the table'	
εἰς/ἐς ('into')	*'into, until, up to'* εἰς Σικελίαν 'into Sicily' ἐς ἠῶ 'until dawn' εἰς ἑκατόν 'up to 100'	*'to the house of'* εἰς Ἅιδου 'to the house of Hades'	

	Accusative	Genitive	Dative
ἐν ('in')		*'at the house of'* ἐν Κροίσου 'In Croesus' house'	*'in, in the power of'* ἐν Σπάρτῃ 'in Sparta' ἐν χειμῶνι 'in winter' ἐν ἐμοί 'in my power'
ἐκ/ἐξ ('from out of')		*'from'* ἐκ Σπάρτης 'from Sparta' ἐκ τῶν παρόντων 'from, with an eye on, present circumstances'	
ἐπί ('at, on')	*'at, against, over'* ἐπὶ βασιλέα 'against, at the king' ἐπὶ πέντε ἔτη 'over five years'	*'on; in the time of; at'* ἐπὶ βωμοῦ 'on the altar' ἐπὶ ἐμοῦ 'in my time' ἐπὶ σχολῆς 'at leisure'	*'on; for the purpose of, because of'* ἐπὶ τῇ θαλάττῃ 'on the sea' ἐπὶ δείπνῳ 'for dinner' ἐπὶ τούτοις 'because of these things, on these conditions'
κατά ('down')	*'down, by; according to'* κατὰ τὸν πόταμον 'down river' κατὰ θάλατταν 'by sea' κατὰ τοὺς νόμους 'according to the laws'	*'down from, beneath, against'* κατὰ τῆς πετρᾶς 'down from the rock' κατὰ χθονός 'beneath the earth' κατὰ ἐμοῦ 'against me'	
μετά ('among')	*'for, after'* μετὰ χρύσον 'for, after gold' μετὰ τὸν πόλεμον 'after the war'	*'with, in company with'* μετὰ τῶν φίλων 'with his friends'	
παρά ('along-side')	*'to, throughout, against'* παρὰ τοὺς φίλους 'to my friends' (house)' παρὰ τὸν ἐνίαυτον 'throughout the year' παρὰ τὸν νόμον 'against the law'	*'from beside, from'* παρὰ τῶν νεῶν 'from beside the ships' παρὰ τῶν μαθητῶν 'from the students'	*'with, near'* παρὰ ἡμῖν 'with us, at our house'
περί ('around, about')	*'about, near'* περὶ τὸ τεῖχος 'near the wall' περὶ τοῦτον τὸν χρόνον 'about this time'	*'concerning'* περὶ πατρός 'concerning father' περὶ πολλοῦ ποιεῖσθαι 'to value highly'	*'about, concerning'* δείσαντες περὶ τῇ στρατιᾷ 'fearing for (concerning) the army'

	Accusative	Genitive	Dative
πρό ('before')		*'in front of, before'* πρὸ τῶν θυρῶν 'in front of the doors' πρὸ δείπνου 'before supper'	
πρός ('to, at, by')	*'towards; with a view to'* πρὸς τὴν πόλιν 'towards the city' πρὸς τὰ παρόντα 'with a view to the present'	*'in name of; from; under the protection of; to the advantage of'* πρὸς θεῶν 'in the name of the gods!' πρὸς Διός 'from Zeus' *or* 'under Zeus' protection' πρὸς ἡμῶν 'to our advantage'	*'by, in addition to'* πρὸς τῷ πυρί 'by the fire' πρὸς τούτῳ 'in addition to this'
σύν ('with the help of')			*'with the help of; in company with'* σὺν τοῖς θεοῖς 'with the help of the gods' σὺν ἡμῖν 'with us'
ὑπέρ ('over')	*'over, exceeding'* ὑπὲρ τὴν θάλατταν 'over the sea' ὑπὲρ δύναμιν 'beyond one's power'	*'on behalf of; over'* ὑπὲρ τῆς πόλεως 'on behalf of the city' ὑπὲρ τῆς κεφαλῆς 'over my head'	
ὑπό ('under')	*'up to and under, at'* ὑπὸ τὰ τείχη 'under the walls' ὑπὸ νύκτα 'at night'	*'under, by'* ὑπὸ τῆς γῆς 'under the earth' ὑπὸ τούτου τοῦ ἀνδρός 'by this man'	

PARTICLES

391.

General remarks[7]

1. Particles are short invariable words which:

   (i) connect an item of utterance to a preceding item, whether that item is uttered by the same speaker or by a different speaker ('and', 'but', 'so …' etc.)

   (ii) qualify an item ('even', 'also', 'anyway', etc.)

---

7 This section was contributed by Sir Kenneth Dover.

(iii) 'colour' an item, expressing what is commonly expressed in spoken English by volume and tone of voice ('he told me!', 'he told me', etc.) and in written by, e.g., italics, exclamation-marks, inverted commas, etc.

ἆρα, ἦ, ἀλλά, καί

2. Four particles – ἆρα, ἦ, ἀλλά, καί – normally come first in the sentence or part of the sentence to which they belong. ἆρα and ἦ introduce questions, e.g.

> ἆρ' ἤκουσας; 'Did you hear?'
> ἀλλὰ τίς σοι διηγεῖτο; ἦ αὐτὸς Σωκράτης; 'But who told you? Socrates himself?'

3. ἀλλά 'but' and καί 'and' are widely used as in English, e.g.

> οὐχ ἡμεῖς ἀλλ' ἐκεῖνοι 'not we, but they'
> ἀλλὰ τίς σοι διηγεῖτο; 'but who told you?'
> ἡμεῖς καὶ ἐκεῖνοι 'we and they'
> καὶ ταῦτ' ἀποκρινάμενος ἀπῆλθεν 'and with that answer he went away'

4. καί may be repeated to give the sense 'both … and …', e.g.

> καὶ ἡμᾶς ἐζήτει καὶ ἐκείνους 'he was looking both for us and for them'

5. καί is also used in the senses 'actually, also, even', etc., and where English raises the volume of the voice, e.g.

> ἐζήτουν καὶ ἐκεῖνον 'I was looking for him too' (or ' … for him also', ' … also for him')
> ἐκεῖνον καὶ ἐζήτουν 'I was (actually) looking for him'
> τί καὶ βούλεσθε; 'What do you (actually) want?' (or, 'What is it that you want?)
> τὰ τοιαῦτα αἰσχρὸν καὶ λέγειν 'it's disgraceful (even) to speak of things like that'
> οὐδὲν ἄν μοι μέλοι εἰ καὶ ἀποθάνοι 'I wouldn't care (even) if he did die'

Post-positives δέ, γάρ, οὖν

6. Most other particles are postpositives, i.e. they cannot come immediately after a pause, and usually come close after the word which does follow the pause. The three most important are δέ, γάρ and οὖν.

7. δέ is translatable by 'and', 'but', or not by anything, according to context; one might call it the 'basic connective' between sentences, e.g.

> τί δ' εἰ ἀποθάνοι; 'But what if he were to die?'
> καθεύδει, ἐγὼ δ' ἀγρυπνῶ 'he's asleep, and/but I'm awake'
> ἀκούσας δ' ἀπῆλθεν '(and) having heard it he went away'

8. When δέ is combined with a negative, the form οὐδέ/μηδέ is used if the preceding item is negative, but otherwise οὐ/μή follows δέ, e.g.

> οὐ ταῦτ' εἶπον οὐδ' ἂν ἐπαινοίην 'that isn't what I said, nor would I commend it' (or ' … and I wouldn't commend it')
> ταῦτ' εἶπον, ὁ δὲ Σωκράτης οὐκ ἐπήνει 'that is what I said, but Socrates did not commend it'

9. οὐδέ/μηδέ is the opposite of καί in some of the senses of §5 above, e.g.

> οὐδ' ἐκεῖνον ἐζήτουν 'I wasn't looking for him either'
> τί ἐρεῖς ἐὰν μηδ' ἀποκρίνηται; 'What will you say if he doesn't even answer?'

10. γάρ introduces the reason for the previous utterance ('for, because'), e.g.
> ἔφευγεν· ἐδίωκον γάρ 'he ran away, for/because they were pursuing him'

11. In a response to a previous speaker γάρ is sometimes translatable as 'Why, …', 'Yes, …', 'No, …', e.g.

> τί γὰρ ἂν ποιοίη; 'Why, what would he do?'
> πῶς γὰρ οὔ; 'Yes, of course' (or 'Yes, indeed'; lit., 'For how not?')
> οὐ γάρ μ' ἐῶσιν 'No, they don't let me'

12. οὖν is the converse of γάρ, introducing the consequence of the previous utterance ('therefore, so, then'), e.g.

> ἐδίωκον· ἔφευγεν οὖν 'they were pursuing him, so he ran away'

13. The consequential sense of οὖν is, however, sometimes very 'faded', so that it approximates to 'then' in the sense 'next', or to 'Well, …' or 'So …' in colloquial English narrative.

Other connectives ἄρα, δῆτα, μήν, τοίνυν

14. Other important particles with a connective sense are ἄρα, δῆτα, μήν and τοίνυν.

15. ἄρα is often translatable as 'then' or 'so', especially (though not only) when the speaker perceives a conclusion to be drawn from a situation or preceding argument, or when he envisages a possibility, e.g.

> οὐκ ἄρ' ἀγαθὸν ὁ πλοῦτος 'so wealth is not a blessing after all'
> ἤκουσα αὐτῶν ὡς ἄρ' οὐδὲν ἔλαβεν 'I'm told by them that he didn't receive anything, it   seems'
> εἰ δ' ἄρα καὶ ἀδικεῖς … 'but if by any chance you are in the wrong …' (or '…   if… actually', 'if… after all')

16. δῆτα is commonest in questions or negations responding to a previous speaker, e.g.

πῶς δῆτ' ἔπραξεν; 'So how did he manage?' (or, 'How did he manage, then?')

οὐ δῆτα 'No indeed!' (according to context, 'No, I won't!', 'No, he didn't!', etc.)

17. μήν is mostly found in combinations with other particles (see below), but note one independent usage with interrogatives and one with negatives, e.g.

(ἀλλά) τί μήν; '(but) what, then(, if not that)?'

οὔτε Καλλίας οὔτε Φιλῖνος οὐ μὴν οὐδὲ Σωκράτης 'neither Kallias nor Philinos nor, indeed, Socrates'

18. τοίνυν introduces an exposition or a stage in an exposition, like English 'Now, ... ', 'Well, now, ...', 'Well, then, ...'

τε

19. τε is a peculiar particle in that it may either connect an item to what precedes or look forward to what follows (the former usage is not very common in prose), e.g.

τέθνηκέ τε 'and he is dead'

ἐγώ τε καὶ σύ '(both) I and you'

20. οὔτε/μήτε is used in pairs or series in the sense 'neither ... nor ...', 'not ... or ...', 'not ..., nor ..., nor ...' e.g.

οὔθ' ἡμᾶς εἶδες οὔτ' ἐκείνους 'you didn't see us or them' (or 'you saw neither us nor them')

γε, δή, μέν, τοι

21. The commonest particles of which the main function is to 'colour' the item with which they occur rather than to connect it with what precedes are γε, δή, μέν and τοι.

22. γε sometimes has a limiting sense, like 'anyway, at least, at any rate' in English, but is used in Greek far more than those expressions in English, e.g.

ἐκεῖνόν γε ἐνίκησας 'you defeated him' (implying 'even if you didn't defeat anyone else' or 'I don't know if you defeated anyone else')

23. γε is also common in responses to a previous speaker's utterance, especially to a question, e.g.

'τί σοι δοκεῖ ποιεῖν;'	'What do you think he's doing?'
'μέμφεσθαί γε τῷ στρατηγῷ.'	'Criticising the general.'
'ἔστι τις ἔνδον;'	'Is anyone in?'
'οὐδείς γε.'	'No, nobody.'

24. Thirdly, γε corresponds to an exclamation-mark with words which convey praise, blame or some other emotional reaction, e.g.

ἀμαθής γ' εἶ 'Why, you are stupid!'

εὖ γε 'Well done!'

25. δή is equivalent to an increased volume of voice on the preceding word, or to an emphatic gesture designed to sustain or revive the hearer's attention. It is used especially with quantitative words ('most', 'many', 'least', 'often', 'only', etc.), with points of time (giving 'then' and 'now' a colouring of 'then at last' and 'just now'), and with expressions such as 'it is obvious' or 'now, consider …' It is rarely translatable. There is one special usage in which it has the effect of showing that the word which it accompanies is quoted from someone else, or represents someone else's way of thinking, and this usually imparts a tone of scepticism or sarcasm.

26. μέν accompanies the first item of a pair, usually when there is a contrast, but when the word which it accompanies is repeated the effect may be cumulative rather than contrastive, e.g.

οἱ μὲν Λακεδαιμόνιοι ἐπαινοῦσιν αὐτόν, τοῖς δὲ Θηβαίοις οὐκ ἀρέσκει 'the Spartans praise him, but he doesn't please the Thebans'

τὰ μὲν μάλ' ἀκριβῶς ἐργάζεται, τὰ δ' ἀμελεῖ 'some things he produces very   carefully, but there are other respects in which he is careless'

πολλοὶ μὲν ἀπέθανον, πολλοὶ δ' ἐζωγρήθησαν 'many were killed and many captured'

27. τοι expresses the speaker's feeling that the hearer's attitude or conduct ought to be affected by what is said: a threatening 'Let me tell you!', a firm but friendly 'do remember' or a gentle 'You do realise, don't you?' Sometimes, however, it conveys little more than 'Look, …',. ' …, you know, …', '…, you see, …' or 'after all' in English.

Particle combinations

28. A very large number of combinations of particles occur, and some of them are written as a single word: γε + οὖν as γοῦν, καί + τοι as καίτοι and μέν + τοι as μέντοι. οὐ + τοι is also written οὔτοι, and οὐ + οὖν as οὔκουν or οὐκοῦν (see §32 below).

29. γοῦν is an emphatic 'at least, at any rate'.

30. καίτοι is an emphatic 'and', sometimes implying 'and yet' (a contrast with what precedes) and sometimes 'and moreover' (the second premise of an argument from which a conclusion is going to be drawn).

31. μέντοι can function as a connective, meaning 'but, however', but also as emphasising a demonstrative or personal pronoun, e.g.

'ἐγώ;' — 'What, me?'

'σὺ μέντοι'   — 'Yes, you!'

32. When the sequence of letters ουκουν occurs, the sense sometimes requires 'therefore … not' but sometimes 'therefore'. The latter sense can often be got

by punctuating the utterance as a question, not as a statement (turning 'so he was not successful' into 'wasn't he successful, then?'), but ancient grammarians recognised a usage οὐκοῦν = οὖν, with οὔκουν (accented on the negative) = οὐ + οὖν.

33. In other combinations the second element is most commonly γάρ, γε, δή, μήν or οὖν.

34. ἀλλά+γάρ may = ἀλλά, e.g.

βουλοίμην ἄν, ἀλλ' οὐ γὰρ οἷός τ' εἰμί 'I'd like to, but I can't'

35. In καί + γάρ, γάρ has its normal sense (§11) and καί as in §5.

36. καί + γε and δέ + γε, usually found in response to a previous speaker, correspond to 'Yes, and …' and 'Yes, but …' respectively.

37. γὰρ δή and μὲν δή are not distinguishable in translation from γάρ and μέν respectively, but καὶ δή imparts a lively tone, 'Look, …!', 'See, …!', sometimes 'And, what's more …'

38. καὶ μήν is an emphatic 'and'; there is considerable overlap of meaning between καὶ δή and καὶ μήν.

39. The combination μὲν οὖν, when it does not combine the usual senses of μέν and οὖν (§§12f., 26) – as it very often does – has a special sense, in which the speaker corrects previous words of his own or of another speaker, e.g.

ὀψὲ λέγω; χθὲς μὲν οὖν καὶ πρῴην 'Did I say "lately"? Why, it was only the other day!' (lit., 'yesterday and the day before yesterday!') (Demosthenes)

This correction often takes the form of suggesting that the previous speaker has not gone far enough, and thus expresses emphatic agreement, e.g.

'οὐ ταῦτά σοι δοκεῖ;'   'Don't you think so?'
'πάνυ μὲν οὖν.'   'Very much so.' (or 'Yes, certainly!')

ὡς (ὥς)

392. This word has a wide range of meanings, which are summarised here:

(i)   = 'as, when, since, because' (+ind. or part.) e.g. ὡς ἀφίκετο, εἰσῆλθεν 'when he came, he entered'; ὡς ἔμοιγε δοκεῖ 'as it seems to me';

(ii)   ='how!' e.g. ὡς καλὰ τὰ δένδρα 'how fine are the trees!';

(iii) = 'that' e.g. ἔλεγεν ὡς 'he said that …' (cf. ὅτι);

(iv)   = 'to, in order to' (+ fut. part.), e.g. εἰσῆλθεν ὡς μαθησόμενος τὰ γενόμενα 'he came in to learn what had happened';

(v)   ='to, in order to' (+ subj./opt.), e.g. εἰσῆλθεν ὡς μάθοι τὰ γενόμενα 'he came in to learn what had happened' (cf. ἵνα);

(vi)   = 'as – as possible' (+ superlatives), e.g. ὡς πλεῖστοι 'as many as possible';

(vii)   = 'to' (+ acc), e.g. ἦλθεν ὡς Φιλόστρατον 'he came to Philostratos' (house)';

(viii)   (as ὥς) = 'so, thus';

(ix)   = 'so as to' (+ inf.; see **396**).

PARTICIPLES

393. The main uses of the participle are as follows:

(i)   as an adjective, when it may best be translated by a relative clause, e.g.

> ἀνὴρ καλῶς πεπαιδευμένος 'a well-educated man', or 'a man who has been well educated'

(ii)   as a noun, when it is used with the definite article, e.g.

> οἱ τρέχοντες 'those who run, runners'

(iii)   to show the aspect of an action, e.g.

> ταῦτ' ἐποίησε βασιλεύων 'he did this *being/while/when he was basileus*'

(iv)   to denote cause, e.g.

> ταῦτ' ἐποίησε [ὡς or ἅτε] βουλόμενος νικῆσαι 'he did this *because he wished to win*'
> (n.b. ὡς and ἅτε are often attached to these usages)

(v)   to denote purpose (usually + future participle), e.g.

> ταῦτ' ἐποίησε (ὡς) νικήσων 'he did this *to win*'

(vi)   conditionally, e.g.

> νικήσας ἀπέφυγεν ἄν 'winning (i.e. *if he had won*) he would have escaped'
> (n.b. negative is μή when such participles are conditional)

(vii)   concessively, when they mean 'although, despite', and are often used with καίπερ, e.g.

> (καίπερ) δυνάμενοι φυγεῖν, ἐμείναμεν 'being able (i.e. although/despite being able) to escape, we stayed'

(viii) The genitive absolute: in all the above cases, the participle and its noun go into the genitive when the clause which they form is not connected grammatically to the rest of the sentence, e.g.

> τῶν πολεμίων ἀπελθόντων, οἱ στρατιῶται ἐστρατοπεδεύσαντο '*the enemy having departed*, the soldiers pitched camp'. The participle clause, expressing the idea of time ('when the enemy...') or cause

('because the enemy…'), has no *grammatical* link with the main verb: so it goes into the genitive. Contrast e.g. ἐρομένῳ δέ μοι ἀπεκρίνατο '[to] me asking, he replied'. Since the speaker replied *to* 'me asking', the participle clause is connected grammatically with the main verb, and goes in the dative.

(ix)   Observe the following idioms:

φθάσας 'sooner' ('anticipating')
λαθών 'secretly' ('escaping notice')
κλαίων 'to one's regret' ('weeping')
ἔχων, φέρων, ἄγων, λαβών, χρώμενος 'with'
τί παθών … ; 'what has one experienced to …? what has made one …?' (lit. 'suffering what?')

(x)   A number of verbs take a participle to complete their meaning. Among these are:

τυγχάνω 'happen, chance, actually to'; e.g. ἔτυχε φυγών 'he actually did escape'
λανθάνω 'escape the notice of'; e.g. ἔλαθέ με φυγών 'I did not see him escaping' (lit. 'he, escaping, did not escape the notice of me')
φθάνω 'anticipate, do something first'; e.g. φθάνω σε φεύγων 'I escape before you'
φαίνομαι 'seem, appear'; e.g. φαίνονται φεύγοντες 'they seem to be in flight (and are)'
δῆλός/φανερός εἰμι 'be obviously, openly'; e.g. δῆλός ἐστι φεύγων 'he is obviously running away'

(xi)   In indirect speech; see **397(iii-iv)**.

INFINITIVES

394. The main uses of the infinitive are as follows:

(i)   to express the English 'to' in certain contexts controlled by verbs, e.g.

ἀγαθόν ἐστι μάχεσθαι 'it is good *to fight*', '*fighting* is good' (where 'fight(ing)' is the subject of the sentence)
βούλομαι μάχεσθαι 'I wish *to fight*' (where 'fight' is the object of 'wish')
κελεύομεν σε μένειν 'we order you *to stay*'
ἐκώλυεν αὐτοὺς ἐλθεῖν 'he prevented them *from going*'
οὐ πέφυκε δουλεύειν 'he is not born *to be a slave*'
ὥρα ἐστὶν ἀπιέναι 'it is time *to depart*'
δεῖ / χρὴ } ἡμᾶς ἐλθεῖν 'it is necessary for us *to go*'

ἔξεστί μοι λέγειν 'it is permitted for me *to speak*'
δοκεῖ εἶναι σοφός 'he seems *to be wise*'
φαίνεται ἀγαθὸς εἶναι 'he appears *to be good*' (but isn't)

(ii)   in certain constructions with adjectives, e.g.

δεινὸς λέγειν 'clever *at speaking*'
δυνατὸς ποιεῖν τοῦτο 'able *to do* this'
ἐπιστήμων λέγειν καὶ σιγᾶν 'knowing *how to speak* and *be silent*'

(iii)   to limit the extent of application of a word, e.g.

λόγοι χρήσιμοι ἀκοῦσαι 'words useful *to hear*'
πρᾶγμα χαλεπὸν ποιεῖν 'an action difficult *to do*'
θαῦμα ἰδέσθαι 'a wonder *to behold*'

(iv)   in certain parenthetical phrases (usually with ὡς/ὅσον), e.g.

ὡς εἰπεῖν 'so *to speak*'
ὡς ἀπεικάσαι '*to make a guess*'
ὀλίγου δεῖν 'almost' (lit. 'to want a little')

(v)   as an imperative, e.g.

μὴ ἤπιος εἶναι 'Don't be soft!'

(vi)   with the definite article, standing as a noun, e.g.

τοῦτό ἐστι τὸ ἀδικεῖν 'this is *injustice*'
διὰ τὸ ξένος εἶναι 'because of his *alienness*'
τοῦ πιεῖν ἐπιθυμία 'desire *for drink*'
τῷ μάχεσθαι '*by fighting*'

(vii)   note the number of possibilities with verbs of prevention or hindrance:

εἴργει σε τοῦτο ποιεῖν
'he prevents you from doing this'
εἴργει σε τοῦ τοῦτο ποιεῖν
εἴργει σε μὴ τοῦτο ποιεῖν
εἴργει σε τοῦ μὴ τοῦτο ποιεῖν
(N.b. τὸ μή is quite common in expressions implying hindrance, prevention, denial.)

(viii)   in indirect speech; see **397(iii-iv)**.

Note
The negative with an infinitive is nearly always μή.

IMPERSONAL VERBS

395.
These verbs have a regular infinitive; but in finite tenses they have forms in 3s. only, and their sole participle is in the neuter accusative s. for use in 'absolute' participle constructions (verbs with a full set of forms use the genitive in absolute constructions, **393[viii]**):

Present	Future	Past	Participle	Infinitive
δεῖ	δεήσει	ἔδει	δέον	δεῖν
ἔξεστι	ἐξέσται	ἐξῆν	ἐξόν	ἐξεῖναι

The subjects of such verbs appear in the accusative or dative; and the verb which follows the impersonal goes into the infinitive, e.g.

> ἔξεστί μοι ἐλθεῖν 'it is possible for me to go'
> δέον με ἐλθεῖν 'it being necessary for me to go' (accusative absolute)
> νομίζω ἐξεῖναι αὐτῷ ἐλθεῖν 'I think [it] to be permitted for him/that he is permitted to go'

The most common impersonal verbs are:

+Acc. and inf.

δεῖ	'must, ought'
χρή	'must, ought'

+Dat. and inf.

ἔξεστι	'it is permitted, possible'
πρέπει	'it is proper'
προσήκει	'it is appropriate'
δοκεῖ	'it seems best' ⎱ these also appear in regular forms and
συμβαίνει	'it happens' ⎰ are not restricted to impersonal use only

RESULT CLAUSES

396. These express the idea 'so that' or 'so ... that' and indicate the result of an action. The 'that' clause is expressed in Greek by ὥστε, which can take either an infinitive (change of subject in the accusative) or an indicative. The infinitive usage is best translated 'as to', but the difference between the two is often marginal, e.g.

> οὕτως ἀνόητός ἐστιν ὥστε ἐπιλανθάνεται τῶν βιβλίων
> 'he is so foolish   that he forgets his books'

ὥστε ἐπιλανθάνεσθαι τῶν βιβλίων
'he is so foolish   as to forget his books'.

These clauses are usually set up by οὕτως 'so', or by a word such as τοσοῦτος, τόσος ('so great', 'so many'), τοῖος ('of such a kind').

397. One can distinguish between three basic types of utterance: statements, questions, and commands (i.e. orders).

These can be quoted directly (when, as a rule, inverted commas will be used; e.g. he said, 'What shall I do? I shall go ...'), or indirectly (e.g. he wondered what to do, and decided that he would go ...).

In Greek, indirect questions and orders are expressed in largely the same way as English; so too are those indirect statements introduced by the Greek ὅτι 'that', but there are a number of verbs which use different methods of expressing indirect statements.

(i) Verbs taking ὅτι (ὡς), and indirect questions

Verbs taking ὅτι, and indirect questions, quote what was originally said, only changing the person, e.g.

ἔλεγεν ὅτι ἀφίξεται 'he said that he would come'

The original statement was 'I shall come'. Changing the person only, Greek writes 'he said that he shall come'; this converts to the English form 'he said that he would come'.

ἤρετο ὅποι Σωκράτης βαίνει 'he asked where Socrates was going'

The original question was 'Where is Socrates going?' This becomes indirectly 'he asked where Socrates is going' (no need to change persons here); English changes this to 'he asked where Socrates was going'.

Note that, in secondary sequence, verbs in indirect statement and question clauses can be turned into the optative without affecting the meaning, e.g.

ἔλεγεν ὅτι ἀφίξοιτο/ἀφίξεται 'He said that he would come'
ἠρόμην ποῖ βαίνοι/βαίνει 'I asked where he was going'

(ii) Indirect orders

Indirect orders are expressed as in English, i.e. by the use of the infinitive, e.g.

κελεύω σε ἀπιέναι 'I order you to depart'

(iii) Accusative + infinitive or participle

More difficult are those cases in which a 'that' clause is expressed in Greek not by ὅτι 'that', but by putting the verb of the 'that' clause into an infinitive form (cf.

Latin accusative and infinitive) or a participle form. There is an English parallel for the infinitive usage here; e.g. 'he knows that I am wise', or 'he knows me to be wise'. In these cases, the infinitive will show the time at which the action took place by its tense, e.g.

> ἔφη με ἐλθεῖν 'he said me to have gone/that I had gone' (orig. 'you went')
> ἔφη με ἰέναι 'he said me to be going/that I was going' (orig. 'you are going')
> ἔφη με ἀφίξεσθαι 'he said me to be about to come/that I would come' (orig. 'you will come')

Some verbs take a participle in the 'that' clause rather than an infinitive, e.g.

> οἶδα σε μῶρον ὄντα 'I know you being stupid/that you are stupid'
> ἐπύθετο Νέαιραν ἀφιξομένην Ἀθήναζε 'he learnt Neaira being about to come/that Neaira would come to Athens'

N.b. all the above examples have put the subject of the 'that' clause into the accusative because the subject of the indirect speech is different from that of the speaker. Where the subject of the 'that' clause is the same as that of the main verb, no subject in the 'that' clause will be stated; or if it is, it will be in the nominative, e.g.

> ἔφη ἐλθεῖν 'he said he had gone' (both 'he's are the same person)
> ἔφη αὐτὸν ἐλθεῖν 'he said that he had gone' (the 'he's are different people)
> οἶδα σοφὸς ὤν 'I know being wise' [nom.], i.e. 'I know that I am wise'; cf. οἶδα σε μῶρον ὄντα 'I know that you are stupid'
> Indirect speech is very common in Greek; and it is very likely suddenly to emerge in a quite unexpected context.
> Watch out for the accusative and infinitive/participle construction *all the time*. When you come across it, begin your translation with the English 'that ...'. This will remind you that you are in indirect speech.

(iv) Verbs taking infinitives and participles

(a) The following verbs generally take the *infinitive* in indirect speech:

φημί	'say that'
οἴομαι	
νομίζω	
ἡγέομαι	'think that'
δοκέω	
ὑπισχνέομαι	'promise to'
ἐλπίζω	'hope to'
γιγνώσκω	'determine how to, recognise how to'
μανθάνω	'learn how to'

οἶδα
ἐπίσταμαι } 'know how to'

Note

The negative with infins. in indirect statements is οὐ, not (as one might expect with infins.) μή' because the negatives in indirect speech reflect the *direct* use.

(b) The following generally take the *participle* in indirect speech:

ἀκούω   'hear that …'
πυνθάνομαι   'ascertain that …'
αἰσθάνομαι   'perceive that …'
οἶδα   'know that …'
γιγνώσκω   'ascertain that …'
ἀγγέλλω   'announce that …'
μανθάνω   'learn that …'

Note the distinction between:

φαίνομαι, δῆλος, φανερός + *participle*, which all mean 'it seems to be the case that', with the strong implication that it really *is* the case; and
φαίνομαι, δῆλος, φανερός + *infinitive*, where the implication is that it is *not* really the case.

TEMPORAL CLAUSES

398.

Definite temporal clauses

(i) 'Definite' temporal clauses express the time at which an event took place. The verb goes into the *indicative*, e.g.

ἕως ἔμενε, ἀπήλθομεν 'while he waited, we left'
ἐπεὶ ἐδίωξαν, ἀπέφυγον οἱ πολέμιοι 'when they pursued, the enemy fled'
ἐμένομεν ἕως ἐκέλευσεν ἡμᾶς ἀπελθεῖν 'we waited until he told us to go'

But πρίν 'before' takes an *infinitive* (change of subject in the accusative), e.g.

πρὶν ἀπελθεῖν, εὔξατο 'before departing, he offered up a prayer'
πρὶν ἡμᾶς ἀπελθεῖν, εὔξατο 'before we departed, he offered up a prayer'

Indefinite temporal clauses

(ii) 'Indefinite' temporal clauses express the idea of generality (i.e. not 'when', but 'whenever'), or of uncertainty about the actual completion of the event which is made to seem to lie in some indefinite future ('if it happens or not, we shall have to see'). In both these cases, the verbs in the temporal clause go into the subjunctive + ἄν in primary sequence, or the plain optative in secondary sequence, e.g.

ἐξίασιν ὅταν βούλωνται 'they go out whenever they wish'
ἐξῆλθον ὅτε βούλοιντο 'they went out whenever they wished'
ἐμένομεν ἕως κελεύοι ἡμᾶς ἀπελθεῖν 'we waited until such time as he should tell us to leave'
μὴ λέγε τοῦτο πρὶν ἂν μάθῃς τὰ γενόμενα 'do not say this before/until you learn what has happened'

Observe that the rules for 'definite' or 'indefinite' utterance apply equally to relative clauses, e.g.

ὅστις ἂν τοῦτο ποιῇ, ἀνόητός ἐστιν 'whoever does this is stupid'
ἐκέλευσεν αὐτὸν ἄγεσθαι ἰατρὸν ὃν βούλοιτο 'he ordered him to bring a doctor, whomever he wanted/he ordered him to bring whichever doctor he wanted'

Note
It must be said that Greek is, as usual, flexible in its usages on this point: sometimes one finds the subjunctive where one would expect the optative, and sometimes ἄν drops out.

PURPOSE CLAUSES

399. A purpose clause indicates an intention in the mind of the speaker, and is often expressed by the English 'in order to', or simply 'to', e.g. 'He has come here in order to insult us', or 'To cross the railway, passengers are asked to use the bridge.'

Subjunctive/optative

Perhaps because an intention is expressed of which the fulfilment is quite uncertain, Greek uses a quasi-indefinite construction in one instance, i.e. ἵνα + subjunctive in primary sequence (no ἄν) and optative in secondary, e.g.

ἀφικνεῖται ἵνα ἡμᾶς πείθῃ 'he is coming to persuade us'
ἀφίκετο ἵνα ἡμᾶς πείθοι 'he came to persuade us'

But Greek also expresses the idea of purpose in two other common ways, i.e.

Participle

(i) ὡς + future participle (lit. 'as intending to '), e.g.

ἀφικνεῖται ὡς ἡμᾶς πείσων 'he is coming to persuade us'

Future indicative

(ii) ὅς + future indicative (lit. 'who will/intends to ')

> ὁ ἀνὴρ ἀφικνεῖται ὃς ἡμᾶς πείσει 'the man is coming to persuade us' (lit. 'who will persuade us')

Notes

(i) ὅπως, ὡς can be used in place of ἵνα.

(ii) When ἵνα takes an indicative, it means 'where'.

VERBS OF FEARING

400.

(i) Fearing *to do* something attracts the infinitive, e.g.

> φοβοῦμαι ἐλθεῖν 'I fear to go'.

(ii) Fearing in case something *may happen in the future* attracts the same sort of construction as purpose clauses, i.e. subjunctive in primary sequence, optative in secondary, e.g.

> φοβοῦμαι μὴ Σωκράτης οὐκ ἔλθῃ 'I am afraid that/lest Socrates may/will not come'
> ἐφοβήθην μὴ Σωκράτης οὐκ ἔλθοι 'I was afraid that/lest Socrates might/ would not come'

Observe the negative in the μή clause is οὐ.

(iii) Fearing that something *has happened already* attracts the simple indicative, e.g.

> φοβούμεθα μὴ ἔπεισεν ἡμᾶς 'we are afraid that he persuaded us'

POTENTIAL ('POLITE') ἄν

401. ἄν with the optative expresses a future action as dependent on remotely possible circumstances or conditions. In its 'polite/potential' use, it is best translated by the English 'may, might, could, would, can, would like to', or 'possibly, perhaps'. But there are times when it is very difficult to differentiate between this 'potential' use and the straight future 'will, shall', e.g.

> λέγοις ἄν μοι 'can you tell me?/would you tell me?/tell me!/would you like to tell me?/will you tell me?'
> δὶς ἐς τὸν αὐτὸν ποταμὸν οὐκ ἂν ἐμβαίης 'you could not/would not/ cannot step twice into the same river'

This 'potential' usage falls into the same category as the conditional usage at **402(i)** below. For this reason it may be called 'potential>conditional'.

CONDITIONALS

402. Conditional sentences (i.e. sentences with an 'if' clause) should be translated by some form of English 'would' or 'should' when they show ἄν in the main clause, as follows:

(i) optatives in the 'if' clause (called the 'protasis') and the main clause (called 'apodosis', or 'payoff'), with ἄν in the apodosis too, make the condition refer to the 'remote' future, and should be translated 'if … were to, … would', e.g.

εἰ κελεύοις, πειθοίμην ἄν 'if you were to order, I would obey'

This is the potential>conditional use of the optative (see **401** above).

(ii) imperfects in the protasis and apodosis, with ἄν in the apodosis, should be translated 'if … were (now), … would' (the 'contrary to fact' present), e.g.

εἴ με ἐκέλευες, ἐπειθόμην ἄν 'if you were (now) ordering me, I would obey'

(iii) aorists in the protasis and apodosis, with ἄν in the apodosis, should be translated 'if … had, … would have' (the 'unfulfilled' past), e.g.

εἴ με ἐκέλευσας, ἐπιθόμην ἄν 'if you had ordered me, I would have obeyed'

Notes

(i) These conditions can be mixed. Greek will then treat each clause on its merits, e.g.

εἴ με ἐκέλευσας, ἐπειθόμην ἄν 'If you had ordered me, I would (now) be obeying.'

(ii) When there is no ἄν, translate normally without 'would/should', e.g.

εἰ ἁμαρτάνεις, μῶρος εἶ 'if you make a mistake, you are a fool'.

(iii) Observe that when a *non*-'would/should' refers to future time, Greek will usually treat the 'if' clause as an indefinite clause (since there can be little certainty about the outcome of a future conditional event) and use ἐάν with subjunctive, e.g.

ἐάν με πείθῃς, οὐκ ἄπειμι 'if you (will) persuade me (but I don't know if you will or not), I shall not go away'.

WISHES

403. Wishes for the future in Greek are expressed by the optative (e.g. ἀπολοίμην 'may I perish!'), or by εἴθε/εἰ γάρ/εἰ + optative, e.g. εἰ γὰρ πείθοιμι τὸν ἄνδρα 'if only I could persuade the man!'

Unattained wishes for the present or past use the imperfect or aorist indicative (cf. unfulfilled conditions, which they closely resemble), e.g.

εἴθε τοῦτο ἐποίει 'if only he were doing this!'
εἰ γὰρ τοῦτο ἐποίησε 'if only he had done this!'

Alternatively, they can be expressed by using a form of ὤφελον + infinitive, e.g.

(εἴθε) ὤφελον ποιεῖν τοῦτο 'would that I were doing this!'
(εἰ γὰρ) ὤφελε ποιῆσαι τοῦτο 'would that I had done this!'

Observe the difference to the tense which the infinitive makes here.
N.b. ἄν is *never* used with wishes.

COMMANDS (ORDERS)

404. Greek uses one set of forms for 2s. person imperatives ('Do this!' 'Do that!') and another for 3rd person orders ('Let him/them do this!') and another for 1st person commands ('Let us do this!'). The 2nd and 3rd person forms appear under the imperative forms in the verb tables.

The distinction between orders using the aorist form and the present form is one of aspect: the aorist form suggests the order applies to a particular instance, the present to a continued or repeated occurrence (cf. 'Pick up that book!' and 'Pick up all the litter!'). But when the order is negative ('Don't do that!' 'Let him not do that!') Greek uses μή + aorist subjunctive to express the aorist aspect, not μή + aorist imperative, e.g.

μὴ ποιήσῃς τοῦτο 'don't do this (once)'
μὴ ποίει τοῦτο 'don't do this (at all, ever)'

Observe also that the subjunctive is used after certain words to express an order or a quasi-order, e.g.

φέρε ποιήσω τοῦτο 'come, let me do this'
βούλει ποιήσω τοῦτο; 'do you wish I should do this?'
ποιήσω here is aor. subj., NOT future.

The plain subjunctive is used to express the idea 'let us ...', e.g.

ἴωμεν 'let us go'

DELIBERATIVES

405. When a first-person question appears in the subjunctive, it carries the idea '(What) am I to ...?', e.g.

ποῖ τράπωμαι; 'Where am I to turn?'

τί γένωμαι; 'What is to become of me?' (lit. 'What am I to become?') If such a 'deliberation' occurs in past time, Greek uses ἔδει + infinitive, i.e. 'what ought I to have …?', e.g.

ποῖ ἔδει με τραπέσθαι; 'Where was I to turn?' (lit. 'Where was it necessary for me to turn?')

If a deliberation in the subjunctive is reported in secondary sequence, it will turn into the optative, e.g.

ἤρετο με ποῖ τράποιτο 'he asked me where he was to turn to'.

SUBJUNCTIVE AND OPTATIVE USAGES COMPARED

406.

SUBJUNCTIVE	OPTATIVE
Main clause	**Main clause**
(i) Hortatory 'Let us ..' e.g. ἴωμεν 'Let's go'	*Wish for future* 'May you …!' (often with εἰ γάρ/εἴθε), e.g. δεινῶς πάθοις 'May you suffer terribly!'
(ii) Deliberative 'What/where (etc.) am I to…?' e.g. ποῖ τρεπῶμαι 'Where am I to turn?'	*Potential/polite* (+ἄν) *'Would you/may you/you will"'!'*, e.g. εἰσέλθοις ἄν 'Would you like to come in?'
(iii) Prohibitions 'Don't…!' (μή + aorist subj.), e.g. μὴ τοῦτο ποιήσῃς 'Don't do this!'	
407 Subordinate clause	**Subordinate clause**
Primary sequence	*Secondary/historic sequence*
(i) Purpose πάρεσμεν ἵνα ἴδωμεν 'We are here in order to see'	*Purpose* παρῆμεν ἵνα ἴδοιμεν 'We were here in order to see'
(ii) Fearing φοβοῦμαι μὴ ἔλθῃ 'I fear that he may come'	*Fearing* ἐφοβούμην μὴ ἔλθοι 'I feared that he might come'
(iii) Indefinite (with ἄν, + subjunctive) ὅστις ἂν ἀκούῃ, μαθήσεται 'Whoever listens will learn' μένε ἕως ἂν καλέσω 'Wait until I call'	*Indefinite* (no ἄν, + optative) ὅστις ἀκούοι, ἔμαθεν 'Whoever listened learnt' ἔμενες ἕως καλέσοιμι 'You waited for me to call'
	(iv) Indirect speech Optative replaces the indicative or subjunctive of what was actually said: εἶπες ὅτι ἀφίκοιντο 'You said that they had arrrived' ('ἀφίκοντο') ἠρόμην τί ποιοῖμεν 'I asked what we were to do' ('τί ποιῶμεν;')

SUBJUNCTIVE	OPTATIVE
(v) Present indefinite/general conditional sentences ἐὰν λέγῃς, ἀκούω 'If ever you [do] speak, I listen'	*Past indefinite/general conditional sentences* εἰ λέγοις, ἤκουον 'If ever you spoke, I listened'
(vi) Future indefinite/general conditional sentences ἐὰν λέγῃς, ἀκούσομαι 'If you [will] speak, I shall listen'	*Future 'remote' conditional sentences* εἰ λέγοις, ἤκουον ἄν 'If ever you were to speak, I would listen' *Note*: the present and past 'would/should' conditions take the *indicative* + ἄν

C Language Surveys[1]

A BRIEF HISTORY OF THE GREEK LANGUAGE

408. Greek belongs to the great family of Indo-European languages. These include English, Welsh, Irish, Latin, Russian, Lithuanian, Albanian, and most modern European languages (notable exceptions being Basque, Finnish, Hungarian and Turkish), as well as Armenian, Persian and the languages of north India. Important extinct languages that belong to the same family include Hittite and Tocharian. Greek has the longest *recorded* history of any of them, running from the fourteenth century B. C. down to the present day. Its apparent similarity to Latin is due, not to any specially close relationship, but to the fact that both languages ultimately derive from the same source and are recorded at an early date; Greek and Latin are both strikingly close to the classical language of India, Sanskrit, and to the language of Darius I and Xerxes, Old Persian.

The earliest record of the Greek language is contained in the clay tablets written in the script called 'Linear B' in the palaces of Knossos, on Crete, and Pylos, Mycenae, Tiryns and Thebes, on the mainland in the fourteenth to thirteenth centuries. This script is not alphabetic but syllabic, i.e. each sign represents not a single sound (e.g. 't', 'p') but a syllable (e.g. 'do', 'sa', 'mu'). Mycenaean (as the language of the Linear B tablets is called) represents an archaic form of the language, but demonstrates firmly that Greek had developed as a separate language – and, indeed, split into dialects – well before this date.

409. The alphabet with which we are familiar (each sign representing a single consonant or vowel) was introduced from Phoenicia (Lebanon), probably in the early eighth century, and this script has been in use in Greece ever since (although the shapes of the letters and their pronunciation have changed). The two great poems of Homer were probably composed during this century, although they contain linguistic and cultural echoes of much earlier ages; and the written form in which we have them is a later form of

---

1 These surveys were contributed for the first edition by members of the Advisory Panel (see *Reading Greek: Text* p. xii). They have been revised for this edition by Professor David Langslow. They remain very largely synchronic – that is, descriptive of Greek as it was in a single period (5th-4th C BC) – but here and there a little more historical explanation has been added in the belief that sometimes a diachronic account (διά + χρόνος 'through time') can illuminate synchronic understanding.

Greek (third century). The earliest inscriptions we possess are mostly brief records of names, but before the end of the eighth century someone had scratched on a vase at Athens a line and a bit of verse (in the same metre as Homer), given here in the spelling we are used to:

ὃς νῦν ὀρχηστῶν πάντων ἀταλώτατα παίζει,
τοῦ τόδε ...

'Who now of all the dancers sports most delicately, this is his ...'

410. The early inscriptions are written in many different scripts and dialects and show that down to c. 300 BC every Greek city had its *own* dialect and often its *own* peculiar form of alphabet. We can group the dialects into four main types:

(i)   West Greek, or Doric, the type spoken by most of Athens' enemies in the Peloponnesian War; it was used in literature for choral lyric poetry

(ii)   Arcadian and Cypriot, without any literary use

(iii) Aeolic, spoken in Thessaly, Boiotia and Lesbos; the personal lyric poetry of Sappho and Alkaios (c. 600) is in a form of Lesbian.

(iv)   Attic-Ionic, two very closely related dialects: Ionic, spoken in Euboia, the islands of the central and east Aegean sea, and on the seaboard of Asia Minor (the west coast of modern Turkey), was used by Homer and all epic poets, and also by Herodotus and writers of scientific prose. Attic, the speech of Athens and Attica, is usually the first dialect met in learning Greek, this course included. This is because texts surviving in Attic vastly outweigh those in other dialects, both in quantity and in literary quality. Attic Greek was used in its purer form by Aristophanes, Plato and the orators, and in modified form by Thucydides and the tragedians, who admitted more Ionic forms (such as θάλασσα 'sea' beside or instead of Attic θάλαττα). With further slight modification in the fourth and third centuries, this Ionic-coloured Attic became the standard language of 'Hellenistic' Greece (i.e. the Greek world after Alexander the Great had vastly extended it eastwards) and subsequently of most of the eastern 'Greek' half of the Roman Empire; this was called ἡ κοινὴ διάλεκτος 'the common speech'. Its grammar and syntax changed little for over a thousand years, though there was some development in vocabulary; but the pronunciation underwent major changes, while retaining the old spellings. Thus a knowledge of Attic will not only enable you to read Athenian literature; it supplies a key to the other dialects used in literature and to the whole of later Greek literature.

411. After Greek-speaking Constantinople – the last outpost of the Roman empire – fell to the Turks in A.D. 1453, Greek was still maintained as the language of the Orthodox Church, and continued to be spoken widely. When Greece was liberated from the ruling Turks in the early nineteenth century, some tried to revive the old language for official purposes, and Greeks today still respect ancient forms as 'more correct' than those they use colloquially. In some respects, some forms of modern Greek are much closer to ancient Greek than, say, Italian is to Latin. But though the difference in pronunciation will prevent you from understanding the spoken language, many public notices will be intelligible, and there is a real sense of continuity in the modern language. For example, some of the signs to be seen on shops and offices in Greece today will be easily understood, such as, παντοπωλεῖον 'general store' (lit. everything-sell-place), or Ἐθνικὴ Τράπεζα τῆς Ἑλλάδος 'National Bank of Greece' (τράπεζα 'table' had already by the fourth century B. C. acquired the sense of 'bank'). A notice sometimes to be seen in parks or woodland reads

ΑΓΑΠΑΤΕ ΤΑ ΔΕΝΔΡΑ 'Be kind to the trees'

Words found on Mycenaean documents (the earliest Greek we know, dateable to c. 1400) but still in use today with only slight change of pronunciation include:

ἔχω 'I have'
θεός 'god'
μέλι 'honey'
παλαιός 'old'

ACTIVE, MIDDLE AND PASSIVE VOICES

412. Grammarians traditionally use the term 'voice' to denote the relation between the subject (in the nominative) and the action denoted by the verb. Many languages, Greek included, have an:

▶ *active* voice, used when the subject is the 'agent', the one performing the action, and the object, if there is one, is the 'patient', the one on the receiving end of the action (e.g. 'Neaira hates Phrastor', 'Socrates deceived the young', etc.); and a

▶ *passive* voice, used when the patient is made the subject and the agent, if expressed, is conveyed in an adverbial phrase usually involving the word 'by' ('Phrastor was hated by Neaira', 'the young were deceived by Socrates').

In addition to these, Greek also has a so-called:

▶ *middle* voice (historically identical with the Latin deponent).

413. Originally, a middle ending indicated that the subject was not only the agent but also the patient or the indirect beneficiary of the action of the verb. This original meaning of the middle can still be seen in a few Greek verbs which in the middle see the agent:

- doing something *to himself* e.g. λούομαι 'I wash myself' vs. λούω 'I wash (someone else)';
- doing something *for himself*, e.g.

(i)   αἱρεῖν means 'to take hold of, seize'; its middle αἱρεῖσθαι means 'to take for oneself, to choose';

(ii) προσάγω means 'bring x (to y)', but προσάγομαι means 'bring x to oneself, to win x over to one's own side';

(iii) the act of engaging in a lawsuit is δικάζω (active), seen from the point of view of the judges, but δικάζομαι (middle) from that of the litigants, who are in it for their own benefit. Consequently, the active forms mean 'give judgment', the middle forms mean 'go to law'.

- In other Greek middle verbs, the old reflexive function is no longer apparent:

(iv) we think that ἕπομαι 'follow' is middle in form because it used to mean 'keep in sight for myself' (the root is ἑπ- from earlier *sek^w-, which is cognate with that of Latin *sequor* 'follow' and English *see*);

(v)   but we cannot account for the intransitive ἔρχομαι 'I go' in these terms; nor of the thoroughly active verb δέχομαι 'I receive'; nor of those verbs which have an active form in the present (e.g. ἀκούω 'hear', βοάω 'shout'), but a middle form in the future (ἀκούσομαι 'I will hear', βοήσομαι 'I will shout') – unless Greeks thought e.g. that, in certain cases like 'hearing' and 'shouting', they would act in the future only in their own interests! Note that many verbs occur only in the middle.

The middle is in fact older than the passive, that is to say, you originally had only active vs. reflexive forms. In the present, imperfect and perfect, the passive was expressed simply by using the middle without any change of form. In the aorist, however, the middle forms are middle only, and the (new) aorist passive was made out of an old intransitive formation in -η- (still seen in e.g. ἐμάνην 'I was mad', ἐχάρην 'I rejoiced'), which is why it has active endings. Note, however, that quite a number of middle verbs (βούλομαι, etc.) use passive forms (but with middle sense) in the aorist (see **324**). The most recent passive tense, the future, was made by adding future middle endings to the stem of the aorist passive.

414. Note the confusion that we have been tiptoeing around – and through! – in this section: we have been trying to say something about middle *functions* (meanings, both original and classical) of middle *forms* (endings). To clarify the matter:

- The definition of 'voice' in the first sentence of this Survey has to do with its *meaning* (the agent doing the action). Often, however, the term 'voice' is also used of just the *endings*: -ω, -εις, -ει etc. are said to be 'active' endings, -ομαι, -ει, -εται etc. to be 'middle' endings.

- The 'active' endings -ω, -εις, -ει etc. are very nearly always active in function, too (with the stunning exception of their use in the aorist passive). But the 'middle' endings are very often used in verbs which have no apparent middle *meaning*: they can be intransitive (like ἔρχομαι 'go', cf. βαίνω 'go', which is *active* in form); or thoroughly active (like δέχομαι 'receive', cf. λαμβάνω, 'take', active in form again).

ASPECT: PRESENT, AORIST AND PERFECT

415. In terms of their meanings (and also to some extent in the way they are formed), the tenses of the Greek verb fall into four *systems:*

- System (i): present (with a past-tense partner, the imperfect)
- System (ii): future
- System (iii): aorist
- System (iv): perfect (with a past-tense partner, the pluperfect, and a future-tense partner, the future perfect).

Each of these systems carries its own particular meaning and this meaning is conveyed in all relevant moods in the system, including the imperative as well as the participle and infinitive. (The future has neither imperative nor subjunctive.)

Of these systems, only one has an exclusively *temporal* force – that is the *future*. Each of the three other systems *may* refer in time to either the present or the past. Observe that in most forms of Greek including Attic, past time is normally marked by the presence of the augment (Myceneaen and Homer are the notable exceptions).

The present ('imperfective') system

416. The present system enables the speaker to report a verbal action as ongoing, incomplete, interruptible. It conveys what is known as the 'imperfective' aspect. By 'imperfective aspect', we mean that the action of the verb (in the present and past) is to be seen as:

▶ a continuing action, a process, e.g. ποιεῖ 'he is (in the process of) making'; ἔτρεχε 'he was (in the process of) running'; *or*
▶ as a process in virtue of its repetition, e.g. ἤστραπτε 'there were several flashes of lightning, it went on lightning for some time'.

The aorist system

417. The aorist system, by contrast, reports the action as one to be seen as:

▶ an event or a fact, not a process, e.g. ἐποίησε 'he made' (often used on vases with the maker's signature); ἤστραψε 'there was (a single flash of) lightning'.

Here it is worth noting that, if the speaker so wishes, he is quite at liberty to regard *any* action as imperfective (i.e. continuing) or aoristic (i.e. having happened as a fact or event). Thus some makers write on their vases ἐποίει 'he was the maker'; and lists of Olympic victors can have ἐνίκα 'he was the victor'.)

It is often stated that the aorist participle refers to *past* time, e.g. ταῦτα εἰπὼν ἀπῆλθε *can* be translated 'having said this he went away'. But this arises naturally from the fact that one action must have preceded the other; it would be equally correct to translate 'saying this he went away'; 'he said this and went away; 'with these words he went away'. That the aorist participle does not *have* to refer to past time is evident from the common phrase ὑπολαβὼν ἔφη 'he said in reply' (not 'having replied'! Strictly, of course, ὑπολαμβάνω means not 'reply' but rather 'take up' [the place in the dialogue]).

The perfect system

'Present' uses of the perfect

418. The perfect is – in origin, and to a large extent still in the classical period – not a past tense but a *present* tense. This is clear from the perfect forms:

● the ending of the 3pl. perfect active is -ασι, cf. e.g. 3pl. pres. τιθέασι 'they are putting';
● the endings of the perfect middle, -μαι, -σαι, -ται, are the same as the present middle endings;
● perfects are regularly used alongside presents, e.g. ἥδομαι [pres.] καὶ γέγηθα [perf.] 'I feel pleasure and joy' (Aristophanes).

The 'presentness' of the original perfect arises because it was used to denote a *state*, in particular a *present* state resulting from a *past* action. This explains why some perfects are used with present meaning, e.g.

● οἶδα 'I have seen (εἶδον), (therefore) I know', μέμνημαι 'I have called to mind, (therefore) I remember', ἐγρήγορα 'I have roused myself, (therefore) I am awake', πέφυκα 'I have been made by nature, (therefore) I am naturally'
● The opposition between action (pres./aor.) and state (perf.) survives in classical Greek in a few verbs such as:
● ἀποθνῄσκει (present)   'he is in the process of dying, i.e. he is on his death-bed'
● ἀπέθανε (aorist) 'he completed the process of dying, i.e. he died,'

- τέθνηκε (perfect) 'he is in the state of being dead, i.e. he is dead,'
- ἐτεθνήκει (pluperfect) 'he was in the state of being dead, i.e. he was [at that time] dead'

(Note that the pluperfect is to the perfect as the imperfect is to the present.)

419. But there are some wrinkles:

(i) Some perfects denoting present states are not so obviously related to a past action, e.g.

γέγηθα 'I am glad', δέδοικα 'I am afraid', εἴωθα 'I am accustomed', ἔοικα 'I seem to —', or (+dat.) 'I resemble';

(ii) A few have present meaning, but are not obviously states, e.g. ἄνωγα 'I order', κέκραγα 'I shout', κέχηνα 'I gape';

(iii) The 'stative' perfect is seen sometimes in the passive, when the verb is rendered better with 'it *is* —ed' than 'it *has been* —ed', e.g. τέτρωται 'he is wounded' (i.e. 'he has received a wound *and still suffers from it*'); γέγραπται 'it is written' (i.e. 'it has been written down *and can still be read*');

(iv) Occasionally, this passive meaning is seen in perfects with *active* endings, e.g. κατέαγε 'it is broken' (κατάγνυ-μι 'break'), πέπηγε 'it is fixed' (πήγνυ-μι 'fix'); even ἑάλωκα 'I am prisoner, I am convicted' (ἁλίσκομαι 'be captured, convicted'); and remember that γίγνομαι, middle in form, has an active perfect, γέγονα.

These uses of the perfect active (of present states, and with intransitive or passive meaning) are vestiges of very ancient uses.

Past uses of the perfect

It is important to note, however, that, alongside these few ancient relics, the perfect (both active and middle/passive) is developing into a past tense already in the fifth century, and by the fourth century can be used in alternation with the aorist, e.g. ἀνήλωκε [perf.] καὶ κατεψεύσατο [aor.] 'he spent and lied' (Demosthenes).

The aspect system at work

The first sentence of Thucydides' history is an excellent example of the aspectual systems at work:

Θουκυδίδης Ἀθηναῖος ξυνέγραψε τὸν πόλεμον τῶν Πελοποννησίων καὶ Ἀθηναίων, ὡς ἐπολέμησαν πρὸς ἀλλήλους, ἀρξάμενος εὐθὺς καθισταμένου

'Thucydides of Athens wrote the history *(event)* of the war between the Peloponnesians and Athenians, how they went to war *(event)* against each other. He began *(event)* as soon as it was starting *(process)*

καὶ ἐλπίσας μέγαν τε ἔσεσθαι καὶ ἀξιολογώτατον τῶν
προγεγενημένων, τεκμαιρόμενος ὅτι ἀκμάζοντές τε ἦσαν ἐς αὐτὸν
ἀμφότεροι παρασκευῇ τῇ πάσῃ καὶ τὸ ἄλλο Ἑλληνικὸν ὁρῶν
ξυνιστάμενον πρὸς ἑκατέρους, τὸ μὲν εὐθύς, τὸ δὲ διανοούμενον.
and had formed the expectation *(event)* that it would be *(future)* important
and more notable than any existing in the past *(perfect),* drawing conclusions *(process)* from the fact that they were undertaking it *(process)* at
the height of their powers *(process)* in every department, and witnessing;
(process) the rest of the Greek nation inclining *(process)* to one side or the
other, some at once, others having only the intention *(process).*'

OPTATIVE

Forms

420. Originally, the optative was formed by adding a suffix (containing -ι-) and
the *past* personal endings to the verbal root or stem (the optative is particularly associated with the past tense in certain constructions. See **299**).
In *athematic* verbs, like δίδωμι, the suffix was:

- -ιη- in the active s.
- -ι- in the active pl.
- -ι- throughout the middle.

The athematic type is seen also in the optative of:

- contract verbs, e.g. ποιοίην, ποιοίης etc. (**373**);
- the aorist passive, e.g. παυθείην, παυθείης etc. (**369**).

In *thematic* verbs, like παύω:

- -ι- was used throughout active and middle, singular and plural, always
  added to the thematic vowel in its *-o-* form.

The thematic type is also seen in the:

- optative of the 1st aorist, where the alpha takes the place of the thematic
  vowel: παύσαιμι, παύσαις etc.

But we still cannot account for the curious alternative endings of the 1st aorist
2s. -ειας, 3s. -ειε(ν) and 3pl. -ειαν (**368**).

Uses

421. In very broadest outline:

> ▶ the indicative is the mood for statements;
> ▶ the subjunctive is the mood for what is *prospective* (i.e. sometime in the future) or imagined ('let us suppose');
> ▶ the optative is the mood for wishes of the speaker or contingencies which are *more remotely prospective.*

This basic force of the optative surfaces in three ways:

(i)   the optative is used to express a *wish for the future,* e.g.

> ἀπολοίμην 'may I perish! Damn me!'
> δοίη τις πέλεκυν 'I wish that someone would give me an axe!'
> γενοίμην αἴετος 'Would I might become an eagle!'

(ii)   the optative with ἄν is used to characterise some event or situation as a *future* possibility (the so-called 'potential>conditional' use of the optative, in which, with trifling exceptions, it is always in Classical Greek accompanied by ἄν). English usually employs for this purpose such words as 'may', 'might', 'can', 'could', 'would', 'should', (sometimes) 'will', e.g.

> λέγοις ἄν 'you might tell me' (i.e. 'please tell me')
> λέγοιμι ἄν ἤδη 'I will tell you now (if you like)'
> εἰ ἐκεῖσε ἔλθοις, ἐγὼ ἄν σοι ἐποίμην 'if you were to go there, I would follow you'
> ἀλλὰ εἴποι τις ἄν ὅτι ... 'but someone may say that ...'

(iii)   in subordinate clauses of various kinds, when the main verb is historic, the optative may replace the subjunctive or the indicative (see **299**).

Note:

(iv)   while a potential>conditional optative virtually always has ἄν accompanying it, the ἄν likes to come *very early* in the clause and may therefore not be adjacent to the verb; or it may be *repeated*, at the start of the clause and with the verb as well.

(v)   the optative usages of types (i) and (iii) never have ἄν, i.e. an optative with ἄν is *always* potential>conditional.

USES OF THE SUBJUNCTIVE

422. As noted in **421** above, the subjunctive mood, in origin and still in the classical period, is used especially of events and situations viewed not as actual but as *prospective* or otherwise imagined. In several constructions, accordingly, the dividing line between the subjunctive and the future indicative can be rather fine; on the whole, the difference is that the future indicative gives an impression of greater definiteness and certainty.

(i) In independent sentences

In independent sentences, the subjunctive is used only:

(a) in first person exhortations (ἴωμεν 'let us go')
(b) in deliberative questions (τί εἴπω; 'what am I to say?')
(c) in prohibitions (aorist only) (μή με ἐπιτρίψῃς, ὦ Ἑρμῆ 'do not destroy me, Hermes')

(ii) In subordinate clauses

The subjunctive is found in many types of subordinate clause which have an indefinite or prospective sense, e.g.

(a) indefinite relative clauses with ἄν (**282–3, 407[iii]**)
(b) indefinite clauses of time, place (etc.) with ἄν (**282, 407[iii, v, vi]**)
(c) conditionals relating to the future (introduced by ἐάν, ἤν, ἄν) (**282, 300, 402, 407[v-vi]**)
(d) 'fear' clauses relating to the future (**293**)
(e) 'purpose' clauses (sometimes with ἄν, though ἵνα 'in order that' never takes ἄν; ἵνα ἄν means 'wherever') (**298**).

Note

(i) Where ἄν accompanies a subjunctive, the particle will almost always come directly after the conjunction or relative introducing the clause (often the two fuse together into one word, e.g. ὅταν, ἐάν, ἐπειδάν).
(ii) In secondary sequence (**299**), the subjunctive in all these subordinate usages is generally replaced by the plain optative; this use of the optative is NOT 'potential', and accordingly there is NO ἄν.

THE USES OF ἄν

423. The particle ἄν has two entirely different fields of usage, which fortunately need never be confused:

▶ in one field the verb associated with ἄν *will always be subjunctive*;
▶ in the other field the verb *will never be subjunctive*.

Originally, the two usages were related, but it is better to treat them quite separately.

Attached to a conjunction or relative pronoun
(with the verb in the subjunctive) →

ἄν has the effect of making the clause *indefinite* (like English '-ever' e.g. 'whoever'), or *prospective* (referring to future contingencies – 'when/if ever that may happen, we don't know' – rather than present facts), e.g.

(a) ἐπειδὴ εἰσῆλθεν, ἐχαίρομεν 'when he came in, we were glad'

This refers to a specific events at a *known* time in the past; hence, indicative.

(b) ἐπειδὰν εἰσέλθῃ, χαιρήσομεν 'when he comes in (whenever that will be), we will be glad'

This refers to an indefinite time in the future; hence, ἄν + subjunctive.

(c) ᾧ τρόπῳ ἐβούλοντο 'in the way they wanted'

This refers to a particular type of treatment that was actually applied.

(d) ᾧ ἄν τρόπῳ βούλωνται 'in whatever way they want'

This gives *carte blanche* to apply any kind of treatment.

(e) εἰ μὴ ἀπέδωκε, διώξομαι αὐτόν 'if he hasn't paid, I'll sue him'

Here the debtor has already *in fact* either paid or defaulted, though the speaker does not know which.

(f) ἐὰν μὴ ἀποδῷ, διώξομαι αὐτόν 'if he doesn't pay, I'll sue him'

Here it is still a matter of speculation whether he will pay or not.
An alternative to (f) is:

(g) εἰ μὴ ἀποδώσει, διώξομαι αὐτόν 'if he is not going to pay, I'll sue him'

This suggests, in contrast with (f), that the speaker has already half-decided that the debtor will *not* pay voluntarily, so the process of law is all the more certain.

Accompanying a verb in the optative
(typically in an independent clause) →

424. ἄν signals that the optative is 'potential>conditional' (see **186**, **402**, **421(ii)**)

Accompanying a verb in a past tense
(impf., aor., plupf. INDICATIVE) →

425. ἄν signals a *hypothetical* statement (or question) based on a condition contrary to fact ('unfulfilled'), e.g.

> εἰ Λακεδαιμόνιοι ταῦτα ἐποίησαν, εὐθὺς ἄν καθειλκύσατε διακοσίας ναῦς 'if the Spartans had done that (which they didn't), you would have launched 200 ships at once'
> εἰ ἄδικος ἦν, οὐκ ἄν ἐνθάδε νῦν ἠγωνιζόμην, ἀλλὰ ἑκὼν ἄν ἔφευγον 'if I were in the wrong (which I am not), I would not now be standing trial here, but would be in voluntary exile'

Observe:

(a) you will sometimes find ἄν accompanying an infinitive or participle. In such cases
(usually in indirect speech), the force of ἄν will be as in **424** or in **425** above, i.e.:

424: potential>conditional, or occasionally **425**: hypothetical

(b) the verb of a clause containing an ἄν of type **423** MUST be *subjunctive,* otherwise the ἄν simply cannot stand.

(c) often in Homer you will find κε or κεν performing just the same functions as ἄν; but the strict principles laid down above for the use of ἄν and of the subjunctives and optatives do not apply in their entirety to Homer, where slightly different rules apply to the use of the moods.

VERBS IN -ω AND VERBS IN -μι

426. Greek verbs are broadly divided into two formal types:

► 'Thematic' verbs like παύω, with 1s. active in -ω and middle in –ομαι. These have a short vowel, ε or ο, *between* the stem and ending, called the 'thematic' vowel. They include the vast majority of classical Greek verbs;

► 'Athematic' verbs like δίδωμι with 1s. active in -μι and middle in -μαι. These add the endings *directly onto* the stem, with *no* intervening vowel. They are in a minority, but are vital since they include very common verbs like 'be' εἰμί, 'go' εἶμι, and 'say' φημί and standard words for 'put' τίθημι, 'give' δίδωμι, 'stand' ἵστημι, 'send' ἵημι and 'show' δείκνυμι.

427. These two classes differ mainly in the present and imperfect (sometimes in the aorist, too), where the conjugation of the -μι verbs is generally less predictable than that of the -ω verbs. A historical explanation may help to clarify the differences.

(i) We know that the original active present endings were *-mi, -si, -ti, -men, -te, -nti.*

(ii) In theory, then, if we add the same set of endings to a thematic and an athematic stem, we should expect φέρ-ω 'I carry' (thematic) and εἶ-μι 'I go' (athematic), both very ancient Indo-European verbs, to conjugate as follows:

	Predicted thematic type in proto-Gk	Attested thematic Gk forms	Predicted athematic type in proto-Gk	Attested athematic Gk forms
1s.	*pher-o-mi*	φέρ-ω	*ei-mi*	εἶμι
2s.	*pher-e-si*	φέρ-εις	*ei-si*	εἶ
3s.	*pher-e-ti*	φέρ-ει	*ei-ti*	εἶσι
1pl.	*pher-o-men*	φέρ-ομεν	*i-men*	ἴμεν
2pl.	*pher-e-te*	φέρ-ετε	*i-te*	ἴτε
3pl.	*pher-o-nti*	φέρ-ουσι (Doric -οντι)	*iy-nti**	ἴᾱσι

*n̥ is 'vocalic', i.e. 'hummed' as in 'risen̲'

This analysis works perfectly in:

(iii)   the 1pl. and 2pl.
(iv)   the thematic 3pl., since -ουσι comes straight from original *-o-nti (cf. -unt in Latin), by the same set of sound-changes that gives (e.g.) dat. pl. λέουσι ('lions') from expected *leont-si.
(v)   the athematic 3pl., since -ᾱσι can be explained agreeably enough as being from *-anti, another regular change;
(vi)   the athematic 1s.;
(vii)   the athematic 2s., since -s- is regularly lost between vowels (see 52);
(viii) the athematic 3s., since -ti in a group of Greek dialects including Attic regularly changes to -si.

The problems lie with the thematic singulars, i.e. can we explain how:

-o-mi   gives   -ω
-e-si   gives   -εις
-e-ti   gives   -ει?

Scholars argue about this. One approach is as follows:

2s: here the -s- has dropped out but been tacked onto the end, to make it look like a respectable 2s. – respectable because there was -s- in the 2s. originally. (This has happened, for example, with δίδως, the 2s. of δίδωμι: originally the 2s. was δίδωσι, but the -σ- dropped out to give δίδωι, and was then added on again to give δίδως.)

3s: here the -t- has dropped out. The reason may be that, since the past ends 2s. -ες, 3s. -ε, the present may have been formed 2s. -εις 3s. -ει to resemble it.

But the whole topic is much disputed.

THE NEGATIVES οὐ AND μή

428. Greek has two negative particles, οὐ and μή, which differ mainly in the contexts in which they are used. Very broadly speaking:

▶ οὐ is used IN STATEMENTS – hence, with the *indicative* (except after 'if') and with all forms of *potential*;

▶ μή is used IN COMMANDS/WISHES – hence, with the *imperative*, with the *optative expressing a wish*, usually with the *subjunctive*, and hence in *conditions* and *purpose-clauses*;

▶ μή (or μή οὐ, with the same meaning) is used with all forms of the INFINITIVE *except in indirect speech, where the negative is the one used in the* direct *context (by the first two rules).*

429. Why should μή be used after 'if', even when the verb is indicative? If you think of εἰ or *if* as meaning 'imagine!' or 'let!', you can see that conditions ('if' clauses) are originally main-clause *commands* or *wishes*: think of those algebra lessons – 'let x = 2, and let y be not greater than 4, then x + y is not greater than 6'. Clearly, here the clause introduced with 'let' is a command, where we expect μή, while the result clause, introduced by 'then', is a statement and hence takes οὐ as its negative. (When conditions refer to the future, of course, the 'if' clause is naturally subjunctive or optative, where your instinctive first choice is μή.)

430. A participle may be negated by either οὐ or μή – and this is one of the few cases where the use of one negative or the other matters for the understanding of the text. You will remember that the participle can 'stand for' various types of clause (see **393**) – including *conditional* clauses (if) and *causal* clauses ('seeing that', 'when', 'because'):

- When the participle is standing for a *conditional* clause, its conditional meaning triggers the use of μή as its negative; in other words, from the reader's point of view, if a participle is negated with μή, translate the participle with 'if'. So:

  τί δράσω τοῦ πατρὸς μὴ εὖ φρονοῦντος (= ἐὰν μὴ εὖ φρονῇ)
  'What shall I do *if* my father is not in his right mind?'

- When the participle is standing for a *causal* clause – 'seeing that' or 'when (as a matter of fact)' – it is negated with οὐ. So:

  τί δράσω τοῦ πατρὸς οὐκ εὖ φρονοῦντος (= ἐπεὶ οὐκ εὖ φρονεῖ)
  'What shall I do, *seeing that* my father is not in his right mind?'

431. You have already seen how, if the same negative is repeated in a clause, the negatives either reinforce or cancel each other (see **75**). The same is true of combinations of different negatives (οὐ μή and μὴ οὐ). Look at the following examples:

(i) μὴ οὐ with an infinitive (common when the main verb is negative) means the same as μή alone, e.g.

   οὐ μισοῦμεν τὰς Ἀθήνας μὴ οὐ μεγάλας εἶναι 'We do not hate Athens (wishing) that it should not be great'

(ii) οὐ μή with subjunctive (usually aorist) or future indicative gives an emphatic version of οὐ with future indicative, i.e. a strong denial or a strong prohibition, e.g.

   οὐ μή ποτε ἁλῶ 'I shall certainly never be caught'
   οὐ μὴ φλυαρήσεις 'Do stop talking nonsense!'

(iii) μὴ οὐ with verbs of fearing:

φοβοῦμαι μὴ οὐ νικήσῃ 'I fear he may not win' ("Let it not be the case
that he does not win!")

MORPHOLOGY OF THE CASES

432. This section gives a brief survey of the *forms* of the cases, the next section
(**437–44**) comments on their *functions*.

Greek has five cases: nominative, vocative, accusative, genitive and dative.
These derive from *eight* cases in the parent language, Indo-European (IE: see
408 above), which has the five of Greek + ablative, locative and instrumental.

> ▶ The Greek *genitive* results from the merger of Indo-European's genitive
> and ablative;
> ▶ The Greek *dative* results from the merger of Indo-European's dative,
> locative and instrumental cases.

This may be expressed as follows:

Case endings and functions

IE: nom., voc., acc., gen., ablative, dat., locative, instrumental
Greek: nom., voc., acc., gen. (absorbs IE abl. function), dat. (absorbs IE loc. and
        instr. functions)

When two or more cases fall together in a language, the resulting single new case
will:

(i) retain *all of the functions* of the several old cases;
(ii) usually have only *one ending*, which it must *choose from the endings* of the
     old cases. So, in Greek, the *dative* forms take sometimes an old dative ending,
     sometimes the locative ending and sometimes the instrumental, as we shall
     see!

433. At first sight, the Greek declensions give the impression of a bewildering
variety of forms. In order to recognise the cases, it is useful to concentrate
on the similarities and to notice that many of the differences are due to later
changes within Greek (changes of vowels, contractions, etc.).

In Indo-European, we can see faint traces of a single set of endings for all
nouns, but even here it is easier to think in terms of three types corresponding
to the three basic types of Greek. The following tables show roughly the prehistoric endings from which the Greek ones you know and love derive. Here
are three simple examples of how it all works:

Table for Type 3 nouns

This table comes first because type 3 nouns add the ending *straight onto* the stem, without any intervening letters.

Example: the stem of πόλις is πολι-. Add the ending -ν to make the acc. s. πόλιν.

Table for Type 2 nouns

These nouns add a vowel (ο or ε) to the stem, and then the ending.

Example: ἄνθρωπ- is the stem, add -ο-, then the ending -ν to make the acc. s. ἄνθρωπον.

Table for Type 1 nouns

As for type 2, except that the intervening vowel is ᾱ.

Example: ἀπορι- is the stem, add -ᾱ-, then add the ending -ν to make the acc. s. ἀπορίᾱν.

Already you can see that, whatever the prehistoric ending-marker of the acc. s. across all three declensions was, it emerged in Greek as -ν. In the three tables below, these prehistoric ending-markers are written in CAPITALS, in the first column – and each table will turn out to have the *same* capitals!

Type 3

434. Type 3 nouns originally had a stem ending in a consonant, or in *-i-*, or in *-u-*.

The stems of **Types 3a, 3b** (πρᾶγμα), **3c** (πλῆθος) and **3d** (τριήρης) originally ended in a *consonant*. Some examples (* indicates a reconstructed form):

- **3a:** λίμην and πατήρ were originally *λιμεν-ς, *πατερ-ς. The ς dropped out and the preceding vowel ε lengthened to η, giving λίμην, πατήρ. λαμπάς and παῖς were originallly *λαμπαδ-ς, *παιδ-ς. With these, the ς remained but the δ dropped out.
- **3b:** πρᾶγμα was originally *πραγματ, but Greek does not allow any consonant at the end of the word except -ς, -ν or -ρ. So the -τ disappeared, leaving πρᾶγμα – the bare stem with zero (i.e. no) ending.
- **3c and d:** like 3b, πλῆθος is in fact the bare stem, with zero ending; so too is τριήρης.
- The stems of **Types 3e** (πόλι-ς, πρέσβυ-ς), **3f** (ἄστυ-) **3g** (βασιλεύ-ς) **and 3h** (ὀφρύ-ς) originally ended in *-i-* or *-u-*.

Prehistoric stem ends in -i-, -u- or a consonant; endings in CAPITALS	Endings in Classical Greek
Singular	
Nom. **-S** after -i- or -u-	same, e.g. πόλι-ς
ZERO after a consonant	same, e.g. λιμήν (zero ending)
ZERO in neuters	same, e.g. πρᾶγμα (zero ending)
Voc. **ZERO**	same, e.g. πόλι (zero ending)
Acc. **-M**	-ν after -ι, -υ e.g. πόλι-ν[2]
	-ᾰ after a consonant[3], e.g. λιμέν-ᾰ
ZERO in neuters	same, e.g. πρᾶγμα (zero ending)
Gen./abl. **-OS** (or **-ES**, or **-S**)	same, e.g. λιμέν-ος[4]
Dat. **-EI**	[lost in type 3 nouns]
Loc. **-I**	same, e.g. λιμέν-ι
Plural	
Nom. **-ES**	same in m. and f., e.g. λιμέν-ες[5]
-A in neuters	same, e.g. πράγματα
Acc. **-NS**	-ς after a vowel, e.g. πόλεις[6]
	- ᾱς after a consonant, e.g. λιμένᾱς[7]
-A in neuters	same, e.g. πράγματα
Gen./abl. **-ŌM**	-ων,[8] e.g. λιμένων
Loc. **-SI**	same, e.g. πόλεσι[9]
Instrum. **-BHIS**	[lost, though appears in Mycenaean]

2 *-m becomes -ν because m is not allowed at the end of a word.

3 *-m or -n can hardly stand after a consonant! It therefore behaves more like a vowel (think of e.g. English 'does**n**'t') and converts into a short α.

4 In many nouns contraction and other changes take place. For example, πλήθους was originally *πληθ-εσ-ος; the -σ- dropped out between vowels (a regular feature: see **52**); and πληθε-ος became by contraction πλήθους. βασίλεως was originally βασιλῆϝ-ος which became βασιλῆ-ος and then βασίλεως, by 'quantitative metathesis', i.e. the long vowel η and the short vowel o change quantities – η becoming ε, o becoming ω!

5 More contractions here: πόλεις from πόλε-ες, βασιλῆς from βασιλῆ(ϝ)-ες, and in the neuter πλήθη, ἄστη from *πλήθε(σ)-α, *ἄστε(ϝ)-α.

6 See footnote 5.

7 See footnote 3 above for ṇ changing to α.

8 For *-m changing to -ν, see footnote 3 above.

9 See **359** for the dat. pl. endings.

Type 2
435.

	Prehistoric stem ends in -o/e-; endings in CAPITALS	Endings in Classical Greek
Singular		
Nom.	-o-S -o-M in neuter	same, e.g. ἄνθρωπ-o-ς -o-ν in neuter, e.g. ἔργ-o-ν
Voc.	*-e-* ZERO	-ε + **zero** e.g. ἄνθρωπ-ε[10]
Acc.	-o-M	same, e.g. ἄνθρωπ-o-ν
Gen./abl.	-o-S-YO [abl. -ōd]	Homeric Greek -oιo > Attic -oυ e.g. ἀνθρώπ-oυ[11]
Dat.	-o-EI > -ŌI	same, e.g. ἀνθρώπ-ῳ
Loc.	-o-I [-e-I]	-oι [-ει][12]
Plural		
Nom.	-o-ES (pronouns -OI) -Ā in neuters	same as *pronouns*, e.g. ἄνθρωπ-oι[13] same (but *short* α), e.g. ἔργ-ᾰ
Acc.	-o-NS -Ā in neuters	-oυς, e.g. ἄνθρωπ-oυς[14] same (but *short* α), e.g. ἔργ-ᾰ
Gen./abl.	o-ŌM	contracted to -ων, e.g. ἀνθρώπ-ων
Loc.	-OISI	same in Ionic, e.g. ἀνθρώπ-oισι
Instrum.	-ŌIS	same in Attic, e.g. ἀνθρώπ-oις

10 The -ε is the vowel at the end of the stem.
11 Prehistoric *-osio lost the *s* (see footnote 4 above) to make -oιo, the Homeric form; then the -*i*- dropped out to make *-oo; and this contracted into -oυ.
12 The *-o-i ending survives in e.g. locative οἴκοι 'at home'.
13 Greek adopted the ending used in Indo-European for *pronouns*, not nouns.
14 The *n of *-o-ns is lost before the final s (see 3a nouns above for more examples), and the o is lengthened to oυ, giving -oυς.

Type 1

436.

	Prehistoric stem ends in -ā-; endings in CAPITALS	Endings in Classical Greek[15]
Singular		
Nom.	-ā + ZERO	same, e.g. ἀπορί-ᾱ (Ionic -η)
Voc.	-ă	replaced by the nom.[16]
Acc.	-ā-M	-ᾱ-ν, e.g. ἀπορί-ᾱ-ν (Ionic -ην)
Gen./abl.	-ā-S	same, e.g. ἀπορί-ᾱ-ς (Ionic -ης)
Dat.	-ā-EI > āi	same, e.g. ἀπορί-ᾳ (Ionic -η): the
Loc.	-ā-I > āi	Greek form could come from either
Plural		
Nom.	-ā-ES > -ās	Greek replaces this with -αι, imitating -οι in Type 2 nouns[17]
Acc.	-ā-NS	-ας, e.g. ἀπορί-ᾱ-ς
Gen./abl.	-ā-S-ŌM	-ᾱ-ων > -ῶν[18]
Loc.	-ā-SI	Greek replaces these with -αις (Ionic
Instrum.	-ā-BHIS	-αισι), imitating -οις (-οισι) from type 2 nouns, e.g. ἀπορί-αις

USE OF THE CASES

Nominative case

437. The most important functions of the nom. are:

(i)   to indicate the subject of a sentence (**7**). Usually, the verb agrees with it in number (an exception in Attic is the *neuter* nom. pl., which can take a s. verb: cf. **35**);

(ii)   as the case for all nouns, adjectives, articles etc. that agree with the subject, either as appositions or as attributes or as complements (see **45–6**);

(iii)   as the citation case (e.g. in lists) or as a title or heading: cf. the numerous inscriptions which start with the phrase τύχη ἀγαθή 'good fortune'.

15 As we can see in Homer, the original *-ā regularly became η (this continues to occur in Ionic Greek). But in Attic the change did not occur after ε, ι, or ρ. Hence ἀπορί-ᾱ, ἡμετέρ-ᾱ, etc.
16 The *-ă form of the vocative does occur in a few Greek words, e.g. Δίκᾰ ('O [personified] Justice' and νύμφᾰ 'O nymph').
17 The -αι ending also clearly distinguished the nom. from the acc.
18 The circumflex accent on -ῶν indicates that it is a contraction of -ᾱ-ων < *-ᾱ-ōm < *-ā-s-ōm.

Accusative case

438. The most important functions of the acc. are:

(i)   as the case used for the direct object of the sentence (**5–7**).

> *Note:* (a) some Greek verbs take *two* accusative objects, e.g. αἰτέω τινά
> τι 'I ask somebody something', κρύπτω σε τοῦτο 'I conceal
> this (from) you', δίδασκέ με τὸν σὸν λόγον 'teach me your
> argument'.
>
> (b) when we find a verb joined to two *independent* accusatives, one
> of the two has predicative value: ἑαυτὸν δεσπότην πεποίηκεν
> 'he has made himself master'.

(ii)   to indicate extent of space or time, e.g.

ἦλθε σταδίους ἑβδομήκοντα 'He went seventy stades' – compare in
English 'he covered seventy stades'.

ἐβασίλευσε πεντήκοντα ἔτεα 'he reigned (for) fifty years', rather like 'he
endured fifty years'.

(iii) to indicate direction or motion towards. In prose this usage calls for a
preposition (εἰς, ἐπί, πρός etc.) or for a construction where the acc. is followed by the particle -δε, e.g. οἴκονδε (also οἴκαδε) 'homewards, home',
Μεγάραδε 'to Megara', Ἀθήναζε = Ἀθήνας + δε 'to Athens').

(iv)   to show the respect in which something is the case, e.g. πόδας ὠκὺς
Ἀχιλλεύς 'Achilles swift in [respect of] his feet', δεινοὶ μάχην 'terrible in
[respect of] battle', etc.

(v)   as (in limited cases) independent adverbs or prepositions, e.g. ἀρχήν 'ini-
tially', τρόπον τινά 'in some way', πρόφασιν + gen. 'on the pretext of',
χάριν + gen. 'for the sake of, on behalf of, on account of'. On the so-called
acc. absolute, see **296, 395**.

Genitive case

439. Some uses of the gen. have been listed at **180(a-e)**. Here it is important
to remember (**432**) that the Greek genitive combines the functions of the
genitive and the ablative in Indo-European. It may be helpful therefore to
distinguish broadly its true genitival uses, on the one hand, and its ablatival
uses, on the other.

Genitive functions

(i)   The archetypal genitive function is to denote:

(a) the *possessor* of someone or something – e.g. ὁ τοῦ Σωκράτους
οἰκέτης 'the slave of [belonging to] Socrates';
(b) a close relative of someone, above all the father – e.g. ὁ Λυσίας ὁ τοῦ
Κεφάλου 'Lysias the [son] of Cephalus'.

(ii)   Hardly less important is the *partitive* function:

    (a) ἡ ἀρχὴ τοῦ πολέμου 'the beginning [part] of the war';

    (b) indicating a part of something which would normally go into the acc., e.g. τῆς γῆς ἔτεμον 'they ravaged [part of] the land' vs. τὴν γῆν πᾶσαν ἔτεμον 'they ravaged [all] the land'. Cf. the use of 'de', 'du' etc. in French – 'j'ai mangé du pain' vs 'j'ai mangé le pain', i.e. all of it.

(iii)   to indicate time during which or (in poetry) place within which; cf. ἡμέρας 'by day', νυκτός 'by night' (see **191** for the difference in meaning between acc., gen and dat. in time constructions). This is a sort of 'partitive' function.

Ablative functions

'Ablative' comes from Latin *ablatus*, a participle of *aufero* meaning 'take, carry away'. So:

(iv)   the genitive is used ablatively in making a comparison: cf. μέλιτος γλυκίων 'sweeter than honey', i.e. taking honey as a point of departure, relatively sweet;

(v)   the genitive is used after prepositions signalling separation or movement away from (cf. ἐκ, ἀπό etc.).

Specialised uses

There are other uses of the genitive where it is harder to say whether the function is originally genitival or ablatival. These include:

(vi)   the so-called genitive absolute construction (ablative absolute in Latin): see **222–3**.

(vii)   gen. of price or value (especially with verbs which mean 'to buy', 'to sell'): ἐργάζεσθαι μισθοῦ 'to work for pay', θανάτου μοι τιμᾷ 'he estimates the penalty in my case as death'; cf. πόσου; 'how much (does it cost)'?;

(viii) gen. of crime (with verbs which mean 'to convict', 'to punish', 'to bring to trial' etc.): cf. ἀσεβείας γράφειν 'to prosecute for impiety', ἀσεβείας φεύγειν 'to be tried for impiety'.

(ix)   As a result of one or other of the functions touched on above, the gen. comes to be associated with many verbs (and in many instances from an English point of view to stand in the direct object position). The most frequent of these include the following:

    to share, to participate in; cf. μέτεστι, μετέχω, κοινωνέω etc.

    to touch, to make contact with, to miss; cf. ἅπτομαι, ἔχομαι, ἁμαρτάνω etc.

    to aim at, to desire; cf. ἐπιθυμέω, ἐράω etc.

    to reach, to obtain; cf. ἐφικνέομαι, τυγχάνω etc.

    to start, to begin; cf. ἄρχω, ἄρχομαι etc.

to remember, to care for, to forget, to despise; cf. μιμνήσκω, φροντίζω, μέλει, ἀμελέω, καταφρονέω etc.

to admire, to be amazed at, to envy; cf. θαυμάζω, ζηλόομαι (with genitive of the thing which one envies)

to hear, to perceive, to come to know [the *gen.* is used of the *source* of the sound, sensation or information, the acc. of the sound etc. itself]; cf. ἀκούω, αἰσθάνομαι, πυνθάνομαι etc.

to rule, to have power over; cf. ἄρχω, κρατέομαι etc.

to need, to lack; cf. ἀπορέω, στερίσκω, δέω, δέομαι etc.

Dative case

440. As noted above, the Greek dative has taken over the functions of three cases in Indo-European: dative, locative (to do with place where/time when) and instrumental. Let us take each of these functions in turn.

'True' dative

(i)   The most frequent dative function is to indicate the indirect object of a verb, where English would normally have a phrase introduced by 'to' or 'for' (cf. **190[a]**): ταῦτα δίδωσιν αὐτοῖς 'he gives these things *to them*', λέγει ταῦτα αὐτοῖς 'he says these things *to them*'.

(ii)   Related to this is the notion of *advantage* or *disadvantage* to or for the noun or pronoun in the dative: ἥδε ἡ ἡμέρα τοῖς Ἕλλησι μεγάλων κακῶν ἄρξει 'this day will be the start of great sorrows *for the Greeks*'.

(iii) Also related to this usage is that of the possessive dative with the verb 'to be' or related verbs: ταῦτά μοί ἐστι/γίγνεται/ὑπάρχει lit. 'these things exist/ come to be/are available *for me*', i.e. 'I have these things'.

(iv)   Notice the possessive nuance in idioms like τί ταῦτ' ἐμοί; τί ἐμοὶ καὶ σοί; literally 'what [are] these things to me?', 'what [is there] to me and you?', i.e. 'what have I to do with …?'

'Locative' dative

441. The locative function of the Greek dative is seen in its use to indicate place *where* or time *when*, nearly always with a preposition, e.g. ἐν Σπάρτῃ 'in Sparta', ἐν τῷ χειμῶνι 'in the winter'. It is rare (and mainly poetic) to find the locatival dative without a preposition, although it does occur even in prose in place-names and time phrases, e.g. Σαλαμῖνι 'in Salamis', τρίτῳ μηνί 'in the third month'.

'Instrumental' dative

442. The Greek dative continues two functions of the old instrumental:

(i)   it may be used (by itself) of the instrument, tool, means or manner in or by which an action is performed: ἐβαλλόμην τοῖς λίθοις 'I was being pelted by/with the stones', ταῖς μαχαίραις κόπτοντες 'smiting them with the swords', σπουδῇ 'in haste', προθυμίᾳ 'with enthusiasm' etc. Note: the simple instrumental dative can sometimes indicate even a *personal agent*, especially with verbal adjectives in -τέος, and when the passive verb is perfect or pluperfect and is used impersonally: ἐμοὶ πέπρακται 'it has been done by me' (normally, of course, the personal agent is expressed with ὑπό + gen.; cf. **221**).

(ii)   it may indicate accompaniment or association (this is sometimes called the 'comitative' dative: Latin *comes*, stem *comit-* 'companion'). This is the use that we find after the preposition σύν 'together with, with the help of', e.g. σὺν τῷ θεῷ 'together with, with the help of, the god'.

Note: a relic of the bare 'comitative' usage is seen in the construction of αὐτός with the dat.: μίαν ναῦν αὐτοῖς ἀνδράσιν εἷλον 'they captured one ship (lit.) along with men themselves, i.e. together with its crew, crew and all'.

The dative with various verbs

443. Some verbs are regularly construed with the dative where English in equivalent sentences would have a direct object or prepositional phrase. The most frequent meanings are:

> to help, to please, to displease, to reproach, to be angry at, to envy: cf. βοηθέω, ἀρέσκω, ἐγκαλέω, ὀργίζομαι, φθονέω etc.
>
> to obey, to serve, to trust, to advise: cf. πείθομαι, δουλεύω, πιστεύω, παραινέω etc.
>
> to meet: cf. ἀπαντάω, περιτυγχάνω etc.
>
> to follow, to accompany, to lead: cf. ἕπομαι, ἀκουλουθέω, ἡγέομαι etc.

Vocative case

444. The vocative is peculiar in terms of its function in that it need not occur in a sentence but can be used on its own in exclamations or when addressing a person or thing (ὦ Ζεῦ, ὦ Δικαιόπολι). Even when it occurs in a sentence, its link with it is tenuous; it could be removed without making the sentence ungrammatical. Its zero ending is eloquent reflection of the fact that it does not assign any function within the sentence to the person or thing called.
In Attic the vocative is normally used after the particle ὦ; absence of ὦ denotes either strong emotion or a desire to keep the person addressed at a distance.

USES OF THE DEFINITE ARTICLE

General features

445. Greek has only one article, ὁ ἡ τό 'the' (the 'definite article'), which – as an adj. – always agrees with its noun in gender, number and case. When English uses 'a' (the 'indefinite article'), Greek uses either the noun without an article or (less often) the indefinite pronoun τις 'a, a certain, some'.

There is a certain amount of agreement between Greek and English use of the definite article, but important differences, too. Here are some of the main ones:

(i)   Greek can (but need not) use the article with personal names and place names: ὁ Σόλων 'Solon', ἡ Ἀσία 'Asia'. Cf. German (*der*) *Michael*, (*der*) *Schuhmacher* (optional), French *la France* (obligatory).

(ii)   Greek can use the article with abstract nouns: ἡ ἀρετή 'courage', ἡ χάρις 'grace' (cf. German *die Liebe*, French *l'amour*).

(iii) Greek uses the article before possessive adjectives: ὁ ἐμὸς οἶκος '[the] my house' (cf. Italian *la mia casa*).

(iv)   In general statements, Greek tends to use the article while English often omits it: αἱ γυναῖκες 'women' (i.e. the class of all women) vs. οἱ Πέρσαι 'the Persians' or 'Persians'.

(v)   Greek does not use the article with nouns used as predicates: νύξ ἡ ἡμέρα ἐγένετο 'the day became night' (νύξ could not have the article).

(vi)   A neat consequence of (iv) and (v) together is a very frequent type of sentence where Greek and English are diametrically opposed, e.g. κυβερνῆται ἄριστοί εἰσιν οἱ ναῦται 'sailors make/are <u>the</u> best captains'.

The article as noun

446. (i) Any Greek adj. can be used as a noun (understanding the reference to be man in the masc., woman in the fem., and thing in the neut.), and the article is no exception – *although it must then be accompanied by an adverb, or a genitival or prepositional phrase, or a particle*, e.g.

ὁ ἄνω 'the man on deck';
αἱ ἐνθάδε 'the women here';
τὰ τῶν Ἀθηναίων, lit. 'the things of the Athenians' (the meaning of τὰ is determined by the context);
οἱ περὶ Ἡράκλειτον 'those round Herakleitos' (i.e. 'Herakleitos and his school');
τὰ ἐν Λακεδαίμονι 'the things/events in Sparta';
and the very common ὁ μὲν … ὁ δέ 'the one … the other'.

(ii) A prominent and important feature of classical Greek is that the article goes much further than other adjectives in being used with almost any kind of word (not only adjectives and adverbs, but also participles, infinitives, whole phrases) to form noun phrases, e.g.

ὁ σοφός 'the wise man';
οἱ αὐτόθι 'those on the spot';
ὁ λέγων 'the man who is speaking';
τὸ θανεῖν 'the fact of dying, death'.

(iii) In this way Greek even introduces the aspectual distinctions of verbs into noun constructions and can distinguish for instance between τὸ θνῄσκειν (the process) and τὸ θανεῖν (the event). The article also allows a noun to be determined by an adverb: ὁ ὀρθῶς κυβερνήτης 'he who is really a pilot, a real pilot'.

(iv) The neuter singular article in particular may be used to form phrases which, though not nouns in origin, are treated as such, e.g.

> τὸ λίαν ἧσσον ἐπαινῶ τοῦ μηδὲν ἄγαν lit. 'I approve "the too much" less than "the nothing in excess" ', i.e. 'I approve of excess less than of moderation';
>
> θαυμαστὸν δέ μοι φαίνεται καὶ τὸ πεισθῆναί τινας lit. 'and amazing it appears to me also *the some people to have been convinced*', i.e. 'and I also find it amazing that some people were convinced.'

While speakers of other languages, including Latin and English, have to cast about for other forms of expression, Greek speakers and writers and philosophers could make almost anything into a neuter singular noun. This device gave the language immense flexibility of syntax and style.

The position of the article

447. (i) Normally the article precedes the noun but notice that in a simple group comprising article, adjective and noun the position of the article will depend on the function of the adj.:

> ὁ σοφὸς ἀνήρ, ὁ ἀνὴρ ὁ σοφός, ἀνὴρ ὁ σοφός (rare) all mean 'the wise man' – a noun phrase, not a complete sentence – as the adj. is 'attributive' (cf. **111**).

> But σοφὸς ὁ ἀνήρ and ὁ ἀνὴρ σοφός mean 'the man is wise'. Here σοφός is used as a predicate (is predicative) and produces a complete sentence, as it contains a predicate.

(ii)   Some adjectives (often originally pronouns) – οὗτος, ὅδε, ἐκεῖνος, πᾶς – take the predicative position:

> οὗτος ὁ ἀνήρ, ὁ ἀνὴρ οὗτος 'this man' (note that οὗτος and ὅδε contain the article as their first element).

Notice, on the other hand, the contrast between ὁ αὐτὸς ἀνήρ 'the same man' and ὁ ἀνὴρ αὐτός, αὐτὸς ὁ ἀνήρ 'the man himself'.

(iii)   Finally, a reminder of masc. ὅς, fem. ἥ in the expressions καὶ ὅς, 'and he ...', ἦ δ' ἥ 'she said'. These forms (orig. *sos, *sā) are demonstrative pronouns closely related to the def. art. They are quite unrelated to the relative pronoun (orig. *yos, *yā). Try to keep them separate in your mind!

448. The following list of prefixes and suffixes attached to nouns, adjectives, adverbs and verbs will help you to determine the meaning of roots or stems which you recognise but the shape of which may be slightly unfamiliar. Following this list of prefixes and suffixes a table of useful common roots/stems is given.

Formation of nouns

The following suffixes will be frequently met:

(i) to denote *actions:*

-σις *f. (3e)* παίδευσις 'training' (παιδεύω)
-σια *f. (1b)* ἐργασία 'work' (ἐργάτης)
-μός *m. (2a)* διωγμός 'pursuit' (διώκω)

(ii) to denote the *result of an action:*

-μα (-ματος) *n. (3b)* πρᾶγμα 'thing (done)' (πράττω)

(iii) to denote *the agent:*

-τήρ *m. (3a)* σωτήρ 'saviour' (σῴζω)
-τωρ *m. (3a)* ῥήτωρ 'orator' (cf. ἐρῶ)
-τής *m. (1d)* ποιητής 'maker, poet' (ποιέω)

(iv) to denote *means or instrument:*

-τρον *n. (2b)* ἄροτρον 'plough' (ἀρόω)

(v) to denote *profession or class of a person:*

-εύς *m. (3g)* ἱερεύς 'priest' (ἱερός)
-της *m. (1d)* πολίτης 'citizen' (πόλις)

(vi) to denote *a quality:*

-ία *f. (1b)* σοφία 'wisdom' (σοφός)
-της (-τητος) *f. (3a)* ἰσότης 'equality' (ἴσος)
-σύνη *f. (1a)* σωφροσύνη 'moderation' (σώφρων)

(vii) to denote *place where an activity occurs:*

-τήριον *n. (2b)* δικαστήριον 'law-court' (δικάστης)
-εῖον *n. (2b)* κουρεῖον 'barber's shop' (κουρεύς)

(viii) to denote a *small example* (familiar, affectionate or contemptuous):

-ιον *n. (2b)* παιδίον 'child' (παῖς)
-ίδιον *n. (2b)* οἰκίδιον 'small house' (οἶκος)
-ίσκος *m. (2a)* νεανίσκος 'youth' (νεανίας)
-ίσκη *f. (1a)* παιδίσκη 'young girl' (παῖς)

(ix) to denote *'son of'* (often used as a personal name, cf. English names in '–son')

-άδης *m. (1d)* Βορεάδης 'son of Boreas' (Βορέας)
-ίδης *m. (1d)* Πριαμίδης 'son of Priam' (Πρίαμος)

(x) to denote *the feminine form:*

-ις (-ιδος) *f. (3a)* νεᾶνις 'young girl' (νεανίας)

Formation of adjectives

449. Adjectives are formed by *composition* (putting two roots together) and *derivation* (by adding suffixes):

Composition

Here two roots are compounded, or juxtaposed, and the meaning is deduced from their combined sense. These roots may derive from *nouns/adjectives* or *verbs* or *prepositions*:

(i)   If the first root is a *noun* or *adjective*, it has:

> either the bare stem, e.g. εὐρύ-πορος, from εὐρύς 'broad'; or
> a vowel -o- added to the stem or replacing the vowel of the stem, e.g. ἀνδρ-ο- φόνος 'man-slaying', cf. ἀνδρ-; ψυχ-ο-πομπός 'escorting souls', cf. ψυχ-ή.

(ii)   If the first root is a *verb,* the verb-form sometimes ends in -ε or -σι, e.g.

> φερέ-νικος 'bringing victory'
> ἑλκεσί-πεπλος 'trailing robes'

(iii)   *Prepositions* are very commonly used in compounds and sometimes have special meanings (see **452** below).

Note especially:

(iv)   the frequent adjective formation with εὐ- 'good', e.g. εὐδαίμων 'having good deities, happy' (ἐύς is still an adjective in Homer, but survived only as the adverb εὖ in Attic)

(v)   the prefix ἀ- or ἀν-, which carries a negative force, e.g. ἄγαμος 'unmarried', ἀνώνυμος 'unnamed'; but beware of the small number of words where ἀ- means 'one and the same, together with', e.g. ἄλοχος 'wife' (lit. 'bedfellow' – λέχος 'bed').

Derivation: adjectival suffixes

450. (i) to denote a *general relationship between the adj. and the base:*

> -ιος: πολέμιος 'enemy' (πόλεμος)
> -ικός, φυσικός 'natural' (φύσις)

(ii)   to denote *material:*

-ινος: λίθινος 'of stone' (λίθος)
-εος or with contraction -ους: χρυσοῦς 'golden' (χρυσός)

(iii)   to denote *inclination,* or *tendency:*

-μων: μνήμων 'mindful' (cf. μέ-μνη-μαι)

(iv)   to denote *aptitude:*

-ιμος: χρήσιμος 'useful' (χράομαι or χρῆσις)

(v)   to denote *passive state* or *capability:*

-τος: σχιστός 'divided' (σχίζω)
      ὁρατός 'visible' (ὁράω)

(vi)   to denote *obligation:*

-τέος: τιμητέος 'that is to be honoured' (τιμάω)

Formation of adverbs

451. Most adjectives form adverbs by:

- Replacing the ending of the nom. with -ως, e.g. κακός – κακῶς, ἀληθής – ἀληθῶς. But:

(i)   Those in -υς replace -υς with -εως, e.g. ἡδύς – ἡδέως.
(ii)   The neuter accusative s. or pl. may be used adverbially as well, e.g. πολύ 'much', μεγάλα 'greatly', μόνον 'alone'.
(iii) Special types are:
       -δόν, -αδόν, -ηδόν, e.g. κυνηδόν 'like a dog', ὁμοθυμαδόν 'unanimously'
       -δήν, -αδήν, e.g. κρυβδήν 'secretly' (cf. κρύπτω 'hide').
(iv)   There are also many adverbs that do not form part of a regular pattern, e.g. τάχα 'quickly', εὐθύς 'at once', παντάπασι 'in every respect'.

Formation of verbs

452. (i) Verbs are formed from nouns (or adjectives) by such suffixes as these:

-άω	τιμάω	'honour'	(τιμή)
-έω	πονέω	'work'	(πόνος)
-όω	δουλόω	'enslave'	(δοῦλος)
-εύω	βασιλεύω	'reign'	(βασιλεύς)
-(ά)ζω	ἀγοράζω	'buy'	(ἀγορά)
-ίζω	πλουτίζω	'enrich'	(πλοῦτος)
-ύνω	μεγαλύνω	'make large'	(μέγας, μεγάλ-)

(ii) These suffixes denote a wish:

| -ιάω | στρατηγιάω | 'to want to be a general' (στρατηγός) |
| -σείω | γελασείω | 'to want to laugh' (γελάω) |

(iii)   Verbs are frequently compounded with prepositions, the sense of which
is sometimes subtle and difficult to render. Apart from their normal senses,
note the following *special* senses of prepositions when used in compounds to
form both verbs and adjectives:

ἀνα-	*withdrawal*	ἀναχωρέω	'retreat'
	repetition	ἀναβιόω	'come to life again'
ἀντι-	*exchange*	ἀντιδίδωμι	'give in return'
	equality	ἀντίθεος	'god-like'
	against	ἀντίδικος	'opponent at law'
ἀπο-	*return*	ἀποδίδωμι	'give back'
	completion	ἀπεργάζομαι	'finish off'
	for the defendant	ἀπολογέομαι	'defend oneself'
δια-	*separation*	διαλύω	'break up'
	disagreement	διαφωνέω	'disagree'
	succession	διαδέχομαι	'take the place of'
	completion	διαπράττω	'accomplish'
ἐπι-	*opposition*	ἐπιστρατεύω	'march against'
	addition	ἐπιμανθάνω	'learn besides'
	superiority	ἐπιβιόω	'survive'
κατα-	*thoroughness*	καταμανθάνω	'learn thoroughly'
	to destruction	καταλύω	'destroy utterly'
μετα-	*change*	μεταγιγνώσκω	'change one's mind, repent'
	share	μέτεστι	'have a share in'
παρα-	*deviation*	παραβαίνω	'overstep, transgress'
περι-	*intensity*	περικαλλής	'very beautiful'
προ-	*abandonment*	προδίδωμι	'betray'
	anteriority	προοράω	'foresee'
ὑπερ-	*excess*	ὑπερβάλλω	'overshoot, exceed'
ὑπο-	*subjection*	ὑπήκοος	'subject'
	moderation	ὑπόλευκος	'whitish'
	stealth	ὑποσπάω	'withdraw secretly'

Changes in root syllables

453. You will have noticed that the root syllables of Greek words are sometimes modified, especially in their vowels. This is familiar in English, where we have such patterns as 'si̲ng', 'sa̲ng', 'su̲ng', 'so̲ng' or 'fo̲ot', 'fe̲et'. The details in Greek are quite complicated, but it is worth noting the patterns in which:

- -ε- is replaced by -o- or by *zero*, i.e. this vowel disappears completely; and
- the *zero* vowel is replaced by α, especially where λ, μ, ν, or ρ are involved.

The following table gives a few examples:

ε	o	**zero**
πέτομαι 'fly'	ποτάομαι 'hover'	πτερόν 'wing'
λείπω 'leave'	λέλοιπα *(perf.)*	ἔλιπον *(aor.)*
φεύγω 'run away'		ἔφυγον *(aor.)* cf. φυγή 'flight'
φέρω 'bring'	-φορος '-bringing'	δίφρος 'chariot' (lit. 'two-carrier')
πατέρα *(acc.)* 'father'	εὐπάτορα (acc.) 'of a noble father'	πατρός *(gen.)* πατράσι *(dat. pl.)*
βέλος 'missile'	βόλος 'cast'	βάλλω 'throw'
τέμνω 'cut'	τόμος 'slice'	ἔταμον *(aor.)*
πένθος 'grief'	πέπονθα 'suffer' *(perf.)*	ἔπαθον *(aor.)*
θείνω 'kill'	φόνος 'murder'	ἔπεφνον *(aor.)*

The last example shows another strange feature, the alternation of θ with φ. Similarly we find τ alternating with π, e.g.

τίς 'who?'	ποῦ 'where?'
τίνω 'pay'	ποινή 'penalty'
πέντε 'five'	πέμπτος 'fifth'

Latin transcriptions

454. The Greek words that have been borrowed into English have normally come by way of Latin; only a few (e.g. 'kudos') are taken directly from the Greek form. Similarly, the proper names of Greek are frequently given a Latin form in English, which is occasionally different from the Greek (e.g. Achilles for Ἀχιλλεύς), although it is increasingly common to find Greek-style rather than Latin-style transcription in modern scholarship on Greek history and Greek literature (e.g. Akhilleus rather than Achilles). For this reason, it is important to know both Greek-style and Latin-style conventions for transcribing from the Greek to the Roman alphabet. Most equivalents are obvious, but the following table sets out the main differences:

Greek letters	Greek-style transcription	Latin-style transcription
θ	th	th
φ	ph	ph
χ	kh	ch
κ	k	c
υ	u	y
ου	ou	ū
αι	ai	ae *or* ē
οι	oi	oe *or* ē
ος	os	us
ον	on	um

Vowel-length is not shown and the corresponding English vowels are often different, since they tend to be lengthened when stressed and shortened when unstressed, e.g. Ὅμηρος becomes 'Hŏmērus', English 'Hōmer'; Σόλων becomes English Sōlŏn. For transcriptions used in this course, see **342**.

D   A Total Greek-English Vocabulary of all Words to be Learnt

FINDING THE LEXICON FORM OF A VERB

The essence is to isolate the present stem, since it is most often this form which will be shown in the lexicon.

(i)   Look at the front of the word, and remove any augment, or reduplication.

> η could be the augmented form of α, ε, η
>
> | η | " | " | αι, ει |
> |---|---|---|---|
> | ην | " | " | αν, εν |
> | ω | " | " | ο |
> | ῳ | " | " | ο ι |
> | ῑ, ῡ | " | " | ι, υ |
> | ει | " | " | ε, ει |

Bear in mind that the augment might be hidden by a prefix such as κατά, ἐκ, πρό, εἰς, ἐν, so check the prefix as well.

> προὔβαλον = προ-έ-βαλον, i.e. προβάλλω
> ἐξέβαλον = ἐκ-έ-βαλον, i.e. ἐκβάλλω
> ἐνέβαλον from ἐν + βάλλω, = ἐμβάλλω

Here is a list of common prefixes, with their various forms:

> | | | |
> |---|---|---|
> | ἀνά ἀν' | ἐν ἐμ- ἐγ- | παρά παρ |
> | ἀπό ἀπ' ἀφ' | ἐπί ἐπ' ἐφ' | πρό προε- πρου- |
> | διά δι' | κατά κατ' καθ' | σύν συμ- συγ- |
> | ἐκ ἐξ | μετά μετ' μεθ' | ὑπό ὑπ' ὑφ' |

(ii) Having made an adjustment for augment/reduplication and prefix, examine the stem and the ending. Remove any personal endings.

(iii) If the remaining stem ends in σ, ξ, ψ, especially if an α follows, it is probably an aorist. Try dropping the σα (e.g. ἔ-λυ-σα = λύω) or converting σ to ζ (ἐ-νόμισ-α = νομίζω). Try restoring a terminal ξ→κ or →ττ (ἔ-πραξ-α = πράττω), and a terminal ψ to π (ἔ-πεμψ-α = πέμπω).

If the stem ends in some form of θη, remember that χ may hide ττ or κ (ἐπράχθην = πράττω), φ may hide π or β (ἐπέμφθην = πέμπω). For common consonant changes, see **359(x).**

(iv)   If there is no augment, check the endings for some sign of σ (ξ, ψ) or ε-
contract in the stem, when it may be future. Check also endings for signs of
participle, infinitive, etc. and remember that the stem you so isolate may be
present or aorist or perfect or future (see **384**).

(v)   If you are still stumped, isolate the stem and look that up in the vocabulary.
Highly irregular stems have been placed there for your peace of mind.

(vi)   Bold square brackets (e.g. **[3A]**) refer to the chapter where the word was
learned.

† = see principal parts at **389**.

†† = these forms appear only with the prefix as shown, but should still be looked
up *without* the prefix at **389**.

* = see **391**.

A

ἀγαγ- *aor. stem of* ἄγω **[7H]**

ἀγαθός ή όν good; noble; courageous **[2B]**

ἄγαλμα (ἀγαλματ-), τό image, statue (3b) **[18D]**

†ἀγγέλλω (ἀγγειλα-) report, announce **[19F]**

ἄγγελος, ὁ messenger (2a) **[17C]**

ἄγε come! (s.) **[3A]**

ἄγομαι bring for oneself, lead; marry **[20B]**

ἀγορά, ἡ gathering (-place); market-place; agora
(1b) **[8A]**

ἀγορεύω speak (in assembly); proclaim **[11A]**

ἄγρη, ἡ hunt (1a) **[19E]**

ἄγροικος ον from the country; boorish **[6A]**

ἀγρός, ὁ field; country (side)(2a) **[11A]**

†ἄγω (ἀγαγ-) lead, bring **[7H]**; live in, be at **[8C]**

εἰρήνην ἄγω live in/be at peace **[8C]**

ἀγών (ἀγων-), ὁ contest; trial (3a) **[12C]**

ἀγωνίζομαι contest, go to law **[12C]**

ἀδελφός, ὁ brother (2a) **[16D]**

ἀδικέω be unjust; commit a crime; wrong **[8B]**

ἀδίκημα (ἀδικηματ-), τό crime, wrong (3b)
[14A]

ἄδικος ον unjust **[5D]**

ἀδύνατος ον impossible **[6B]**

†ᾄδω = ἀείδω **[8B]**

ἀεί always **[1J]**

†ἀείδω sing **[8B]**

ἀέκων = ἄκων **[19B]**

ἀθάνατος ον immortal **[11A]**

'Αθήναζε to Athens **[12F]**

'Αθῆναι, αἱ Athens (1a) **[6B]**

'Αθηναῖος, ὁ Athenian (2a) **[2B]**

'Αθήνησι at Athens **[12I]**

ἄθλιος ᾱ ον pathetic, miserable, wretched **[15C]**

ἀθροίζω gather, collect **[18D]**

ἀθῡμέω be downhearted, gloomy, disheartened
[16B]

ἀθῡμίᾱ, ἡ lack of spirit, depression (1b) **[16G]**

αἰδώς, ἡ respect for others, shame (acc. αἰδῶ;
gen. αἰδοῦς; dat. αἰδοῖ) **[18E]**

αἰεί = ἀεί **[20A]**

αἱρέομαι (ἑλ-) choose **[11C]**

†αἱρέω (ἑλ-) take, capture; convict **[9I]**

†αἰσθάνομαι (αἰσθ-) perceive, notice (+ acc. or
gen.) **[11C]**

αἰσχρός ᾱ όν ugly (of people); base, shameful
(comp. αἰσχίων; sup. αἴσχιστος) **[13G]**

†αἰσχῡνομαι be ashamed, feel shame (before)
[12E]

αἰτέω ask (for) **[9I]**

αἰτίᾱ, ἡ reason, cause; responsibility (1b) **[5C]**

αἴτιος ᾱ ον responsible (for), guilty (of) (+ gen.)
[5A]

αἰχμή, ἡ spear-point (1a) **[19D]**

ἀκήκοα *perf. of* ἀκούω **[13I]**

ἀκηκοώς υῖα ός (-οτ-) *perf. part. of* ἀκούω

ἀκοή, ἡ hearing (1a) **[16B]**

ἀκολουθέω follow, accompany (+ dat.) **[17C]**

ἀκόσμητος ον unprovided for **[18C]**

†ἀκούω hear **[1C-D]**; listen (to) (+ gen. of person,
gen. or acc. of thing) (fut. ἀκούσομαι) **[9H]**

ἀκρῑβῶς accurately, closely **[1E-F]**

ἀκρόπολις, ἡ Acropolis, citadel (3e) **[1A-B]**; **[18C]**

ἄκῡρος ον invalid **[14C]**

ἄκων ἄκουσα ἆκον (ἄκοντ-) unwilling(ly) **[11B]**
ἀλ- *aor. stem of* ἀλίσκομαι
ἀλήθεια, ἡ truth (1b) **[7A]**
ἀληθῆ, τά the truth **[1D]**
†ἀλίσκομαι (ἀλ-) be convicted; be caught **[16F]**
*ἀλλά but **[1C]**
ἀλλήλους each other, one another (2a) **[3C]**
ἄλλος η ο other, the rest of **[3C]**
ἄλλος … ἄλλον one … another **[12A]**
ἀλλότριος ᾱ ον someone else's; alien **[12D]**
*ἀλλ' οὖν well anyway; however that may be **[16B]**
ἄλλως otherwise; in vain **[17E]**
ἄλογος ον speechless; without reason **[18C]**
ἅμα at the same time **[2C]**
ἀμαθής ές ignorant **[6D]**
†ἁμαρτάνω (ἁμαρτ-) err; do wrong; make a mistake **[13H]**; miss (+ gen.) **[19F]**
ἅμαρτε 3rd s. (str.) aor of ἁμαρτάνω *(no augment)*
ἀμείβομαι answer, reply to (+ acc.) **[19D]**
ἀμείνων ἄμεινον (ἀμεινον-) better **[9E]**
ἀμελής ές uncaring **[10E]**
ἀμήχανος ον impossible, impracticable **[18C]**
†ἀμῡ́νω keep off, withstand **[18B]**
ἀμφέρχομαι (ἀμφηλυθ-) surround (+ acc.) **[20C]**
ἀμφίπολος, ἡ handmaiden (2a) **[20C]**
ἀμφότερος ᾱ ον both **[9I]**
ἄν (+ ind.) *conditional;* (+ opt.) *potential>conditional* **[8A-C, 12G]**; (+ subj.) *indefinite* **[14]**
ἀναβαίνω (ἀναβα-) go up, come up **[1A-G]**
ἀναβάς (ἀναβαντ-) *aor. part. of* ἀναβαίνω
ἀναγκάζω force, compel **[10B]**
ἀναγκαῖος ᾱ ον necessary **[17Λ]**
ἀνάγκη, ἡ necessity (1a) **[7B]**
ἀνάγκη ἐστί it is obligatory (for x [acc. or dat.] to – [inf.]) **[7B]**
ἀναιρέω (ἀνελ-) pick up **[7G]**
ἀναίτιος ον innocent **[16H]**
ἀναλαμβάνω (ἀναλαβ-) take back, up **[13B]**
†ἀνᾱλίσκω (ἀνᾱλωσα-) spend, use, kill **[18B]**
ἀναμένω (ἀναμείνα-) wait, hold on **[9F]**
ἄναξ (ἀνακτ-), ὁ lord, prince, king (3a) **[9D]**
ἀναπείθω persuade over to one's side **[9C]**
ἄνασσα, ἡ princess (1c) **[20E]**
ἀναχωρέω retreat **[2D]**

ἀνδρεῖος ᾱ ον brave, manly **[7D]**
ἄνεμος, ὁ wind (2a) **[20F]**
ἀνέστην I stood up (*aor. of* ἀνίσταμαι)
ἀνέστηκα I am standing (*perf. of* ἀνίσταμαι)
ἀνεστώς ῶσα ός (ἀνεστωτ-) standing (*perf. part. of* ἀνίσταμαι)
ἄνευ (+ gen.) without **[11B]**
†ἀνέχομαι put up with (+ gen.) **[18E]**
ἀνήρ (ἀνδρ-), ὁ man (3a) **[3A-B]**
ἄνθρωπος, ὁ man, fellow (2a) **[1G]**; ἡ, woman **[13F]**
ἀνίσταμαι (ἀναστα-) get up, stand up, emigrate **[8B]**
ἀνόητος ον foolish **[17E]**
ἀνομίᾱ, ἡ lawlessness (1b) **[4C]**
ἀντί (+ gen.) instead of, for **[16H]**
ἀντίδικος, ὁ contestant in lawsuit (2a) **[12C]**
ἄνω above **[9B]**
ἄξιος ᾱ ον worth, worthy of (+ gen.) **[8C]**
ἄοπλος ον unarmed **[18C]**
ἀπαγγέλλω (ἀπαγγειλα-) announce, report **[17B]**
ἀπαγορεύω (ἀπειπ-) forbid **[17A]**
ἀπάγω (ἀπαγαγ-) lead, take away **[4C]**
ἄπαις (ἀπαιδ-) childless **[13B]**
ἀπαιτέω demand (X [acc.] from Y [acc.]) **[16D]**
ἀπάνευθε(ν) afar off **[20G]**
ἅπᾱς ἅπᾱσα ἅπαν (ἁπαντ-) all, the whole of **[10A]**
ἀπέβην aor. of ἀποβαίνω
ἀπέδωκα aor. of ἀποδίδωμι
ἀπέθανον aor. of ἀποθνῄσκω
ἄπειμι be absent **[16D]**
ἄπειρος ον inexperienced in (+ gen.) **[13E]**
ἀπελεύθερ-ος, -ᾱ, ὁ, ἡ freedman, freedwoman (2a) **[16A]**
ἀπελθ- *aor. stem of* ἀπέρχομαι
ἀπέρχομαι (ἀπελθ-) go away, depart **[6C]**
ἀπέχομαι (ἀποσχ-) refrain, keep away from (+ gen.) **[10A]**
ἀπῆλθον aor. of ἀπέρχομαι
ἀπιέναι inf. of ἀπέρχομαι/ἄπειμι
ἄπιθι imper. of ἀπέρχομαι/ἄπειμι
ἀπικνέομαι = ἀφικνέομαι
ἀπιών οὖσα όν (ἀπιοντ-) aor. part. of ἀπέρχομαι/ἄπειμι
ἀπό (+ gen.) from, away from **[1G]**
ἀποβαίνω (ἀποβα-) leave, depart **[7G]**

ἀποβλέπω look steadfastly at (and away from everything else) [11A]

ἀποδίδωμι (ἀποδο-) give back, return [13A]

ἀποδο- *aor. stem of* ἀποδίδωμι

ἀποδραμ- *aor. stem of* ἀποτρέχω

ἀποδώσειν fut. inf. of ἀποδίδωμι

ἀποθαν- *aor. stem of* ἀποθνῄσκω

†ἀποθνῄσκω (ἀποθαν-) die [1A-G]

ἀποκρῑ́νομαι (ἀποκρῑνα-) answer [7D]

ἀπόκρισις, ἡ reply, answer (3e) [17C]

ἀποκτείνω (ἀποκτεινα-) kill [4D]

ἀπολαβ- *aor. stem of* ἀπολαμβάνω

ἀπολαμβάνω take [16H]

ἀπολεσα- *aor. stem of* ἀπόλλῡμι

ἀπολέ-ω I shall kill, ruin, destroy [8C]

†ἀπόλλῡμι (ἀπολεσα-) kill, ruin, destroy; mid./pass. be killed (aor. ἀπωλόμην) [11B]; perf. I have been killed, I am done for (ἀπόλωλα)

ἀπολογέομαι make a speech in defence, defend oneself [9H]

ἀπολογίᾱ, ἡ speech in one's defence (1b) [9I]

ἀπολ- *aor. stem of* ἀπόλλῡμαι

ἀπολῡ́ω acquit, release [9J]

ἀπόλωλα *perf. of* ἀπόλλυμαι I am lost [13H]

ἀποπέμπω send away, divorce [13A]

ἀπορέω have no resources, be at a loss [2B]

ἀπορίᾱ, ἡ lack of provisions, perplexity (1b) [2]

ἀποτρέχω (ἀποδραμ-) run away, run off [9E]

ἀποφαίνω reveal, show [7B]

ἀποφέρω (ἀπενεγκ-) carry back [17A]

ἀποφεύγω (ἀποφυγ-) escape, run off [4C]

ἀποχωρέω go away, depart [1A-G]

ἀποψηφίζομαι vote against; reject [13D]; acquit (+ gen.) [14B]

ἅπτομαι touch (+ gen.) [20E]

†ἅπτω light, fasten, fix [5B]

ἀπώλεσα *aor. of* ἀπόλλῡμι

*ἄρα then, consequently (*marking an inference*) [6D]; straightaway [20A]

*ἆρα = ? (direct q.) [1B]

ἀργύριον, τό silver, money (2b) [12H]

†ἀρέσκω, please (+ dat.) [11C]

ἀρετή, ἡ courage, excellence, quality (1a) [7D]

ἄριστος η ον best, very good [1J]

†ἁρπάζω seize, plunder, snatch [17C]

ἄρτι just now, recently [10B]

ἀρχή, ἡ beginning, start [12C]; rule, office, position [13E]; board of magistrates (1a)

ἄρχομαι (mid.) begin (+ gen.) [9G]; (+ inf./part.) [9I]; (pass.) be ruled over [11C]

†ἄρχω rule (+ gen.) [11C]; begin (+ gen.) [12E]

ἄρχων (ἀρχοντ-), ὁ archon (3a) [13F]

ἀσέβεια, ἡ irreverence to the gods (1b) [4D]

ἀσεβέω (εἰς) commit sacrilege upon [12D]

ἀσεβής ές impious, unholy [13E]

ἀσθένεια, ἡ illness, weakness (1b) [13C]

ἀσθενέω be ill, fall ill [13C]

ἀσθενής ές weak, ill [18A]

ἀσπάζομαι greet, welcome [12A]

ἀστή, ἡ female citizen (1a) [12F]

ἀστός, ὁ male citizen (2a) [12F]

ἄστυ, τό city (3f) [4A-B]

ἀσφαλής ές safe, secure [20A]

ἀτάρ but [9F]

ἅτε since, seeing that (+ part.) [18D]

ἀτῑμάζω hold in dishonour, dishonour [4B]

ἀτῑμίᾱ, ἡ loss of citizen rights (1b) [12E]

ἄτῑμος ον deprived of citizen rights [12D]

αὖ again, moreover [9I]

αὐδάω speak, say [20G]

αὖθις again [2C]

αὐλή, ἡ courtyard (1a) [17A]

αὔριον tomorrow [5D]

αὐτάρ but, then [20G]

αὐτίκα at once [17D]

αὐτόν ήν ό him, her, it, them [4D]

αὐτός ή ό self [7H]

ὁ αὐτός the same [7H]

ἀφαιρέομαι (ἀφελ-) take X (acc.) from Y (acc.) [12D]; claim

ἀφειλόμην *aor. of* ἀφαιρέομαι

ἀφεῖναι aor. inf. of ἀφίημι

††ἀφέλκω (ἀφελκυσα-) drag off [4D]

ἀφελ- *aor. stem of* ἀφαιρέομαι

††ἀφῑ́ημι (ἀφε-) release, let go [17A]

†ἀφικνέομαι (ἀφῑκ-) arrive, come [3A]

ἀφῑκόμην *aor. of* ἀφικνέομαι

ἀφίσταμαι relinquish claim to (+ gen.), revolt from (+ gen.) [13A]

B

βαδίζω walk, go (fut. βαδιοῦμαι) [10A]

βαθέως deeply [1E-F]

βαθύς εῖα ύ deep **[5A]**

†βαίνω (βα-) go, come, walk **[1A-B]**

†βάλλω (βαλ-) hit, throw **[19F]**; βάλλ' εἰς
κόρακας go to hell! **[6A]**

βάρβαρος, ὁ barbarian, foreigner (2a) **[2C]**

βάρος, τό weight, burden (3c) **[15C]**

βαρύς εῖα ύ heavy, weighty **[5A]**; βαρέως φέρω
take badly, find hard to bear **[9C]**

βασιλεύς, ὁ king **[4D]**; king archon (3g) **[13E]**

βασιλεύω be king, be king archon; be queen

βέβαιος (ᾱ) ον secure **[2B]**

βέλτιστος η ον best **[8A]**

βελτῑων βέλτῑον (βελτῑον-) better **[8A]**

βιάζομαι use force **[6C]**

βίος, ὁ life; means, livelihood (2a) **[5A]**

βλέπω look (at) **[1C-D]**

βληθείς εῖσα έν (βληθεντ-) aor. part. pass. of
βάλλω

βοάω shout (for) **[3D]**

βοή, ἡ shout (1a) **[2]**

βοήθεια, ἡ help, rescue operation (1b) **[16C]**

βοηθέω run to help (+ dat.) **[1E-F]**

βουλεύομαι discuss, take advice **[17E]**

βουλευτής, ὁ member of council (1d) **[16F]**

βουλή, ἡ council (1a) **[13F]**

†βούλομαι wish, want **[7A]**

βραδέως slowly **[2B]**

βραχύς εῖα ύ short, brief **[16B]**

βροτός, ὁ mortal, man (2a) **[20E]**

βωμός, ὁ altar (2a) **[4D]**

Γ

'γαθέ = ἀγαθέ

γαῖα (1c) = γῆ, ἡ (1a) **[20E]**

†γαμέω (γημα-) marry **[13D]**

γάμος, ὁ marriage (2a) **[5A]**

*γάρ for **[1C]**; *γάρ δή really, I assure you **[7B]**

*γε at least (denotes some sort of reservation)
[1G, 5D]

γεγένημαι perf. of γίγνομαι **[13H]**

γεγενημένα, τά events, occurrences (2b) (perf.
part. of γίγνομαι) **[16B]**

γέγονα perf. of γίγνομαι (part. γεγονώς or
γεγώς) **[19F]**

γείτων (γειτον-), ὁ neighbour (3a) **[3A-B]**

†γελάω (γελασα-) laugh **[7F]**

γεν- aor. stem of γίγνομαι

γένεσις, ἡ birth (3e) **[18A]**

γενναῖος ᾱ ον noble, fine **[15A]**

γεννήτης, ὁ member of a genos (1d) **[13C]**

γένος, τό genos **[13C]**; race, kind (3c)

γέρων (γεροντ-), ὁ old man (3a) **[6D]**

γεῦμα (γευματ-), τό taste, sample (3b) **[11C]**

γεύομαι taste **[11C]**

γεωργός, ὁ farmer (2a) **[4A]**

γῆ, ἡ land, earth (1a) **[1A-B]**

γημα- aor. stem of γαμέω

†γίγνομαι (γεν-) become, be born, happen, arise
[2]

†γιγνώσκω (γνο-) know, think, resolve **[1I]**

γίνομαι = γίγνομαι **[19C]**

γλαυκῶπις (γλαυκωπιδ-), ἡ grey-eyed **[20C]**

γλυκύς εῖα ύ sweet **[10E]**

γνήσιος ᾱ ον legitimate, genuine **[13C]**

γνούς γνοῦσα γνόν (γνοντ-) aor. part. of
γιγνώσκω

γνώμη, ἡ judgment, mind, purpose, plan (1a)
[6D]

*γοῦν at any rate **[10E]**

γοῦνα, τά knees (2b) (sometimes γούνατα [3b])
[20D]

γραῦς (γρα-), ἡ old woman (3a; but acc. s. γραῦν;
acc. pl. γραῦς) **[10B]**

γραφή, ἡ indictment, charge, case (1a) **[9H]**
γραφὴν γράφομαι indict x (acc.) on charge of
γ (gen.) **[9H]**

γράφομαι indict, charge **[9H]**

†γράφ-ω propose (a decree); write **[16C]**

γυνή (γυναικ-), ἡ woman, wife (3a) **[4A]**

Δ

δαίμων (δαιμον-), ὁ god, demon (3a) **[4A]**

†δάκνω (δακ-) bite, worry **[6A]**

δάκρυον, τό tear (2b) **[15C]**

δακρύω weep **[15B]**

*δέ and, but **[1A]**

δεήσει fut. of δεῖ

†δεῖ it is necessary for x (acc.) to – (inf.) **[7B]**

†δείκνῡμι (δειξα-) show **[16E]**

δεινός ή όν terrible, dire, astonishing, clever
[3B]; clever at (+ inf.) **[9F]**

δέκα ten **[17C]**

δέμνια, τά bed, bedding (2b) **[20A]**

δένδρον, τό tree (2b) **[18B]**

δεξιά, ἡ right hand (1b) **[6D]**

δεξιός ᾱ όν right-hand **[6D]**; clever **[8C]**

†δέομαι need, ask, beg for (+ gen.) **[10E]**

δέον it being necessary **[16C]**

δέρμα (δερματ-), τό skin (3b) **[18B]**

δεσμός, ὁ bond (2a) **[18E]**

δέσποινα, ἡ mistress (1c) **[15A]**

δεσπότης, ὁ master (1d) **[4B]**

δεῦρο here, over here **[1B]**

†δέχομαι receive **[5D]**

*δή then, indeed **[3E]**

δῆλος η ον clear, obvious **[1H]**

δηλόω show, reveal **[1E-F]**

δημιουργικός ή όν technical, of a workman **[18E]**

δημιουργός, ὁ craftsman, workman, expert, (2a) **[18E]**

δῆμος, ὁ people **[6B]**; deme **[8B]** (2a)

δήπου of course, surely **[7D]**

*δῆτα then **[6D]**

διά (+ acc.) because of **[2D]**; (+ gen.) through **[8C]**; διὰ τί; why? **[1G]**

διαβαίνω (διαβα-) cross **[7H]**

διαβάλλω (διαβαλ-) slander **[7A]**

διαβολή, ἡ slander (1a) **[7C]**

διάκειμαι be in x (adv.) state, mood **[16G]**

διακρῑνω (διακρῑνα-) judge between, decide **[14D]**

διακωλύω prevent **[16F]**

διαλέγομαι converse **[5A]**

διαλείπω (διαλιπ-) leave **[16D]**

διανοέομαι intend, plan **[5C]**

διάνοια, ἡ intention, plan (1b) **[5C]**

διαπράττομαι (διαπραξα-) do, perform, act **[13G]**

διατίθημι (διαθε-) dispose, put x (acc.) in y (adv.) state **[17B]**

διατριβή, ἡ delay, pastime, discussion, way of life (1a) **[17C]**

διατρῑβω pass time, waste time **[12H]**

διαφέρω differ from (gen.); make a difference; be superior to (gen.) **[12B]**

διαφεύγω (διαφυγ-) get away, flee **[17A]**

††διαφθείρω (διαφθειρα-) destroy; kill **[4B]**; corrupt **[7C]**

διαφυγή, ἡ means of escape, flight (1a) **[18B]**

διδάσκαλος, ὁ teacher (2a) **[7E]**

†διδάσκω teach **[5D]**

†δίδωμι (δο-) give, grant **[10E]**

δίκην δίδωμι be punished, pay the penalty **[13I]**

διεξέρχομαι (διεξελθ-) go through, relate (fut. διέξειμι) **[16A]**

διέρχομαι (διελθ-) go through, relate **[2]**

διεφθάρμην plup. pass. of διαφθείρω **[19A]**

διηγέομαι explain, relate, go through **[14B]**

δικάζω be a juror; make a judgment **[9C]**

δίκαιος ᾱ ον just **[5D]**

δικαιοσύνη, ἡ justice (1a) **[18E]**

δικανικός ή όν judicial **[12A]**

δικαστήριον, τό law-court (2b) **[8B]**

δικαστής, ὁ juror, dikast (1d) **[8B]**

δίκη, ἡ lawsuit; justice; penalty (1a) **[5A]**; fine, case **[17C]**

δίκην δίδωμι be punished, pay the penalty **[13I]**

δίκην λαμβάνω punish, exact one's due from (παρά + gen.) **[5A]**

διοικέω administer, run **[13F]**

δῖος ᾱ ον godlike **[20C]**

διότι because **[5A]**

διώκω pursue **[1C-D]**; prosecute **[9H]**

δο- *aor. stem of* δίδωμι

δοκεῖ it seems a good idea to x (dat.) to do y (inf.); x (dat.) decides to – (inf.) **[9A-E, 10A]**

δοκέω seem, consider (self) to be **[7C]**

δόμοι, οἱ house, home (2a) **[15A]**

δόξα, ἡ reputation, opinion (1c) **[7A]**

δοῦλος, ὁ slave (2a) **[4C]**

δουλόομαι enslave (for oneself), make x a slave **[2A-D]**

δούς δοῦσα δόν (δοντ-) *aor. part. of* δίδωμι

δρᾶμα (δρᾱματ-), τό play, drama (3b) **[9A]**

δραχμή, ἡ drachma (coin) *(pay for two days' attendance at* ekklesia) (1a) **[11B]**

†δράω (δρᾱσα-) do, act **[6D]**

†δύναμαι be able **[7H]**

δύναμις, ἡ power, ability, faculty (3e) **[18A]**

δυνατός ή όν able, possible **[18B]**

δύο two **[7H]**

δύω sink **[1G]**

δυστυχής ές unlucky **[5A]**

δῶκαν *3rd pl. aor. of* δίδωμι

δωρέω bestow, give as a gift **[18C]**

δῶρον, τό gift, bribe (2b) **[10B]**

E

ἐ- augment (*remove this and try again under stem of verb*)

ἐάν (+ subj.) if (ever) [14C]

ἑαυτόν ἥν ὁ himself/herself/itself [7A]

ἐάω allow [9F]

ἐγγράφω enrol, enlist, register [13C]

ἐγγυάω engage, promise [13A]

ἐγγύς nearby [3C]; near + gen. [8C]

ἐγκλείω shut in, lock in [9E]

ἔγνων aor. of γιγνώσκω

ἐγώ I [1B]

ἔγωγε I at least, for my part [1D]

ἐδόθην aor. pass. of δίδωμι

ἔδομαι fut. of ἐσθίω

ἔδωκα aor. of δίδωμι

ἐθέλω (ἐθελησα-) wish, want [9H]

ἔθεσαν 3rd pl. aor. of τίθημι

ἔθηκα aor. of τίθημι

ἔθος, τό manner, habit (3c) [13E]

εἰ if [6D]

εἶ 2nd s. of εἰμί, εἶμι

εἰᾶσα- aor. stem ἐάω

εἰδείην opt. of οἶδα

εἰδέναι inf. of οἶδα

εἶδον aor. of ὁράω

εἰδώς εἰδυῖα εἰδός (εἰδοτ-) knowing (part. of
    οἶδα) [7C]

εἶεν very well, then! [11B]

εἴθε (+ opt.) I wish that! would that! if only!
    [12G]

εἰκός probable, reasonable, fair [12E]

εἴκοσι(ν) twenty [16F]

εἰκότως reasonably, rightly [13G]

εἴληφα perf. of λαμβάνω [13H]

εἰλόμην aor. of αἱρέομαι

εἰμαρμένος η ον allotted, appointed [18C]

εἵματα, τά clothes (3b) [20B]

†εἰμί be [1J]

†εἶμι I shall go (inf. ἰέναι; impf. ᾖα I went) [7C]

εἶναι to be (inf. of εἰμί)

εἰπ- aor. stem of λέγω

εἰπέ speak! tell me! [3C]

εἶπον aor. of λέγω

εἴρηκα I have said (perf. act. of λέγω)

εἴρημαι I have been said (perf. pass. of λέγω)
    [13H]

εἰρήνη, ἡ peace (1a) [8C]

    εἰρήνην ἄγω live in, be at peace [8C]

εἰς (+ acc.) to, into, onto [1G]

εἷς μία ἕν (ἑν-) one [18E]

εἰσαγγελίᾶ, ἡ impeachment (1b) [16G]

εἰσαγγέλλω (εἰσαγγειλα-) impeach [16F]

εἰσάγω (εἰσαγαγ-) introduce [12D]

εἰσβαίνω I go onto, on board [1C-D]

εἰσεληλυθώς υἶα ός (-οτ-) perf. part. of
    εἰσέρχομαι

εἰσελθ- aor. stem of εἰσέρχομαι

εἰσέρχομαι (εἰσελθ-) enter [5D]

εἰσήγαγον aor. of εἰσάγω

εἰσῄα impf. of εἰσέρχομαι/εἴσειμι

εἰσῆλθον aor. of εἰσέρχομαι

εἰσιδ- aor. stem of εἰσοράω

εἰσιέναι inf. of εἰσέρχομαι/εἴσειμι F

εἰσιών οὖσα όν (-οντ-) aor. part. of εἰσέρχομαι/
    εἴσειμι

εἴσομαι fut. of οἶδα

εἰσοράω (εἰσιδ-) behold, look at [20E]

εἰσπεσ- aor. stem of εἰσπίπτω

εἰσπίπτω (εἰσπεσ-) fall into, on [15B]

εἰσφέρω (εἰσενεγκ-) bring, carry in [5A]

εἶτα then, next [6C]

εἴτε … εἴτε whether ... or [12B]

εἶχον impf. of ἔχω

ἐκ (+ gen.) out of [1G]

ἕκαστος η ον each [14B]

ἑκάτερος ᾱ ον each/both (of two)

ἐκβαλ- aor. stem of ἐκβάλλω

ἐκβάλλω (ἐκβαλ-) throw out [6A]; divorce
    [13A]; break down, break open [17A]

ἐκβληθείς εἶσα ἕν (-εντ-) aor. part. pass. of
    ἐκβάλλω

ἐκδέχομαι receive in turn [7F]

ἐκδίδωμι (ἐκδο-) give in marriage [13A]

ἐκδο- aor. stem of ἐκδίδωμι

ἐκδύομαι undress [10E]

ἐκεῖ there [16G]

ἐκεῖνος η ο that, (s)he [3C-E]

ἐκεινοσί that there (pointing)

ἐκεῖσε there, (to) there [8A]

ἐκκλησίᾱ, ἡ assembly, ekklesia (1b) [8B]

ἐκπέμπω send out, divorce [13B]

ἐκπεσ – aor. stem of ἐκπίπτω

ἐκπίπτω (ἐκπεσ-) be thrown out, divorced
    [13A]

ἐκπορίζω supply, provide [18B]

††ἐκτίνω (ἐκτεισ-) pay [17C]

ἐκτρέχω (ἐκδραμ-) run out [9G]

ἐκφέρω (ἐξενεγκ-) carry out; (often: carry out for burial) [9F]

ἐκφεύγω (ἐκφυγ-) escape [9E]

ἐκφορέω carry off [17C]

ἐκφυγ- aor. stem of ἐκφεύγω

ἑκών οὖσα όν (ἑκοντ-) willing(ly) [13C]

ἔλαβον aor. of λαμβάνω

ἔλαθον aor. of λανθάνω

ἐλάττων ἔλᾶττον (ἐλᾶττον-) smaller; fewer; less [13I]

ἔλαχον aor. of λαγχάνω

ἔλεγχος, ὁ examination, refutation (2a) [14E]

ἐλέγχω refute, argue against [14C]

ἑλ- aor. stem of αἱρέω/ομαι

ἐλευθερίᾶ, ἡ freedom (1b) [2]

ἐλεύθερος ᾶ ον free [2D]

ἐλευθερόω set free [2]

ἐλήλυθα perf. of ἔρχομαι [14A]

ἐλήφθην aor. pass. of λαμβάνω

ἐλθέ come! (s.) [1A-G]

ἐλθ- aor. stem of ἔρχομαι

ἔλιπον aor. of λείπω

Ἑλλάς (Ἑλλαδ-), ἡ Greece (3a) [14A]

Ἕλλην (Ἑλλην-), ὁ Greek (3a) [1J]

†ἐλπίζω hope, expect (+ fut. inf.) [9I]

ἐλπίς (ἐλπιδ-), ἡ hope, expectation (3a) [12I]

ἔμαθον aor. of μανθάνω

ἐμαυτόν ήν myself [6D]

ἐμβαίνω (ἐμβα-) embark [3E]

ἔμεινα aor. of μένω

ἐμεωυτόν = ἐμαυτόν [19B]

ἔμμεναι = εἶναι [20F]

ἐμός ή όν my, mine [2C]

ἔμπειρος ον skilled, experienced [1I]

ἐμπεσ- aor. stem of ἐμπίπτω

ἐμπίπτω (ἐμπεσ-) (ἐν) (εἰς) fall into, on, upon [7F]

ἐμπόριον, τό market-hall, trading-post (2b)

ἐμφανής ές open, obvious [13E]

ἐν (+ dat.) in, on, among [1G]; (+ gen.) in the house of [19B]

  ἐν τούτῳ meanwhile [8A]

ἑν- stem of εἷς one

ἐναντίον (+ gen.) opposite, in front of [8C]

ἔνδον inside [5D]

ἐνεγκ- aor. stem of φέρω

ἔνειμι be in [5B]

ἕνεκα (+ gen.) because, for the sake of (usually follows its noun) [9G]

ἐνέπεσον aor. of ἐμπίπτω

ἐνέχυρον, τό security, pledge (2b) [16F]

ἔνθα there [15B]; where [19F]

ἐνθάδε here [9F]

ἐνθῡμέομαι take to heart, be angry at [16H]

ἑνί = ἑν [20B]

ἐνταῦθα here, at this point [9D]

ἐντεῦθεν from then, from there [7B]

ἐντίθημι (ἐνθε-) place in, put in [17B]

ἐντυγχάνω (ἐντυχ-) meet with, come upon (+ dat.) [9A-E] [12A]

ἐξ = ἐκ

ἐξάγω (ἐξαγαγ-) lead, bring out [9E]

ἐξαίφνης suddenly [10B]

ἐξαπατάω deceive, trick [9J]

ἐξέβαλον aor. ἐκβάλλω

ἐξεδόθην aor. pass. of ἐκδίδωμι

ἐξέδωκα aor. act. of ἐκδίδωμι

ἐξελέγχω convict, refute, expose [13A]

ἐξελθ- aor. stem of ἐξέρχομαι

ἐξέρχομαι (ἐξελθ-) go out, come out [9C]

ἔξεστι it is possible for x (dat.) to – (inf.) [9F]

ἐξετάζω question closely [7C]

ἐξευρ- aor. stem of ἐξευρίσκω

ἐξευρίσκω (ἐξευρ-) find out [6C]

ἐξῆλθον aor. of ἐξέρχομαι

ἐξήνεγκα 1st. aor. of ἐκφέρω

ἐξιέναι inf. of ἐξέρχομαι/ἔξειμι

ἐξόν it being permitted, possible [16C]

ἔξω (+ gen.) outside [16A]

ἔοικα seem; resemble (+ dat.)

ἔοικε it seems, is reasonable [16A]; it is right for (+ dat.) [14F]; [20B]

ἐπαγγέλλω (ἐπαγγειλα-) order [17D]

ἔπαθον aor. of πάσχω

††ἐπαινέω (ἐπαινεσα-) praise, agree [7F]

ἐπανελθ- aor. stem of ἐπανέρχομαι

ἐπανέρχομαι (ἐπανελθ-) return [7H]

ἐπανῆλθον aor. of ἐπανέρχομαι

ἐπεί since [8C]; when [9C]

ἐπειδάν (+ subj.) when(ever) [14C]

ἐπειδή when [2D]; since, because [3C]

ἐπεισέρχομαι (ἐπεισελθ-) attack [17A]

ἔπειτα then, next [1A]

ἐπείτε when, since [19B]

ἐπέρχομαι (ἐπελθ-) go against, attack [2]

ἐπέσχον *aor. of* ἐπέχω

ἐπέχω (ἐπισχ-) hold on, restrain, check [16B]

ἐπί (+ acc.) against, at, to [2D]; (+ gen.) on [8C]; in the time of [19D]; (+ dat.) at, near, on [16F]; for the purpose of [14A]

ἐπιδείκνῡμι (ἐπιδειξα-) prove, show, demonstrate [13C]

ἐπιδημέω come to town, be in town [12I]

ἐπιεικής ἐς reasonable, moderate, fair [16G]

ἐπιθόμην *aor. of* πείθομαι

ἐπιθῡμέω desire, yearn for (+ gen.) [16B]

ἐπικαλέομαι call upon (to witness) [4D]

ἐπιλανθάνομαι (ἐπιλαθ-) forget (+ gen.) [12G]

ἐπιμέλεια, ἡ concern, care (1b) [14E]

ἐπιμελέομαι care for (+ gen.) [13B]

ἐπιμελής ἐς careful [14B]

ἐπισκοπέομαι (ἐπισκεψα-) review [18A]

†ἐπίσταμαι know how to (+ inf.); understand [9J]

ἐπισχ- *aor. stem* ἐπέχω

ἐπιτήδειος ᾱ ον suitable, useful for [16B]

ἐπιχειρέω undertake, set to work [18D]

†ἕπομαι (σπ-) follow (+ dat.) [7G]

ἔπος, τό word (3c) (uncontr. pl. ἔπεα) [19C]

ἐρ- *see* ἐρωτάω *or* ἐρέω

†ἐργάζομαι work, perform [12I]

ἔργον, τό task, job (2b) [1I]

ἐρέω *fut. of* λέγω

ἔρημος ον empty, deserted, devoid of [13B]

†ἔρχομαι (ἐλθ-) go, come [2]

†ἐρωτάω (ἐρ-) ask [3A]

ἐς = εἰς [20B]

ἐσθής (ἐσθητ-), ἡ clothing (3a) [18D]

†ἐσθίω (φαγ-) eat [9F]

ἐσθλός ή όν fine, noble, good [15C]

ἔσομαι *fut. of* εἰμί (be) (3rd s. ἔσται) [12Ι]

ἑσπόμην *aor. of* ἕπομαι [7G]

ἔσσι – εἶ you (s.) are [20E]

ἔσται 3rd s. *fut. of* εἰμί (be)

ἔσταν they stopped (3rd pl. *aor. of* ἵσταμαι)

ἐστερημένος η ον *perf. part. pass. of* στερέω [19B]

ἑστηκώς υῖα ός (-οτ-) standing (*perf. part. of* ἵσταμαι)

ἔσχατος η ον worst, furthest, last [12D]

ἔσχον *aor. of* ἔχω

ἑταίρᾱ, ἡ prostitute, courtesan (1b) [12F]

ἑταῖρος, ὁ male companion (2a) [12F]

ἕτερος ᾱ ον one (or the other) of two [6D]

ἕτερος … ἕτερον one … another [12A]

ἔτι still, yet [3D]

ἔτι καὶ νῦν even now, still now [4A]

ἕτοιμος η ον ready (to) (+ inf.) [8C]

ἔτος, τό year (3c) [17D]

ἐτραπόμην *aor. of* τρέπομαι

ἔτυχον *aor. of* τυγχάνω

εὖ well [3B]

εὖ ποιέω treat well, do good to [12C]

εὖ πρᾱττω fare well, be prosperous [19E]

εὐδαίμων εὔδαιμον (εὐδαιμον-) happy, rich, blessed by the gods [8B]

εὐθύς at once, straightaway [7F]; straight towards (+ gen.) [16A]

εὔνοια, ἡ good will (1b) [12B]

εὔνους ουν well-disposed [11B]

εὐπλόκαμος ον with pretty hair [20F]

εὐπορίᾱ, ἡ abundance, means (1b) [18C]

εὐπρεπής ἐς seemly, proper, becoming [15A]

εὑρ- *aor. stem of* εὑρίσκω

εὕρηκα *perf. of* εὑρίσκω

†εὑρίσκω (εὑρ-) find, come upon [7C]

εὐρύς εῖα ύ broad, wide [20G]

εὐσεβέω act righteously [13I]

εὐτυχής ἐς fortunate, lucky [15B]

εὔφρων εὔφρον well-disposed [4A-B]

εὐχή, ἡ prayer (1a) [3E]

εὔχομαι pray [3E]

ἐφ' = ἐπί

ἐφάνην *aor. of* φαίνομαι

ἔφην *impf. of* φημί

ἐφοπλίζω equip, get ready [20B]

ἔφῡν be naturally (*aor. of* φύομαι)

ἔχθρᾱ, ἡ enmity, hostility (1b) [12C]

ἐχθρός, ὁ enemy (2a)

ἐχθρός ᾱ όν hostile, enemy [12C]

†ἔχω (σχ-) have, hold [1A-G]; (+ adv.) be in X [adv.] condition [13B]

ἐν νῷ ἔχω have in mind, intend

ἐών = ὤν being [19B]

ἑώρᾱ 3rd s. *impf. of* ὁράω

ἕως, ἡ dawn [20B]

ἕως (+ ἄν + subj.) until [16G]; until, while (+ ind.); (+ opt.) until [17A]

ἑωυτόν = ἑαυτόν [19B]

Z

Ζεύς (Δι-), ὁ Zeus (3a) **[3C-E]**

ζημίᾱ, ἡ fine(1b) **[13A]**

ζημιόω fine, penalise, punish **[16F]**

ζητέω look for, seek **[3D]**

ζῷον, τό animal, creature, living thing (2b) **[18B]**

H

ἤ – augment (if not under ἤ – look under ἀ – or ἐ -)

ἤ or **[1J]**; than **[7A]**

ἦ 1st s. past of εἰμί (be)

ἤ or **[20E]**

ἦ δ' ὅς he said **[7D]**

ᾖα impf. of ἔρχομαι/εἶμι

ἡγεμών (ἡγεμον-), ὁ leader (3a) **[8A]**

ἡγέομαι lead (+ dat.) **[8C]**; think, consider **[8A]**

ἠδέ and **[20F]**

ᾔδει 3rd s. past of οἶδα

ᾔδεσαν 3rd pl. past οἶδα

ἡδέως with pleasure, sweetly **[2A]**

ἤδη by now, now, already **[2A]**

ἤδη past of οἶδα

ἥδιστος most pleasant (sup. of ἡδύς) **[11C]**

†ἥδομαι enjoy, be pleased with (+ dat.) **[7D]**

ἡδονή, ἡ pleasure (1a) **[8C]**

ἡδύς εῖα ύ sweet, pleasant (sup. ἥδιστος) **[5A]**

ἥκιστα least of all, no, not **[16H]**

ἥκω come, have come **[11A]**

ἦλθον aor. of ἔρχομαι/εἶμι

ἥλιος, ὁ sun (2a) **[6C]**

ἦμαρ (ἡματ-), τό day (3b) **[20E]**

ἡμεῖς we **[1C]**

ἦμεν 1st pl. past of εἰμί

ἡμέρᾱ, ἡ day (1b) **[9A-E]**

ἡμέτερος ᾱ ον our **[1G]**

ἡμίονος, ὁ mule (2a) **[9E]**

ἦν 3rd s. past of εἰμί

ἦν δ' ἐγώ I said **[7D]**

ἤνεγκον aor. of φέρω

ἠπιστάμην impf. of ἐπίσταμαι **[13A]**

Ἡρακλῆς, ὁ Herakles (3d uncontr.) **[8C]**

ἠρόμην aor. of ἐρωτάω

ἦσαν 3rd pl. past of εἰμί

ἦσθα 2nd s. past of εἰμί

ᾐσθόμην aor. of αἰσθάνομαι

ἡσυχάζω be quiet, keep quiet **[2C]**

ἡσυχίᾱ, ἡ quiet, peace (1b) **[2]**

ἥσυχος η ον quiet, peaceful **[9B]**

ἦτε 2nd pl. past of εἰμί or 2nd pl. subj. of εἰμί

ἥττων ἧττον (ἡττον-) lesser, weaker **[6D]**

ηὗρον aor. of εὑρίσκω

ἠώς, ἡ (= ἕως, ἡ) dawn (acc. ἠῶ; gen. ἠοῦς; dat. ἠοῖ) **[20B]**

Θ

θάλαμος, ὁ bedchamber (2a) **[15B]**

θάλαττα, ἡ sea (1c) **[1A-G]**

θαν- aor. stem of θνῄσκω

θάνατος, ὁ death (2a) **[9I]**

θαυμάζω wonder at **[6B]**

θε- aor. stem of τίθημι

θεᾱ̄, ἡ goddess (1b) **[2]**

θεάομαι watch, gaze at **[3B]**

θεᾱτής, ὁ spectator, (pl.) audience (1d) **[9A]**

θεῖος ᾱ ον divine **[18D]**

θεῖτο 3rd s. aor. opt. of τίθεμαι

θέμενος η ον aor. part. of τίθεμαι

θεός, ὁ ἡ god (2a) **[4B]**

θεράπαινα, ἡ maidservant (1c) **[17A]**

θεραπεύω look after, tend **[13C]**

θεράπων (θεραποντ-), ὁ servant (3a) **[17B]**

θές place! set! put! (aor. imper. [s.] of τίθημι)

θέσθαι aor. inf. of τίθεμαι

θέω run **[19F]**

θῆκε(ν) 3rd s. aor. of τίθημι (no augment)

θηρίον, τό beast (2b) **[18D]**

θήσεσθε 2nd pl. fut. of τίθεμαι

†θνῄσκω (θαν-) die **[15A]**

θνητός ή όν mortal **[4B]**

θορυβέω make a disturbance, din **[11A]**

θόρυβος, ὁ noise, din, clamour, hustle and bustle (2a) **[3B]**

θυγάτηρ (θυγατ[ε]ρ-), ἡ daughter (3a) **[12D]**

θῡμός, ὁ heart; anger (2a) **[20C]**

θύρᾱ, ἡ door (1b) **[3D]**

θυσίᾱ, ἡ sacrifice (1b) **[3E]**

θύω sacrifice **[3E]**

θώμεθα 1st pl. aor. subj. of τίθεμαι

θωπεύω flatter

I

ἰᾱτρικός ή όν medical, of healing **[18E]**

ἰᾱτρός, ὁ doctor (2a) **[17D]**

ἰδ- aor. stem of ὁράω

ἰδιώτης, ὁ layman, private citizen (1d) **[18E]**

ἴδον *1st s. aor. of* ὁράω (*no augment*)

ἰδού look! here! hey! **[3A]**

ἰέναι *inf. of* ἔρχομαι/εἶμι

ἱερά, τά rites, sacrifices (2b) **[13E]**

ἱερόν, τό sanctuary (2b) **[4C]**

ἴθι *imper. s. of* ἔρχομαι/εἶμι

ἱκανός ή όν sufficient; able to (+ inf.) **[18B]**; capable of (+ inf.) **[14D]**

ἱκάνω come, come to/upon (+ acc.) **[20D]**

ἱκετεύω beg, supplicate **[13F]**

ἱκέτης, ὁ suppliant (1d) **[4C]**

†ἱκνέομαι (ῐκ-) come to, arrive at **[20E]**

ἱκόμην *aor. of* ἱκνέομαι

ἱμάτιον, τό cloak (2b) **[12A]**

ἴμεν = ἰέναι **[20D]**

ἵνα (+ subj./opt.) in order to/that **[16D]**; (+ indic.) where

ἵππος, ὁ horse (2a) **[5A]**

ἴσᾱσι(ν) *3rd pl. of* οἶδα

ἴσμεν *1st pl. of* οἶδα

ἴστε *2nd pl. of* οἶδα†

†ἵστημι (στησ-) set up, raise

ἵσταμαι (στα-) stand **[15A]**

ἰσχυρός ά όν strong, powerful **[13H]**

ἴσως perhaps **[7A]**

ἴω *subj. of* ἔρχομαι/εἶμι

ἰών ἰοῦσα ἰόν (ἰοντ-) *part. of* ἔρχομαι/εἶμι

K

κάδ = κατά **[20G]**

καθαίρω (καθηρα-) cleanse, purify **[19F]**

καθέστηκα I have been put (*perf. of* καθίσταμαι) **[13H]**

καθεστώς ῶσα ός (καθεστωτ-) having been made (*perf. part. of* καθίσταμαι)

καθεύδω sleep **[3D]**

††κάθημαι be seated **[16B]**

καθίζομαι sit down **[9C]**

καθίζω sit down **[9C]**

καθίσταμαι (καταστα-) be placed, put, made **[12D]**

καθίστημι (καταστησα-) set up, make, place, put X (acc.) in (εἰς) Y **[12D]**

καθοράω (κατιδ-) see, look down on **[8A]**

*κ*αί and **[1A]**; also **[1B]**, even

τε ... *καί* both A and B

*καὶ γάρ in fact; yes, certainly **[12C]**

*καὶ δή and really; as a matter of fact; look! let us suppose **[13A]**

*καὶ δὴ καί moreover **[5D]**

*καὶ μήν what's more; look! **[12B]**; yes, and; and anyway

καίπερ although, despite (+ part.) **[6A]**

*καίτοι and yet **[10D]**

κακοδαίμων κακόδαιμον (κακοδαιμον-) unlucky, dogged by an evil daimon **[4A-B]**

κακός ή όν bad, evil, cowardly, mean, lowly **[1G]**
    κακὰ (κακῶς) ποιέω treat badly, do harm to **[5B]**

κακῶς badly, evilly **[1E-F]**

καλεσα- *aor. stem of* καλέω

†καλέω (καλεσα-) call, summon **[3D]**

κάλλιστος η ον most (very) fine, good, beautiful **[2C]**

καλός ή όν beautiful, good **[1A-B]**

καλῶς well, finely, beautifully **[1E-F]**

κάρη (καρητ-), τό head (Attic κάρᾱ [κρατ-], τό [3b]) **[20G]**

κατά (+ acc.) in, on, by, according to **[3C]**; down, throughout, in relation to **[12B]**; (+ gen.) below **[15A]**; down from, against **[20G]**

καταβαίνω (καταβα-) go down, come down **[1C-D]**

καταδικάζω condemn; convict X (gen.) of Y (acc.) **[9I]**

καταδίκη, ἡ fine (1a) **[16H]**

καταθε- *aor. stem of* κατατίθημι

καταθνῄσκω (καταθαν-) die away **[15A]**

κατακλίνομαι lie down **[10D]**

καταλαβ- *aor. stem of* καταλαμβάνω

καταλαμβάνω (καταλαβ-) overtake, come across, seize **[7H]**

καταλέγω (κατειπ-) recite, list **[12G]**

καταλείπω (καταλιπ) leave behind, bequeath **[14A]**

καταλήψομαι *fut. of* καταλαμβάνω

καταλύω bring to an end, finish **[10A]**

καταμαρτυρέω give evidence against (gen.) **[13D]**

καταστάς ᾶσα άν (κατασταντ-) being placed, put (*aor. part. of* καθίσταμαι)

καταστῆναι to be put (*aor. inf. of* καθίσταμαι)

καταστήσομαι *fut. of* καθίσταμαι

κατατίθημι (καταθε-) put down, pay, perform [12I]

καταφέρω (κατενεγκ-) carry down [17C]

καταφρονέω despise, look down on (+ gen.) [12E]

κατεγγυάω demand securities from (+ acc.) [13A]

κατέλαβον *aor. of* καταλαμβάνω

κατέλιπον *aor. of* καταλείπω

κατέστην I was put (*aor. of* καθίσταμαι)

κατέστησα I put (*aor. of* καθίστημι)

κατηγορέω prosecute X (gen.) on charge of Y (acc.) [9H]

κατηγορίᾱ, ἡ speech for the prosecution (1b) [9H]

κατήγορος, ὁ prosecutor (2a) [12B]

κατθανών *aor. part. of* καταθνήσκω

κατιδ- *aor. stem of* καθοράω

κάτω below [11A]

κε (κεν) = ἄν (*enclitic*) [20A]

†κεῖμαι lie, be placed, be made [17B]

κεῖνος η ο = ἐκεῖνος [20E]

κέλευσαν *3rd pl. aor. of* κελεύω (*no augment*)

κέλευσε *3rd s. aor. of* κελεύω (*no augment*)

κελευστής, ὁ boatswain (1d) [3D]

κελεύω order [3E]

κεν = κε [20A]

κεφαλή, ἡ head (1a) [6A]

κῆρυξ (κηρυκ-), ὁ herald (3a) [4D]

κηρῡ́ττω announce, proclaim [11A]

κινδῡνεύω be in danger, run a risk; be likely to (+ inf.) [17C]

κίνδῡνος, ὁ danger (2a) [3A]

κλαίω (κλαυσ-) weep [15C]

κλείω close, shut [17A]

κλέπτης, ὁ thief (1d) [9I]

κλέπτω steal [6D]

κληθείς εἶσα ἐν (κληθεντ-) *aor. part. pass. of* καλέω

κλοπή, ἡ theft (1a) [18C]

κλύον *3rd pl. aor. of* κλύω (no augment)

κλῦτε *2nd pl. imper. of* κλύω

κλύω hear [15A]

κοινός ή όν common, shared [16D]

κοῖος = ποῖος

κολάζω punish [5B]

κομίζομαι collect [16D]

κόπτω knock (on); cut [5D]

κόραξ (κορακ-), ὁ crow (3a)

βάλλ' εἰς κόρακας go to hell!

κόρη, ἡ maiden, girl, daughter (1a) [13A]

κόσμος, ὁ decoration, ornament; order; universe (2a) [15A]

κοτε = ποτε

κου = που [19F]

κούρη, ἡ = κόρη, ἡ girl, daughter (1a) [20A]

κρατέω hold sway, power over (+ gen.) [4A]

κρείττων κρεῖττον (κρειττον-) stronger, greater [6D]

κρῑ́νω (κρῑνα-) judge, decide [13F]

κρίσις, ἡ judgment, decision; dispute; trial (3e) [16F]

κτάομαι acquire, get, gain [15B]

κτείνω (κτεινα-) kill [18E]

κτῆμα (κτηματ-), τό possession (3b) [7H]

κυβερνήτης, ὁ captain, helmsman (1d) [1G]

κῡ́ριος ᾱ ον able, with power, sovereign, by right [14A]

κύων (κυν-), ὁ dog (3a) [9H]

κωλῡ́ω prevent, stop [4B]

κως = πως

Λ

λαβ- *aor. stem of* λαμβάνω

λαγχάνω (λαχ-) obtain by lot; run as a candidate for office [13C]
   δίκην λαγχάνω bring suit against

λαθ- *aor. stem of* λανθάνω

Λακεδαιμόνιος, ὁ Spartan (2a) [3C]

λαμβάνομαι (λαβ-) take hold of (+ gen.) [8C]

λαμβάνω (λαβ-) take, capture [3C]
   δίκην λαμβάνω punish, exact one's due from (παρά + gen.)

λαμπάς (λαμπαδ-), ἡ torch (3a) [3A-B]

λανθάνω (λαθ-) escape notice of x (acc.) –ing (nom. part.) [4D]

λᾱός, ὁ people, inhabitant (2a) [20F]

λαχ- *aor. stem of* λαγχάνω

λέγω (εἰπ-) speak, say, tell, mean [1A-G]

λείπω (λιπ-) leave, abandon [13C]

λέληθε *3rd s. perf. of* λανθάνω

λέμβος, ὁ boat, life-boat (2a) [1G]

ληφθ- *aor. pass. stem of* λαμβάνω

λήψομαι *fut. of* λαμβάνω

λίθος, ὁ stone (2a) [11C]

λιμήν (λιμεν-), ὁ harbour (3a) [3A-B]

λίσσομαι beseech **[20D]**

λογίζομαι calculate, reckon, consider **[7B]**

λογισμός, ὁ calculation (2a) **[13B]**

λόγος, ὁ story, tale **[2C]**; speech, word **[3C]**; reason, argument **[5D]** (2a)

λοιπός ή όν left, remaining **[17B]**

λούω wash (mid. wash oneself) **[20F]**

λύω release **[6A]**

M

μά by! (+ acc.) **[4C]**

μαθ- *aor. stem of* μανθάνω

μαθήσομαι *fut. of* μανθάνω

μαθητής, ὁ student (1d) **[5D]**

μακρός ᾱ όν large, big, long **[15A]**

μάλα very, quite, virtually **[16H]**

μάλιστα (μάλα) especially, particularly; yes **[4B]**

μᾶλλον (μάλα) ... ἤ more, rather than **[13I]**

μανθάνω (μαθ-) learn, understand **[3C]**

μαρτυρέω give evidence, bear witness **[13D]**

μαρτυρίᾱ, ἡ evidence, testimony (1b) **[12G]**

μαρτύρομαι invoke, call to witness **[19F]**

μάρτυς (μαρτυρ-), ὁ witness (3a) **[9H]**

μάχη, ἡ fight, battle (1a) **[7G]**

μάχομαι (μαχεσ-) fight **[2]**

μεγάλοιο *gen. s. m. of* μέγας

μέγας μεγάλη μέγα (μεγαλ-) great, big **[3C-E]**

μέγεθος, τό size (3c) **[20E]**

μέγιστος η ον greatest (sup. of μέγας) **[8B]**

μέθες *2nd s. aor. imper. of* μεθίημι

μεθίημι (μεθε-) allow, let go **[19D]**

μείζων μεῖζον (μειζον-) greater (comp. of μέγας) **[8B]**

μέλᾱς αινα αν (μελαν-) black **[9D]**

μέλει x (dat.) is concerned about (+ gen.) **[14C]**

μέλλω be about to (+ fut. inf.); hesitate; intend (+ pres. inf.) **[9J]**

μέμφομαι blame, criticise, find fault with (+ acc. or dat.) **[10D]**

*μέν ... δέ on one hand ... on the other **[1E]**

*μέντοι however, but **[7G]**

μένω (μεινα-) remain, wait for **[1C-D]**

μέρος, τό share, part (3c) **[9H]**

μετά (+ acc.) after **[7H]**; (+ gen.) with **[8C]**; (+ dat.) among, in company with **[20B]**

μεταυδάω speak to **[20G]**

μετελθ- *aor. stem of* μετέρχομαι **[20G]**

μετέρχομαι (μετελθ-) send for, chase after **[16F]**; go among (+ dat.); attack (+ dat. or μετά + acc.) **[20G]**

μετέχω share in (+ gen.) **[14B]**

μετίημι = μεθίημι **[19D]**

μέτριος ᾱ ον moderate, reasonable, fair **[16F]**

μή (+ imper.) don't! **[1C]**; not **[7C]**; (+ aor. subj.) don't! **[16B]**

μηδαμῶς not at all, in no way **[10D]**

*μηδέ ... μηδέ neither ... nor **[12A]**

μηδείς μηδεμία μηδέν (μηδεν-) no, no one **[10E]**

μηκέτι no longer **[9E]**

*μήτε ... μήτε neither ... nor **[11B]**

μήτηρ (μητ(ε)ρ-), ἡ mother (3a) **[10D]**

μηχανάομαι devise, contrive **[18A]**

μηχανή, ἡ device, plan (1a) **[10A]**

μιαρός ᾱ όν foul, polluted **[9E]**

μῑκρός ᾱ όν small, short, little **[12F]**

†μιμνήσκομαι (μνησθ-) remember, mention **[17D]**

μιν him, her (acc.) (*enclitic*) **[19A]**

μισέω hate **[4D]**

μισθός, ὁ pay (2a) **[14A]**

μῖσος, τό hatred (3c) **[13B]**

μνᾶ, ἡ mina (100 drachmas) (1b) **[13A]**

μνείᾱ, ἡ mention (1b) **[12G]**

μνημονεύω remember **[12G]**

μνησθ- *aor. stem of* μιμνήσκομαι

μόνος η ον alone **[8C]**

μόνον only, merely

οὐ μόνον ... ἀλλὰ καί not only ... but also

μῦθος, ὁ word, story (2a) **[20B]**

μῶν surely not? **[8B]**

μῶρος ᾱ ον stupid, foolish **[11]**

N

ναί yes **[1I]**

ναυμαχίᾱ, ἡ naval battle (1b) **[2]**

ναῦς, ἡ ship (3 irr.) **[1J]**; **[3C-E]**

ναύτης, ὁ sailor (1d) **[1A-B]**

ναυτικός ή όν naval **[3C]**

νεᾱνίᾱς, ὁ young man (1d) **[5B]**

νεᾱνίσκος, ὁ young man (2a) **[7D]**

νεηνίης, ὁ = νεᾱνίᾱς, ὁ **[19C]**

νειμα- *aor. stem of* νέμω

νεκρός, ὁ corpse (2a) **[4B]**

†νέμω (νειμα-) distribute, allot, assign **[18A]**

νέος ᾱ ον young [5B]
νεώριον, τό dockyard [1A-B]
νή by! (+ acc.) [4A]
νῆσος, ἡ island (2a) [3A]
'νθρωπε = ἄνθρωπε
νῑκάω win, defeat [2B]
νῑκη, ἡ victory, conquest (1a) [2]
νοέω plan, devise [20C]; think, mean, intend,
   notice [7B]
νομή, ἡ distribution (1a) [18C]
νομίζομαι be accustomed [19B]
†νομίζω acknowledge, think x (acc.) to be y
   (acc. or acc. + inf.) [7G]
νόμος, ὁ law, convention (2a) [4B]
νοσέω be sick [13C]
νόσος, ἡ illness, plague, disease (2a) [4B]
νοῦς, ὁ (νόος, contr.) mind, sense (2a) [5C]
   ἐν νῷ ἔχω have in mind, intend [6A]
νυ = νυν [20C]
νυν now, then (enclitic) [8C]
νῦν now [1G]
νύξ (νυκτ-), ἡ night (3a) [3A-B]

Ξ

ξεῖνος = ξένος
ξένη, ἡ foreign woman (1a)
ξένος, ὁ foreigner, guest, host (2a) [4C]

O

ὁ ἡ τό the [1A-B]; in Ionic = he, she, it [20D]
ὁ αὐτός the same
*ὁ δέ and/but he [11C]
*ὁ μέν... ὁ δέ one... another [8C]
ὅ τι; what? (sometimes in reply to τί;) [9F]
ὅδε ἥδε τόδε this [9J]
ὁδί this here (pointing)
ὁδοιπόρος, ὁ traveller (2a) [11B]
ὁδός, ἡ road, way (2a) [11B]
ὅθεν from where [5C-D]; [16C]
οἱ = αὐτῷ to him, her (dat.) (Ionic) [19A]
οἷ (to) where [5C-D] [13E]
†οἶδα know [1J]
   χάριν οἶδα be grateful to (+ dat.)
οἴκαδε homewards [3B]
οἶκε = ἔοικε resemble, be like (+ dat.) [19D]
οἰκεῖος, ὁ relative (2a) [13B]
οἰκεῖος ᾱ ον related, domestic, family [13B]

οἰκέτης, ὁ house-slave (1d) [5B]
οἰκέω dwell (in), live [7H]
οἴκημα (οἰκηματ-), τό dwelling (3b) [18C]
οἴκησις, ἡ dwelling (3e) [4A-B]
οἰκίᾱ, ἡ house (1b) [3B]
οἰκία, τά palace (2b) [19F]
οἰκίδιον, τό small house (2b) [12I]
οἴκοι at home [3D]
οἴκόνδε home, homewards [20E]
οἶκος, ὁ household, house (2a) [15C]
οἰκός = εἰκός reasonable [19F]
οἰκτῑρω (οἰκτῑρα-) pity [8B]
†οἶμαι think [7C]
οἴμοι alas! oh dear! [1F]
οἷος ᾱ ον what a! what sort of a! [10C]
   οἷός τ' εἰμί be able to (+ inf.) [12D]
οἴχομαι be off, depart [17B]
ὁκόθεν = ὁπόθεν [19B]
ὀλ- aor. stem of ὄλλῡμαι
ὀλεσα- aor. stem of ὄλλῡμι
ὀλίγος η ον small, few [4A]
ὀλίγωρος ον contemptuous [14B]
ὄλλῡμαι (aor. ὠλόμην) be killed, die, perish
   [11B]
†ὄλλῡμι (ὀλεσα-) destroy, kill [11B]
ὅλος η ον whole of [5A]
ὀλοφῡρομαι lament [4D]
†ὄμνῡμι (ὀμοσα-) swear [13C]
ὅμοιος ᾱ ον like, similar to (+ dat.) [9E]
ὁμολογέω agree [7E]
ὁμόνοια, ἡ agreement, harmony (1b) [2]
ὅμως nevertheless, however [9F]
ὄνειρος, ὁ dream (2a) [19A]
ὄνομα (ὀνοματ-), τό name (3b) [9B]
ὀξύς εῖα ύ sharp, bitter, shrill [11C]
ὅπλα, τά weapons, arms (2b) [3B]
ὁπόθεν from where [5C-D]; [19B]
ὅποι to where [5C-D]
ὁποῖος ᾱ ον of what kind [13E]
ὁπόσος η ον how many, how great [6C]
ὁπόταν whenever (+ subj.) [16D]
ὁπότε when [5C-D]; whenever (+ opt.) [16E]
ὅπου where [5C-D, 6B]
ὅπως how (answer to πῶς;) [11A]; how (indir. q.)
   [5C-D]
   (+ fut. ind.) see to it that [12G]
   (+ subj. or opt.) = ἵνα in order to/that [18B]

†ὁράω (ἰδ -) see [1E-F]
ὀργή, ἡ anger (1a) [13B]
ὀργίζομαι grow angry with (+ dat.) [12H]
ὄρεος = ὄρους, gen. of ὄρος, τό
ὀρθός ή όν straight, correct, right [4C]
ὅρκος, ὁ oath (2a) [12B]
ὁρμάομαι charge, set off [17A]
ὄρος, τό mountain (3c) [19F]
ὅς ἥ ὅ who, what, which [10E]
ὅσος η ον how great! [2B]; as much/many as [11B]
ὅσπερ ἥπερ ὅπερ who/which indeed [10E]
ὅστις ἥτις ὅτι (ὅπ) who(ever), which(ever) [10E]
ὅταν (+ subj.) whenever [14E]
ὅτε when [5C-D, 6A]
ὅτι that [1H]; because [9J]
οὐ (οὐκ, οὐχ) no, not [1C]
οὐ μόνον … ἀλλὰ καί not only … but also [12C]
οὗ where (at) [16D]
οὐδαμῶς in no way, not at all [10A]
οὐδέ and not, not even [3C]
οὐδέν nothing [1D]
οὐδείς οὐδεμία οὐδέν (οὐδεν-) no, no one, nothing [4A-B]
οὐδέποτε never [5C]
οὐδέπω not yet [5A]
οὐκ = οὐ no, not
οὐκέτι no longer [2D]
*οὐκοῦν therefore [7E]
*οὔκουν not… therefore [7E]
*οὖν therefore [1D]
οὔνομα = ὄνομα, τό [19B]
οὗπερ where [17A]
οὔποτε never [15C]
οὔπω not yet [5A]
οὐρανός, ὁ sky, heavens (2a) [6B]
οὐσίᾱ, ἡ property, wealth (1b) [16D]
*οὔτε … οὔτε neither . .. nor [5D]
οὖτις (οὖτιν-) no one [15C]
οὗτος αὕτη τοῦτο this; (s)he, it [3C-E]
    οὗτος hey there! you there! [6D]
οὑτοσί this here (pointing)
οὕτως/οὕτω thus, so; in this way [2D]
οὐχ = οὐ
†ὀφείλω owe [5A]
ὀφθαλμός, ὁ eye (2a) [20E]
ὄφρα (+ subj./opt.) = ἵνα (+ ind./subj./opt.) [20G]; while, until

ὄψις, ἡ vision, sight (3e) [19D]

Π

παθ- aor. stem of πάσχω
πάθος, τό suffering, experience (3c) [8B] ἁ
παιδίον, τό child, slave (2b) [9I]
παιδοποιέομαι beget, have children [12F]
παίζω play, joke at (πρός + acc.) [1H]
παῖς (παιδ-), ὁ, ἡ child; son; boy; slave (3a) [3A-B]
πάλαι long ago [19F]
παλαιός ᾱ όν ancient, of old, old [13B]
πάλιν back, again [7H]
πανταχοῦ everywhere [8B] ἁ
παντελῶς completely, outright [14D]
*πάνυ very (much); at all [6D]
*πάνυ μὲν οὖν certainly, of course [16B]
πανύστατος η ον for the very last time [15A]
πάρα = πάρεστι(ν) [19E]
πάρ = παρά [20G]
παρά (+ acc.) along, beside [2A]; against, to; compared with; except [12D]
    (+ gen.) from [9I]
    (+ dat.) with, beside, in the presence of [10B]
πάρα = πάρεστι it is possible for (+ dat.)
παραγίγνομαι (παραγεν-) be present, turn up at (+ dat.) [17B]
παραδίδωμι (παραδο-) hand over [16C]
παραδώσειν fut. inf. of παραδίδωμι
παραιτέομαι beg [18A]
παράκειμαι lie, be placed beside (+ dat.) [17B]
παραλαβ- aor. stem of παραλαμβάνω
παραλαμβάνω (παραλαβ-) take, receive from [12I]; undertake [19D]
παρασκευάζω prepare, equip [16C]
παρασκευή, ἡ preparation, equipping; force (1a) [11C]
παρασχ- aor. stem of παρέχω
παρεγενόμην aor. of παραγίγνομαι
πάρειμι be at hand, be present (+ dat.) [7B]
παρέλαβον aor. of παραλαμβάνω
παρελθ- aor. stem of παρέρχομαι
παρέρχομαι (παρελθ-) pass, go by, come forward [11A]
πάρεστι it is possible for (+ dat.) [19E]
παρέχω (παρασχ-) give to, provide [9E]
πρᾱγματα παρέχω cause trouble (to) [9E]
παρθένος, ἡ maiden (2a) [20G]

Παρθενών, ὁ the Parthenon (3a) **[1A-B]**

πάριτε *2nd pl. imper. of* παρέρχομαι/πάρειμι

παριών οὖσα όν (-οντ-) *aor. part. of* παρέρχομαι

παροράω (παριδ-) notice **[19D]**

παρών οὖσα όν (παροντ-) *aor. part. of* πάρειμι

πᾶς πᾶσα πᾶν (παντ-) all **[9G]**
   ὁ πᾶς the whole of **[9G]**

†πάσχω (παθ-) suffer, experience **[4D]**

πατήρ (πατ[ε]ρ-), ὁ father (3a) **[5A]**

πατρίς (πατριδ-), ἡ fatherland (3a) **[3A-B]**

πατρῷος ᾱ ον ancestral, of one's father **[15A]**

παύομαι stop, cease (+ part.) **[4D]**; cease from
   (+ gen.) **[10D]**

παύω stop x (acc.) from y (ἐκ + gen.); stop
   X (acc.) doing Y (acc. part.) **[5B]**

πείθομαι (πιθ-) trust, obey **[5B]**; believe **[6B]**
   (+ dat.)

πείθω persuade **[5D]**

πειράομαι (πειρᾱσα-) test, try **[7C]**

πείσομαι *fut. of* πάσχω *or* πείθομαι

†πέμπω send **[8A]**

πένης (πενητ-) poor man (3a); (adj.) poor **[12G]**

πενίᾱ, ἡ poverty (1b) **[12D]**

πεντήκοντα fifty **[17B]**

περί (+ acc.) about, concerning **[1I]**
   (+ gen.) about, around **[8C]**
   (+ dat.) in, on **[20E]**; about **[18E]**

περιφανής ές very clear, obvious **[13D]**

πεσ- *aor. stem of* πίπτω

πέφῡκα tend naturally to (*perf. of* φύομαι)

πηδάω leap, jump **[6C]**

πιθ- *aor. stem of* πείθομαι

†πῑνω (πι-) drink **[17B]**

†πίπτω (πεσ-) fall, die **[2B]**

πιστεύω trust (+ dat.) **[12C]**

πιστός ή όν reliable, trustworthy, faithful **[17A]**

πλεῖστος η ον very much, most (sup. of πολύς)
   [16D]

πλέον more (adv.) (comp. of πολύς) **[16G]**

†πλέω (πλευσα-) sail **[1A-G]**

πλέως ᾱ ων full of (+ gen.) **[8C]**

πλῆθος, τό number, crowd; the people (3c) **[4A-B]**

πλήν (+ gen.) except **[9G]**

πλησίον nearby, (+ gen.) near **[9C]**

πλησίος ᾱ ον near, close to (+ gen.) **[17C]**

πλοῖον, τό vessel, ship (2b) **[1A-B]**

πλούσιος ᾱ ον rich, wealthy **[12G]**

πλΰνω wash **[20B]**

πόθεν; from where? **[3A, 5C-D]**; ποθεν from
   somewhere **[5C-D]**

ποῖ; where to? **[1E]** ; ποι to somewhere **[5C-D]**

ποιέομαι make **[8C]**

ποιέω make, do **[1E-F]**
   κακά (κακῶς) ποιέω treat badly, harm

ποιητής, ὁ poet (1d) **[7B]**

ποιμήν (ποιμεν-), ὁ shepherd (3a) **[17A]**

ποῖος ᾱ ον; what sort of? **[10E]**

πολεμέω make war **[11B]**

πολεμικός ή όν of war, military, martial **[18D]**

πολέμιοι, οἱ the enemy (2a) **[2D]**

πολέμιος ᾱ ον hostile, enemy **[2D]**

πόλεμος, ὁ war (2a) **[2D]**

πόλις, ἡ city, city-state (3e) **[4A-B]**

πολῑτείᾱ, ἡ state, constitution (1b) **[13G]**

πολῑτεύομαι be a citizen **[13G]**

πολίτης, ὁ citizen (1d) **[8A]**

πολῑτικός ή όν political, to do with the πόλις
   [18C]

πολῖτις (πολῑτιδ -), ἡ female citizen (3a) **[14C]**

πολλά many things **[1I]**

πολλάκις many times, often **[7C]**

πολύς πολλή πολύ (πολλ-) much, many **[3C-E]**
   πολύ (adv.) much **[9H]**

πονηρός ά όν wicked, wretched **[9B]**

πόντος, ὁ sea (2a) **[20F]**

πορεύομαι march, journey, go **[3B]**

πορίζω provide, offer **[18B]**

πόρνη, ἡ prostitute (1a) **[14D]**

πόρρω far, afar off **[6C]**

Ποσειδῶν (Ποσειδων-), ὁ Poseidon, god of sea
   (3a) (voc. Πόσειδον; acc. Ποσειδῶ) **[5C]**

πόσις, ὁ husband, spouse (3e) **[15A]**

ποταμοῖο *gen. s. of* ποταμός

ποταμός, ὁ river (2a) **[7H]**

ποτε once, ever (*enclitic*) **[5C-D, 7B]**

πότε when? **[5C-D]**

πότερον … ἤ whether … or **[2C]**

πότερος ᾱ ον; which (of two)? **[6D]**

που somewhere, anywhere (*enclitic*) **[5C-D]**;
   [20E]

ποῦ; where? **[1F, 5C-D]**

πούς (ποδ-), ὁ foot (3a) **[6A]**

πρᾶγμα (πρᾱγματ-), τό thing, matter, affair; (pl.)
   troubles (3b) **[4A-B]**

πράγματα παρέχω cause trouble
πρᾶξις, ἡ fact, action (3e) [13E]
†πράττω do, perform, fare [13E]
    εὖ πράττω fare well, be prosperous
πρέσβεις, οἱ ambassadors (3e) [4D]
πρεσβευτής, ὁ ambassador (1d) [4D]
πρεσβύτερος ᾱ ον older, rather old [17A]
πρίν (+ inf.) before [13B]
πρὶν ἄν (+ subj.) until [17B]
πρίν (+ opt.) until [17B]
πρό (+ gen.) before, in front of [19F]
προάγω lead on [16G]
πρόβατον, τό sheep (2b) [17B]
πρόγονος, ὁ forebear, ancestor (2a) [13G]
προδίδωμι (προδο-) betray [15B]
προδο- aor. stem of προδίδωμι
προθῡμέομαι be ready, eager [16B]
πρόθῡμος ον ready, eager, willing [13B]
προίξ (προικ-), ἡ dowry (3a) [13A]
πρός (+ acc.) to, towards [1G]
    (+ gen.) in the name/under the protection of
    [9H]
    (+ dat.) in addition to, near [9A-E]; [16C];
    [17A]
    (adverbial) in addition [18C]
προσαγορεύω address, speak to [10C]
προσάπτω give, attach to (+ dat.) [18B]
προσδραμ- aor. stem of προστρέχω
προσεῖπον I spoke x (acc.) to y (acc.)
    (προσέειπον Ionic) [20B]
προσελθ- aor. stem of προσέρχομαι
προσέρχομαι (προσελθ-) go/come towards,
    advance [2]
προσέχω bring near, apply to
    προσέχω τὸν νοῦν pay attention to (+ dat.)
    [12B]
προσήκει it is fitting for x (dat.) to – (+ inf.)
    [18E]
προσῆλθον aor. of προσέρχομαι
πρόσθεν previously; before (+ gen.) [20G]
προσιών οὖσα όν (προσιοντ-) aor. part. of
    προσέρχομαι/πρόσειμι
προσκαλέω summon, call [17B]
προσλέγω (προσειπ-) address [15C]
προσπίτνω fall upon, embrace [15A]
προστάττω (προσταξα-) order (+ dat.) [18A]
προστρέχω (προσδραμ-) run towards [8A]

προτείνω stretch out [19F]
προτεραῖος ᾱ ον of the previous day [17C]
πρότερον formerly, previously [12D]
πρότερος ᾱ ον first (of two); previous [12D]
προτρέπω urge on, impel [7D]
πρύτανις, ὁ prytanis (3e) [11A]
πρῶτον first, at first [6C]
πρῶτος η ον first [6C]
πυθ- aor. stem of πυνθάνομαι
πύλη, ἡ gate (1a) [16A]
†πυνθάνομαι (πυθ-) learn, hear, get to know [13F]
πῦρ (πυρ-), τό fire (3b) [9G]
πυρά, τά fire-signal (2b) [3A]
πυρά, ἡ funeral pyre (1b) [4B]
πύργος, ὁ tower (2a) [17C]
πω yet (enclitic) [20E]
†πωλέω sell [9E]
πως somehow (enclitic) [5C, C-D]
πῶς; how? [5C-D]
*πῶς γὰρ οὔ; of course [1J]

P

ῥᾴδιος ᾱ ον easy [6A]
ῥᾳδίως easily [6A]
ῥᾷστος η ον very easy [17D]
ῥαψῳδός, ὁ rhapsode (2a) [1A-B]; [1H]
ῥήτωρ (ῥητορ-), ὁ orator, politician (3a) [8B]
†ῥίπτω throw [1A-G]

Σ

σαφῶς clearly [1E-F]; [1H]
σεαυτόν yourself (s.) [1E]
σελήνη, ἡ moon (1a) [6D]
σέο = σοῦ of you [19D]
σεῦ = σοῦ of you
σημαίνω (σημην-) tell, signal [19F]
σημεῖον, τό sign, signal (2b) [7H]
σῑγάω be quiet [11A]
σιδηρέος η ον of iron, metal [19D]
σῖτος, ὁ food (2a) (pl. σῖτα, τά [2b]) [8C]
σιωπάω be silent [2C]
†σκέπτομαι examine, look carefully at [16B]
σκεύη, τά gear, furniture [4A-B]; ship's gear (3c)
    [16C]
σκοπέομαι look at, consider
†σκοπέω consider, examine [2C]
ομῑκρός ά όν small, short, little [12F]

σός σή σόν your (s.) **[6D]**
σοφίᾱ, ἡ wisdom (1b) **[7A]**
σοφιστής, ὁ sophist, thinker (1d) **[5D]**
σοφός ή όν wise, clever **[5D]**
†σπένδω pour a libation **[3E]**
σπεύδω hurry **[3A]**
σπονδαί, αἱ treaty, truce (1a) **[8C]**
σπονδή, ἡ libation (1a) **[3E]**
σπουδάζω be concerned; do seriously **[12E]**
σπουδαῖος ᾱ ον serious, important **[12E]**
σπουδή, ἡ zeal, haste, seriousness (1a) **[10C]**
στᾱ́ς στᾶσα στᾱ́ν (σταντ-) standing (*aor. part. of* ἵσταμαι)
στείχω go, come **[15C]**
στένω groan **[9E]**
στερέω deprive of **[19B]**
στή = ἔστη he/she stood (*aor. of* ἵσταμαι) (*no augment*)
στῆθ' = στῆτε
στῆτε stand! (*2nd pl. imper. aor. of* ἵσταμαι)
στόμα (στοματ-), τό mouth (3b) **[16F]**
στρατηγός, ὁ general (2a) **[1J]**
στρατιᾱ́, ἡ army (1b) **[2]**
στρωμνή, ἡ bed (1a) **[18B]**
σύ you (s.) **[1B]**
συγγεγένημαι *perf. of* συγγίγνομαι
συγγένεια, ἡ kinship (1b) **[18D]**
συγγενής, ὁ relation (3d) **[8C]**
συγγίγνομαι (συγγεν-) be with, have intercourse, dealings with (+ dat.) **[12G]**
συγγνώμη, ἡ pardon, forgiveness (1a)
συγγνώμην ἔχω forgive, pardon **[9J]**
συγκόπτω beat up, strike (*aor. pass.* συνεκόπην) **[17C]**
συγχωρέω agree with, to; yield to (+ dat.) **[16F]**
συλλέγω collect, gather **[16G]**
συμβουλεύομαι discuss with (+ dat.) **[17E]**
συμβουλή, ἡ discussion, recommendation (1a) **[18E]**
συμμαχός, ὁ ally (2a) **[16C]**
συμπέμπω send with (+ dat.) **[19C]**
συμπροθῡμέομαι share enthusiasm of (+ dat.) **[17E]**
συμφορά, ἡ disaster, mishap, occurrence (1b) **[16A]**
συμφορή = συμφορᾱ́
σύν (+ dat.) with the help of **[9A-E]**; together with **[18C]**

συνέρχομαι (συνελθ-) come together **[12F]**
συνῆλθον *aor. of* συνέρχομαι
συνοικέω live with, together (+ dat.) **[10B]**
συντυγχάνω (συντυχ-) meet with (+ dat.) **[16A]**
σφεῖς they (Attic σφᾶς σφῶν σφίσι) (Ionic σφεῖς σφέας σφέων σφι) **[19D]**
σφι to them (dat. of σφεῖς) **[19D]**
σφόδρα very much, exceedingly **[17C]**
σχ- *aor. stem of* ἔχω/ἔχομαι
σχεδόν near, nearly, almost **[5A]**
σχολή, ἡ leisure (1a) **[16B]**
†σῴζω save, keep safe **[1A-G]**
Σωκράτης, ὁ Socrates (3d) **[6C]**
σῶμα (σωματ-), τό body, person (3b) **[14A]**
σῶος ᾱ ον safe **[1G]**
σωτήρ (σωτηρ-), ὁ saviour (3a) **[3A-B]**
σωτηρίᾱ, ἡ safety (1b) **[1A-G]**
σωφροσύνη, ἡ good sense, moderation (1a) **[18E]**
σώφρων (σωφρον-) sensible, temperate, modest, chaste, discreet, prudent, law-abiding, disciplined **[15B]**

T

τάλας αινα αν wretched, unhappy **[9D]**
τᾶν my dear chap (condescending) **[8C]**
τάξις, ἡ order, rank, battle-array (3e) **[4A-B]**
ταχέως quickly **[2D]**
τάχος, τό speed (3c) **[18A]**
*τε … καί both … and **[1A]**
τεῖχος, τό wall (of a city) (3c) **[10C]**
τεκμαίρομαι conclude, infer **[16G]**; assign, ordain
τεκμήριον, τό evidence, proof (2b) **[12F]**
τέκνον, τό child (2b) **[15A]**
τελευτάω die, end, finish **[17D]**
τέλος in the end, finally **[2B]**
τευ = τινος **[19D]**
τέχνη, ἡ skill, art, expertise (1a) **[3C]**
τήμερον today **[6D]**
τι a, something (*enclitic*) **[2D]**
τί; what? **[1D]** why? **[6C]**
†τίθημι (θε-) put, place **[6C] [12F]**
†τίκτω (τεκ-) bear, give birth to **[15A]**
τῑμάω honour **[4B]**; value, reckon **[17B]**; (+ dat.) fine **[12D]**
τῑμή, ἡ privilege, honour (1a) **[14D]**

τίμημα (τῑμηματ-), τό fine (3b) [12D]

τῑμωρέομαι take revenge on [12C]

τῑμωρίᾱ, ἡ revenge, vengeance (1b) [12C]

τις τι (τιν-) a certain, someone (enclitic) [4A-B]

τίς τί (τίν-); who? what? which? [1B]

τίτθη, ἡ nurse (1a) [17B]

*τοι then (inference) [10D]

τοι = σοι [19D]

τοί = οἵ (relative) [20E]

*τοίνυν well then (resuming argument) [12H]

τοι-όσδε ἥδε όνδε of this kind [19E]

τοι-οῦτος αὕτη οὗτο of this kind, of such a kind [9B]

τοῖσι = τοῖς [19B]

τόλμα, ἡ daring (1c) [2]

τολμάω dare, be daring, undertake [2D]

τοσοῦτος αὕτη οὗτο so great [12D]

τότε then [5A]

τούτῳ dat. of οὗτος
   ἐν τούτῳ meanwhile, during this

τράπεζα, ἡ bank (1c) [17B]

τραπ- aor. stem of τρέπομαι

τρεῖς τρία three [11C]

τρέπομαι (τραπ-) turn (self), turn in flight [4D]

†τρέπω cause to turn, put to flight

†τρέφω (θρεψα-) rear, raise, feed, nourish [14D]

†τρέχω (δραμ-) run [3D]

τριηραρχέω serve as a trierarch [16C]

τριήραρχος, ὁ trierarch (2a) [3D]

τριήρης, ἡ trireme (3d) [11B]

τρόπος, ὁ way, manner (2a) [12H]

τροφή, ἡ food, nourishment (1a) [18B]

†τυγχάνω (τυχ-) chance, happen (to be –ing + nom. part.); be actually –ing (+ nom. part.) [4D]; (+ gen.) hit, chance/happen on, be subject to [9I]

†τύπτω strike, hit [4B]

τυχ- aor. stem of τυγχάνω

τύχη, ἡ chance, good/bad fortune (1a) [12A]

Υ

ὑβρίζω treat violently, disgracefully [13A]; humiliate

ὕβρις, ἡ aggression, violence, insult, humiliation (3e) [4D]

ὑβριστής, ὁ violent, criminal person (1d) [16A]

ὕδωρ (ὑδατ-), τό water (3b) [15A]

υἱός, ὁ son (2a; also, except for acc. s., like m. forms of γλυκύς) [5A]

ὑμεῖς you (pl.) [1D]

ὑμέτερος ᾱ ον your (when 'you' is more than one person) [7H]

ὑπακούω reply, answer; obey (+ dat.) [16E]

ὑπάρχω be, be sufficient [19E]; begin (+ gen.) [12C]

ὑπέρ (+ gen.) for, on behalf of [8C]

ὑπηρέτης, ὁ servant, slave (1d) [4D]

†ὑπισχνέομαι (ὑποσχ-) promise (to) (+ fut. inf.) [16H]

ὕπνος, ὁ sleep (2a) [19D]

ὑπό (+ acc.) under, along under, up under [16A] (+ gen.) by, at the hand of [8C] (+ dat.) under, beneath [15A]

ὑποδέχομαι welcome, entertain [19E]

ὑπόλοιπος ον remaining [17C]

ὗς, ὁ boar (3h) [19D]

ὑστεραῖος ᾱ ον of the next day [17C]

ὕστερον later, further [9J]

ὕστερος ᾱ ον later, last (of two) [9J]

ὑφ' = ὑπό

ὑφαιρέομαι (ὑφελ-) steal, take for oneself by stealth [9I]

Φ

φαίνομαι (φαν-) appear, seem [3B]; seem (to be) (+ nom. part.) [4D]; seem to be but not really to be (+ inf.) [13F]

†φαίνω (φην-) reveal, declare, indict [13H]

φάμενος η ον aor. part. mid. of φημί (ἐφάμην)
   οὐ φάμενος saying … not, refusing

φάναι inf. of φημί

φανερός ᾱ όν clear, obvious [12F]

φάνη 3rd s. aor. of φαίνομαι (no augment)

φάσθ' you say (2nd pl. mid. of φημί)

φάσκω allege, claim, assert [13G]

φάτο he spoke (3rd s. aor. mid. of φημί)

φέρε come! [9B]

†φέρω (ἐνεγκ-) carry [4B]; bear, endure [17D]; lead [17A]
   χαλεπῶς φέρω be angry, displeased at

†φεύγω (φυγ-) run off, flee [1C-D]; be a defendant, be on trial [9H]

φεύξομαι fut. of φεύγω

†φημί/ἔφην I say/I said [7F]

φής you say [5B]

φήσω *fut. of* φημί

φήσειεν *3rd s. aor. opt. of* φημί

†φθάνω (φθασ-) anticipate x (acc.) by/in –ing (nom. part.) [4D]

φιλέω love, kiss [5C]; be used to (+ inf.) [11B]

φιλίᾱ, ἡ friendship (1b) [18E]

φίλος, ὁ friend (2a) [1A-G]

φίλος η ον dear; one's own

φιλοσοφίᾱ, ἡ philosophy (1b) [7D]

φιλόσοφος, ὁ philosopher (2a) [8C]

φίλτατος η ον most dear (sup. of φίλος) [10C]

φοβέομαι fear, be afraid of, respect [2] φοβέομαι μή (+ subj.) fear that, lest [16B]; (+ opt.) [16H]

φοβερός ᾱ́ όν terrible, frightening [18C]

φόβος, ὁ fear (2a) [4B]

φόνος, ὁ murder (2a) [17D]

φράζω utter, mention, talk [16D]

φρᾱ́τηρ (φρᾱτερ-), ὁ member of phratry (3a) [13B]

φρήν (φρεν-), ἡ heart, mind (3a) [20C]

φρονέω think, consider [20D]

φροντίζω think, worry [1A-G]

φροντίς (φροντιδ-), ἡ thought, care, concern (3a) [6A]

φυγή, ἡ flight (1a) [18A]

φύγον *1st s. aor. of* φεύγω (*no augment*)

φυλακή, ἡ guard (1a) [18C]

φύλαξ (φυλακ-), ὁ, ἡ guard (3a) [10C]

φυλάττω guard (Ionic φυλάσσω) [7G]

φύσις, ἡ nature, character, temperament (3e) [13A]

†φῦ́ω bear; mid. grow; (aor. mid.) ἔφῡν be naturally; (perf.) πέφῡκα be inclined by nature [13H]

φωνέω speak, utter [7H]

φωνή, ἡ voice, language, speech (1a) [7H]

φῶς (φωτ-), τό light (3b) [18C]

φώς (φωτ-), ὁ man, mortal (3a) [20F]

Χ

χαῖρε greetings! hello! [8A] farewell!

†χαίρω (χαρ-) rejoice [20A]

χαλεπός ή όν difficult, hard [8C]

χαλεπῶς φέρω be angry, displeased at [13F]

χαλκοῦς ῆ οῦν of bronze [17A]

χαρίζομαι oblige, please; be dear to (+ dat.) [19E]

χάρις (χαριτ-), ἡ reciprocal action, thanks, grace, (3a) [16B]
    χάριν οἶδα be grateful to (+ dat.) [16B]

χειμών (χειμων-), ὁ winter, storm (3a) [18B]

χείρ (χειρ-), ἡ hand (3a) [8A]

χείρων χεῖρον (χειρον-) worse (comp. of κακός) [8C]

χθές yesterday [17D]

χῑ́λιοι αι α thousand [17C]

χορός, ὁ dance; chorus (2a) [20E]

†χράομαι use, employ (+ dat.) [9E]

χρέα, τά debts (3c uncontr.) [5B]

†χρή it is necessary for x (acc.) to – (infin.) [9F]

χρῆμα (χρηματ-), τό thing (3b) [19B]

χρήματα, τά money (3b) [5A]

χρηματίζω do business [11B]

χρῆσθαι *pres. inf. of* χράομαι

χρήσιμος η ον profitable, useful [6D]

χρηστός ή όν good, fine, serviceable [5B]

χρῆται *3rd s. pres. of* χράομαι

χρόα *acc. of* χρώς [20D]

χροΐ *dat. of* χρώς [20D]

χρόνος, ὁ time (2a) [8B]

χροός *gen. of* χρώς [20D]

χρύσεος η ον golden [20G]

χρώς (χρωτ-), ὁ flesh, skin, body (3a) [15A] (Ionic acc. χρόα; gen. χροός; dat. χροΐ [20D])

χωρέω go, come [3A]

χώρη, ἡ land (1a) (*Attic* χώρᾱ, ἡ [1b]) [19C]

χωρίον, τό place; space; region [6C]; farm (2b) [16A]

χωρίς apart, separately (from) (+ gen.) [16D]

Ψ

ψευδής ές false, lying [12D]

ψεύδομαι lie, tell lies [13F]

ψευδῶς falsely [2C]

ψηφίζομαι vote [10E]

ψήφισμα (ψηφισματ-), τό decree (3b) [12D]

ψῆφος, ἡ vote, voting-pebble (2a) [9H]

ψῡχή ἡ soul, life (1a) [17C]

Ω

ὠ- *augment* (*if not under* ὠ- *look under* ὀ-)
ὤ what …! (+ gen.) [4D]
ὦ O (+ voc./nom.) (*addressing someone*) [1B]
ὧδε thus, as follows [18E]
ὠθέω push, shove [12A]
ὠλόμην *aor. of* ὄλλυμαι
ᾤμην *impf. of* οἶμαι
ὦμος, ὁ shoulder (2a) [20G]
ὤν οὖσα ὄν (ὀντ-) *part. of* εἰμί
ὦν = οὖν [19C]

†ὠνέομαι (πρια-) buy [16C]
ὡς how! [1C, 5C-D]; as [6A]; that [7B]
    (+ acc.) towards, to the house of [12F]
    (+ fut. part.) in order to [13B]
    (+ sup.) as – as possible [16C]
    (+ subj./opt.) = ἵνα in order to/that [20C]
ὥς thus, so [20A]
ὥσπερ like, as [2D]
ὥστε so that, with the result that, consequently
    (+ inf./indic.) [16C]

LIST OF PROPER NAMES

Most names of people(s) and all names of places will be found in the running
vocabularies where they occur. The names which recur several times and are not
repeated in the running vocabularies are listed here for convenience of reference.

Ἄδμητ-ος, ὁ Admetos (2a) (husband of Alkestis)
Ἄδρηστ-ος, ὁ Adrastos (2a) ('Unable to escape'; member of the Phrygian royal
    family and suppliant of Croesus)
Ἀθήν-η/-ᾶ, ἡ Athene (1a/b) (goddess of craftsmanship and protectress of
    Odysseus)
Ἀλκίνο-ος, ὁ Alkinoos (2a) (king of the Phaiakians and father of Nausikaa)
Ἀμφί-θε-ος, ὁ Amphitheos (2a) ('God on both sides'; goes to Sparta to get
    Dikaiopolis' private peace-treaty)
Ἀπολλόδωρ-ος, ὁ Apollodoros (2a) (prosecutor of Neaira and Stephanos; friend
    of Aristarkhos)
Ἀπόλλων (Ἀπολλων-), ὁ Apollo (3a: but voc. usu. Ἄπολλον; acc. Ἀπόλλω)
    (god of prophecy, with oracular shrine at Delphi)
Ἀρίσταρχ-ος, ὁ Aristarkhos (2a) (friend of Apollodoros, narrator of his legal
    troubles at the hands of Theophemos and Euergos)
Ἀφροδίτ-η, ἡ Aphrodite (1a) (goddess of love; used often as synonym for sexual
    pleasure)
Βδελυκλέων (Βδελυκλεων), ὁ Bdelykleon (3a) ('Loathe-Kleon'; son of
    Philokleon)
Δικαιόπολις, ὁ Dikaiopolis (3e) ('Just citizen'; Attic farmer in search of peace)
Διονυσόδωρ-ος, ὁ Dionysodoros (2a) (sophist, brother of Euthydemos)
Ἐπιμηθ-εύς, ὁ Epimetheus (3g) ('Aftersight'; brother of Prometheus)
Ἑρμ-ῆς, ὁ Hermes (Id) (Zeus' messenger)
Εὐεργίδ-ης, ὁ Euergides (1d) (experienced dikast)
Εὔεργ-ος, ὁ Euergos (2a) (brother of Theophemos and his helper in seizing
    Aristarkhos' goods)
Εὐθύδημ-ος, ὁ Euthydemos (2a) (sophist, brother of Dionysodoros)

Θεογέν-ης, ὁ Theogenes (3d) (*basileus archon* and for a short time husband of Phano)

Θεόφημ-ος, ὁ Theophemos (2a) (enemy of Aristarkhos and responsible for the seizure of his goods)

Ἴλῑσ-ός, ὁ river Ilisos (2a) (see map, *Text*, p. 19)

Κῑνησί-ᾱς, ὁ Kinesias (1d) ('Sexually active'; husband of Myrrhine)

Κλεινί-ᾱς, ὁ Kleinias (1d) (a young friend of Socrates)

Κλεονῑκ-η, ἡ Kleonike (1a) (friend and fellow-conspirator of Lysistrata)

Κροῖσ-ος, ὁ Croesus (2a) (king of Lydia) (see map, *Text*, p. 157)

Κωμί-ᾱς, ὁ Komias (1d) (experienced dikast)

Λάβης (Λαβητ-), ὁ Labes (3a) ('Grabber'; dog indicted on a charge of stealing cheese)

Λῡδ-οί, οἱ Lydians (2a) (Croesus' people) (see map, *Text*, p. 157)

Λυσί-ᾱς, ὁ Lysias (1d) (the famous orator, lover of Metaneira)

Λῡσιστράτ-η, ἡ Lysistrata (1a) ('Destroyer of the army'; prime-mover of the women's sex-strike)

Μετάνειρ-α, ἡ Metaneira (1b) (a slave and prostitute in Nikarete's brothel, loved by Lysias)

Μυρρίν-η, ἡ Myrrhine (1a) (friend of Lysistrata and wife of Kinesias)

Μῡσ-οί, οἱ Mysians (2a) (see map, *Text*, p. 157)

Ναυσικά-ᾱ, ἡ Nausikaa (1b) (unmarried daughter of Alkinoos, king of the Phaiakians)

Νέαιρ-α, ἡ Neaira (1b) ('wife' of Stephanos; indicted by Apollodoros for living with Stephanos as his wife and pretending that her children were citizens)

Νῑκαρέτ-η, ἡ Nikarete (1a) (brothel-keeper; former owner of Neaira)

Ξανθί-ᾱς, ὁ Xanthias (1d) (slave of Bdelykleon)

Ὀδυ(σ)σ-εύς, ὁ Odysseus (3g) (cunning Greek hero, who wandered for ten years after the Trojan War before finally returning to Ithaka, his kingdom)

Ὅμηρ-ος, ὁ Homer (2a) (epic poet, author of the *Iliad* and the Odyssey)

Πεισ-έταιρ-ος, ὁ Peisetairos (2a) ('Persuade-friend'; friend of Dikaiopolis; plans to leave Athens with Euelpides)

Περικλ-ῆς, ὁ Pericles (3d: uncontr.) (political leader in Athens during the mid-fifth century)

Προμηθ-εύς, ὁ Prometheus (3g) ('Foresight'; brother of Epimetheus)

Πῶλ-ος, ὁ Polos (2a) (a rower on board a trireme)

Στέφαν-ος, ὁ Stephanos (2a) ('husband' of Neaira; indicted by Apollodoros for living with a foreigner as his wife and trying to pass off her children as citizens)

Στρεψιάδ-ης, ὁ Strepsiades (1d) ('Twist and turn'; debt-ridden farmer, father of Pheidippides)

Στρῡμόδωρ-ος, ὁ Strymodoros (2a) (inexperienced dikast)

Σωσί-ᾱς, ὁ Sosias (1d) (slave of Bdelykleon)

Φαίηκ-ες, οἱ Phaiakians (3a) (Alkinoos' people)

Φαν-ώ, ἡ Phano (acc. Φαν-ώ; gen. Φαν-οῦς; dat. Φαν-οῖ) (daughter of Neaira; married to Phrastor, then Theogenes)

Φειδιππίδ-ης, ὁ Pheidippides (1d) ('Son of Pheidon and horse'; chariot-racing, horse-mad son of Strepsiades)

Φιλοκλέων (Φιλοκλεων-), ὁ Philokleon (3a) ('Love-Kleon'; jury-service-loving father of Bdelykleon)

Φράστωρ (Φραστορ-), ὁ Phrastor (3a) (for a time husband of Phano)

Φρῡνίων (Φρῡνιων-), ὁ Phrynion (3a) (former lover of Neaira, from whom Stephanos rescued her)

Χαιρεφῶν (Χαιρεφωντ-), ὁ Khairephon (3a) (good friend of Socrates)

E   English–Greek Vocabulary

NOTES

(a) This vocabulary has been compiled from all the words needed to complete successfully all the English-Greek Exercises in *Reading Greek*. If you find difficulty with a particular phrase, look in this vocabulary under the main word in the phrase. You will normally find some helpful suggestions as to how to tackle it. Remember that you may often have to rethink the English phrasing, particularly in the prose passages.

Please note that this vocabulary is for use with the Exercises in this book. It may be misleading to apply it to other prose exercises.

(b) Remember, especially if you try the prose passages, that Greek uses many more connecting and other particles than English. Try to use at least μέν ... δέ, δέ, ἀλλά, γάρ, δή and οὖν in your writing, all of which you will meet very often in your reading. You should also consult **391**.

a (certain) τις τι (τιν-)
able, be able δύναμαι (+ inf.)
about περί (+ acc./gen.)
according to κατά (+ acc.)
account, on x's ὑπέρ (+ gen.)
accurately ἀκρῑβῶς
acquit ἀπολύω
actually *indicating definite statement: use indicative verb*
advocate ἀντίδικος, ὁ (2a)
afraid of, be φοβέ-ομαι (+ acc.)
afraid that, be φοβέ-ομαι μή + subj./opt.
    afraid that ... not μή ... οὐ
after μετά (+ acc.)
afterwards, not long οὐ διὰ πολλοῦ
again αὖθις
against one's will ἄκων ἄκουσα ἆκον (ἄκοντ-)
agree ὁμολογέω
all πᾶς πᾶσα πᾶν (παντ-)
all sorts of *use* πᾶς
at all πάνυ *or omit*

allow ἐάω (ἐᾱσα-)
already ἤδη
although καίπερ + part., *or* plain part.
always ἀεί
amazed, be θαυμάζω
Amazon Ἀμαζών (Ἀμαζον-), ἡ (3a)
ambassador πρεσβευτής, ὁ (1d)
and καί
and yet καίτοι
angry, be made ὀργίζομαι (aor. ὠργίσθην)
announce, make an announcement κηρύττω
another ἄλλος η ο
answer ἀποκρίνομαι (ἀποκρῑνα-)
anyone *in negative sentence use* οὐδείς οὐδεμία οὐδέν (οὐδεν-); *if no neg., use* τις
any such thing τι τοιοῦτο
Apollodoros Ἀπολλόδωρος, ὁ (2a)
appear φαίνομαι; δοκέω
archon ἄρχων (ἀρχοντ-), ὁ (3a)
argument λόγος, ὁ (2a)
arrive ἀφικνέομαι (ἀφῑκ-)

as *use* ὤν οὖσα ὄν (ὀντ-); ὡς + ind.; ὡς
  + noun
as – as possible ὡς + sup. adv. /adj.
ask ἐρωτάω (ἐρ-)
ask for αἰτέω
assembly ἐκκλησίᾱ, ἡ (1b)
astounded at, be θαυμάζω (+ acc.)
at εἰς (+ acc.)
at once εὐθύς
at the hands of ὑπό (+ gen.)
Athenian Ἀθηναῖος, ὁ (2a)
attention, pay *use aor. of* ἀκούω; προσέχω τὸν
  νοῦν (+ dat.)

bad κακός ἡ όν
bank τράπεζα, ἡ (1c)
Bdelykleon Βδελυκλέων (-εων-), ὁ (3a)
be εἰμί
bear φέρω
  find hard to bear βαρέως φέρω (fut. οἴσω)
because διότι
because of διά (+ acc.)
become γίγνομαι (γεν-)
before πρίν (+ inf.)
  do x before y, φθάνω y (acc.)
  doing x (nom. part.)
begin ἄρχομαι (+ gen. or part.); ὑπάρχω (+ gen.)
behalf of, on ὑπέρ (+ gen.)
beloved *use pass. of* φιλέω
best ἄριστος η ον
better, feel συλλέγω ἐμαυτόν (1st pl. ἡμᾶς
  αὐτούς)
big μέγας μεγάλη μέγα (μεγαλ-)
boat πλοῖον, τό (2b)
body νεκρός, ὁ (2a)
boy παῖς (παιδ-), ὁ (3a)
bribe δῶρον, τό (2b)
bring ἄγω (ἀγαγ-)
bring out ἐκφέρω (ἐξενεγκ-)
bring to an end καταλύω
bumpkin ἄγροικος ον
business, move χρηματίζω (fut. χρηματιῶ: έω
  contr.)
but ἀλλά (*first word*); δέ (*second word*)
by κατά (+ acc.)
  by land κατὰ γῆν
  by! (oath) νή (+ acc.)

by (agent) ὑπό (+ gen.)

call upon ἐπικαλέομαι
captain κυβερνήτης, ὁ (1d)
capture αἱρέω (ἑλ-) (fut. αἱρήσω); καταλαμβάνω
  (-λαβ-) (fut. -λήψομαι)
carefully ἀκρῑβῶς
carry out ἐκφορέω
cast (a vote) τίθεμαι (θε-)
caught, be ἁλίσκομαι (ἁλ-)
charge, make a γραφὴν γράφομαι (γραψα-)
chase διώκω
child παιδίον, τό (2b)
childless person ἄπαις (ἀπαιδ-), ὁ (3a)
citizen ἀστός, ὁ (2a)
city πόλις, ἡ (3e)
claim φάσκω (fut. φήσω)
clear δῆλος η ον
  it is clear that δῆλόν ἐστιν ὅτι
clearly, be δῆλός ἐστι (+ nom. part.); *or use*
  δῆλόν ἐστιν ὅτι
clever σοφός ἡ όν
closely (= nearby) πλησίον
collect λαμβάνω (λαβ-)
come ἔρχομαι (ἐλθ-)
  have come ἥκω
come! ἐλθέ
come across καταλαμβάνω (καταλαβ-)
come forward προσέρχομαι (προσελθ-)
  (to address assembly) παρέρχομαι
  (παρελθ-)
come in(to) εἰσέρχομαι (εἰσελθ-)
come on! ἄγε δή
come upon εὑρίσκω (εὑρ-)
conceive διανοέομαι
condemn x (person) to y (punishment)
  καταδικάζω x (gen.) to y (acc.)
consequently ὥστε
consider σκοπέω
contest ἀγωνίζομαι
converse (with) διαλέγομαι (πρός + acc.)
corpse νεκρός, ὁ (2a)
corrupt διαφθείρω
council βουλή, ἡ (1a)
countryside ἀγροί, οἱ (2a)
court(-room) δικαστήριον, τό (2b)
cowardly κακός ἡ όν

creditor χρήστης, ὁ (1d)

cross διαβαίνω

danger κίνδῡνος, ὁ (2a)

danger (of), be in κινδῡνεύω (περί + acc.)

daughter θυγάτηρ (θυγατ(ε)ρ-), ἡ (3a)

dear φίλος η ον

death θάνατος, ὁ (2a)

debts χρέα, τά (3c uncontr.)

deceive ἐξαπατάω

decree ψήφισμα, τό (3b)

deed ἔργον, τό (2b); or use n. pl. adjectives

defeat νῑκάω (νῑκησα-)

defence speech ἀπολογίᾱ, ἡ (1b)

   make a defence speech ἀπολογέομαι

defendant φεύγων (φευγοντ-), ὁ (3a)

demand κελεύω

depart ἀπέρχομαι (ἀπελθ-)

deposited, be κεῖμαι

despair ἀπορίᾱ, ἡ (1b)

   be in despair ἀπορέω

destroy διαφθείρω; ἀπόλλῡμι

die ἀποθνῄσκω (ἀποθαν-)

difficult χαλεπός ή όν

Dikaiopolis Δικαιόπολις, ὁ (3e)

dikast δικαστής, ὁ (1d)

din θόρυβος, ὁ (2a)

Dionysodoros Διονῡσόδωρος, ὁ (2a)

discover (ἐξ)ευρίσκω ([ἐξ]ευρ-)

disdainful ὀλίγωρος ον

disease νόσος, ἡ (2a)

dishonour ἀτῑμάζω

divorce ἐκβάλλω (ἐκβαλ-); ἐκπέμπω

do ποιέω; δράω (δρᾱσα-); πράττω

dog κύων (κυν-), ὁ (3a)

don't μή + imperative; μή + aor. subj.

door θύρᾱ, ἡ (1b)

downhearted, be ἀθῡμέω (ἀθῡμησα-)

draft γράφω

drag away ἀφέλκω

duty translate 'must'

easy ῥᾴδιος ᾱ ον

   most easy ῥᾷστος η ον

end, bring to an καταλύω

enemies πολέμιοι, οἱ (2a)

enmity ἔχθρᾱ, ἡ (1b)

enough ... to οὕτω ... ὥστε + inf.

enter εἰσέρχομαι (εἰσελθ-) (εἰς + acc.)

equip παρασκευάζω

equipment σκεύη, τά (3c); or use τά + gen. (of what it belongs to)

escape ἀποφεύγω (ἀποφυγ-)

Euelpides Εὐελπίδης, ὁ (1d)

ever ποτε (enclitic); in indef. sentences add ἄν to conjunction and use subj. verb

everything translate 'all (things)'

evidence τεκμήριον, τό (2b)

evil κακός ή όν

except πλήν (+ gen.)

expect ἐλπίζω (+ fut. inf.)

experience πάθος, τό (3c)

experienced (in) ἔμπειρος ον (περί + acc.)

face the prospect of μέλλω (+ fut. inf.)

fall πῑπτω

fall ill ἀσθενέω

family οἰκεῖοι, οἱ (2a)

farmer γεωργός, ὁ (2a)

father πατήρ (πατ[ε]ρ-), ὁ (3a)

feel better συλλέγω ἐμαυτόν (1st pl. ἡμᾶς αὐτούς)

fetch out ἐκφέρω (fut. ἐξοίσω)

few ὀλίγοι αι α

fifty πεντήκοντα

fight μάχομαι (μαχεσα-) (with, against) πρός (+ acc.)

finally τέλος

find εὑρίσκω (εὑρ-)

find out πυνθάνομαι (πυθ-)

fine τῑμημα (τῑμηματ-), τό (3b)

fine (adj.) καλός ή όν

fire πῦρ (πυρ-), τό (3b)

flatter θωπεύω

follow ἕπομαι (σπ-) (+ dat.); (= accompany) ἀκολουθέω (+ dat.)

fool(ish) μῶρος ᾱ ον

for = because γάρ (second word)

for = on behalf of (prep.) ὑπέρ (+ gen.)

force ἀναγκάζω (ἀναγκασ-)

forefather πρόγονος, ὁ (2a)

fortunate εὐδαίμων εὔδαιμον (εὐδαιμον-)

free ἐλεύθερος ᾱ ον

freedom ἐλευθερίᾱ, ἡ (1b)

friend φίλος, ὁ (2a); φίλη, ἡ (1a)
furniture σκεύη, τά (3c)

gaze out (into) ἀποβλέπω (εἰς + acc.)
gear σκεύη, τά (3c)
general στρατηγός, ὁ (2a)
get λαμβάνω (λαβ-)
get back κομίζομαι
get hold of λαμβάνομαι (+ gen.)
get into καθίσταμαι (καταστα-) (εἰς + acc.)
get up ἀναβαίνω (ἀναβα-)
give δίδωμι (δο-)
glance βλέπω (aorist aspect)
go ἔρχομαι (ἐλθ-) (fut. εἶμι; subj. ἴω; perf.
   ἐλήλυθα)
go away (off) ἀπέρχομαι (ἀπελθ-)
going to, be μέλλω (+ fut. inf.)
go up to προσέρχομαι (-ελθ-) (πρός + acc.)
god θεός, ὁ (2a)
good καλός ή όν; χρηστός ή όν; ἀγαθός ή όν or
   translate as adverb, 'well'
grab λαμβάνομαι (λαβ-) (+ gen.)
great μέγας μεγάλη μέγα (μεγαλ-)
govern πολῑτεύομαι
grievously μεγάλα
guard φυλάττω
guard φύλαξ (φυλακ-), ὁ ἡ (3a)

hand χείρ (χειρ-), ἡ (3a); at the hands of ὑπό
   (+ gen.)
hand over παραδίδωμι (παραδο-)
happen (to be) τυγχάνω (τυχ-) (+ nom. part.)
happen, occur γίγνομαι (γεν-) (perf. γεγένημαι)
harbour λιμήν (λιμεν-), ὁ (3a)
hard, find hard to bear βαρέως φέρω (fut. οἴσω)
hate μισέω
hated by the gods κακοδαίμων κακόδαιμον
   (κακοδαιμον-)
have ἔχω (σχ-); ἐστί (+ dat.)
have in mind ἐν νῷ ἔχω
have to δεῖ X (person who 'has to', acc.) to Y (inf.)
hear ἀκούω (ἀκουσα-)
here ἐνθάδε
home(wards) οἴκαδε
hope ἐλπίζω (+ fut. inf.)
horse ἵππος, ὁ (2a)
house οἰκίᾱ, ἡ (1b)

how? πῶς;
how (indir. q.) πῶς, ὅπως
how big ὅσος η ον, ὁπόσος η ον
hullo! χαῖρε
husband ἀνήρ (ἀνδρ-), ὁ (3a)

I ἐγώ (emphatic; or just 1st s. of verb)
idea γνώμη, ἡ (1a)
it seems a good idea to δοκεῖ to X (dat.) to do Y
   (inf.)
if εἰ
if (fut. time) ἐάν (+ subj.)
if... were –, ... would – εἰ + opt., opt. + ἄν
if... were –ing, ... would [now] be –ing εἰ
   + impf., impf. + ἄν
if... had –ed,. .. would have –ed εἰ + aor., aor.
   + ἄν
if not εἰ μή
if only εἴθε, εἰ γάρ (+ opt.)
ignoramus ἀμαθής ές
ill, be ill ἀσθενέω
impious, be ἀσεβέω
in ἐν (+ dat.); inside ἔνδον (adv.); be in, be
   present πάρειμι
inclined to, be naturally πέφῡκα (+ inf.)
inhabit οἰκέω
intend μέλλω (+ fut. inf.)
intending to ὡς (+ fut. part.)
into εἰς (+ acc.)
itself (reflexive) ἑαυτόν ἑαυτήν ἑαυτό

job ἔργον, τό (2b)
judge δικάζω; give, pass judgment δικάζω
juror δικαστής, ὁ (1d)
just δίκαιος α ον
justly δικαίως

Khairedemos Χαιρέδημος, ὁ (2a)
kill ἀποκτείνω (ἀποκτειν-)
king (king archon) βασιλεύς, ὁ (3g)
knock (on) κόπτω (+ acc.); gave a knock use
   aorist
know γιγνώσκω; οἶδα (part. εἰδώς; inf. εἰδέναι)

lady γυνή (γυναικ-), ἡ (3a)
Lampito Λαμπιτώ, ἡ (voc. Λαμπιτοῖ)
land γῆ, ἡ (1a); by land κατὰ γῆν

large μέγας μεγάλη μέγα (μεγαλ-)
last, at last τέλος
laugh γελάω (γελασα-)
law νόμος, ὁ (2a)
law-court δικαστήριον, τό (2b)
learn μανθάνω (μαθ-)
leave ἀπέρχομαι (ἀπελθ-) (ἀπό + gen.)
legal *translate* 'of the court'
legitimate γνήσιος ᾱ ον
lct ἐάω (ἐᾱσα-); *or use 3rd person imper. or 1st pl. subj.*
life ψυχή, ἡ (1a)
like φιλέω (φιλησα-)
liking, be to one's ἀρέσκει (+ dat.)
listen (to) ἀκούω (+ gen./acc. of thing)
live (in) οἰκέω (+ acc.)
live together συνοικέω
live with συνοικέω (+ dat.)
lock in ἐγκλείω (ἐν + dat.)
long after, not οὐ διὰ πολλοῦ
look (at) βλέπω (εἰς/πρός + acc.)
look! ἰδού (s.)
look after θεραπεύω
look for ζητέω
lot, a *use* πολλά
a lot of πολύς πολλή πολύ (πολλ-)
loud μέγας
very loud μέγιστος η ον
love φιλέω
love of wisdom φιλοσοφίᾱ, ἡ (1b)

maidservant θεράπαινα, ἡ (1c)
make ποιέομαι
man ἄνθρωπος, ὁ (2a); ἀνήρ (ἀνδρ-), ὁ (3a)
managed to (x) *use aorist of* (x)
many πολλοί αἱ ά
marry γαμέω (γημα-)
matter πρᾶγμα (πρᾱγματ-), τό (3b)
messenger ἄγγελος, ὁ (2a)
mind, have in ἐν νῷ ἔχω
mistreat κακά (κακῶς) ποιέω (+ acc.)
mock (at) παίζω (πρός + acc.)
money χρήματα, τά (3b)
mother μήτηρ (μητ(ε)ρ-), ἡ (3a)
move business χρηματίζω (fut. χρηματιῶ: -έω contr.)
much πολύς πολλή πολύ (πολλ-)

mule ἡμίονος, ὁ (2a)
must δεῖ x (*person who* 'must') (acc.) do y (inf.)
my ἐμός ή όν
myself *use* αὐτός

name ὄνομα (ὀνοματ-), τό (3b)
naturally inclined, to be πέφῡκα (+ inf.)
Neaira Νέαιρα, ἡ (1b)
necessary, it is δεῖ (past ἔδει) for x (acc.) to y (inf.)
neighbour γείτων (γειτον-), ὁ (3a)
neither *if it means 'and not' use* οὐδέ (*phrased so that another* οὐ *precedes it*)
neither ... nor οὔτε ... οὔτε
never οὐδέποτε
new *use* ἄλλος η ο
news ('the news') *omit in translating*
next day τῇ ὑστεραίᾳ
not οὐ, οὐκ, οὐχ (*accented* οὔ *at end of sentence*) (with infinitives) μή, *except in indirect speech*
notice *use* οὐ λανθάνω (λαθ-) ('x [nom.] does not escape the notice of y [acc.] doing z [nom. part.]')
notice of, take προσέχω τὸν νοῦν (+ dat.)
number πλῆθος, τό (3c)

oath ὅρκος, ὁ (2a)
obediently *use part. of* πείθομαι
obey πείθομαι (+ dat.)
obliged *use* δέον (acc. absol.) ('x [acc.] being obliged to y [inf.]')
be obliged, compelled to ἀνάγκη ἐστί for x (acc.) to y (inf.)
obviously δῆλόν ἐστιν ὅτι
old man γέρων (γεροντ-), ὁ (3a)
old woman γραῦς (γρα-), ἡ (3a irr.)
on *may indicate aorist aspect* (e.g. 'on seeing him')
on (preposition) κατά (+ acc.)
once, once and for all *may indicate aorist aspect* (e.g. 'stop that once and for all!'); *or, use* γίγνομαι (γεν-) (e.g. 'once friends'); *or use a gen. absolute* (e.g. 'once this had happened, ...')
once, at *see* at once
only μόνον
or ἤ
order, give orders κελεύω (κελευσα-)

our ἡμέτερος ᾱ ον
out of ἐκ (+ gen.)
out with it! *use aor. imper. of* λέγω
owe ὀφείλω

peace εἰρήνη, ἡ (1a)
Peisetairos Πεισέταιρος, ὁ (2a)
people δῆμος, ὁ (2a); πλῆθος, τό (3c)
perform διαπράττομαι
perplexed, be ἀπορέω (ἀπορησα-)
Persian Πέρσης, ὁ (1d)
persuade πείθω (πεισα-)
persuasion *use the verb*
Phano Φανώ, ἡ (acc. Φανώ; gen. Φανοῦς)
Philokleon Φιλοκλέων (-εων-), ὁ (3a)
Philoxenos Φιλόξενος, ὁ (2a)
Phrastor Φράστωρ (Φραστορ-), ὁ (3a)
Phrynion Φρῡνίων (Φρῡνιων-), ὁ (3a)
pick up ἀναιρέω (ἀνελ-); ἐκδέχομαι (ἐκδεξα-)
pious, be εὐσεβέω
Piraeus Πειραιεύς, ὁ (3g)
place χωρίον, τό (2b)
plague νόσος, ἡ (2a)
plan γνώμη, ἡ (1a); μηχανή, ἡ (1a)
plan, make a μηχανὴν ποιέομαι
pleasure, with ἡδέως
poet ποιητής, ὁ (1d)
politician ῥήτωρ (ῥητορ-), ὁ (3a)
poor condition πονηρῶς
position *turn qualifying adj. into noun*
possession κτῆμα (κτηματ-), τό (3b)
possible for, it is ἔξεστι for x (dat.) to Y (inf.)
   since it is possible ἔξον
praise ἐπαινέω (ἐπαινεσα-)
promise in marriage ἐγγυάω
property *use* τά + *gen. of person who owns it*
prosecute κατηγορέω
prosecution κατηγορίᾱ, ἡ (1b)
prosecutor κατήγορος, ὁ (2a); διώκων
   (διωκοντ-), ὁ (3a)
prospect of, face the μέλλω (+ fut. inf.)
prostitute ἑταίρᾱ, ἡ (1b)
prove δηλόω
prytaneis πρυτάνεις, οἱ (3e)
punish κολάζω
pursue διώκω
pursuer διώκων (διωκοντ-), ὁ (3a)

put down κατατίθημι (καταθε-)
put in(to) καθίστημι (καταστησα-) X (acc.) in(to)
   Y (εἰς + acc.)
   be put into καθίσταμαι (καταστα-)
put x into such a Y state, condition διατίθημι
   (διαθε-) x (acc.) οὕτω Y (adv.)

question … closely ἐξετάζω
quickly ταχέως
quiet, keep ἡσυχάζω

reason, for what διὰ τί; τί βουλόμενος;
   for x (gen.) reason ἕνεκα (*prep. after noun*)
receive δέχομαι (δεξα-)
recover ἀνίσταμαι
refrain ἀπέχομαι (fut. ἀφέξομαι) (from) (+ gen.)
relate διέρχομαι (διελθ-)
remember μνημονεύω
rescue-force βοήθεια, ἡ (1b)
responsible (for) αἴτιος ᾱ ον (+ gen.)
retreat ἀναχωρέω
return ἐπανέρχομαι (-ελθ-)
rhapsode ῥαψῳδός, ὁ (2a)
rich εὐδαίμων εὔδαιμον (εὐδαίμον-)
risk κινδῡνεύω (+ inf.)
river ποταμός, ὁ (2a)
rogue ὑβριστής, ὁ (1d)
rule ἄρχω
run τρέχω
run away φεύγω
run off φεύγω
run out ἐκτρέχω (ἐκδραμ-)
run towards προστρέχω (-δραμ-) (πρός + acc.)

sacrifice θύω
   make sacrifices θυσίᾱς θύω
safe σῶος ᾱ ον
sail πλέω
sailor ναύτης, ὁ (1d)
same ὁ αὐτός, ἡ αὐτή, τὸ αὐτό
say (that) λέγω *(εἰπ-)* + ὅτι; φημί + acc./nom.
   + inf.
   I said ἦν δ’ ἐγώ
Scythian Σκύθης, ὁ (1d)
sea θάλαττα, ἡ (1c)
   by sea κατὰ θάλατταν
sea-battle ναυμαχίᾱ, ἡ (1b)

see ὁράω (ἰδ-)
    don't you see? use λανθάνω (e.g. 'doing
    Y [nom. part.] does he avoid your notice?'
    — translating 'your notice' as 'you' [acc.])
seem δοκέω
seem a good idea δοκεῖ to x (dat.) to y (inf.)
seize λαμβάνω (λαβ-)
sell πωλέω
serious βαρύς εῖα ύ
set up ποιέομαι
share μέρος, τό (3c)
sheep πρόβατον, τό (2b)
ship πλοῖον, τό (2b); ναῦς, ἡ (3 irr.)
short (of time) ὀλίγος η ον
should use ἄν + opt.
shout βοάω
    gave a shout use aorist
shout, shouting βοή, ἡ (1a)
show δηλόω; ἀποφαίνω
shut in ἐγκλείω (ἐγκλεισα-)
since use ὤν οὖσα ὄν (ὀντ-) or participle
sit (down) καθίζω; καθίζομαι
slander διαβάλλω
slave δοῦλος, ὁ (2a); δούλη, ἡ (1a); ὑπηρέτης, ὁ
    (1d); παῖς (παιδ-), ὁ (3a)
sleep καθεύδω
slowly βραδέως
so οὖν (second word)
so that (intent) ἵνα + subj./opt.
someone τις (τιν-)
son υἱός, ὁ (2a/3e)
soon as possible, as ὡς τάχιστα
sophist σοφιστής, ὁ (1d)
space χωρίον, τό (2b)
Spartan Λακεδαιμόνιος, ὁ (2a)
speak λέγω
speak in assembly ἀγορεύω
speak up! use aor. imper.
spectator θεᾱτής, ὁ (1d)
steal ὑφαιρέομαι (ὑφελ-)
Stephanos Στέφανος, ὁ (2a)
stop (doing) παύομαι (+ part.)
stop (someone doing) παύω (acc. + part.)
    (put a stop to) παύω (+ acc.)
stranger ξένος, ὁ (2a)
strike τύπτω
student μαθητής, ὁ (1d)

stupid μῶρος ᾱ ον
such/so ... that οὕτω ... ὥστε + inf./ind.
suffer πάσχω (παθ-)
suit δίκη, ἡ (1a); γραφή, ἡ (1a); ἀγών (ἀγων-),
    ὁ (3a)
sun ἥλιος, ὁ (2a)
suppliant ἱκέτης, ὁ (1d)
sure βέβαιος ον
sway, hold κρατέω
swear ὄμνῡμι (ὀμοσα-)
sweetly ἡδέως

take λαμβάνω (λαβ-)
take back ἀναλαμβάνω (ἀναλαβ-) (fut.
    ἀναλήψομαι)
take off ἄγω
take up ἐκδέχομαι
talk διαλέγομαι
teach διδάσκω (διδαξα-)
teacher διδάσκαλος, ὁ (2a)
tell λέγω (εἰπ-)
tell me! εἰπέ μοι (s.)
terrible δεινός ή όν
than ἤ
that (conj.) ὅτι
that (adj.) ἐκεῖνος η ο
    so that (expressing a result) ὥστε + inf./ind.
their (belonging to subject) ἑαυτῶν
them αὐτούς αὐτάς
themselves αὐτοί αὐταί; (acc. reflexive) ἑαυτούς
then δή (emphasising previous word)
then, from then on ἐντεῦθεν
Theogenes Θευγένης, ὁ (3d)
Theophemos Θεόφημος, ὁ (2a)
there, over there ἐκεῖ
therefore οὖν (second word)
they ἐκεῖνοι/οὗτοι
thief κλέπτης, ὁ (1d)
thing πρᾶγμα (πρᾱγματ-), τό (3b); or use n. of
    adj. or pronoun
this οὗτος αὕτη τοῦτο
though use ὤν οὖσα ὄν (ὀντ-) or καίπερ + part.
throw out ἐκβάλλω (ἐκβαλ-)
time χρόνος, ὁ (2a)
to (intention) ὡς + fut. part; ἵνα + subj./opt.
to, towards πρός (+ acc); εἰς (+ acc.)
    (of persons) ὡς (+ acc.)

tolerable μέτριος ᾱ ον

too καί

torch λαμπάς (λαμπαδ-), ἡ (3a)

towards πρός (+ acc.)

town, be in ἐπιδημέω

travel πορεύομαι

trial ἀγών (ἀγων-), ὁ (3a)

trierarch τριήραρχος, ὁ (2a)

trireme τριήρης, ἡ (3d)

trouble use κίνδῡνος, ὁ (2a)

truce σπονδαί, αἱ (1a)

truth ἀληθῆ, τά; ἀλήθεια, ἡ (1b)

try πειράομαι (πειρᾱσα-) + inf.

uncaring ἀμελής ές

unhappy κακοδαίμων κακόδαιμον (κακοδαιμον-)

unjust ἄδικος ον

unlucky κακοδαίμων κακόδαιμον (κακοδαιμον-)

until ἕως ἄν + subj. (*primary*); ἕως + opt. (*past*);
    ἕως + ind. (*definite*);
    (= before) πρὶν ἄν + subj. (*primary*); πρίν
    + opt. (*past*)

urge on προτρέπω

use χράομαι (+ dat.)

used to *use imperfect*

useful χρήσιμος η ον

vengeance on,
    take τῑμωρέομαι (+ acc.)

very ('this very thing') αὐτὸ τοῦτο

victorious, be νῑκάω

virtue ἀρετή, ἡ (1a)

vote ψῆφος, ἡ (2a)

wait μένω (fut. μενῶ: -έω contr.)

wall τεῖχος, τό (3c)

want (to) βούλομαι (+ inf.); ἐθέλω (ἐθελησα-)

war πόλεμος, ὁ (2a)

way τρόπος, ὁ (2a)

we ἡμεῖς (*or just 1st pl. of verb*)

well εὖ

well-disposed (to) εὔνους ουν (+ dat.)

what? ὅ τι; (*reply to question* τί;)

what (indir. q.) ὅστις ἥτις ὅ τι

what sort of ὁποῖος ᾱ ον

whatever ὅστις ἄν, ἥτις ἄν, ὅ τι ἄν

when ὅτε, ἐπειδή, ἐπεί, ὁπότε

when(ever) (indef.) ἐπειδάν, ὅταν, ὁπόταν

where? ποῦ;

where (indir. q.) ποῦ, ὅπου

where(ever) (indef.) ὅπου ἄν + subj. (*primary*);
    ὅπου + opt. (*past*)

where to? ποῖ;

whether ... or πότερον ... ἤ

which *use* ὤν οὖσα ὄν (ὀντ-) *or* ὅς ἥ ὅ (relative)

while *use* μέν ... δέ ('on the one hand [μέν] X is
    happening, while [δέ] Y ...'); *or use gen. abs.*

while, a ὀλίγον χρόνον

who? τίς; τί; (τίν-)

who *use* ὤν οὖσα ὄν (ὀντ-); *or* ὅς ἥ ὅ (relative)

why? διὰ τί; τί; τί παθών; τί βουλόμενος;

wicked πονηρός ᾱ όν

wife γυνή (γυναικ-), ἡ (3a)

will, against one's ἄκων ἄκουσα ἄκον (ἀκοντ-)

win νῑκάω (νῑκησα-)

wisdom σοφίᾱ, ἡ (1b)

wise σοφός ή όν

wish βούλομαι

with (= by means of) *use dative case*

without being seen by, *use* λανθάνω + *acc.*
    + *nom. part.*

woman γυνή (γυναικ-), ἡ (3a)

word λόγος, ὁ (2a)

worry φροντίζω

worth ἄξιος ᾱ ον (+ gen.)

would *use imperfect or* ἄν + *opt.*

wrong ἀδικέω (ἀδικησα-)

yes ναί; *or just repeat question as statement*

yet, and yet καίτοι

yokel ἄγροικος ον

you (s.) σύ (*or 2nd s. of verb*)
    (pl.) ὑμεῖς (*or 2nd pl. of verb*)

young νέος ᾱ ον

young man νεᾱνίας, ὁ (1d); νεᾱνίσκος, ὁ (2a)

your (s.) σός σή σόν
    (pl.) ὑμέτερος ᾱ ον

zeal σπουδή, ἡ (1a)

Zeus Ζεύς (Δι-), ὁ (3a)

F   The Grammatical Index to *Reading Greek*

Except where *Grammar* + page number is given, references are to numbered paragraphs. **1–339** are to be found in the running *Grammar* for *Sections* 1–20, **340–407** in the *Reference Grammar*, and **408–54** in the *Language Surveys*.

hiatus, **343(vii)(b)**
Homeric dialect, main features of, **337, 349–52**

iambic trimeter, **289–90**
imperative
    summary of endings of, **384**
    summary of usages, **404**
    pres. active, **18–21, 206, 367**
    pres. active contract, **26–7, 373–4**
    pres. middle of regular and contracted verbs,
        52–4, 206, 367–74
    first and second aorist imperative active,
        198–9, 206, 368, 370
    first and second aorist imperative middle,
198–9, 206, 368, 370
    aorist passive, **321, 369**
    perf. active, **372**
    perf. middle and passive, **372**
    of irregular verbs, **206, 207, 322–3**
    3rd person imperatives, **206–7**
    1st person – subjunctive, **303, 404, 406(i),
        422(i)(a)**
    negation – μή + pres. imp., **21,**
μή + aor. subj., **292, 406(iii)**
    aspect of pres. and aor. imp., **200, 340, 415–7**
imperfect tense
    indic. active, regular and contracted, **101, 106,
        375**
    indic. middle, regular and contracted, **102,
        107, 375**
    passive, **220, 375**
    in pres. 'contrary to fact' conditions, **242,
        402(ii), 425**
'imperfective', **416–7**
impersonal verbs, **395**
    δεῖ, **153, 296, 395**
    ἔξεστι, **202, 296, 395**
indefinite adjective/pronoun
    inflection of τις, τι, **83, 363**
    inflection of ὅστις, **219, 360**
indefinite adverb, **125**
indefinite constructions, **398(ii)**
    with subj., **282, 407(iii, v, vi), 422(ii)(a–c),
        423**
    with opt., **300, 407(iii, v, vi), 421(iii)**
    relative clauses, **282**
    temporal clauses, **282, 398**

with ἕως, **304, 307, 312(ii), 407(iii), 423(f)**
with πρίν, **311–2, 398(ii)**
indirect commands, **397(ii)**
indirect object, dat. of, **190(a), 440(i)**
indirect questions, **125, 148(c), 397(i), 406(iii),
    407(iv)**
indirect statements
    survey of, **397**
    verbs introducing, **235, 397**
    acc. + inf., **235–6, 397(iii-iv)**
    tense of inf., **236**
    nom. + inf., **236, 397(iii)**
    acc. + participle, **247, 340(ii), 397(iii)**
    opt. in secondary sequence, **265, 340(iii),
        397(i), 407(iv), 422(ii)**
    οὐ φημί, **336**
    ὅτι **148, 397(i)**, ὡς **397(i)**
infinitives
    summary of endings, **384**
    summary of main uses of, **394**
    pres. active and middle, **150, 367**
    pres. of contracted vbs., **151, 373–4**
    first and second aor., active, middle, **195–6,
        368, 370**
    aor. passive, **249, 369**
    root aorists, **209(c)**
    fut. active, middle, **208, 371**
    fut. passive, **248, 371**
    perf. active, middle, passive, **270, 372**
    inf. of irregular vbs., **152**
    Homeric inf. endings, **337(e)**
    negative with, **152(b), 235(a), 257, 394n.,
        397(iv)n., 428**
    aspect of pres. and aor. inf., **197**
    acc. + inf. in indirect statement, **235–6, 397**
    vbs. + inf., **153, 202, 394, 395, 397(ii, iv[a]),
        ἐπίσταμαι + inf., 210; 397(iv)(a)**
    adj. + inf., **203, 394(ii-iii)**
    fut., with vbs. of hoping, promising etc., **208(c)**
    πρίν + inf., **252, 398(i)**
    τό + inf., as noun, **257–8, 394(vi), 446(ii-iii)**
    in result clause, **315, 317, 396**
    in parenthetical phrases, **394(iv)**
    as imperative, **394(v)**
    with vbs. of prevention, hindrance, **394(vii)**
    with verbs of fearing, **293, 400(i)**
instrument, dat. of, **197(c), 221, 442**

INDEX OF GREEK WORDS

All nouns/adjectives and verbs are also summarised in the Reference Grammar
ad. loc.

ποῦ etc. **125**
πρᾶγμα declined **77**; cf. **356**; historically **434**
πρέπει **395**
πρέσβυς declined **79**, cf. **356**; contrasted with
 ὀφρύς **143**
πρίν with infin. 'before' **252**, **398**; 'until' + ἄν
 311–12, **398(ii)**
πρό **390**
πρός **390**
προσάγω active/middle **413(ii)**
προσήκει **395**
πυνθάνομαι with participle in reported speech
 247, **397(iv)**
πῶς etc. **125**

ῥᾴδιος comp. **365**
ρει rule **37**, **56**

σιωπάω future **119**
σοφός comp. and sup. **154–9**; comp. and sup.
 adverbs **225**
σύ declined **68**, cf. **360**; emphatic forms **68 (a-b)**
συμβαίνει **395**
σύν **390**
Σωκράτης declined **127**, cf. **356**
σωτήρ voc. **204**

ταχύς comp. **365**, **366**
τε … τε, τε … καί **41**, **42**, **51**, **391.19**
τε (Homer) **352**
-τέος usages **294–5**
τέτταρες declined **319**
τίθημι most pres. fut. imperf. and aor. act. mid.
 and pass. forms **237**; compared with δίδωμι
 238;
τιμάω pres. part. act. **91**; imperf. indic. act. **106**;
 future indic. act. **115**; aor. indic. act. **133**;
 pres. opt. act. **185**; third-person pres. imperat.
 act. and mid. **206**; perf. ind. act. **261**; pres.
 subjunctive act., mid. and pass. **278**; cf. **377**
τί meaning 'why?' **147**; + part. **188**; deliberatives
 405, **406(ii)**, **422(i)(b)**
τίς; τις declension and usage **83–5**, cf. **361**, **363**,
 393(ix)
τοι (Homer) **352**, Attic **391.27**
τοίνυν **391.18**
τρεῖς declined **319**

τρέχω strong aorist stem-change **146**
τριήρης declined **127**; voc. **204**, cf. **356**
τυγχάνω with participle **95**, **393(x)**; strong aorist
 stem-change **146**; + gen. **439(ix)**

υἱός declined **215**, cf. **357**
ὑπέρ **390**
ὑπισχνέομαι with fut. infin **208**, **397(iv)**
ὑπό **221**, **390**

φαίνομαι with participle **95**; perf. ind. act. **261**;
 393(x), **394(i)**, **397(iv)**
φάσκω pres. part. **168**; + infin. **235**
φέρε + subjunc., **404**
φέρω act. and mid. distinction **124**; princ. parts
 211; perf. **273**
φεύγω future **119**; + gen. of prosecution **439(viii)**
φημί pres. indic., inf. and part., past indic. **168**;
 pres. opt. **227**; + infin. **235**; imperat. **323**; οὐ
 φημί **336**; cf. **388**; **397(iv)**
φθάνω with participle **95**, **393(ix-x)**
-φι termination **349(ii)**
φοβέομαι pres. part. middle **93**; imperf. indic.
 mid. **107**; pres. infin. mid. **151**; with object,
 infin. and μή + subjun. **293**; with μή + opt.
 305; pass. in form in the aor. **324**; **400**; **407(ii)**

χαίρω pass. in form in the aor. **324**, **413(v)**
χάρις acc. s. **67(f)**
χείρ dat. pl. **359(ix)**
χράομαι + dat. **190(e)**
χρή **394(i)**, **395**

ὤν οὖσα ὄν declension **87**; usage **88**; cf. **364**
ὡς with fut. part. 'in order to' **251**; 'as – as' **297**;
 392, **394(iv)**
ὥστε in 'result' usages **315–7**, **396**
ὤφελον expressing wish for the past **244**, **403**